CENTURY 21®
ACCOUNTING

ROBERT M. SWANSON

Professor of Business Education and Office Administration
College of Business
Ball State University
Muncie, Indiana

LEWIS D. BOYNTON

Professor Emeritus
Formerly Chairman, Department of Business Education
Central Connecticut State College
New Britain, Connecticut

KENTON E. ROSS

Chairman, Department of Accounting
College of Business Administration
University of North Florida
Jacksonville, Florida

ROBERT D. HANSON

Chairman, Department of Business Education
Central Michigan University
Mount Pleasant, Michigan

Published by

B27 **SOUTH-WESTERN PUBLISHING CO.**

CINCINNATI   WEST CHICAGO, ILL.   DALLAS   PELHAM MANOR, N.Y.
PALO ALTO, CALIF.

CENTURY 21®

ACCOUNTING

 Advanced Course

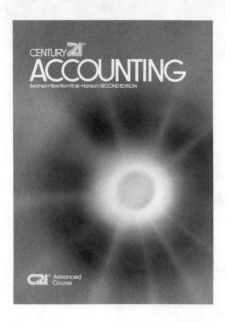

CENTURY 21
ACCOUNTING
Swanson•Boynton•Ross•Hanson/SECOND EDITION

C21 Advanced Course

ON THE COVER

The cover of this book portrays the brilliance of a laser beam and symbolizes the future of accounting at the dawning of a new and exciting century. This spirit is captured in CENTURY 21 ACCOUNTING. The design element represents a cross section view of a laser beam now being used in increasingly prominent ways in business, industry, and medicine. Continuing experiments with a laser beam promise even broader applications, perhaps in accounting, in this micro/electronic era.

The design element gives the impression of a beginning, of emergence, of development that is appropriate for a student exploring careers and starting a foundation for an occupation. The colors dramatically represent a wide spectrum of career opportunities for the student of accounting in Century 21.

ISBN: 0-538-02270-1

Library of Congress Catalog Card Number: 77-73288

2 3 4 5 6 7 8 9 10 11 12 13 14 15 16 17 18 19 20 K 5 4 3 2 1 0 9 8

Printed in the United States of America

Preface

This advanced course is the second volume of a two-year set of texts for high school accounting. This text has evolved from a highly successful series started 75 years ago. Each new edition in the series has led the way in providing easily understood learning materials. The series has been useful in preparing accounting students for the present and providing a basis for vocations in the future. This second volume is designed primarily for students with determined career objectives in the accounting profession.

FROM THE KNOWN TO THE UNKNOWN

Learning moves most successfully when the learner starts with what is already mastered — what is already known. In using this advanced text, students begin with a review of what was learned in the first year of accounting study. Each chapter builds on what students already know. New learning is developed gradually throughout the text. Thus, students start with what is already known and proceed to the unknown. In each topic studied, students will find much with which they are already familiar. The expanded depth and scope of the topics will provide appropriate challenges.

CAREER EDUCATION IN ACCOUNTING

Entry-level accounting jobs commonly are clerical and machine oriented for recently graduated high school students. To begin the second year of accounting study, students are introduced to an accounting career ladder showing opportunities for progress. For many of the accounting positions, the completion of high school accounting is sufficient for entry-level positions in the profession. For the upper rungs of the career ladder, individuals need additional formal education and/or accounting experience. Chapter 1 outlines the opportunities in accounting on the career ladder. The remainder of the text provides the learning needed for the entry-level positions and the basis for further accounting study.

This advanced course is designed for students who have one or more of the following objectives:

1. To become accounting clerks or accountants' assistants upon graduation from high school.
2. To go to college and major in accounting or some other phase of business administration. Major collegiate areas such as marketing, management, and finance usually require some knowledge of accounting theory and practice.
3. To broaden and improve knowledge about business procedures and the use of accounting records.
4. To understand better the relationship between automated data processing and manual processing of accounting data.

FEATURES OF THIS REVISION

Through the years, teachers and students alike have generally approved of the content and organization of the advanced course text. For this reason, the successful features of the series have been retained in this revision. However, in response to suggestions from teachers, professional accountants, and students, important changes have been made where needed.

1. *New organization.* The content and chapters have been reorganized to emphasize the work of various accounting clerks. Part 2 emphasizes work done by general accounting clerks. Parts 4 and 5 emphasize work done by various specialized accounting clerks. Part 6 has been completely rewritten to emphasize the work of coding clerks in the processing of accounting data by automated means. Part 8 emphasizes the work of accounting clerks in a cost accounting situation. Parts 9 and 10 emphasize some of the kinds of work done by individuals in advanced career positions such as junior and assistant accountants. The thrust of the entire reorganization is plainly established in Part 1, a chapter on accounting careers.

2. *Simulations.* Simulations have proven to be a very popular learning device. The completely rewritten simulations help students apply the principles and procedures learned in the separate chapters of the text. In addition, students are provided with two projects somewhat like mini-simulations that are shorter than the regular simulations. Project 1 (in Part 2) is a review of the principles and procedures studied in a first year of accounting. Project 2 (in Part 5) is based on the work of a payroll clerk.

3. *Flexibility.* Most parts of the text consist of 1, 2, or 3 chapters each. This arrangement provides more convenient testing points. After students have completed Part 5, the remainder of the parts can be studied in any order that the teachers and students think is best. The short parts make it possible to omit those not needed in local situations and to substitute other activities which are needed. As an example, Part 2, a review, can easily be omitted for students who recently completed a first year of accounting with great success.

4. *Automation.* A development in business today is to have separate departments for accounting and automated data processing. Some businesses

have an internal data processing department that serves the entire business. Other businesses use an outside ADP service center. In either situation, the work is essentially the same in preparing accounting data for automated data processing. Part 6 (Chapters 12, 13, and 14) emphasizes the work of coding clerks in preparing data for the automated data processing department or service center. The emphasis in Part 6 is on the handling of data rather than on the manipulation of machines. Students with special career interests in automated data processing need to enroll in separate ADP courses in addition to the study of accounting.

5. *New topics.* A new introductory chapter on accounting careers (Chapter 1) has been added. This chapter provides students with information about accounting career possibilities as well as some guidance in the formal education needed. A new chapter on cash accounting (Chapter 24) has also been added. Many businesses operate on a cash basis without many transactions for sales on account or purchases on account. In addition, most social organizations operate strictly on a cash basis. A knowledge of cash-basis accounting is needed in today's world.

REDEFINING ACCOUNTING VALUES

The accounting profession has organized the Financial Accounting Standards Board. The goal of the Board on a national level is to define certain procedures and rules for keeping and reporting accounting data. Much of the need for stricter definitions of accounting values arises because of the demands of the federal government. Businesses must report net income and net worth each year. Based on the reports, income taxes are figured and management decisions are made.

A great amount of the work of the Financial Accounting Standards Board to date has been related to establishing values of assets and reporting items on financial statements. For example, should merchandise inventory be valued at the cost price or the replacement cost? Should plant assets be recorded at the original cost value or at the current replacement cost? However, once these decisions have been made, most of the accounting procedures for recording the data are the same as before. Therefore, the nature of the work of accounting clerks may not change much, but the dollar values they record can change because of the work of the Board.

CENTURY 21 ACCOUNTING, Advanced Course, presents principles and concepts that are in agreement with Statements of Financial Accounting issued by the FASB, and with the Accounting Principles Board Opinions issued by the APB before being replaced by the FASB.

AUTOMATION AND ACCOUNTING

The increased demand for data by federal and state governments has increased the quantity and kind of data that most businesses must record and report. One way to speed the recording and reporting of accounting data is to employ more persons. A second way to speed the work is to utilize automated equipment. A third way is a combination of the first two. In the past twenty years the increased use of automated equipment in accounting has been dramatic. At the same time, the federal government's census reports show a steady increase in the number of accountants and accounting clerks. Based on these findings, there appears to be a continuing need for persons employed to process accounting data manually. The outlook for the future in accounting is bright.

ACKNOWLEDGEMENTS

Seventy-five years of successful accounting texts reflect the combined efforts of many authors, editors, teachers, students, and professional accounting personnel. Suggestions for improvements to 20th CENTURY BOOKKEEPING AND ACCOUNTING and its successor CENTURY 21 ACCOUNTING have come from many people and many sources. The revisions have been evolutionary rather than revolutionary from one edition to the next. The authors express sincere appreciation to all who have helped in making this revision. The authors especially thank those professional teachers and students who have suggested changes that have produced improvements.

Robert M. Swanson
Lewis D. Boynton
Kenton E. Ross
Robert D. Hanson

Contents

PART 9   JUNIOR ACCOUNTANTS

PART 10   ASSISTANT ACCOUNTANTS

ACCOUNTING CAREERS

THE ACCOUNTING PROFESSION REQUIRES EDUCATION.
Accounting is a profession—the fastest growing profession in the
United States. Currently, over 2,000,000 persons are employed
at various levels in the accounting profession, with a demand
for approximately 160,000 additional people each year through
1985. The satisfactory completion of high school accounting
courses is sufficient preparation for many of the beginning jobs
on the accounting career ladder. Education beyond high school
is generally required, however, to begin employment at one of
the higher rungs on the accounting career ladder. Many of the
successful people doing accounting work acquired their initial
training by taking high school accounting.

Preparing for a career in accounting requires careful planning.
Part 1 of this textbook describes the (a) areas of employment,
(b) career opportunities, (c) accounting positions, (d) entry-
level jobs, (e) advancement-level jobs, and (f) minimum
educational requirements.

Wang Laboratories, Inc.

Dennison Manufacturing Company

Accounting as an Occupation

Choosing a career is one of the important steps in every person's life. Young people seeking careers that are challenging, interesting, and rewarding should consider the field of accounting. The study of accounting in high school is the first step in acquiring the necessary skills for starting an accounting career.

ACCOUNTING PROFESSION

Jobs in the accounting profession vary greatly. An accounting employee who gathers, classifies, records, posts, and summarizes accounting data is called an accounting clerk. An accounting clerk may also be known as a bookkeeper in some businesses. An accounting employee who interprets, analyzes, and collects data for management decision making is called an accountant. An accountant may also supervise the work of accounting clerks. In businesses that have a small volume of business transactions, one person may have the responsibility for keeping the accounting records. As the volume of accounting data increases, a number of people are usually employed to do the accounting work. Regardless of business size or number of business transactions, there is a continuous need for people to gather, classify, record, and interpret financial information for management. Employment in the accounting profession is generally in one of the following areas: governmental accounting, public accounting, or private accounting.

Governmental accounting

In governmental accounting a person works for federal, state, or local governmental agencies. The Treasury Department and the Internal Revenue Service are examples of governmental agencies with continuous needs for people in accounting.

Public accounting

In public accounting, a person may work independently or as a member of a public accounting firm. Public accountants sell services to individuals or businesses. For example, a doctor may use the services of an individual accountant or accounting firm. A public accountant who has the required education and experience and passes a required examination may become a Certified Public Accountant (CPA). The CPA certificate signifies professional status in public accounting.

Public accountants perform a variety of duties. They may do all of the accounting for a business. They may check and verify the accounting records for businesses that have their own accountants. Also, public accountants may be asked to review all accounting procedures and suggest ways to increase profits. Many individuals and businesses employ public accountants to prepare income tax reports and to prepare, analyze, and interpret financial statements.

Private accounting

In private accounting, a person is employed by a private business or institution. The work in private accounting is similar in nature to that of public accounting. However, in private accounting the person works as an employee for only one business.

CAREER OPPORTUNITIES

According to the U.S. Department of Labor there are over 2,000,000 people employed in the accounting field. Of this number about 700,000 are employed as accountants and about 1,500,000 are employed as bookkeepers or accounting clerks. The bookkeeping worker classification includes all accounting clerks.

Labor projections show that there will be a demand for about 42,000 additional accountants each year through 1985. These projections further show that there will be a demand for about 120,000 new bookkeeping workers each year through 1985. Also, there will be an increasing demand for additional persons trained to work with automated equipment. In many businesses, the accounting clerks, accountants, and data processing workers combine to complete the total accounting work. The demand for automated data processing workers is in addition to the projections for accounting or bookkeeping occupations.

ACCOUNTING POSITIONS

Jobs on which beginning workers start without any experience are called entry-level jobs. Some entry-level jobs do not require any specific skills or education. Jobs of this nature require on-the-job training by the employer. Other entry-level jobs require specific skills to qualify for the first position. To qualify as a beginning worker in accounting, for example, specific skills, aptitudes, and abilities are required. Entry-level jobs vary depending on the amount of formal education required. For example, accountants normally require greater skills than accounting clerks.

The series of jobs that a person may move through in a career is called a career ladder. Each step on a career ladder requires more skill and carries more responsibility than the step before. Moving up the career ladder is usually possible within the same company. Jobs on the career ladder that a person may advance to after gaining experience or additional training are called advancement-level jobs. How long a person will have to work at an entry-level job depends on the person and the job itself. An employee who does well on an entry-level job will normally be considered for advancement as experience is gained and other jobs open up. Additional education or on-the-job training usually speeds the movement up the career ladder. Sometimes advancement is only possible by moving to another business.

Job titles and descriptions for the variety of positions available in the accounting field vary depending on level of responsibility and locality. The job titles described in this chapter are found in the *Dictionary of Occupational Titles* and the *1976–77 Occupational Handbook* published by the federal government. Also included are selected job titles and descriptions that appeared in classified help wanted advertisements in such newspapers as: *Chicago Tribune, Denver Post, Detroit Free Press, Miami Herald, New York Times*, and *San Francisco Chronicle*.

> The classified advertisements in local and surrounding area newspapers should be checked. Also, local employment agencies and the high school placement office have current listings of job openings and requirements for accounting positions.

Accounting clerks

Small and medium sized businesses do not have the volume or complexity of business transactions as do large businesses. Therefore, these businesses do not hire as many people to handle the accounting procedures. In a small business one person may be responsible for the recording of business transactions and the completion of a trial balance. In medium sized businesses two or more people may be needed to perform these functions. The accounting procedures in large businesses are more complex and specialized. The accounting positions are likewise more specialized. Many larger businesses maintain their accounting records on a departmental basis with one or more persons handling specific types of transactions. Depending on the volume and complexity of business transactions, accounting clerks may be further classified as either general accounting clerks or specialized accounting clerks.

General accounting clerks. A person who verifies and records accounting transactions, posts data to ledgers, and completes the books through the trial balance is called a general accounting clerk. A general accounting clerk may also be classified as a general bookkeeper. Businesses that employ only general accounting clerks also may employ public accountants to prepare financial statements and interpret the accounting records for management.

Specialized accounting clerks. An accounting employee who checks, records, posts, and prepares reports for specific types of business transactions is called a specialized accounting clerk. Specialized accounting clerks are often classified according to the type of accounting transactions for which they are responsible. Businesses that employ specialized accounting clerks will also employ their own accountant or a public accountant to prepare and interpret financial statements, and to prepare income tax reports. The most common types of specialized accounting clerks are:

1. Purchases and cash payments clerk — checks, records, and posts transactions related to purchases and cash payments. A cash payments clerk may also be responsible for the reconciliation of bank statements. A person working in this position may also be known as an accounts payable clerk.
2. Sales and cash receipts clerk — checks, records, and posts transactions related to sales and cash receipts. A person working in this position may also be known as an accounts receivable clerk. An accounts receivable clerk may also be responsible for the preparation of customers' statements of account.
3. Inventory clerk — determines the value of inventories. An inventory clerk may also be responsible for preparing reports related to inventory control.
4. Payroll clerk — prepares and records the payroll.
5. Voucher clerk — prepares the records for a voucher accounting system.
6. Coding clerk — manually records accounting data on forms in preparation for computer processing.
7. Cost accounting clerk — records direct and indirect costs, prepares cost sheets, and records entries related to costs.

Educational requirements for accounting clerks. Entry-level jobs for accounting clerks on the accounting career ladder are shown on page 7.

The educational requirements for accounting clerks vary depending on the size of the business and the level of responsibility. In small businesses a person who has successfully completed the first-year high school accounting course meets the minimum qualifications for starting an accounting career as a general accounting clerk. To obtain an entry-level

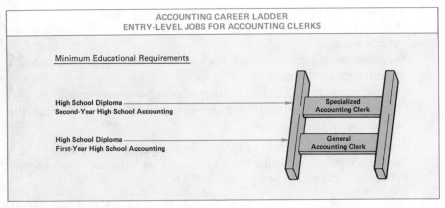

ACCOUNTING CAREER LADDER
ENTRY-LEVEL JOBS FOR ACCOUNTING CLERKS

Minimum Educational Requirements

High School Diploma
Second-Year High School Accounting → Specialized Accounting Clerk

High School Diploma
First-Year High School Accounting → General Accounting Clerk

Accounting career ladder entry-level jobs for accounting clerks

job as a specialized accounting clerk, a second-year high school account-ing course is generally required as the minimum educational prepara-tion. Besides studying accounting in high school, individuals should also study typewriting, business mathematics, and other related business courses.

Some small businesses may require that a general accounting clerk be qualified to prepare financial statements at the close of a fiscal period. Therefore, students planning to begin their accounting career in a small business should be prepared to handle all phases of the accounting cycle. If a general accounting clerk prepares financial statements, a pub-lic accountant is normally employed to check and verify the accounting records. The public accountant may also interpret the financial state-ments and prepare income tax reports.

Part 2 of this textbook includes the basic skills required for entry-level jobs as general accounting clerks. This part reviews the basic accounting procedures developed in the first-year course. Upon completion of Part 2, students will have reviewed procedures to:

1. Record and post business transactions.
2. Complete journals at the end of the month.
3. Prepare a trial balance on a work sheet.
4. Plan adjustments and complete a work sheet.
5. Prepare financial statements.
6. Record and post adjusting and closing entries.
7. Prepare a post-closing trial balance.

Parts 4, 5, 6, and 8 of this textbook include the basic skills required for employment as a specialized accounting clerk. Upon successful comple-tion of these parts, students will be able to:

1. Record and post transactions related to departmental purchases, cash payments, sales, cash receipts, and payroll.
2. Reconcile bank statements.
3. Determine the value of inventories.

4. Maintain payroll records.
5. Prepare vouchers and prepare and post from a voucher register and a check register.
6. Record business transactions on a special form in preparation for computer processing.
7. Prepare forms to check the accuracy of computer processing.
8. Prepare cost accounting records for merchandising and manufacturing businesses.

Some businesses seeking a specialized accounting clerk may require that prospective candidates have experience as a general accounting clerk or as a specialized accounting clerk.

Employment ads for accounting clerks. The chart below shows the types of employment ads for accounting clerks that are representative of those appearing in the classified sections of newspapers.

Classified ads for accounting clerks

ACCOUNTING CLERK	ACCOUNTING CLERK	ACCOUNTS SUPERVISOR
Accounting clerk position open with fast growing food distributor. Experience in batching receivables for computer input and edit lists necessary. General office skills, typing, and familiarity with data processing a plus.	Person with good math aptitude, previous experience in the field of accounting helpful but will consider good beginner.	Accounts supervisor to supervise nine people in accounts payable. Retail experience. Paid benefits.
	Growing mortgage bank in suburb has an opening for a general bookkeeper (general accounting clerk). Hours are flexible. Must be able to handle full service books thru trial balance.	**CODING CLERK** Coding clerk needed to process data for computer input. Experience necessary.
Area business needs an efficient bookkeeper (general accounting clerk). Experienced in posting general ledger thru trial balance. Must maintain all journals plus related detail work.		
Accounting Clerk General accounting clerk for hotel dining room operation. Must be skilled thru trial balance. Restaurant experience helpful.	**A/R CLERK** Immediate opening for conscientious, detail-minded person for checking and auditing accounts receivable. Good salary and company benefits.	Need one year of accounting experience or equivalency in training for this spot. You'll prepare data for computer input, process credit info and all accompanying reports.
ACCOUNTING CLERK Present job dull and routine? Want a challenge and a chance for growth? Like friendly people? Then see us. We have an opening for beginner in accounting. Some knowledge of bookkeeping or accounting necessary. Must be a good typist. Good pay and excellent benefits.	**A/R Clerk** Publishing company accounting department has openings for accounts receivable clerk to handle advertising, billing, and coding; train as backup in cash and miscellaneous accounting jobs.	**PAYROLL CLERK** Immediate opening for a take charge individual to handle payroll on ADP system for 150 employees. Good salary and company benefits.
	ACCOUNTS PAYABLE AND RECEIVABLE CLERK. Rapidly expanding chemical company has opening for person who is looking for a career and wants to grow with us.	**Supervisor** Supervise a 5 person office. A good accounting background required. Medium sized pharmaceutical company.

Career advancement for accounting clerks. The advancement-level jobs for accounting clerks on the accounting career ladder are shown below.

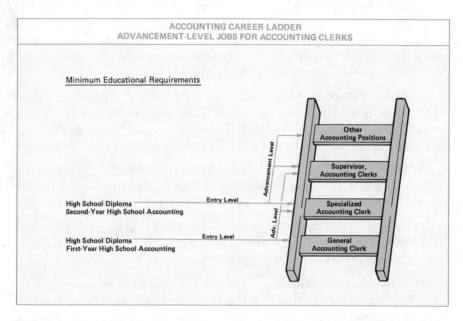

ACCOUNTING CAREER LADDER
ADVANCEMENT-LEVEL JOBS FOR ACCOUNTING CLERKS

Minimum Educational Requirements

Other
Accounting Positions

Supervisor,
Accounting Clerks

High School Diploma
Second-Year High School Accounting — Entry Level

Specialized
Accounting Clerk

Advancement Level

Adv. Level

High School Diploma
First-Year High School Accounting — Entry Level

General
Accounting Clerk

Accounting career ladder advancement-level jobs for accounting clerks

A general accounting clerk may advance to the position of specialized accounting clerk and to a supervisory position. Advancement would normally be the result of on-the-job experience, on-the-job training, or additional formal education beyond high school. To obtain these positions an individual may have to move to a larger business. As the volume of business transactions increases, accounting work becomes more specialized. Larger businesses may use more classifications for their accounting staff than general accounting clerks. They classify those persons responsible for gathering, classifying, recording, and summarizing particular types of accounting data as specialized accounting clerks.

Specialized accounting clerks with from one to five years accounting experience may advance to a supervisory position or to other accounting positions requiring more specialized skills. Advancement in most businesses is possible without the need for additional formal education beyond high school. Advancement is usually faster, however, when additional courses in accounting or related business courses are taken. Adult evening schools, community colleges, universities, and independent business colleges usually offer classes at night for employed persons unable to attend classes during the day. Many businesses encourage additional education and will pay the cost of tuition for their employees.

Many persons with some accounting education beyond the high school level may start as specialized accounting clerks. However, these individuals may quickly advance to supervisory or other accounting positions.

Accountants

Accountants prepare, analyze, and interpret financial statements. They also collect data for management decision making. An accountant may also supervise the work of accounting clerks and other accountants with less experience or responsibility. Accountants may be classified according to level of responsibility or specialization.

Junior accountant. A person who handles general accounting procedures, including accounting for uncollectible accounts, plant assets, and prepaid items and accruals is called a junior accountant. A junior accountant may also be classified as a full-charge bookkeeper.

Assistant accountant. A person who handles all aspects of the accounting cycle, has a working knowledge of cost accounting, and prepares reports for management is called an assistant accountant.

Specialized accountant. A person who works in a particular area within the accounting system, such as auditing, tax work, cost accounting, or budgeting, is called a specialized accountant.

Professional accountant. A person who works with all aspects of accounting, including auditing, budgeting, financial statement analysis, taxes, and accounting systems is called a professional accountant. A professional accountant will normally have received the CPA certificate.

Educational requirements for accountants. The entry-level jobs for accountants on the accounting career ladder are shown below.

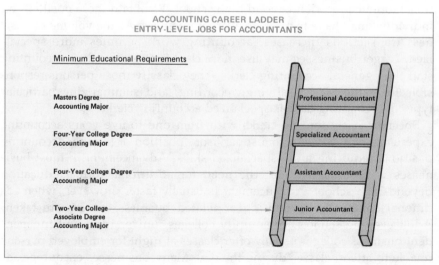

Accounting career ladder entry-level jobs for accountants

To be prepared for an entry-level job as a junior accountant, a person should have completed at least two years of college and received the associate degree. The major emphasis in the two-year college program should be in accounting and business related courses.

To qualify for an entry-level job as an assistant accountant or a specialized accountant, a person should have completed a four-year college degree with a major in accounting. To be prepared for an entry-level job as a professional accountant, a masters degree (usually five years of college) may be required.

Career advancement for accountants. The advancement-level jobs for accountants on the accounting career ladder are shown below.

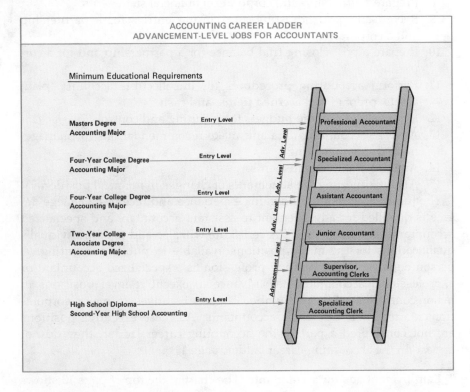

Accounting career ladder advancement-level jobs for accountants

A person with two years of high school accounting plus related business courses has the foundation for starting an accounting career as a specialized accounting clerk. Advancement to the position of junior accountant and assistant accountant is available after gaining considerable accounting experience or on-the-job training.

Parts 3, 7, 9, and 10 of this textbook include those skills required for specialized accounting clerks to advance to the level of junior accountant and assistant accountant. Upon successful completion of these parts, students will be able to:

1. Record and post transactions for starting a partnership and starting a corporation.
2. Record and post transactions for admitting a new partner in a partnership and issuing new stock in a corporation.

3. Record and post transactions for terminating a partnership.
4. Divide partnership and corporation earnings.
5. Prepare a distribution of net income statement for a partnership and a stockholders' equity statement for a corporation.
6. Prepare a trial balance for a partnership and a corporation on a work sheet.
7. Plan adjustments and complete a work sheet for a partnership and a corporation.
8. Prepare partnership and corporation financial statements.
9. Record and post adjusting and closing entries for a partnership and a corporation.
10. Prepare a post-closing trial balance for a partnership and for a corporation.
11. Perform accounting procedures for uncollectible accounts, plant assets, prepaid and accrued items, and cash.
12. Analyze and prepare budgets for planning and control.
13. Analyze accounting data and make recommendations for management decision making.
14. Analyze financial statements.
15. Analyze and prepare statements of changes in financial position.

The junior accountant who gains experience and receives a college degree is qualified for advancement to assistant accountant and specialized accountant. Obtaining the CPA certificate will also add to an individual's qualifications for the many positions available in public accounting. A person entering the accounting profession as a specialized accountant or a professional accountant may advance to executive-level positions in major companies. A large number of top executives in major corporations started their careers as accountants. As these executive positions are not considered a part of the accounting career ladder, they do not appear on the accounting career ladder, page 11.

Employment ads for accountants. The chart at the top of page 13 shows the types of employment ads for accountants that are representative of those appearing in the classified sections of newspapers.

SUMMARY

The entry-level jobs for people preparing for a career in accounting are summarized at the bottom of page 13.

Each entry-level job in the accounting career ladder requires specific skills and abilities. These skills and abilities are directly related to the amount of formal education in accounting an individual has obtained. The more formal education in accounting an individual has completed, the higher the entry-level job will be on the career ladder.

ACCOUNTANT

Degreed accountant with detail experience to take responsibility for accounting department. Excellent opportunity and future. EDP experience a plus, but not required.

Accountant

Accountant with a minimum of 2 years experience in public accounting for 9-person local CPA firm. Must be loyal, conscientious, and dedicated.

ACCOUNTANT

Have immediate opening for a staff accountant with tax background.

Challenging position with diversified growth company. Primary responsibility will be gathering data for financial presentations. Some experience in real estate development preferred.

Accountant

Recently or soon to be degreed individual with 2 or more years experience in standard and job cost related to manufacturing. Must be a self starter willing to work with details and in other accounting areas. Data processing background a plus.

ASSISTANT ACCOUNTANT

Independent worker needed to assist accountant in manufacturing company. Gain experience in all aspects of accounting with emphasis on EDP systems transition and financial analysis. Advancement potential is excellent.

Assistant accountant needed to supervise billing.

Assistant Accountant

Join the largest firm in its industry. You will assist the manager in consolidations, financial statements, and more.

AUDITOR

Auditor to travel. Degree and hospitality experience necessary. Exciting company, benefits, and opportunity for right individual.

JUNIOR ACCOUNTANT

Junior accountant with 2 years bookkeeping experience. Prefer some college accounting. Full benefits including company paid pension plan and profit sharing.

Junior accountant for construction company, fluent in Spanish and English. Minimum 1 year experience. Light secretarial duties required.

Junior Accountant

Junior accountant to maintain and evaluate standard cost systems, and prepare monthly cost analysis. Must have a college degree in accounting and 1 year experience in cost accounting.

Classified ads for accountants

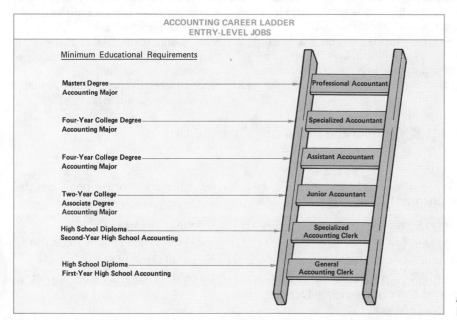

Accounting career ladder entry-level jobs

Using Career Planning Terms

✦ What is the meaning of each of the following?

- accounting clerk
- accountant
- entry-level jobs
- career ladder

- advancement-level jobs
- general accounting clerk
- specialized accounting clerk
- junior accountant

- assistant accountant
- specialized accountant
- professional accountant

Questions for Career Planning

1. What is the first step in acquiring the necessary skills for starting an accounting career?
2. For whom does a person in the governmental accounting area work?
3. For whom does a person in public accounting work?
4. What are some of the duties that a person working in public accounting might be required to perform?
5. For whom does a person in private accounting work?
6. What are the two types of accounting clerks?
7. Why do businesses that employ primarily general accounting clerks also employ a public accountant?
8. Why do businesses that employ specialized accounting clerks also employ their own accountant or a public accountant?
9. What other job title is often given to a purchases and cash payments clerk?
10. What other job title is often given to a sales and cash receipts clerk?
11. How much formal education is required of a person starting an accounting career as a general accounting clerk?
12. How much formal education is required to obtain an entry-level job as a specialized accounting clerk?
13. What career advancement is available to a person who starts employment as a general accounting clerk?
14. What factors help the career advancement of general accounting clerks?
15. Why do larger businesses classify employees responsible for gathering, classifying, recording, and summarizing accounting data by titles other than general accounting clerks?
16. What career advancement is available to a person who starts employment as a specialized accounting clerk?
17. What are the four classifications of accountants?
18. How much formal education is required to obtain an entry-level job as a junior accountant?
19. How much formal education is required to obtain an entry-level job as either an assistant accountant or a specialized accountant?
20. How much formal education is required to obtain an entry-level job as a professional accountant?
21. What career advancement is available to a junior accountant?

Problems for Career Planning

PROBLEM 1-1 Educational planning for entry-level accounting jobs

Listed below are the various levels of education for the accounting positions described in Chapter 1.

a. Masters Degree
   Accounting Major
b. Four-Year College Degree
   Accounting Major
c. Two-Year College Associate Degree
   Accounting Major

d. High School Diploma
   Second-Year High School Accounting
e. High School Diploma
   First-Year High School Accounting

Instructions: ☐ **1.** On a sheet of paper prepare a form similar to the following:

Education	Entry-Level Job
a. Masters Degree, Accounting Major	

☐ **2.** List each level of education given on page 14 on the form.

☐ **3.** Write the name of the entry-level job(s) for each level of education.

PROBLEM 1-2 Advancement-level accounting jobs

Listed below are selected entry-level accounting positions.

a. Specialized accounting clerk   c. Specialized accountant
b. Junior accountant

Instructions: ☐ **1.** On a sheet of paper prepare a form similar to the following:

Entry-Level Jobs	Advancement-Level Jobs
a. Specialized Accounting Clerk	

☐ **2.** List each entry-level job given above on the form.

☐ **3.** Write the names of all advancement-level jobs for each entry-level job (no additional formal education).

PROBLEM 1-3 Analyzing classified want ads

Given below are classified want ads for accounting that appeared in selected newspapers.

a. Accounts receivable clerk. Growing chemical company has opening for person who is looking for a career and wants to grow with us.
b. Excellent opportunity for individual with payroll experience who can work independently. Typing ability and good figure aptitude mandatory, as well as a knowledge of calculators and adding machines.
c. Bookkeeper [general accounting clerk] through trial balance. One person office. Some typewriting. Must be reliable and able to assume responsibility.
d. Full-charge bookkeeper [junior accountant] to handle complete set of books, prepare financial statements and other accounting reports. Must have 3–5 years minimum experience.
e. Auditor to travel. Degree and hospitality experience necessary. Exciting company, benefits and opportunity for right individual.

Instructions: ☐ **1.** For each of the classified ads, answer the following questions:

1. Would the position be considered an entry-level or an advancement-level job?
2. What would be the minimum level of education required of a person to qualify for the position?
3. What related skills or abilities other than accounting are required or desired?

PART 2

GENERAL ACCOUNTING CLERKS

ACCOUNTING PROCEDURES VARY LITTLE. The basic accounting procedures used in various businesses are generally the same regardless of the accounting system used. Some variations in the records may be necessary because of the nature of a specific business. However, the work of a general accounting clerk tends to be the same in all businesses.

MERCHANDISING BUSINESSES SELL GOODS. Many businesses, both large and small, sell goods to customers. Part 2 of this textbook reviews basic accounting records kept by a general accounting clerk for a merchandising business. The records include special journals, a general ledger, and subsidiary ledgers.

GENERAL ACCOUNTING CLERKS RECORD TRANSACTIONS. The general accounting clerk for *Village Gift Shop* records transactions in a four-column general journal and in special journals (sales, purchases, cash receipts, and cash payments). The entries in the journals are posted to a general ledger (using four-column ledger forms) and to an accounts receivable and an accounts payable ledger (using three-column ledger forms). The end-of-fiscal-period work includes the preparation of an eight-column work sheet, an income statement, a capital statement, a balance sheet, and a post-closing trial balance.

Part 2 of this textbook is a general review of accounting procedures learned by students in the first-year study of accounting.

VILLAGE GIFT SHOP
CHART OF ACCOUNTS

Balance Sheet Accounts

(1) ASSETS	Account Number
11 *Current Assets*	
Cash	111
Petty Cash	112
Accounts Receivable	113
Allowance for Uncollectible Accounts	113.1
Notes Receivable	114
Merchandise Inventory	115
Supplies	116
Prepaid Insurance	117
Interest Receivable	118
12 *Plant Assets*	
Equipment	121
Accumulated Depreciation — Equipment	121.1

(2) LIABILITIES	
21 *Current Liabilities*	
Accounts Payable	211
Notes Payable	212
Employees Income Tax Payable — Federal	213
FICA Tax Payable	214
Unemployment Tax Payable — Federal	215
Unemployment Tax Payable — State	216
Sales Tax Payable	217
Interest Payable	218

(3) CAPITAL	
Mildred Gunweld, Capital	311
Mildred Gunweld, Drawing	312
Income Summary	313

Income Statement Accounts

(4) OPERATING REVENUE	Account Number
Sales	411
Sales Returns and Allowances	411.1

(5) COST OF MERCHANDISE	
Purchases	511
Purchases Returns and Allowances	511.1

(6) OPERATING EXPENSES	
Bad Debts Expense	611
Depreciation Expense — Equipment	612
Insurance Expense	613
Miscellaneous Expense	614
Payroll Taxes Expense	615
Rent Expense	616
Salary Expense	617
Supplies Expense	618

(7) OTHER REVENUE	
Interest Income	711

(8) OTHER EXPENSE	
Interest Expense	811

While most charts of accounts have the same general organization, there is no rigid sequence of accounts within the divisions of general ledgers that is considered the one acceptable sequence. Therefore, charts of accounts differ from business to business. The chart of accounts for Village Gift Shop is illustrated above for ready reference in your study of Part 2 of this textbook.

Recording Phase of Accounting

2

A manager needs financial information to make wise decisions, control daily activities, and make plans for future operations of a business. Business financial records are also needed in preparing various tax reports.

Detailed facts of any kind are called data. The recording, sorting, classifying, calculating, summarizing, and reporting of data is called data processing. Processing financial data using pen, ink, and simple office machines is called manual accounting. Processing financial data using specialized accounting machines is called machine accounting. Processing financial data using automated machines is called automated data processing. Automated data processing restricted solely to accounting activities is sometimes known as automated accounting.

Few businesses use only one method of processing data. Even businesses using automated equipment also use some manual and machine methods as part of the total accounting system. Regardless of the method or the equipment used, the basic accounting principles are the same in each system.

SOME BASIC ACCOUNTING CONCEPTS

Two basic accounting principles common to all double-entry accounting systems are: (1) The total value of the things a business owns (the assets) is equal to the total claims against those assets (the equities). The equities are commonly divided into claims by outsiders (liabilities) and claims by the owners (capital). (2) The debits equal the credits in each business transaction.

Fundamental accounting equation

The total value of all things owned by a business is the total value of its assets. Creditors have claims (liabilities) against the value of the business assets for the amount owed to them. The value of assets remaining

19

after the liabilities are deducted is the claim of the owners of the business (capital).

A statement of the relationship between the assets, the liabilities, and the capital of a business is called the fundamental accounting equation. The fundamental accounting equation may be stated as *assets = equities*. The claims against the assets of a business are called equities. However, the equation is usually stated as:

ASSETS = LIABILITIES + CAPITAL

The fundamental accounting equation is the basic concept on which all double-entry accounting systems are built.

Principles of debit and credit

Accounting records show the value and changes in value of each asset and liability, and in the owner's capital. An accounting form used to sort and summarize the changes caused by business transactions is called an account. Terms used by accountants to describe increases and decreases in values recorded in accounts are "debit" and "credit."

The difference between the total debits and credits in an account is called the account balance. Each business transaction causes a change in the balance of two or more accounts. Increases in an account balance are recorded on the balance side of the account. Decreases in an account balance are recorded on the side opposite to the balance side of the account. Therefore, an accountant must know which is the balance side of each account.

There are six *major* kinds of accounts as shown on the chart of accounts, page 18: assets, liabilities, capital, revenue, cost, and expenses. Asset, cost, and expense accounts have *debit* balances. Liability, capital, and revenue accounts have *credit* balances. The chart below summarizes the concepts of debit and credit as applied to account balances.

ACCOUNTS WITH DEBIT BALANCES Asset, Cost, Expense		ACCOUNTS WITH CREDIT BALANCES Liability, Owner's Capital, Revenue	
+ Debit Side	− Credit Side	− Debit Side	+ Credit Side
Balance side Increased on the balance side	Decreased on side opposite to the balance side	Decreased on side opposite to the balance side	Balance side Increased on the balance side

BASIC RECORDS OF TRANSACTIONS

Data about business transactions are found on the original business papers, in journals, and in ledgers.

Source documents

A business paper prepared when a business transaction occurs and from which an entry is made is called a source document. Common source documents include check stubs, receipts, cash register tapes, invoices, and memorandums.

A source document describes in detail the data about a transaction. From the data on the source document, an accounting clerk analyzes the transaction into its debit and credit parts. The data are recorded in a book of original entry. Finally, the source document is filed for future reference.

Journals

The first book in which the records of a business transaction are written is called a journal. Some businesses may use a single journal in which all transactions can be recorded. Other businesses may use two or more journals. Each business plans its journals to fit its own needs.

A journal with two amount columns in which all kinds of entries can be recorded is called a general journal. Although all transactions can be recorded in a general journal, few businesses use only a general journal.

A multicolumn journal in which all transactions of a business can be recorded is called a combination journal. Many small businesses, with only one or two persons doing all of the accounting work, find that the single combination journal is all that is needed. A combination journal has special amount columns for recording the most common business transactions.

A journal in which only one kind of business transaction is recorded is called a special journal. Any business, large or small, may use special journals. When a business uses special journals, the business also uses a general journal for the miscellaneous entries that cannot be recorded in any of the special journals. Sometimes a general journal may have more than two amount columns.

The Village Gift Shop, described in Chapters 2 and 3, uses special journals and a four-column general journal in which to record transactions. The journals kept by the Village Gift Shop's general accounting clerk are:

Purchases journal — for all entries for purchases of merchandise on account.

Sales journal — for all entries for sales of merchandise on account.

Cash payments journal — for all entries involving a payment of cash.

Cash receipts journal — for all entries involving a receipt of cash.

General journal — for all entries that are not to be recorded in a special journal.

These journals are described in detail later in this chapter.

Ledgers

The data recorded in journals are arranged in chronological order according to the date on which the transactions occurred. Periodically data are sorted into accounts to summarize the changes. A group of accounts is called a ledger. A ledger that contains all the accounts needed to prepare financial statements is called a general ledger. The arrangement of accounts in the general ledger of the Village Gift Shop is shown in the chart of accounts, page 18. A ledger that is summarized in a single general ledger account is called a subsidiary ledger. A general ledger account that summarizes a subsidiary ledger is called a controlling account.

The Village Gift Shop has two subsidiary ledgers and two controlling accounts:

Subsidiary Ledgers	Controlling Accounts	Acct. No.
Accounts Receivable Ledger	Accounts Receivable	113
Accounts Payable Ledger	Accounts Payable	211

JOURNALIZING TRANSACTIONS RELATED TO THE PURCHASE OF MERCHANDISE

Merchandise may be purchased for cash or on account. When merchandise is purchased on account, cash payments are made to creditors some time after the date of the purchase. Merchandise that is not satisfactory may be returned for credit. Sometimes a note may be issued to a creditor to obtain an extension of time in which to pay.

Purchase of merchandise for cash

January 3, 1978. Issued a check for cash purchase of merchandise, $213.00. Check No. 102.

Purchases	511
213.00	

Cash	111
	213.00

The cost account **Purchases** is debited and the asset account **Cash** is credited for $213.00.

The entry made by the general accounting clerk for this purchase of merchandise transaction is shown on Line 1 of the cash payments journal below.

					GENERAL		ACCOUNTS PAYABLE DEBIT	CASH CREDIT	
	DATE	ACCOUNT TITLE	CK. NO.	POST. REF.	DEBIT	CREDIT			
1	*1978 Jan. 3*	*Purchases*	*102*		*213 00*			*213 00*	1
2									2
3									3

CASH PAYMENTS JOURNAL — PAGE 23

Entry to record purchase of merchandise for cash

The debit amount, $213.00, is recorded in the General Debit column, and the name of the account, Purchases, is written in the Account Title column. The amount is also written in the Cash Credit column. The name of the credit account, Cash, is not written in the Account Title column because it already appears in the credit column heading.

Purchase of merchandise on account

January 3, 1978. Purchased merchandise on account from Norma's Candle House, $367.25. Purchase Invoice No. 108.

GENERAL LEDGER

Purchases	511
367.25	

Accounts Payable	211
	367.25

ACCOUNTS PAYABLE LEDGER
Norma's Candle House

	367.25

The cost account Purchases is debited and the liability account Accounts Payable is credited for $367.25. The creditor's account, Norma's Candle House, is also credited for the same amount as the controlling account, Accounts Payable.

The entry made by the general accounting clerk for this transaction is shown on Line 1 of the purchases journal below.

	DATE	ACCOUNT CREDITED	PURCH. NO.	POST. REF.	PURCHASES, DR. ACCTS. PAY. CR.	
1	1978 Jan. 3	Norma's Candle House	108		367 25	1
2	17	Odle Company	109		402 75	2
22	31	Total			8799 03	22
23					8799 03	23

PURCHASES JOURNAL   PAGE *18*

Entry to record purchase of merchandise on account

The Village Gift Shop uses a purchases journal with a single special amount column. Any amounts recorded in this single column are both a debit to Purchases and a credit to Accounts Payable. This entry and the account titles are shown by the amount column heading. Because the titles of both accounts appear in the amount column heading, no account titles need to be written in the Account Credited column. However, the name of the subsidiary ledger account, Norma's Candle House, is written in the Account Credited column.

Purchases returns and allowances

Merchandise may be returned to a seller because it is unsatisfactory or is not what was ordered. When merchandise is returned, the seller usually gives credit to the buyer.

January 19, 1978. Returned merchandise to Odle Company, $14.25. Debit Memorandum No. 21.

GENERAL LEDGER

Accounts Payable	211
14.25	

Purchases Returns and Allowances	511.1
	14.25

ACCOUNTS PAYABLE LEDGER

Odle Company

14.25	

The liability account Accounts Payable is debited and the contra account, Purchases Returns and Allowances, is credited for $14.25. The creditor's account is also debited for the same amount as the controlling account.

An account representing a deduction from another general ledger account is called a contra account. **Purchases Returns and Allowances** is a contra account. It represents a deduction from the purchases account. Sometimes a contra cost account is known as a minus cost account.

The Village Gift Shop records most of its transactions in special journals. Only one kind of transaction is recorded in each special journal. A purchases returns and allowances transaction does not belong in any of the special journals used by Village Gift Shop. Therefore, this entry is recorded in a general journal.

The January 19 transaction for purchases returns and allowances is shown on Lines 1–3 of the general journal below. The amount of the debit, $14.25, is written in the Accounts Payable Debit column. The name of the account is shown in the column heading, so the account title is not written in the Account Title column. The name of the subsidiary ledger account, **Odle Company**, *is* written in the Account Title column. The credit amount, $14.25, is written on the next line in the General

GENERAL JOURNAL   PAGE *15*

	ACCOUNTS PAYABLE DEBIT	GENERAL DEBIT	DATE	ACCOUNT TITLE	POST. REF.	GENERAL CREDIT	ACCOUNTS RECEIV. CREDIT	
1	14.25		1978 Jan. 19	Odle Company				1
2				Purchases Ret. + Allow.		14.25		2
3				Debit Memo. No. 21.				3
4	300.00		21	Dixie Supply Co.				4
5				Notes Payable		300.00		5
6				Memorandum No. 32.				6
26		35.00	28	Sales Returns and Allow.				26
27		1.40		Sales Tax Payable				27
28				Cora Rickles			36.40	28
29				Credit Memo. No. 43.				29
30		200.00	31	Notes Receivable				30
31				Gerald Augburn			200.00	31
32				Memorandum No. 36.				32
33		72.68	31	Payroll Taxes Expense				33
34				FICA Tax Payable		47.40		34
35				Unemploy. Tax Pay.-Fed.		3.95		35
36				Unemploy. Tax Pay.-State		21.33		36
37				Memorandum No. 37.				37
38	521.50	725.36	31	Totals		66.21	580.65	38

Four-column general journal

Credit column because there is no special amount column for purchases returns and allowances. The name of the account, Purchases Returns and Allowances, is written in the Account Title column, indented about one-half inch (about 1.3 centimeters). The source document for this transaction, Debit Memo. No. 21, is written on the next line, indented an additional one-half inch (a total of about 2.5 centimeters).

Cash payment on account

January 4, 1978. Issued a check to Party Novelties Company for payment of Purchase Invoice No. 105, $122.04. Check No. 103.

GENERAL LEDGER

Accounts Payable	211
122.04	

Cash	111
	122.04

ACCOUNTS PAYABLE LEDGER

Party Novelties Company

122.04

The liability account Accounts Payable is debited and the asset account Cash is credited for $122.04. The creditor's account, Party Novelties Company, is also debited for the same amount as the controlling account.

The entry for this transaction in the cash payments journal is shown below.

					GENERAL		ACCOUNTS PAYABLE DEBIT	CASH CREDIT	
	DATE	ACCOUNT TITLE	CK. NO.	POST. REF.	DEBIT	CREDIT			
1	*1978 Jan. 3*	*Purchases*	*102*		*213 00*			*213 00*	1
2	*4*	*Party Novelties Company*	*103*				*122 04*	*122 04*	2

CASH PAYMENTS JOURNAL — PAGE *23*

Entry to record cash payment on account

The amount debited to Accounts Payable, $122.04, is recorded in the Accounts Payable Debit column. The credit to Cash is recorded in the Cash Credit column. The names of both accounts appear in the amount column headings. Therefore, no account title is written in the Account Title column. However, the name of the subsidiary ledger account, Party Novelties Company, *is* written in the Account Title column.

Issuing a note payable

Promissory notes that a business issues to creditors are called notes payable. Most notes are payable within a short period of time, usually less than a year. A business issues a note payable (a) to obtain additional time in which to pay an amount owed to a creditor, (b) to borrow money, or (c) to purchase merchandise or some other asset.

When a note payable is issued, the amount charged to Notes Payable is the amount of the note. If there is interest to be paid on a note, the interest is recorded either when actually paid or at the end of the fiscal period.

January 21, 1978. Issued a 30-day, 6% note to Dixie Supply Company for an extension of time to pay, $300.00. Memorandum No. 32.

GENERAL LEDGER

Accounts Payable	211
300.00	

Notes Payable	212
	300.00

ACCOUNTS PAYABLE LEDGER

Dixie Supply Company	
300.00	

The liability account Accounts Payable is debited and the liability account Notes Payable is credited for the amount of the note, $300.00. The subsidiary ledger account, Dixie Supply Company, is also debited for the same amount as the controlling account.

This entry is shown on Lines 4–6 of the general journal, page 24. The debit to Accounts Payable, $300.00, is written in the Accounts Payable Debit column. The name of the creditor, Dixie Supply Company, is written in the Account Title column. On the next line, the credit amount is written in the General Credit column. The name of the general ledger account, Notes Payable, is written in the Account Title column, indented about one-half inch (about 1.3 centimeters). On the next line, indented another one-half inch (a total of about 2.5 centimeters), the name of the source document, Memorandum No. 32, is written to complete the entry.

Paying a note payable

When a note payable is due, the borrower must pay both the amount of the note plus any interest due. On November 6, 1977, Village Gift Shop issued a 6%, 60-day note payable to a creditor. The note is paid on January 5, 1978.

January 5, 1978. Paid a note payable due today, $100.00, plus interest of $1.00; total, $101.00. Check No. 104.

Notes Payable	212
100.00	

Interest Expense	811
1.00	

Cash	111
	101.00

If a business has many notes payable, a notes payable register is usually kept. When this is done, each note is numbered to help keep track of all the notes. Village Gift Shop issues very few notes. For this reason, a notes payable register is not kept and notes are not numbered.

The liability account Notes Payable is debited for the amount of the note, $100.00. The expense account Interest Expense is debited for $1.00. The asset account Cash is credited for the total amount paid, $101.00.

The general accounting clerk records this transaction as shown on Lines 3 and 4 of the cash payments journal below.

					GENERAL		ACCOUNTS PAYABLE DEBIT	CASH CREDIT	
					1	2	3	4	
	DATE	ACCOUNT TITLE	CK. NO.	POST. REF.	DEBIT	CREDIT			
3	5	Notes Payable	104		100 00			101 00	3
4		Interest Expense				1 00			4

CASH PAYMENTS JOURNAL   PAGE 23

Entry to record paying a note payable

The debit to Notes Payable, $100.00, is written in the General Debit column. The name of the general ledger account, Notes Payable, is written in the Account Title column. The debit to Interest Expense, $1.00, is written on the next line in the General Debit column. The name of the account, Interest Expense, is written in the Account Title column. The credit to Cash, $101.00, is written in the Cash Credit column. A bracket is placed in the Date column to show that the data on Lines 3 and 4 belong to the same entry.

JOURNALIZING TRANSACTIONS RELATED TO THE SALE OF MERCHANDISE

Merchandise may be sold for cash or on account. When merchandise is sold on account, cash is received from customers some time after the date of the sale. Any merchandise that is not satisfactory may be returned for credit. Also, a note is sometimes received from a charge customer to obtain an extension of time in which to pay.

Sale of merchandise for cash

January 7, 1978. Cash sales for the week, $2,238.15, plus sales tax of $89.53; total, $2,327.68. Cash Register Tape No. 7.

Cash is increased by the total amount received, Sales Tax Payable is increased by the amount of tax collected, and the revenue account Sales is increased by the amount of merchandise sold. Therefore, Cash is debited for $2,327.68; Sales Tax Payable is credited for $89.53; and Sales is credited for $2,238.15.

The entry made by the general accounting clerk for this transaction is shown on Line 2 of the cash receipts journal below.

Cash	111
2,327.68	

Sales Tax Payable	217
	89.53

Sales	411
	2,238.15

CASH RECEIPTS JOURNAL — PAGE 19

DATE	ACCOUNT TITLE	Doc. No.	Post. Ref.	GENERAL DEBIT	GENERAL CREDIT	SALES CREDIT	SALES TAX PAYABLE CREDIT	ACCOUNTS RECEIVABLE CREDIT	CASH DEBIT	
1978 Jan. 1	Balance on hand, $9,105.02		✓							1
7	✓	37	✓			2238 15	8953		232768	2 ✔
9	Ronald Wynkowski	254						11865	11865	3 ✔
{ 28	Notes Receivable	263			9000				9090	21 ✔
	Interest Income				90					22
31	✓	731	✓			44233	1769		46002	23
31	Totals			9090	1023195	40928	422060	1495278		24
				9090	1023195	40928	422060	1495273		

Cash receipts journal

The debit to Cash, $2,327.68, is written in the Cash Debit column. The credit to Sales Tax Payable, $89.53, is written in the Sales Tax Payable Credit column. The credit to Sales, $2,238.15, is written in the Sales Credit column. The titles of all accounts affected by this transaction are included in the amount column headings. Therefore, a check mark is placed in the Account Title column to show that nothing needs to be written for this transaction. A check mark is placed in the Post. Ref. column to indicate no individual amounts are to be posted from the entry on this line.

Sale of merchandise on account

GENERAL LEDGER

Accounts Receivable	113
65.52	

Sales Tax Payable	217
	2.52

Sales	411
	63.00

ACCOUNTS RECEIVABLE LEDGER

Ronald Wynkowski

65.52	

January 2, 1978. Sold merchandise on account to Ronald Wynkowski, $63.00, plus sales tax, $2.52; total, $65.52. Sales Invoice No. 163.

The asset account Accounts Receivable is debited for $65.52. The liability account Sales Tax Payable is credited for $2.52. The revenue account Sales is credited for $63.00. In the subsidiary ledger, Ronald Wynkowski's account is debited for the same amount as the controlling account.

The general accounting clerk records this transaction as shown on Line 1 of the sales journal below.

		SALES JOURNAL				PAGE *14*	
					1	2	3
	DATE	ACCOUNT DEBITED	SALE NO.	POST. REF.	ACCOUNTS RECEIVABLE DEBIT	SALES TAX PAYABLE CREDIT	SALES CREDIT
1	1978 Jan. 2	Ronald Wynkowski	163		6552	252	6300	1
2	4	Gary Youngblood	164		5163	199	4964	2
28		31 Totals			487658	18756	468902	28
29								29

Sales journal

The debit to Accounts Receivable, $65.52, is written in the Accounts Receivable Debit column. The name of the charge customer, Ronald Wynkowski, is written in the Account Debited column. The credit to Sales Tax Payable, $2.52, is written in the Sales Tax Payable Credit column. The credit to Sales, $63.00, is written in the Sales Credit column.

Not all states and cities charge a sales tax. When this is true, the entry is a debit to Accounts Receivable and a credit to Sales. Under these circumstances, a business may use a sales journal with only one amount column similar to the purchases journal shown on page 23. The single amount column in the sales journal would have the double heading: Accounts Receivable Debit; Sales Credit.

29

Sales returns and allowances

The Village Gift Shop has a policy that customers may return for credit any merchandise that proves unsatisfactory. To summarize data about the total amount of merchandise returned, Village Gift Shop records sales returns and allowances in a contra revenue account titled Sales Returns and Allowances.

January 28, 1978. Granted credit to Cora Rickles for merchandise returned by her, $35.00, plus sales tax on the returned merchandise, $1.40; total $36.40. Credit Memorandum No. 43.

GENERAL LEDGER

Sales Returns and Allowances	411.1
35.00	

Sales Tax Payable	217
1.40	

Accounts Receivable	113
	36.40

ACCOUNTS RECEIVABLE LEDGER
Cora Rickles

	36.40

The contra account, Sales Returns and Allowances, is debited, $35.00, and the liability account Sales Tax Payable is debited, $1.40. The asset account Accounts Receivable is credited, $36.40. The customer's account, Cora Rickles, is also credited for the same amount as the controlling account, $36.40.

The entry to record this transaction is shown on Lines 26–29 of the general journal, page 24.

The debit to Sales Returns and Allowances, $35.00, is written on the first line of the entry in the General Debit column. The name of the account is written in the Account Title column. On the next line, the debit to Sales Tax Payable is written in the General Debit column. The name of the account is written in the Account Title column. On the next line, the credit to Accounts Receivable is written in the Accounts Receivable Credit column. The charge customer's name is written in the Account Title column indented about one-half inch (about 1.3 centimeters). On the next line, the source document, Credit Memo. No. 43, is written in the Account Title column, indented about another one-half inch (a total of about 2.5 centimeters).

> If a cash customer returns merchandise for a cash refund, an entry is made in the cash payments journal. The entry would include a debit to Sales Returns and Allowances, a debit to Sales Tax Payable, and a credit to Cash.

Cash received on account

January 9, 1978. Received cash on account from Ronald Wynkowski, $118.65. Receipt No. 54.

GENERAL LEDGER

Cash	111
118.65	

Accounts Receivable	113
	118.65

ACCOUNTS RECEIVABLE LEDGER
Ronald Wynkowski

	118.65

The asset account Cash is debited and the asset account Accounts Receivable is credited for $118.65. The charge customer's account, Ronald Wynkowski, is also credited for the same amount as the controlling account.

The entry to record this transaction is shown on Line 3 of the cash receipts journal, page 27. The debit to Cash, $118.65, is written in the Cash Debit column. The credit to Accounts Receivable, $118.65, is written in the Accounts Receivable Credit column. The name of the charge customer, Ronald Wynkowski, is written in the Account Title column.

Receiving a note receivable on account

Promissory notes that a business receives are called notes receivable. Except for the accounts affected, recording notes receivable is similar to recording notes payable.

GENERAL LEDGER

Notes Receivable	114
200.00	

Accounts Receivable	113
	200.00

ACCOUNTS RECEIVABLE LEDGER

Gerald Augburn	
	200.00

January 31, 1978. Received a 6%, 60-day note from Gerald Augburn, for an extension of time on his account, $200.00. Memorandum No. 36.

The asset account Notes Receivable is debited and the asset account Accounts Receivable is credited for the amount of the note, $200.00. The charge customer's account is also credited for the same amount as the controlling account.

The entry to record this transaction is shown on Lines 30–32 of the general journal, page 24.

The debit to Notes Receivable, $200.00, is written on the first line in the General Debit column. The name of the account, Notes Receivable, is written in the Account Title column. The credit to Accounts Receivable, $200.00, is written on the next line in the Accounts Receivable Credit column. The name of the charge customer, Gerald Augburn, is written in the Account Title column indented about one-half inch (about 1.3 centimeters). The name of the source document, Memorandum No. 36, is written on the next line in the Account Title column, indented about another one-half inch (a total of about 2.5 centimeters).

Receiving cash for a note receivable

January 28, 1978. Received cash from Darwood Alton for his note receivable, $90.00, plus interest, $0.90; total, $90.90. Receipt No. 63.

Cash	111
90.90	

Interest Income	711
	.90

Notes Receivable	114
	90.00

The asset account Cash is debited for the total received, $90.90. The revenue account Interest Income is credited for the amount of interest received, $0.90. The value of the note, $90.00, is credited to the asset account Notes Receivable.

The entry for this transaction is shown on Lines 21–22 of the cash receipts journal, page 27. The debit to Cash, $90.90, is written on Line 21 in the Cash Debit column.

The credit to Notes Receivable, $90.00, is written on the same line in the General Credit column. The name of the account, Notes Receivable, is written on the same line in the Account Title column. The credit to Interest Income, $0.90, is written on the next line in the General Credit column. The name of the account, Interest Income, is written on the same line in the Account Title column. A bracket is placed in the Date column to show that the data on Lines 21 and 22 are part of the same entry.

CASH PAYMENTS FOR OTHER TRANSACTIONS

A business pays cash for transactions other than payments to creditors for purchases of merchandise on account. Cash may also be paid for such things as expenses, withdrawals by the owner, supplies, and petty cash expenditures.

Cash payment for an expense

January 5, 1978. Paid cash for January rent, $500.00.	Rent Expense	616
Check No. 105.	500.00	
	Cash	111
		500.00

The expense account Rent Expense is debited and the asset account Cash is credited for $500.00.

The general accounting clerk records this transaction as shown on Line 5 of the cash payments journal, below.

CASH PAYMENTS JOURNAL   PAGE 23

				1	2	3	4	
	DATE	ACCOUNT TITLE	CK. NO.	POST. REF.	GENERAL DEBIT	GENERAL CREDIT	ACCOUNTS PAYABLE DEBIT	CASH CREDIT	
1	*1978 Jan. 3*	*Purchases*	102		21300			21300	1
2	4	*Party Novelties Company*	103				12204	12204	2
3	5	*Notes Payable*	104		10000			10100	3
4		*Interest Expense*			100				4
5	5	*Rent Expense*	105		50000			50000	5
6	6	*Mildred Gunweld, Drawing*	106		33500			33500	6
7	6	*Supplies*	107		2500			2500	7
29	31	*Supplies*	128		1500			7000	29
30		*Miscellaneous Expense*			5500				30
31	31	*Salary Expense*	129		79000			63107	31
32		*Empl. Inc. Tax Pay.-Federal*				11153			32
33		*FICA Tax Payable*				4740			33
34	31	*Totals*			107 41 05	317 86	847470	1889789	34
35									35

Cash payments journal

The debit, $500.00, is written in the General Debit column. The name of the account, Rent Expense, is written in the Account Title column. The credit, $500.00, is written on the same line in the Cash Credit column.

Cash withdrawal

From time to time a business owner may take amounts of assets out of a business. Assets taken out of a business by the owner reduce the amount of capital. However, withdrawals are usually recorded in a separate capital account. This separate general ledger capital account enables the owner to see readily how much is withdrawn compared to the income earned by the business.

January 6, 1978. Issued a check to the owner, Mildred Gunweld, for a cash withdrawal, $335.00. Check No. 106.

Mildred Gunweld, Drawing 312
335.00

Cash	111
	335.00

The capital account Mildred Gunweld, Drawing is debited and the asset account Cash is credited for $335.00.

The entry for this transaction is shown on Line 6 of the cash payments journal, page 31. The debit, $335.00, is written in the General Debit column. The name of the account, Mildred Gunweld, Drawing, is written in the Account Title column. The credit, $335.00, is written on the same line in the Cash Credit column.

Cash payment to buy supplies

January 6, 1978. Issued a check for supplies, $25.00. Check No. 107.

Supplies	116
25.00	

Cash	111
	25.00

The asset account Supplies is debited and the asset account Cash is credited for $25.00.

The entry for this transaction is shown on Line 7 of the cash payments journal, page 31. The debit, $25.00, is written in the General Debit column. The name of the account, Supplies, is written in the Account Title column. The credit, $25.00, is written on the same line in the Cash Credit column.

Cash payment to replenish petty cash

Village Gift Shop deposits all cash receipts in the bank at the end of each business day. However, some money is kept on hand for making small payments and for making change at the cash register. An amount of cash kept on hand for making small payments is called a petty cash fund. The Village Gift Shop has a petty cash fund of $200.00.

The petty cash fund should be replenished whenever the amount of the fund becomes low. The Village Gift Shop replenishes petty cash whenever the actual amount of petty cash on hand is $50.00 or below. A check is written for the amount spent. The check is cashed at the bank and the cash placed in the fund. The fund is always replenished at the end of each month regardless of the amount on hand at that time. In this way, all the expenditures are recorded each month.

January 31, 1978. Issued a check to replenish the petty cash fund. Charge the following accounts: Supplies, $15.00; Miscellaneous Expense, $55.00; total, $70.00. Check No. 128.

Supplies is debited for $15.00; Miscellaneous Expense is debited for $55.00; and Cash is credited for $70.00. When the amount, $70.00, is placed in the petty cash fund, it will bring the fund back up to the established amount, $200.00.

The entry for this transaction is shown on Lines 29–30 of the cash payments journal, page 31. The debit, $15.00, is written in the General Debit column, and Supplies is written in the Account Title column. The debit, $55.00, is written on the next line in the General Debit column, and Miscellaneous Supplies is written in the Account Title column. The credit, $70.00, is written in the Cash Credit column. A bracket is placed in the Date column to show that Lines 29 and 30 are part of the same entry.

Supplies	116
15.00	

Miscellaneous Expense	614
55.00	

Cash	111
	70.00

COMPLETING JOURNALS AT THE END OF THE MONTH

At the end of a month, all journals are footed, proved, and ruled to prepare them for posting. In addition, cash is proved.

Footing, proving, and ruling special journals

The general accounting clerk foots and rules the purchases journal as shown on page 23. Because there is only one amount column, the single total represents both a debit to Purchases and a credit to Accounts Payable. The check for equality of debits and credits is to read carefully the amount column to assure that the total is correct.

The cash payments journal, page 31, has been footed and ruled. To check the equality of debits and credits, the sum of the debit totals is compared to the sum of the credit totals:

Total, General Debit column..................................	$10,741.05	
Total, General Credit column...............................		$ 317.86
Total, Accounts Payable Debit column....................	8,474.70	
Total, Cash Credit column		18,897.89
Sum of Debits and Credits....................................	$19,215.75	$19,215.75

The sum of the debit column totals is the same as the sum of the credit column totals, $19,215.75. The cash payments journal is proved.

The sales journal, page 28, the cash receipts journal, page 27, and the general journal, page 24, are also shown after being footed and ruled. These three journals are proved in the same way described above for the cash payments journal.

Proving cash

Determining that the amount of cash on hand agrees with the amount of cash shown in the accounting records is called proving cash. The procedure used by the general accounting clerk to prove cash is:

Balance of cash on hand, beginning of month
(Shown on Line 1 of cash receipts journal, page 27).............. $ 9,105.02
Plus, cash received
(Total of Cash Debit column, Line 24, cash receipts journal,
page 27) 14,952.73
Equals a total.. $24,057.75
Minus cash paid
(Total of Cash Credit column, Line 34, cash payments journal,
page 31) 18,897.89
Equals, balance of cash on hand, end of month...................... $ 5,159.86

The cash balance figured above, $5,159.86, is the same as shown on the last used check stub of the checkbook for the Village Gift Shop. When these two balances agree, cash is proved.

POSTING TO THE LEDGERS

Transferring entries in journals to accounts in ledgers is called posting. Individual amounts are posted from journals periodically. The Village Gift Shop posts individual items at least once each week. Totals of amount columns in journals are posted at the end of each month.

The Village Gift Shop uses a four-column account form in its general ledger. The account form is shown on page 35. The business uses a three-column account form for its subsidiary ledgers. The account form for the accounts payable ledger is shown on page 35. Because the account form shown is for use in an accounts payable ledger, it has a Credit Balance column. The same account form in an accounts receivable ledger has a Debit Balance column.

Posting individual items from journals to ledgers

All amounts in General Debit and General Credit columns in any journal are posted individually to the accounts named in the Account Title column. For example, the illustration on the next page shows the posting of Line 1 of the cash payments journal.

After the data from Line 1 of the journal shown on page 35 are posted, the account number, 511, is written in the Post. Ref. column of the journal. This last step provides a means of tracing the posting to the ledger, and also provides a check that the data on the line have been posted.

All amounts in special amount columns for accounts payable are posted individually to the creditors' accounts in the accounts payable

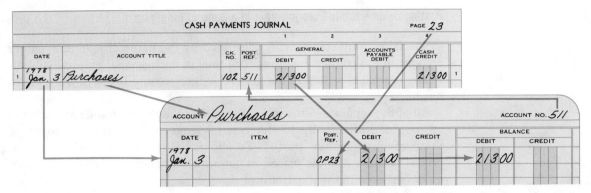

Posting individual items from the cash
payments journal to the general ledger

subsidiary ledger. For example, Line 1 of the general journal is shown
below posted to a creditor's account in the accounts payable ledger.

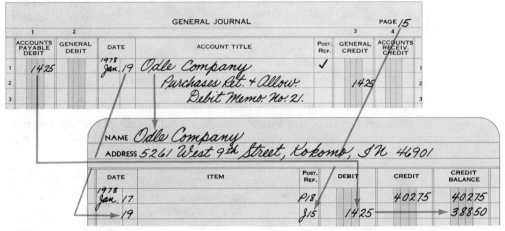

Posting individual items from the general journal
to the accounts payable ledger

The amount is not posted from the Accounts Payable Debit column of
the general journal to the controlling account, Accounts Payable, in the
general ledger. The amounts are posted to this account as a column total
at the end of a month. Posting totals is described later in this chapter.

All amounts in special amount columns for accounts receivable are
posted individually to charge customers' accounts in the accounts receivable subsidiary ledger.

To keep the amounts in order by date in the accounts, the general
accounting clerk posts individually from the journals in the following
order: sales journal, purchases journal, general journal, cash receipts
journal, and cash payments journal. Individual items are usually posted
before the journals are ruled at the end of the month. The Village Gift
Shop posts individual items once a week. However, other businesses,
with many more transactions, may post daily.

Posting column totals from journals to a general ledger

Special amount columns are identified by the name of a general ledger account in the column heading. The total of each special amount column in any journal is posted to the general ledger account listed in the column heading.

All of the separate items in a General Debit or a General Credit column are posted individually to the general ledger. Therefore, the totals of these columns are not posted. To show that the column totals are not posted, a check mark is placed in parentheses below the total. This check mark is shown in the illustration below.

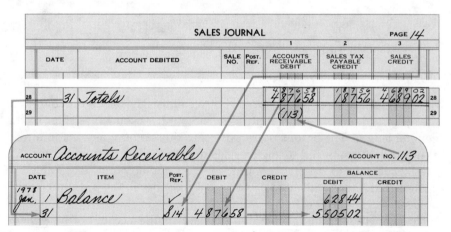

Four-column general journal totaled, ruled, and posted

Totals of special amount columns in any journal *are* posted to the accounts listed in the column headings. The total of one of the sales journal special amount columns, Accounts Receivable Debit, is shown below posted to the accounts receivable account.

Posting column totals from sales journal to general ledger

Posting of totals from all journals follows the same procedures as described for the Accounts Receivable Debit column of the sales journal. The totals of special amount columns are posted in the same order as for individual item posting: sales journal, purchases journal, general journal, cash receipts journal, and cash payments journal.

Proving the accuracy of posting to the subsidiary ledgers

The account balances of all accounts in a subsidiary ledger are listed and totaled. The total of this list is compared to the balance of the controlling account in the general ledger. A list of the balance due from each charge customer and the total due from all charge customers is called a schedule of accounts receivable. The schedule of accounts receivable prepared on January 31, 1978, is shown below.

Village Gift Shop Schedule of Accounts Receivable January 31, 1978		
Darwood Alton	4345	
Mary Cassidy	10141	
Richard Mullins	38194	
Cora Rickles	21945	
Ronald Wrynkowski	2520	
Gary Youngblood	13232	
Total Accounts Receivable		90377

Schedule of accounts receivable

The accounts receivable ledger also contains an account for Gerald Augburn. The account balance was zero on January 31, 1978. Therefore, the account is not listed on the schedule of accounts receivable.

A list of the balance owed to each creditor and the total owed to all creditors is called a schedule of accounts payable. The schedule of accounts payable is prepared from data in the accounts payable subsidiary ledger. The schedule of accounts payable prepared by the general accounting clerk on January 31, 1978, is shown below.

Village Gift Shop Schedule of Accounts Payable January 31, 1978		
Alberta's Leather Goods	16146	
Franklin Company	13900	
Newman Card Company	18000	
Norma's Candle House	27573	
Odle Company	18850	
Party Novelties Company	16731	
Total Accounts Payable		111200

Schedule of accounts payable

The accounts payable subsidiary ledger also contains an account for Dixie Supply Company. However, the balance of this creditor's account on January 31, 1978, was zero. Therefore, the account is not listed on the schedule of accounts payable.

The balances of the general ledger controlling accounts are compared with the totals on the schedules. The two amounts must be the same. The balance of the accounts receivable account is $903.77 which is the same as the total on the schedule. The posting to the accounts receivable ledger is proved to be in balance. The balance of the controlling account, Accounts Payable, is $1,112.00 which is the same as the total on the schedule of accounts payable. The posting to the accounts payable ledger is proved to be in balance.

Proving the accuracy of posting to the general ledger

If the equality of debits and credits is maintained in the journals, and if the posting is done correctly, debits will equal credits in the general ledger accounts. The proof of the equality of the debits and the credits in the general ledger is called a trial balance.

A trial balance may be prepared in many ways. Three of these ways are: (1) *On an adding machine*. All the debit account balances are added and all the credit account balances are added. The total of the debit balances must equal the total of the credit balances. (2) *On a separate trial balance form*. A list is prepared of all the general account titles and account balances, with the debit balances in one column and the credit balances in another column. The two columns are added, and the totals must be the same. (3) *On a work sheet*. Using the first two amount columns on a work sheet, a list is prepared similar to the one described in (2) above. The totals of the two columns must be the same.

The general accounting clerk for the Village Gift Shop uses an adding machine to prepare an informal trial balance on adding machine tape. If the tape totals show that the debit balances equal the credit balances, a trial balance is prepared on a work sheet as shown on the next page.

The trial balance prepared on a work sheet for Village Gift Shop shows that the debit balances and the credit balances both total $81,973.01. The general ledger is proved because the debits equal the credits in the ledger. Therefore, the posting is assumed to be correct.

Using Business Terms

✦ What is the meaning of each of the following?

- data
- data processing
- manual accounting
- machine accounting
- automated data processing
- fundamental accounting equation
- equities
- account
- account balance

- source document
- journal
- general journal
- combination journal
- special journal
- ledger
- general ledger
- subsidiary ledger
- controlling account

- contra account
- notes payable
- notes receivable
- petty cash fund
- proving cash
- posting
- schedule of accounts receivable
- schedule of accounts payable
- trial balance

Village Gift Shop
Work Sheet
For Month Ended January 31, 1978

	ACCT. NO.	TRIAL BALANCE		ADJUSTMENTS		INCOME STATEMENT		BALANCE SHEET	
		DEBIT	CREDIT	DEBIT	CREDIT	DEBIT	CREDIT	DEBIT	CREDIT
1 Cash	111	515986							
2 Petty Cash	112	20000							
3 Accounts Receivable	113	90377							
4 Allow. for Uncoll. Acct.	113.1		7940						
5 Notes Receivable	114	55000							
6 Merchandise Inventory	115	3658500							
7 Supplies	116	58700							
8 Prepaid Insurance	117	37290							
9 Interest Receivable	118								
10 Equipment	121	480000							
11 Accum. Depr.- Equip.	121.1		115400						
12 Accounts Payable	211		111200						
13 Notes Payable	212		45000						
14 Emp. Inc. Tax Pay.- Fed.	213		22306						
15 FICA Tax Payable	214		18960						
16 Unempl. Tax Pay.- Fed.	215		790						
17 Unempl. Tax Pay. State	216		4266						
18 Sales Tax Payable	217		58561						
19 Interest Payable	218								
20 Mildred Gunweld, Cap.	311		4309471						
21 Mildred Gunweld, Draw.	312	67000							
22 Income Summary	313								
23 Sales	411		3492097						
24 Sales Returns + Allow.	411.1	36578							
25 Purchases	511	2936403							
26 Purchases Ret. + Allow.	511.1		11220						
27 Bad Debts Expense	611								
28 Depr. Exp.- Equipment	612								
29 Insurance Expense	613								
30 Miscellaneous Exp.	614	18831							
31 Payroll Taxes Expense	615	14536							
32 Rent Expense	616	50000							
33 Salary Expense	617	158000							
34 Supplies Expense	618								
35 Interest Income	711		90						
36 Interest Expense	811	100							
37		8197301	8197301						

Trial balance recorded on a work sheet

1. Why does the manager of a business need detailed financial information?
2. How is the accounting equation usually stated?
3. What kind of account balance do each of the following normally have: Assets? Liabilities? Capital?
4. What kind of account balance do each of the following normally have: Costs? Expenses? Revenues?
5. The account balances for which kinds of accounts normally are increased on the debit side?

6. The account balances for which kinds of accounts normally are decreased on the debit side?

7. What kind of transactions are recorded in each of the following journals? Purchases journal? Sales journal? Cash payments journal? Cash receipts journal? General journal?

8. The Village Gift Shop uses two subsidiary ledgers. What are the names of each of these ledgers and the title of each controlling account?

9. In the entry, page 22, to record the cash purchase of merchandise, why is the account title "Purchases" written in the Account Title column, but the account title "Cash" is not?

10. In the entry, page 26, to record the payment of a note payable, why is a bracket placed in the Date column?

11. In the entry for January 7, Line 2 of the cash receipts journal, page 27, why is a check mark placed in the Account Title column?

12. How is cash proved?

13. From what amount columns in any journal are individual items posted separately?

14. For what amount columns in any journal are column totals posted?

15. How is the accuracy of posting to subsidiary ledgers proved?

16. How is the accuracy of posting to the general ledger proved?

Cases for Management Decision

CASE 1 Antonio Paras plans to open a roadside ice cream business this summer. For his accounting system he plans to use special journals similar to those described in Chapter 2. However, he does *not* plan to use a general journal. He says that the cash payments journal has both a general debit and a general credit column and can be used to record any entry normally placed in a general journal. His wife, Carmen, believes that he still needs to use a general journal. With whom do you agree? Explain why.

CASE 2 In his business, Mr. Lem Chang collects a state sales tax for all merchandise sold. When recording the sale, Mr. Chang journalizes only the amount for the merchandise sold. He places the amount of sales tax collected in a special box next to the cash register. At the end of the day, when depositing cash receipts, Mr. Chang deposits in a special checking account the amount collected for sales tax. When he must pay this amount to the state, he writes a check on the special checking account. Do you agree with his methods of handling sales tax? Explain your answer.

Processing Business Data: Journals, Ledgers, and Trial Balance

SCOPE OF PROJECT 1, PARTS A AND B

Project 1 presents the accounting cycle for a small merchandising business. The project is divided into two parts:

PART A, following Chapter 2, includes journalizing, posting, and preparing a trial balance.

PART B, following Chapter 3, includes completing a work sheet, preparing financial statements, recording and posting adjusting and closing entries, and preparing a post-closing trial balance.

Project 1 includes the accounting work for a single month, December of the current year. The fiscal year for the business is January 1 to December 31. During the fiscal year, statements are prepared monthly. On December 31, the end of the fiscal year, the books are closed and the financial statements are prepared for the year.

THE BUSINESS

Lori Del Bianco owns and manages a retail book store called Discount-Books. You are the general accounting clerk employed by the business. Most sales are for cash, but a few sales are made to charge customers. All sales are subject to a 5% sales tax collected from customers by the business for payment to the state.

Books of account

The journals used by Discount-Books are: a purchases journal similar to the one shown on page 23; a sales journal, page 28; a cash payments journal, page 31; a cash receipts journal, page 27; and a general journal, page 24.

The ledgers used by Discount-Books are: a general ledger, an accounts receivable ledger, and an accounts payable ledger.

In the working papers that accompany this text, the accounts in ledgers are opened and account balances are entered for all three ledgers. If you are using the working papers, skip Instructions 1, 2, and 3 that follow. **41**

Opening accounts in the general ledger

Instructions: 1. Open the accounts given below in the general ledger of Discount-Books. No entries have been made in the merchandise inventory account or the capital account during the first eleven months of the year. Therefore, date the balances of these two accounts January 1 of the current year. Date the balances of the other accounts December 1 of the current year.

Account Titles	Acct. No.	Debit Balances	Credit Balances
Cash	111	$ 2,965.05	
Petty Cash	112	200.00	
Accounts Receivable	113	636.47	
Allowance for Uncollectible Accounts	113.1		$ 18.73
Notes Receivable	114	550.00	
Merchandise Inventory	115	26,292.00	
Supplies	116	721.98	
Prepaid Insurance	117	784.00	
Interest Receivable	118	——	
Store Equipment	131	5,100.00	
Accumulated Depreciation — Store Equipment	131.1		343.00
Accounts Payable	211		4,015.73
Notes Payable	212		300.00
Employees Income Tax Payable — Federal	213		67.20
FICA Tax Payable	214		34.65
Unemployment Tax Payable — Federal	215		5.78
Unemployment Tax Payable — State	216		31.19
Sales Tax Payable	217		290.58
Interest Payable	218		——
Lori Del Bianco, Capital	311		26,936.27
Lori Del Bianco, Drawing	312	5,900.00	
Income Summary	313	——	
Sales	411		69,741.46
Sales Returns and Allowances	411.1	912.90	
Purchases	511	38,177.62	
Purchases Returns and Allowances	511.1		915.32
Bad Debts Expense	611	——	
Depreciation Expense — Store Equipment	612	——	
Insurance Expense	613	——	
Miscellaneous Expense	614	836.62	
Payroll Taxes Expense	615	1,368.27	
Rent Expense	616	4,400.00	
Salary Expense	617	13,860.00	
Supplies Expense	618	——	
Interest Income	711		11.00
Interest Expense	811	6.00	

Opening customers' accounts in the accounts receivable ledger

Instructions: 2. Open accounts in the accounts receivable ledger for Discount-Books frcm the list below. Record the balances for those accounts where given. Date the balances December 1 of the current year.

Customers' Names and Addresses	Account Balances
Sarah Billings, 3132 Stine Road, Camden, NJ 08104............................	$ 51.50
Eva Browning, 3761 Sutton Road, Camden, NJ 08104	141.80
Edgar Cziraky, 4229 Windway Drive, Camden, NJ 08105..................	42.00
Eli Epstein, 214 Downing Place, Camden, NJ 08103	——
Ramona Lopez, 620 Popular Street, Camden, NJ 08104.....................	119.45
Roman Lopez, 6924 Wilson Avenue, Camden, NJ 08103	74.35
Goldie Masters, 5721 Wilton Street, Camden, NJ 08105....................	207.37
Paul Richardson, 4907 Wentworth Street, Camden, NJ 08105.............	——

Opening creditors' accounts in the accounts payable ledger

Instructions: 3. Open accounts in the accounts payable ledger for Discount-Books from the list below. Record the balances for those accounts where given. Date the balances December 1 of the current year.

Creditors' Names and Addresses	Account Balances
Booker Press, Inc., 611 Amsterdam Avenue, New York, NY 10024	$ 893.00
Dennison Supply Co., 694 Everest Street, Camden, NJ 08102.............	184.00
Eastman Press, 719 West 5th Street, New Rochelle, NY 10802	718.00
Holmes Publishing Co., 6949 Elton Drive, Chicago, IL 60644.............	1,451.73
Peterson Books, 57 Union Square West, New York, NY 10003	——
Sutton's, Inc., 2494 London Road, New Rochelle, NY 10804..............	769.00

Recording transactions

Instructions: 4. Record the following transactions for December of the current year. Use the following journals with the page numbers as shown: purchases journal, page 12; sales journal, page 16; cash payments journal, page 14; cash receipts journal, page 15; and general journal, page 7.

In the following transactions, the source documents have been abbreviated as: check, Ck; memorandum, M; purchase invoice, P; receipt, R; sales invoice, S; cash register tape, T; credit memo, CM; debit memo, DM.

December   1. Record the memorandum entry for the beginning cash balance, $2,965.05.

2. Paid December rent, $400.00. Ck258.

2. Received on account from Edgar Cziraky, $42.00. R199.

December   **3.** Received from Ms. Del Bianco, the owner, an additional investment in the business, $1,000.00. R200.
    4. Paid on account to Holmes Publishing Co., $1,451.73. Ck259.
    5. Sold merchandise on account to Eli Epstein, $23.92, plus sales tax, $1.20. S190.
    5. Paid on account to Dennison Supply Co., $184.00. Ck260.
    6. Purchased merchandise on account from Peterson Books, $963.00. P213.
    6. Received on account from Goldie Masters, $207.37. R201.
    7. Received for cash sales, $1,112.50, including $1,059.52 for merchandise and $52.98 sales tax. T7.

Posting: Post each amount that is to be posted individually. (Items in the Accounts Receivable, Accounts Payable, and General columns of any of the five journals. Column totals are not posted until the end of the month.) Post from the journals in the following order: sales journal, purchases journal, general journal, cash receipts journal, and cash payments journal.

December   **9.** Paid to the Mutual Home Bank (a federal government depository) $101.85 for employees income tax payable, $67.20, and FICA tax payable, $34.65. Ck261.
    9. Paid state division of taxes for sales tax payable, $290.58. Ck262.
    10. Paid Bassett Brothers Company for supplies bought for cash, $26.50. Ck263.
    10. Paid for a note payable due this date, $75.74, including $75.00 for the note and $0.74 for interest. Ck264.
    11. Paid amount owed to Eastman Press, $718.00. Ck265.
    11. Received on account from Sarah Billings, $51.50. R202.
    12. Issued a credit memo to Eli Epstein for merchandise returned by him, $5.00, plus sales tax, $0.25, for a total of $5.25. CM33.
    13. Sold merchandise on account to Paul Richardson, $46.75, plus sales tax, $2.34, for a total of $49.09. S191.
    13. Paid Settles' News Company for cash purchase of merchandise, $174.57. Ck266.
    14. Received for cash sales of merchandise, $1,351.70, including $1,287.33 for merchandise plus $64.37 sales tax. T14.

Posting: Post items that are to be posted individually from the five journals.

December   **16.** Paid amount owed to Peterson Books, $963.00. Ck267.
    17. Purchased merchandise on account from Sutton's, Inc., $359.55. P214.
    17. Received on account from Ramona Lopez, $119.45. R203.
    17. Sold merchandise on account to Sarah Billings, $20.75, plus sales tax, $1.04, for a total of $21.79. S192.
    18. Paid *Newark Evening Globe* for newspaper advertising, $50.00. Ck268.
    19. Sold merchandise on account to Goldie Masters, $16.00, plus sales tax, $0.80, for a total of $16.80. S193.
    20. Issued a debit memo to Sutton's, Inc., for merchandise returned to them, $23.75. DM49.
    21. Received a 60-day, 6% note from Eva Browning to apply on account, $141.80. M22.

December 21. Received for cash sales of merchandise, $1,070.79, including $1,019.80 for merchandise and $50.99 for sales tax. T21.

Posting: Post the items that are to be posted individually.

December 23. Sold merchandise on account to Edgar Cziraky, $58.00, plus sales tax, $2.90, for a total of $60.90. S194.
   24. Sold merchandise on account to Paul Richardson, $13.60, plus sales tax of $0.68, for a total of $14.28. S195.
   27. Issued a 4%, 90-day note to Booker Press in payment of the amount owed to them, $893.00. M23.
   27. Purchased merchandise on account from Holmes Publishing Co., $349.66. P215.
   27. Paid amount owed to Sutton's, Inc., $769.00. Ck269.
   28. Received for cash sales of merchandise, $1,297.38, including $1,235.60 for merchandise plus $61.78 sales tax. T28.
   30. Paid Ms. Del Bianco, owner, for personal use, $300.00. Ck270.
   30. Paid Bell Telephone Company for telephone service, $44.46. Ck271.
   30. Purchased merchandise on account from Eastman Press, $678.00. P216.
   31. Paid City Gas and Electric Company for electric service, $165.01. Ck272.
   31. Paid monthly payroll, $1,008.00, including salary expense, $1,260.00, less deductions for: employees income tax, $176.40, and FICA tax, $75.60. Ck273.

Record this payroll entry in the cash payments journal as follows:

	DATE	ACCOUNT TITLE	CK. NO.	POST. REF.	GENERAL DEBIT	GENERAL CREDIT	ACCOUNTS PAYABLE DEBIT	CASH CREDIT	
		CASH PAYMENTS JOURNAL			1	2	3	PAGE 14	
								4	
18	31 Salary Expense		273		126000			100800	18
19		Empl. Inc. Tax Pay. - Federal					17640		19
20		FICA Tax Payable					7560		20
21									21

   31. Record employer's payroll taxes on the December 31 payroll: FICA tax, $75.60; federal unemployment tax, $6.30; and state unemployment tax, $34.02. M24.

Record this entry in the general journal as follows:

	ACCOUNTS PAYABLE DEBIT	GENERAL DEBIT	DATE	ACCOUNT TITLE	POST. REF.	GENERAL CREDIT	ACCOUNTS RECEIV. CREDIT	
	1	2		GENERAL JOURNAL		3	PAGE 7	
							4	
14		11592	31	Payroll Taxes Expense				14
15				FICA Tax Payable		7560		15
16				Unempl. Tax Pay. - Fed.		630		16
17				Unempl. Tax Pay. - State		3402		17
18				Memorandum No. 24				18
19								19

December 31. Paid a refund to a cash customer who returned merchandise: Debit Sales Returns and Allowances, $15.00; debit Sales Tax Payable, $0.75; and credit Cash, $15.75. Ck274.
   31. Replenished petty cash: Supplies, $19.00; Miscellaneous Expense, $24.00. Ck275.
   31. Received for cash sales of merchandise, $241.76, including $230.25 for merchandise plus $11.51 sales tax. T31.

Posting: Post the items that are to be posted individually.

Completing the journals

Instructions: 5. Foot the amount columns of all the journals. Prove the equality of debits and credits in the journals.

   6. Prove cash. The checkbook balance is $2,678.31.

   7. Total and rule the five journals.

Complete the posting from the journals

Instructions: 8. Post the totals of all amount columns that are to be posted. Post the journals in this order: sales journal, purchases journal, general journal, cash receipts journal, and cash payments journal.

Preparing schedules of subsidiary ledgers

Instructions: 9. Prepare a schedule of accounts receivable. Compare the total of the schedule with the balance of the controlling account, Accounts Receivable. The two amounts must be the same.

   10. Prepare a schedule of accounts payable. Compare the total of the schedule with the balance of the controlling account, Accounts Payable. The two amounts must be the same.

Preparing a trial balance

Instructions: 11. Prepare a trial balance of the general ledger accounts. Prepare the trial balance in the Trial Balance columns of a work sheet. List all the accounts in the general ledger whether the accounts have balances or not.

   If you are using the working papers accompanying this text, the account titles and account numbers have already been entered on the work sheet for you. You have only to record the account balances from the general ledger.

   The five journals, the three ledgers, and the trial balance prepared in Part A of Project 1 are needed to complete Part B of Project 1. Part B is at the end of Chapter 3.

Summarizing and Reporting Phase of Accounting

The ledgers of a business contain valuable financial data that are considered by the owners in making business decisions. To help owners make decisions, accountants periodically summarize and report financial data to the owners.

The length of time for which an analysis of business operations is made is called a fiscal period. Usually the fiscal period is twelve months long. However, it may be six months, three months, or only one month long. The length of a fiscal period depends on how often a specific business needs to analyze its accounting data.

For tax purposes, businesses must always report financial data for a fiscal year. Many businesses begin the tax fiscal period on January 1 of each year. Other businesses may begin the fiscal year on the first day of another month. This is done so that the end-of-year work can be completed during a period of little business activity. However, once a business has selected the beginning date of a tax fiscal period, that period may not be changed in succeeding years without permission from the Internal Revenue Service.

WORK SHEET

Reports of a business should be planned before they are prepared in final form. An analysis paper on which the financial condition of a business is conveniently summarized is called a work sheet. The work sheet of the Village Gift Shop for the month ended January 31, 1978, is shown on page 48.

Trial balance columns of a work sheet

The trial balance is prepared from data in the general ledger accounts. The general accounting clerk lists all general ledger accounts on the work sheet in the order in which they appear in the general ledger. The account balances are written in the Trial Balance Debit and Credit columns. The equality of debits and credits is proved by adding the two Trial Balance columns.

The procedure for preparing a trial balance for the Village Gift Shop is described in detail in Chapter 2.

Village Gift Shop
Work Sheet
For Month Ended January 31, 1978

#	ACCOUNT TITLE	ACCT. NO.	TRIAL BALANCE DEBIT	TRIAL BALANCE CREDIT	ADJUSTMENTS DEBIT	ADJUSTMENTS CREDIT	INCOME STATEMENT DEBIT	INCOME STATEMENT CREDIT	BALANCE SHEET DEBIT	BALANCE SHEET CREDIT
1	Cash	111	515986						515986	
2	Petty Cash	112	20000						20000	
3	Accounts Receivable	113	90377						90377	
4	Allow. for Uncoll. Acct.	113.1		7940		(a) 2594				10534
5	Notes Receivable	114	55000						55000	
6	Merchandise Inventory	115	3658500		(b) 3505600	(b) 3658500			3505600	
7	Supplies	116	58700			(c) 32720			25980	
8	Prepaid Insurance	117	37290			(d) 24521			12769	
9	Interest Receivable	118			(g) 475				475	
10	Equipment	121	480000						480000	
11	Accum. Depr.-Equip.	121.1		115400		(f) 5700				121100
12	Accounts Payable	211		111200						111200
13	Notes Payable	212		45000						45000
14	Emp. Inc. Tax Pay.-Fed.	213		22306						22306
15	FICA Tax Payable	214		18960						18960
16	Unempl. Tax Pay.-Fed.	215		790						790
17	Unempl. Tax Pay. State	216		4266						4266
18	Sales Tax Payable	217		58561						58561
19	Interest Payable	218				(h) 225				225
20	Mildred Gunweld, Cap.	311		4309471						4309471
21	Mildred Gunweld, Draw.	312	67000						67000	
22	Income Summary	313			(b) 3658500	(a) 3505600	3658500	3505600		
23	Sales	411		3492097				3492097		
24	Sales Returns + Allow.	411.1	36578				36578			
25	Purchases	511	2936403				2936403			
26	Purchases Ret. + Allow.	511.1		11220				11220		
27	Bad Debts Expense	611			(a) 2594		2594			
28	Depr. Exp.-Equipment	612			(f) 5700		5700			
29	Insurance Expense	613			(d) 24521		24521			
30	Miscellaneous Exp.	614	18831				18831			
31	Payroll Taxes Expense	615	14536				14536			
32	Rent Expense	616	50000				50000			
33	Salary Expense	617	158000				158000			
34	Supplies Expense	618			(c) 32720		32720			
35	Interest Income	711		90		(g) 475		565		
36	Interest Expense	811	100		(h) 225		325			
37			8197301	8197301	7230335	7230335	6938708	7009482	4773187	4702413
38	Net Income						70774			70774
39							7009482	7009482	4773187	4773187

Work sheet

Adjustments columns of the work sheet

At the end of a fiscal period, certain general ledger accounts need to be brought up-to-date. Before journal entries are made to bring accounts up-to-date, adjustments are planned in the Adjustments columns of a work sheet. Each adjustment has a debit part and a credit part. Therefore, two or more accounts are affected by each adjustment.

Adjustment for bad debts expense. Occasionally, merchandise will be sold on account to a customer who later is unable to pay the amount owed. Amounts that cannot be collected from charge customers are an expense of a business. The Village Gift Shop has found that approximately 0.6% of its total charge sales will not be collected.

The total charge sales for January, 1978, were $4,323.24. The estimated bad debts expense for January is $25.94 ($4,323.24 × .006 = $25.94).

Bad Debts Expense is debited for the additional estimated amount of bad debts for January. Allowance for Uncollectible Accounts is credited for the same amount.

Bad Debts Expense	611
25.94	

Allowance for Uncollectible Accounts is a contra asset account. The account represents a deduction from the asset account Accounts Receivable. The balance of Allowance for Uncollectible Accounts represents the total estimated

Allowance for Uncollectible Accounts	113.1
	25.94

amount that the business believes will not be collected from charge customers. This estimated amount cannot be deducted from the balance of Accounts Receivable until it is known which customer will not pay. Therefore, the estimated amount is recorded in a separate account.

The adjustment for bad debts expense is shown on the work sheet, page 48, Lines 4 and 27.

> When the adjustment is recorded in the Adjustments columns of the work sheet, a small letter (a) is written before both amounts. The small letter helps in locating the two parts of the entry. Similar identification is made for the other adjustments on the work sheet, using succeeding letters of the alphabet. The adjustments are assigned the small letters in the same order they are planned on the work sheet.

Adjustment for beginning merchandise inventory. The merchandise inventory account has a debit balance of $36,585.00, as shown on the trial balance, page 48. This balance is the value of the inventory at the beginning of the month. During the month some of this inventory is sold, and additional merchandise is purchased. At the end of January, 1978, Village Gift Shop determines that its ending merchandise inventory balance is $35,056.00. This is determined by making an actual count of the merchandise still on hand.

Income Summary	313
36,585.00	

To remove the old beginning inventory from Merchandise Inventory, the account is credited for $36,585.00. Income Summary is debited for $36,585.00.

Merchandise Inventory	115
	36,585.00

The income summary account is a temporary capital account. The account is used only at the end of a fiscal period. This account provides a means of summarizing all costs, expenses, and revenues in the ledger.

The adjustment for beginning merchandise inventory is shown on the work sheet, page 48, Lines 6 and 22. The entry is identified with the small letter (b).

Adjustment for ending merchandise inventory. The amount of the ending merchandise inventory should be the balance of the account at the end of January, 1978.

Merchandise Inventory	115
35,056.00	

Income Summary	313
	35,056.00

Merchandise Inventory is debited for the amount of the ending inventory, $35,056.00. The income summary account is credited for the same amount. When the two adjustments for merchandise inventory are journalized and posted, the merchandise inventory account will show an up-to-date balance of $35,056.00.

The adjustment for the ending merchandise inventory is shown on the work sheet, page 48, Lines 6 and 22. The data are identified with the small letter (c).

Adjustment for supplies. The balance of the supplies account as shown on the trial balance represents two things: (1) the balance at the beginning of the month, plus (2) the value of supplies bought during the month. The balance does not reflect the value of any supplies used during the month.

An inventory taken at the end of January shows that the value of the remaining supplies is $259.80. The difference between the balance of the supplies account, $587.00, and the value of the inventory, $259.80, is the value of the supplies used during the month, $327.20.

	Supplies Expense	618
Adj.	327.20	

	Supplies	116
Bal.	587.00	Adj. 327.20

Supplies Expense is debited for $327.20, the amount of supplies expense for the month. Supplies is credited for $327.20 to reduce the balance to its up-to-date amount.

The adjustment for supplies expense is shown on the work sheet, page 48, Lines 7 and 34. The adjustment is identified on the work sheet with the small letter (d).

Adjustment for prepaid insurance. The balance of the prepaid insurance account on the work sheet trial balance, page 48, is $372.90. A check of the insurance records shows that the amount of prepaid insurance remaining at the end of January is $127.69. The difference between the account balance and the amount remaining at the end of the month is $245.21, the amount of insurance premium used up in January ($372.90 − 127.69 = $245.21).

	Insurance Expense	613
Adj.	245.21	

	Prepaid Insurance	117
Bal.	372.90	Adj. 245.21

Insurance Expense is debited for the amount of January's expense, $245.21. Prepaid Insurance is credited for the same amount to bring its balance up-to-date.

This adjustment is shown on the work sheet, page 48, Lines 8 and 29. The adjustment is identified with the small letter (e).

Adjustment for depreciation of equipment. The amount that equipment depreciates is an estimate on the records. The actual depreciation is not known until a plant asset is disposed of. Therefore, a separate account is used in which to record the estimated depreciation. Village Gift Shop estimates that the equipment depreciates $57.00 during January, 1978.

Depreciation Expense — Equipment is debited for $57.00. The contra asset account, Accumulated Depreciation — Equipment, is credited for the same amount. The total estimated accumulated depreciation after the adjustment is $1,211.00 ($1,154.00 + 57.00).

Depreciation Expense — Equipment	612
Adj. 57.00	

Accumulated Depreciation — Equipment	121.1
	Bal. 1,154.00
	Adj. 57.00

This adjustment is shown on the work sheet, page 48, Lines 11 and 28, identified with the small letter (f).

Adjustments for interest on notes. At the end of a fiscal period, interest may be owed but not yet paid on notes payable. Also, interest may be due but not yet received on notes receivable.

Interest receivable. At the end of January, 1978, an inspection of the notes receivable shows that $4.75 in interest has been earned, is due, but not yet received. Interest Receivable is debited for $4.75 and Interest Income is credited for the same amount. This adjustment is shown on the work sheet, page 48, Lines 9 and 35, identified with (g).

Interest Receivable	118
Adj. 4.75	

Interest Income	711
	Bal. .90
	Adj. 4.75

Interest payable. At the end of January, 1978, an inspection of the records for notes payable shows that $2.25 interest is owed but not yet paid. Interest Expense is debited and Interest Payable is credited for $2.25. This adjustment is shown on the work sheet, page 48, Lines 19 and 36, identified with (h).

Interest Expense	811
Bal. 1.00	
Adj. 2.25	

Interest Payable	218
	Adj. 2.25

Proving and ruling the Adjustments columns on a work sheet. After all the adjustments are recorded on the work sheet, the Adjustments Debit and Credit columns are totaled. If the totals of these two columns are the same, the equality of debits and credits has been maintained. The work sheet, page 48, shows the Adjustments columns totaled and ruled.

Income Statement and Balance Sheet columns on a work sheet

To aid in preparing financial statements, the up-to-date balances of accounts are sorted on the work sheet. The asset, liability, and capital accounts are extended to the Balance Sheet columns. The balance of the income summary account, and all revenue, cost, and expense accounts are extended to the Income Statement columns. For the income summary account, a balance is not determined. Rather, the two figures to be recorded in the account, because of adjustments, are both extended to the Income Statement columns. This procedure is shown on the work sheet, page 48, Line 22. Both of these figures are needed when preparing the income statement from data on the work sheet.

Figuring the net income on a work sheet. The net income is found from data in the Income Statement columns of the work sheet. The two columns are totaled as shown on the work sheet, page 48, Line 37. Using these two totals, the net income is found:

Total of Income Statement Credit column.............................. $70,094.82
Less total of Income Statement Debit column 69,387.08
Equals amount of net income.. $ 707.74

Completing the work sheet. The amount of net income, $707.74, is written in the Income Statement Debit column on the line immediately below the Debit column total. The words, *Net Income*, are written in the Account Title column on the same line as the amount. The same amount, $707.74, is written on the same line in the Balance Sheet Credit column. The four columns, Income Statement Debit and Credit, and Balance Sheet Debit and Credit, are totaled and ruled as shown on the work sheet, page 48, Line 39.

The totals of the two Income Statement columns are compared. The two totals should now be the same. As shown on the work sheet, page 48, Line 39, the two totals, $70,094.82, are the same. The two totals of the Balance Sheet columns are also compared. The two totals, $47,731.87, are the same. Equality of debits and credits has been maintained. The arithmetic on the work sheet is assumed to be correct.

INCOME STATEMENT

A report showing the revenue, costs, expenses, and the net income or net loss for a fiscal period is called an income statement. The income statement prepared by the general accounting clerk for Village Gift Shop for January, 1978, is shown on page 53. The data to prepare this statement are obtained from the Income Statement Debit and Credit columns of the work sheet, page 48.

CAPITAL STATEMENT

A report that summarizes the changes in the owner's capital account since the beginning of the fiscal period is called a capital statement. The capital statement for the Village Gift Shop is shown on page 53. The data

```
                            Village Gift Shop
                            Income Statement
                      For Month Ended January 31, 1978


Operating Revenue:
  Sales . . . . . . . . . . . . . . . . . .        $34,920.97
  Less Sales Returns and Allowances . . . . . . .      365.78
  Net Sales . . . . . . . . . . . . . . .                         $34,555.19

Cost of Merchandise Sold:
  Merchandise Inventory, January 1, 1978 . . . .   $36,585.00
  Purchases . . . . . . . . . . . . . . .  $29,364.03
  Less Purchases Returns and Allowances . . . . .     112.20
  Net Purchases . . . . . . . . . . . . .              29,251.83
  Total Cost of Merchandise Available for Sale .     $65,836.83
  Less Merchandise Inventory, January 31, 1978 .      35,056.00
  Cost of Merchandise Sold . . . . . . . . . .                     30,780.83

Gross Profit on Operations . . . . . . . . . .                    $ 3,774.36

Operating Expenses:
  Bad Debts Expense . . . . . . . . . . . . .      $     25.94
  Depreciation Expense--Equipment . . . . . . . .        57.00
  Insurance Expense . . . . . . . . . . . . . .         245.21
  Miscellaneous Expense . . . . . . . . . . . .         188.31
  Payroll Taxes Expense . . . . . . . . . . . .         145.36
  Rent Expense . . . . . . . . . . . . . .               500.00
  Salary Expense . . . . . . . . . . . . . .           1,580.00
  Supplies Expense . . . . . . . . . . . . .             327.20
  Total Operating Expenses . . . . . . . . . .                     3,069.02

Income from Operations . . . . . . . . . . . . .                 $   705.34

Other Revenue:
  Interest Income . . . . . . . . . . . . . .       $      5.65

Other Expense:
  Interest Expense . . . . . . . . . . . . .                3.25

Net Addition . . . . . . . . . . . . . . . . .                         2.40

Net Income . . . . . . . . . . . . . . . . .                     $   707.74
```

Income statement

used to prepare the capital statement are obtained from the owner's capital account, from the owner's drawing account, and from the Balance Sheet columns of the work sheet.

Capital statement

```
                            Village Gift Shop
                            Capital Statement
                      For Month Ended January 31, 1978


  Mildred Gunweld, Capital, January 1, 1978 . . . .  $42,094.71
  Plus Additional Investment . . . . . . . . . .       1,000.00

  Total . . . . . . . . . . . . . . . . . . .                      $43,094.71

  Net Income for January, 1978 . . . . . . . . .  $   707.74
  Less Withdrawals for January, 1978 . . . . . .      670.00

  Net Increase in Capital . . . . . . . . . . .                        37.74

  Mildred Gunweld, Capital, January 31, 1978 . . .                $43,132.45
```

On January 31, 1978, Mildred Gunweld has capital totaling $43,132.45 in the Village Gift Shop. This amount, shown on the capital statement, page 53, is used again on the balance sheet, shown below.

In some businesses, the facts on the capital statement may be shown as part of the balance sheet. When this is done, the capital section of the balance sheet contains the same data as shown on page 53 for the capital statement.

BALANCE SHEET

Balance sheet

A report showing what is owned (assets), what is owed (liabilities), and what a business is worth (capital) on a specific date is called a balance sheet. The balance sheet of the Village Gift Shop is shown below.

```
                          Village Gift Shop
                           Balance Sheet
                           January 31, 1978
```

ASSETS

Current Assets:		
Cash		$ 5,159.86
Petty Cash		200.00
Accounts Receivable	$903.77	
Less Allowance for Uncollectible Accounts	105.34	798.43
Notes Receivable		550.00
Merchandise Inventory		35,056.00
Supplies		259.80
Prepaid Insurance		127.69
Interest Receivable		4.75
Total Current Assets		$42,156.53
Plant Assets:		
Equipment		$ 4,800.00
Less Accumulated Depreciation--Equipment		1,211.00
Total Plant Assets		3,589.00
Total Assets		$45,745.53

LIABILITIES

Current Liabilities:	
Accounts Payable	$ 1,112.00
Notes Payable	450.00
Employees Income Tax Payable--Federal	223.06
FICA Tax Payable	189.60
Unemployment Tax Payable--Federal	7.90
Unemployment Tax Payable--State	42.66
Sales Tax Payable	585.61
Interest Payable	2.25
Total Current Liabilities	$ 2,613.08

CAPITAL

Mildred Gunweld, Capital	43,132.45
Total Liabilities and Capital	$45,745.53

The balance sheet is prepared from data in the Balance Sheet Debit and Credit columns of the work sheet, page 48, and from the capital statement, page 53. Because the total assets equal the total liabilities and capital, the balance sheet is said to be in balance.

ADJUSTING ENTRIES

All changes in ledger accounts are based on entries posted from a journal. Journal entries made to bring general ledger accounts up-to-date are called adjusting entries.

Adjusting entries are recorded in the general journal. The data for the adjusting entries are taken from the Adjustments columns of the work sheet, page 48. The adjusting entries prepared by Village Gift Shop's general accounting clerk on January 31, 1978, are shown below.

| | GENERAL JOURNAL | | | | PAGE 16 | |
| 1 | 2 | | | 3 | 4 | |
ACCOUNTS PAYABLE DEBIT	GENERAL DEBIT	DATE	ACCOUNT TITLE	POST. REF.	GENERAL CREDIT	ACCOUNTS RECEIV. CREDIT
			Adjusting Entries			
	2594	1978 Jan. 31	Bad Debts Expense			
			Allow. for Uncoll. Accts.		2594	
	365 85 00	31	Income Summary			
			Merchandise Inventory		3658500	
	350 56 00	31	Merchandise Inventory			
			Income Summary		3505600	
	327 20	31	Supplies Expense			
			Supplies		32720	
	245 21	31	Insurance Expense			
			Prepaid Insurance		24521	
	57 00	31	Depreciation Expense—Equip.			
			Accum. Depr.—Equip.		5700	
	2 25	31	Interest Expense			
			Interest Payable		225	
	4 75	31	Interest Receivable			
			Interest Income		475	

Adjusting entries

The words, *Adjusting Entries*, are written in the Account Title column to identify the group of entries that follows. In this way, a source does not have to be indicated for each adjusting entry.

CLOSING ENTRIES

At the end of each fiscal period, journal entries are made to transfer the balances of the revenue, cost, and expense accounts to the income summary account. Also, entries are made to transfer the balance of the drawing account to the capital account and to record the net income or net loss in the capital account. A journal entry that transfers a balance from one account to another is called a closing entry.

The data for the closing entries are taken from the Income Statement columns of the work sheet, page 48. The closing entries prepared by Village Gift Shop's general accounting clerk on January 31, 1978, are shown below.

ACCOUNTS PAYABLE DEBIT	GENERAL DEBIT	DATE	ACCOUNT TITLE	POST. REF.	GENERAL CREDIT	ACCOUNTS RECEIV. CREDIT	
			GENERAL JOURNAL PAGE *16*				
18			*Closing Entries*				18
19	3492097	31	*Sales*				19
20	11220		*Purchases Returns & Allow.*				20
21	565		*Interest Income*				21
22			*Income Summary*		3503882		22
23	3280208	31	*Income Summary*				23
24			*Sales Returns & Allow.*		36578		24
25			*Purchases*		2936403		25
26			*Bad Debts Expense*		2594		26
27			*Depreciation Exp. Equip.*		5700		27
28			*Insurance Expense*		24521		28
29			*Miscellaneous Expense*		18831		29
30			*Payroll Taxes Expense*		14536		30
31			*Rent Expense*		50000		31
32			*Salary Expense*		158000		32
33			*Supplies Expense*		32720		33
34			*Interest Expense*		325		34
35	70774	31	*Income Summary*				35
36			*Mildred Gunweld, Capital*		70774		36
37	67000	31	*Mildred Gunweld, Capital*				37
38			*Mildred Gunweld, Drawing*		67000		38
39							39
40							40

Closing entries

The first closing entry, Lines 19 to 22, closes all the income statement accounts with credit balances. The second closing entry, Lines 23 to 34, closes all income statement accounts with debit balances. The third closing entry, Lines 35 to 36, records the net income in the capital account and closes the income summary account. The fourth closing entry, Lines 37 to 38, closes the owner's drawing account into the capital account.

As a result of the four closing entries, only balance sheet accounts (assets, liabilities, and capital) show balances at the end of the fiscal period. All other accounts are closed and begin the next fiscal period with a zero balance. In this way, revenue, cost, and expense accounts for one fiscal period are not confused with the same data for the next fiscal period.

POST-CLOSING TRIAL BALANCE

The debits always equal the credits in the general ledger accounts if the records are kept correctly. To prove the equality of debits and credits in the general ledger after all posting has been completed, a trial balance is prepared. This procedure is described in Chapter 2 and at the beginning of this chapter.

To prove the equality of debits and credits in the general ledger accounts after the adjusting and closing entries are posted, a trial balance is also prepared. A trial balance prepared after the adjusting and closing entries have been posted is called a post-closing trial balance. The post-closing trial balance of the Village Gift Shop is shown below.

Village Gift Shop
Post-Closing Trial Balance
January 31, 1978

ACCOUNT TITLE	ACCT. NO.	DEBIT	CREDIT
Cash	111	5159 86	
Petty Cash	112	200 00	
Accounts Receivable	113	903 77	
Allowance for Uncollectible Accounts	113.1		105 34
Notes Receivable	114	550 00	
Merchandise Inventory	115	35056 00	
Supplies	116	259 80	
Prepaid Insurance	117	127 69	
Interest Receivable	118	4 75	
Equipment	121	4800 00	
Accumulated Depreciation — Equipment	121.1		1211 00
Accounts Payable	211		1112 00
Notes Payable	212		450 00
Employees Income Tax Payable — Federal	213		223 06
FICA Tax Payable	214		189 60
Unemployment Tax Payable — Federal	215		7 90
Unemployment Tax Payable — State	216		42 66
Sales Tax Payable	217		585 61
Interest Payable	218		2 25
Mildred Gunweld, Capital	311		43132 45
		47061 87	47061 87

Post-closing trial balance

The total of the debit balances is the same as the total of the credit balances, $47,061.87. The equality of debits and credits has been maintained in the general ledger. The post-closing trial balance provides a final check that all the work of adjusting and closing the general ledger has been completed accurately. The general ledger is in balance and ready for the entries of the next fiscal period.

SUMMARY OF THE ACCOUNTING CYCLE

Chapters 2 and 3 are a review of the accounting procedures used by the Village Gift Shop. The procedures used for the monthly fiscal period ended January 31, 1978, are followed for each month of the year. The complete series of activities involved in double-entry accounting for a fiscal period is called the accounting cycle. The accounting cycle begins with the source documents and ends with the post-closing trial balance. The flowchart on page 59 illustrates the steps in the accounting cycle.

Using Business Terms

✦ What is the meaning of each of the following?

- fiscal period
- work sheet
- income statement
- capital statement
- balance sheet
- adjusting entries
- closing entry
- post-closing trial balance
- accounting cycle

Questions for Individual Study

1. On what date during a year may a fiscal period begin?
2. Why is a work sheet prepared?
3. What two accounts are affected by each of the adjusting entries listed below?
   a. Bad debts expense
   b. Merchandise inventory
   c. Supplies
   d. Prepaid insurance
   e. Interest on notes receivable earned but not yet received
   f. Interest on notes payable owed but not yet paid
4. How is the net income or net loss figured from information on a work sheet?

5. Where on a work sheet are data needed for each of the following financial statements found?
   a. Income Statement
   b. Balance Sheet
6. Where are the data needed to prepare the adjusting entries found?
7. Where are the data needed to prepare the closing entries found?
8. In what journal does Village Gift Shop record the adjusting and closing entries?
9. Why are closing entries made at the end of a fiscal period?
10. Why is a post-closing trial balance prepared?

Cases for Management Decision

CASE 1 To obtain financial data very often on which to base business decisions, Willard Petrovitch prepares the following items at the end of each week: work sheet, income statement, capital statement, balance sheet, adjusting and closing entries, and post-closing trial balance. Mr. Petrovitch carefully studies the financial statements to determine if business is increasing this week as compared to last week. What, in your opinion, are the advantages and disadvantages of this procedure?

CASE 2 Marty Muldoon does not make an adjustment for bad debts expense at the end of a fiscal period. Instead, after making every possible attempt to collect from a charge customer, Mr. Muldoon declares the account a bad debt and debits Bad Debts Expense and credits Accounts Receivable. This may occur many, many months after the sale on account to the charge customer has been made. Is this procedure acceptable? Explain your answer.

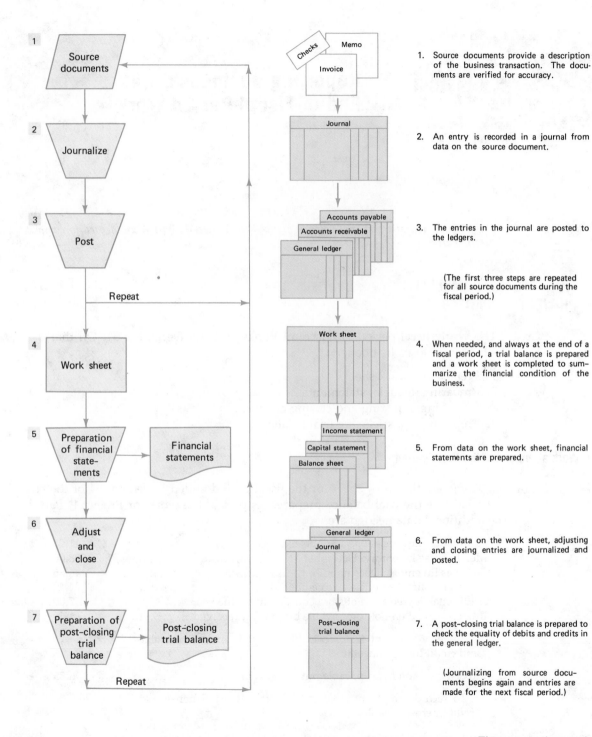

1. Source documents provide a description of the business transaction. The documents are verified for accuracy.

2. An entry is recorded in a journal from data on the source document.

3. The entries in the journal are posted to the ledgers.

   (The first three steps are repeated for all source documents during the fiscal period.)

4. When needed, and always at the end of a fiscal period, a trial balance is prepared and a work sheet is completed to summarize the financial condition of the business.

5. From data on the work sheet, financial statements are prepared.

6. From data on the work sheet, adjusting and closing entries are journalized and posted.

7. A post-closing trial balance is prepared to check the equality of debits and credits in the general ledger.

   (Journalizing from source documents begins again and entries are made for the next fiscal period.)

The accounting cycle

Reporting Business Data: End-of-Fiscal-Period Work

The journals, ledgers, and trial balance prepared in Project 1, Part A are needed to complete Project 1, Part B.

WORK TO BE COMPLETED PROJECT 1, PART B

The yearly fiscal period of Discount-Books ends on December 31. On that date the business closes its books by:

1. Preparing a work sheet.
2. Preparing financial statements.
3. Recording adjusting and closing entries.
4. Preparing a post-closing trial balance.

Work at the end of the fiscal period

Instructions: 1. Complete the work sheet for the fiscal period ended December 31 of the current year. Use the trial balance prepared as part of the work for Project 1, Part A. The additional data needed are:

Additional allowance for bad debts expense.................................	$ 11.28
Merchandise Inventory, December 31	25,098.00
Supplies Inventory, December 31	146.65
Value of insurance policies, December 31	204.40
Additional depreciation of store equipment for the year	467.00
Interest earned on notes receivable but not yet received.................	4.10

To record the interest receivable, debit Interest Receivable and credit Interest Income.

Interest owed on notes payable but not yet paid	6.85

To record the interest payable, debit Interest Expense and credit Interest Payable.

Compare your work sheet with the work sheet shown on page 48.

2. Prepare an income statement from the data on the work sheet. Compare your income statement with the one shown on page 53.

Since the income statement is prepared for a fiscal year, the beginning merchandise inventory is dated January 1 of the current year.

3. Prepare a capital statement from data on the work sheet. Use data in the owner's capital account in the general ledger, also. Compare your capital statement with the one shown on page 53.

4. Prepare a balance sheet from the data on the work sheet. Compare your balance sheet with the one shown on page 54.

5. Record in the general journal, page 8, the adjusting and closing entries. Obtain the data for these entries from the work sheet. Compare your work with the adjusting and closing entries shown on pages 55 and 56.

6. Post the adjusting and closing entries to the general ledger.

7. Prepare a post-closing trial balance from the data in the general ledger. Compare your post-closing trial balance with the one shown on page 57.

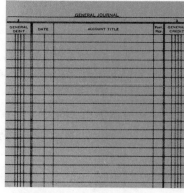
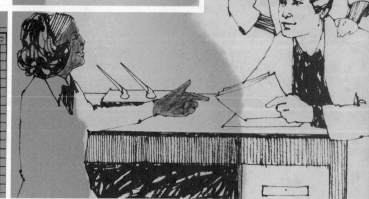

3

PARTNERSHIP ACCOUNTING

CAPITAL ACCOUNTS DIFFER. The accounting procedures for a sole proprietorship are reviewed in Part 2 of this textbook. The same procedures apply to most partnerships. The major difference in the accounting records for the two kinds of business organizations is in the general ledger accounts for capital. In a sole proprietorship, one capital account and one drawing account are kept for the single owner. In a partnership, a capital account and a drawing account are kept for each partner.

NET INCOME OR NET LOSS IS DISTRIBUTED. In a sole proprietorship, the single owner is entitled to all of the net income or net loss of the business. In a partnership, the net income or net loss is divided among the several partners. The division of net income or net loss is stated in the partnership agreement.

Part 3 of this textbook describes those features of the records for a partnership that are different from those of a sole proprietorship.

CHART OF ACCOUNTS

Balance Sheet Accounts

	Account Number
(1000) ASSETS	

(1100) *Current Assets*

Cash	1101
Petty Cash	1102
Accounts Receivable	1103
Allowance for Uncollectible Accounts	1103.1
Notes Receivable	1104
Merchandise Inventory	1105
Supplies	1106
Prepaid Insurance	1107
Interest Receivable	1108

(1200) *Plant Assets*

Equipment	1201
Accumulated Depreciation — Equipment	1201.1

(2000) LIABILITIES

(2100) *Current Liabilities*

Accounts Payable	2101
Notes Payable	2102
Employees Income Tax Payable — Federal	2103
FICA Tax Payable	2104
Unemployment Tax Payable — Federal	2105
Unemployment Tax Payable — State	2106
Sales Tax Payable	2107
Interest Payable	2108

(3000) CAPITAL

Coleen O'Brien, Capital	3101
Coleen O'Brien, Drawing	3102
Terry Moore, Capital	3201
Terry Moore, Drawing	3202
Income Summary	3901

Income Statement Accounts

	Account Number
(4000) OPERATING REVENUE	
Sales	4001
Sales Returns and Allowances	4001.1

(5000) COST OF MERCHANDISE

Purchases	5001
Purchases Returns and Allowances	5001.1

(6000) OPERATING EXPENSES

(6100) *Selling Expenses*

Advertising Expense	6101
Delivery Expense	6102
Miscellaneous Expense — Sales	6103
Salary Expense — Sales	6104

(6200) *Administrative Expenses*

Bad Debts Expense	6201
Depreciation Expense — Equipment	6202
Insurance Expense	6203
Miscellaneous Expense — Administrative	6204
Payroll Taxes Expense	6205
Rent Expense	6206
Salary Expense — Administrative	6207
Supplies Expense	6208

(7000) OTHER REVENUE

Interest Income	7001

(8000) OTHER EXPENSE

Interest Expense	8001

The partnership of O'Brien and Moore uses a four-digit numbering system for the general ledger accounts. This system permits adding more accounts in each division without running out of account numbers.

Forming a Partnership

4

A business that is owned by one person is called a sole proprietorship. In another common type of business organization the ownership is shared by more than one person. A form of business organization in which two or more persons operate as co-owners of a business is called a partnership. Each member of a partnership is called a partner.

There are some differences in the way that proprietorships and partnerships are organized and operated. However, except for the handling of the capital accounts, the day-to-day accounting procedures of these two types of business organizations are the same.

NATURE OF A PARTNERSHIP

The organization of partnerships and the accounting problems peculiar to this form of business are described in Chapters 4, 5, and 6.

Advantages of a partnership

A partnership has several advantages when compared to a sole proprietorship. Two or more persons may have more capital to invest in a business than does a single owner. A partnership combines the business skills of more than one person. As a result of combining capital and abilities, the partners anticipate increased efficiency and greater profits than if each operated a separate business.

Disadvantages of a partnership

Because a partnership is based on a contract between two or more persons, the partnership has a limited life. A partnership is ended by the death or withdrawal of any one of the partners. When one partner dies the remaining partners may immediately form a new partnership.

Each partner is personally liable by law for all the debts of the partnership. If a partnership is unable to pay its debts, creditors may require one or all of the partners to use personal assets to settle the debts.

Under normal circumstances, each partner has the right to enter into the management of the business. Every partner is an agent of the partnership and can bind it to any contract within the scope of the business. The right of all partners to contract for the partnership is called mutual agency. Each partner can be held responsible for the debts of the firm. Poor judgment on the part of one partner may result not only in loss of profit for all partners, but also in possible loss of their personal assets.

In spite of the disadvantages of partnerships, the large number in operation proves that partnerships are a popular and a successful form of business organization. The increased efficiency and profits possible as compared to the sole proprietorship usually outweigh the disadvantages of the partnership form of business.

The partnership agreement

A written agreement that sets forth the various conditions under which a partnership is to operate is called the articles of partnership. Legally, the partnership agreement may be written or oral. In order to avoid disagreements about what was agreed upon, the contract should be in writing.

The laws of the various states do not require that the agreement be in any special form. A partnership agreement, however, should include the following:

1. The names of the partners.
2. The nature and scope of the business that the partnership will engage in.
3. The name and location of the business.
4. The investment of each partner and each partner's equity in the partnership property.
5. The duties of each partner and the limitations on the activities of each partner.
6. The salary of each partner, the provisions for distributing profits and losses, and the provisions for withdrawing profits or investments.
7. The provisions for keeping records of the partnership.
8. The length of time that the partnership is to run.
9. The provisions for dissolving the partnership.

STARTING A PARTNERSHIP

Coleen O'Brien and Terry Moore decide to form a partnership to operate a wholesale candy business. Ms. O'Brien has been operating a candy business as a sole proprietorship. Mr. Moore has been working as a salesperson.

Forming a partnership

With the assistance of an attorney, Ms. O'Brien and Mr. Moore draw up the partnership agreement shown below. The agreement is prepared in triplicate and signed by both partners. Each partner receives a copy of the agreement for personal files and the third copy becomes part of the records of the partnership.

Articles of partnership

ARTICLES OF PARTNERSHIP

THIS CONTRACT, made and entered into on the second day of January, 1978, by and between Terry Moore and Coleen O'Brien, of Charleston, South Carolina.

WITNESSETH: That the said parties have this date formed a partnership for the purpose of engaging in and conducting a wholesale candy business under the following stipulations, which are a part of this contract:

FIRST: The business is to be conducted under the firm name of O'Brien and Moore, located at 927 Washington Drive, Charleston, South Carolina 29406.

SECOND: The investments are as follows: Coleen O'Brien, the capital in her candy business, located at 927 Washington Drive, Charleston, South Carolina, as shown by her balance sheet of December 31, 1977. Terry Moore, cash equal to one half of the investment of Coleen O'Brien.

THIRD: Coleen O'Brien is to devote her entire time and attention to the business and is to engage in no other business enterprise without the written consent of Terry Moore. Coleen O'Brien is to have general supervision and operation of the business. Terry Moore will participate in the general policy-making decisions and will participate in the sales operations of the business.

FOURTH: During the operation of this partnership, no partner is to become surety or bondsman for anyone without the written consent of the other partner.

FIFTH: Coleen O'Brien is to receive a salary of $10,000.00 a year and Terry Moore a salary of $8,000.00 a year. Each partner is to receive an annual 5% interest on investment. At the end of each fiscal period, the net income or loss, after the salaries have been paid and the interest has been allowed, is to be shared equally.

SIXTH: No partner is to withdraw assets in excess of the agreed upon salary without written consent of the other partner.

SEVENTH: The investment and all transactions completed in the operation of the business are to be recorded in books of accounts in accordance with standard accounting procedures. These books of account are to be open for the inspection of either partner at all times.

EIGHTH: In case of the death or the legal disability of either partner, the capital (equity) of the partners is to be determined as of the time of the death or the disability of the one partner. The continuing partner is to have the option to buy the interest of the deceased or incapacitated partner at book value.

NINTH: The said partnership is to continue for a term of ten years from January 2, 1978, unless the partners mutually agree in writing to a shorter period. Either partner may terminate this contract by giving the other partner written notice at least 90 days prior to the date of termination.

TENTH: At the conclusion of this contract, unless it is mutually agreed to continue the operation of the partnership under a new contract, the assets of the partnership, after all liabilities are paid, are to be divided in proportion to the equity recorded in each partner's capital account on that date.

IN WITNESS WHEREOF, the parties aforesaid have hereunto set their hands and affixed their seals on the day and year written.

Signed__*Coleen O'Brien*_____ (Seal) Date__*Jan. 2, 1978*_____

Signed_*Terry Moore*_____ (Seal) Date__*Jan. 2, 1978*____

Determining the kind and amount of a partner's investment

Usually the values assigned to assets invested by a partner are the fair market values agreed to by the partners on the date of transfer to the partnership. A partner may invest assets other than cash if the other partners agree. The value assigned to the invested assets may or may not be the same as the value recorded on the books of the partner making the investment. In any case, the values assigned must be agreed to by all the partners.

According to the articles of partnership, page 67, Ms. O'Brien is to invest the capital of her existing candy business. In order to show the amount of her investment, Ms. O'Brien prepares the balance sheet shown below.

```
                          O'Brien Candy Company
                             Balance Sheet
                           December 31, 1977


                    ASSETS

Current Assets:
  Cash  . . . . . . . . . . . . . . . . . . . .      $ 6,675.96
  Petty Cash . . . . . . . . . . . . . . . .             200.00
  Accounts Receivable . . . . . . . . . . . .  $10,263.50
    Less Allowance for Uncollectible Accounts . . .    256.60     10,006.90
  Notes Receivable . . . . . . . . . . . . . .         2,150.00
  Merchandise Inventory . . . . . . . . . . .         28,218.60
  Supplies . . . . . . . . . . . . . . . . . .           201.60
  Prepaid Insurance . . . . . . . . . . . . .            249.50
  Total Current Assets . . . . . . . . . . . .                   $47,702.56

Plant Assets:
  Equipment . . . . . . . . . . . . . . . . .  $26,755.00
    Less Accumulated Depreciation--Equipment  . . .    3,544.00
  Total Plant Assets . . . . . . . . . . . . .                    23,211.00

Total Assets . . . . . . . . . . . . . . . . .                   $70,913.56


                    LIABILITIES

Current Liabilities:
  Accounts Payable . . . . . . . . . . . . . .       $ 9,113.56
  Notes Payable . . . . . . . . . . . . . . .          2,800.00
  Total Current Liabilities . . . . . . . . .                    $11,913.56


                    CAPITAL

Coleen O'Brien, Capital . . . . . . . . . . .                     59,000.00

Total Liabilities and Capital . . . . . . . .                    $70,913.56
```

Balance sheet of a sole proprietorship being invested in a partnership

Based on the second item in the articles of partnership, page 67, Ms. O'Brien is to invest her present equity in her existing candy business, $59,000.00. Mr. Moore is to invest cash equal to one half of the value of Ms. O'Brien's investment, $29,500.00.

Opening entries for a partnership

The opening entries for a partnership are similar to the opening entries for a sole proprietorship. In a partnership, however, a separate entry is made to record the investment of each partner. Also, a separate capital account is kept for each partner.

Opening entries for investment of cash and other assets. When a partnership is being started with investments of cash and other assets, the opening entries are recorded in a general journal. These entries provide a complete entry with all data in one journal.

The two opening entries to illustrate the start of the partnership of O'Brien and Moore are shown below.

ACCOUNTS PAYABLE DEBIT	GENERAL DEBIT	DATE	ACCOUNT TITLE	POST. REF.	GENERAL CREDIT	ACCOUNTS RECEIV. CREDIT
	667596	1973 Jan. 2	Cash	1101		
	20000		Petty Cash	1102		
	1026350		Accounts Receivable	1103		
	215000		Notes Receivable	1104		
	2821860		Merchandise Inventory	1105		
	20160		Supplies	1106		
	24950		Prepaid Insurance	1107		
	2675500		Equipment	1201		
			Allow. for Uncoll. Accts.	1103.1	25660	
			Accum. Depr.- Equip.	1201.1	354400	
			Accounts Payable	2101	911356	
			Notes Payable	2102	280000	
			Coleen O'Brien, Capital	3101	5900000	
			Memorandum No. 1.			
	2950000	2	Cash	1101		
			Terry Moore, Capital	3201	2950000	
			Memorandum No. 1.			

GENERAL JOURNAL — PAGE 1

Opening entries of a partnership

The source document for the opening entries shown above is a memorandum to which is attached the partnership's copy of the articles of partnership. These entries are posted to the accounts in the new general ledger of the partnership. From a schedule of accounts receivable, the account balances are entered in the new accounts receivable ledger. From a schedule of accounts payable, the account balances are entered in the new accounts payable ledger.

Entering the initial cash investments in a cash receipts journal. When the posting of the two opening entries, above, is completed, the cash account has two debits, $6,675.96 and $29,500.00. The total of these two cash investments, $36,175.96, is written as a memorandum entry on Line 1 of the new cash receipts journal.

Beginning cash balance shown in the cash receipts journal of a partnership

The memorandum entry is made in the cash receipts journal to aid in proving cash at the end of a month.

Partnership capital accounts

There are two accounts for each partner in the capital section of the general ledger. One account represents the partner's investment and is the partner's capital account. The other account represents the partner's personal account and is the partner's drawing account.

Partner's capital account. After the opening entries of O'Brien and Moore have been posted, each partner's capital account shows the total initial investment of the partner in the partnership. The capital accounts in the general ledger are shown below.

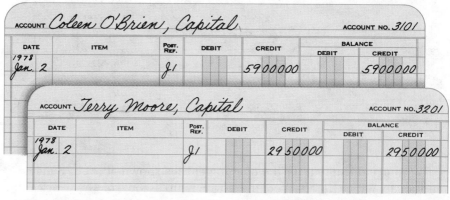

Capital accounts of a partnership

The capital accounts should show each partner's equity in the business. At the end of each fiscal period the capital accounts, therefore, should be debited for losses or credited for net income of the business in the ratio stated in the articles of partnership.

Partner's drawing account. Temporary changes in capital are recorded in drawing accounts. Thus, when a partner withdraws cash or merchandise, these amounts are charged to a drawing account. This procedure is the same as that followed for sole proprietorships.

Withdrawals by partners are frequently the cause of disagreements. For this reason, some partners include statements much like the sixth paragraph, page 67, which states, "No partner is to withdraw assets in excess of the agreed upon salary without written consent of the other partner." Thus, a partner could not withdraw most of an investment from the business without consent of the other partner.

ADMITTING A NEW PARTNER

Any change in the number of partners dissolves a partnership. If one partner dies, the partnership is dissolved. Also, an agreement to admit an additional partner dissolves the existing partnership and a new one must be created. The admission of a new partner requires the approval of all partners of the existing partnership. A new partnership agreement is also required for the newly created partnership.

When a new partner is admitted, the accounting records of the old partnership are often continued. As a result, an opening entry for a new set of records is not needed. The entry for the admission of a new partner, however, must show clearly (a) the amount of investment by the new partner, and (b) any change the admission of a new partner has on the capital accounts of the other partners.

Admission of a partner with no increase in capital

A partner may be admitted to an existing partnership without an increase in the amount of total capital. Paul Long and James Miller are partners in the operation of a retail grocery. David Myer has had considerable experience in the grocery business and desires to become a partner. Mr. Long and Mr. Miller agree that Mr. Myer will be a valuable addition to the business, but they do not feel that there is a need for more capital in the business. On February 1 they agree to accept Mr. Myer as a partner. He is to pay $10,000.00 to each of the two existing partners and receive in return a one-third interest in the business.

The capital accounts for Miller and Long both show balances of $30,000.00. They therefore agree that each partner will sell one third of his capital to Mr. Myer. The entry in a general journal to record the transfer of a one-third interest to Mr. Myer is shown below.

1 ACCOUNTS PAYABLE DEBIT	2 GENERAL DEBIT	DATE	ACCOUNT TITLE	POST. REF.	3 GENERAL CREDIT	4 ACCOUNTS RECEIV. CREDIT	
	10 000 00	*1978* Feb. 1	Paul Long, Capital	3101			1
	10 000 00		James Miller, Capital	3201			2
			David Myer, Capital	3301	20 000 00		3
			Memorandum No. 1.				4

GENERAL JOURNAL   PAGE 2

Admission of a partner with no increase in capital

The cash is paid by Mr. Myer directly to Mr. Long and Mr. Miller and does not affect the partnership's assets. The only entry required is to adjust the capital accounts.

The debit of $10,000.00 to each of the capital accounts for Mr. Long and Mr. Miller reduces their capital by one third. The credit of $20,000.00 to Mr. Myer's capital account records his one-third interest in the partnership. The effect of this entry is shown in the T accounts below.

Paul Long, Capital	3101		James Miller, Capital	3201
2/1 10,000.00	Bal. 30,000.00	2/1 10,000.00	Bal. 30,000.00

David Myer, Capital	3301
	2/1 20,000.00

Admission of a partner by investment

Ann Downing and Janet Crocker are equal partners in a beauty shop. On August 1 each partner has a capital investment of $9,000.00 in the partnership. The partners believe that having more capital for expansion and adding another person to share in the operation of the business will increase profits. They therefore agree to sell Lee Ann Mosler a one-fourth interest in the business for $6,000.00.

When Miss Mosler invests $6,000.00, the total capital is $24,000.00. Her capital of $6,000.00 is therefore one fourth of the total capital. There is no change in the amount of total capital of the original two partners. Therefore, the only entry required is to record Miss Mosler's investment. Her investment is shown in the cash receipts journal below.

					GENERAL		SALES CREDIT	ACCOUNTS RECEIVABLE CREDIT	CASH DEBIT
					1	2	3	4	5
DATE	ACCOUNT TITLE	DOC. NO.	POST. REF.		DEBIT	CREDIT			
1978 aug. 1	*Lee Ann Mosler, Capital*	21	3301			600000			600000

CASH RECEIPTS JOURNAL   PAGE 8

Cash investment of a new partner

Because no new accounting records are needed, opening entries are not needed. The investment of Miss Mosler can be recorded in the existing cash receipts journal.

The effect of the investment by Miss Mosler on the partners' capital accounts is shown in the T accounts below.

Ann Downing, Capital	3101		Janet Crocker, Capital	3201
	Bal. 9,000.00		Bal. 9,000.00

Lee Ann Mosler, Capital	3301
	8/1 6,000.00

Admission of a new partner with an interest greater than the investment

Donald Dayton and Joseph Royal are partners in a dairy supply business. The capital of each of the existing partners is $5,500.00. On May 1 the partnership of Dayton and Royal is in need of additional cash. The existing partners agree to admit Thomas Wilson as a partner and give him a one-third interest if he will invest $4,000.00.

After Mr. Wilson invests $4,000.00, the total capital is $15,000.00. A one-third interest in this total capital is $5,000.00. The entry to record Mr. Wilson's investment is shown in the cash receipts journal below.

					GENERAL		SALES CREDIT	SALES TAX PAYABLE CREDIT	ACCOUNTS RECEIVABLE CREDIT	CASH DEBIT
DATE	ACCOUNT TITLE	Doc. No.	Post. Ref.	DEBIT	CREDIT					
1978 May 1	Thomas Wilson, Capital	R38	3301		4000 00					4000 00

CASH RECEIPTS JOURNAL — PAGE 9

Cash investment of a new partner

Mr. Wilson's capital account will have a balance of $4,000.00 when the entry above is posted. His account needs $1,000.00 more to equal his $5,000.00, one-third interest in the total capital. According to the articles of partnership, Mr. Dayton and Mr. Royal share equally in profits and losses. The distribution of capital in this situation is also based on the same ratio. Therefore, each of the two original partners must transfer $500.00 of their original capital to Mr. Wilson.

The entry to transfer $1,000.00 capital into Mr. Wilson's capital account is shown in the general journal below.

ACCOUNTS PAYABLE DEBIT	GENERAL DEBIT	DATE	ACCOUNT TITLE	Post. Ref.	GENERAL CREDIT	ACCOUNTS RECEIV. CREDIT
	500 00	1978 May 1	Donald Dayton, Capital	3101		
	500 00		Joseph Royal, Capital	3201		
			Thomas Wilson, Capital	3301	1000 00	
			Memorandum No. 42.			

GENERAL JOURNAL — PAGE 5

Transfer of capital to a partner admitted with interest greater than investment

After the entries in the cash receipts and general journals are posted, the effect on the capital accounts is shown in the T accounts below.

The balance of each capital account represents a one-third share of the total capital, $5,000.00.

Donald Dayton, Capital 3101	
5/1 Transfer 500.00	4/31 Bal. 5,500.00

Joseph Royal, Capital 3201	
5/1 Transfer 500.00	4/31 Bal. 5,500.00

Thomas Wilson, Capital 3301	
	5/1 Invest. 4,000.00
	5/1 Transfer 1,000.00

Allowance for goodwill to partners when a new partner is admitted

Judy Hall and Anthony Giovani are partners in an existing partnership. Each partner has a capital of $13,000.00. Manuel Cruiz offers to invest $15,000.00 for a one-third interest in the business. Ms. Hall and Mr. Giovani agree to admit Mr. Cruiz on October 1.

If Mr. Cruiz is willing to pay $15,000.00 for a one-third interest, he evidently believes that the firm is worth three times that amount, $45,000.00. After Mr. Cruiz invests $15,000.00, the total capital of the business will be $41,000.00. The value of the total capital should be $4,000.00 more than will be shown on the records. The value of a business in excess of the total capital of the original owners is called goodwill. The amount of goodwill should be recorded in an asset account with the title Goodwill.

> The asset Goodwill is not a tangible item and is referred to as an intangible asset. The value of an intangible asset is definitely fixed only when it is purchased or sold. An intangible asset should never be recorded unless it is actually purchased or sold. The value of the intangible asset, Goodwill, should be charged off as an expense over a period of years. Good accounting practice dictates that goodwill be written off the records in a relatively few years. Income tax regulations do not permit recording an expense for goodwill written off in figuring taxable income for tax reporting purposes. Therefore, goodwill is often reported as a write-off to the partners' capital.

The entries to record the investment of Mr. Cruiz and to record the goodwill created by his admission as a partner are shown below.

			CASH RECEIPTS JOURNAL							PAGE 10
				1	2	3	4	5	6	
DATE	ACCOUNT TITLE	Doc. No.	Post. Ref.	GENERAL DEBIT	GENERAL CREDIT	SALES CREDIT	SALES TAX PAYABLE CREDIT	ACCOUNTS RECEIVABLE CREDIT	CASH DEBIT	
1973 Oct. 1	Manuel Cruiz, Capital	R54	3301		1500000				1500000	1
										2

Recording an investment allowance for goodwill when new partner is admitted

			GENERAL JOURNAL				PAGE 11
1	2				3	4	
ACCOUNTS PAYABLE DEBIT	GENERAL DEBIT	DATE	ACCOUNT TITLE	Post. Ref.	GENERAL CREDIT	ACCOUNTS RECEIV. CREDIT	
	400000	*1973* Oct. 1	Goodwill	1109			1
			Judy Hall, Capital	3101	200000		2
			Anthony Giovani, Capital	3201	200000		3
			Memorandum No. 21.				4
							5

The cash receipts journal entry shows the investment made by Mr. Cruiz. The general journal entry records the goodwill and divides it equally between Ms. Hall and Mr. Giovani.

The effect of these entries is to give each partner a one-third interest in the total capital, as shown in the T accounts below.

Judy Hall, Capital	3101
	Bal. 13,000.00
	10/1 2,000.00

Anthony Giovani, Capital	3201
	Bal. 13,000.00
	10/1 2,000.00

Manuel Cruiz, Capital	3301
	10/1 15,000.00

Goodwill	1109
10/1 4,000.00	

TERMINATING A PARTNERSHIP

A partnership may be terminated or go out of business for many reasons. These reasons are:

1. Withdrawal of a partner from the business.
2. Termination of the partnership agreement. The partnership agreement may be terminated by mutual agreement of the partners. Also, the articles of partnership may state a specific date on which the partnership is to be terminated.
3. Death of one of the partners.
4. Failure or bankruptcy of the business.

When a partnership is terminated, (a) the assets are sold, (b) the liabilities are paid, and (c) the remaining cash is distributed to the partners according to their capital. The process of selling assets, paying liabilities, and distributing the remaining cash to the owners of a business is called liquidation.

When a partnership is liquidated, the sale of assets may result in a loss. This loss is distributed to the partners in the same ratio as a profit would be.

On April 29, 1978, Woodruff and Miller decide to dissolve their partnership. On that date, the records are as shown below in the abbreviated trial balance.

```
                    Woodruff and Miller
                       Trial Balance
                      April 29, 1978

    Cash . . . . . . . . . . . .   $ 5,000.00
    Other Assets . . . . . . . .     6,000.00
    Total Liabilities  . . . . .                  $ 2,000.00
    Joan Woodruff, Capital . . .                    5,000.00
    Alice Miller, Capital  . . .                    4,000.00

                                   $11,000.00     $11,000.00
```

Abbreviated trial balance

The procedure for liquidating the partnership is as follows:

(a) The partnership's other assets are sold for $6,000.00 cash. The effect of this sale is shown in the T accounts below.

Cash	1101		Other Assets	1000
Bal. 5,000.00		Bal. 6,000.00	(a) 6,000.00
(a) 6,000.00			

(b) The liabilities, $2,000.00, are paid. The payment of the liabilities affects the general ledger accounts as shown below.

Cash	1101		Liabilities	2000
Bal. 5,000.00	(b) 2,000.00	(b) 2,000.00	Bal. 2,000.00
(a) 6,000.00			

(c) The remaining cash, $9,000.00, is distributed to the two partners. The remaining cash is distributed according to the amount of capital each partner has at the time the partnership is liquidated. The remaining cash, $9,000.00, is the same as the total remaining capital, $5,000.00 + $4,000.00 = $9,000.00. Therefore, each partner's share of the remaining cash is equal to her capital. The effect of distributing the remaining cash to the partners is shown in the T accounts below.

Cash	1101		Joan Woodruff, Capital	3101
Bal. 5,000.00	(b) 2,000.00	(c) 5,000.00	Bal. 5,000.00
(a) 6,000.00	(c) 9,000.00		

	Alice Miller, Capital	3201
(c) 4,000.00	Bal. 4,000.00

After the remaining cash is distributed to the partners, all of the general ledger accounts are closed. Once the journal entries have been made and posted, liquidation of the partnership is completed.

Using Business Terms

✦ What is the meaning of each of the following?

- sole proprietorship
- partnership
- partner
- mutual agency
- articles of partnership
- goodwill
- liquidation

Questions for Individual Study

1. What advantages does a partnership have as compared to a sole proprietorship?

2. What are some disadvantages of the partnership form of business?

3. Why should a partnership agreement be in writing?

4. From the articles of partnership, page 67, answer the following:
   a. What is the nature of the business?
   b. What is the investment of each partner?
   c. What are the general duties of each partner?
   d. How will the partners be paid for their services and investments?
   e. For how long will the partnership continue under this agreement?
   f. What must be done if either partner wishes to terminate the agreement before 10 years?

5. Why did Coleen O'Brien have to prepare the balance sheet, page 68, and Terry Moore did not, when they were setting up the accounting records for their new partnership?
6. How does the capital section of the general ledger differ for a partnership as compared to a sole proprietorship?
7. Why did the articles of partnership, page 67, contain the sixth paragraph?
8. When Mr. Myer was admitted to the partnership, page 71, why was no record made of the cash paid by Mr. Myer?
9. Why was a debit of $500.00 made to the capital accounts of Mr. Dayton and Mr. Royal when Mr. Wilson was admitted to the partnership, page 73?
10. Why was goodwill created by the admission of Mr. Cruiz to the partnership, page 74?
11. What happens to a loss resulting from the liquidation of a partnership?

Cases for Management Decision

CASE 1 Jerry Stobach and Marty Messina are partners in the operation of a service garage. Mr. Stobach contracts to purchase a tow truck without consulting Mr. Messina. Mr. Messina refuses to accept the new truck because Mr. Stobach did not tell him of the purchase, and therefore he had not agreed to the purchase. The seller of the truck sues the partnership for payment. Will the partnership have to pay? Explain.

CASE 2 Leo Hadesty and James Achenbach both operate individual hardware stores in a small town. Mr. Hadesty believes that by merging the two businesses into a partnership both men can make more profit. If you were Mr. Achenbach, what factors would you consider before deciding to form a partnership with Mr. Hadesty?

CASE 3 Marva Battle operates a women's clothing store. She decides to establish a men's department. Evald Johnson is willing to enter a partnership with Mrs. Battle and to manage the men's department of the business. Mrs. Battle suggests that she continue the business as a sole proprietorship and engage Mr. Johnson on a salary to manage the men's department. (1) What are the advantages and disadvantages of admitting Mr. Johnson as a partner? and (2) What are the advantages and disadvantages of employing Mr. Johnson on a salary?

CASE 4 Jerry Wood and Jane Hodge are partners in the operation of a home decorating business. The business has not been profitable, and the two partners agree to terminate the partnership. At the time of the liquidation, the capital accounts show a balance of $10,000.00 for Mr. Wood and $15,000.00 for Miss Hodge. After all the noncash assets are sold and all liabilities paid, the cash balance is $10,000.00.

(a) What is the amount of gain or loss from liquidating the business?
(b) If the two partners share income or loss according to their investments, how much of the income or loss will each partner receive?
(c) How will the cash on hand, $10,000.00, be divided between the two partners?

PROBLEM 4-1 Forming a partnership; assets and liabilities invested by one partner, and only cash invested by another partner

Problems for Applying Concepts

On April 1 of the current year, Ruth Tolson and Kai Wong, pharmacists, form a partnership for the purpose of operating a drugstore. Ms. Wong has been operating a small drugstore as a sole proprietorship. The partnership is to assume the assets and liabilities of her business. Ms. Tolson invests cash equal to the capital investment of Ms. Wong. Ms. Wong's trial balance on March 31 appears on page 78.

Kai Wong
Trial Balance
March 31, 19—

Cash..	10	273	12				
Accounts Receivable	2	449	39				
Allowance for Uncollectible Accounts					48	97	
Merchandise Inventory..............................	17	193	51				
Supplies..		438	42				
Equipment...	8	275	00				
Accumulated Depreciation — Equipment.....				2	026	00	
Accounts Payable				5	819	22	
Kai Wong, Capital				30	735	25	
	38	629	44	38	629	44	

Instructions: ☐ **1.** Record on page 1 of a general journal the opening entry for Ms. Wong. M1.

☐ **2.** Record the opening entry for Ms. Tolson. M2.

PROBLEM 4-2 Admission of a new partner with no increase in partnership capital

Manfreid Heinrichs and Minda Dario are partners in a real estate business. Each has an investment of $8,250.00. The partners agree to admit Mary Mahoney as a third partner. The agreement is that the original partners will sell Ms. Mahoney an equal part of their invested capital to give her a one-third share of the partnership.

Instructions: Use the current date and record on page 8 of a general journal the journal entry for the admission of Ms. Mahoney as a partner. M1. The cash payment is between the individuals and is not recorded on the partnership books.

PROBLEM 4-3 Admission of a partner by investment

Alice Anderson and Elmer Baker are partners in a stationery store. Each partner has invested $8,600.00 in the business. Dianne Moorstein is allowed to join the partnership by investing $8,600.00 cash. Ms. Moorstein is given a one-third interest in the partnership.

Instructions: Use the current date and page 1 of a cash receipts journal. Record the entry for Ms. Moorstein's investment. R61.

PROBLEM 4-4 Admission of a partner with an interest greater than investment made

Kenneth Ward, Ted Holland, and Russell Track each have $10,000.00 invested in a partnership. Charles Owens is admitted as a fourth partner. Mr. Owens invests $6,000.00 cash and is given a one-fourth interest in the partnership.

Instructions: □ 1. Use the current date and page 5 of a cash receipts journal. Record the entry for Mr. Owens' investment. R18.

□ 2. Use page 16 of a general journal. Record the entry to transfer the necessary amounts to the new partner's capital account to give him one fourth of the total capital in the partnership. M12.

PROBLEM 4-5 Admission of a partner with an allowance for goodwill to the other partners

Jane Downing and Alberta Johnson are partners. Each partner has an investment of $13,000.00 in the partnership. Fred Richards is admitted as an additional partner. Mr. Richards invests $16,000.00 cash for a one-third interest in the partnership. Goodwill is valued at $6,000.00.

Instructions: Use the current date, page 17 of a general journal, and page 15 of a cash receipts journal. Record the entries for the admission of Fred Richards. R1; M1.

MASTERY PROBLEM 4-M Opening entries for a merger of two sole proprietorships into a partnership

On May 1 of the current year Frank Thomas and Bertha Miller form a partnership to consolidate their two real estate offices. The partnership takes over the assets and liabilities of each partner's former business. The post-closing trial balances on April 30 for the two sole proprietorships are shown below and on page 80.

Instructions: □ 1. Record on page 1 of a general journal the opening entry for the investment of Mr. Thomas. M1. (The entry is similar to the first entry shown on page 69.)

□ 2. Record the opening entry for the investment of Miss Miller. M2.

Frank Thomas
Post-Closing Trial Balance
April 30, 19--

Cash	2 002 83	
Accounts Receivable	2 003 65	
Allowance for Uncollectible Accounts		31 13
Prepaid Insurance	99 00	
Supplies	154 66	
Office Equipment	1 014 75	
Accumulated Depreciation — Office Equipment		264 77
Automobile	2 365 00	
Accumulated Depreciation — Automobile		580 00
Accounts Payable		220 33
Frank Thomas, Capital		6 543 66
	7 639 89	7 639 89

Bertha Miller
Post-Closing Trial Balance
April 30, 19--

Cash...	1 804	00		
Accounts Receivable	1 100	00		
Allowance for Uncollectible Accounts			55	00
Prepaid Insurance...	44	00		
Supplies..	88	20		
Office Equipment	1 056	00		
Accumulated Depreciation — Office Equipment..............			264	00
Automobile	2 530	00		
Accumulated Depreciation — Automobile......................			632	50
Notes Payable..			440	00
Accounts Payable			101	64
Bertha Miller, Capital..			5 129	06
	6 622	20	6 622	20

**BONUS
PROBLEM 4-B** ● Liquidating a partnership

Hal Polson and Willard Youngman are partners in a small lawn care business. On July 1 of the current year, the two partners decide to dissolve the partnership and liquidate the business. The trial balance for the partnership on July 1 is below:

Ace Lawn Care Business
Trial Balance
July 1, 19--

Cash...	2 803	96		
Supplies..	216	53		
Equipment...	1 420	65		
Accumulated Depreciation — Equipment......................			370	68
Accounts Payable			142	31
Hal Polson, Capital...			1 840	02
Willard Youngman, Capital...			2 088	13
	4 441	14	4 441	14

On July 2 of the current year the supplies are sold for $150.00 cash. The equipment is sold for $1,000.00 cash. The creditors are paid in full.

Instructions: □ **1.** Use the date of July 2 of the current year and page 15 of a cash receipts journal. Record the entries for the receipt of $1,150.00 cash for the sale of assets. (Profits and losses are distributed equally to the two partners.) R74.

□ **2.** In a cash payments journal, page 12, record payment of the liabilities. Ck37.

□ **3.** In the cash payments journal record the distribution of the remaining cash to the two partners, according to their remaining capital. Ck38 and Ck39.

Dividing Partnership Earnings

The articles of partnership include a statement about the amount of each partner's capital investment and the contribution of personal services. If a partnership agreement does not include a statement about how earnings are to be divided among the partners, the law requires that the net income or loss be shared equally. This is true regardless of the partners' differences in investment, ability, or amount of time devoted to the partnership business.

The most common ways of figuring each partner's share of net income or loss are:

1. Give an equal amount to each partner.
2. Use an agreed upon ratio such as 60% to one partner and 40% to the other.
3. Use the ratio of each partner's capital investment to the total capital.
4. Allow interest on each partner's capital investment.
5. Allow salaries to one or more of the partners. Sometimes all the partners receive a salary.
6. Use a combination of two or more of the above methods.

DIVISION OF NET INCOME OR LOSS ACCORDING TO A FIXED RATIO

Next to sharing equally, the easiest way to divide a partnership's net income or loss is to give each partner a stated fraction of the total. This arrangement is common when one of the partners contributes more capital or services than the other partners.

John Apple and LeRoy Waterson form a partnership to run a retail fast food business. Mr. Apple has had several successful years operating a similar business. Mr. Waterson is inexperienced in this field. Each partner invests $50,000.00 in the partnership. Because of Mr. Apple's experience, the partnership agreement includes a statement that net income or loss is to be divided two thirds to Mr. Apple and one third to Mr. Waterson — a ratio of 2 to 1.

At the close of the first year of business for Apple and Waterson, the net income for the year is $12,000.00. Mr. Apple receives two thirds of the net income, or $8,000.00. Mr. Waterson receives one third of the net income, or $4,000.00. A closing entry is made to record each partner's share of the net income. The effect of the closing entry is shown in the T accounts at the left.

Income Summary	3901
(a) 12,000.00	Bal. 12,000.00

John Apple, Capital	3101
	(a) 8,000.00

LeRoy Waterson, Capital	3201
	(a) 4,000.00

If the partnership has a loss of $600.00, the loss would be divided as: John Apple — two thirds of the loss, $400.00; LeRoy Waterson — one third of the loss, $200.00.

DIVISION OF NET INCOME OR LOSS ACCORDING TO THE RATIO OF CAPITAL INVESTMENTS

Raymond Delmonico and Wanda Mason are partners in a bookstore. Mr. Delmonico invested $31,500.00 and Mrs. Mason invested $21,000.00. The total investment of the two partners is $52,500.00.

The net income or loss of the partnership is to be divided according to the ratio of each partner's capital investment to the total investment. Therefore, Mr. Delmonico receives 60% of the net income or loss ($31,500.00 ÷ $52,500.00), and Mrs. Mason receives 40% of the net income or loss ($21,000.00 ÷ $52,500.00).

On December 31, 1978, the partnership of Delmonico and Mason has a net income of $6,300.00. Mr. Delmonico receives 60% of the net income, $3,780.00, and Mrs. Mason receives 40%, $2,520.00. The effect on the capital accounts is shown in the T accounts at the left.

Income Summary	3901
(a) 6,300.00	Bal. 6,300.00

Raymond Delmonico, Capital	3101
	(a) 3,780.00

Wanda Mason, Capital	3201
	(a) 2,520.00

If the partnership of Delmonico and Mason has a net loss of $500.00 during the fiscal period, the net loss would be divided as: Mr. Delmonico (60%), $300.00; Mrs. Mason (40%), $200.00.

DIVISION OF NET INCOME OR LOSS WHEN INTEREST IS ALLOWED ON CAPITAL INVESTMENTS

The investments in the Lee-Ann Shoppe, a partnership, are shown below:

Ann Wehle...	$36,000.00
Lee Jacobson...	12,000.00
Total investment	$48,000.00

Both partners devote all their time to the operation of the business. The partners agree that a division of net income solely on the basis of investments will not be fair, because Miss Wehle has invested much more than Mr. Jacobson. Therefore, the partners agree to allow each partner interest at the rate of 6% per year on capital investment. The remaining net income or loss will be divided equally between the two partners.

Distribution of net income statement

A financial statement that shows in detail the distribution of the net income or loss to each partner is called a distribution of net income statement. On June 30, 1978, the end of a fiscal period for the partnership, the net income for the business is $12,500.00. The distribution of net income statement prepared on that date is shown below.

```
                          Lee-Ann Shoppe
                 Distribution of Net Income Statement
                    For Year Ended June 30, 1978


   Ann Wehle:

       6% Interest on Capital   . . . . . $2,160.00
       1/2 of Remaining Net Income . . .   4,810.00
       Total Share of Net Income . . . .              $ 6,970.00

   Lee Jacobson:

       6% Interest on Capital   . . . . . $  720.00
       1/2 of Remaining Net Income . . .   4,810.00
       Total Share of Net Income . . . .                5,530.00

   Total Net Income . . . . . . . . .                 $12,500.00
```

Effect of closing entries when interest is allowed on investment

The Lee-Ann Shoppe makes a closing entry to record net income in the partners' capital accounts taking into consideration (a) the amount of interest allowed to each partner; and (b) the remaining net income or loss after interest is allowed.

The amount to be charged as interest to each partner's account is figured as:

$$\text{Miss Wehle:} \quad \$36,000.00 \times 6\% = \$2,160.00$$
$$\text{Mr. Jacobson:} \quad \$12,000.00 \times 6\% = \underline{720.00}$$
$$\text{Total interest allowed} \dots \dots \dots \$2,880.00$$

The amount of remaining net income to be allowed to each partner is figured as:

Total net income $12,500.00

Less interest allowed 2,880.00

Equals remaining net income..................................... $ 9,620.00

The net income is divided equally between the two partners. Therefore, each partner receives one half, $4,810.00, of the remaining net income. The distribution of the net income is shown in the table below.

Partner	Interest allowed	Share of remaining net income	Total share
Wehle Jacobson	$2,160.00 720.00	$4,810.00 4,810.00	$6,970.00 5,530.00

The effect of the closing entry is shown in the T accounts below.

	Income Summary	3901	
(a)	12,500.00	Bal.	12,500.00

Ann Wehle, Capital	3101		Lee Jacobson, Capital	3201
Bal.	36,000.00		Bal.	12,000.00
(a)	6,970.00		(a)	5,530.00

Effect of closing entries when there is a net loss and interest is allowed on investments

When interest is allowed on partners' investments, the interest is credited to the partners whether there is a net income or loss. If the net income is less than the interest allowed, Income Summary has a debit balance after the interest is recorded. If there is a net loss, the debit balance of Income Summary is increased after the interest is recorded.

For example, if the Lee-Ann Shoppe had shown a net loss on June 30, 1978, of $1,600.00, the distribution would be:

Net loss.. $1,600.00
Plus interest on investments.. 2,880.00
Equals total deficit to be charged to capital...................... $4,480.00

The distribution of net income statement would be:

```
                        Lee-Ann Shoppe
                Distribution of Net Income Statement
                    For Year Ended June 30, 1978


    Ann Wehle:

        6% Interest on Capital  . . . . .  $2,160.00
        1/2 of Deficit  . . . . . . . .    2,240.00
        Total Share of Net Loss . . . . .             $    80.00

    Lee Jacobson:

        6% Interest on Capital  . . . . .  $  720.00
        1/2 of Deficit  . . . . . . . . .   2,240.00
        Total Share of Net Loss . . . . .              1,520.00

    Total Net Loss . . . . . . . . . .                $1,600.00
```

The effect of a closing entry for distributing the net loss to the partners' capital accounts is shown in the T accounts below.

Income Summary	3901	
Bal. 1,600.00	(a)	1,600.00

Ann Wehle, Capital	3101
(a) 80.00	Bal. 36,000.00

Lee Jacobson, Capital	3201
(a) 1,520.00	Bal. 12,000.00

DIVISION OF NET INCOME OR LOSS WHEN SALARIES ARE ALLOWED TO PARTNERS

Partners' salaries may be recorded as either (a) expenses of the business, or (b) withdrawals in anticipation of net income. When partners' salaries are recorded as expenses, an expense account Partners' Salaries is debited each time the salaries are paid. At the end of a fiscal period, this account, like other expenses, is closed into Income Summary.

Many businesses, however, prefer to treat partners' salaries as withdrawals instead of as expenses. One of the major reasons for this preference is that the Internal Revenue Service has ruled that partners' salaries are *not* expenses of the business for income tax purposes.

Effect of closing entries when there is a net income and salaries are allowed

A partnership has the following investments: Jack Middleton, $25,000.00, and Larry Long, $25,000.00. Mr. Middleton has more experience than Mr. Long in the kind of business the partnership operates. The partners agree that Mr. Middleton is to receive an annual salary of $9,600.00 and the remaining net income or loss is to be shared equally. The distribution of net income statement on December 31, 1977, for a total net income of $14,000.00, is shown below.

```
                          Middleton and Long
                 Distribution of Net Income Statement
                    For Year Ended December 31, 1977


Jack Middleton:

    Salary for the Year  . . . . . .    $9,600.00
    1/2 of Remaining Net Income  . .     2,200.00
    Total Share of Net Income  . . .                 $11,800.00

Larry Long:

    1/2 of Remaining Net Income  . .                   2,200.00

Total Net Income  . . . . . . . . .                 $14,000.00
```

The amounts for the distribution of net income are figured as:

Amount of net income $14,000.00
Less partners' salaries paid... 9,600.00
Equals remaining net income...................................... $ 4,400.00

The remaining net income, $4,400.00, is divided equally between the partners. Therefore, Mr. Middleton receives a total of $11,800.00, and Mr. Long receives a total of $2,200.00.

The effect of the closing entry, based on the data in the distribution of net income statement, page 85, is shown in the T accounts below.

Income Summary 3901	
(a) 14,000.00	Bal. 14,000.00

Jack Middleton, Capital 3101		Larry Long, Capital 3201	
	Bal. 25,000.00		Bal. 25,000.00
	(a) 11,800.00		(a) 2,200.00

Effect of closing entries when the salary allowed is more than the net income

On December 31, 1978, the records of the partnership, Middleton and Long, showed a net income of $8,000.00. The distribution of net income statement is shown below.

```
                    Middleton and Long
              Distribution of Net Income Statement
                For Year Ended December 31, 1978


Jack Middleton:

      Salary for the Year . . . . . . .   $9,600.00
      1/2 of Deficit . . . . . . . . .       800.00
      Total Share of Net Income . . . .              $8,800.00

Larry Long:

      1/2 of Deficit . . . . . . . . .                 800.00

Total Net Income . . . . . . . . . .                 $8,000.00
```

The amounts for the distribution of net income statement are figured as:

Net income before salaries allowed............................... $8,000.00
Less salary for Mr. Middleton 9,600.00
Equals remaining deficit $1,600.00

The deficit is divided equally between the two partners. Therefore, each partner is to receive $800.00 of the deficit. Mr. Middleton receives a share of $8,800.00, and Mr. Long receives $800.00 of the deficit.

The effect of the closing entry on the partnership capital accounts is shown in the T accounts below.

```
                    Income Summary      3901
            (a)        8,000.00  Bal.     8,000.00
```

```
    Jack Middleton, Capital  3101              Larry Long, Capital    3201
            Bal.     25,000.00   (a)           800.00  Bal.    25,000.00
            (a)       8,800.00
```

As a result of this closing entry, Mr. Middleton's capital account is increased by $8,800.00. Mr. Long's capital account is decreased by $800.00.

DIVISION OF NET INCOME OR LOSS WHEN INTEREST IS ALLOWED AND SALARIES ARE PAID TO PARTNERS

The following items are included in the articles of partnership for O'Brien and Moore, described on page 67, Chapter 4.

1. Investments: Coleen O'Brien, $59,000.00; Terry Moore, $29,500.00.
2. Each partner is to receive interest of 5% on investment.
3. Salaries: Ms. O'Brien, $10,000.00; Mr. Moore, $8,000.00.

The net income for the fiscal year ended December 31, 1978, is $24,175.00. The table below shows the distribution of this net income.

Partner	Interest on investment	Salaries	Equal share of remaining income	Total share
O'Brien	$2,950.00	$10,000.00	$875.00	$13,825.00
Moore	1,475.00	8,000.00	875.00	10,350.00

The interest on investment is figured as:

O'Brien: $59,000.00 × 5% = $2,950.00
Moore: 29,500.00 × 5% = 1,475.00

The amount of remaining net income after salaries and interest, is figured as:

Total interest on investment for both partners .... $ 4,425.00
Total salaries allowed to both partners 18,000.00
Total interest and salaries $22,425.00

Total net income, $24,175.00, *less* total interest and salaries, $22,425.00, *equals* remaining net income, $1,750.00. One half of the remaining net income, $875.00, is to be distributed to each partner. Therefore, Ms. O'Brien receives a share of $13,825.00, and Mr. Moore receives $10,350.00.

The distribution of net income statement prepared from this data is shown below.

```
                          O'Brien and Moore
                  Distribution of Net Income Statement
                     For Year Ended December 31, 1978


        Coleen O'Brien:

             5% Interest on Investment . . . .   $ 2,950.00
             Salary for the Year . . . . . . .    10,000.00
             1/2 of Remaining Net Income . . .       875.00
             Total Share of Net Income . . . .               $13,825.00

        Terry Moore:

             5% Interest on Investment . . . .   $ 1,475.00
             Salary for the Year . . . . . . .     8,000.00
             1/2 of Remaining Net Income . . .       875.00
             Total Share of Net Income . . . .               10,350.00

        Total Net Income . . . . . . . . .                   $24,175.00
```

The general journal entry to record the distribution of the net income is shown below.

ACCOUNTS PAYABLE DEBIT	GENERAL DEBIT	DATE	ACCOUNT TITLE	POST. REF.	GENERAL CREDIT	ACCOUNTS RECEIV. CREDIT	
22		2417500	31	Income Summary	3901			22
23				Coleen O'Brien, Capital	3101	1382500		23
24				Terry Moore, Capital	3201	1035000		24
25								25
26								26

GENERAL JOURNAL   PAGE 14

The effect of the closing entry on the partners' capital accounts is shown in the T accounts below.

Income Summary	3901
(a) 24,175.00	Bal. 24,175.00

Coleen O'Brien, Capital 3101		Terry Moore, Capital 3201
Bal. 59,000.00		Bal. 29,500.00
(a) 13,825.00		(a) 10,350.00

✦ What is the meaning of the following?

     • distribution of net income statement

1. If the articles of partnership do not include a statement about how net income or loss is to be shared by the partners, how is it distributed?

2. What are the six most common ways of sharing net income or loss in a partnership?

3. If a partnership has net income of $10,000.00, and Partner A has an investment of $60,000.00, and Partner B has an investment of $40,000.00, and:
   a. There is no agreement in the articles of partnership on sharing net income or loss, how much does each partner receive?
   b. There is an agreement to share income or loss: Partner A, 80%, and Partner B, 20%, how much does each partner receive?
   c. There is an agreement to share the net income or loss on a ratio of each partner's investment to the total capital, how much does each partner receive?

4. In a partnership, Partner A has an investment of $60,000.00; Partner B has an investment of $40,000.00. Each partner is to receive 6% interest on capital investment and share equally in the remaining net income or loss. How much will each partner receive if the net income is $10,000.00?

5. In a partnership, Partner A has an investment of $25,000.00; Partner B has an investment of $75,000.00. Each partner is to receive a salary of $4,000.00 and 5% interest on capital investment. If the net income for the year is $10,000.00, how much does each partner receive?

6. In a partnership, Partner A is to receive a salary of $5,000.00; Partner B is to receive a salary of $3,000.00. Both partners are to receive 4% interest on capital investments. The remainder of the net income or loss is to be shared equally. Capital for the partners is: Partner A, $100,000.00; Partner B, $80,000.00. The net loss for the period is $4,000.00. How much of the loss is shared by each partner?

7. In question 5 above, what accounts are debited and credited, and for what amounts, to close the income summary account and to record each partner's share of the net income?

8. In question 6 above, what accounts are debited and credited, and for what amounts, to close the income summary account and to record each partner's share of the net loss?

CASE 1 Jean Stucky and Lorrie Braun enter into a partnership agreement. As part of the agreement, Mrs. Stucky is to invest $65,000.00 and Ms. Braun is to invest $35,000.00. Mrs. Stucky wants a statement to be included in the articles of partnership that net income and loss will be shared on a ratio of Mrs. Stucky's 65 to Ms. Braun's 35. Ms. Braun does not believe that any statement needs to be included about the sharing of net income and loss. Which partner is correct? Explain your answer.

CASE 2 Milton Case has $15,000.00 to invest in a business. Manuela Truilijo has $25,000.00 to invest. Ms. Truilijo has about 20 years experience in a business similar to the one in which the partnership will engage, but cannot spend much time actively participating in the business. Mr. Case will spend all his time working in the business activities of the partnership. What method of distributing net income or loss would be best for this partnership? Explain your answer.

PROBLEM 5-1   Recording division of net income and net loss according to ratio of capital investments

Elaine Blair and Rita Busch are partners in a retail flower shop. Ms. Blair invested $10,000.00 and Mrs. Busch invested $5,000.00. The articles of partnership include the items listed on page 90.

a. All net income or loss is divided according to the partners' initial capital investments.

b. Interest on investments or salaries are *not* paid to the partners.

The income statements show the following for:

1977 — net income of $21,000.00.
1978 — net loss of $900.00.

Instructions: □ **1.** Use page 12 of a general journal and the date December 31, 1977. Record the closing entry to close the income summary account and distribute the net income for the year.

□ **2.** Use the same page of a general journal and the date December 31, 1978. Record the closing entry to close the income summary account and distribute the net loss for the year.

PROBLEM 5-2 Recording and reporting the division of net income when interest is allowed on capital

A partnership, Anderson and Bottsford, has the following investments recorded in the partners' capital accounts on June 30 of the current year: Ted Anderson, $32,000.00; Mischell Bottsford, $19,000.00. The partnership agreement includes the statement that partners are to receive 8% interest on their investments. The remaining net income or loss is to be distributed equally. The income statement for the fiscal year ended June 30 shows a net income of $6,100.00.

Instructions: □ **1.** Prepare a distribution of net income statement dated June 30 of the current year.

□ **2.** Use page 6 of a general journal and the date of June 30 of the current year. Record the entry to close the income summary account and distribute the net income to the partners' capital accounts.

PROBLEM 5-3 Net income less than interest on investments

The partnership, Sampson-Southland-Salis, formed by John Sampson, Kermit Southland, and Charlene Salis has the following investments: Sampson, $80,000.00; Southland, $10,000.00; and Salis, $35,000.00. The articles of partnership include a statement that each partner is to receive interest on invested capital at the rate of 5%. The remaining net income or loss is to be divided equally. The income statement for the fiscal year ended December 31 of the current year shows a net income of $5,350.00.

Instructions: □ **1.** Prepare a distribution of net income statement dated December 31 of the current year.

□ **2.** Use page 18 of a general journal. Record the entry to close the income summary account and distribute the net income to the partners' capital accounts.

PROBLEM 5-4   Recording the division of net income
                                      allowing salaries to partners

Pauline Terry and Mildred Newsome own a business known as Northside Realty. Their partnership agreement includes a statement that Ms. Terry is to receive a monthly salary of $800.00 (or $9,600.00 per year). Miss Newsome is to receive a monthly salary of $500.00. The remaining net income or loss is to be divided equally. On March 31 of the current year, the income statement for the fiscal year shows a net income of $24,000.00. The partners' salaries are treated as withdrawals.

Instructions: □ **1.** Prepare a distribution of net income statement.

□ **2.** Use page 8 of a general journal. Record the entry to close the income summary account and distribute the net income to the partners' capital accounts.

MASTERY   Recording the distribution of net income
PROBLEM 5-M   by a combination of methods

Optional
Problems

On December 31 of the current year, the investments in the partnership of Shao and Cheng are: Arlene Shao, $36,300.00; Liu Wong Cheng, $24,200.00. The income summary account has a credit balance of $18,440.00 after all the revenue, cost, and expense accounts have been closed. The articles of partnership include a statement that each partner is to receive an 8% interest on capital invested. In addition, Mrs. Shao is to receive a monthly salary of $500.00. Miss Cheng is to receive a monthly salary of $300.00. The remaining net income or loss is to be divided equally. The partners' salaries are treated as withdrawals.

Instructions: □ **1.** Prepare a distribution of net income statement dated for the fiscal year ended December 31 of the current year.

□ **2.** Use page 22 of a general journal. Record the entry to close the income summary account and distribute the net income or loss to the partners' capital accounts.

BONUS   Net income less than allowances
PROBLEM 5-B   for interest and salaries

Assume that in Mastery Problem 5-M there is a credit balance of $14,000.00 in the income summary account, instead of $18,440.00.

Instructions: □ **1.** Prepare a distribution of net income statement.

□ **2.** Use page 22 of a general journal. Record the entry to close the income summary account and distribute the net income or loss to the partners' capital accounts.

6

End-of-Fiscal-Period Work for a Partnership

The end-of-fiscal-period work for a partnership is similar to that for a sole proprietorship. However, on the balance sheet and the capital statement of a partnership the capital for each partner is listed separately. In addition to the usual financial statements prepared for sole proprietorships, a distribution of net income statement is prepared for partnerships.

WORK SHEET FOR A PARTNERSHIP

The partnership of O'Brien and Moore, described in Chapters 4 and 5, operates a wholesale candy business. The chart of accounts used by the partnership is shown on page 64.

Preparing a trial balance on a work sheet

At the end of the yearly fiscal period, December 31, 1978, a trial balance is prepared on work sheet paper for the partnership of O'Brien and Moore. All the account titles and account numbers are listed on the trial balance in the same order as they appear on the chart of accounts. The trial balance prepared for O'Brien and Moore is shown in the Trial Balance columns of the work sheet, page 93.

Data needed for adjustments on the work sheet

At the end of the yearly fiscal period, the accountant for O'Brien and Moore obtains the data needed for adjusting general ledger accounts.

Interest earned but not received on notes receivable	$ 51.63
Merchandise inventory, December 31, 1978	49,947.92
Supplies inventory, December 31, 1978	227.30
Value of prepaid insurance, December 31, 1978	679.00
Interest owed on notes payable but not yet paid	20.00
Additional bad debts expense to be recorded	221.00
Depreciation expense on equipment to be recorded	1,565.00

O'Brien and Moore
Work Sheet
For Year Ended December 31, 1978

#	ACCOUNT TITLE	ACCT. NO.	TRIAL BALANCE DEBIT	TRIAL BALANCE CREDIT	ADJUSTMENTS DEBIT	ADJUSTMENTS CREDIT	INCOME STATEMENT DEBIT	INCOME STATEMENT CREDIT	BALANCE SHEET DEBIT	BALANCE SHEET CREDIT	
1	Cash	1101	679268						679268		1
2	Petty Cash	1102	20000						20000		2
3	Accounts Receivable	1103	1472076						1472076		3
4	Allow. for Uncoll. Accts.	1103.1		14680		(g)22100				36780	4
5	Notes Receivable	1104	147500						147500		5
6	Merchandise Inventory	1105	4573689		(c)4994792	(b)4573689			4994792		6
7	Supplies	1106	257022			(d)234292			22730		7
8	Prepaid Insurance	1107	272000			(e)204100			67900		8
9	Interest Receivable	1108			(a)5163				5163		9
10	Equipment	1201	3912700						3912700		10
11	Accum. Depr.-Equip.	1201.1		354400		(h)156500				510900	11
12	Accounts Payable	2101		415290						415290	12
13	Notes Payable	2102		240000						240000	13
14	Employees Inc. Tax Pay.-Fed.	2103		67515						67515	14
15	FICA Tax Payable	2104		57870						57870	15
16	Unempl. Tax Pay.-Fed.	2105		2411						2411	16
17	Unempl. Tax Pay.-State	2106		13021						13021	17
18	Sales Tax Payable	2107		149842						149842	18
19	Interest Payable	2108				(f)2000				2000	19
20	Coleen O'Brien, Capital	3101		5900000						5900000	20
21	Coleen O'Brien, Drawing	3102	816000						816000		21
22	Terry Moore, Capital	3201		2950000						2950000	22
23	Terry Moore, Drawing	3202	625000						625000		23
24	Income Summary	3901			(b)4573689	(c)4994792	4573689	4994792			24
25	Sales	4001		35962250				35962250			25
26	Sales Returns + Allow.	4001.1	157210				157210				26
27	Purchases	5001	25409640				25409640				27
28	Purchases Ret. + Allow.	5001.1		326160				326160			28
29	Advertising Expense	6101	224800				224800				29
30	Delivery Expense	6102	466500				466500				30
31	Misc. Expense-Sales	6103	31728				31728				31
32	Salary Expense-Sales	6104	4761600				4761600				32
33	Bad Debts Expense	6201			(g)22100		22100				33
34	Depr. Expense-Equip.	6202			(h)156500		156500				34
35	Insurance Expense	6203			(e)204100		204100				35
36	Misc. Exp.-Admin.	6204	228874				228874				36
37	Payroll Taxes Expense	6205	532407				532407				37
38	Rent Expense	6206	840000				840000				38
39	Salary Expense-Admin.	6207	1025425				1025425				39
40	Supplies Expense	6208			(d)234292		234292				40
41	Interest Income	7001				(a)5163		5163			41
42	Interest Expense	8001			(f)2000		2000				42
43			44453439	44453439	10192636	10192636	38870865	41288365	12763129	10345629	43
44	Net Income						2417500			2417500	44
45							41288365	41288365	12763129	12763129	45
46											46

Completed eight-column work sheet

Analyzing adjustments on the work sheet

The adjustments are recorded in the Adjustments columns of the work sheet. Each adjustment has a debit part and a credit part; therefore, two or more accounts are affected by each adjustment.

Interest on notes receivable. The interest earned on notes receivable, but not yet received, is still revenue for the fiscal period in which it is earned. The amount of interest to be received, $51.63, is shown on the financial statements. The entry to record this interest income is a debit to Interest Receivable and a credit to Interest Income for $51.63.

> The recording of income earned but not yet received is described in greater detail in Chapter 23.

Merchandise inventory. Two adjustments are made for merchandise inventory:

1. To transfer the balance of the beginning merchandise inventory, $45,736.89, to the income summary account. The entry is a debit to Income Summary and a credit to Merchandise Inventory.
2. To record the ending merchandise inventory, $49,947.92, in the merchandise inventory account. The entry is a debit to Merchandise Inventory and a credit to Income Summary.

Supplies inventory. The supplies account shows a balance of $2,570.22 in the trial balance. A physical count of the supplies on hand shows that the balance should be $227.30. The difference between these two figures, $2,342.92, is the amount of supplies expense for the fiscal period. The adjusting entry is a debit to Supplies Expense and a credit to Supplies for $2,342.92.

Prepaid insurance. The prepaid insurance account shows a balance of $2,720.00 in the trial balance. A check of the insurance policies and records shows that the unused portion of the prepaid insurance is $679.00. The difference between these two figures, $2,041.00, is the amount of insurance expense for the fiscal period. The adjusting entry is a debit to Insurance Expense and a credit to Prepaid Insurance for $2,041.00.

Interest owed on notes payable. On December 31, 1978, the partnership has some notes payable outstanding which will be paid in the 1979 fiscal year. However, some of the interest on these notes, $20.00, was an expense for the time in 1978 that the notes were held by creditors. An adjusting entry must be made to record that interest expense which applies to the 1978 fiscal year. The adjusting entry is a debit to Interest Expense and a credit to Interest Payable for $20.00.

> The recording of expenses incurred but not paid at the end of a fiscal period is described in greater detail in Chapter 23.

Bad debts expense. Using past experience as a guide, the accountant for O'Brien and Moore has determined that the amount of allowance made for uncollectible accounts should be increased by $221.00. The adjusting entry is a debit to Bad Debts Expense and a credit to Allowance for Uncollectible Accounts for $221.00.

> The calculating and recording of bad debts expense is described in more detail in Chapter 21.

Depreciation expense. Based on the expected life and trade-in value of the plant assets on hand, December 31, 1978, the accountant for O'Brien and Moore figures that the additional depreciation to be recorded is $1,565.00. The adjusting entry to record the depreciation is a debit to Depreciation Expense — Equipment and a credit to Accumulated Depreciation — Equipment for $1,565.00.

> The calculating and recording of depreciation on various kinds of plant assets is described in greater detail in Chapter 22.

The adjustments made on December 31, 1978, for O'Brien and Moore are shown in the Adjustments columns of the work sheet, page 93.

Completing the work sheet

The work sheet for a partnership is completed in the usual way. All the amounts in the Trial Balance columns and the Adjustments columns are extended to the Income Statement columns and Balance Sheet columns. The net income or loss is figured in the usual way and recorded in the Income Statement and Balance Sheet columns.

The completed work sheet for the O'Brien and Moore partnership is shown on page 93. The form and procedures used for the O'Brien and Moore partnership are the same as those used to prepare the work sheet for the Village Gift Shop, Chapter 3, page 48.

PARTNERSHIP FINANCIAL STATEMENTS

A partnership prepares the same three financial statements prepared by a sole proprietorship: income statement, capital statement, and balance sheet. In addition, a partnership usually prepares a distribution of net income statement to show how the net income or loss is divided among the partners.

Income statement

The income statement for O'Brien and Moore is shown on the next page. This income statement is different from the income statement prepared for the Village Gift Shop, Chapter 3, page 53. The partnership has divided the operating expenses into two classifications: selling expenses and administrative expenses. Those operating expenses directly related to the selling of merchandise are called selling expenses. Those operating expenses that are entirely or partly related to the administrative or non-selling activities are called administrative expenses. Not all expenses can be neatly placed in either the selling or administrative classification. For example, depreciation expense might apply to equipment used for both selling and administrative activities. If an operating expense cannot be clearly classified solely as a selling expense, the expense is listed under administrative expenses.

```
                        O'Brien and Moore
                        Income Statement
                  For Year Ended December 31, 1978


Operating Revenue:
  Sales . . . . . . . . . . . . . . . . . . . . .    $359,622.50
  Less Sales Returns and Allowances . . . . . . .       1,572.10
  Net Sales . . . . . . . . . . . . . . . . . .                     $358,050.40

Cost of Merchandise Sold:
  Merchandise Inventory, January 1, 1978 . . . .     $ 45,736.89
  Purchases . . . . . . . . . . . . . . . . . .    $254,096.40
  Less Purchases Returns and Allowances . . . . .      3,261.60
  Net Purchases . . . . . . . . . . . . . . . .                       250,834.80
  Total Cost of Merchandise Available for Sale  .                   $296,571.69
  Less Merchandise Inventory, December 31, 1978 .                     49,947.92
  Cost of Merchandise Sold . . . . . . . . . . .                                   246,623.77

Gross Profit on Operations . . . . . . . . . . .                                  $111,426.63

Operating Expenses:
  Selling Expenses:
    Advertising Expense . . . . . . . . . . . . .    $   2,248.00
    Delivery Expense . . . . . . . . . . . . . .         4,665.00
    Miscellaneous Expense--Sales . . . . . . . .           317.28
    Salary Expense--Sales . . . . . . . . . . . .       47,616.00
    Total Selling Expenses . . . . . . . . . . .                   $ 54,846.28

  Administrative Expenses:
    Bad Debts Expense . . . . . . . . . . . . . .    $     221.00
    Depreciation Expense--Equipment . . . . . . .        1,565.00
    Insurance Expense . . . . . . . . . . . . . .        2,041.00
    Miscellaneous Expense--Administrative . . . .        2,288.74
    Payroll Taxes Expense . . . . . . . . . . . .        5,324.07
    Rent Expense . . . . . . . . . . . . . . . .         8,400.00
    Salary Expense--Administrative . . . . . . .        10,254.25
    Supplies Expense . . . . . . . . . . . . . .         2,342.92
    Total Administrative Expenses . . . . . . . .                    32,436.98
  Total Operating Expenses . . . . . . . . . . .                                   87,283.26

Income from Operations . . . . . . . . . . . . .                                  $ 24,143.37

Other Revenue:
  Interest Income . . . . . . . . . . . . . . . .    $      51.63

Other Expense:
  Interest Expense . . . . . . . . . . . . . . .            20.00

Net Addition . . . . . . . . . . . . . . . . . .                                       31.63

Net Income . . . . . . . . . . . . . . . . . . .                                  $ 24,175.00
```

Partnership income statement

Distribution of net income statement

The distribution of net income statement for O'Brien and Moore is described and illustrated in Chapter 5, pages 87 to 88. The total amount of net income shown on the distribution of net income statement, page 88, is the same as the amount of net income shown on the work sheet, page 93.

Capital statement

The capital statement for the partnership of O'Brien and Moore, prepared on December 31, 1978, is shown below.

```
                          O'Brien and Moore
                          Capital Statement
                    For Year Ended December 31, 1978


    Coleen O'Brien:
                                                          $59,000.00
        Capital, January 1, 1978 . . . . . . . .
        Share of Net Income . . . . . . . . . .  $13,825.00
            Less Withdrawals . . . . . . . . . .    8,160.00
        Net Increase in Capital . . . . . . . .                5,665.00
        Present Capital, December 31, 1978 . . .                        $64,665.00

    Terry Moore:
                                                          $29,500.00
        Capital, January 1, 1978 . . . . . . . .
        Share of Net Income . . . . . . . . . .  $10,350.00
            Less Withdrawals . . . . . . . . . .    6,250.00
        Net Increase in Capital . . . . . . . .                4,100.00
        Present Capital, December 31, 1978 . . .                          33,600.00

    Total Capital, December 31, 1978 . . . . . .                        $98,265.00
```

Partnership capital statement

The capital statement for O'Brien and Moore is similar to the capital statement for Village Gift Shop shown in Chapter 3, page 53. The major difference is that there are data for each partner on the capital statement of O'Brien and Moore. The net income for the owner of Village Gift Shop is found on the work sheet for the shop. The share of net income for each of the partners in O'Brien and Moore is found on the distribution of net income statement for the partnership, page 88. The amount of each partner's withdrawals is found on the work sheet, page 93, and the capital statement above.

If a net loss should be incurred, each partner's share of the net loss will be *added* to withdrawals. The total of the net loss and withdrawals for each partner is *subtracted* from beginning capital to find the amount of the present capital at the end of a fiscal period.

Balance sheet

The balance sheet for a partnership is similar to that for a sole proprietorship. The balance sheet of a sole proprietorship, page 54 in Chapter 3, shows a single amount of capital for the single owner. The balance sheet of a partnership, shown below, includes the capital for each partner in the capital section. The capital amounts for the partners are totaled to show the total capital for the partnership. The data for the capital section of the partnership balance sheet are obtained from the capital statement, page 97. The data for the remainder of the balance sheet are obtained from the work sheet, page 93.

O'Brien and Moore
Balance Sheet
December 31, 1978

ASSETS

Current Assets:			
Cash			$ 6,792.68
Petty Cash			200.00
Accounts Receivable		$14,720.76	
Less Allowance for Uncollectible Accounts		367.80	14,352.96
Notes Receivable			1,475.00
Merchandise Inventory			49,947.92
Supplies			227.30
Prepaid Insurance			679.00
Interest Receivable			51.63
Total Current Assets			$ 73,726.49
Plant Assets:			
Equipment		$39,127.00	
Less Accumulated Depreciation--Equipment		5,109.00	
Total Plant Assets			34,018.00
Total Assets			$107,744.49

LIABILITIES

Current Liabilities:		
Accounts Payable	$ 4,152.90	
Notes Payable	2,400.00	
Employees Income Tax Payable--Federal	675.15	
FICA Tax Payable	578.70	
Unemployment Tax Payable--Federal	24.11	
Unemployment Tax Payable--State	130.21	
Sales Tax Payable	1,498.42	
Interest Payable	20.00	
Total Current Liabilities		$ 9,479.49

CAPITAL

Coleen O'Brien, Capital	$64,665.00	
Terry Moore, Capital	33,600.00	
Total Capital		98,265.00
Total Liabilities and Capital		$107,744.49

Partnership balance sheet

ADJUSTING ENTRIES FOR A PARTNERSHIP

The adjusting entries for a partnership are essentially the same as those for a sole proprietorship. The data for the adjusting entries are taken from the Adjustments columns of the work sheet, page 93. The adjusting entries for the partnership of O'Brien and Moore, on December 31, 1978, are shown below.

ACCOUNTS PAYABLE DEBIT	GENERAL DEBIT	DATE	ACCOUNT TITLE	POST. REF.	GENERAL CREDIT	ACCOUNTS RECEIV. CREDIT	
			GENERAL JOURNAL		PAGE 13		
			Adjusting Entries				1
	5163	1978 Dec. 31	Interest Receivable	1108			2
			Interest Income	7001	5163		3
	4573689	31	Income Summary	3901			4
			Merchandise Inventory	1105	4573689		5
	4994792	31	Merchandise Inventory	1105			6
			Income Summary	3901	4994792		7
	234292	31	Supplies Expense	6208			8
			Supplies	1106	234292		9
	204100	31	Insurance Expense	6203			10
			Prepaid Insurance	1107	204100		11
	2000	31	Interest Expense	8001			12
			Interest Payable	2108	2000		13
	22100	31	Bad Debts Expense	6201			14
			Allow. for Uncoll. Accts.	1103.1	22100		15
	156500	31	Depreciation Exp.—Equip.	6202			16
			Accum. Depr.—Equip.	1201.1	156500		17
							18

Adjusting entries for a partnership

CLOSING ENTRIES FOR A PARTNERSHIP

The closing entries for a partnership are similar to those for a sole proprietorship. The major difference is that separate entries are made for each partner to record the distribution of net income or loss and to close the partners' drawing accounts.

The closing entries for O'Brien and Moore are shown on page 100.

Data for the closing entries, are obtained from the following sources:

1. *Lines 1 to 21:* The Income Statement columns of the work sheet, page 93.
2. *Lines 22 to 24:* The distribution of net income statement, page 88. The procedure and source is described in Chapter 5, pages 87 to 88.
3. *Lines 25 to 28:* From the Balance Sheet columns of the work sheet, page 93.

ACCOUNTS PAYABLE DEBIT	GENERAL DEBIT	DATE	ACCOUNT TITLE	POST. REF.	GENERAL CREDIT	ACCOUNTS RECEIV. CREDIT
			GENERAL JOURNAL PAGE 14			
			Closing Entries			
	35962250	1978 Dec. 31	Sales	4001		
	326160		Purchases Returns & Allow.	5001.1		
	5163		Interest Income	7001		
			Income Summary	3901	36293573	
	34297176	31	Income Summary	3901		
			Sales Returns & Allow.	4001.1	157210	
			Purchases	5001	25409640	
			Advertising Expense	6101	224800	
			Delivery Expense	6102	466500	
			Misc. Exp.-Sales	6103	31728	
			Salary Expense-Sales	6104	4761600	
			Bad Debts Expense	6201	22100	
			Depr. Expense-Equip.	6202	156500	
			Insurance Expense	6203	204100	
			Misc. Exp.-Administrative	6204	228874	
			Payroll Taxes Expense	6205	532407	
			Rent Expense	6206	840000	
			Salary Exp.-Administrative	6207	1025425	
			Supplies Expense	6208	234292	
			Interest Expense	8001	2000	
	2417500	31	Income Summary	3901		
			Coleen O'Brien, Capital	3101	1382500	
			Terry Moore, Capital	3201	1035000	
	816000	31	Coleen O'Brien, Capital	3101		
			Coleen O'Brien, Drawing	3102	816000	
	625000	31	Terry Moore, Capital	3201		
			Terry Moore, Drawing	3202	625000	

From work sheet

From distribution of net income statement

From work sheet

Closing entries for a partnership

The effect of the closing entries on the partners' capital accounts is shown in the T accounts below.

Coleen O'Brien, Capital 3101			Terry Moore, Capital 3201		
Drawing	8,160.00	Bal. 59,000.00	Drawing	6,250.00	Bal. 29,500.00
		Closing 13,825.00			Closing 10,350.00

Coleen O'Brien, Drawing 3102			Terry Moore, Drawing 3202		
Bal.	8,160.00	To Cap. 8,160.00	Bal.	6,250.00	To Cap. 6,250.00

POST-CLOSING TRIAL BALANCE FOR A PARTNERSHIP

After the closing entries are posted, the only accounts that have balances are the asset, liability, and capital accounts. To prove the accuracy of the work at the end of the fiscal period, a post-closing trial balance is prepared. The post-closing trial balance must be in balance; that is, the total of the debit balances will equal the total of the credit balances.

The form of the post-closing trial balance for the partnership O'Brien and Moore will be the same as the one prepared for the Village Gift Shop, page 57. The exception will be that the present balance of the capital accounts for both partners will be listed.

PARTNERS' FEDERAL INCOME TAXES

Partners are not considered to be employees of the business they own. Instead, they are classified by federal laws as self-employed persons.

Federal income taxes for partners

Partnerships are not taxed as business units. Instead, the partners themselves must report and pay income taxes on the income they receive from their partnership. The income is reported on the partners' individual, personal income tax returns. A partner's share of the partnership net income must be reported, whether or not any or all of it has been withdrawn from the business during the year. Thus, the total share of net income or loss shown on the distribution of net income statement is the amount reported by each partner.

In those states which have individual income tax laws, the regulations are similar to those for the federal government.

FICA tax

Although partners are self-employed persons, they are still entitled to old-age, survivors, and disability insurance benefits. Partners are entitled to the same benefits as employees of the business. The partners can qualify for the FICA benefits by paying a FICA tax directly to the federal government. The rate of the FICA tax for self-employed persons changes from time to time. A partner or other self-employed person who wishes to pay FICA taxes and qualify for the benefits should check with the local social security office.

Both the income tax and the FICA tax are personal expenses of self-employed persons. These payments do not appear on the records of the business as expenses. The payments are made by the individuals and not by the business.

Retirement benefits

Federal tax regulations make it possible for a self-employed person to establish a retirement fund and pay into it regularly. The amount that may be paid into the fund, and the effect of the payment on reporting annual income tax is established by federal tax regulations. A self-employed person who wishes to establish a retirement fund under these regulations should check with the nearest federal Internal Revenue Service office. Payment into a retirement fund under these regulations is a personal payment by the self-employed person. The payment is not recorded on the books of the business as an expense of the business.

Using
Business
Terms

✦ What is the meaning of each of the following?

• selling expenses   • administrative expenses

Questions
for
Individual
Study

1. What financial statement is prepared for a partnership that is not prepared for a sole proprietorship?
2. How do the procedures for preparing a trial balance for a partnership compare to the procedures for preparing a trial balance for a sole proprietorship?
3. For each of the following adjustments made on the work sheet for O'Brien and Moore, page 93, how are the accounts affected:
   a. Interest earned on notes but not received?
   b. Merchandise inventory?
   c. Supplies inventory?
   d. Prepaid insurance balance?
   e. Interest owed on notes payable?
   f. Bad debts expense?
   g. Depreciation expense?
4. In what way does the income statement form for O'Brien and Moore,

page 96, differ from the income statement form for Village Gift Shop, page 53?
5. In what way does the capital statement for O'Brien and Moore, page 97, differ from the capital statement for Village Gift Shop, page 53?
6. In what way does the balance sheet for O'Brien and Moore, page 98, differ from the balance sheet for Village Gift Shop, page 54?
7. How do the adjusting entries for a partnership compare to those for a sole proprietorship?
8. How do the closing entries for a partnership compare to those for a sole proprietorship?
9. Why is it that partners' income taxes, FICA taxes, and salaries are not charged to expense accounts on the records of O'Brien and Moore?

Cases for
Manage-
ment
Decision

CASE 1 The partnership of Harrison and Washington records partners' salaries by debiting Partners' Salaries and crediting Cash. What effect will this method have on the income tax reports filed by the individual partners for their personal taxes?

CASE 2 In the situation described above in Case 1, a public accountant advises the partners of Harrison and Washington to continue to record the salaries for partners in an account titled Partners' Salaries. In this way, the accountant claims, the partnership will pay less income taxes because the expense for partners' salaries will reduce the amount of net income earned by the partnership. Mr. Harrison states that he does not believe this is true. With whom do you agree? Why?

CASE 3 The partnership of Mulligan and Foster has as part of the partnership agreement a statement that 5% interest will be paid on each partner's capital investment. At the end of the 1978 fiscal year there is insufficient net income to pay the 5% interest. For this reason, the accountant for the partnership does not record the 5% interest. Do you agree or disagree with the accountant's procedures? Why?

PROBLEM 6-1 End-of-fiscal-period work for a partnership

If you are not using the workbook correlating with this textbook complete Review Problem 6-R 1 instead of Problem 6-1.

The trial balance for the Doyle and Beezer partnership is given on work sheet paper in the workbook.

Instructions: □ **1.** Using December 31 of the current year as the date, complete the work sheet for the partnership. The additional data needed are:

Interest earned on notes receivable but not yet received, $12.94
Allowance for uncollectible accounts, an additional $74.29
Merchandise inventory, $87,127.51
Supplies inventory, $355.06
Value of insurance policies on hand, $1,970.00
Additional depreciation expense for the year, $1,188.75
Interest owed on notes payable but not yet paid, $52.93

□ **2.** Prepare an income statement.

□ **3.** Prepare a distribution of net income statement. (The partnership agreement includes yearly salaries of $8,600.00 for Patti Doyle and $5,700.00 for Don Beezer; 5% interest per year on each partner's capital as of the *beginning* of the year; and remaining income or loss to be shared equally. No additional investments have been made during the year.)

□ **4.** Prepare a capital statement. (No additional investment has been made during the year by either partner.)

□ **5.** Prepare a balance sheet.

□ **6.** Use page 25 of a general journal. Record the adjusting entries.

□ **7.** Use page 26 of a general journal. Record the closing entries.

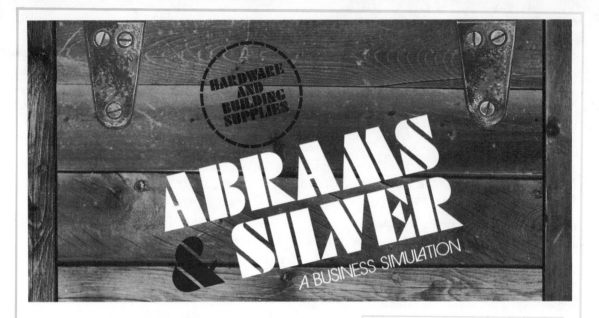

You are ready to apply the accounting principles discussed and illustrated in this textbook to the realistic situations included in the Abrams and Silver business simulation. The set covers the transactions completed by a partnership specializing in hardware and building supplies. The books shown above are used in the accounting system. A block flowchart of the accounting cycle is shown on page 105. A pictorial flowchart of the accounting system is shown on pages 106 and 107.

(The narrative is provided in the set available from the publisher.)

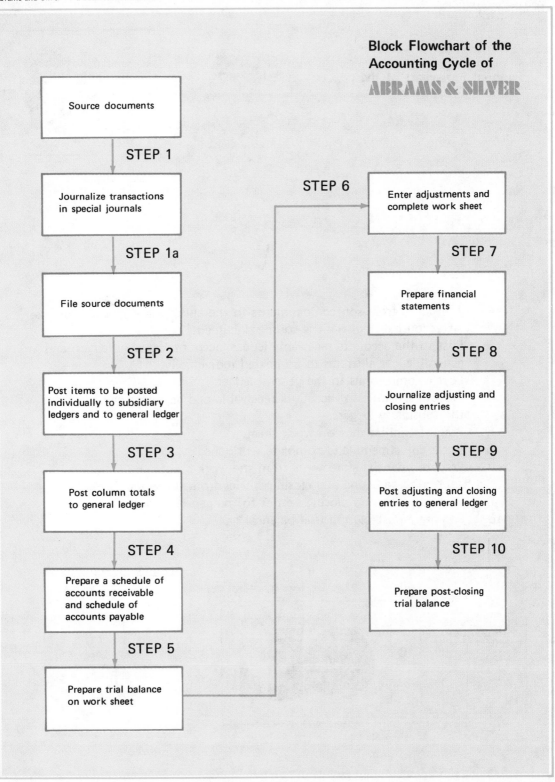

Block Flowchart of the Accounting Cycle of ABRAMS & SILVER

Source documents

STEP 1

Journalize transactions in special journals

STEP 1a

File source documents

STEP 2

Post items to be posted individually to subsidiary ledgers and to general ledger

STEP 3

Post column totals to general ledger

STEP 4

Prepare a schedule of accounts receivable and schedule of accounts payable

STEP 5

Prepare trial balance on work sheet

STEP 6

Enter adjustments and complete work sheet

STEP 7

Prepare financial statements

STEP 8

Journalize adjusting and closing entries

STEP 9

Post adjusting and closing entries to general ledger

STEP 10

Prepare post-closing trial balance

Pictorial Flowchart of the Accounting Cycle of

ABRAMS & SILVER

Source documents

1   Journalize from source documents to the appropriate special journals.
1a   After journalizing, file the source documents.
2   Post to the accounts receivable ledger, accounts payable ledger, and general ledger all items to be posted individually.
3   Post column totals to the general ledger.
4   Prepare schedules of accounts receivable and accounts payable from the subsidiary ledgers.
5   Prepare trial balance on work sheet.
6   Enter adjustments and complete work sheet.
7   Prepare financial statements from the work sheet.
8   Journalize adjusting and closing entries from the work sheet.
9   Post adjusting and closing entries to the general ledger.
10   Prepare a post-closing trial balance.

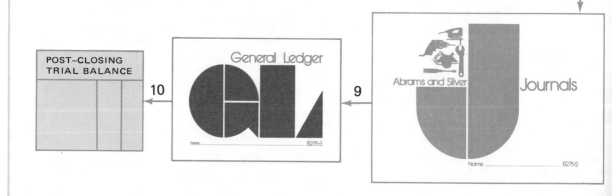

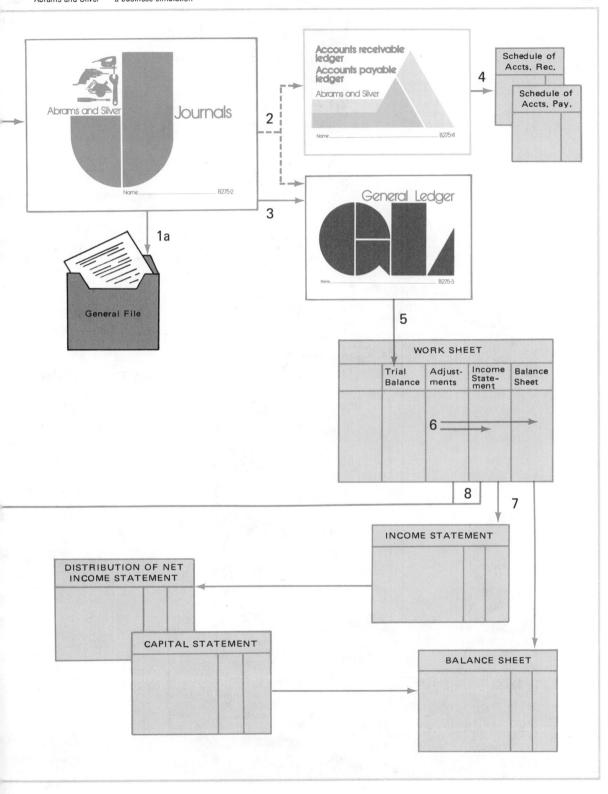

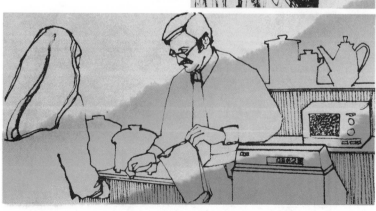

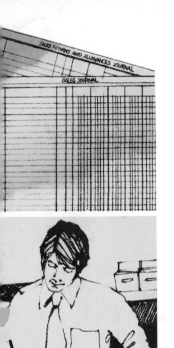

SPECIALIZED ACCOUNTING CLERKS

SOME BUSINESSES USE DEPARTMENTAL ACCOUNTING SYSTEMS. Businesses often organize their merchandise activities and their accounting records by departments for management efficiency. Specialized accounting clerks are employed to check, record, post, and prepare reports for specific types of business transactions. The scope and nature of the work of specialized accounting clerks vary from business to business.

Part 4 of this textbook describes the departmental accounting system used by *Amaros*, a merchandising business. The six departmental journals maintained are: (a) the purchases journal, (b) the purchases returns and allowances journal, (c) the cash payments journal, (d) the sales journal, (e) the sales returns and allowances journal, and (f) the cash receipts journal. Procedures for determining the value of inventories, estimating ending inventories, and preparing an interim departmental statement of gross profit are also described.

AMAROS
CHART OF ACCOUNTS

Balance Sheet Accounts

(1) ASSETS	Account Number
11 *Current Assets*	
Cash	111
Petty Cash	112
Accounts Receivable	113
Allowance for Uncollectible Accounts	113.1
Merchandise Inventory — Floor Covering	114
Merchandise Inventory — Paint	115
Merchandise Inventory — Wallpaper	116
Supplies	117
Prepaid Insurance	118
12 *Plant Assets*	
Delivery Equipment	121
Accumulated Depreciation — Delivery Equipment	121.1
Store Equipment	122
Accumulated Depreciation — Store Equipment	122.1

(2) LIABILITIES	
Accounts Payable	211
Salaries Payable	212
Employees Income Tax Payable — Federal	213
Employees Income Tax Payable — State	214
FICA Tax Payable	215
Unemployment Tax Payable — Federal	216
Unemployment Tax Payable — State	217
Hospital Insurance Payable	218
Group Life Insurance Payable	219
Sales Tax Payable	220

(3) CAPITAL	
Alex Amaro, Capital	311
Alex Amaro, Drawing	312
Income Summary	313

Income Statement Accounts

(4) OPERATING REVENUE	Account Number
Sales — Floor Covering	411
Sales Returns and Allowances — Floor Covering	411.1
Sales — Paint	412
Sales Returns and Allowances — Paint	412.1
Sales — Wallpaper	413
Sales Returns and Allowances — Wallpaper	413.1

(5) COST OF MERCHANDISE	
Purchases — Floor Covering	511
Purchases Returns and Allowances — Floor Covering	511.1
Purchases Discount — Floor Covering	511.2
Purchases — Paint	512
Purchases Returns and Allowances — Paint	512.1
Purchases — Wallpaper	513
Purchases Returns and Allowances — Wallpaper	513.1

(6) OPERATING EXPENSES	
Advertising Expense	611
Bad Debts Expense	612
Delivery Expense	613
Depreciation Expense — Delivery Equipment	614
Depreciation Expense — Store Equipment	615
Insurance Expense	616
Miscellaneous Expense	617
Payroll Taxes Expense	618
Rent Expense	619
Salary Expense — Administrative	620
Salary Expense — Floor Covering Sales	621
Salary Expense — Paint Sales	622
Salary Expense — Wallpaper Sales	623
Supplies Expense	624

(7) OTHER REVENUE	
Telephone Income	711

The chart of accounts for Amaros is illustrated above for ready reference in your study of Chapters 7—10 of this textbook.

Purchases and Cash Payments Clerk

The owner of a business makes management decisions about the efficiency of each phase of the business. To help make these decisions, the owner needs information about the kinds of merchandise that are producing the greatest or the least profit. A business with two or more departments needs accounting data to show how well each department is doing. An accounting system showing accounting data for two or more departments is called a departmental accounting system.

Department stores, home improvement centers, shoe stores, furniture stores, and garages with both sales and repair, are examples of firms that commonly organize on a departmental basis. A department store, for example, may have departments such as toys, jewelry, hardware, furniture, and women's and men's clothing.

Alex Amaro owns and operates a home improvement center called Amaros. Amaros has three departments: (a) Floor Covering, (b) Paint, and (c) Wallpaper. Mr. Amaro wishes to know the gross profit for each department in the business. For this reason, the accounting records must include separate departmental accounts for transactions affecting purchases and sales of merchandise. The separate departmental accounts for Amaros are shown in Sections (1), (4), (5), and (6) on the chart of accounts on page 110.

ACCOUNTING DEPARTMENT

The organization and the number of employees in an accounting department depends on the size of the business and the amount of accounting data to be recorded. The organization of Amaros' accounting department is shown on page 112.

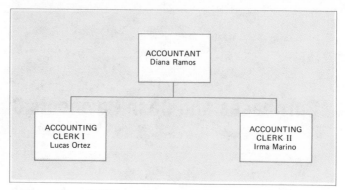

The specific responsibilities of persons in Amaros' accounting department are:

Accountant

1. Supervises persons in the accounting department.
2. Approves and signs all checks.
3. Prepares federal and state tax reports.
4. Prepares and analyzes financial statements.
5. Prepares general accounting recommendations for Mr. Amaro.
6. Records and posts entries in general journal.

Accounting Clerk I

1. Records and posts purchases of merchandise on account.
2. Records and posts purchases returns and allowances.
3. Prepares checks for the accountant's approval and signature.
4. Records and posts cash payments.
5. Reconciles bank statement.
6. Prepares and records payroll.

Accounting Clerk II

1. Records and posts sales of merchandise on account.
2. Records and posts sales returns and allowances.
3. Records and posts cash receipts.
4. Prepares statements to customers.
5. Maintains inventory records by department.

DEPARTMENTAL PURCHASES ON ACCOUNT

Recording purchases of merchandise on account for a departmentalized business is the same as for a business with a single department except for the following:

1. A notation is placed on each purchase invoice showing to which department the purchase applies.
2. The purchases journal has a separate Purchases Debit column for each department.

The source document for each entry in the departmental purchases journal is a purchase invoice. Usually each invoice received by Amaros is for only one department: either Floor Covering, Paint, or Wallpaper. Occasionally, however, merchandise for more than one department may be included on a single invoice.

The first invoice received in September, 1978, is shown below.

Allied Paint Company		INVOICE NO. **26428**	DATE AUGUST 29, 1978

SOLD TO	AMAROS 8240 JACKSON STREET DENVER, CO 80211	SHIP TO	AMAROS 8240 JACKSON STREET DENVER, CO 80211

BUYER ORDER NO.	CARRIER	TERMS OF SALE	SOLD BY
693	MASON TRUCKING CO.	NET 30 DAYS	SMITHFIELD

QUANTITY	DESCRIPTION	UNIT PRICE	AMOUNT
24	#4260 PAINT, 1 LITER	2.77	66.48 ✓
36	#4262 PAINT, 2 LITERS	5.68	204.48 ✓
18	#4280 PAINT, 2 LITERS	5.68	102.24 ✓
36	#6240 PAINT, 4 LITERS	7.40	266.40 ✓

Pur. Inv. No. 352
Received 9/2/78
Wallpaper (513)
Paint (512)
Floor Covering (511)
$639.60

THANK YOU!

644 Central Avenue
Golden, CO 80401

INVOICE TOTAL
639.60

Purchase invoice

As each invoice is received by Amaros, Lucas Ortez, Accounting Clerk I, stamps a form on the invoice. In the stamped form shown above, Mr. Ortez writes the following:

1. The purchase invoice number assigned to the invoice by Amaros, 352.
2. The date on which the invoice is received, 9/2/78.
3. The amount to be charged to the purchases account for each department, Paint, $639.60.

> September 2, 1978. Purchased paint on account from Allied Paint Company, $639.60. Purchase Invoice No. 352.

The cost account Purchases — Paint is debited and the liability account Accounts Payable is credited for $639.60. The creditor's account, Allied Paint Company, is also credited for the same amount as the controlling account, Accounts Payable.

GENERAL LEDGER

Purchases — Paint	512
639.60	

Accounts Payable	211
	639.60

ACCOUNTS PAYABLE LEDGER

Allied Paint Company	
	639.60

Departmental purchases journal

The purchases journal used by Amaros has special Purchases Debit columns for each of the three departments: Floor Covering, Paint, and Wallpaper. The departmental purchases journal for September, 1978, with both account names and account numbers at the top of the amount columns, is shown below.

The small number in parentheses in the amount column headings, such as Floor Covering (511), is the account number. This number aids the accounting clerk in finding the account in the general ledger when the column totals are posted.

| | DATE | ACCOUNT CREDITED | PURCH. NO. | POST. REF. | ACCOUNTS PAYABLE CREDIT (211) | PURCHASES DEBIT | | |
						FLR. COVER. (511)	PAINT (512)	WALLPAPER (513)
1	1978 Sept. 2	Allied Paint Co.	352	✓	639 60		639 60	
2	5	Mission Paint + Wallpaper Co.	353	✓	574 20		436 20	138 00
3	5	Acme Quality Paints	354	✓	183 20		183 20	
4	5	Tri-State Carpeting Co.	355	✓	1840 00	1840 00		
5	6	Devoe Wallpaper Co.	356	✓	89 30			89 30
6	6	A + G Floors, Inc.	357	✓	960 00	960 00		
7	7	Western Floor Covering	358	✓	1360 00	1360 00		
8	7	Alba Wallpaper	359	✓	134 20			134 20
24	26	Acme Quality Paints	375	✓	316 40		316 40	
25	27	Veloz Carpeting	376	✓	760 20	760 20		
26	30	Totals			9840 30	5660 80	3140 60	1038 90
27					(211)	(511)	(512)	(513)

PURCHASES JOURNAL   PAGE 8

The details of each invoice are recorded by Mr. Ortez on one line in the departmental purchases journal. The total amount of the invoice is written in the Accounts Payable Credit column. The amount to be debited to Purchases for each department is written in the appropriate departmental Debit column. The number of the purchase invoice is written in the Purch. No. column. (Since only purchase invoice numbers are recorded in this column, an identifying letter with the purchase invoice number is not necessary.) The name of the creditor, Allied Paint Co., is written in the Account Credited column.

After each purchase invoice is recorded, the invoice is filed in an unpaid invoices file under the date on which payment should be made. The invoice, which is recorded on Line 1 of the journal above with the September 2 date of receipt, is actually dated August 29, 1978. Payment is due in 30 days with no discount allowed. Therefore the invoice is filed under the date of September 28, 1978. If a discount can be earned by early payment, the invoice is filed under the last date on which the payment can be made and the discount still be taken.

Posting from the departmental purchases journal

Amaros keeps accounts with creditors in an accounts payable ledger. The individual amounts in the Accounts Payable Credit column of the departmental purchases journal are posted daily by Mr. Ortez to the appropriate creditors' accounts. *P8* is written in the Post. Ref. column of the ledger account to indicate that the posting came from page 8 of the purchases journal. A check mark is placed in the Post. Ref. column of the purchases journal to indicate the completion of the posting.

At the end of the month, the departmental purchases journal is footed, proved, totaled, and ruled. The total of each amount column is posted to the general ledger account named in the column heading. The number of the account to which the total of each column is posted is written in parentheses immediately below the total to show that the amount has been posted. The illustration on page 114 shows the departmental purchases journal after all posting has been completed.

Handling transportation charges on purchases

When a business purchases merchandise, there are usually transportation charges for delivering the merchandise to the buyer. When the seller pays the transportation charges and treats them as an expense, the records of the purchaser are not involved. When, however, transportation charges on purchases are paid by the buyer, such transportation charges become part of the cost of the merchandise.

When transportation charges on purchases are paid by the buyer, one of two different ways described below is often used to record these charges.

1. The seller pays the transportation company, and the amount of the transportation charge is shown on the invoice to the buyer. The charges are paid by the buyer to the seller as part of the total purchase invoice.
2. The charges are paid by the buyer to the transportation company. The charges are not shown on the purchase invoice.

In either case, all transportation charges on purchased merchandise are debited to an appropriate purchases account.

Some businesses find it inconvenient to determine which department or departments should be debited for each bill for transportation charges. In such cases, all transportation charges may be debited to an account called Transportation on Purchases, or Freight-In, or a similar title. At the end of the fiscal period, the balance of this account is distributed to the departmental purchases accounts. The amounts to be charged to each department may be distributed in any one of several ways. Often distribution is made in proportion to the dollar volume of purchases in each department.

All transportation charges for purchases on account transactions at Amaros are paid by the seller. Therefore, the accounting records of Amaros are not affected by transportation costs.

DEPARTMENTAL PURCHASES RETURNS AND ALLOWANCES

The details of a purchases return or allowance may be stated in a letter, or the buyer may use a debit memorandum. Amaros uses a debit memorandum when returning merchandise or requesting an adjustment.

A debit memorandum issued in September is shown below.

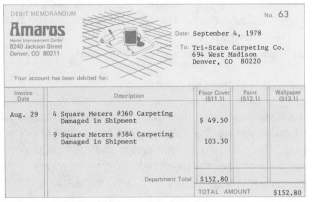

Debit memorandum
for purchases returns
and allowances

Mr. Ortez prepares all debit memorandums for Amaros. The debit memorandums are used as the source documents for purchases returns and allowances transactions.

Some buyers wait for written notice from the seller before journalizing a purchases return or allowance. This written notice is usually in the form of a credit memorandum received from the seller. When this procedure is followed, the buyer uses the credit memorandum from the seller as the source document for the transaction.

September 4, 1978. Returned damaged carpeting to Tri-State Carpeting Co., $152.80. Debit Memorandum No. 63.

GENERAL LEDGER

Accounts Payable   211
152.80 |

Purchases Returns and
Allowances — Floor Covering 511.1
| 152.80

ACCOUNTS PAYABLE LEDGER

Tri-State Carpeting Co.
152.80 |

The liability account Accounts Payable is debited and Purchases Returns and Allowances — Floor Covering is credited for $152.80. The creditor's account in the accounts payable ledger is also debited for the same amount as the controlling account.

Departmental purchases returns and allowances journal

Amaros records all purchases returns and allowances in a special departmental purchases returns and allowances journal. The journal has a Purchases Returns and Allowances Credit column for each of the three departments. Amaros' departmental purchases returns and allowances journal is shown below.

DATE	ACCOUNT DEBITED	DEBIT MEMO. NO.	POST. REF.	ACCOUNTS PAYABLE DEBIT (211)	PURCHASES RETURNS AND ALLOWANCES CREDIT		
					FLR. COVER. (511.1)	PAINT (512.1)	WALLPAPER (513.1)
1973 Sept. 4	Tri-State Carpeting Co.	63	✓	15280	15280		
8	Alba Wallpaper	64	✓	3200			3200
13	Acme Quality Paints	65	✓	6320		6320	
19	Allied Paint Co.	66	✓	3860		3860	
23	Mission Paint + Wallpaper Co.	67	✓	6240			6240
26	Western Floor Covering	68	✓	36280	36280		
31	Devoe Wallpaper Co.	69	✓	1850			1850
				73030	51560	10180	11290
31	Totals			73030	51560	10180	11290
				(211)	(511.1)	(512.1)	(513.1)

Departmental purchases returns and allowances journal

Mr. Ortez records the details of each debit memorandum on one line of the purchases returns and allowances journal. The amount of the debit memorandum is written in the Accounts Payable Debit column. The amount to be credited to Purchases Returns and Allowances for each department is written in the appropriate departmental column. The number of the debit memorandum is written in the Debit Memo. No. column. (An identifying letter is not necessary.) The name of the creditor is written in the Account Debited column.

After the debit memorandum is recorded, the memorandum is attached to the purchase invoice to which it applies. The two documents are filed in the unpaid invoices file. When the invoice is to be paid, details of the decrease in the amount owed because of the debit memorandum are readily available.

Posting from the departmental purchases returns and allowances journal

The departmental purchases returns and allowances journal is posted in the same manner as the departmental purchases journal. The individual amounts in the Accounts Payable Debit column are posted daily by Mr. Ortez to the creditor's account named in the Account Debited column. *PR9* is written in the Post. Ref. column of the ledger account to indicate that the posting came from page 9 of the purchases returns and allowances journal. A check mark is placed in the Post. Ref. column of the journal to indicate the completion of the posting.

Sometimes a purchases return or allowance is made after a creditor has been paid in full. This situation might happen if an invoice is paid very soon after it is received in order to take advantage of the discount. When this happens, the creditor's account after posting has a debit balance instead of a normal credit balance.

A balance in an account that is opposite to the kind of balance that the account normally has is called a contra balance. In manual accounting, a contra balance is usually shown by drawing a circle around the amount in the account. In machine accounting, a contra balance is usually printed in red. Typists often show contra balances by typing these balances in parentheses.

At the end of the month, a departmental purchases returns and allowances journal is footed, proved, totaled, and ruled. The total of each amount column is posted to the general ledger account named in the column heading. To show completion of the posting, the account number is written in parentheses immediately below the total. All posting has been completed for the departmental purchases returns and allowances journal, page 117.

In the chart of accounts, page 110, the account numbers for the departmental purchases returns and allowances accounts contain decimals. An account with a decimal is a deduction from the account having the same number without the decimal. For example, Account No. 511.1, Purchases Returns and Allowances — Floor Covering, is a deduction from Account No. 511, Purchases — Floor Covering. An account that is a deduction from another account is known as a contra account.

DEPARTMENTAL CASH PAYMENTS

GENERAL LEDGER

Accounts Payable	211
1,260.00	

Purchases Discount — Floor Covering	511.2
	25.20

Cash	111
	1,234.80

ACCOUNTS PAYABLE LEDGER

Veloz Carpeting	
1,260.00	

All cash payments are made by check except for small payments that are made from a petty cash fund. The check stubs are the source documents from which entries are made in the cash payments journal.

September 1, 1978. Paid on account to Veloz Carpeting, $1,234.80, covering Purchase Invoice No. 340 for $1,260.00 less a 2% discount. Check No. 730.

The liability account Accounts Payable is debited for $1,260.00, and the contra account, Purchases Discount — Floor Covering, is credited for $25.20. Cash is credited for $1,234.80. The creditor's account in the accounts payable ledger, Veloz Carpeting, is also debited for the same amount as the controlling account.

Departmental cash payments journal

Amaros' cash payments journal is shown below. The journal has two debit columns: General Debit and Accounts Payable Debit. The journal also has three credit columns: General Credit, Purchases Discount — Floor Covering Credit, and Cash Credit. Amaros does not receive any discounts on purchases of paint or wallpaper. As a result, only one purchases discount column is needed.

		CASH PAYMENTS JOURNAL						**PAGE 9**
			1	2	3	4	5	
DATE	ACCOUNT TITLE	CK. NO. / POST. REF.	GENERAL DEBIT	GENERAL CREDIT	ACCOUNTS PAYABLE DEBIT (211)	PURCHASES DISCOUNT — FLR. COVER. CREDIT (511.2)	CASH CREDIT (111)	
1978 Sept. 1	Veloz Carpeting	730 ✓			1260 00	25 20	1234 80	1
1	Rent Expense	731 619	900 00				900 00	2
1	Miscellaneous Expense	732 617	86 50				86 50	3
4	Allied Paint Co.	733 ✓			639 60		639 60	4
4	Acme Quality Paints	734 ✓			183 20		183 20	5
5	Prepaid Insurance	735 118	165 00				165 00	6
5	Supplies	736 117	83 00				83 00	7
5	Advertising Expense	737 611	68 50				68 50	8
28	Delivery Expense	831 613	88 40				88 40	18
29	Totals		6880 30	536 60	11730 82	88 40	17686 12	19
			6880 30	836 60	11730 82	88 40	17686 12	
			(✓)	(✓)	(211)	(511.2)	(111)	20

Departmental cash payments journal

When a business receives discounts on purchases for several departments, a special purchases discount column is used for each department.

Mr. Ortez records the data from each check stub in Amaros' cash payments journal. The entry on Line 1 above shows the cash payment to Veloz Carpeting in which there is a cash discount. The entry on Line 4 shows a cash payment on account for which there is no cash discount.

Posting from the departmental cash payments journal

Mr. Ortez posts daily each individual amount in the General Debit and General Credit columns of the cash payments journal to the general ledger. Also, each individual amount in the Accounts Payable Debit column is posted daily to the accounts payable ledger. In the Post. Ref. columns of the ledger accounts, the source of the posting is shown by writing the journal page, *CP9*.

At the end of the month, the cash payments journal is footed, proved, totaled, and ruled. Then the totals of the special columns are posted by Mr. Ortez to their respective accounts in the general ledger. The account number is written in parentheses immediately below the total. A check mark is written in parentheses below the totals of the General Debit column and the General Credit column. The departmental cash payments journal, page 119, is shown after all posting has been completed.

A schedule of accounts payable is prepared each time the totals of all journals are posted in order to check the accuracy of the posting.

BANK STATEMENT

Banks keep detailed records of their depositors' checking accounts. The records show all deposits received from the depositor, all checks cashed by the bank against the account, and miscellaneous charges made against the account. Miscellaneous charges include such items as charges for stopping payment on checks, for collecting notes, and for checking account service charges.

Banks in different parts of the country have different ways of figuring the bank service charge. Some banks omit the charge if the depositor has a large balance in the checking account.

A report sent by the bank to a depositor showing the deposits, withdrawals, charges, and ending bank balance is called a bank statement. Most banks send monthly statements to depositors. With the statement, the bank includes the canceled checks listed on the statement.

On October 3, 1978, Amaros received the monthly bank statement shown below.

American Security Bank

Denver, Colorado 80213

AMAROS
8240 JACKSON STREET
DENVER, CO 80211

ACCOUNT NUMBER

382-32816

STATEMENT DATE

SEPT. 30, 1978

BALANCE LAST STATEMENT	TOTAL AMOUNT CHECKS	NUMBER OF CHECKS	NUMBER OF DEPOSITS	TOTAL AMOUNT DEPOSITS	SERVICE CHARGE
2,937.04	17,681.95	51	26	18,909.83	4.17

CHECKS		DEPOSITS	DATE			BALANCE
1,234.80	900.00	1,656.40	9	1	78	2,937.04
86.50			9	4	78	2,458.64
639.60	183.20	1,573.60	9	4	78	2,372.14
165.00	83.00	974.63	9	5	78	3,122.94
68.50			9	6	78	3,849.57
			9	6	78	3,781.07
286.75	733.88		9	29	78	4,164.92
4.17SC			9	29	78	4,160.75

KEY: SC - SERVICE CHARGE   OD - OVERDRAFT   CM - CREDIT MEMO
       EC - ERROR CORRECTED   RCC - RETURNED CHECK CHARGE DM - DEBIT MEMO

Bank statement

The last amount, $4,160.75, in the column headed "Balance" is the bank balance of the checking account for Amaros on September 29, 1978.

Reconciling the bank statement

Banks request depositors to report at once any errors found on the bank statements sent to them. Each depositor, therefore, should immediately check the bank statement for accuracy. The bank balance is compared with the checkbook balance. The process of bringing the bank balance and the check-stub balance into agreement is called reconciling the bank statement.

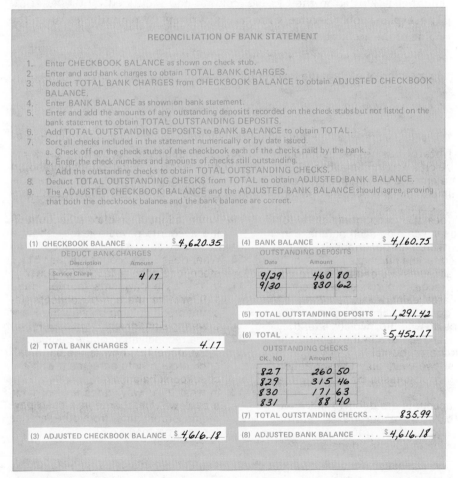

RECONCILIATION OF BANK STATEMENT

1. Enter CHECKBOOK BALANCE as shown on check stub.
2. Enter and add bank charges to obtain TOTAL BANK CHARGES.
3. Deduct TOTAL BANK CHARGES from CHECKBOOK BALANCE to obtain ADJUSTED CHECKBOOK BALANCE.
4. Enter BANK BALANCE as shown on bank statement.
5. Enter and add the amounts of any outstanding deposits recorded on the check stubs but not listed on the bank statement to obtain TOTAL OUTSTANDING DEPOSITS.
6. Add TOTAL OUTSTANDING DEPOSITS to BANK BALANCE to obtain TOTAL.
7. Sort all checks included in the statement numerically or by date issued.
   a. Check off on the check stubs of the checkbook each of the checks paid by the bank.
   b. Enter the check numbers and amounts of checks still outstanding.
   c. Add the outstanding checks to obtain TOTAL OUTSTANDING CHECKS.
8. Deduct TOTAL OUTSTANDING CHECKS from TOTAL to obtain ADJUSTED BANK BALANCE.
9. The ADJUSTED CHECKBOOK BALANCE and the ADJUSTED BANK BALANCE should agree, proving that both the checkbook balance and the bank balance are correct.

| (1) CHECKBOOK BALANCE | $ 4,620.35 |
| DEDUCT BANK CHARGES | |

Description	Amount
Service Charge	4 17

| (2) TOTAL BANK CHARGES | 4.17 |
| (3) ADJUSTED CHECKBOOK BALANCE | $ 4,616.18 |

| (4) BANK BALANCE | $ 4,160.75 |
| OUTSTANDING DEPOSITS | |

Date	Amount
9/29	460 80
9/30	830 62

| (5) TOTAL OUTSTANDING DEPOSITS | 1,291.42 |
| (6) TOTAL | $ 5,452.17 |

OUTSTANDING CHECKS

CK. NO.	Amount
827	260 50
829	315 46
830	171 63
831	88 40

| (7) TOTAL OUTSTANDING CHECKS | 835.99 |
| (8) ADJUSTED BANK BALANCE | $ 4,616.18 |

Printed form for reconciliation of bank statement

Lucas Ortez, Accounting Clerk I, uses the steps and the form printed on the back of the bank statement when reconciling the bank statement each month. The reconciliation of Amaros' September bank statement is shown above. The adjusted checkbook balance and the adjusted bank balance, $4,616.18, must be the same.

Recording bank charges in a journal

Any bank charges listed on a bank statement are considered cash payments made to the bank. Even though no check is issued for these payments, the amount of the bank charges is recorded in the cash payments journal. Amaros records bank charges as a miscellaneous expense.

The entry to record the bank service charge for September, 1978, is entered in the cash payments journal for October. Miscellaneous Expense is debited and Cash is credited for $4.17. There is no check stub to serve as a source document for this entry. Therefore, a memorandum is prepared showing the details of the service charge. The memorandum number is written in the Ck. No. column and identified by the letter *M*. The explanation "Service Charge" is written in parentheses after the name of the account debited.

Using Business Terms

✦ What is the meaning of each of the following?

- departmental accounting system
- contra balance
- bank statement
- reconciling the bank statement

Questions for Individual Study

1. What types of businesses commonly organize on a departmental basis?
2. What determines the organization and the number of employees in an accounting department?
3. How does the accounting clerk for Amaros indicate on each purchase invoice which department is to be charged for the purchase?
4. What accounts are debited and credited to record a purchase on account for Amaros' paint department?
5. What does the accounting clerk for Amaros do with the invoices after they have been recorded in the departmental purchases journal?
6. In what two ways may transportation costs on purchases be paid by the buyer?
7. What accounts are debited and credited to record a purchases returns and allowances transaction for Amaros' floor covering department?

8. What does the accounting clerk for Amaros do with a debit memorandum after it has been recorded in the purchases returns and allowances journal? Why?
9. When might a creditor's account in the accounts payable ledger show a debit instead of a credit balance?
10. What does the account number 511.1 mean for a general ledger account?
11. In the cash payments journal, page 119, why is there a purchases discount credit column only for the Floor Covering Department?
12. In the reconciliation of the bank statement, page 121, how is the bank balance brought into agreement with the checkbook balance?
13. In what three ways does the entry for a bank service charge in a cash payments journal differ from other entries for cash payments?

Cases for Management Decision

CASE 1 Ms. Maria Valdez owns and operates a shoe store. Her records are kept in much the same way as described in Chapters 2 and 3 for the Village Gift Shop. Periodically, she has an outside accountant check her records to assure that they are correct and to prepare end-of-fiscal-period statements. The accountant recommends that Ms. Valdez change her accounting records to a departmental basis. The accountant recommends that she have separate revenue accounts and cost accounts for the three types of merchandise sold — men's shoes, women's shoes, and children's shoes. What are the advantages and the disadvantages of the proposed plan?

CASE 2 The Valley Hardware Store is considering a plan to improve efficiency and take advantage of all purchases discounts. The plan is to use a combined purchase order and check. A check for the amount shown on the purchase order less any available purchases discount is to be attached to and sent with each purchase order. What are the advantages and the disadvantages of this plan?

CASE 3 John Elijah owns and manages a small engine repair business. He has found that his bank statement and his checkbook reconcile without error month after month. In order to save time spent reconciling his bank statement each month, Mr. Elijah decides to make the reconciliation once each six months. Mrs. Elijah, who helps with the accounting for the business, objects to this practice. Who is right? Why?

PROBLEM 7-1 Recording purchases on account and purchases returns and allowances for a departmental business

Problems for Applying Concepts

Figuero's Supermarket has three departments: Grocery, Meat, and Produce. The selected transactions listed below were completed during October of the current year.

Instructions: □ **1.** Record the following transactions on page 9 of a purchases journal and on page 6 of a purchases returns and allowances journal similar to those shown on pages 114 and 117.

Oct. 2. Purchased produce on account from Valle Farms, Inc., $802.31. P61.
4. Purchased groceries on account from Bristol Grocery Company, $879.85. P62.
6. Returned produce received in poor condition to Valle Farms, Inc., $56.50. DM36.
9. Returned groceries received in poor condition to Bristol Grocery Company, $59.75. DM37.
10. Purchased merchandise on account from Lucero's Supply: groceries, $1,071.47; meat, $230.38. P63.
10. Purchased produce on account from Valle Farms, Inc., $861.50. P64.
16. Purchased meat on account from Lucero's Supply, $493.53. P65.
18. Purchased groceries on account from DeCamp Wholesale, $162.10. P66.
19. Returned meat received in poor condition to Lucero's Supply, $63.50. DM38.
20. Purchased groceries on account from Bristol Grocery Company, $330.32. P67.
24. Purchased merchandise on account from Lucero's Supply: groceries, $307.85; meat, $407.51. P68.
27. Returned groceries received in poor condition to Bristol Grocery Company, $52.75. DM39.
31. Purchased produce on account from Valle Farms, Inc., $603.06. P69.

Instructions: ◻ **2.** Foot all amount columns of the purchases journal, prove the equality of debits and credits, and total and rule the journal.

◻ **3.** Foot all columns of the purchases returns and allowances journal, prove the equality of debits and credits, and total and rule the journal.

The journals prepared in this problem will be needed to complete Problem 7-2.

PROBLEM 7-2 Posting the purchases records of a departmental business

The journals prepared in Problem 7-1 are needed to complete this problem.

Instructions: ◻ **1.** Open the following accounts in a general ledger. Allow three lines for each account.

Accounts Payable................	211	Purchases Returns and	
Purchases — Grocery............	511	Allowances — Meat..........	512.1
Purchases Returns and		Purchases — Produce	513
Allowances — Grocery.......	511.1	Purchases Returns and	
Purchases — Meat	512	Allowances — Produce	513.1

Instructions: ◻ **2.** Open accounts in an accounts payable ledger for each of the following creditors. Allow four lines for each account.

Bristol Grocery Company, 386 Bryden Avenue, Denver, CO 80214
DeCamp Wholesale, 4122 Beach Street, Boulder, CO 80302
Lucero's Supply, 6255 Pickard Lane, Denver, CO 80214
Valle Farms, Inc., 228 Andre Circle, Greeley, CO 80631

Instructions: ◻ **3.** Post the individual items from the two journals to the subsidiary ledger accounts. Use *PR* and the page number in the Post. Ref. column to indicate postings from the purchases returns and allowances journal.

◻ **4.** Post the column totals to the general ledger accounts.

PROBLEM 7-3 Recording cash payments of a departmental business

Varela's sells women's and men's shoes. The business keeps its records on a departmental basis. During the month of November of the current year, Varela's made the selected cash payments listed below.

The cash payments journal of Varela's has the following amount columns: General Debit; General Credit; Accounts Payable Debit (211); Purchases Discount — Women's Shoes Credit (511.2); Purchases Discount — Men's Shoes Credit (512.2); and Cash Credit (111). Expenses for which account titles are not given should be debited to Miscellaneous Expense.

Instructions: ◻ **1.** Record the selected cash payments transactions, page 125, on page 9 of the cash payments journal.

Nov. 1. Paid November rent, $500.00. Ck246.
  3. Paid telephone bill, $73.60. Ck247.
  7. Paid on account to Denslow Distributors, $1,311.75, covering invoice for men's shoes, dated October 10, for $1,325.00 less a 1% discount. Ck248.
  9. Paid on account to Pillote Manufacturing, $1,434.23, covering invoice for women's shoes, dated October 13, for $1,463.50 less a 2% discount. Ck249.
  10. Paid advertising expense, $110.25. Ck250.
  13. Paid on account to Angula Manufacturing, $1,648.95. No discount. Ck251.
  16. Bought supplies for cash from Tapia Supply, $93.20. Ck252.
  20. Purchased men's shoes for cash from Herandez Shoe Wholesalers, $263.45. Ck253.
  22. Paid on account to Moreno Shoes, $630.73, covering invoice for men's shoes dated October 25, for $643.60 less a 2% discount. Ck254.
  24. Paid on account to Abernathy Shoe Wholesalers, $1,449.16, covering invoice for women's shoes, dated October 26, for $1,463.80 less a 1% discount. Ck255.
  27. Paid delivery expense, $78.50. Ck256.
  28. Paid on account to Ashley Shoes, $957.12, covering invoice for women's shoes, dated October 30, for $976.65 less a 2% discount. Ck257.
  30. As shown on the bank statement received today, a service charge of $4.33 has been made by the bank. M21.

Instructions: □ **2.** Foot the amount columns in the cash payments journal and prove the equality of debits and credits.

□ **3.** Total and rule the cash payments journal.

PROBLEM 7-4 Reconciling a bank statement

On December 5 of the current year Butler's Sport Center received its bank statement from American Trust Bank. With the statement were the store's canceled checks and a charge slip showing that a service charge of $5.13 had been deducted from the account.

Instructions: □ **1.** Record the service charge on page 13 of a cash payments journal similar to the one shown on page 119. M26.

□ **2.** Prepare a reconciliation of the bank statement in the same form as that shown on page 121.

(a) The balance shown on the bank statement was $1,966.34.
(b) A December 5 deposit of $255.75 was not shown on the bank statement.
(c) Outstanding checks were: No. 321, $186.35; No. 332, $83.76; No. 338, $283.50; No. 339, $85.16.
(d) The checkbook balance at the close of business on December 5 was $1,588.45. This balance was before the bank service charge had been deducted.

MASTERY
PROBLEM 7-M   Recording purchases and cash payments
of a departmental business

Pernell's operates two departments: Furniture and Appliances. The purchases journal used by the store is similar to the one shown on page 114 except that there are only two departments. The cash payments journal is similar to the one shown on page 119 except that there is a purchases discount column for each of the two departments.

All purchases of merchandise on account are subject to a 2% cash discount if payment is made within 10 days.

Instructions: □ **1.** Record the following selected transactions for January of the current year on page 7 of a purchases journal and on page 9 of a cash payments journal.

Jan. 2. Paid January rent, $600.00. Ck433.
      3. Purchased furniture on account from Sykes Furniture, $3,422.00. P313.
      3. Paid advertising expense, $65.25. Ck434.
      5. Purchased appliances on account from Iznaga Wholesalers, $733.50. P314.
      7. Purchased appliances on account from Rivas, Inc., $866.48. P315.
      8. Purchased furniture on account from Roundfield Furniture Company, $2,375.00. P316.
    10. Purchased furniture on account from Sykes Furniture, $1,155.00. P317.
    11. Paid on account to Sykes Furniture, $3,353.56, covering P313 for $3,422.00 less discount. Ck435.
    14. Bought supplies for cash from Ellis Supply Company, $43.25. Ck436.
    14. Purchased appliances on account from Zapata Corporation, $844.50. P318.
    15. Paid on account to Iznaga Wholesalers, $718.83, covering P314 for $733.50 less discount. Ck437.
    15. Received the bank statement showing the service charge for the checking account, $4.16. M3.
    16. Purchased appliances on account from Rivas, Inc., $748.35. P319.
    16. Paid on account to Rivas, Inc., $849.15, covering P315 for $866.48 less discount. Ck438.
    17. Paid on account to Roundfield Furniture Company, $2,327.50, covering P316 for $2,375.00 less discount. Ck439.
    18. Purchased appliances on account from Apodaca Appliances, $413.50. P320.
    19. Paid on account to Sykes Furniture, $1,131.90, covering P317 for $1,155.00 less discount. Ck440.
    22. Purchased furniture on account from Hodges Furniture, $622.00. P321.
    23. Paid miscellaneous expense, $31.25. Ck441.
    24. Paid on account to Zapata Corporation, $827.61, covering P318 for $844.50 less discount. Ck442.
    25. Purchased appliances on account from Iznaga Wholesalers, $313.75. P322.
    28. Paid on account to Apodaca Appliances, $405.23, covering P320 for $413.50 less discount. Ck443.

Jan. 31. Paid on account to Rivas, Inc., $748.35, covering P319. Through error, this invoice was not paid during the discount period and therefore the full amount of the invoice has to be paid. Ck444.

31. Replenished the petty cash fund, $83.50. The accounts debited are: Supplies, $33.80; Advertising Expense, $24.30; Delivery Expense, $13.75; Miscellaneous Expense, $11.65. Ck445.

Instructions: ☐ **2.** Foot the columns in the two journals. Prove the equality of debits and credits in each journal.

☐ **3.** Total and rule the two journals.

**BONUS
PROBLEM 7-B** Recording purchases at net amount and using the account Discounts Lost

Introductory remarks: Some businesses record purchases at the net amount to be paid when the cash discount is taken. For example, merchandise is purchased for $200.00 with a 2% discount allowed if the account is paid within 10 days. The discount will reduce the price from $200.00 to $196.00. To record this purchase on account transaction, Purchases is debited for $196.00 and Accounts Payable is credited for $196.00. When the account is paid, Accounts Payable is debited for $196.00 and Cash is credited for $196.00.

If the discount period expires before payment is made, then the entry in the cash payments journal for the example above would be: Accounts Payable debited for $196.00, Discounts Lost debited for $4.00, and Cash credited for $200.00. Because almost all cash discounts are taken, there are few entries involving the discounts lost account. For this reason, no special amount column is provided for the account in the cash payments journal. Instead, the amounts debited to this account are recorded in the General Debit column.

Instructions: ☐ **1.** Record the selected transactions in Mastery Problem 7-M. Use page 8 of a purchases journal similar to the one shown on page 114 except that there are two departments: Furniture and Appliances. Use page 11 of a cash payments journal with four amount columns: General Debit, General Credit, Accounts Payable Debit, and Cash Credit.

☐ **2.** Foot the two journals. Prove the equality of debits and credits in the purchases journal and the cash payments journal.

☐ **3.** Total and rule the two journals.

8

Sales and Cash Receipts Clerk

The major reason for using a departmental accounting system is to determine the gross profit for each department. Departmental accounting helps a business determine (1) if each department is earning its way or (2) if effort is needed to improve the operations of a department. To determine the gross profit for each department, the records of departmental sales and departmental inventory as well as departmental purchases are necessary.

DEPARTMENTAL SALES ON ACCOUNT

When a sale on account is made by Amaros, a salesclerk prepares a sales invoice in duplicate. The sales invoice shows the amount sold from each department and the total amount of the sale. A sales invoice for a charge sale made by Amaros in the month of September is shown below.

Amaros
Home Improvement Center
8240 Jackson Street
Denver, CO 80211

SALES INVOICE

INVOICE NO. 316

SOLD TO: Harold Jackson
1365 Jefferson Street
Denver, CO 80211

TERMS: 30 days

DATE: Sept. 1, 1978

Quant.	Description	Unit Price	Item Amount Floor Covering	Item Amount Paint	Item Amount Wallpaper
6	630 cm # 312 wallpaper	3.95			23.70
8	630 cm # 620 wallpaper	4.50			36.00
	Department Total				$ 59.70
	Invoice Total				$ 59.70
	Sales Tax				2.39
	Total Amount				$ 62.09

Sales invoice for a sale on account

The original copy of the sales invoice is given to the customer when the merchandise is delivered or picked up. The duplicate copy is kept by Amaros as the source document for journalizing the transaction.

> September 1, 1978. Sold wallpaper on account to Harold Jackson, $59.70, plus sales tax, $2.39; total, $62.09. Sales Invoice No. 316.

The asset account Accounts Receivable is debited for $62.09. The liability account Sales Tax Payable is credited for $2.39. The revenue account Sales — Wallpaper is credited for $59.70. The charge customer's account in the subsidiary ledger, Harold Jackson, is debited for the same amount as the controlling account.

Departmental sales journal

Amaros keeps a record of all sales according to the department making the sale. The sales journal has special Sales Credit columns for each of the three departments: Floor Covering, Paint, and Wallpaper. The departmental sales journal of Amaros for September is shown below.

GENERAL LEDGER

Accounts Receivable	113
62.09	

Sales Tax Payable	220
	2.39

Sales — Wallpaper	413
	59.70

ACCOUNTS RECEIVABLE LEDGER

Harold Jackson

62.09

SALES JOURNAL   PAGE 13

	DATE	ACCOUNT DEBITED	SALE No.	Post. Ref.	ACCOUNTS RECEIVABLE DEBIT (113)	SALES TAX PAYABLE CREDIT (220)	FLR. COVER. (411)	PAINT (412)	WALLPAPER (413)	
1	1978 Sept. 1	Harold Jackson	316	✓	6209	239			5970	1
2	2	Jamie Owens	317	✓	191360	7360	184000			2
3	2	Rita Bauer	318	✓	12506	481		8350	3675	3
4	2	Larry Pitt	319	✓	81120	3120	78000			4
5	2	John Young	320	✓	1742	67		1675		5
32	31	Carol Bush	438	✓	5278 1220984	203 46961	786083	3250 224080	1825 163860	32
33	31	Totals			1220984	46961	786083	224080	163860	33
34					(113)	(220)	(411)	(412)	(413)	34
35										35

Irma Marino, Accounting Clerk II, records each sales invoice on one line of the departmental sales journal. The sales invoice, page 128, is recorded on Line 1 of the departmental sales journal above. The total amount of the sale is written in the Accounts Receivable Debit column. The sales tax is written in the Sales Tax Payable Credit column. The sales amount for each department is written in the appropriate Sales Credit column. The name of the customer is written in the Account Debited column. The number of the sales invoice is written in the Sale No. column to identify the source document. After the invoice is recorded, Ms. Marino files the invoice for future reference.

Departmental sales journal

Posting from the departmental sales journal

Amaros keeps accounts with charge customers in an accounts receivable ledger. The individual amounts in the Accounts Receivable Debit column of the departmental sales journal are posted daily by Ms. Marino to the appropriate customers' accounts. *S13* is written in the Post. Ref. column of the ledger account to indicate that the posting came from page 13 of the sales journal. A check mark is placed in the Post. Ref. column of the sales journal to show the completion of the posting.

At the end of the month, the departmental sales journal is footed, proved, totaled, and ruled by Ms. Marino. The total of each amount column is posted to the general ledger account named in the column heading. The number of the account to which the total of each column is posted is written in parentheses immediately below the total. The illustration, page 129, is the departmental sales journal after all posting has been completed.

Transportation on sales

Amaros pays for all delivery of merchandise to its customers. The cost of the delivery is recorded as a debit to Delivery Expense and as a credit to Cash. The customers are not charged for this delivery service.

Some businesses charge the cost of delivery service to the customers. When this is done, the delivery charge is included on the sales invoice and the amount is credited to an account called Transportation on Sales. At the time the sale is made, Transportation on Sales is credited and the customer's account is debited. At the time the delivery firm is paid for its services, Transportation on Sales is debited and Cash is credited. The debit and the credit to the transportation on sales account cancel each other. In this way the delivery cost does not become an expense to the seller.

> If the firm does charge delivery costs to customers, the departmental sales journal has a special amount column for Transportation on Sales Credit.

DEPARTMENTAL SALES RETURNS AND ALLOWANCES

The return of goods for which a customer is allowed credit on account or is given a cash refund is called a sales return. Credit given to a customer for part of the sales price of goods, when these goods are not returned, is called a sales allowance. The seller usually confirms in writing the amount of a sales return or a sales allowance.

Amaros confirms each of its sales returns and allowances by preparing a credit memorandum in duplicate. A credit memorandum for a sales return issued by Amaros in September is shown on page 131.

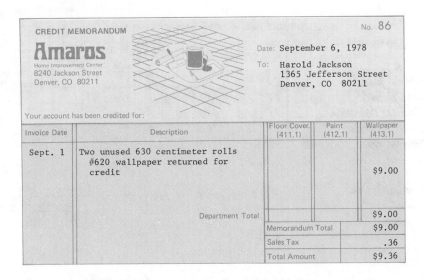

CREDIT MEMORANDUM   No. 86

Amaros
Home Improvement Center
8240 Jackson Street
Denver, CO 80211

Date: September 6, 1978

To: Harold Jackson
     1365 Jefferson Street
     Denver, CO 80211

Your account has been credited for:

Invoice Date	Description	Floor Cover. (411.1)	Paint (412.1)	Wallpaper (413.1)
Sept. 1	Two unused 630 centimeter rolls #620 wallpaper returned for credit			$9.00
	Department Total			$9.00
	Memorandum Total			$9.00
	Sales Tax			.36
	Total Amount			$9.36

Credit memorandum for sales returns and allowances

The original copy of the credit memorandum is given to the customer when merchandise is returned or an adjustment is made. The duplicate copy is kept by Amaros as the source document for journalizing the transaction.

September 6, 1978. Granted credit to Harold Jackson for unused wallpaper returned by him, $9.00, plus sales tax on the returned wallpaper, $.36. Credit Memorandum No. 86.

The liability account Sales Tax Payable is debited for $.36. The contra account, Sales Returns and Allowances, is debited for $9.00. The asset account Accounts Receivable is credited for $9.36. The customer's account, Harold Jackson, is credited for the same amount as the controlling account, $9.36.

GENERAL LEDGER

Sales Tax Payable   220
.36

Sales Returns and
Allowances — Wallpaper 413.1
9.00

Accounts Receivable   113
                          9.36

ACCOUNTS RECEIVABLE LEDGER

Harold Jackson
                          9.36

Departmental sales returns and allowances journal

Amaros records all sales returns and allowances in a special departmental sales returns and allowances journal. The journal provides a Sales Returns and Allowances Debit column for each of the three departments. The departmental sales returns and allowances journal for September, 1978, is shown on page 132.

Ms. Marino records the details of each credit memorandum on one line of the sales returns and allowances journal. The credit memorandum above is shown recorded on Line 1 of the departmental sales returns and allowances journal, page 132. The amount of the credit memorandum is written in the Accounts Receivable Credit column. The amount of sales tax charged to the sale is written in the Sales Tax Payable Debit column.

	DATE	ACCOUNT CREDITED	CREDIT MEMO. No.	POST. REF.	ACCOUNTS RECEIVABLE CREDIT (113)	SALES TAX PAYABLE DEBIT (220)	SALES RETURNS AND ALLOW. DEBIT		
							FLR. COVER. (411.1)	PAINT (412.1)	WALLPAPER (413.1)
1	1978 Sept. 6	Harold Jackson	86	✓	936	36			900
2	9	Larry Pitt	87	✓	1690	65	1625		
3	11	Jamie Owens	88	✓	10400	400	10000		
4	18	Alice Lamas	89	✓	2054	79		1125	850
5	20	Henry Soto	90	✓	7800	300	7500		
6	25	Norma Vega	91	✓	515	20			495
19	30	Holly Dorna	104	✓	286	11		275	
					31247	1202	22500	4360	3186
20	30	Totals			31247	1202	22500	4360	3185
21					(113)	(220)	(411.1)	(412.1)	(413.1)

Departmental sales returns and allowances journal

The amount to be debited to Sales Returns and Allowances for each department is written in the appropriate departmental column. The number of the credit memorandum is written in the Credit Memo. No. column. The name of the customer is written in the Account Credited column.

After the credit memorandum is recorded, the memorandum is attached to the sales invoice to which it applies. The two papers are filed in the sales invoice file.

Posting from the departmental sales returns and allowances journal

The individual amounts in the Accounts Receivable Credit column are posted daily by Ms. Marino to the customer's account named in the Account Credited column. *SR4* is written in the Post. Ref. column of the ledger account to show that the posting came from page 4 of the sales returns and allowances journal. A check mark is placed in the Post. Ref. column of the sales returns and allowances journal to show the completion of the posting.

Sometimes a sales return or allowance is made after a customer has paid the account in full. When this happens the customer's account has a credit balance instead of the normal debit balance. This credit balance in the customer's account reduces the amount to be collected for future sales on account.

At the end of the month, the departmental sales returns and allowances journal is footed, proved, totaled, and ruled by Ms. Marino. The total of each amount column is posted to the general ledger account named in the column heading. The number of the account to which the total of each column is posted is written in parentheses immediately below the total. The departmental sales returns and allowances journal above is shown after all posting has been completed.

DEPARTMENTAL CASH RECEIPTS

In addition to keeping a record of the charge sales for each department, Amaros keeps a record of the cash sales for each department. The cash receipts journal has special amount columns for recording cash sales for each department.

Departmental cash receipts journal

The cash receipts journal of Amaros has a special Sales Credit column for each of its three departments: Floor Covering, Paint, and Wallpaper.

Amaros has credit terms of net 30 days and does not give a cash discount for early payment. For this reason, the receipt of cash on account from a customer does not involve sales discount. Therefore, no special amount columns for sales discount are required in the cash receipts journal. The departmental cash receipts journal for the month of September is shown below.

	DATE	ACCOUNT TITLE	Doc. No.	Post. Ref.	GENERAL CREDIT	ACCOUNTS RECEIVABLE CREDIT (113)	SALES TAX PAYABLE CREDIT (220)	SALES CREDIT FLR. COVER. (411)	SALES CREDIT PAINT (412)	SALES CREDIT WALLPAPER (413)	CASH DEBIT (111)	
1	1978 Sept. 1	Balance on hand, $2,932.82		✓								1
2	2	✓	J2	✓			3746	76000	8350	9300	97396	2
3	2	Norma Vega	R36	✓		4683					4683	3
4	2	Telephone Income	R37	711	636						636	4
23	30	✓	J90	✓			2944	62500	6840	4250	76534	23
24	30	Totals			2560	468171	56409	934650	283000	192575	1937365	24
25					(✓)	(113)	(220)	(411)	(412)	(413)	(111)	25

Departmental cash receipts journal

Irma Marino, Accounting Clerk II, records all entries in the departmental cash receipts journal. She also posts from the journal to the appropriate accounts in the general ledger and the subsidiary ledger.

Recording a memorandum entry. The balance of the cash account in the general ledger of Amaros on September 1, 1978, is $2,932.82. This amount is used whenever cash is proved during the month. A notation is made each month on the first line of the cash receipts journal to show the amount of cash on hand. The memorandum entry for the beginning cash balance is shown on Line 1 of the departmental cash receipts journal above. Because the memorandum entry is not posted, a check mark is placed in the Post. Ref. column.

Recording cash sales. The source document for cash sales is a cash register tape.

GENERAL LEDGER

Cash	111
973.96	

Sales Tax Payable	220
	37.46

Sales — Floor Covering	411
	760.00

Sales — Paint	412
	83.50

Sales — Wallpaper	413
	93.00

September 2, 1978. Cash sales for September 1–2: Floor Covering, $760.00; Paint, $83.50; Wallpaper, $93.00; plus sales taxes of $37.46; total, $973.96. Cash Register Tape No. 2.

The asset account Cash is debited for the total amount received, $973.96. The liability account Sales Tax Payable is credited for the total amount of sales tax charged on sales, $37.46. The departmental revenue accounts are credited for the total amount of departmental sales made: Sales — Floor Covering, $760.00; Sales — Paint, $83.50; Sales — Wallpaper, $93.00.

The entry for the cash sales for September 1–2 is shown on Line 2 of the cash receipts journal, page 133. The total amount of cash sales, $973.96, is recorded in the Cash Debit column. The amount of cash sales for each department is recorded in the appropriate Departmental Sales Credit column: Floor Covering, $760.00; Paint, $83.50; and Wallpaper, $93.00. The amount of sales tax charged, $37.46, on the cash sales of September 1–2 is recorded in the Sales Tax Payable Credit column. *T2* is recorded in the Doc. No. column to show that the cash register tape of September 2 is the source document for this entry. Both the debit part and the credit parts of this transaction are recorded in special amount columns. A check mark is placed in the Account Title column to show that no account title needs to be written for this entry. A check mark is also placed in the Post. Ref. column to show that no individual items on this line need to be posted.

Recording a receipt of cash from a charge customer. Amaros prepares a receipt as the source document for cash received on account.

GENERAL LEDGER

Cash	111
46.83	

Accounts Receivable	113
	46.83

ACCOUNTS RECEIVABLE LEDGER

Norma Vega	
	46.83

September 2, 1978. Received cash on account from Norma Vega, $46.83. Receipt No. 36.

The asset account Cash is debited and the asset account Accounts Receivable is credited for $46.83. The charge customer's account, Norma Vega, is also credited for the same amount as the controlling account.

The entry for this transaction is shown on Line 3 of the cash receipts journal, page 133. The amount of cash received, $46.83, is recorded in the Cash Debit column and in the Accounts Receivable Credit column. *R36* is recorded in the Doc. No. column to show the source document for this entry. The name of the customer, Norma Vega, is written in the Account Title column.

Recording a receipt of miscellaneous revenue. A pay telephone is located in the store for the convenience of customers. Amaros receives a percentage of the total amount collected from users of the pay telephone. A receipt is prepared as the source document for miscellaneous revenue.

> September 2, 1978. Received cash for telephone income, $6.36. Receipt No. 37.

GENERAL LEDGER

Cash	111
6.36	

Telephone Income	711
	6.36

The asset account Cash is debited and the revenue account Telephone Income is credited for $6.36.

The entry for this transaction is shown on Line 4 of the cash receipts journal, page 133. The amount of the cash received, $6.36, is recorded in the Cash Debit column and in the General Credit column. R37 is recorded in the Doc. No. column to show the source document for this entry. Telephone Income is written in the Account Title column.

Recording COD sales. When cash will be collected for the entire sale at the time the merchandise is delivered, the terms are said to be COD. The letters COD mean Collect On Delivery or Cash On Delivery. A sale in which cash is collected at the time the merchandise is delivered is called a COD sale. The most common reasons for using the COD method of selling are:

1. A business may operate on a strictly cash basis even when merchandise is to be delivered to a customer.
2. A business may make additional sales to a customer whose maximum amount of credit has been exceeded.
3. A business may make sales to a customer before the customer's credit rating can be checked and established.
4. A business may increase sales by providing this service.

As with most businesses, Amaros considers COD sales as cash sales. When COD merchandise is delivered and the cash received, the transaction is recorded in the same way as all cash sales transactions. No entry is made until the cash is received.

The entry on Line 2 of the cash receipts journal, page 133, is for the cash sales of September 1–2, 1978. The totals in this entry include both the cash sales made at Amaros' place of business and the COD sales. A separate entry for COD sales is not made.

Sometimes Amaros cannot deliver COD merchandise because: (1) the customer is not home, or (2) the customer refuses to accept the merchandise or to pay the COD amount. When this happens, the merchandise is returned to the store and no entry is made. No entry is made because no transaction has been completed.

Posting from the departmental cash receipts journal

Each individual amount in the General Credit column of the cash receipts journal is posted daily to the appropriate account in the general ledger. The account number is written in the Post. Ref. column of the journal. Each individual amount in the Accounts Receivable Credit column is posted daily to the appropriate customer's account in the accounts receivable ledger. A check mark is placed in the Post. Ref. column of the journal. In the Post. Ref. columns of the ledger accounts, the source of posting is indicated by writing the journal page number, *CR18*.

At the end of the month, after the cash receipts journal has been ruled, the totals of the special columns are posted to the general ledger. The number of the account to which the total of each special column is posted is written in parentheses immediately below the total. A check mark is written in parentheses below the total of the General Credit column to indicate that this total is not to be posted. The illustration on page 133 shows the departmental cash receipts journal after all posting has been completed.

A schedule of accounts receivable should be prepared each time the totals of the journals are posted in order to check the accuracy of the posting.

CUSTOMER'S STATEMENT OF ACCOUNT

A form that shows the charges to a customer's account, the amounts credited to the account, and the balance of the account is called a statement of account. Irma Marino, Accounting Clerk II, sends a statement of account once a month to each charge customer. The statement of account is a reminder to the customer to pay the account. The statement also gives the customer an opportunity to check the accuracy of the statement. In this way, a proof of the work of the accounting department is made. A statement of account is shown below.

Amaros
Home Improvement Center
8240 Jackson Street
Denver, CO 80211

STATEMENT OF ACCOUNT

Sandra Jefferson
1830 Elm Street
Denver, CO   80213

DATE September 30, 1978

DATE	DEBITS	CREDITS	BALANCE
1978			
Sept. 2			$46.50
4	$39.66		86.16
9		$46.50	39.66
20	8.83		48.49
25	12.11		60.60

Statement of account

✦ What is the meaning of each of the following?

- sales return
- sales allowance
- COD sale
- statement of account

1. What use can an owner of a departmental business make of data about the gross profit of each department?
2. What three types of records are necessary to determine departmental gross profit?
3. What use is made of the two copies of the sales invoice prepared by Amaros?
4. What special sales amount columns are provided in the departmental sales journal of Amaros on page 129?
5. When merchandise sold on account comes from more than one department, what accounts are debited and credited?
6. What use is made of the two copies of the credit memorandum prepared by Amaros for sales returns or allowances?
7. When merchandise is returned by a charge customer, what accounts are debited and credited?

8. When might a customer's account in the ledger have a credit balance instead of the normal debit balance?
9. Why is the balance of the cash account on September 1 recorded in the Account Title column of the cash receipts journal on page 133?
10. What is the source document for recording cash sales in the departmental cash receipts journal of Amaros?
11. Why is a check mark written in parentheses below the total of the General Credit column of the cash receipts journal on page 133?
12. What are the principal reasons why businesses sell merchandise on COD terms?
13. How does Amaros record COD sales?
14. Why is it advisable to send a monthly statement of account to each charge customer?

CASE 1 Louis Montano owns and operates an office specialties store that carries a full line of office machines, office furniture, and office supplies. His accounting records are not kept on a departmental basis. Eva Miller, his accountant, recommends that he should reorganize his records on a departmental basis. Do you agree with his accountant's advice? Why?

CASE 2 The Westlane Department Store specializes in clothing for men, women, and children. All accounting records except sales returns and allowances are kept on a departmental basis. When merchandise is returned by a customer or an allowance is granted, a general journal entry is made debiting the appropriate departmental sales account and crediting Accounts Receivable and the customer's account. Do you agree or disagree with this accounting procedure? Why?

PROBLEM 8-1   Recording sales on account and sales returns and allowances for a departmental business

The Mission Building and Supply Company has three departments: Hardware, Paint, and Wallpaper. The selected transactions listed on page 138 were completed during October of the current year.

Instructions: □ **1.** Record the following transactions on page 12 of a sales journal and on page 7 of a sales returns and allowances journal similar to those shown on page 129 and page 132.

Oct. 2. Sold paint to Cindy Acker, $41.35, plus sales tax, $1.65; total, $43.00. S281.

4. Sold wallpaper to Bertha Perez, $33.50, plus sales tax, $1.34; total, $34.84. S282.

9. Sold hardware to Stanley Evans, $16.25, plus sales tax, $.65; total, $16.90. S283.

12. Granted credit to Bertha Perez for unused wallpaper returned by her, $8.00, plus sales tax on the returned wallpaper, $.32; total, $8.32. CM83.

12. Granted credit to Stanley Evans for defective hardware returned by him, $3.25, plus sales tax on returned hardware, $.13; total, $3.38. CM84.

16. Sold wallpaper to Bertha Perez, $63.00, plus sales tax, $2.52; total, $65.52. S284.

18. Sold paint to Cindy Acker, $46.00, plus sales tax, $1.84; total, $47.84. S285.

20. Sold paint to Stanley Evans, $88.50, plus sales tax, $3.54; total, $92.04. S286.

23. Granted credit to Cindy Acker for unused paint returned by her, $9.75, plus sales tax on returned paint, $.39; total, $10.14. CM85.

26. Sold hardware to Jose Sotela, $65.00, plus sales tax, $2.60; total, $67.60. S287.

28. Granted credit to Stanley Evans for unused paint returned by him, $6.60, plus sales tax on returned paint, $.26; total $6.86. CM86.

31. Sold wallpaper to Jose Sotela, $47.35, plus sales tax, $1.89; total, $49.24. S288.

Instructions: □ **2.** Foot the amount columns of the sales journal, prove the equality of debits and credits, and total and rule the journal.

□ **3.** Foot the amount columns of the sales returns and allowances journal, prove the equality of debits and credits, and total and rule the journal.

The journals prepared in this problem will be needed to complete Problem 8-2.

PROBLEM 8-2 Posting the sales records of a departmental business

The journals prepared in Problem 8-1 are needed to complete this problem.

Instructions: □ **1.** Open the following accounts in a general ledger. Allow three lines for each account.

Accounts Receivable	113	Sales Returns and Allowances —	
Sales Tax Payable	220	Paint	412.1
Sales — Hardware	411	Sales — Wallpaper	413
Sales Returns and Allowances —		Sales Returns and Allowances —	
Hardware	411.1	Wallpaper	413.1
Sales — Paint	412		

Instructions: ◻ **2.** Open accounts in an accounts receivable ledger for each of the following charge customers. Allow four lines for each account.

> Cindy Acker, 286 7th Avenue South, Denver, CO 80212
> Stanley Evans, 3339 Jefferson Street, Boulder, CO 80302
> Bertha Perez, 3862 Cedar Avenue, Denver, CO 80211
> Jose Sotela, 5137 Madison Avenue, Greeley, CO 80631

Instructions: ◻ **3.** Post the individual items from the two journals to the subsidiary ledger accounts. Use *SR* in the Post. Ref. column to show postings from the sales returns and allowances journal.

◻ **4.** Post the column totals to the general ledger accounts.

PROBLEM 8-3 Recording cash receipts transactions in a departmental cash receipts journal

Tafoya Food Market has three departments: Grocery, Meat, and Produce. The cash receipts journal is the same as the one shown on page 133 except that the three Sales Credit columns are for Grocery (411), Meat (412), and Produce (413). The selected cash receipts transactions listed below were completed during November of the current year.

Instructions: ◻ **1.** Record the following cash receipts transactions on page 11 of a cash receipts journal similar to the one shown on page 133.

Nov. 1. Recorded the cash balance on November 1 as a memorandum entry in the cash receipts journal, $2,846.33.
   1. Received on account from Pleasant View Inn, $230.45. R62.
   4. Received on account from Juan Soto, $180.68. R63.
   4. Cash sales for November 1–4: Grocery, $273.40; Meat, $279.83; Produce, $163.50; plus sales taxes of $28.67; total, $745.40. T4.
   7. Received on account from Valley Motel, $387.40. R64.
   9. Received on account from Shanty Creek Lodge, $160.39. R65.
   11. Cash sales for November 6–11: Grocery, $386.59; Meat, $333.48; Produce, $224.60; plus sales taxes of $37.79; total, $982.46. T11.
   14. Received on account from Flor Salazan, $28.25. R66.
   18. Cash sales for November 13–18: Grocery, $336.49; Meat, $279.58; Produce, $291.40; plus sales taxes of $36.30; total, $943.77. T18.
   21. Received on account from Mountain Inn, $218.58. R67.
   25. Cash sales for November 20–25: Grocery, $392.30; Meat, $315.87; Produce, $247.43; plus sales taxes of $38.22; total, $993.82. T25.
   28. Received on account from Central Motel, $36.29. R68.
   30. Received from the telephone company for share of public telephone receipts, $7.26. R69.
   30. Cash sales for November 27–30: Grocery, $258.60; Meat, $235.27; Produce, $147.20; plus sales taxes of $25.64; total, $666.71. T30.

Instructions: ◻ **2.** Foot the amount columns of the cash receipts journal and prove the equality of debits and credits.

◻ **3.** Total and rule the cash receipts journal.

MASTERY PROBLEM 8-M Recording sales and cash receipts of a departmental business

The Downtowner, a clothing store, has two departments: Women's Clothing and Men's Clothing. The selected sales and cash receipts transactions listed below were completed during December of the current year.

Instructions: ◻ **1.** Record the following selected transactions on page 8 of a sales journal similar to the one shown on page 129 and on page 10 of a cash receipts journal similar to the one shown on page 133.

Dec. 1. Recorded the cash balance on December 1 as a memorandum entry in the cash receipts journal, $2,635.79.
1. Sold women's clothing on account to Alvinia Hunter, $18.95, plus sales tax, $.76; total, $19.71. S241.
2. Sold men's clothing on account to Celso Salinas, $28.50, plus sales tax, $1.14; total, $29.64. S242.
2. Cash sales for December 1–2: Women's Clothing, $312.42; Men's Clothing, $286.39; plus sales taxes of $23.95; total, $622.76. T2.
4. Received cash on account from Celso Salinas in full payment of S242. R674.
6. Sold men's clothing on account to Gloria Vines, $75.00, plus sales tax, $3.00; total, $78.00. S243.
9. Cash sales for December 4–9: Women's Clothing, $883.50; Men's Clothing, $996.00; plus sales taxes of $75.18; total, $1,954.68. T9.
14. Sold men's clothing on account to Elias Vanquez, $22.50, plus sales tax, $.90; total, $23.40. S244.
16. Received cash on account from Alvinia Hunter in full payment of S241. R675.
16. Cash sales for December 11–16: Women's Clothing, $934.00; Men's Clothing, $913.00; plus sales taxes of $73.88; total, $1,920.88. T16.
23. Cash sales for December 18–23: Women's Clothing, $1,025.75; Men's Clothing, $987.40; plus sales taxes of $80.53; total $2,093.68. T23.
27. Received cash on account from Gloria Vines in full payment of S243. R676.
28. Sold on account to Lidia Banvelos: Women's Clothing, $32.00; Men's Clothing, $15.00; plus sales tax of $1.88; total, $48.88. S245.
30. Cash sales for December 26–30: Women's Clothing, $648.35; Men's Clothing, $550.00; plus sales taxes of $47.93; total, $1,246.28. T30.

Instructions: ◻ **2.** Foot the amount columns in both journals. Prove the equality of debits and credits in each journal.

◻ **3.** Total and rule both journals.

| **BONUS** | **PROBLEM 8-B** | Recording sales, cash receipts, and cash discounts for a departmental business |

Assume that the Downtowner, the business described in Problem 8-M, is located in a state that does not levy a sales tax on retail sales. Also assume that the Downtowner allows a 1% discount when a charge customer pays the account before the end of the month.

Use a cash receipts journal similar to the one shown on page 133 with the following changes:

1. Delete the special amount column for Sales Tax Payable Credit.
2. Add special amount columns for Sales Discount Debit — Women's Clothing and Sales Discount Debit — Men's Clothing.

Use a sales journal similar to the one shown on page 129, but delete the special Sales Tax Payable Credit column.

Instructions: □ **1.** Record the transactions shown in Problem 8-M in the sales journal and in the cash receipts journal. Do not record any sales taxes. For each transaction in which cash is received on account, figure the amount of cash discount allowed and include it in the transaction. For example, the entry for December 4 is in payment of the amount of Sales Invoice No. 242. The amount of the sale, $28.50 (no sales tax is charged), less a 1% discount of $.29, equals total cash received of $28.21.

□ **2.** Foot the amount columns in both journals and prove the equality of debits and credits in each journal.

□ **3.** Total and rule both journals.

9

Inventory Control Clerk

A business needs adequate records to control merchandise inventory. The sale of merchandise for more than the purchase price provides the major source of revenue for a merchandising business. A business therefore needs controls that help maintain a merchandise inventory of sufficient quantity, variety, and price.

The value of the merchandise on hand is reported at the end of a fiscal period on both the balance sheet and the income statement. An error in determining the value of the merchandise inventory will cause the current assets and capital reported on the balance sheet to be misstated. The inventory value error will also cause a misstatement of the gross profit and net income reported on the income statement.

An efficient system of inventory control is important, regardless of whether the accounting records are kept on a departmental or a nondepartmental basis.

IMPORTANCE OF CONTROLLING THE QUANTITY OF MERCHANDISE INVENTORY

Frequent analyses of purchases, sales, and inventory records are necessary to make the best decisions about the size of merchandise inventory to maintain. Many businesses fail because too much or too little merchandise inventory is kept on hand. Sometimes the wrong merchandise is kept on hand. If the merchandise is not sold to customers, revenues decrease. In addition, greater expense results from storing merchandise that does not sell well or does not sell at all.

Effects of a merchandise inventory that is larger than needed

A merchandise inventory that is larger than needed may decrease the net income of a business for the following reasons:

1. Store and warehouse space occupied by the unneeded part of the inventory is often expensive.
2. Part of the capital invested in the excess inventory could be invested to a better advantage in income-producing securities.
3. Taxes and insurance premiums must be paid on the excess merchandise inventory.
4. The excess merchandise may become obsolete and unsaleable.

Effects of a merchandise inventory that is smaller than needed

A merchandise inventory that is smaller than needed may decrease the net income of a business for the following reasons:

1. If items wanted by customers are not on hand, sales will be lost.
2. If there is insufficient variety of merchandise that customers want, sales will be lost to competitors.
3. When merchandise is reordered often and in small quantities, the cost is usually higher than if orders are placed for larger quantities.

TYPES OF INVENTORY CONTROL SYSTEMS

A merchandising business needs to know the quantity of merchandise on hand. The two principal methods used to determine the quantity of each type of merchandise on hand are:

1. By counting, weighing, or measuring each kind of merchandise on hand.
2. By keeping a continuous daily record of the increase, the decrease, and the balance of each kind of merchandise on hand.

A merchandise inventory that is determined by counting, weighing, or measuring the items of merchandise on hand is called a periodic inventory. A periodic inventory is sometimes known as a physical inventory. A merchandise inventory that is determined by keeping a continuous record of the increase, the decrease, and the balance on hand is called a perpetual inventory. A perpetual inventory is sometimes known as a book inventory.

Periodic inventory

Taking a periodic inventory is usually a large task. Therefore, periodic inventories are taken infrequently, such as once a year. Businesses usually arrange to take an annual periodic inventory at a time of the year when stock is at its lowest point. For example, a department store may take a periodic inventory at the end of January. The amount of merchandise on hand is low because of Christmas sales. The January clearance sales have been held, and few purchases of additional merchandise are made in January. All of these activities make the merchandise inventory low at the end of January.

Amaros takes its periodic inventory of departmental merchandise during the last week of December. Amaros has found from past experience that relatively few sales are made during that week. Few customers start home improvement projects during the holiday season. Also, the stock of merchandise is relatively low at that time.

Taking a periodic inventory using manual methods. Amaros uses manual methods in taking its periodic inventory. A form is used to record the important data about the merchandise inventory in each department — Floor Covering, Paint, and Wallpaper. The form has space to record stock number, unit of count, number of units on hand, unit cost price, and the total value of the items on hand. The form used by Amaros is shown at the left.

AMAROS
Merchandise Inventory

Sheet No. __2__

Date __December 31, 1977__   Department __Floor Covering__

Stock No.	Unit of Count	No. of Units on Hand	Unit Cost Price	Total Value
6212	Sq. Meters (m²)	20	9.00	180.00
6213	Sq. Meters (m²)	50	7.50	375.00
6215	Sq. Meters (m²)	30	12.00	360.00
6216	Sq. Meters (m²)	100	8.00	800.00
8640	Sq. Meters (m²)	60	7.00	420.00
8696	Sq. Meters (m²)	200	6.50	1,300.00
				$24,196.75

Inventory record sheet

Irma Marino, Accounting Clerk II, types in data for the Stock No. column and the Unit of Count column before the count is begun. The employees taking the periodic inventory in each department write the actual count in the No. of Units on Hand column. The inventory record sheets are then sent to the accounting department where Ms. Marino completes the two columns, Unit Cost Price and Total Value.

Taking a periodic inventory using automated equipment. The use of automated equipment can speed the process of completing the inventory sheets. For example, before the inventory is taken, a punched card is prepared for each kind of merchandise in stock. One form of punched card for a periodic inventory is shown on page 145.

Data are punched in the cards for the stock number, unit of count, and unit cost price. Space is provided to record manually the periodic count of units on hand. The person making the count uses a special pencil to mark quantity on the card. The cards are next fed into a computer, which "reads" the quantity and the unit cost and makes the necessary calculations. The computer also punches holes in the cards for the total values, and then prints a complete record of the periodic inventory.

Punched card for periodic inventory

Perpetual inventory

Some businesses keep inventory records that will show at any time the quantity on hand for each kind of merchandise. A form used to show each kind of merchandise, the quantity received, the quantity issued, and the balance on hand is called a stock record. The form may also be known as an inventory card. The form is often printed on a card. An entire file of stock records for all the merchandise on hand is called a stock ledger. Sometimes the inventory cards are kept in metal containers known as tubs.

The principal purpose of the perpetual inventory system is to give the business owner continuous day-to-day information as to the quantity of each kind of merchandise on hand. On each stock record is shown the minimum balance that is allowed before a reorder must be placed. When the minimum balance is reached, the inventory clerk notifies management so that additional merchandise can be ordered. The minimum level is the amount of merchandise that will last until merchandise can be received from the suppliers. Daily reports showing the amount of merchandise on hand may be necessary to determine when to reorder specific items that are selling rapidly. These daily reports may be prepared from data on perpetual inventory records. A business may find the expense too great to obtain the data by a daily inventory.

Perpetual inventory using manual methods. When a perpetual inventory of merchandise is kept, entries are made on stock records to show:

1. Increases in the quantity on hand when additional merchandise is received.
2. Decreases in the quantity on hand when merchandise is sold.
3. The balance on hand after each increase or decrease is recorded.

A stock record in card form is shown on page 146.

Description _Electric Typewriter_						Stock No. _C460_
Maximum _10_			Minimum _4_			Location _Aisle 2_
PURCHASES			SALES			BALANCE
DATE	PURCHASE ORDER NO.	QUANTITY	DATE	SALES INVOICE NO.	QUANTITY	QUANTITY
1978 Jan. 1						6
			1978 Jan. 18	4387	2	4
Jan. 19	633	6				10
			Feb. 3	4705	2	8

Stock record card

Usually a stock record shows quantity but not value of merchandise.

A separate stock record card is prepared for each kind of merchandise carried in stock. Each time additional merchandise is received, an entry is recorded in the Purchases columns and the balance on hand is updated in the Balance column. Each time merchandise is sold, an entry is recorded in the Sales columns and the balance is updated. The quantity of a particular kind of merchandise can be obtained quickly by referring to the last amount in the Balance column of the stock record card.

A high volume business needing perpetual inventory records to make business decisions normally uses automated equipment to maintain a continuous record of merchandise inventory.

Perpetual inventory using automated equipment. Using automated equipment greatly decreases the time and the effort required to maintain a perpetual inventory. For example, data relating to purchases and sales are fed into the computer. The computer is programmed to update the inventory records immediately. The computer also prints a daily record of items in low supply that need to be reordered. When a complete listing of the inventory is required, the computer can furnish a printed record of the updated inventory in a very short time.

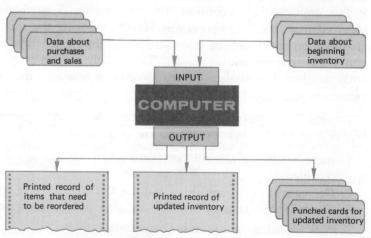

Flowchart showing use of electronic computer for keeping a perpetual inventory

Advantages of using a computer to keep a perpetual inventory are: (1) the speed with which the work can be handled, and (2) the greater accuracy of the inventory records.

Perpetual inventory using a cash register and automated equipment. Merchandising businesses keeping a perpetual inventory on an electronic computer may also use a specially designed cash register as part of the system. Each item of merchandise has a code number on the price tag. The code number is recorded on the cash register at the same time the sale is recorded. As a result, a punched paper tape is prepared inside the cash register with a coded record of items sold. At the end of the day, the punched paper tape is used to bring the perpetual inventory in the computer up to date.

Specially designed cash registers may also be connected directly to a computer. As the sale is recorded on a cash register, the data are fed directly to the computer. Thus, the inventory records are brought up to date immediately.

Checking the accuracy of the perpetual merchandise inventory. When a perpetual inventory is kept manually, errors may be made in recording amounts or in making computations. Also, some of the stock record cards may be incorrect because merchandise is taken from stock and not recorded on the stock record cards. A customary practice is to take a periodic inventory at least once a year and to compare the data thus obtained with the perpetual inventory records. If errors are discovered, they are corrected on the stock record cards.

PRICING THE MERCHANDISE INVENTORY AT COST

Cost prices are often not recorded on the inventory sheets at the time the periodic inventory is taken. After the quantities of merchandise on hand are counted, the inventory clerk uses either purchase invoices or recent catalogs to find the cost prices. The prices are recorded on the inventory sheets, the necessary extensions are made, and the total value of the inventory is found at cost prices.

Many retail businesses selling a small number of high-cost items, however, mark both the selling price and the original cost price of each article of merchandise on the price tag. The price tag is attached to the merchandise. When the merchandise is counted for a periodic inventory, the cost shown on the price tag is also recorded on the inventory sheet.

Cost price listed in code on price tags

When marking the cost price on a price tag, a customary practice is to use a code. The use of a code makes it difficult for a customer to interpret

PURCHASING   X
1 2 3 4 5 6 7 8 9 0   repeat

$60.00

CUGX

Stock# 834

Price tag with cost
shown in code

the data and know the cost price. The personnel of the business, however, can read the code and use the data.

The code should have ten different letters to represent the ten digits. The ten-letter code at the left can be easily remembered.

Whenever a digit is repeated in the price, the letter "X" is used. For example, the cost price $122.00 is written in code as PUXGX. The price tag at the left shows the selling price, $60.00, and the cost price, $42.00 (in code: CUGX). The Stock No., 834, is also shown on the price tag. Businesses that use automated equipment for inventory control often record both the stock number and the price on the cash register for each sale.

Pricing the inventory by the first-in, first-out method

For a periodic inventory at the end of a fiscal period, Amaros assumes that the merchandise purchased first is also the merchandise sold first. Amaros also assumes that the ending inventory consists of the most recently purchased merchandise. Only the most recent invoices for purchases are used in pricing each item on the inventory sheets. For example, the most recently received cans of paint are placed on the shelves behind the older cans. Therefore, the merchandise purchased first is also the merchandise sold first. The same procedure is used in the floor covering and wallpaper departments.

The first-in, first-out method is frequently abbreviated as *fifo* (the first letter of each of the four words). On December 31, a periodic count of one style of carpeting from the floor covering department showed 80 square meters on hand. The cost records for this carpeting showed the following data:

	Units	Unit Cost
January 1, beginning inventory	20 Sq. Meters	$ 8.00
January 17, purchases	30 Sq. Meters	8.00
April 13, purchases	30 Sq. Meters	10.00
July 27, purchases	50 Sq. Meters	10.00
November 10, purchases	50 Sq. Meters	12.00

Under the fifo method, the 80 units are priced at the most recent costs. The most recent costs are $12.00 and $10.00. The computations are summarized below.

Most recent costs, November 10, 50 units @ $12.00	$600.00
Next most recent costs, July 27, 30 units @ $10.00	300.00
Total value of 80 units	$900.00

On the inventory sheets the 80 square meters of merchandise would therefore be shown as having a total value of $900.00.

Pricing the inventory by the last-in, first-out method

The last-in, first-out method is frequently abbreviated as *lifo*. In the lifo method of pricing the inventory, the inventory is priced at the amount paid for the merchandise purchased first. This method is based on the idea that the most recent costs of merchandise should be charged against the current revenue.

Under the lifo method, each item on the inventory sheets is priced according to the earliest prices paid for each kind of merchandise. If the 80 square meters described on page 148 were priced by the lifo method, the value would be figured as follows:

Earliest costs, January 1, 20 units @ $8.00 .... $160.00
Next earliest costs, January 17, 30 units @ $8.00............................ 240.00
Next earliest costs, April 13, 30 units @ $10.00............................. 300.00

Total value of 80 units... $700.00

On the inventory sheets, the 80 units of this kind of merchandise would therefore be shown as having a total value of $700.00.

Comparison of fifo and lifo pricing methods

The figures above show the 80 square meters of carpeting priced under the fifo and lifo methods during a year of rising prices. To show the effect of falling prices, assume that the cost figures are reversed as shown below.

	Units	Unit Cost
January 1, beginning inventory	20 Sq. Meters	$12.00
January 17, purchases	30 Sq. Meters	10.00
April 13, purchases	30 Sq. Meters	10.00
July 27, purchases	50 Sq. Meters	8.00
November 10, purchases	50 Sq. Meters	8.00

Under the fifo method, the 80 units are priced at the most recent costs. The most recent costs are $8.00 and $8.00. The computations are summarized below.

Most recent costs, November 10, 50 units @ $8.00......................... $400.00
Next most recent costs, July 27, 30 units @ $8.00.......................... 240.00

Total value of 80 units... $640.00

Under the lifo method, the 80 units are priced at the earliest prices. The earliest prices are $12.00 and $10.00. The computations are summarized below.

Earliest costs, January 1, 20 units @ $12.00.................................. $240.00
Next earliest costs, January 17, 30 units @ $10.00 .... 300.00
Next earliest costs, April 13, 30 units @ $10.00............................. 300.00

Total value of 80 units... $840.00

A comparison of the fifo and lifo methods in determining gross profit with net sales of $1,200.00 is shown below.

	RISING PRICES				FALLING PRICES			
	FIFO		LIFO		FIFO		LIFO	
Revenue:								
Net Sales		$1,200.00		$1,200.00		$1,200.00		$1,200.00
Cost of Merchandise Sold:								
Merchandise Inventory, January 1 .	$ 160.00		$ 160.00		$ 240.00		$ 240.00	
Net Purchases	1,640.00		1,640.00		1,400.00		1,400.00	
Merchandise Available for Sale. . . .	1,800.00		1,800.00		1,640.00		1,640.00	
Less Ending Inventory, January 31.	900.00		700.00		640.00		840.00	
Cost of Merchandise Sold		900.00		1,100.00		1,000.00		800.00
Gross Profit on Sales		$ 300.00		$ 100.00		$ 200.00		$ 400.00

In a year of rising prices, the fifo method gives the highest possible valuation and the lifo method gives the lowest possible valuation of the ending inventory. Therefore, the fifo method gives the highest and the lifo method gives the lowest net income during a year when prices are rising.

In a year of falling prices, the fifo method gives the lowest possible valuation and the lifo method gives the highest possible valuation of the ending inventory. Therefore, the fifo method gives the lowest and the lifo method gives the highest net income during a year of falling prices. Both methods assume a periodic inventory count.

PRICING THE INVENTORY AT LOWER OF COST OR MARKET

Another inventory pricing method uses both the cost price and the market price of each item of merchandise. This method follows the well-established tradition that if the value of items in an inventory declines, the loss should be recognized even though the merchandise has not been sold.

When this practice in accounting is applied to the pricing of each item in the inventory, the rules to follow are:

1. When the cost price is lower than the current market price, use the cost price.
2. When the market price is lower than the cost price, use the market price.

When the "lower of cost or market" method is used, the inventory sheet has three price columns:

1. One column to record the cost price of each item.
2. One column to record the market price of each item.
3. One column to record the total value of all identical items using either the market price or the cost price, whichever is lower.

One form of inventory sheet using this inventory pricing method is shown below.

Beechmont Company			DEPT. Games		
MERCHANDISE INVENTORY					
DATE December 31, 1978			SHEET NO. 2		
Stock No.	Unit of Count	No. of Units on Hand	Unit Price		Value at Lower of Cost or Market
			Cost	Market	
G1010	Each	24	$ 6.00	$ 4.00	$ 96.00
G1022	Set	40	8.00	9.60	320.00
G1031	Dozen	87	7.95	9.95	691.65
G1035	Each	15	1.85	1.85	27.75
G1040	Each	23	18.20	11.60	266.80
G1050	Dozen	12	20.00	18.75	225.00
G1062	Set	48	1.29	1.50	61.92
G3012	Each	151	5.95	5.75	868.25
G3050	Dozen	40	3.00	3.10	120.00
G3089	Each	10	109.95	116.50	1,099.50
G3110	Each	5	29.95	27.75	138.75
					$9,387.54

Inventory sheet for pricing at lower of cost or market

The first item on the inventory sheet above, G1010, has a lower market price, $4.00, than the cost price, $6.00. Therefore, the market price is used for this item on the inventory sheet. The number of items on hand, 24, times the price to be used, $4.00, equals the value, $96.00. The value, $96.00, is recorded in the column headed "Value at Lower of Cost or Market."

Each business decides which method to use in pricing merchandise inventory. However, the method selected (fifo, lifo, lower of cost or market) is used consistently from year to year. The Internal Revenue Service requires that a business use the same method from year to year. If a business wishes to change inventory pricing methods, permission of the IRS must be obtained.

DEPARTMENTAL FINANCIAL STATEMENTS

A departmentalized business prepares the same financial statements as a nondepartmentalized business: an income statement, a capital statement, and a balance sheet. These statements are prepared in the same form as similar statements for a nondepartmentalized business. A departmentalized business usually also prepares a statement of gross profit to show how each department is doing. A statement prepared at the end of a fiscal period, showing the gross profit for each department, is called a departmental statement of gross profit.

Managers also need to know how each department is doing on a monthly basis even though the fiscal period is more than a month. Therefore, a departmental statement of gross profit is often prepared at the end of each month. A statement showing the gross profit for each department for a portion of a fiscal period is called an interim departmental statement of gross profit.

In the preparation of the interim departmental statement of gross profit, values for both the beginning and the ending merchandise inventory are needed. As the ending inventory for each month becomes the beginning inventory for the next month, both beginning and ending merchandise inventory must be figured monthly. If a perpetual inventory is kept, the value of the merchandise inventory is relatively easy to determine at any time. However, a monthly periodic inventory would require a physical count of the merchandise at the end of each month. A perpetual or periodic inventory may not be practical. When neither a perpetual nor a monthly periodic inventory is taken, the value of the ending merchandise inventory is estimated.

Estimating the value of ending merchandise inventory

Estimating the ending inventory by using previous years' percent of gross profit on sales is called the gross profit method of estimating an inventory. Amaros prepares an interim departmental statement of gross profit at the end of each month. The gross profit method of estimating the ending merchandise inventory is used. To estimate the ending merchandise inventory on September 30, 1978, Ms. Marino obtains the following data:

Beginning inventory, January 1, 1978 .... $ 28,140.00
Net purchases for the period, January 1 to September 30......... 89,536.20
Net sales for the period, January 1 to September 30............... 139,665.68
Gross profit on sales (percentage based on records of previous
    years' operations) .... 30% of sales

The three steps in estimating the ending merchandise inventory for the floor covering department on September 30, 1978, are:

1. Determine the value of the cost of merchandise available for sale.

Beginning inventory, January 1 .... $ 28,140.00
Plus net purchases, January 1 to September 30................... 89,536.20
Equals value of merchandise available for sale $117,676.20

2. Determine the estimated value of the cost of merchandise sold.

Net sales for January 1 to September 30........................... $139,665.68
Less estimated gross profit on sales ($139,665.68 × 30%) 41,899.70
Equals estimated cost of merchandise sold........................ $ 97,765.98

3. Subtract the estimated cost of merchandise sold from the value of the merchandise available for sale to determine the estimated ending merchandise inventory.

Merchandise available for sale (from step 1) $117,676.20
Less estimated cost of merchandise sold (from step 2) 97,765.98
Equals estimated ending merchandise inventory .... $ 19,910.22

The estimated merchandise inventory for the floor covering department on September 30, 1978, is $19,910.22. This value is used on the interim departmental statement of gross profit. The same procedure is used to find the estimated ending inventory for the paint department and the wallpaper department.

An estimated inventory is admittedly not completely accurate. The rate of gross profit on sales may not be exactly the percentage used. Also, some merchandise may have been stolen or damaged. However, the estimated ending inventory is close enough to the correct amount to be usable for the interim departmental statement of gross profit.

Interim departmental statement of gross profit

Amaros' interim departmental statement of gross profit prepared on September 30, 1978, is shown below. The data for each department are organized in a form similar to the first part of an income statement for a fiscal period. The beginning inventory recorded for each department is the estimated ending inventory from the interim departmental statement of gross profit for August 31, 1978.

> The value of the ending inventory reported on Amaros' financial statements at the end of a fiscal period is obtained by taking a periodic inventory.

Amaros
Interim Departmental Statement of Gross Profit
For Month Ended September 30, 1978

	FLOOR COVERING		PAINT		WALLPAPER		TOTAL	
Revenue:								
Net Sales		$16,982.33		$5,067.20		$3,532.50		$25,582.03
Cost of Merchandise Sold:								
Estimated Mdse. Inv., Sept. 1	$26,741.06		$10,300.00		$6,140.30		$43,181.36	
Net Purchases	5,056.80		3,038.80		926.00		9,021.60	
Merchandise Available for Sale.	31,797.86		13,338.80		7,066.30		52,202.96	
Less Estimated End. Inv., Sept. 30. .	19,910.22		10,559.26		4,593.55		35,063.03	
Cost of Merchandise Sold		11,887.64		2,779.54		2,472.75		17,139.93
Gross Profit on Sales		$ 5,094.69		$2,287.66		$1,059.75		$ 8,442.10

Interim departmental statement of gross profit

✦ What is the meaning of each of the following?

- periodic inventory
- perpetual inventory
- stock record
- stock ledger

- departmental statement of gross profit
- interim departmental statement of gross profit

- gross profit method of estimating an inventory

Using Business Terms

1. What is the major source of revenue for a merchandising business?
2. What effect does an error in determining the value of the merchandise inventory have on the balance sheet and income statement?
3. If the merchandise inventory is larger than needed, what effect may this have on the net income of the business? Why?
4. If the inventory is smaller than needed, what effect may this have on the net income of the business? Why?
5. What two methods can be used to determine the quantity of each item of merchandise on hand?
6. When should a periodic inventory be taken?
7. Under what business conditions should a perpetual inventory be kept?
8. When a perpetual inventory is kept, how may the balance on hand of a specific kind of merchandise be determined?
9. What are the advantages of using a computer to keep a perpetual inventory?
10. How is the accuracy of a perpetual inventory checked? How often is it checked?

11. When the fifo method of pricing inventory is used, how is the value of each kind of merchandise determined?
12. When the lifo method of pricing inventory is used, how is the value of each kind of merchandise determined?
13. In a year of rising prices, which inventory pricing method, fifo or lifo, gives the highest net income?
14. In a year of falling prices, which inventory pricing method, fifo or lifo, gives the highest net income?
15. What inventory pricing method follows the well-established tradition that if the value of items in an inventory declines, the loss should be recognized even though the merchandise has not been sold?
16. What type of financial statements are prepared by a departmentalized business?
17. When neither a perpetual nor a monthly periodic inventory is taken, how is the ending merchandise inventory determined for the interim departmental statement of gross profit?

CASE 1 The Midstate Sporting Goods Co. uses the lifo method of pricing its merchandise inventory. The owner is considering a change to the fifo method. Prices have increased steadily for the past three years. If the change is made, what effect will it have on (1) the amount of net income as shown by the income statement, (2) the amount of income taxes to be paid, and (3) the quantity of each item of merchandise that must be kept in stock? Why?

CASE 2 Samuel Reyies owns and manages the Reyies Hardware Store. He has many small and large items of merchandise in his store. He has always taken a periodic inventory at the end of a fiscal year. However, he has not kept a perpetual inventory as he believes it would cost more than it is worth. At the same time he wishes he had a reasonably accurate inventory at the end of each month so that he can prepare interim statements to help him in making decisions about his business. What would you recommend?

CASE 3 The ALBA Company has three departments. The company keeps its accounting records on a departmental basis. Departmental statements of gross profit are prepared for each department at the end of each month. The owner also would like to be able to compare net profit by departments. To do this, a portion of the operating expenses must be listed for each department. How might the ALBA Company determine how much of the operating expenses to charge to each department?

PROBLEM 9-1   Pricing an inventory by the fifo and lifo methods

Problems
for
Applying
Concepts

The inventory clerk of Trienda Appliance Center obtained the following information from the records of the business concerning the purchases of refrigerators during the current year.

Model	Beginning Inventory Jan. 1	First Purchase	Second Purchase	Third Purchase	Inventory Count Dec. 31
630	6 @ $218	6 @ $223	4 @ $233	5 @ $236	4
631	3 @ $269	5 @ $274	4 @ $278	4 @ $268	6
632	4 @ $325	4 @ $325	2 @ $342	3 @ $354	4
730	1 @ $418	6 @ $409	4 @ $426	6 @ $433	8
731	3 @ $460	4 @ $467	3 @ $473	2 @ $486	6
732	4 @ $515	8 @ $488	5 @ $523	3 @ $534	5

Instructions: □ **1.** Use an inventory sheet that has the following column headings:

Model	Number of Units on Hand	Unit Cost	Value

□ **2.** Figure the total amount of the inventory on December 31 according to the *fifo* method. Proceed as follows:

(a) Record the model number and the number of units of each model on hand on December 31.

(b) Record the unit cost of each model. If more than one unit cost must be used, list the number of units on hand with the unit cost applicable to each on separate lines.

(c) Figure the total value of each model and write the amount in the Value column.

(d) Add the Value column to determine the total amount of the inventory.

□ **3.** On another inventory sheet, figure the total amount of the inventory according to the *lifo* method. Follow the steps given in Instruction 2.

□ **4.** Compare the total amount of the inventory obtained in Instructions 2 and 3. Which method, *fifo* or *lifo*, resulted in the lower total amount for the inventory?

PROBLEM 9-2   Pricing the inventory at lower of cost or market

The Sotelo Co. attaches a price tag to all pieces of merchandise. The price tag shows both the selling price and the cost price. The cost price is shown according to the code at the right.

MONEY TALKS	R
1 2 3 4 5 6 7 8 9 0	Repeat

The information shown below was prepared by the inventory clerk at the time a periodic inventory was taken on December 31 of the current year.

Stock No.	No. of Units on Hand	Unit Cost in Code	Current Market Price
A3	8	ARYS	$ 83.00
A6	12	KMSR	90.00
C8	4	MYOYO	156.00
D1	12	MKYSR	189.00
D9	14	OSOLR	204.00
F3	6	MANET	182.00
F5	8	OESRR	261.00

Instructions: □ **1.** Copy the information from the table above on an inventory sheet with column headings as follows:

1	2	3	4	5	6
Stock No.	No. of Units on Hand	Unit Cost Price	Current Market Price	Unit Price To Be Used	Value

When recording the unit cost price in Column 3, convert the code to dollar amounts.

□ **2.** Decide which cost price, unit cost or current market, is to be used for each kind of merchandise. Write the price you select in Column 5.

□ **3.** Figure the value of each kind of merchandise; write the amount in Column 6.

□ **4.** Total Column 6 and determine the amount of the ending inventory.

PROBLEM 9-3 Preparing an interim departmental statement of gross profit

Lucio's has three departments: Hardware, Furniture, and Appliances. The accounting clerk obtained the following data from the accounting records at the end of January of the current year.

Beginning inventory, January 1: Appliance Department $23,400.00
                                 Furniture Department 64,700.00
                                 Hardware Department............................. 38,500.00

Net purchases for January: Appliance Department................................. $ 3,150.00
                           Furniture Department.................................. 8,920.00
                           Hardware Department 3,270.00

Net sales for January: Appliance Department.. $ 6,890.00
                       Furniture Department.. 10,940.00
                       Hardware Department 8,360.00

Gross profit on sales (percentage based on records of previous years' operations) ....25% of sales

Instructions: □ **1.** Estimate the value of the ending inventory for January of the current year for each department. Use the gross profit method of estimating an inventory.

□ **2.** Prepare an interim departmental statement of gross profit for the month ended January 31 of the current year.

| MASTERY PROBLEM 9-M | | Preparing an interim departmental statement of gross profit | Optional Problems |

Westside Shoe Store has two departments: Women's Shoes and Men's Shoes. The accounting clerk obtained the following data from the accounting records at the end of January of the current year.

Beginning inventory, January 1: Women's Shoe Department......................	$18,650.00
Men's Shoe Department	19,380.00
Net purchases for January: Women's Shoe Department	$ 1,380.00
Men's Shoe Department.................................	1,620.00
Net sales for January: Women's Shoe Department.................................	$ 7,320.00
Men's Shoe Department	8,640.00
Gross profit on sales: Women's Shoe Department ....30% of sales	
Men's Shoe Department...25% of sales	

Instructions: □ **1.** Estimate the value of the ending inventory for January of the current year for each department. Use the gross profit method of estimating an inventory.

□ **2.** Prepare an interim departmental statement of gross profit for the month ended January 31 of the current year.

| BONUS PROBLEM 9-B | | Estimating the value of merchandise destroyed by fire |

The entire stock of merchandise of Southern Automotive Supply was destroyed by fire on March 17. From accounting records that were not destroyed by the fire, the following data were obtained:

Beginning merchandise inventory, January 1..	$51,470.00
Net purchases from January 1 to March 17...	39,200.00
Sales from January 1 to March 17	62,450.00

In a special sale held in January, the amount of the sales was $18,000.00. The average gross profit on the merchandise sold at this time was 15% of sales. The balance of the sales was made with a gross profit rate of 30% on the net sales.

Instructions: Estimate the value of the merchandise that was destroyed by the fire. Use the gross profit method of estimating an inventory.

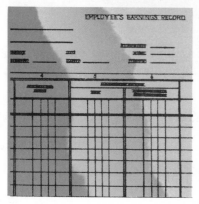

CUSTOM FLOOR COVERINGS

PART 5

SPECIALIZED ACCOUNTING CLERKS (Continued)

PAYROLL RECORDS ARE ESSENTIAL. Employers are required by law to withhold certain taxes from the earnings of their employees. Employers must also pay the government certain additional taxes on the earnings of their employees. Accurate payroll records are essential as the basis for preparing required reports and paying payroll taxes levied by federal, state, and local governments.

VOUCHER SYSTEMS CONTROL CASH. Accounting systems provide checks and safeguards on the use of cash and other assets to aid management in making decisions and planning for the future. As cash is the asset most often used and misused, a system of controlling cash is of great importance. A voucher system provides a systematic plan for controlling cash payments and for fixing responsibility for the handling of cash.

Part 5 of this textbook describes both a departmental payroll system and a departmental voucher system.

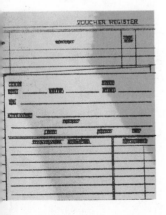

ZAPADA COMPANY

CHART OF ACCOUNTS

Balance Sheet Accounts

(1) ASSETS	Account Number
11 *Current Assets*	
Cash	111
Petty Cash	112
Accounts Receivable	113
Allowance for Uncollectible Accounts	113.1
Merchandise Inventory — Sportsware	114
Merchandise Inventory — Games	115
Office Supplies	116
Store Supplies	117
Prepaid Insurance	118
12 *Plant Assets*	
Delivery Equipment	121
Accumulated Depreciation — Delivery Equipment	121.1
Store Equipment	122
Accumulated Depreciation — Store Equipment	122.1

(2) LIABILITIES

21 *Current Liabilities*	
Vouchers Payable	211
Salaries Payable	212
Employees Income Tax Payable — Federal	213
Employees Income Tax Payable — State	214
FICA Tax Payable	215
Unemployment Tax Payable — Federal	216
Unemployment Tax Payable — State	217
Sales Tax Payable	218

(3) CAPITAL

A. T. Zapada, Capital	311
A. T. Zapada, Drawing	312
Income Summary	313

Income Statement Accounts

(4) OPERATING REVENUE	Account Number
Sales — Sportsware	411
Sales Returns and Allowances — Sportsware	411.1
Sales — Games	412
Sales Returns and Allowances — Games	412.1

(5) COST OF MERCHANDISE

Purchases — Sportsware	511
Purchases Returns and Allowances — Sportsware	511.1
Purchases Discount — Sportsware	511.2
Purchases — Games	512
Purchases Returns and Allowances — Games	512.1
Purchases Discount — Games	512.2

(6) OPERATING EXPENSES

Advertising Expense	611
Bad Debts Expense	612
Delivery Expense	613
Depreciation Expense — Delivery Equipment	614
Depreciation Expense — Store Equipment	615
Insurance Expense	616
Miscellaneous Expense — Administrative	617
Miscellaneous Expense — Sales	618
Office Supplies Expense	619
Payroll Taxes Expense	620
Rent Expense	621
Salary Expense — Administrative	622
Salary Expense — Delivery	623
Salary Expense — Games Sales	624
Salary Expense — Sportsware Sales	625
Store Supplies Expense	626

(7) OTHER REVENUE

Telephone Income	711

The chart of accounts for Zapada Company is illustrated above
for ready reference in your study of Chapter 11 of this textbook.

The chart of accounts to be used as you study Chapter 10 is shown on page 110.

10 Payroll Clerk

Businesses that have employees must keep accurate payroll records. Various federal, state, and local laws require both the employee and the employer to pay certain taxes on employees' earnings. The employer is required to withhold income taxes from the employees' earnings for each pay period. The employer must report to the government the amount of the taxes withheld from employees. A business, therefore, must keep records of each employee's earnings, the amount withheld for taxes, and the amount received in the paycheck. The payroll records must also show the total amount of taxes that the business must pay on its payroll.

A business is told by federal, state, and local governments what payroll information is to be reported. However, each business may decide what system of payroll accounting to use as the basis for these reports. A business protects itself by keeping complete and accurate payroll records showing all required information.

PREPARING THE DEPARTMENTAL PAYROLL

In addition to his duties as Accounting Clerk I, Lucas Ortez is the payroll clerk for Amaros. The departmentalized accounting system of Amaros shows the amount of payroll expense for each department.

Types of employee earnings

Employees may be paid by the number of pieces produced, by the hour, on a weekly or monthly basis, or on a yearly basis. Earnings paid on an hourly or piecework basis are often called wages. Earnings paid on a weekly, biweekly, semi-monthly, monthly, or yearly basis are often called salary. In actual practice, the terms *wages* and *salary* are used interchangeably. The unit of measure most often used for payroll is time. The employee's pay is usually stated as a rate per hour, day, week, month, or year. Pay is sometimes based on pieces produced per unit of time.

The basic salary or wage of an employee may be supplemented by other types of earnings. For example, in addition to a basic monthly salary an employee may receive commissions, cost-of-living adjustments, a share of profits, or bonuses.

Amaros has three types of employee earnings. First, hourly wages are paid each week to salesclerks and accounting department employees. Second, weekly salaries are paid to the supervisors of each of the three departments. Third, monthly commissions are also paid to each of the departmental supervisors.

Payroll time card

Amaros is open 6 days a week from 8:30 a.m. until 5:30 p.m. Employees, however, usually work only a 5-day week of 40 hours. The days worked during the week vary so that enough employees are available for each of the six days the business is open. For example, one employee may work Monday through Friday; whereas, another employee may work Tuesday through Saturday.

The salesclerks and the accounting employees of Amaros are paid an hourly wage for the regular 40-hour work week. All time worked on Sundays and holidays and in excess of 8 hours a day (provided 40 regular hours are worked) is considered overtime. Employees are paid 1½ times the regular hourly rate for overtime hours. Amaros uses an electric time clock to keep a record of the regular and overtime hours worked by each employee paid an hourly wage.

Payroll time card

In a time-clock system a payroll time card is inserted in the time clock each time an employee arrives for work and leaves work. The time clock records on the payroll time card the starting and stopping time for each work day.

The time card at the left is for Hilda Alonzo. The card shows that Ms. Alonzo worked a total of 40 *regular* hours for the week ending September 30. Her lunch period is from 1 to 2 p.m. daily. Her time card also shows that she worked 3 *overtime* hours — 2 on Wednesday and 1 on Friday.

At the end of the week, Mr. Ortez figured the number of hours worked by Hilda Alonzo to be 43 hours. Using the number of hours worked, Mr. Ortez figured Ms. Alonzo's weekly earnings, $178.00. The total pay due an employee before deductions for a pay period is called total earnings. The hours worked and the total earnings are marked on the time card by Mr. Ortez. Total earnings are sometimes known as gross pay or gross earnings. In figuring Ms. Alonzo's regular wages, Mr. Ortez multiplied the 40 regular hours by the base pay rate of $4.00 per hour. Next, the 3 overtime hours are multiplied by the overtime rate of $6.00 (1½ × $4.00). The regular wages, $160.00, plus the overtime wages, $18.00, equals the total earnings, $178.00.

Commissions record

The supervisors for each of the three sales departments, floor covering, paint, and wallpaper, are paid a regular weekly salary. They are not paid for overtime because their hours are not as regular as the salesclerks. To compensate for supervisory duties and to encourage efforts that increase sales, each departmental supervisor is paid a monthly commission on the net sales. The monthly commission is based on a percentage of net sales. Because the sales volume and the unit cost of the merchandise in the three departments vary, the commission rates also vary. The commission rates used are:

Floor Covering Department	1% of Net Sales
Paint Department	2% of Net Sales
Wallpaper Department	3% of Net Sales

At the end of each month, Mr. Ortez records on a special form the data necessary to figure the commissions for each departmental supervisor. A form used to summarize sales by department for the purpose of figuring commissions is called a commissions record. A commissions record is designed according to the particular needs of the business. Amaros' commissions record form is shown below.

General information is recorded at the top of the form. The charge sales for the month, $7,860.83, are obtained from Column 3, Line 33, of the sales journal, page 129. The cash sales for the month, $9,346.50, are obtained from Column 4, Line 24, of the cash receipts journal, page 133. The sales returns and allowances for the month, $225.00, are obtained from Column 3, Line 20, of the sales returns and allowances journal, page 132. The commissions on net sales are figured as follows: Net Sales, $16,982.33, times the commissions rate, 1%, equals the commission for Ms. Calvo, $169.82.

COMMISSIONS RECORD

Employee Name *Calvo, Eva*   Commission _1_ %

Employee Number ___11___   Month *September*   Year *1978*

Dept. *Floor Covering*   Regular Weekly Salary *$180.00*

Sales		
Charge Sales	$7,860.83	
Cash Sales	9,346.50	
Total Gross Sales	$17,207.33	
Less Sales Returns and Allowances	225.00	
Net Sales		$16,982.33
Commission on Net Sales		$169.82

Commissions record

Payroll deductions

Two federal taxes are withheld from an employee's pay: income withholding tax and FICA tax. FICA tax is also known as social security tax.

FICA are the initials for the Federal Insurance Contributions Act. Since 1966, the FICA tax also includes hospital insurance commonly referred to as medicare.

Some cities and states also require that employers deduct amounts from employees' earnings for income and other taxes. In some businesses, an employee may have other deductions, such as group life insurance, hospital insurance, pension plans, and savings deposits.

> The laws for handling state and city income taxes and other withholdings vary. Therefore, each employer needs to be familiar with the local and state regulations.

Amaros makes deductions from its employees' pay for federal income tax, FICA tax, state income tax, hospital insurance, and group life insurance.

Payroll register

A business form on which details about an entire payroll are recorded is called a payroll register. A payroll register summarizes the payroll for one pay period. A register also shows the totals of the amounts earned, the amounts withheld, and the cash paid out for all employees.

Amaros pays its employees once a week. The store prepares a separate payroll register for each week's payroll. Amaros' payroll register for the week ended September 30, 1978, is shown below and on page 165.

Recording basic employee data in a payroll register. The last day of the payroll week, September 30, is entered at the top of the payroll register. The date of payment, October 3, is also entered at the top of the payroll register. The difference of several days between the end of the pay period and the date of payment is necessary to prepare the payroll records and the payroll checks.

	EMPL. NO.	EMPLOYEE'S NAME	MARITAL STATUS	NO. OF EXEMPTIONS	TOTAL HOURS	EARNINGS				
						REGULAR	OVERTIME	COMMISSION	TOTAL	
1	8	Alonzo, Hilda	M	3	43	160 00	18 00		178 00	1
2	11	Calvo, Eva	S	1	—	180 00		169 82	349 82	2
3	3	Gorthy, John	S	1	40	140 00			140 00	3
4	6	Marino, Irma	M	2	41	200 00	7 50		207 50	4
5	13	Mesa, David	M	4	—	170 00		100 54	270 54	5
11	4	Torrez, Delia	S	1	—	175 00		105 98	280 98	11
12	16	Walker, Frank	M	4	44	144 00	21 60		165 60	12
13						2009 00	70 20	376 34	2455 54	13
14										14

WEEK ENDED *September 30, 1978* PAYROLL REGISTER

Payroll register (left page)

Mr. Ortez, the payroll clerk, also fills in basic data about each employee: Employee No., Employee Name, Marital Status, and No. of Exemptions. The basic data are taken from personnel records kept for each employee. The basic data for Hilda Alonzo are shown on Line 1, Columns 1–4, of the payroll register, page 164.

> For each person supported, including the employee, the employee is entitled to a reduction in the amount on which the income tax is figured. A deduction from total earnings for each person legally supported by a taxpayer is called an exemption.

Recording data from time cards in the payroll register. The information on each time card about hours worked and earnings is recorded in the payroll register on the line with the employee's name. The entry on Line 1, Columns 5–9, of the payroll register, page 164, shows the information from Hilda Alonzo's time card.

Recording data from commissions record in the payroll register. The entry on Line 2 in the payroll register below and on page 164 shows the information from Eva Calvo's commissions record for September, page 163. Departmental supervisors do not account for their hourly time on a time card. Therefore, a line is drawn through the Total Hours column, Column 5, in the payroll register. The weekly salary of each departmental supervisor remains the same for each pay period. Therefore, the amount of weekly salary is recorded in the Regular Earnings column, Column 6. At the end of the month, the commissions from the commissions record are entered in the Commissions Earnings column, Column 8. The Regular Earnings, Column 6, and the Commissions Earnings, Column 8, are added together to determine Total Earnings for the pay period.

Recording departmental and administrative salaries in the payroll register. The time card and the commissions record show the department to

DATE OF PAYMENT *October 3, 1978*   PAYROLL REGISTER

	DEPARTMENT			ADMIN. SALARIES	DEDUCTIONS					PAID		
	FLOOR COVERING	PAINT	WALLPAPER		FEDERAL INCOME TAX	STATE INCOME TAX	FICA TAX	OTHER	TOTAL	NET PAY	CK. NO.	
1	17800				1530	263	1068	H 560	3421	14379	214	1
2	34982				6950	980	2099	H 380 / B 350	10759	24223	215	2
3			14000		1930	318	840	H 380	3468	10532	216	3
4				20750	2410	356	1245	H 560 / B 350	4921	15829	217	4
5		27054			3110	413	1623	H 560	5706	21348	218	5
11				28098	5180	763	1686	H 380	8009	20089	224	11
12				16560	1040	138	994	H 560	2732	13828	225	12
13	52782	56054	59658	77060	31850	4265	14733	H 5060 / B 1000	56908	188646		13
14												14

Payroll register (right page)

be charged for each employee's salary. The salary is entered in Columns 10–12 of the payroll register, page 165, according to the department in which the employee works. The salary for each of the non-sales employees, such as the employees in the accounting department, are entered in the Admin. Salaries column, Column 13.

The entry on Line 1, Column 10, of the payroll register, page 165, shows that Hilda Alonzo's salary is charged to the floor covering department. The entry on Line 4, Column 13, shows that Irma Marino's salary is charged to the administrative salaries.

Recording deductions for federal income tax on employees. The amount of federal income tax to be withheld from each employee's pay is determined from withholding tables furnished by the federal government. Part of an income tax withholding table for a weekly payroll period is shown on page 167.

> Tax regulations may be changed from time to time. The regulations used in this textbook are those in effect at the time the materials for this book were written.

The amount of federal income tax to be withheld is based on the total earnings of an employee. The amounts withheld depend on the marital status of an employee and the number of exemptions claimed. For example, Hilda Alonzo's total earnings for the week ended September 30 are $178.00. Hilda is married and claims 3 exemptions. Mr. Ortez, the payroll clerk, finds the amount of total earnings in the two columns at the left of the tax table for married persons, page 167. Total earnings of $178.00 is in the category of "at least 170 but less than 180." The amount to be withheld is found on the same line in the column at the right with the 3 at the top. The amount to be withheld is $15.30. This deduction for federal income tax is recorded on Line 1, Column 14, of the payroll register, page 165.

Recording deductions for state income tax on employees. The State of Colorado has an income tax on the total earnings of its residents. The amount of state income tax to be withheld from the earnings of employees is usually determined from a printed tax table furnished by the state. The payroll clerk determines from the state income tax withholding table that Ms. Alonzo's deduction for state income tax for the week ended September 30 is $2.63. This deduction for state income tax is entered on Line 1, Column 15, of the payroll register, page 165.

> Some cities levy an income tax on the earnings of those who work within the city. The tax rate and the amount of earnings on which the tax is levied vary from city to city.

Recording deductions for FICA tax on employees. The FICA tax is based on employee earnings paid in a calendar year. Congress sets the

INCOME TAX WITHHOLDING TABLES

SINGLE Persons — WEEKLY Payroll Period

And the wages are—		And the number of withholding allowances claimed is—										
At least	But less than	0	1	2	3	4	5	6	7	8	9	10 or more
		The amount of income tax to be withheld shall be—										
$120	$125	$18.00	$14.90	$12.00	$9.20	$6.40	$4.10	$1.80	$0	$0	$0	$0
125	130	19.20	15.90	13.00	10.20	7.30	4.90	2.60	.20	0	0	0
130	135	20.30	17.00	14.00	11.20	8.30	5.70	3.40	1.00	0	0	0
135	140	21.50	18.20	15.00	12.20	9.30	6.50	4.20	1.80	0	0	0
140	145	22.60	19.30	16.00	13.20	10.30	7.40	5.00	2.60	.30	0	0
145	150	23.80	20.50	17.10	14.20	11.30	8.40	5.80	3.40	1.10	0	0
150	160	25.50	22.20	18.90	15.70	12.80	9.90	7.00	4.60	2.30	0	0
160	170	27.80	24.50	21.20	17.80	14.80	11.90	9.00	6.20	3.90	1.60	0
170	180	30.10	26.80	23.50	20.10	16.80	13.90	11.00	8.10	5.50	3.20	.90
180	190	32.40	29.10	25.80	22.40	19.10	15.90	13.00	10.10	7.20	4.80	2.50
190	200	34.50	31.40	28.10	24.70	21.40	18.10	15.00	12.10	9.20	6.40	4.10
200	210	36.60	33.50	30.40	27.00	23.70	20.40	17.10	14.10	11.20	8.30	5.70
210	220	38.70	35.60	32.60	29.30	26.00	22.70	19.40	16.10	13.20	10.30	7.50
220	230	40.80	37.70	34.70	31.60	28.30	25.00	21.70	18.40	15.20	12.30	9.50
230	240	42.90	39.80	36.80	33.80	30.60	27.30	24.00	20.70	17.40	14.30	11.50
240	250	45.20	41.90	38.90	35.90	32.80	29.60	26.30	23.00	19.70	16.30	13.50
250	260	47.80	44.00	41.00	38.00	34.90	31.90	28.60	25.30	22.00	18.60	15.50
260	270	50.40	46.60	43.10	40.10	37.00	34.00	30.90	27.60	24.30	20.90	17.60
270	280	53.00	49.20	45.50	42.20	39.10	36.10	33.10	29.90	26.60	23.20	19.90
280	290	55.80	51.80	48.10	44.30	41.20	38.20	35.20	32.10	28.90	25.50	22.20
290	300	58.80	54.50	50.70	46.90	43.30	40.30	37.30	34.20	31.20	27.80	24.50
300	310	61.80	57.50	53.30	49.50	45.80	42.40	39.40	36.30	33.30	30.10	26.80
310	320	64.80	60.50	56.20	52.10	48.40	44.60	41.50	38.40	35.40	32.40	29.10
320	330	67.80	63.50	59.20	54.80	51.00	47.20	43.60	40.50	37.50	34.50	31.40
330	340	70.80	66.50	62.20	57.80	53.60	49.80	46.10	42.60	39.60	36.60	33.60
340	350	73.80	69.50	65.20	60.80	56.50	52.40	48.70	44.90	41.70	38.70	35.70
350	360	77.40	72.50	68.20	63.80	59.50	55.20	51.30	47.50	43.80	40.80	37.80
360	370	81.00	75.80	71.20	66.80	62.50	58.20	53.90	50.10	46.40	42.90	39.90
370	380	84.60	79.40	74.20	69.80	65.50	61.20	56.90	52.70	49.00	45.20	42.00
380	390	88.20	83.00	77.80	72.80	68.50	64.20	59.90	55.50	51.60	47.80	44.10

MARRIED Persons — WEEKLY Payroll Period

And the wages are—		And the number of withholding allowances claimed is—										
At least	But less than	0	1	2	3	4	5	6	7	8	9	10 or more
		The amount of income tax to be withheld shall be—										
135	140	16.40	13.60	10.70	7.80	5.40	2.90	.50	0	0	0	0
140	145	17.40	14.60	11.70	8.80	6.20	3.80	1.30	0	0	0	0
145	150	18.40	15.60	12.70	9.80	7.10	4.60	2.20	0	0	0	0
150	160	19.90	17.10	14.20	11.30	8.40	5.90	3.50	1.00	0	0	0
160	170	21.90	19.10	16.20	13.30	10.40	7.60	5.20	2.70	.30	0	0
170	180	23.90	21.10	18.20	15.30	12.40	9.50	6.90	4.40	2.00	0	0
180	190	25.60	23.10	20.20	17.30	14.40	11.50	8.60	6.10	3.70	1.20	0
190	200	27.30	24.80	22.20	19.30	16.40	13.50	10.60	7.80	5.40	2.90	.50
200	210	29.00	26.50	24.10	21.30	18.40	15.50	12.60	9.80	7.10	4.60	2.20
210	220	30.70	28.20	25.80	23.30	20.40	17.50	14.60	11.80	8.90	6.30	3.90
220	230	32.40	29.90	27.50	25.00	22.40	19.50	16.60	13.80	10.90	8.00	5.60
230	240	34.10	31.60	29.20	26.70	24.30	21.50	18.60	15.80	12.90	10.00	7.30
240	250	35.80	33.30	30.90	28.40	26.00	23.50	20.60	17.80	14.90	12.00	9.10
250	260	37.50	35.00	32.60	30.10	27.70	25.20	22.60	19.80	16.90	14.00	11.10
260	270	39.20	36.70	34.30	31.80	29.40	26.90	24.50	21.80	18.90	16.00	13.10
270	280	41.70	38.40	36.00	33.50	31.10	28.60	26.20	23.70	20.90	18.00	15.10
280	290	44.20	40.60	37.70	35.20	32.80	30.30	27.90	25.40	22.90	20.00	17.10
290	300	46.70	43.10	39.50	36.90	34.50	32.00	29.60	27.10	24.70	22.00	19.10
300	310	49.20	45.60	42.00	38.60	36.20	33.70	31.30	28.80	26.40	23.90	21.10
310	320	51.70	48.10	44.50	40.90	37.90	35.40	33.00	30.50	28.10	25.60	23.10

Section of income tax withholding tables for weekly payroll period

tax base and the tax rates for FICA tax. An act of Congress can change the base and rate at any time. The accounting principles involved, however, are the same regardless of changes in tax bases and tax rates. Therefore, a rate of 6% on a maximum salary of $15,000.00, or a maximum annual FICA tax of $900.00, is assumed for all payroll calculations in this textbook.

The total salary of Hilda Alonzo for the week ended September 30 is subject to the FICA tax. The amount of salary, $178.00, is multiplied by the tax rate, 6%, to figure the amount of tax to be withheld, $10.68. This deduction for FICA tax is entered on Line 1, Column 16, of the payroll register, page 165.

Recording other deductions for employees. Besides deductions for income taxes and FICA tax, some employees have two other deductions:

1. Hospital Insurance. This deduction is $3.80 for each insured single employee and $5.60 for each insured married employee. The deduction for hospital insurance is written in Column 17 of the payroll register, page 165. The deduction for hospital insurance is identified by writing the initial *H* in front of the amount in Column 17.
2. Group Life Insurance. This deduction may vary from one employee to the next. The amount of the deduction depends on the insurance coverage desired by an employee. The amount of this deduction for group life insurance is written in Column 17 of the payroll register, page 165. The deduction is identified by writing the initial *G* in front of the amount in Column 17.

On Line 1, Column 17, of the payroll register, page 165, the payroll clerk enters the amount of hospital insurance, $5.60, to be withheld from Ms. Alonzo's earnings. Ms. Alonzo is not enrolled in the group life insurance program. Therefore, no amount is written on Line 1, Column 17, for group life insurance.

Figuring net pay for employees. After all deductions are recorded in the payroll register, Mr. Ortez adds the amounts for deductions and writes the total in Column 18. He then figures the net amount to be paid by subtracting the total deductions, Column 18, from the total earnings, Column 9. For example, on Line 1 of the payroll register, pages 164–165, the net pay for Hilda Alonzo is: Total earnings, $178.00, *less* total deductions, $34.21, *equals* net pay, $143.79. The amount of net pay, $143.79, is written on Line 1, Column 19, of the payroll register.

Proving the accuracy of a payroll register. When the net pay has been entered for all employees, Mr. Ortez totals each of the amount columns in the payroll register. The accuracy of the payroll register is proved by: Total earnings, Column 9, $2,455.54, *less* total deductions, Column 18, $569.08, *equals* total of all net pay, Column 19, $1,886.46. After the payroll register is proved, a double line is ruled below the totals across all amount columns.

Employee's earnings record

Amaros must make a report to the federal government and to the state government each quarter of the year. The report shows the taxable wages that each employee earned and the amount of taxes withheld. The detailed information about all wages paid to each employee is brought together in one record. A business form showing detailed information about wage and salary payments made to one specific employee is called an employee's earnings record. The total earnings and the deductions for each employee shown on each payroll register are summarized on one line of that employee's earnings record. A separate employee's earnings record is prepared for each quarter for each employee.

Amaros keeps its employee's earnings records on printed sheets, using one sheet for each quarter. The employee's earnings record for Hilda Alonzo during the third quarter of 1978 is shown on pages 170 and 171.

The totals for the first and second quarters have been recorded on Lines 1 and 2. The September 30 payroll entry is shown on Line 15.

The Cumulative Total column, Column 4, shows the employee's total earnings for the year to date after each entry is made in the earnings record. The cumulative total shows readily when the employee's total earnings have reached the amount beyond which certain payroll taxes do not apply. Columns 5 and 6 show the earnings to which FICA tax and unemployment compensation tax apply. FICA tax is based on the first $15,000.00 of earnings. Hilda Alonzo's total earnings for the year to date have not exceeded $15,000.00. Therefore, FICA tax applies to all of her earnings for the third quarter. Unemployment compensation tax is based on the first $4,200.00 of earnings. Ms. Alonzo's earnings reached $4,200.00 before the end of the second quarter. Therefore, unemployment compensation tax does not apply after that pay period.

> The unemployment compensation tax is levied on and paid by the employer only, as described later in this chapter. Therefore, the amount of the unemployment tax does not appear on the employee's earnings record.

The amounts in the Deductions and Paid columns, Columns 7–12, of the employee's earnings record, page 171, are recorded each week by the payroll clerk. The amounts are obtained from Columns 14–19 of the payroll register, page 165.

Totals for the third quarter are entered on Line 17 of the form. These totals are for the 13 weeks of the third quarter only and do not include the totals for the first and second quarters. The third quarter totals are used to make the third quarterly report to the government.

> The totals for the first three quarters will be recorded on the first three lines of the employee's earnings record for the fourth quarter. The form for the final quarter provides space for entering the totals for the fourth quarter as well as for entering the yearly totals.

EMPLOYEE'S EARNINGS RECORD

NAME __Alonzo, Hilda__

ADDRESS __8340 Central Avenue, Denver, CO 80211__

MALE _____ MARRIED __X__ NUMBER OF _____ PAY _____ PER HOUR __X__

FEMALE __X__ SINGLE _____ EXEMPTIONS __3__ RATE __$4.00__ WEEK _____ MONTH _____

	1 PAY PERIOD	2	3 TOTAL EARNINGS	4 CUMULATIVE TOTAL	5 TAXABLE EARNINGS	6
	QUARTER	DATE ENDED			FICA	UNEMPLOYMENT COMPENSATION
1	FIRST	TOTALS	2296 00	2296 00	2296 00	2296 00
2	SECOND	TOTALS	2278 00	4574 00	2278 00	1904 00
3	THIRD	7/8	160 00	4734 00	160 00	
4		7/15	172 00	4906 00	172 00	
5		7/22	160 00	5066 00	160 00	
6		7/29	178 00	5244 00	178 00	
7		8/5	172 00	5416 00	172 00	
8		8/12	160 00	5576 00	160 00	
9		8/19	160 00	5736 00	160 00	
10		8/26	160 00	5896 00	160 00	
11		9/2	178 00	6074 00	178 00	
12		9/9	172 00	6246 00	172 00	
13		9/16	160 00	6406 00	160 00	
14		9/23	160 00	6566 00	160 00	
15		9/30	178 00	6744 00	178 00	
16						
17	THIRD	TOTALS	2170 00		2170 00	

Employee's earnings record (left page)

PAYING THE DEPARTMENTAL PAYROLL

Amaros pays its employees weekly by check. A special payroll bank account and special payroll checks are used.

Payroll bank account

After the payroll register for a weekly payroll has been completed by Mr. Ortez, the payroll clerk, the payroll is approved by Diana Ramos, accountant. A regular check is written in favor of Payroll for the total net amount to be paid to the employees. This check is deposited in a special payroll bank account against which payroll checks are written for the individual employees.

The special payroll bank account does not appear in the general ledger or on the chart of accounts. The amount of the weekly deposit to the payroll bank account equals exactly the sum of the week's salary payments. Therefore, the special payroll bank account balance is reduced to zero as soon as all employees have cashed their payroll checks. Because the special payroll bank account has a balance only until all payroll checks are cashed, no special account is needed in the general ledger.

FOR QUARTER ENDING September 30, 1978

EMPLOYEE NO. 8   SOC. SEC. NO. 363-06-2114

DATE EMPLOYED July 1, 1976   OCCUPATION Salesclerk

DATE EMPLOYMENT TERMINATED _____   DEPARTMENT Floor Covering

	7	8	9	10	11	12
	FEDERAL INCOME TAX	STATE INCOME TAX	FICA TAX	OTHER	TOTAL	NET AMOUNT PAID
1	196 90	33 90	137 76	472 80	441 36	1854 64
2	194 90	33 61	136 68	472 80	437 99	1840 01
3	13 30	2 34	9 60	H 5 60	30 84	129 16
4	15 30	2 61	10 32	H 5 60	33 83	138 17
5	13 30	2 34	9 60	H 5 60	30 84	129 16
6	15 30	2 63	10 68	H 5 60	34 21	143 79
7	15 30	2 61	10 32	H 5 60	33 83	138 17
8	13 30	2 34	9 60	H 5 60	30 84	129 16
9	13 30	2 34	9 60	H 5 60	30 84	129 16
10	13 30	2 34	9 60	H 5 60	30 84	129 16
11	15 30	2 63	10 68	H 5 60	34 21	143 79
12	15 30	2 61	10 32	H 5 60	33 83	138 17
13	13 30	2 34	9 60	H 5 60	30 84	129 16
14	13 30	2 34	9 60	H 5 60	30 84	129 16
15	15 30	2 63	10 68	H 5 60	34 21	143 79
16						
17	184 90	32 10	130 20	H 72 80	420 00	1750 00

Employee's earnings record (right page)

Payroll checks

Amaros uses a special payroll check form. The payroll check has a detachable stub showing total earnings for the pay period, deductions, and net amount paid. The detached stub is the employee's record.

Diana Ramos, accountant, prepares and signs the individual payroll checks. The information for the individual payroll checks is taken from the payroll register. Hilda Alonzo's payroll check for the pay period ended September 30, 1978, is shown below.

PERIOD ENDED	9	30	19 78		**Amaros** 8240 Jackson Street	No. 214
					Home Improvement Center Denver, CO 80211	23-311 / 1020

October 3 19 78

EARNINGS $ 178 00

REGULAR.... $ 160.00
OVERTIME .. $ 18.00

Pay to the order of   Hilda Alonzo $ 143.79

DEDUCTIONS $ 34 21

One hundred forty-three 79/100-------------------- Dollars

FED. INC. TAX. $ 15.30
STATE INC. TAX $ 2.63
FICA TAX ... $ 10.68
OTHER ..... $ 5.60H

ASB AMERICAN SECURITY BANK

Denver, CO 80213

Amaros

Diana Ramos

NET PAY $ 143 79

⑆1020⑉0311⑆ 083⑈10395⑉

Payroll check with detachable stub

To complete the records, the payroll check number for each employee is written on the same line as the employee's name in Column 20 of the payroll register, page 165.

Automatic check deposit

An employee may authorize an employer to deposit payroll checks in a specified bank. The procedure of depositing payroll checks directly to an employee's checking account in a specified bank is called an automatic check deposit. After the deposit has been recorded, the bank sends the employee a deposit receipt. The use of automatic check deposit for payroll does not change the accounting procedures for recording payroll.

RECORDING THE DEPARTMENTAL PAYROLL

Two journal entries are needed to record payroll. First, an entry is made in the cash payments journal to record the payment of the payroll. Second, an entry is made in the general journal to record the employer's payroll taxes.

Journalizing payment of a payroll

A check is written for the total net amount of a payroll. The check stub is the source document for journalizing the payroll data in the cash payments journal.

> *October 3, 1978. Paid weekly payroll ended September 30, $1,886.46, covering:*
> *Salaries – administrative, $770.60.*
> *Salaries – floor covering sales, $527.82.*
> *Salaries – paint sales, $560.54.*
> *Salaries – wallpaper sales, $596.58.*
> *Less deductions of:*
> *Employees income tax – federal, $318.50.*
> *Employees income tax – state, $42.65.*
> *FICA tax, $147.33.*
> *Hospital insurance, $50.60.*
> *Group life insurance, $10.00.*
> *Check No. 834.*

The effects of this weekly payroll transaction are analyzed in the T accounts on page 173.

Cash is credited for the net amount paid to employees, $1,886.46. Five liability accounts are credited for the amounts deducted from employees' salaries: Employees Income Tax Payable — Federal, $318.50; Employees Income Tax Payable — State, $42.65; FICA Tax Payable, $147.33; Hospital Insurance Payable, $50.60; and Group Life Insurance Payable, $10.00. Four salary expense accounts are debited: Salary Expense — Administrative, $770.60; Salary Expense — Floor Covering Sales, $527.82; Salary Expense — Paint Sales, $560.54; and Salary Expense — Wallpaper Sales, $596.58.

GENERAL LEDGER

Cash	111		Group Life Insurance Payable	219
	1,886.46			10.00

Employees Income Tax Payable — Federal	213		Salary Expense — Administrative	620
	318.50		770.60	

Employees Income Tax Payable — State	214		Salary Expense — Floor Covering Sales	621
	42.65		527.82	

FICA Tax Payable	215		Salary Expense — Paint Sales	622
	147.33		560.54	

Hospital Insurance Payable	218		Salary Expense — Wallpaper Sales	623
	50.60		596.58	

The weekly payroll transaction for the pay period ended September 30 is shown in the cash payments journal below.

						GENERAL		ACCOUNTS PAYABLE DEBIT (211)	PURCHASES DISCOUNT — FLR. COVER. CREDIT (511.2)	CASH CREDIT (111)	
	DATE	ACCOUNT TITLE	CK. NO.	POST. REF.		DEBIT	CREDIT				
1	1978 Oct. 3	Salary Expense-Administrative	834			77060				188646	1
2		Salary Exp.-Floor Covering Sales				52782					2
3		Salary Expense-Paint Sales				56054					3
4		Salary Expense-Wallpaper Sales				59658					4
5		Employees Income Tax Pay.-Federal					31850				5
6		Employees Income Tax Pay.-State					4265				6
7		FICA Tax Payable					14733				7
8		Hospital Insurance Payable					5060				8
9		Group Life Insurance Pay.					1000				9
10											10

Entry to record payroll

Figuring the employer's payroll taxes

Employers as well as employees must pay FICA taxes. Employers also must pay federal and state unemployment taxes. These funds are used to pay qualified workers cash benefits for limited periods of unemployment.

In a few states employees also have their earnings taxed for state unemployment taxes. Employees do not pay federal unemployment taxes.

The payroll taxes expense of the employer is based on a percentage of employee earnings. The employer's FICA tax is figured at the same rate and on the same earnings used in figuring the FICA tax for employees. The federal unemployment tax is 0.5% on the first $4,2000.00 of each employee's earnings for a calendar year. The state unemployment tax rates vary among states. In most states the tax is based on the first $4,200.00 of each employee's earnings. Also, in nearly all states employers may secure a reduction from the maximum rate if they provide steady employment for their employees.

> The rate of 2.7% on the first $4,200.00 of each employee's earnings is a common amount for employers to pay for their state unemployment tax. Therefore, this rate is used in this textbook.

Diana Ramos, accountant, figures the employer's payroll taxes. The payroll register, pages 164 and 165, shows that $147.33 was withheld from employees' salaries for the FICA tax. As the employer pays the same amount of FICA tax as employees, Amaros' FICA tax is also $147.33. The amount of unemployment tax for the September 30 payroll is figured by checking the total line of Column 6, headed Unemployment Compensation, Line 15, of each employee's earnings record. All employees of Amaros had earned more than $4,200.00 by the September 30 payroll. Therefore, no unemployment taxes are paid for this period.

> A journal entry that includes unemployment taxes is shown on Lines 14–18 of the general journal, page 45.

Journalizing the employer's payroll taxes

The source document for the entry to record the employer's payroll taxes is a memorandum prepared by Ms. Ramos. The memorandum shows all the details of the employer's taxes on the current payroll. To record the employer's payroll taxes on the September 30 payroll, Ms. Ramos makes the entry shown in the general journal below.

	DATE	ACCOUNT TITLE	POST. REF.	DEBIT	CREDIT	
		GENERAL JOURNAL			PAGE *16*	
1	*1978* Oct. 3	Payroll Taxes Expense		147 33		1
2		FICA Tax Payable			147 33	2
3		Memorandum No. 56.				3
4						4

Entry to record employer's payroll taxes

Payroll Taxes Expense is debited for $147.33. FICA Tax Payable is credited for $147.33, the amount owed to the federal government.

REPORTING AND PAYING PAYROLL TAXES LIABILITIES

Employers must pay to the federal, state, and local governments all payroll taxes withheld from employees' salaries. Employers also must pay payroll taxes that are expenses of the employer. Each employer is required by law to make various reports and payments at specified times.

Employer's withholding tax statement to employees

Each employer must furnish employees with copies of an annual statement showing their total earnings and the amounts withheld for taxes. This statement is made on Form W-2 furnished by the Internal Revenue Service. Six copies of Form W-2 are prepared by Ms. Ramos. One copy is sent to the Internal Revenue Service. One copy is sent to state, city, or local departments. One copy is for the employer's records. Three copies are given to each employee. One copy is filed with the employee's federal income tax return, and one copy is filed with the employee's state or local income tax return. The third copy is kept for the employee's personal records. Hilda Alonzo's copy of Form W-2, prepared by Ms. Ramos, for the year 1978 is shown below.

	Wage and Tax Statement 1978		
28-3339524 Amaros 8240 Jackson Street Denver, CO 80211	Type or print EMPLOYER'S name, address, ZIP code and Federal identifying number.	Copy C For employee's records	
		Employer's State identifying number 40-2648301	
Employee's social security number 363-06-2114	1 Federal income tax withheld 771.60	2 Wages, tips, and other compensation 9,022.00	3 FICA employee tax withheld 541.32	4 Total FICA wages
Type or print Employee's name, address, and ZIP code below. (Name must aline with arrow)		5 Was employee covered by a qualified pension plan, etc.? Yes	6	7
Hilda Alonzo 8340 Central Avenue Denver, CO 80213		8 State or local tax withheld 133.22	9 State or local wages 9,022.00	10 State or locality Colorado
		11 State or local tax withheld	12 State or local wages	13 State or locality
Form **W-2** This information is being furnished to the Internal Revenue Service.			Department of the Treasury—Internal Revenue Service

Form W-2, Wage and Tax Statement

The withholding tax statement furnished to each employee of Amaros shows the total wages paid during the calendar year. The statement also shows the FICA wages (if not the same as total wages), the amounts withheld for FICA tax, federal income tax, and state income tax. An employee must attach a copy of the W-2 form to personal income tax reports as evidence of earnings and tax withholdings.

Reporting and paying the liability for employees' federal income tax and for FICA tax

Each employer must make quarterly reports to the federal government of the amounts withheld from employees' pay for federal income tax and FICA tax. The quarterly reports must also show the employer's share of the FICA tax. In addition to the quarterly reports, the employer is required to make a summary report of all quarters at the end of the year. Payment of the liabilities for these taxes must be made at stated times, depending on the amount involved. The federal government publishes rules informing employers how often and in what form tax reports and tax payments must be made.

When Amaros pays the federal government the amount owed for employees' federal income tax and for FICA tax, an entry is made in the cash payments journal. The liability accounts Employees Income Tax Payable — Federal and FICA Tax Payable are debited for the appropriate amounts. Cash is credited for the total tax payment.

Reporting and paying the liability for employees' state income tax

Each employer must make quarterly reports to the state government showing the amounts withheld for state income tax. An annual summary report also must be filed by the employer. Instructions are provided by the state government about the forms to be used and how often payment is to be made.

> Rules regarding reporting and paying state or city income tax are not the same in each state or city. Therefore, the employer must know the rules for the state or city involved.

When Amaros pays the state government the amount owed for employees' state income tax, an entry is made in the cash payments journal. The liability account Employees Income Tax Payable — State is debited and Cash is credited for the amount of the tax payment.

Reporting and paying the liability for federal and state unemployment taxes

Each employer must make reports and payments to the federal and state governments for federal and state unemployment taxes. The times for payment are specified by law. Federal rules require only an annual report for federal unemployment taxes. Payments of the federal unemployment tax, however, must be made more often depending on the amount involved. State requirements vary for reporting and paying state unemployment tax. In general employers are required to make reports and payments quarterly.

When Amaros pays the amounts owed for federal and state unemployment taxes, an entry is made in the cash payments journal. For federal unemployment tax, Unemployment Tax Payable — Federal is debited and Cash is credited for the amount of the payment. For state unemployment tax, Unemployment Tax Payable — State is debited and Cash is credited for the amount of the payment.

MORE EFFICIENT METHODS FOR HANDLING PAYROLL WORK

Payroll work tends to be repetitive and to follow routine procedures. Therefore, payroll departments are often the first offices where faster procedures are adopted. Such procedures include:

1. The use of a pegboard, applying the write-it-once principle. This method is done by aligning payroll forms on a pegboard. When the forms are aligned, the information written on the check is also written on the employee's earnings record and the payroll register at the same time.
2. The use of accounting machines to speed up the recording of payroll information. The payroll forms are aligned similar to the manual procedure mentioned above. The operator uses an accounting machine to record the information once and it carries through to two or three other forms.
3. The use of automated data processing equipment whereby the basic payroll data about each employee are stored on magnetic disk or magnetic tape. The payroll data for each pay period are punched into cards. The cards are read by the automated equipment, and the payroll is automatically computed and recorded, and paychecks are produced.

✦ What is the meaning of each of the following?

- wages
- salary
- total earnings
- commissions record
- payroll register
- exemption
- employee's earnings record
- automatic check deposit

Using Business Terms

1. Why should every business have an efficient payroll system?
2. What three types of employee earnings does Amaros have?
3. How did the payroll clerk determine Hilda Alonzo's total earnings on the time card shown on page 162?
4. Why are Amaros' departmental sales supervisors not paid overtime?
5. How are Amaros' departmental sales supervisors compensated for their supervisory and overtime duties?
6. What are the two federal taxes that are withheld from an employee's pay?
7. What deductions does Amaros make from its employees' pay?
8. What is the purpose of the payroll register?
9. What information is recorded in the Earnings columns, Columns 6–9, of the payroll register shown on pages 164–165?
10. How is the net pay for each employee determined?
11. How is the accuracy of the payroll register proved?
12. Why is an employee's earnings record kept for each employee?

Questions for Individual Study

13. What is the purpose of the Cumulative Total column of the employee's earnings record, pages 170–171?
14. How does the special payroll bank account of Amaros operate?
15. What salary expense accounts are debited in the entry in the cash payments journal on page 173?

16. For what payroll taxes must the employer make contributions?
17. What three methods for handling payroll work are more efficient than those described for Amaros?

Cases for Management Decision

CASE 1 Steve Backus owns and operates the Eastland Sports Center. The accounting records are kept on a departmental basis for all accounts in the general ledger that affect gross profit on sales. The operating expenses connected with sales are not kept on a departmental basis. As the salary expense is the largest single selling expense, Mr. Backus recommends that the accounting department consider setting up special sales salary expense accounts for each of the departments. The salespersons do not work totally in individual departments. They have the responsibility of selling merchandise in all departments. The accountant feels that it would not be feasible to identify sales salary expenses by department. Therefore, the decision was made to continue using one sales salary expense account for all departments. Do you agree or disagree with the decision? Why?

CASE 2 Amaros uses one account, Payroll Taxes Expense, in which to record all of the expenses for FICA tax, federal unemployment tax, and state unemployment tax for the business. Haroldson's, Inc., uses three expense accounts — FICA Tax Expense, Federal Unemployment Tax Expense, and State Unemployment Tax Expense — when recording the three payroll tax expenses for the business. What are the advantages of each procedure?

Problems for Applying Concepts

PROBLEM 10-1 Preparing a payroll register and recording the payroll entries

The Ashley Company has two sales departments: Television Department and Stereo Department. Salesclerks and employees in the accounting department are paid on an hourly basis and receive 1½ times the regular hourly pay rate for all hours worked over 40 each week. Departmental supervisors are paid on a weekly basis and receive monthly commissions of 1% of net sales. Payroll data about the 11 employees for the week ended December 2 of the current year are shown at the top of page 179.

All earnings on the December 2 payroll are subject to FICA tax. Unemployment compensation taxes do not apply to this payroll. The November commissions are paid with the December 2 payroll.

Instructions: □ **1.** Prepare a commissions record for each departmental supervisor, similar to the one on page 163, for the month of November. Additional data needed are:

(a) Television Department: charge sales, $6,463.30; cash sales, $8,746.20; sales returns and allowances, $218.60.
(b) Stereo Department: charge sales, $6,133.80; cash sales, $7,922.50; sales returns and allowances, $188.25.

Empl. No.	Name	Job Title	Dept.	Marital Status	Number of Exemptions	Total Hours Worked	Regular Hourly Pay Rate	Weekly Wages
1	Andrews, Stephanie	Salesclerk	TV	S	1	40	$3.00	
2	Blair, Vincent	Salesclerk	Stereo	S	1	43	$3.00	
3	Carnes, Gary	Supervisor	Stereo	M	2	—	——	$150.00
4	Dobbins, Amber	Salesclerk	TV	S	1	42	$3.00	
5	Irvine, Anita	Supervisor	TV	M	3	—	——	$150.00
6	Jacobs, Wayne	Salesclerk	TV	M	2	40	$3.50	
7	Kennedy, Kaye	Salesclerk	Stereo	S	1	44	$3.50	
8	Martinez, Celia	Payroll Clerk	Acct.	S	1	42	$3.50	
9	Maya, Carlos	Salesclerk	Stereo	M	2	43	$3.80	
10	Rocca, Juan	Salesclerk	Stereo	M	3	41	$3.80	
11	Sabin, Amy	Accountant	Acct.	M	2	44	$4.00	

Instructions: ☐ **2.** Prepare a payroll register, similar to the one on pages 164 and 165, for the week ended December 2. Additional data needed are:

(a) A deduction is to be made from each employee's pay for federal income tax. Use the appropriate income tax withholding table on page 167.

(b) A deduction of 3% is to be made from each employee's pay for state income tax.

(c) A deduction of 6% is to be made from each employee's pay for FICA tax.

(d) A deduction of $5.00 is to be made from each single employee's pay and a deduction of $7.20 is to be made from each married employee's pay for hospital insurance.

☐ **3.** Make the entry on page 9 of a cash payments journal like the one on page 173 to record the payroll for the week ended December 2. Check No. 582 for the net amount of the payroll has been issued and deposited in the special payroll bank account.

☐ **4.** Make an entry on page 19 of a general journal like the one on page 174 to record the employer's payroll taxes expense on the December 2 payroll. The FICA tax rate for the employer is 6%. M33.

☐ **5.** Complete the payroll register by inserting the payroll check numbers, beginning with Ck133.

PROBLEM 10-2   ● Preparing an employee's earnings record

The hours worked by Rose Harria for the 13 weeks in the quarterly period July through September of the current year are given on page 180. Also included are the deductions for hospital insurance (H) and U.S. savings bonds (B).

Week Ended	Regular Hours	Overtime Hours	Other Deductions	Week Ended	Regular Hours	Overtime Hours	Other Deductions
7/7	40	2	H $9.25	8/25	39	—	
7/14	40	—		9/1	40	1	H $9.25
7/21	40	3	B $18.75	9/8	40	4	
7/28	38	—		9/15	40	—	B $18.75
8/4	40	4	H $9.25	9/22	36	—	
8/11	40	—		9/29	40	3	
8/18	40	—	B $18.75				

Instructions: Prepare an employee's earnings record, similar to the one shown on pages 170 and 171, for Rose Harria for the third quarter of the current year. Additional data needed to complete the record are as follows:

(a) Miss Harria's address is 3920 East Concord, Oakwood, OH 45873.

(b) Miss Harria is single and claims one exemption.

(c) Miss Harria's hourly pay rate is $3.80 for regular time and $5.70 for overtime.

(d) Miss Harria's employee number is 46.

(e) Miss Harria was employed on October 10, 1977.

(f) Miss Harria's social security number is 504-44-2648.

(g) Miss Harria is employed as a departmental supervisor.

(h) Miss Harria's earnings and deductions for the current year prior to the week ended July 7 were as follows:

	1st Quarter	2nd Quarter
Total earnings	$2,360.00	$2,286.00
Cumulative total	2,360.00	4,646.00
Taxable earnings:		
FICA	2,360.00	2,286.00
Unemployment compensation	2,360.00	1,840.00
Deductions:		
Federal income tax	378.30	348.40
State income tax	47.20	45.72
FICA tax	141.60	137.16
Other:		
Hospital insurance	27.75	27.75
U.S. savings bonds	56.25	56.25
Total deductions	651.10	615.28
Net amount paid	1,708.90	1,670.72

(i) Taxable earnings are:

(1) FICA — earnings not in excess of $15,000.00.

(2) Unemployment compensation — earnings not in excess of $4,200.00.

(j) In addition to Miss Harria's deductions for hospital insurance and savings bonds, the following deductions for taxes should be made.

(1) A deduction for federal income tax. (Use the appropriate income tax withholding table on page 167 to find each of her weekly deductions.)

(2) A deduction for state income tax of 2% of her total earnings each week.

(3) A deduction for FICA tax of 6% of her total earnings each week.

Departmentalized Accounting

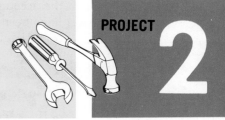

PROJECT 2

Project 2 reviews departmentalized accounting procedures of a merchandising business for a single month, including:

1. Recording and posting transactions using special departmental journals.
2. Preparing a bank reconciliation.
3. Estimating ending merchandise inventories.
4. Preparing an interim departmental statement of gross profit.

THE BUSINESS

Lewis Haynes owns and manages a retail store, Haynes Hardware. The store has three departments: hardware, houseware, and sporting goods. Both cash sales and charge sales are made. All sales are subject to a 5% sales tax collected from customers.

The fiscal year for the business is January 1 to December 31. During the fiscal year, an interim departmental statement of gross profit is prepared monthly. On December 31, the end of the fiscal year, the books are closed and annual financial statements prepared. Therefore, an income statement, capital statement, and balance sheet are not prepared at the end of each month.

Books of account

The journals used by Haynes Hardware are: a purchases journal similar to the one shown on page 114; a purchases returns and allowances journal, page 117; a cash payments journal, page 119; a sales journal, page 129; a sales returns and allowances journal, page 132; a cash receipts journal, page 133; and a general journal, page 174.

The ledgers used by Haynes Hardware are: a general ledger, an accounts receivable ledger, and an accounts payable ledger.

In the working papers that accompany this textbook, the accounts in ledgers are opened and account balances are entered for all three ledgers. If you are using the working papers, skip Instructions 1, 2, and 3 that follow.

Opening accounts in the general ledger

Instructions: **1.** Open the accounts given below in the general ledger of Haynes Hardware. No entries have been made in the merchandise inventory accounts or the capital account since the beginning of the fiscal year. Therefore, date the balances of these four accounts January 1. Date the balances of the other accounts May 1 of the current year.

Account Titles	Acct. No.	Debit Balances	Credit Balances
Cash	111	$ 8,386.20	
Petty Cash	112	100.00	
Accounts Receivable	113	2,665.30	
Merchandise Inventory — Hardware	114	21,133.50	
Merchandise Inventory — Houseware	115	18,644.30	
Merchandise Inventory — Sporting Goods	116	19,386.15	
Store Supplies	117	347.60	
Office Supplies	118	263.75	
Accounts Payable	211		$ 4,388.75
Employees Income Tax Payable — Federal	212		893.60
Employees Income Tax Payable — State	213		201.40
FICA Tax Payable	214		775.20
Sales Tax Payable	215		984.33
Unemployment Tax Payable — Federal	216		32.30
Unemployment Tax Payable — State	217		174.42
Lewis Haynes, Capital	311		55,793.25
Lewis Haynes, Drawing	312	2,048.00	
Sales — Hardware	411		35,360.80
Sales Returns and Allowances — Hardware	411.1	247.60	
Sales — Houseware	412		29,841.20
Sales Returns and Allowances — Houseware	412.1	166.40	
Sales — Sporting Goods	413		33,252.80
Sales Returns and Allowances — Sporting Goods	413.1	147.75	
Purchases — Hardware	511	23,265.20	
Purchases Returns and Allowances — Hardware	511.1		386.45
Purchases Discount — Hardware	511.2		225.30
Purchases — Houseware	512	16,846.33	
Purchases Returns and Allowances — Houseware	512.1		382.70
Purchases Discount — Houseware	512.2		196.93
Purchases — Sporting Goods	513	19,366.55	
Purchases Returns and Allowances — Sporting Goods	513.1		355.20
Advertising Expense	611	381.66	
Delivery Expense	612	42.30	
Miscellaneous Expense	613	98.40	
Payroll Taxes Expense	614	2,300.64	
Rent Expense	615	2,400.00	
Salary Expense — Administrative	616	7,093.60	
Salary Expense — Hardware	617	6,848.20	
Salary Expense — Houseware	618	6,744.80	
Salary Expense — Sporting Goods	619	4,320.40	

Opening customers' accounts in the accounts receivable ledger

Instructions: 2. Open the following accounts in the accounts receivable ledger. Record the balances on May 1 of the current year.

Customers' Names and Addresses	Account Balances
Carmella Acosta, 2216 Drake Road, Carson, NM 87517	$ 68.40
Audrey Argo, 484 Pickard Street, Carson, NM 87517	93.40
Kathy Bross, 1325 East River Road, Carson, NM 87517	269.60
Keith Egner, 685 South Haven, Carson, NM 87517	48.63
Thelma Grady, 353 West Jackson Street, Carson, NM 87517	116.25
Sue Lundy, 4414 Hamden Avenue, Carson, NM 87517	406.62
Thea Mims, 184 Riverview, Carson, NM 87517	83.20
Jay Ridgemont, 1483 Chestnut Street, Carson, NM 87517	1,260.40
Miriam Verdin, 2261 East Jackson Street, Carson, NM 87517	186.20
Dorothy Zumbiel, 881 North Haven, Carson, NM 87517	132.60

Opening creditors' accounts in the accounts payable ledger

Instructions: 3. Open the following accounts in the accounts payable ledger. Record the balances on May 1 of the current year.

Creditors' Names and Addresses	Account Balances
Ashbrook Houseware, 3336 Commercial, Albuquerque, NM 88114	$891.15
Hastings Supply, 1536 Main Street, Rogers, NM 88132	694.20
Horvath Sports Equipment, 2271 Chester, Albuquerque, NM 88114 ...	683.40
L & M Hardware, 5633 Walnut, Fresno, CA 93702	539.90
Lyman Houseware, 466 Beech Avenue, Golden, CO 80401	235.00
Tanaka Hardware, 3381 Bellows, Sonora, CA 96091	719.30
Vega Sporting Goods, 1643 West High Street, Lubbock, TX 79400	625.80

Recording transactions

Instructions: 4. Record the following transactions for May of the current year. Use the following journals with the page numbers as shown: purchases journal, page 14; purchases returns and allowances journal, page 6; cash payments journal, page 12; sales journal, page 15; sales returns and allowances journal, page 6; cash receipts journal, page 16; and general journal, page 3.

In the following transactions, the source documents have been abbreviated as: check, Ck; memorandum, M; purchase invoice, P; receipt, R; sales invoice, S; cash register tape, T; credit memo, CM; debit memo, DM.

May

1. Recorded the cash balance on May 1 as a memorandum entry in the cash receipts journal, $8,386.20.
1. Paid May rent, $600.00. Ck413.

May
1. Paid the *Daily Times News* for advertising, $78.20. Ck414.
1. Purchased sporting goods on account from Horvath Sports Equipment, $619.23. P268.
1. Received on account from Dorothy Zumbiel, $132.60. R168.
2. Sold sporting goods on account to Kathy Bross, $181.73, plus sales tax, $9.09; total, $190.82. S286.
2. Sold houseware on account to Thea Mims, $15.74, plus sales tax, $0.79; total, $16.53. S287.
3. Purchased merchandise on account from Hastings Supply: hardware, $652.20; sporting goods, $1,286.00. P269.
3. Purchased houseware on account from Ashbrook Houseware, $260.75. P270.
3. Received on account from Thea Mims, $83.20. R169.
4. Granted credit to Thea Mims for houseware returned, $15.74, plus sales tax on the returned merchandise, $0.79; total, $16.53. CM72.
5. Purchased hardware on account from Tanaka Hardware, $2,480.00. P271.
5. Paid on account to Horvath Sports Equipment, $683.40, no discount. Ck415.
5. Returned hardware to Tanaka Hardware, $36.00. DM83.
6. Sold houseware on account to Miriam Verdin, $85.44, plus sales tax, $4.27; total $89.71. S288.
6. Cash sales for May 1–6: hardware, $1,938.20; houseware, $1,646.00; sporting goods, $1,738.20; plus sales tax of $266.12; total, $5,588.52. T6.
8. Purchased houseware on account from Lyman Houseware, $2,643.20. P272.
8. Received on account from Keith Egner, $48.63. R170.

Posting: Post each amount that is to be posted individually. (Items in the Accounts Receivable, Accounts Payable, and General columns of the journals. Column totals are not posted until the end of the month.) Post the journals in the following order: sales journal, sales returns and allowances journal, purchases journal, purchases returns and allowances journal, general journal, cash receipts journal, and cash payments journal.

May
9. Sold hardware on account to Carmella Acosta, $133.92, plus sales tax, $6.70; total, $140.62. S289.
9. Granted credit to Miriam Verdin for houseware returned, $22.56, plus sales tax on the returned merchandise, $1.13; total, $23.69. CM73.
9. Paid on account to L & M Hardware, $260.09, covering invoice for $265.40 less a 2% discount. Ck416.
9. Returned sporting goods to Horvath Sports Equipment, $168.20. DM84.
10. Sold houseware on account to Dorothy Zumbiel, $252.48, plus sales tax, $12.62; total, $265.10. S290.
11. Purchased sporting goods on account from Vega Sporting Goods, $3,611.30. P273.
11. Received on account from Thelma Grady, $116.25. R171.
12. Paid on account to Ashbrook Houseware, $1,146.68, covering beginning balance of $891.15, no discount, and invoice for $260.75 less a 2% discount. Ck417.
13. Sold hardware on account to Jay Ridgemont, $38.25, plus sales tax, $1.91; total, $40.16. S291.

May **13.** Cash sales for May 8–13: hardware, $2,060.00; houseware, $1,730.35; sporting goods, $1,840.00; plus sales tax of $281.52; total, $5,911.87. T13.

15. Paid on account to Hastings Supply, $168.80, no discount. Ck418.

Posting: Post items that are to be posted individually from the journals.

May **16.** Purchased hardware on account from L & M Hardware, $2,738.00. P274.

16. Returned houseware to Ashbrook Houseware, $74.60. DM85.

16. Granted credit to Jay Ridgemont for hardware returned, $18.72, plus sales tax on the returned merchandise, $0.94; total, $19.66. CM74.

17. Sold sporting goods on account to Audrey Argo, $65.76, plus sales tax, $3.29; total, $69.05. S292.

17. Received on account from Carmella Acosta, $68.40. R172.

17. Paid on account to Vega Sporting Goods, $625.80, no discount. Ck419.

18. Sold hardware on account to Thea Mims, $134.35, plus sales tax, $6.72; total, $141.07. S293.

19. Purchased houseware on account from Ashbrook Houseware, $2,960.30. P275.

20. Cash sales for May 15–20: hardware, $2,036.80; houseware, $1,810.00; sporting goods, $1,782.60; plus sales tax of $281.47; total, $5,910.87. T20.

22. Sold sporting goods on account to Keith Egner, $345.60, plus sales tax, $17.28; total, $362.88. S294.

Posting: Post items that are to be posted individually from the journals.

May **23.** Purchased merchandise on account from Tanaka Hardware: hardware, $1,546.30, sporting goods, $930.50. P276.

23. Paid on account to Lyman Houseware, $230.30, covering invoice for $235.00 less a 2% discount. Ck420.

23. Received on account from Kathy Bross, $269.60. R173.

23. Granted credit to Audrey Argo for sporting goods returned, $31.20, plus sales tax on the returned merchandise, $1.56; total, $32.76. CM75.

24. Returned hardware to L & M Hardware, $82.00. DM86.

24. Received on account from Miriam Verdin, $186.20. R174.

25. Sold hardware on account to Thelma Grady, $44.35, plus sales tax, $2.22; total, $46.57. S295.

26. Purchased houseware on account from Lyman Houseware, $2,327.00. P277.

26. Returned houseware to Lyman Houseware, $41.00. DM87.

26. Paid on account to Tanaka Hardware, $719.30, no discount. Ck421.

26. Granted credit to Thelma Grady for hardware returned, $44.35, plus sales tax on the returned merchandise, $2.22; total, $46.57. CM76.

27. Cash sales for May 22–27: hardware, $1,983.40; houseware, $1,546.20; sporting goods, $1,860.80, plus sales tax of $269.52; total, $5,659.92. T27.

29. Sold houseware on account to Sue Lundy, $26.40, plus sales tax, $1.32; total, $27.72. S296.

30. Received bank statement dated May 27. Prepare a reconciliation of the bank statement in the same form as that shown on page 121. Additional data needed are given on page 186.

(a) The checkbook balance at the close of business on May 27 is $27,849.69.

(b) The May 27 balance on the bank statement is $23,130.54. The bank statement shows a service charge of $8.83.

(c) A deposit of $5,659.92 is not shown on the bank statement.

(d) Outstanding checks are: No. 420, $230.30; No. 421, $719.30.

May

30. As shown on the bank statement received on May 30, a service charge of $8.83 had been made by the bank. M11.

30. Purchased hardware on account from Hastings Supply, $2,646.20. P278.

30. Received on account from Audrey Argo, $93.40. R175.

30. Returned hardware to Tanaka Hardware, $374.00. DM88.

31. Paid monthly payroll ended May 31, $4,787.37, covering: Salary Expense — Administrative, $1,773.40; Salary Expense — Hardware, $1,688.20; Salary Expense — Houseware, $1,736.20; Salary Expense — Sporting Goods, $1,032.60; less deductions of Employees Income Tax — Federal, $882.30; Employees Income Tax — State, $186.91; FICA Tax, $373.82. Ck422.

31. Recorded employer's payroll taxes on the May 31 payroll: FICA Tax, $373.82; federal unemployment tax, $31.15; state unemployment tax, $168.22. M12.

31. Replenished petty cash: Store Supplies, $13.00; Office Supplies, $21.00; Delivery Expense, $6.75; Miscellaneous Expense, $16.30. Ck423.

31. Cash sales for May 29–31: hardware, $1,031.30; houseware, $763.60; sporting goods, $943.40, plus sales tax of $136.92; total, $2,875.22. T31.

Posting: Post items that are to be posted individually from the journals.

Completing the journals

Instructions: 5. Foot the amount columns of all journals. Prove the equality of debits and credits in the journals.

6. Prove cash. The checkbook balance is $25,965.06.

7. Total and rule the journals.

8. Post the totals of all amount columns that are to be posted. Post the journals in the following order: sales journal, sales returns and allowances journal, purchases journal, purchases returns and allowances journal, general journal, cash receipts journal, and cash payments journal.

Preparing interim departmental statement of gross profit

Instructions: 9. Estimate the value of the ending inventory for May of the current year for each department. Use the gross profit method of estimating an inventory. The gross profit on sales, percentage based on records of previous years' operations, is 20%.

10. Prepare an interim departmental statement of gross profit for month ended May 31 of the current year. The estimated beginning inventories on May 1 are:

Hardware department	$13,130.20
Houseware department	9,002.01
Sporting goods department	9,551.99

Voucher System Clerk 11

The cash account is affected by business transactions more often than any other general ledger account. Also, the cash account is more often subject to misuse. A procedure is needed that places accounting controls on cash.

One control procedure used by many businesses is to require that all cash payments be approved by someone in authority. In small businesses, one person, usually the owner or manager, approves cash payments before they are made. In large businesses, more than one person may have the right to approve cash payments. Department managers in a departmentalized business may also have to approve payment for goods and services bought by their own departments.

When several persons have the right to approve cash payments, a plan to control the payments is of great importance. A common plan for controlling cash payments when several persons are authorized to approve cash payments is through the use of a voucher system.

VOUCHER SYSTEM

A business form that shows the approval for a cash payment by an authorized person is called a voucher. Any business paper used as authority for an accounting entry is often referred to as a voucher. When the voucher system is used, however, the word *voucher* applies only to the approval form used for a cash payment.

A system for controlling cash payments in which a voucher is prepared and approved before a cash payment is made is called a voucher system. The person who prepares and records vouchers is called a voucher clerk. The journal in which vouchers are recorded when a voucher system is used is called a voucher register. The form of cash payments journal used in a voucher system is called a check register.

The major steps in using a voucher system are:

☐ 1 Verify the amounts and data on the invoice.
☐ 2 Determine the accounts to be debited and credited and prepare a voucher.
☐ 3 Obtain approval of the voucher.
☐ 4 Record the voucher in the voucher register and make a notation of the recording on the voucher.
☐ 5 File the unpaid voucher in an "unpaid vouchers file" according to the due date on which payment is to be made.
☐ 6 On the due date, obtain approval and issue a check for the amount of the voucher. Make a notation of the payment on the voucher.
☐ 7 File the paid voucher in the "paid vouchers file."
☐ 8 Record the check in the check register. Make a notation of the payment in the voucher register.

PREPARING VOUCHERS

The Zapada Company, a wholesale sporting goods business, uses a voucher system to control all cash payments. For each cash payment to be made a voucher is prepared.

Verifying the invoice

When an invoice is received by the Zapada Company, an invoice verification form is stamped on the invoice as shown below.

The invoice is verified for such details as quantities received, terms, prices, and amounts. The account or accounts to be debited and credited are also shown. The person doing each part of this work initials the verification form to show the responsibility for that part.

Verification of invoice

Preparing the voucher

The verified invoice is sent to the accounting department where a voucher clerk prepares a voucher. The voucher prepared for the verified invoice, page 188, is at the right.

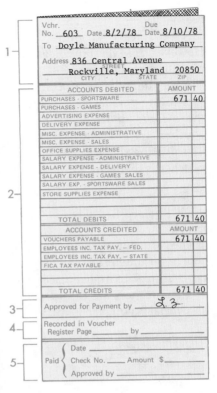

Outside of voucher for an invoice

The voucher clerk completes Section 1 of the voucher. The data entered are: the voucher number; the date on which the voucher is being prepared; the date on which payment is to be made; and the name and address of the business to which the money is to be paid.

> Vouchers are numbered consecutively to identify the vouchers and to assure that all vouchers have been accounted for.

In Section 2 of the voucher, the voucher clerk records the accounts and amounts to be debited and credited, the total debits, and the total credits. Account titles not printed on the voucher form are written on the blank lines in the debit or the credit section.

August 2, 1978. Purchased sportsware on account from Doyle Manufacturing Company, $671.40. Voucher No. 603.

The cost account **Purchases — Sportsware** is debited and the liability account **Vouchers Payable** is credited, $671.40.

Purchases — Sportsware	511
671.40	

Vouchers Payable	211
	671.40

> In a voucher system, **Vouchers Payable** is used as the liability account rather than **Accounts Payable**. Also, no accounts payable ledger is kept. The unpaid vouchers file shows the amounts owed. The paid vouchers file shows the amounts that have been paid.

The inside of a voucher, shown on page 198, contains space for other details about the transaction. The invoice is placed inside the voucher jacket. In the case of Voucher No. 603 above, all the details are contained on the invoice used to prepare the voucher. Therefore, the invoice is placed inside the voucher and no further data need be recorded on the inside of the voucher.

The voucher is folded and becomes a folder in which related documents can be placed. For this reason, the voucher is sometimes referred to as a voucher jacket. The voucher jackets provide a cover or file of uniform size for all invoices and other documents of various sizes that are received.

A separate voucher is usually prepared for each invoice received. However, if several invoices are received at the same time from the same creditor, some businesses combine all invoices into one voucher.

After the voucher is completed by the voucher clerk, the voucher is sent to the person who is authorized to approve it. Luis Zapada, one of the owners of the Zapada Company, is the person who authorizes vouchers for the company. He checks the voucher and indicates approval by initialing the voucher in Section 3 shown on page 189. The approved voucher is then sent to the accounting department to be recorded.

VOUCHER REGISTER

The voucher clerk for the Zapada Company uses each voucher as a source document for an entry in the voucher register. The voucher register is similar to and replaces the purchases journal described in Chapter 7. The vouchers are recorded in numerical order. A missing number will show that a voucher is missing.

	DATE	CREDITOR	VCHR. NO.	PAID DATE	CK. NO.	VOUCHERS PAYABLE CREDIT	
1	*1978* Aug 2	Doyle Manufacturing Company	603	Aug 10	741	671 40	1
2	3	Ellison Motors	604			4300 00	2
3	4	Maya's Inc.	605	Aug. 11	742	583 60	3
4	7	Pernell and Company	606			106 75	4
5	7	Marshall Company	607			736 30	5
6	8	Moreno's, Inc.	608	See Vchr. No. 611		88 00	6
7	10	Calvo Supply	609			36 20	7
8	11	Santos, Inc.	610	Aug. 21	748	380 45	8
9	12	Moreno's, Inc.	611			50 00	9
10							10
22	28	Payroll	633	Aug. 28	757	2393 75	22
23							23
24							24
25							25
26							26
27							27
28							28
29	31	Petty Cash	634	Aug. 31	758	47 60	29
30							30
31	31	Totals				9981 20 / 9981 20	31
32						(211)	32

PAGE 24   VOUCHER REGISTER

Voucher register (left page)

The voucher register used by the Zapada Company is shown below and on page 190. In the voucher register, special Purchases Debit columns are used for each department: Sportsware and Games. When vouchers are recorded that affect accounts for which there are no special amount columns, amounts are recorded in the General columns.

When a voucher is paid, the date and the check number are written in the Paid columns of the voucher register. This gives the voucher clerk a cross-reference from the voucher register to the check register.

Recording a voucher in the special amount columns of the voucher register

The entry on Line 1 of the voucher register below is for Voucher No. 603, page 189. The date of the voucher, 1978, Aug. 2, is written in the Date column. The name of the creditor, Doyle Manufacturing Company, is written in the Creditor column. The number of the voucher, 603, is written in the Vchr. No. column. The total amount to be paid for this voucher, $671.40, is written in the Vouchers Payable Credit column. As the total amount of the voucher is debited to Purchases — Sportsware, $671.40 is also written in the Purchases Debit — Sportsware Dept. column.

FOR MONTH OF *August* 19 **78**							**PAGE** *24*			
2	3	4	5			6	7			
DISTRIBUTION					**GENERAL**					
PURCHASES DEBIT		**STORE SUPPLIES DEBIT**	**OFFICE SUPPLIES DEBIT**	**ACCOUNT**		**POST REF.**	**DEBIT**	**CREDIT**		
SPORTSWRE. DEPT.	**GAMES DEPT.**									
1	67140									1
2					*Delivery Equipment*	121	430000			2
3		58360								3
4		10675								4
5	41085	32545								5
6		8800								6
7				3620						7
8	38045									8
9					*Vouchers Payable*	211	8800			9
10					*Purch. Rets. + Allow.-Games*	512.1		3800		10
22					*Salary Exp.-Admin.*	622	116000			22
23					*Salary Exp.-Delivery*	623	30000			23
24					*Salary Exp.-Games Sales*	624	52500			24
25					*Salary Exp.-Sportswre. Sales*	625	110000			25
26					*Empl. Inc. Tax Pay.-Fed.*	213		41360		26
27					*Empl. Inc. Tax Pay.-State*	214		9255		27
28					*FICA Tax Payable*	215		18510		28
29					*Advertising Expense*	611	2470			29
30					*Misc. Expense-Sales*	618	2290			30
31	169315	141020	4630	3620			752060	72525		31
	169315	141020	4630	3620			752060	72525		
32	(511)	(512)	(117)	(116)			(✓)	(✓)		32

Voucher register (right page)

After recording Voucher No. 603 in the voucher register, the voucher clerk makes a notation in Section 4 on the outside of the voucher. The illustration at the left shows that Voucher No. 603 was recorded on page 24 of the voucher register. The voucher clerk initials the voucher in this section to show who recorded the entry. The voucher is then filed in an unpaid vouchers file according to the due date on which payment must be made.

4 — ☐ Recorded in Voucher
Register Page **24** by *Q.R.Q.*

Voucher clerk's notation on the voucher to show that the voucher has been recorded

Recording a voucher in the General columns of the voucher register

August 3, 1978. Bought used delivery truck on account from Ellison Motors, $4,300.00. Voucher No. 604.

Delivery Equipment	121
4,300.00	

Vouchers Payable	211
	4,300.00

The plant asset account Delivery Equipment is debited and the liability account Vouchers Payable is credited, $4,300.00.

From the data on Voucher No. 604, the voucher clerk for the Zapada Company makes the entry shown on Line 2 of the voucher register, pages 190 and 191. The total amount of the voucher, $4,300.00, is written in the Vouchers Payable Credit column. There is no special amount column in which to record a debit to the delivery equipment account. To record the debit, the name of the general ledger account, Delivery Equipment, is written in the General Account column. The amount, $4,300.00, is written in the General Debit column.

Posting from the voucher register

The only items posted individually from the voucher register are those recorded in the General Debit or General Credit columns. As each amount is posted periodically to the general ledger, the account number is written in the Post. Ref. column of the voucher register.

At the end of each month, the amount columns of the voucher register are footed, and the equality of debits and credits is proved. The voucher register is then totaled and ruled. The voucher register on pages 190 and 191 is shown footed, totaled, and ruled.

The totals of the special amount columns are posted to the general ledger accounts named in the column headings. The number of the account to which each special amount column total is posted is written in parentheses below the total. Check marks are placed below the totals of the General Debit and General Credit columns to show that these totals are not posted.

PAYING VOUCHERS

When a voucher system is used, each voucher is paid by a check. Each day the voucher clerk removes from the unpaid vouchers file the vouchers that are to be paid that day. A check is prepared for the amount of each voucher less any deductions for cash discounts. Checks are issued only for approved vouchers.

Preparing the voucher check

A check with space on it for writing the purpose of the payment is called a voucher check. A voucher check is shown below.

Voucher No. 603		
IN PAYMENT OF:		
Invoice No. 31956		
$671.40		
Less 2% disc. Sptswr. Dept.	13.43	
TOTAL	$657.97	
Zapada Company		

ZAPADA Company
705 Leeswood Road   Augusta, GA 30903

NO. **741**

64—1204
611

Date August 10, 1978

Pay To The Order Of Doyle Manufacturing Company $ 657.97

Six hundred fifty-seven 97/100 ------------------------------ Dollars

COASTAL BANK
Augusta, GA 30903

A. T. Zapada

⑆0611⑆1204⑆   372⑈1238⑈

Voucher check

Voucher checks can be used when a voucher system is not used. For example, the check shown on page 171, Chapter 10, is a voucher check used for payroll.

The check above is issued by the Zapada Company in payment of Voucher No. 603. The main portion of the check is prepared in the usual manner. In the space provided for the voucher data, the voucher clerk records:

1. The voucher number.
2. The invoice number.
3. The amount of the invoice.
4. The amount of the discount, if any.
5. The net amount for which the check is written.

Recording the payment on the voucher

After a check in payment of a voucher is written, a notation is made in Section 5 on the outside of the voucher. The notation made on Voucher No. 603 is shown at the right. The notation shows that Check No. 741 was issued on August 10, 1978, in payment of the voucher. The check was approved and signed by A. T. Zapada.

5—
Date August 10, 1978
Paid { Check No. 741 Amount $ 657.97
Approved by A. T. Zapada

Notation on the voucher to show that the voucher has been paid

After a notation of the payment is made on a voucher, the voucher is filed in numerical order in the paid vouchers file. The voucher is then available for future reference if necessary.

CHECK REGISTER

The check register used by the Zapada Company is shown below. The check register is similar to and replaces the cash payments journal described in Chapter 7.

		CHECK REGISTER							PAGE 28
					1	2	3	4	5 6
DATE	IN FAVOR OF	CK. NO.	VCHR. NO.	VOUCHERS PAYABLE DEBIT	PURCH. DISCOUNT CR. SPORTSWRE DEPT.	GAMES DEPT.	CASH CREDIT	BANK DEPOSITS	BALANCE
1978 Aug. 10	Brought Forward	✓		234062	1627	983	231452		934026
10	Doyle Manufacturing Co	741	603	67140	1343		65797		868229
11	Maya's Inc.	742	605	58360		1167	57193		811036
14	Payroll	743	612	239375			239375		571661
14	Balboa Company	744	602	14625		293	14332		557329
14	Deposit	✓						91520	648849
28	Payroll	757	633	239375			239375		854093
31	Petty Cash	758	634	4760			4760		849333
31	Deposit	✓						106028	955361
31	Totals			1218722	2970	2443	1213309		955361
				1218722	2970	2443	1213309		
				(211)	(511.2)	(512.2)	(111)		

Check register

Some businesses have bank accounts in more than one bank. In such cases, a separate account is often kept in the general ledger for each bank account. A separate check register is sometimes kept for each bank account. However, a single check register may be used with separate amount columns for each bank account. The Zapada Company has only one bank account and uses a single check register.

A voucher check is written for each voucher at the time the voucher is paid. The Zapada Company prepares each voucher check in duplicate. The duplicate copy is the source document for the entry in the check register. The voucher clerk records each check in the check register in numerical order. Any missing check numbers must be accounted for.

Each check is recorded in a check register as a debit to Vouchers Payable and a credit to Cash. If there is a discount for prompt payment, the amount is recorded as a credit in the appropriate departmental Purch. Discount Cr. column. In a voucher system, these accounts are the only ones in the general ledger that are affected by cash payments transactions. All other accounts were debited or credited when the voucher was recorded in the voucher register. Therefore, special amount columns are used in a check register for Vouchers Payable Debit, Purchases Discount Credit for each department, and Cash Credit.

Recording checks in the check register

On August 10, 1978, the Zapada Company's voucher clerk forwarded the debit column totals, the credit column totals, and the bank balance. These column totals are forwarded from page 27 to page 28 of the check register of the Zapada Company. The amounts brought forward are shown on Line 1 of the check register on page 194.

August 10, 1978. Paid Voucher No. 603, $671.40, less Purchases Discount of $13.43. Check No. 741.

The liability account **Vouchers Payable** is debited for $671.40, and the contra account, **Purchases Discount — Sportsware**, is credited for $13.43. **Cash** is credited for $657.97.

Vouchers Payable	211
671.40	

Purchases Discount — Sportsware	511.2
	13.43

Cash	111
	657.97

The entry to record this check is shown on Line 2 of the check register, page 194. The date, 10, is entered in the Date column. The name of the payee, Doyle Manufacturing Company, is written in the In Favor Of column. The check number, 741, is written in the Ck. No. column, and the voucher number, 603, is written in the Vchr. No. column. The total amount of the voucher, $671.40, is written in the Vouchers Payable Debit column. The amount of the discount, $13.43, is written in the Purch. Discount Cr. — Sportsware column. The amount of the check, $657.97, is written in the Cash Credit column. The amount of the check is subtracted from the balance shown in the Bank Balance column on Line 1. The amount of the new balance, $8,682.29, is written in the Bank Balance column on Line 2.

After the check has been recorded in the check register, a notation is made in the voucher register. On Line 1 of the voucher register, page 190, a notation is made in the Paid columns for the payment of Voucher No. 603. The date of payment, Aug. 10, is written in the Paid Date column. The check number, 741, is written in the Paid Ck. No. column.

Recording deposits in the check register

The check register shown on page 194 has two columns with the heading *Bank*. These two columns are used to keep an up-to-date record of the amount of cash in the bank account. The Bank Deposits column is used to record the amounts deposited in the bank account. The Bank Balance column is used to show the balance in the bank account after each check is issued and after each deposit is made. When this form of check register is used, maintaining a record of deposits and a bank balance on check stubs is not necessary.

On August 14, 1978, the Zapada Company made a deposit of $915.20 in its bank account. The memorandum entry to record this deposit is shown on Line 6 of the check register on page 194. The date, 14, is written in the Date column. The word *Deposit* is written in the In Favor Of column. A check mark is placed in the Vchr. No. column to show that no voucher is used for this memorandum entry. The amount of the deposit, $915.20, is written in the Bank Deposits column. The amount of the deposit is then added to the previous bank balance shown in the Bank Balance column on Line 5. The new bank balance, $6,488.49, is written in the Bank Balance column on Line 6.

Posting from the check register

The check register used by the Zapada Company has only special amount columns. Individual items in the check register are not posted. At the end of the month, amount columns are footed, the equality of debits and credits is proved, and the check register is totaled and ruled. The check register for the Zapada Company, page 194, is shown footed, totaled, and ruled at the end of August, 1978.

The totals of the special amount columns are posted to the general ledger accounts named in the column headings. The number of the account to which each special amount column total is posted is written in parentheses below the total.

The Bank Deposits column and the Bank Balance column are used only to show the balance upon which checks can be written. These columns, therefore, are neither totaled nor ruled.

APPLICATION OF THE VOUCHER SYSTEM TO SELECTED BUSINESS TRANSACTIONS

For the transactions described previously in this chapter, a voucher was prepared from an invoice and each voucher was paid in full when due. Some transactions, however, require slightly different procedures. Examples are purchases returns and allowances, payroll payments, petty cash replenishments, and partial payments of vouchers.

Recording purchases returns and allowances when the voucher system is used

A purchases returns and allowances transaction reduces the total amount owed on an invoice. The voucher for the original invoice must be changed to show the reduction in the amount owed.

> *August 12, 1978. Issued Debit Memorandum No. 64 to Moreno's, Inc., for the return of merchandise purchased for the Games Department, $38.00. Canceled Voucher No. 608 and issued Voucher No. 611.*

The liability account Vouchers Payable is debited for the amount of Voucher No. 608, $88.00, and credited for the amount of the new Voucher No. 611, $50.00. The contra account, Purchases Returns and Allowances — Games, is credited for $38.00. In recording the change in the amount owed on Voucher No. 608 because of the return, the voucher clerk proceeds as follows:

Vouchers Payable	211
88.00	88.00
	50.00

| Purchases Returns and | |
| Allowances — Games | 512.1 |

1. Removes Voucher No. 608 from the unpaid vouchers file. Writes *Canceled* across the outside of the voucher.
2. Prepares a new voucher and has it approved. Voucher No. 611 is prepared for the amount of the new balance, $50.00 (original voucher amount, $88.00, less the amount of the purchases return, $38.00). The canceled copy of Voucher No. 608, the original invoice, and the debit memorandum are placed inside the voucher jacket for the new Voucher No. 611.
3. Writes the notation *See Vchr. No. 611* in the Paid columns of the voucher register on the line for the canceled Voucher No. 608. This notation is shown on Line 6 of the voucher register, page 190.
4. Records the new voucher in the voucher register. This entry is shown on Lines 9 and 10 of the voucher register, pages 190 and 191. Vouchers Payable is debited in the General Debit column for $88.00 to cancel Voucher No. 608. Purchases Returns and Allowances — Games Dept. is credited in the General Credit column for $38.00 to record the decrease in the cost of purchases. Vouchers Payable is credited in the Vouchers Payable Credit column for $50.00 ($88.00 − $38.00) to record the amount owed for the new Voucher No. 611.
5. Files Voucher No. 611 in the unpaid vouchers file under the due date.

Paying the payroll when the voucher system is used

The Zapada Company pays its employees every two weeks. A payroll register is prepared to show the details of each payroll. This payroll register is the source of data for the payroll voucher.

When the voucher for the August 28, 1978, payroll is prepared, the data from the payroll register are recorded in summary form on the inside of the voucher as shown on page 198. The outside of the voucher for the August 28 payroll is then completed as shown on page 198.

The Zapada Company uses four salary expense accounts: Salary Expense — Administrative, Salary Expense — Delivery, Salary Expense — Games Sales, and Salary Expense — Sportsware Sales. The salary amounts for each account are shown on the outside of Voucher No. 633. Salary Expense — Administrative is debited for $1,160.00; Salary Expense — Delivery is debited for $300.00; Salary Expense — Games Sales is debited for $525.00; and Salary Expense — Sportsware Sales is debited for $1,100.00. The four debit

VOUCHER

ZAPADA Company

Vchr.
No. 633 Date August 28 19 78 Terms _____ Due August 28 19 78

To Payroll

Address _____

City _____ State _____ Zip _____

For the following: Attach all invoices or other papers permanently to voucher.

DATE	VOUCHER DETAILS		AMOUNT
Aug. 28			
	Payroll for period ended 8/28/78		
	Salary Expense--Administrative	$1,160.00	
	Salary Expense--Delivery	300.00	
	Salary Expense--Games Sales	525.00	
	Salary Expense--Sportsware Sales	1,100.00	$3,085.00
	Deductions:		
	Employees Inc. Tax Pay.--Federal	$ 413.60	
	Employees Inc. Tax Pay.--State	92.55	
	FICA Tax Payable	185.10	691.25
	Net cash payment		$2,393.75

Approved by *Luis Zapada*

Inside of voucher for a payroll

Vchr.
No. 633 Date 8/28/78 Due Date 8/28/78

To Payroll

Address _____
STREET

CITY   STATE   ZIP

ACCOUNTS DEBITED	AMOUNT	
PURCHASES - SPORTSWARE		
PURCHASES - GAMES		
ADVERTISING EXPENSE		
DELIVERY EXPENSE		
MISC. EXPENSE - ADMINISTRATIVE		
MISC. EXPENSE - SALES		
OFFICE SUPPLIES EXPENSE		
SALARY EXPENSE - ADMINISTRATIVE	1,160	00
SALARY EXPENSE - DELIVERY	300	00
SALARY EXPENSE - GAMES SALES	525	00
SALARY EXP. - SPORTSWARE SALES	1,100	00
STORE SUPPLIES EXPENSE		
TOTAL DEBITS	3,085	00
ACCOUNTS CREDITED	AMOUNT	
VOUCHERS PAYABLE	2,393	75
EMPLOYEES INC. TAX PAY. – FED.	413	60
EMPLOYEES INC. TAX PAY. – STATE	92	55
FICA TAX PAYABLE	185	10
TOTAL CREDITS	3,085	00

Approved for Payment by *LZ*

Recorded in Voucher
Register Page 24 by *O.R.O.*

Paid { Date *August 28, 1978*
Check No. 757 Amount $ *2,393.75*
Approved by *Art Zapada* }

Outside of voucher for a payroll

items are added and the total, $3,085.00, is entered on the Total Debits line. **Vouchers Payable** is credited for $2,393.75, the net amount of the payroll to be paid to the employees. **Employees Income Tax Payable — Federal** is credited for $413.60, **Employees Income Tax Payable — State** is credited for $92.55, and **FICA Tax Payable** is credited for $185.10. These amounts are the withholdings from the employees' salaries for these taxes. The four credits are added and the total, $3,085.00, is entered on the Total Credits line. The total debits on each voucher must equal the total credits.

The voucher is approved for payment by Luis Zapada, who signs the inside of the voucher and initials the outside of Section 3. The approved voucher is sent to the accounting department to be recorded in the voucher register. The entry to record Voucher No. 633 for the August 28 payroll is on Lines 22–28 of the voucher register, pages 190 and 191. After this entry is recorded in the voucher register, the voucher clerk makes a notation of the recording on the outside of Voucher No. 633 in Section 4. The voucher register page number and the clerk's initials are recorded.

Since Voucher No. 633 is to be paid immediately, the voucher is not placed in the unpaid vouchers file. Rather, Check No. 757 is issued for the payroll voucher. The paid section of Voucher No. 633 is completed. The paid voucher is then filed in the paid vouchers file.

The entry to record Check No. 757 is shown on Line 19 of the check register, page 194. Vouchers Payable is debited and Cash is credited for $2,393.75. The date of the check and the check number are written on Line 22 in the Paid columns of the voucher register, page 190.

A general journal entry is required to record the employer's payroll taxes as described in Chapter 10, page 174. When quarterly payments are due the government for the employees' and employer's payroll taxes, a voucher is prepared and approved. The approved voucher is sent to the accounting department to be recorded in the voucher register. A check is then issued for the voucher and is recorded in the check register.

Replenishing petty cash when the voucher system is used

When the petty cash fund is established, a voucher is prepared and a check is issued. When the fund needs to be replenished, the cashier for the petty cash fund submits a statement of expenditures to the voucher clerk. The voucher clerk prepares a voucher, has the voucher approved, and records the data in the voucher register.

Lines 29–30 of the voucher register, pages 190–191, show the entry for Voucher No. 634 to replenish petty cash on August 31, 1978. The debits for the entry are recorded in the General Debit column. Vouchers Payable is credited for an amount equal to the total of all the debits in this entry. The account names are written in the General Account column.

The entry to record Check No. 758, issued in payment of Voucher No. 634, is shown on Line 20 of the check register, page 194. The check is drawn in favor of *Petty Cash*. The cashier for the petty cash fund cashes the check and places the money in the petty cash drawer.

Recording a partial payment of a voucher when the voucher system is used

Some accountants prefer to cancel the original voucher when a partial payment is made. In place of the original voucher, a new voucher is prepared for the balance still due. A notation is placed on the original voucher and in the voucher register whenever a partial payment is made.

When large purchases, such as those for equipment, are made, a business often agrees to pay in a series of installments. A separate voucher is prepared for each installment. The invoice is placed inside the first voucher. A brief description is written on the inside of the other vouchers. A complete list of all voucher numbers in the series is placed inside each voucher. Thus, the voucher clerk can easily locate any of the installment vouchers. Each voucher is recorded separately in the voucher register and is filed in the unpaid vouchers file according to its due date. As each installment is paid, the voucher for that installment is removed from the unpaid vouchers file. The proper notation is made on the voucher, and the voucher is filed in the paid vouchers file.

SUMMARY OF THE ADVANTAGES OF THE VOUCHER SYSTEM

The voucher system of controlling cash payments has many advantages for large businesses that make many expenditures. Some of these advantages are:

1. The responsibility for authorizing and approving all expenditures is centralized in a few persons.
2. The voucher jacket provides a convenient method of filing invoices for reference. This is especially true when the invoices received from creditors may be of different sizes.
3. The filing of vouchers according to their due dates facilitates the payment of invoices within the discount periods.
4. The paid vouchers file and the unpaid vouchers file replace the accounts payable ledger.
5. The voucher system eliminates all posting to creditors' accounts.
6. A check register used as part of the voucher system makes it possible to eliminate the keeping of check stubs. The check register combines the records of a cash payments journal and the check stubs.

Using Business Terms

✦ What is the meaning of each of the following?

- voucher
- voucher system
- voucher clerk
- voucher register
- check register
- voucher check

Questions for Individual Study

1. What are the major steps in using a voucher system?
2. Why are vouchers numbered consecutively?
3. In a voucher system what liability account is used in place of accounts payable?
4. What ledger is usually not kept when a voucher system is used?
5. When an invoice is received for merchandise purchased on account, which accounts are debited and credited in a voucher system?
6. What is done with an invoice after it has been used to prepare a voucher?
7. What journal does the voucher register replace when a voucher system is used?
8. How are vouchers that affect accounts for which no special amount columns are used recorded in the voucher register?
9. In the voucher register shown on page 190, why is there no entry in the Paid columns on Line 2?

10. In the voucher register, pages 190–191, which amount columns are posted individually?
11. What five things does the Zapada Company include in the voucher space on its voucher checks?
12. What journal does the check register replace in a voucher system?
13. Why are no amounts posted individually from any of the columns in the check register used by the Zapada Company?
14. When a check register contains a Bank Deposits column and a Bank Balance column, why is it not necessary to maintain a check-stub record of checks issued?
15. How is the change in the amount owed on a voucher because of a purchases return recorded?
16. What is the source of data for the payroll voucher?
17. What are six advantages of the voucher system?

CASE 1 Romona Angulo owns and operates two women's sportswear stores. Miss Angulo keeps most of the accounting records herself, but she employs a public accountant part time to assist her. Miss Angulo is considering using a voucher system for her business. What questions should she answer in deciding whether to install a voucher system?

CASE 2 Juan Salazar owns a hardware store. He uses a voucher system that involves the following steps: (1) When an invoice is received, it is verified and a voucher is prepared for it. (2) The voucher is filed in an unpaid vouchers file under the due date. (3) When the voucher is due, a check is issued, a notation of the payment is made on the voucher, and it is filed in the paid vouchers file. (4) The check issued is recorded in a cash payments journal. Mr. Salazar does not record the voucher in any journal. The check is recorded as the only entry. For example, if the invoice received is for purchases and the voucher is paid with a discount, the entry made in the cash payments journal debits Purchases, credits Purchases Discount, and credits Cash.

What are the advantages and the disadvantages of this procedure?

PROBLEM 11-1 Recording transactions when a voucher system is used

The Panopio Company has two departments: Toys Department and Games Department. The company uses a voucher register similar to the one shown on pages 190 and 191 and a check register similar to the one shown on page 194.

Instructions: □ 1. Record the following transactions completed during October of the current year. Use page 14 of a voucher register and page 11 of a check register. Source documents are abbreviated as: check, Ck; debit memorandum, DM; voucher, V.

Oct. 1. Recorded the cash balance on October 1 as a memorandum entry in the check register, $13,284.00.

2. Purchased merchandise on account from Dotson Company as follows: Toys Department, $196.45; Games Department, $263.00. V516.

4. Purchased merchandise on account from Tandoc Company as follows: Toys Department, $496.50; Games Department, $1,460.30. V517.

4. Bought supplies from Reyies Supply as follows: store supplies, $63.00; office supplies, $26.40. V518.

4. Paid Voucher No. 518, $89.40; no discount. Ck283.

6. Issued DM112 to Dotson Company, for the return of merchandise purchased for Toys Department, $36.00. Canceled V516 and issued V519.

10. Paid V519, $423.45, less purchases discount as follows: Toys Department, $1.60; Games Department, $2.63. Ck284.

11. Bought supplies from Morales Company as follows: store supplies, $93.70; office supplies, $78.50. V520.

13. Paid V517, $1,956.80. No discount. Ck285.

16. Made a deposit in the bank, $6,263.70.

16. Purchased merchandise on account from Squire Company as follows: Toys Department, $836.20; Games Department, $916.36. V521.

Oct. 19. Paid V521, $1,752.56, less purchases discount as follows: Toys Department $16.72; Games Department, $18.33. Ck286.

26. Paid V520, $172.20; no discount. Ck287.

27. Bought gasoline and oil for the delivery truck from Greg's Service Station, $93.00. V522. (Delivery Expense)

27. Paid V522, $93.00; no discount. Ck288.

30. Made a deposit in the bank, $5,843.93.

31. The payroll register for the month showed the following: Salary Expense — Delivery, $600.00; Salary Expense — Sales, $1,965.80; Salary Expense — Administrative, $940.75; Employees Income Tax Payable — Federal, $574.60; Employees Income Tax Payable — State, $144.38; FICA Tax Payable, $210.39. V523.

31. Paid V523, $2,577.18. Ck289.

31. Replenished the petty cash fund as follows: Store Supplies, $13.50; Office Supplies, $8.20; Delivery Expense, $26.33; Miscellaneous Expense — Sales, $11.00; Miscellaneous Expense — Administrative, $4.25. V524.

31. Paid V524, $63.28. Ck290.

Instructions: □ **2.** Foot, prove, total, and rule the voucher register and the check register.

Optional Problems

MASTERY PROBLEM 11-M		Recording transactions in a voucher register and a check register

The Nevarez Company uses a voucher system. The company is not departmentalized and therefore maintains only one account for purchases, one account for purchases returns and allowances, and one account for purchases discount.

Instructions: □ **1.** Record the following transactions completed during November of the current year. Use page 19 of a voucher register and page 17 of a check register. The voucher register has only one Purchases Debit column, and the check register has only one Purchases Discount Credit column. Source documents are abbreviated as: check, Ck; voucher, V.

All purchases of merchandise on account are subject to a 2% cash discount if paid within 10 days. No cash discounts are allowed on other payments.

Nov. 1. Recorded the cash balance on November 1 as a memorandum entry in the check register, $8,863.70.

2. Purchased merchandise on account from Meir Company, $286.00. V423.

9. Purchased merchandise on account from Casas Co., $1,283.60. V424.

9. Made a deposit in the bank, $2,688.33.

12. Paid V423 less discount. Ck376.

19. Purchased merchandise on account from Plouff Company, $436.19. V425.

20. Made a deposit in the bank, $2,648.52.

22. Bought supplies from Terrell Supply as follows: store supplies, $213.00; office supplies, $53.60. V426.

22. Paid V426, $266.60; no discount. Ck377.

Nov. 26. Paid V424. Since this voucher was not paid within the discount period, no discount is to be taken. Ck378.

28. Received a statement from Quick Delivery Service for delivery expenses for the month, $287.50. V427.

28. Paid V427; no discount. Ck379.

28. Paid V425 less discount. Ck380.

29. Purchased merchandise on account from Casas Co., $658.20. V428.

29. Paid V428 less discount. Ck381.

30. The payroll register for the month showed the following: Salary Expense — Store, $3,486.30; Salary Expense — Administrative, $1,455.30; Employees Income Tax Payable — Federal, $618.36; Employees Income Tax Payable — State, $133.82; FICA Tax Payable, $296.50. V429.

30. Paid V429. Ck382.

30. Replenished the petty cash fund as follows: Store Supplies, $13.25; Office Supplies, $9.20; Advertising Expense, $18.00; Delivery Expense, $21.00; Miscellaneous Expense — Administrative, $26.40. V430.

30. Paid V430. Ck383.

30. Made a deposit in the bank, $2,267.48.

Instructions: □ **2.** Foot, prove, total, and rule the voucher register and the check register.

BONUS PROBLEM 11-B Recording transactions when a voucher system is used

Recording invoices at the net amount to be paid. Some businesses make a practice of paying all invoices within the discount period. These businesses can record invoices at the net amount to be paid at the time the invoice is received. For example, an invoice for $1,000.00, terms 2/10, n/30, would be recorded at $980.00. At the time the voucher is prepared and is recorded in the voucher register, Purchases is debited for $980.00 and Vouchers Payable is credited for the same amount. The amount of the purchases discount is not recorded.

If for any reason the invoice is not paid within the discount period and the discount is lost, an account titled Discounts Lost is debited for the amount of the discount lost. For example, if the invoice described above were not paid within the 10-day discount period, a total of $1,000.00 would have to be paid. The entry would be a debit to Vouchers Payable for $980.00, a debit to Discounts Lost for $20.00, and a credit to Cash for the amount of the check, $1,000.00.

When this system is used the check register has special amount columns with the headings Vouchers Payable Debit, Discounts Lost Debit, and Cash Credit.

Instructions: □ **1.** Use the transactions and information given in Mastery Problem 11-M. In the check register, record the beginning cash balance, $8,863.70.

□ **2.** Record the transactions for November on page 23 of a voucher register and on page 18 of a check register. Record all vouchers at the net amount to be paid. If the discount is lost, record this in the check register at the time the voucher is paid.

□ **3.** Foot, prove, total, and rule the voucher register and the check register.

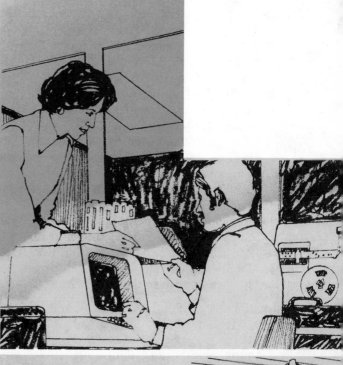

Harrod's
fine department stores

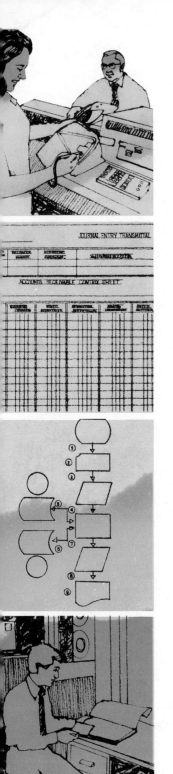

AUTOMATED ACCOUNTING— CODING CLERKS

MANY BUSINESSES USE AUTOMATED ACCOUNTING SYSTEMS. The use of automated data processing procedures for the processing of accounting data is growing rapidly in business. Part 6 of this textbook illustrates and describes the automated accounting procedures used by *Harrod's*, a merchandising business. The organization and role of an accounting department that utilizes automated data processing procedures are presented. Coding clerks record accounting data on journal entry transmittals in preparation for computer processing. The data on the journal entry transmittals are summarized on batch control sheets to facilitate an accuracy check of the data processed by the computer. The preparation of control sheets for accounts payable and accounts receivable is also presented.

Part 6 of this textbook describes the procedures followed by the data processing department to process the accounting data. The accounting reports produced by a computer are illustrated and described.

HARROD'S
CHART OF ACCOUNTS
GENERAL LEDGER

Account Number	ASSETS	Account Number	OPERATING REVENUE
	Current Assets	41 01000	Sales
11 01000	Cash	41 02000	Sales Returns and Allowances
11 02000	Petty Cash		
11 03000	Accounts Receivable		**COST OF MERCHANDISE**
11 04000	Allowance for Uncollectible Accounts	51 01000	Purchases
11 05000	Merchandise Inventory	51 02000	Purchases Returns and Allowances
11 06000	Store Supplies	51 03000	Purchases Discount
11 07000	Office Supplies		
11 08000	Prepaid Insurance		**OPERATING EXPENSES**
		61 01000	Bad Debts Expense
	Plant Assets	61 02000	Depreciation Expense—Office Equipment
12 01000	Store Equipment	61 02500	Depreciation Expense—Store Equipment
12 02000	Accumulated Depreciation—Store Equipment	61 03000	Insurance Expense
12 03000	Office Equipment	61 04000	Miscellaneous Expense
12 04000	Accumulated Depreciation—Office Equipment	61 05000	Office Supplies Expense
		61 06000	Payroll Taxes Expense
	LIABILITIES	61 07000	Rent Expense
	Current Liabilities	61 08000	Salary Expense
21 01000	Accounts Payable	61 09000	Store Supplies Expense
21 02000	Employees Income Tax Payable—Federal		
21 03000	Payroll Taxes Payable		
21 04000	Sales Tax Payable		
	CAPITAL		
31 01000	Saad Arrifay, Capital		
31 02000	Saad Arrifay, Drawing		
31 03000	Income Summary		

CHART OF ACCOUNTS
SUBSIDIARY LEDGERS

Accounts Receivable

Customer Number	Customer Name	Customer Number	Customer Name
10 00100	Nancy Adams	10 01100	Donna Morey
10 00200	Ronald Adams	10 01200	Karla Owen
10 00300	Mildred Adkins	10 01300	Sammy Pitt
10 00400	Tammie Bauer	10 01350	Doris Price
10 00412	Carol Beard	10 01400	John Ramos
10 00425	Rita Bess	10 01500	Roberto Valdez
10 00450	Patricia Burns	10 01550	Jody Vincent
10 00500	Larry Bush	10 01575	Leroy Wallace
10 00600	Arthur Cooper	10 01600	Virginia Whitney
10 00650	David Cotter	10 01700	Robert Wysong
10 00700	Bernice Durfee	10 01800	Dennis Young
10 00800	Connie Faber	10 01900	Judith Zimmer
10 00825	Janet Goldberg		
10 00850	Robert Hayes		
10 00900	Olga Heinrich		
10 00950	Janice Kline		
10 00975	John LaRose		
10 01000	Wilfred Martin		

Accounts Payable

Creditor Number	Creditor Name
20 00100	Agren Manufacturing Co.
20 00200	American Furniture Co.
20 00300	Baldwin Supply
20 00350	Calvo Fashions
20 00400	Daniels Advertising Agency
20 00500	Greene Giftware
20 00550	Lee Floor Coverings
20 00575	Mackie Men's Apparel
20 00600	Miles Supply
20 00700	Oatley Footwear
20 00750	Ramos Fashions
20 00800	Stark Giftware
20 00900	Tobias Sporting Goods
20 01000	Trost Manufacturing
20 01100	Villara Office Equipment
20 01200	Wagner Supply
20 01300	Witt Electrical
20 01400	Yates Suppliers

The charts of accounts for Harrod's general and subsidiary ledgers
are illustrated above for ready reference as you study Part 6 of this textbook.

Recording Daily Transactions

12

The recording, sorting, classifying, calculating, summarizing, storing, and reporting of facts is known as data processing. An organized set of procedures for handling information is called a system. The accounting cycle of a business requires that data be recorded in a journal, sorted in a ledger, summarized in a trial balance, and reported in the financial statements. Therefore, the accounting cycle procedures are considered a data processing system.

A data processing system in which most of the work is done by hand is known as a manual data processing system. Most manual data processing systems combine manual work with some mechanization. A manual system may include the use of common office machines such as typewriters, adding machines, and calculators.

As the amount of data increases, a faster and more efficient data processing system becomes necessary. One way to handle more data is to reduce the number of times the same information is recorded. Another way to speed the handling of data is to utilize special data processing machines.

The process of doing most of the work by machines with a minimum amount of human effort is called automation. A system using automated machines to process data is called an automated data processing system. Automated data processing is often abbreviated ADP.

THE AUTOMATED DATA PROCESSING SYSTEM

A group of interconnected electronic machines capable of processing data according to stored instructions is called a computer. Computers can store vast amounts of data, perform rapid calculations, and print the results. A system using a computer to process data is called an electronic data processing system. An electronic data processing (EDP) system is the most common type of automated data processing system.

Both large and small businesses make use of computers to store and process accounting information. Specially trained persons operate the computer. Therefore, the accountant does not have to be a computer specialist. However, when a business uses an EDP system, the accountant needs to understand the basic concepts of the system. The accountant must master the same basic accounting principles whether using a manual or an automated data processing system. An automated data processing system does not change the basic accounting principles. Only the tools and methods change. A computer performs the routine and repetitive operations.

An EDP system follows four steps to complete the accounting cycle:

1. Input
2. Processing
3. Storage
4. Output

When an EDP system is used, data must be converted into a form that can be processed by automated equipment. Data received for processing are called input. The physical forms in which data are prepared for processing by automated machines are called input media. Input media may be in the form of magnetic tape or paper tape as well as punched cards. Other forms of input media are magnetic ink characters, optical mark forms, and magnetic disk. However, the punched card is the most widely used form of input media.

Working with data according to precise procedures is called processing. Before data can be processed by a computer, step-by-step instructions for doing each job must be prepared. A set of instructions followed by a computer to process data is called a computer program. The computer program is stored in the computer. A person who prepares a computer program is called a programmer. A programmer needs special training in electronic data processing.

Filing or holding data until they are needed is called storage. The physical forms of the data being stored are called storage media. An EDP system may utilize magnetic or paper tape, punched cards, or magnetic disks as storage media. The magnetic disk is the most common form of storage media for accounting information.

The results of processing in a data processing system are called output. The physical forms of the data produced in a data processing system are called output media. Some examples of output media are printed reports and processed data recorded on magnetic tape, paper tape, punched cards, or magnetic disks.

A diagram of an EDP system is shown on page 209. Humans must place the input media in the input unit. From that point on, the data are processed automatically to the output stage with no human assistance. The output is then used by humans.

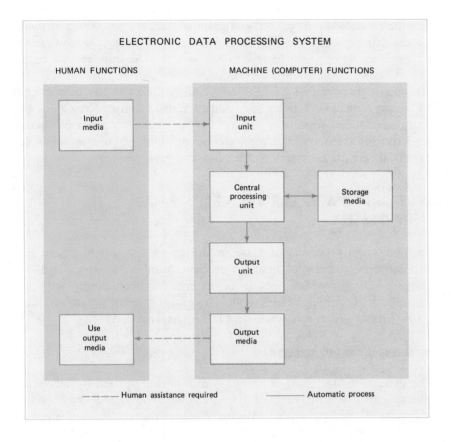

ELECTRONIC DATA PROCESSING SYSTEM

HUMAN FUNCTIONS   MACHINE (COMPUTER) FUNCTIONS

------ Human assistance required   ——— Automatic process

Diagram of an electronic data processing system

ORGANIZATION OF THE ACCOUNTING DEPARTMENT

Saad Arrifay owns and operates a department store called Harrod's. Because of the volume of business and the records to be kept, Mr. Arrifay utilizes an EDP system for the processing of accounting data. Personnel specially trained to operate the EDP system are employed in the data processing department. The organization of the accounting department is shown at the right.

The accountant supervises the operating procedures and the flow of data in the accounting department. The accountant also makes recommendations to management based on the analysis of the business and financial records produced by the data processing department.

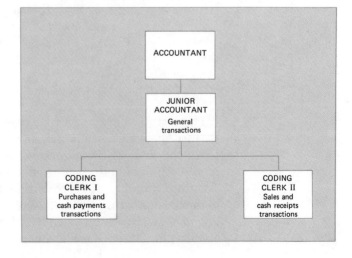

The junior accountant (a) records general transactions, (b) distributes the workload between the two coding clerks, (c) checks the accuracy of the work completed, and (d) submits the recorded transactions to the data processing department for processing.

The major responsibility of the two coding clerks is the recording of daily accounting transactions for computer processing. The clerks also prepare specialized reports requested by the junior accountant. Coding Clerk I records transactions for purchases and cash payments, and Coding Clerk II records transactions for sales and cash receipts.

NUMBERING SYSTEM FOR THE CHART OF ACCOUNTS IN AN EDP SYSTEM

To the human processor of data, an alphabetic account name, such as Cash, is more meaningful than an account number, such as 11 01000. However, EDP machines operate faster and more efficiently with numeric data than with alphabetic data. Therefore, account names are identified by account numbers when an EDP system is used.

General ledger chart of accounts

The general ledger chart of accounts numbering system includes (a) a numeric listing within each division, (b) a predesigned order within each division, and (c) enough digits to allow the addition of new accounts. Each business numbers its accounts according to its particular needs. Harrod's accounting system uses seven-digit account numbers. A breakdown of this seven-digit numbering system is shown below.

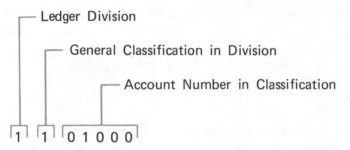

Account number for cash

The first digit of the account code identifies the major divisions of the balance sheet and income statement groups. The second digit further divides the general classifications. For example, the second digit allows identification of both current assets (11 00000) and plant assets (12 00000). The third through the seventh digits provide identification of accounts in each division of the ledger. A part of Harrod's general ledger chart of accounts is shown on page 211. The complete general ledger chart of accounts for Harrod's is shown on page 206.

```
                              HARROD'S
                         CHART OF ACCOUNTS
                          GENERAL LEDGER
```

Account Number	ASSETS	Account Number	OPERATING REVENUE
	Current Assets	41 01000	Sales
11 01000	Cash	41 02000	Sales Returns and
11 02000	Petty Cash		Allowances
11 03000	Accounts Receivable		
11 04000	Allowance for Uncollectible		COST OF MERCHANDISE
	Accounts	51 01000	Purchases
11 05000	Merchandise Inventory	51 02000	Purchases Returns and
11 06000	Store Supplies		Allowances
11 07000	Office Supplies		
11 08000	Prepaid Insurance		

Partial chart of accounts for Harrod's general ledger

Adding new accounts to the general ledger chart of accounts

The numbering system for EDP systems must contain enough digits to allow addition of new accounts without changing the numbering sequence of existing accounts. New accounts are assigned the unused middle number between two existing accounts. For example, if a new account Office Supplies is to be inserted between Merchandise Inventory (Account Number 11 05000) and Prepaid Insurance (11 06000), the new account number is 11 05500. If a new account Store Supplies is to be inserted between Merchandise Inventory (Account Number 11 05000) and Office Supplies (11 05500), the new account number is 11 05250.

Merchandise Inventory	11 05000
OFFICE SUPPLIES	11 05500
Prepaid Insurance	11 06000

Merchandise Inventory	11 05000
STORE SUPPLIES	11 05250
Office Supplies	11 05500

New accounts that are added after the last account in a division are assigned the next one-thousand number. For example, if the Salary Expense (Account Number 61 08000) is the last expense account and a new account Store Supplies Expense is added, the new account number is 61 09000.

Salary Expense	61 08000
STORE SUPPLIES EXPENSE	61 09000

Chart of accounts for subsidiary ledgers

The accounts in the subsidiary ledgers are also assigned account numbers in an EDP system. Harrod's accounting system also uses a seven-digit account number for its subsidiary ledgers. A breakdown of the seven-digit numbering system for the subsidiary ledgers is shown on page 212.

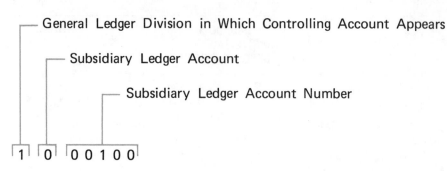

General Ledger Division in Which Controlling Account Appears

Subsidiary Ledger Account

Subsidiary Ledger Account Number

Account number for
account in subsidiary
ledger

1 0 0 0 1 0 0

The first digit of the account number identifies the division in which
the controlling account appears in the general ledger. The 0 in the second
position of the account number identifies that the account appears in the
subsidiary ledgers. The third through the seventh digits provide account
identification. Accounts are assigned by hundreds beginning with the
fifth position. This procedure makes it possible to assign numbers in
alphabetic order and to allow the addition of new accounts without
changing the existing alphabetic order. A partial chart of accounts for the
subsidiary ledgers of Harrod's is shown below. The complete chart of
accounts for Harrod's subsidiary ledgers is given on page 206.

	HARROD'S CHART OF ACCOUNTS SUBSIDIARY LEDGERS		
Accounts Receivable		Accounts Payable	
Customer Number	Customer Name	Creditor Number	Creditor Name
10 00100	Nancy Adams	20 00100	Agren Manufacturing Co.
10 00200	Ronald Adams	20 00200	American Furniture Co.
10 00300	Mildred Adkins	20 00300	Baldwin Supply

Partial chart of
accounts for Harrod's
subsidiary ledgers

For the customer number 10 00100, the 1 (first digit) shows that the
controlling account is an asset (Accounts Receivable) and the 0 (second
digit) shows that the account is located in a subsidiary ledger (in this
case the accounts receivable ledger). For the creditor number 20 00100,
the 2 (first digit) shows that the controlling account is a liability (Accounts Payable) and the 0 (second digit) shows that the account is located
in a subsidiary ledger (in this case the accounts payable ledger).

Adding new accounts to subsidiary ledgers

The procedure for adding new accounts to subsidiary ledgers is the
same as for the general ledger. New accounts to be added between two
existing accounts are assigned the unused middle number. For example,

the new account **Thomas Adams** is added to the accounts receivable ledger. The proper alphabetic position of this account is between the accounts of Ronald Adams (Customer Number 10 00200) and Mildred Adkins (Customer Number 10 00300). The unused middle number, 10 00250, is assigned to the account of Thomas Adams.

Ronald Adams	10 00200
THOMAS ADAMS	10 00250
Mildred Adkins	10 00300

If no exact middle number is available, either of the two numbers closest to the middle is used. The middle number between 10 00600 and 10 00625, for example, is 10 00612.5. The number 10 00612.5 contains eight digits and cannot be assigned in a seven-digit numbering system. Therefore, either 10 00612 or 10 00613 is used.

RECORDING DAILY TRANSACTIONS IN AN EDP SYSTEM

In an EDP system, daily transactions must be converted to an input media that can be read and processed by machines. Harrod's uses punched cards as the input media for all accounting data processed by the data processing department. The accounting department sends the data for the daily transactions to the data processing department where the data are punched into cards on a card punch machine.

The transactions could be punched directly from data on source documents. However, Harrod's prefers to keep all original source documents in the accounting department. Therefore, data about transactions are written on a special form which is then sent to the data processing department. A special form used in an EDP system for recording data about transactions is called a journal entry transmittal. A journal entry transmittal is also known as a transaction transmittal. The format of the journal entry transmittal is designed according to the needs of the particular business. Harrod's uses one journal entry transmittal to record all of its transactions. The form is shown on page 215.

The advantages of using a journal entry transmittal are:

1. All source documents are kept in the accounting department. This method reduces the possibility of losing source documents.
2. The card punch operator can read the data from single sheets set up in an arrangement matching that on the punched cards. This procedure is faster than reading the data from source documents of different sizes and format.

Each evening, at the close of a business day, the source documents are collected by the accounting department. In the morning of the next business day, the junior accountant (a) sorts the source documents by transaction categories and (b) gives the appropriate source documents to the two coding clerks for recording on journal entry transmittals.

Grouping of transactions

Before transactions are recorded on journal entry transmittals, the source documents are manually sorted by categories or groups. For example, all purchases of merchandise on account are sorted into one group, all cash payments in a second group, all sales of merchandise on account in a third group, and all cash receipts in a fourth group. The process of sorting transactions by similar groups is called batching. One combined entry is made for each group of batched transactions. For example, all purchases of merchandise on account transactions are recorded in only one entry to the purchases account — the total of all purchases on account.

Recording purchases on account in an EDP system

Harrod's has the following purchases on account transactions for November 1, 1978:

> November 1, 1978. *Total purchases on account, $2,679.00, from the following:*
>
> *Baldwin Supply, $485.00. Purchase Invoice No. 743.*
> *Greene Giftware, $359.00. Purchase Invoice No. 744.*
> *Ramos Fashions, $1,200.00. Purchase Invoice No. 745.*
> *Stark Giftware, $260.00. Purchase Invoice No. 746.*
> *Trost Manufacturing, $375.00. Purchase Invoice No. 747.*

GENERAL LEDGER

Purchases	51 01000
2,679.00	

Accounts Payable	21 01000
	2,679.00

ACCOUNTS PAYABLE LEDGER

Baldwin Supply	20 00300
	485.00

Greene Giftware	20 00500
	359.00

Ramos Fashions	20 00750
	1,200.00

Stark Giftware	20 00800
	260.00

Trost Manufacturing	20 01000
	375.00

Analyzing the total daily purchases on account transactions. The T accounts at the left show the effect of all the purchases on account transactions for November 1, 1978.

One combined entry is made each day for all the purchase invoices. As shown in the T accounts at the left, Purchases is debited for the total, $2,679.00. Accounts Payable is credited for the same amount.

Each creditor's account in the accounts payable ledger is credited for the amount of the individual purchase invoice. The total of all the credits made in the accounts payable ledger is the same as the amount credited to the controlling account, Accounts Payable, $2,679.00.

Recording purchases on account transactions on a journal entry transmittal. The combined entry for all purchases on account for November 1, 1978, is shown on Lines 1–6 of the journal entry transmittal shown on page 215.

JOURNAL ENTRY TRANSMITTAL

DATE 11 / 01 / 78   PAGE 1 OF 1 PAGES

	Bch. No.	Jr. No.	Ety. No.	Document Number	Account Number	Explanation	Debit	Credit	
1	1	10	1		5101000	Purchase of Merchandise on Account	267900		1
2			2	7432	000300			48500	2
3			3	7442	000500			35900	3
4			4	7452	000750			120000	4
5			5	7462	000800			26000	5
6			6	7472	001000			37500	6
7	2	20	1	8626	1107000	General Cash Payments	120000		7
8			2	8631	107000		3600		8
9			3	8646	104000		8200		9
10			4		1101000			131800	10
11	3	20	1	8652	000100	Cash Payments on Account	48000		11
12			2	8662	000200		87500		12
13			3	8672	000800		55000		13
14			4	8682	001400		75000		14
15			5		5103000			3335	15
16			6		1101000			262165	16
40									40

JOURNAL NUMBERS

PURCHASES = 10   CASH RECEIPTS = 40
CASH PAYMENTS = 20   GENERAL = 50
SALES = 30

PREPARED BY
Sally Smith

The data for batch 1, purchases on account, are recorded on the journal entry transmittal as follows:

Column 1. Record the batch number once for each batch. Lines 1–6 contain data for the first batch. The number for this batch is 1. The batch number is recorded in Column 1, Line 1.

Column 2. Record the journal number once for each batch. The journal number is found in the box at the bottom of the transmittal. The journal number for any purchases transaction is 10. This journal number is recorded once in Column 2 on Line 1 for all of batch 1.

Column 3. Record the entry number. Each line of every batch is numbered consecutively beginning with the number 1. For batch 1, there are six entries. On Line 1 write the beginning number, 1. As the data are recorded on succeeding lines for this batch, write consecutive numbers.

Column 4. Record the document numbers. The documents for batch 1 are the purchase invoices. On Line 1, since there is no related source document, no document number is recorded in Column 4. However, on the succeeding lines of batch 1, the purchase invoice numbers (such as 743, 744, 745) are recorded on the same line as the creditors' account numbers to which the invoices apply.

Column 5. Record the number of the account affected. On Line 1, record 51 01000, the account number for **Purchases**. (The account numbers

Journal entry transmittal for purchases and cash payments

are on the charts of accounts, page 206.) As data are recorded on succeeding lines of the batch, record the numbers of the accounts affected.

Column 6. Write a brief description of the batch data. For batch 1, the description recorded is Purchases of Merchandise on Account. Filling in this column is optional. A written description is not necessary for computer processing. Account names are stored on magnetic disk storage. Therefore, no account names need to be written on any of the journal entry transmittal forms. Accounts are identified and processed by account number.

Column 7. Write the debit amount. When the amount on a line is to be debited to an account, write the amount in the debit column, Column 7. If the amount is not a debit, leave the column blank on that line. For Line 1 of the form, the debit amount, $2,679.00, is written in Column 7.

Column 8. Write the credit amount. When the amount on a line is to be credited to an account, write the amount in the credit column, Column 8. If the amount is not a credit, leave the column blank on that line. For Lines 2–6, the credit amounts are written in Column 8.

The computer is programmed to total automatically all the credits for Journal Number 10 in Column 8. The total is automatically credited to Accounts Payable. Therefore, no entry is made in batch 1 for this credit.

Recording general cash payments in an EDP system

General cash payments are all payments except those to creditors. Harrod's had the following general cash payments on November 1, 1978:

November 1, 1978. Total general cash payments, $1,318.00, are:

November rent, $1,200.00. Check No. 862.
Office supplies, $36.00. Check No. 863.
Telephone bill, $82.00. Check No. 864.

GENERAL LEDGER

Rent Expense	61 07000
1,200.00	

Office Supplies	11 07000
36.00	

Miscellaneous Expense	61 04000
82.00	

Cash	11 01000
	1,318.00

Analyzing the total general cash payments transactions. The T accounts at the left show the effect of all the general cash payments transactions for November 1, 1978.

Each of the accounts affected by a cash payment is debited. Cash is credited for the total of all the general cash payments, $1,318.00.

Recording general cash payments on a journal entry transmittal. The combined entry to record all the general cash payments transactions is shown on Lines 7–10 of the form, page 215. The general data are recorded in each of the columns in the same way as data were recorded for batch 1. The steps described on pages 215 to 216 are used in writing the data in each of the columns on the form. The single credit to Cash, $1,318.00, is shown in Column 8, Line 10. The batch is the second one recorded on the form, so it is labeled batch 2 in Column 1. The journal entry number, 20, is found by referring to the box at the bottom of the form. The total of all amounts written in Column 7 for batch 2 is the same as the amount written in Column 8, $1,318.00.

Recording cash payments on account in an EDP system

Harrod's has the following cash payments on account transactions for November 1, 1978:

> *November 1, 1978. Total cash payments on account, $2,621.65, to the following:*
> *Agren Manufacturing Co., $470.40, covering a purchase invoice of $480.00 less a discount of $9.60. Check No. 865.*
> *American Furniture Co., $866.25, covering a purchase invoice of $875.00 less a discount of $8.75. Check No. 866.*
> *Stark Giftware, $550.00, covering a purchase invoice of $550.00, no discount. Check No. 867.*
> *Yates Suppliers, $735.00, covering a purchase invoice of $750.00 less a discount of $15.00. Check No. 868.*

Analyzing the total daily cash payments on account transactions. The T accounts at the right show the effect of all cash payments on account for November 1, 1978.

In the general ledger, Accounts Payable is debited for the total of the purchase invoices paid, $2,655.00. Purchases Discount is credited for the total of all discounts allowed, $33.35. Cash is credited for the total of all checks issued, $2,621.65.

Recording cash payments on account on a journal entry transmittal. The combined entry for all cash payments on account for November 1, 1978, is shown on Lines 11–16 of the form, page 215. In Column 1, Line 11, the batch number, 3, is written. This is the third batch recorded on this transmittal for November 1, 1978. The journal number, 20, is written on Line 11 in Column 2. In Column 5, the account number for each creditor is written on the line with the data for each creditor.

The computer is programmed to total automatically all the debits for Journal Number 20 in Column 7. The total, $2,655.00, is recorded automatically as a debit to Accounts Payable in the general ledger. Therefore, no data are recorded in batch 3 for the debit to Accounts Payable.

GENERAL LEDGER

Accounts Payable 21 01000

| 2,655.00 | |

Purchases Discount 51 03000

| | 33.35 |

Cash 11 01000

| | 2,621.65 |

ACCOUNTS PAYABLE LEDGER

Agren Manufacturing Co. 20 00100

| 480.00 | |

American Furniture Co. 20 00200

| 875.00 | |

Stark Giftware 20 00800

| 550.00 | |

Yates Suppliers 20 01400

| 750.00 | |

The general cash payments transactions and the cash payments on account transactions are recorded in separate batches. This procedure makes it easier to identify the cash payments on account transactions which affect a subsidiary ledger.

After all the data are recorded on a page of a journal entry transmittal, the coding clerk does the following:

1. Places the date in the space provided at the top-left of the page, 11/01/78.
2. Indicates the page number at the top-right of the form, page 1 of 1 pages.

> If two pages had been required for these three batches, the first page would be numbered page 1 of 2 pages. The second page is numbered page 2 of 2 pages. This numbering system helps keep all pages together. The system also helps assure a person using the data that all the pages have been accounted for.

Batch control sheet for purchases and cash payments

The general ledger and subsidiary ledgers are stored on magnetic disk storage in the data processing department. Data stored on magnetic disks are not visible. Therefore, the accountant has no means of visually checking the accuracy of the data. The accuracy of the data stored is only as accurate as the data entered into the computer through input media.

The accuracy of the input media must be assured in automated accounting systems. Input media is prepared from the data on the journal entry transmittal. A common practice is to maintain a separate record of totals that summarizes the data on the journal entry transmittal. This record is used as a basis for proving the accuracy of the data sent to the data processing department for processing. The totals of selected individual columns on the journal entry transmittal used to check the accuracy of the input media in an EDP system are called summary totals. Summary totals are also known as control totals. A meaningless number or total used solely to check the accuracy of work in an EDP system is called a hash total. Hash totals have no particular significance in themselves.

A special form which summarizes data recorded on a journal entry transmittal through the use of totals is called a batch control sheet. The data on the batch control sheet provide summary totals of the entries recorded on the journal entry transmittal. The number and format of the batch control sheets are determined by the type of business and the arrangement of the data on the journal entry transmittal. Harrod's uses one batch control sheet. The same batch control sheet is used by the coding clerks and the junior accountant to summarize (a) the purchases and cash payments (described in this chapter), (b) the sales and cash receipts (described in Chapter 13), and (c) the general transactions (described in Chapter 13). Space is provided on the batch control sheet to designate the type of journal entries that are represented by the summary totals.

After all transactions for the previous day have been recorded on the journal entry transmittal, a batch control sheet is prepared. The batch control sheet for the November 1, 1978, purchases and cash payments is shown below. The data shown for each of the lines of the batch control sheet are obtained from the journal entry transmittal, page 215.

BATCH CONTROL SHEET	
DATE *11/01/78*	
1	TOTAL NUMBER OF BATCHES	*3*
2	TOTAL NUMBER OF TRANSACTION ENTRIES	*16*
3	TOTAL OF DOCUMENT NUMBERS	*9,780*
4	TOTAL OF ACCOUNT NUMBERS	*43,729,850*
5	TOTAL DEBITS	*$6,652.00*
6	TOTAL CREDITS	*$6,652.00*

CONTROL TOTALS FOR: ✓ Purchases ✓ Cash Payments ___ Sales ___ Cash Receipts ___ General

PREPARED BY *Sally Smith*

Batch control sheet for purchases and cash payments

The steps in completing the batch control sheet from the data on the journal entry transmittal are:

☐ **1** Write the date, 11/01/78.

☐ **2** Write the number of batches. The batch number column, Column 1, shows there were 3 batches.

☐ **3** Write the total number of transaction entries. This total is obtained by adding the total number of entries, Column 3, for each batch of data. Batch 1 had 6 entries, batch 2 had 4 entries, and batch 3 had 6 entries for a total of 16 entries.

☐ **4** Write the total of document numbers. This total is obtained by adding all entries in the document number column, Column 4.

☐ **5** Write the total of account numbers. This total is obtained by adding all entries in the account number column, Column 5.

☐ **6** Write the total of the debits. This total is obtained by adding all entries in the debit column, Column 7.

☐ **7** Write the total of the credits. This total is obtained by adding all entries in the credit column, Column 8.

☐ **8** Place a check mark (√) next to the type of data the control totals summarize.

The completed journal entry transmittal and batch control sheet for purchases and cash payments are given to the junior accountant. The coding clerk then files the source documents.

The junior accountant checks the accuracy of the data recorded on the two forms by re-adding the columns on the journal entry transmittal that are summarized on the batch control sheet. The coding clerk who records sales and cash receipts (described in Chapter 13) also gives the completed journal entry transmittal and batch control sheet to the junior accountant for the same type of accuracy check.

The junior accountant prepares the journal entry transmittal and batch control sheet for general transactions (described in Chapter 13). The completed forms for general transactions are given to one of the coding clerks to be checked for accuracy. The coding clerk re-adds the columns of the journal entry transmittal that are summarized on the batch control sheet. The two forms are then returned to the junior accountant.

After all transactions have been recorded and checked for accuracy, the junior accountant prepares control sheets for the subsidiary ledgers (described in Chapter 13). All journal entry transmittals and batch control sheets are then sent to the data processing department.

SUMMARY

A summary of the steps necessary to record purchases of merchandise on account and cash payments for Harrod's is shown in the block diagram on page 221.

Using Business Terms

✦ What is the meaning of each of the following?

- system
- automation
- automated data processing system
- computer
- electronic data processing system
- input
- input media

- processing
- computer program
- programmer
- storage
- storage media
- output

- output media
- journal entry transmittal
- batching
- summary totals
- hash total
- batch control sheet

Questions for Individual Study

1. What are two ways to increase the speed and efficiency of a data processing system?
2. What is the most common type of automated data processing system?
3. Does the accountant have to be a computer specialist in order to utilize an EDP system?
4. Does an automated data processing

system change the basic accounting principles?
5. What are some of the forms of input media used by an electronic data processing system?
6. What is the most widely used form of input media?
7. What type of storage media may be used by an EDP system?

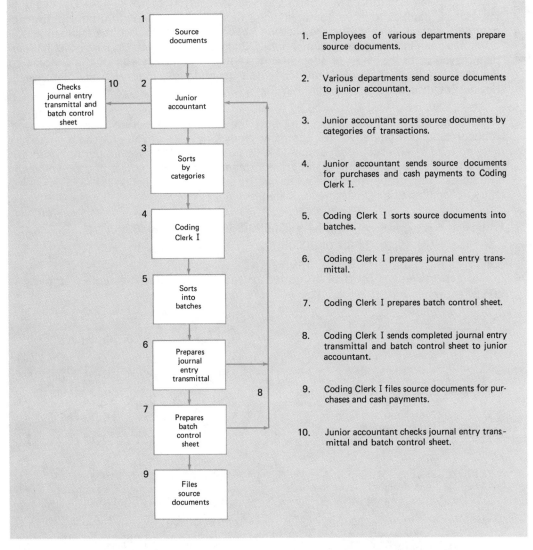

1. Employees of various departments prepare source documents.

2. Various departments send source documents to junior accountant.

3. Junior accountant sorts source documents by categories of transactions.

4. Junior accountant sends source documents for purchases and cash payments to Coding Clerk I.

5. Coding Clerk I sorts source documents into batches.

6. Coding Clerk I prepares journal entry transmittal.

7. Coding Clerk I prepares batch control sheet.

8. Coding Clerk I sends completed journal entry transmittal and batch control sheet to junior accountant.

9. Coding Clerk I files source documents for purchases and cash payments.

10. Junior accountant checks journal entry transmittal and batch control sheet.

8. What is the most common form of storage media for accounting data?
9. What type of output media is used in an EDP system?
10. Why are accounts identified by account numbers in an automated data processing system?
11. What are the two advantages of using a journal entry transmittal for the journalizing of daily transactions for an automated accounting system?
12. What is the source document for the journal entry for a purchase of merchandise on account?

13. What is the source document for a cash payment?
14. How many batches may be recorded on the journal entry transmittal for purchases of merchandise on account and cash payments?
15. Why is the journal number recorded on the journal entry transmittal?
16. Why isn't the account name written on the journal entry transmittal?
17. Why are the journal entry transmittals and batch control sheets sent to the junior accountant rather than directly to the data processing department?

Cases for
Manage-
ment
Decision

CASE 1 Howell Enterprises will be changing from a manual to an automated accounting system. Randy Romero, coding clerk, has been instructed to design a numbering system for the chart of accounts of the accounts receivable subsidiary ledger. Howell Enterprises has 93 accounts in the ledger. Mr. Romero designed a two-digit numbering system, numbering the accounts from 01–93. Will the numbering system designed by Mr. Romero meet the current and future needs of the automated accounting system for Howell Enterprises?

CASE 2 Mary Hayes is coding clerk for the Johnson Supply Company. The company uses an automated accounting system. Ms. Hayes has the responsibility of recording purchases and cash payments on a journal entry transmittal. She is instructed to batch the transactions before recording the entries. She asks why the batching procedure is used in an EDP system but not used in a manual accounting system. How would you respond to this question?

Problems
for
Applying
Concepts

PROBLEM 12-1 Adding new accounts to the general ledger chart of accounts

The general ledger chart of accounts for the Garcia Office Systems Company is given below.

Account Number	ASSETS	Account Number	OPERATING REVENUE
	Current Assets	41 01000	Sales
11 01000	Cash	41 02000	Sales Returns and Allowances
11 02000	Accounts Receivable		
11 03000	Allowance for Uncollectible Accounts		COST OF MERCHANDISE
11 04000	Merchandise Inventory	51 01000	Purchases
11 04500	Office Supplies	51 02000	Purchases Returns and Allowances
11 05000	Prepaid Insurance	51 03000	Purchases Discount
	Plant Assets		OPERATING EXPENSES
12 01000	Store Equipment	61 01000	Bad Debts Expense
12 02000	Accumulated Depreciation — Store Equipment	61 02000	Depreciation Expense — Store Equipment
		61 03000	Insurance Expense
	LIABILITIES	61 04000	Miscellaneous Expense
	Current Liabilities	61 05000	Office Supplies Expense
21 01000	Accounts Payable	61 05500	Payroll Taxes Expense
21 02000	FICA Tax Payable	61 05750	Rent Expense
21 03000	Sales Tax Payable	61 06000	Salary Expense
	CAPITAL		
31 01000	Teresa Garcia, Capital		
31 02000	Income Summary		

Instructions: ☐ **1.** On a sheet of paper copy the names of the new accounts listed on page 223 that are being added to the above general ledger chart of accounts.

☐ **2.** Assign account numbers to the new accounts. Refer to the charts of accounts shown on pages 160 and 206 for the proper order of general ledger accounts. Use the "unused middle number" method of assigning new account numbers.

Petty Cash	Unemployment Tax Payable—Federal
Store Supplies	Unemployment Tax Payable—State
Office Equipment	Teresa Garcia, Drawing
Accumulated Depreciation—	Depreciation Expense—
Office Equipment	Office Equipment
Employees Income Tax Payable—Federal	Store Supplies Expense

☐ **3.** On a second sheet of paper prepare a new chart of accounts for the general ledger. Include the new accounts with their respective account numbers.

The chart of accounts parepared in Instruction 3 will be needed to complete Problems 13-1, 13-2, 14-1, and 14-2.

PROBLEM 12-2 Adding new accounts to the chart of accounts for the subsidiary ledgers

The chart of accounts for the subsidiary ledgers of Garcia Office Systems Company is given below.

Customer Number	Customer Name	Creditor Number	Creditor Name
10 00100	Carl Anderson	20 00100	Alba Office Equipment Co.
10 00200	Donna Bedford	20 00150	Balboa Supply
10 00250	Jamie Casas	20 00200	Dixon Stationery Co.
10 00300	Joanna Durfee	20 00300	Hunter Machines
10 00400	Kim Ellis	20 00325	Lopez Enterprises
10 00450	Eva Gilbert	20 00350	Mackie Office Furniture
10 00500	Dave Hammond	20 00400	Morates Office Supply
10 00600	Gloria Jenkins	20 00450	Tovar, Inc.
10 00650	Phyllis Kline	20 00500	Vasquez Word Processing
10 00700	Anthony Morey		
10 00750	Julio Valdez		
10 00800	Frederick Walsh		
10 00900	Pamela Werner		
10 01000	John Zackery		
10 01100	Miriam Zech		

Instructions: ☐ **1.** On a sheet of paper copy the names of the following new accounts that are being added to the above subsidiary ledgers.

Accounts Receivable	Accounts Payable
Marcia Cooper	Casey Manufacturing
Cynthia Harris	Lee Office Systems
William Livingston	Rabelo Office Supplies
Susan Trent	
Alex Unger	
Timothy Voiers	
Elena Zapata	

▢ **2.** Assign account numbers to the new accounts. Use the "unused middle number" method of assigning new account numbers.

▢ **3.** On a second sheet of paper prepare a new chart of accounts for the subsidiary ledgers. Include the new accounts with their respective account numbers.

The chart of accounts prepared in Instruction 3 will be needed to complete Problems 13-1 and 13-2.

PROBLEM 12-3 ### Recording purchases and cash payments for an automated accounting system

The Garcia Office Systems Company completed the following purchases and cash payments transactions on November 16 of the current year. All transactions are arranged by groups before being recorded.

Nov. 16. Summary of purchases of merchandise on account, total of $1,258.00; purchased merchandise on account from:
Balboa Supply, $368.00. P832.
Hunter Machines, $240.00. P833.
Lopez Enterprises, $650.00. P834.

Nov. 16. Summary of general cash payments, total of $1,192.00; paid cash for:
Office Supplies, $225.00. Ck544.
Store Equipment, $967.00. Ck545.

Nov. 16. Summary of cash payments on account, total of $1,464.00; paid cash on account to:
Alba Office Equipment Co., $318.50, covering purchase invoice for $325.00 less a 2% discount. Ck546.
Dixon Stationery Co., $132.30, covering purchase invoice for $135.00 less a 2% discount. Ck547.
Tovar, Inc., $82.00, no discount. Ck548.
Vasquez Word Processing, $931.20, covering purchase invoice for $960.00 less a 3% discount. Ck549.

Instructions: ▢ **1.** Record the purchases and cash payments on a journal entry transmittal. Use the account numbers from the chart of accounts for Garcia Office Systems illustrated in Problems 12-1 and 12-2, pages 222 and 223. Include a description of each data batch in the explanation column.

▢ **2.** Prepare a batch control sheet for the purchases and cash payments.

The journal entry transmittal prepared in Instruction 1 will be needed to complete Problem 13-3.

**MASTERY
PROBLEM 12-M** Recording purchases for an
automated accounting system

Moreno's Fashion Center completed the following purchases of merchandise on
account on December 14 of the current year.

Dec. 14. Summary of purchases of merchandise on account, total of $2,309.00;
purchased merchandise on account from:
Alvarez Menswear, $675.00. P655.
Becker Fashions, $350.00. P656.
Irvine Ladies' Fashions, $745.00. P657.
Nolan Clothing, $136.00. P658.
Williams Footwear, $403.00. P659.

Instructions: ◻ **1.** Record the purchases of merchandise on account on a journal
entry transmittal. The account numbers needed to complete the journal entry transmittal are given below.

Purchases	51 01000	Irvine Ladies' Fashions	20 00700
Alvarez Menswear	20 00200	Nolan Clothing	20 00950
Becker Fashions	20 00350	Williams Footwear	20 01200

◻ **2.** Prepare a batch control sheet for the purchases of merchandise on account.

**BONUS
PROBLEM 12-B** Recording general cash payments for
an automated accounting system

Gilbert's completed the following general cash payments on December 1 of the
current year.

Dec. 1. Summary of general cash payments, total of $1,232.00; paid cash for:
Store Supplies, $63.00. Ck584.
Office Supplies, $32.00. Ck585.
Prepaid Insurance, $325.00. Ck586.
Rent Expense, $800.00. Ck587.
Miscellaneous Expense, $12.00. Ck588.

Instructions: ◻ **1.** Record the general cash payments on a journal entry transmittal. The account numbers needed to complete the journal entry transmittal are given
below.

Cash	11 01000	Prepaid Insurance	11 07000
Store Supplies	11 05000	Miscellaneous Expense	61 05000
Office Supplies	11 06000	Rent Expense	61 07000

◻ **2.** Prepare a batch control sheet for the general cash payments.

13

Recording Daily Transactions (Continued)

The automated procedures used by Harrod's to record purchases on account and cash payments are described in Chapter 12. The methods for recording sales on account, cash receipts, and other general business transactions are described in this chapter.

RECORDING SALES AND CASH RECEIPTS

The sales invoice is used by Harrod's as the source document for all sales on account. The source documents for cash receipts are (a) a receipt prepared for each cash receipt on account and (b) a cash register tape for total cash sales for the day.

Each evening, at the end of a business day, the sales and cash receipts source documents are collected by the accounting department. In the morning of the next business day, the junior accountant sorts the source documents by transaction categories. The junior accountant then gives the source documents to Coding Clerk II. The coding clerk sorts the source documents into batches for sales and cash receipts. The data from the source documents are then recorded on a journal entry transmittal.

Recording sales on account in an EDP system

Harrod's has the following sales of merchandise on account for November 1, 1978:

> November 1, 1978. Sales on account, $492.00, plus sales tax of $19.68, to the following:
> Ronald Adams, $36.00, plus sales tax of $1.44. Sales Invoice No. 923.
> Carol Beard, $88.00, plus sales tax of $3.52. Sales Invoice No. 924.
> Connie Faber, $300.00, plus sales tax of $12.00. Sales Invoice No. 925.
> John Ramos, $68.00, plus sales tax of $2.72. Sales Invoice No. 926.

Analyzing sales on account transactions. The effect of the sales on account transactions on the general ledger accounts is shown in the T accounts at the right.

Accounts Receivable is debited for the total amount to be collected from charge customers, $511.68. Sales Tax Payable is credited for the total amount of sales tax, $19.68. Sales is credited for the total amount of sales on account, $492.00.

The individual accounts for charge customers affected by the November 1, 1978, sales on account are debited in the accounts receivable ledger. The total of all debits in the subsidiary ledger, $511.68 is equal to the debit to the accounts receivable account in the general ledger.

Recording sales on account on a journal entry transmittal. The sales on account for November 1, 1978, are shown recorded on the form below, Lines 1–6.

The sales on account are the first batch recorded on the form shown below. Therefore, the batch number, 1, is recorded on Line 1 in Column 1. The journal number, 30, is recorded once on Line 1 in Column 2 for batch 1. The number is obtained from the box at the bottom of the form. The number 30 is the number for all entries that

GENERAL LEDGER

Accounts Receivable 11 03000
511.68 |

Sales Tax Payable 21 04000
| 19.68

Sales 41 01000
| 492.00

ACCOUNTS RECEIVABLE LEDGER

Ronald Adams 10 00200
37.44 |

Carol Beard 10 00412
91.52 |

Connie Faber 10 00800
312.00 |

John Ramos 10 01400
70.72 |

Journal entry transmittal for sales and cash receipts

should appear in the sales journal. The entry numbers are recorded from 1 to 6 in Column 3 for batch 1. The document numbers, sales invoices 923–926, are recorded on Lines 1–4 on the same line as the data for each of the charge customers. No document number is recorded on Lines 5 and 6. The numbers of accounts affected are recorded on each line in Column 5. The account numbers are found by referring to Harrod's charts of accounts, page 206. A brief description of the batch, Sales of Merchandise on Account, is written on Line 1 in Column 6. This identifies the kind of transactions recorded in batch 1. The debit amounts are written in Column 7; the credit amounts, in Column 8.

The computer is programmed to add automatically the amounts debited to individual accounts receivable as listed in Column 7. This total is automatically debited by the computer to Accounts Receivable in the general ledger. Therefore, no entry is recorded in batch 1 for the debit to Accounts Receivable.

Recording cash received on account in an EDP system

Harrod's has the following cash received on account transactions for November 1, 1978:

> *November 1, 1978. Summary of cash received on account, $422.38, from the following:*
> *Nancy Adams, $138.52. Receipt No. 566.*
> *Janice Kline, $74.38. Receipt No. 567.*
> *Doris Price, $82.66. Receipt No. 568.*
> *Dennis Young, $126.82. Receipt No. 569.*

GENERAL LEDGER

Cash	11 01000
422.38	

Accounts Receivable	11 03000
	422.38

ACCOUNTS RECEIVABLE LEDGER

Nancy Adams	10 00100
	138.52

Janice Kline	10 00950
	74.38

Doris Price	10 01350
	82.66

Dennis Young	10 01800
	126.82

Analyzing cash received on account transactions. The effect of the cash received on account transactions is shown in the T accounts at the left.

Cash is debited for the total amount of cash received on account, $422.38. Accounts Receivable is credited for the same amount.

Each of the individual charge customers' accounts affected is credited in the accounts receivable ledger. The total of all the credits to individual accounts in the accounts receivable ledger is the same as the credit to the controlling account in the general ledger, $422.38.

Recording cash received on account on a journal entry transmittal. The cash received on account transactions for November 1, 1978, are shown recorded on Lines 7–11 of the form, page 227.

In Column 1, Line 7, the batch number, 2, is written. In Column 2, on Line 7, the journal number, 40, is written. The journal number 40 is used for all cash receipts transactions. This number is found by referring to the box at the bottom of the form. The entry numbers, 1–5, are recorded in Column 3. The numbers of the receipts are recorded in Column 4 on Lines 8–11. No document number is recorded for Line 7. The account numbers are recorded in Column 5. The account numbers are found by referring to the charts of accounts, page 206. On Line 7, in Column 6, a brief description, Cash Received on Account, is written to identify the kind of transactions recorded in batch 2. The debit amounts are recorded in Column 7 and the credit amounts in Column 8.

The computer is programmed to add automatically all the credits to individual charge customers' accounts listed in Column 8. This total is automatically credited by the computer to Accounts Receivable in the general ledger. Therefore, no entry is recorded in batch 2 for the credit to Accounts Receivable.

Recording cash sales transactions in an EDP system

Harrod's has the following cash sales for November 1, 1978:

November 1, 1978. Cash sales for the day, $1,288.00, plus sales tax of $51.52. Cash Register Tape No. 263.

When a business has a large number of cash sales each day, the cash sales are recorded daily. However, if the amount of cash sales is small, a business may record the cash sales only once a week.

Analyzing cash sales transactions. The effect of the cash sales transactions for November 1, 1978, is shown in the T accounts at the right.

Cash is debited for the total amount of cash received, $1,339.52. Sales Tax Payable is credited for the amount of sales tax collected on cash sales, $51.52. Sales is credited for the amount of cash sales, $1,288.00.

GENERAL LEDGER

Cash	11 01000
1,339.52	

Sales Tax Payable	21 04000
	51.52

Sales	41 01000
	1,288.00

Recording cash sales on a journal entry transmittal. The cash sales for November 1, 1978, are shown recorded on Lines 12–14 of the form, page 227.

The batch number, 3, is recorded on Line 12 in Column 1. The journal number, 40, is recorded on Line 12, in Column 2. The entry numbers, 1–3, are recorded on the three lines in Column 3. The document number, 263, is recorded on Line 12 in Column 4. This one reference to the source document is sufficient for all the entries in batch 3. The account numbers for each line are recorded in Column 5. The account numbers are found by referring to the charts of accounts, page 206. A brief description, Cash Sales, is written on Line 12 in Column 6 to identify the kind of entry recorded. The debit amount is written in Column 7 and the credit amounts are written in Column 8.

Batch control sheet for sales and cash receipts

After all transactions for the previous day have been recorded on the journal entry transmittal, the coding clerk prepares a batch control sheet for sales and cash receipts. The batch control sheet provides summary totals of the entries recorded on the journal entry transmittal. The batch control sheet for the November 1, 1978, sales and cash receipts is shown below.

BATCH CONTROL SHEET

DATE ___11/01/78___

1	TOTAL NUMBER OF BATCHES	3
2	TOTAL NUMBER OF TRANSACTION ENTRIES	14
3	TOTAL OF DOCUMENT NUMBERS	6,231
4	TOTAL OF ACCOUNT NUMBERS	22,619,012
5	TOTAL DEBITS	$2,273.58
6	TOTAL CREDITS	$2,273.58

CONTROL TOTALS FOR: _____ Purchases   ✓ Cash Receipts   _____ General   _____ Cash Payments   ✓ Sales

PREPARED BY

Mike Fields

Batch control sheet for sales and cash receipts

The data necessary to complete the batch control sheet shown above are obtained from the journal entry transmittal on page 227. The steps in completing the batch control sheet from the journal entry transmittal are:

☐ **1**   Write the date, 11/01/78.

☐ **2**   Write the number of batches. The batch number column, Column 1, shows there were 3 batches.

☐ **3**   Write the total number of transaction entries. This total is obtained by adding the total number of entries for each batch of data from Column 3.

☐ **4**   Write the total of document numbers. This total is obtained by adding all entries in the document number column, Column 4.

☐ **5**   Write the total of account numbers. This total is obtained by adding all entries in the account number column, Column 5.

☐ **6**   Write the total of debits. This total is obtained by adding all entries in the debit column, Column 7.

☐ **7** Write the total of credits. This total is obtained by adding all entries in the credit column, Column 8.

☐ **8** Place a check mark (√) next to the type of data the control totals are summarizing.

The completed journal entry transmittals and batch control sheets for each day are sent to the junior accountant by the coding clerk. Then the coding clerk files the source documents. The complete set of procedures for recording sales and cash receipts is shown below in block diagram form.

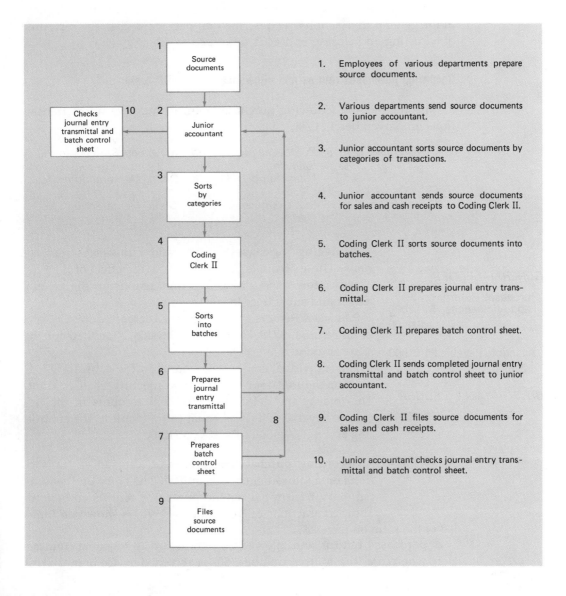

1. Employees of various departments prepare source documents.

2. Various departments send source documents to junior accountant.

3. Junior accountant sorts source documents by categories of transactions.

4. Junior accountant sends source documents for sales and cash receipts to Coding Clerk II.

5. Coding Clerk II sorts source documents into batches.

6. Coding Clerk II prepares journal entry transmittal.

7. Coding Clerk II prepares batch control sheet.

8. Coding Clerk II sends completed journal entry transmittal and batch control sheet to junior accountant.

9. Coding Clerk II files source documents for sales and cash receipts.

10. Junior accountant checks journal entry transmittal and batch control sheet.

RECORDING GENERAL TRANSACTIONS

The junior accountant at Harrod's has the responsibility for the following six types of general transactions:

1. Purchases returns and allowances on account.
2. Supplies bought on account.
3. Withdrawal of merchandise by the owner for personal use.
4. Sales returns and allowances on account.
5. Correcting entries affecting customers' accounts.
6. Adjusting and closing entries.

The source documents for general transactions are memorandums. Five of the general transactions are described on pages 232–234. The recording of adjusting and closing entries is described in Chapter 14.

Recording purchases returns and allowances in an EDP system

Harrod's has the following purchases returns and allowances transactions on November 1, 1978:

> *November 1, 1978. Purchases returns and allowances, $218.00, to the following:*
> *Miles Supply, $130.00. Debit Memorandum No. 235.*
> *Stark Giftware, $88.00. Debit Memorandum No. 236.*

GENERAL LEDGER

Purchases Returns
and Allowances 51 02000

	218.00

Accounts Payable 21 01000

218.00	

ACCOUNTS PAYABLE LEDGER

Miles Supply   20 00600

130.00	

Stark Giftware 20 00800

88.00	

Analyzing purchases returns and allowances transactions. The T accounts at the left show the effect of the purchases returns and allowances transactions on the general ledger and subsidiary ledger accounts.

Purchases Returns and Allowances is credited for the total of all returns, $218.00. Accounts Payable is debited for the same amount.

The individual creditor's accounts in the subsidiary ledger are debited for the amounts affecting each account. The total of the debits to individual accounts in the Accounts Payable Ledger is equal to the debit to the controlling account, Accounts Payable, $218.00.

Recording purchases returns and allowances transactions on a journal entry transmittal. The entry on the journal entry transmittal for the purchases returns and allowances transactions of November 1, 1978, is shown on Lines 1–3 of the form on page 233.

A purchases returns and allowances transaction is a general transaction. Therefore, the journal number, 50, is recorded in Column 2. This number is found in the box at the bottom of the form. Recording the entry for purchases returns and allowances follows the same procedures as described previously in this chapter and in Chapter 12.

	Bch. No.	Jr. No.	Ety. No.	DOCUMENT NUMBER	ACCOUNT NUMBER	EXPLANATION	DEBIT	CREDIT	
	1	2	3	4	5	6	7	8	
1	150	1		2352	00006 00	Purchases Returns & Allowances	13000		1
2		2		2362	00008 00		8800		2
3		3			5102000			21800	3
4	250	1		1106	000	Supplies bought on Account	11100		4
5		2		5162	001200			9300	5
6		3		5172	001400			1800	6
7	350	1		5183	102000	Withdrawal of Merchandise	5000		7
8		2			5101000			5000	8
9	450	1		4102	000	Sales Returns & Allowances	6200		9
10		2			2104000		248		10
11		3		3861	000900			4160	11
12		4		3871	001700			2288	12
13	550	1		5191	001400	Correcting Entry	5400		13
14		2			1000975			5400	14
15									15
16									16
17									17
18									18
40									40

DATE 11 / 01 / 78   JOURNAL ENTRY TRANSMITTAL   PAGE 1 OF 1 PAGES

JOURNAL NUMBERS

PURCHASES = 10   CASH RECEIPTS = 40
CASH PAYMENTS = 20   GENERAL = 50
SALES = 30

PREPARED BY

Carol Severson

Journal entry transmittal for general transactions

Recording buying of supplies on account in an EDP system

Harrod's has the following transactions for buying supplies on account on November 1, 1978:

> November 1, 1978. Bought store supplies on account, $111.00, from the following:
> Wagner Supply, $93.00. Memorandum No. 516.
> Yates Suppliers, $18.00. Memorandum No. 517.

The effect of these transactions on the ledger accounts is shown in the T accounts at the right.

These transactions are shown recorded on Lines 4–6 of the form above.

GENERAL LEDGER

Store Supplies	11 06000
111.00	

Accounts Payable	21 01000
	111.00

ACCOUNTS PAYABLE LEDGER

Wagner Supply	20 01200
	93.00

Yates Suppliers	20 01400
	18.00

Recording withdrawals of merchandise in an EDP system

Harrod's has the following transaction for the withdrawal of merchandise by the owner on November 1, 1978:

GENERAL LEDGER

Saad Arrifay,
Drawing   31 02000

50.00

Purchases   51 01000

50.00

November 1, 1978. Saad Arrifay, owner, withdrew merchandise for personal use, $50.00. Memorandum No. 518.

The effect of this transaction on the ledger accounts is shown in the T accounts at the left.

This transaction is shown recorded on Lines 7–8 of the form on page 233.

Recording sales returns and allowances in an EDP system

GENERAL LEDGER

Sales Returns
and Allowances 41 02000

62.00

Sales Tax Payable 21 04000

2.48

Accounts Receivable 11 03000

64.48

ACCOUNTS RECEIVABLE LEDGER

Olga Heinrich   10 00900

41.60

Robert Wysong   10 01700

22.88

Harrod's has the following sales returns and allowances transactions on November 1, 1978:

November 1, 1978. Sales returns and allowances, $62.00, plus sales taxes of $2.48, from the following:
Olga Heinrich, $40.00, plus sales tax of $1.60. Credit Memorandum No. 386.
Robert Wysong, $22.00, plus sales tax of $0.88. Credit Memorandum No. 387.

The effect of these transactions on the ledger accounts is shown in the T accounts at the left.

These transactions are shown recorded on Lines 9–12 of the form, page 233.

Recording a correcting entry in an EDP system

Harrod's had the following correcting entry on November 1, 1978:

ACCOUNTS RECEIVABLE LEDGER

John Ramos   10 01400

54.00

John LaRose   10 00975

54.00   54.00

November 1, 1978. Discovered that a sale on account to John Ramos was incorrectly charged to the account of John La Rose, $54.00. Memorandum No. 519.

The effect of this correcting entry on the ledger accounts is shown in the T accounts at the left. No accounts in the general ledger are affected by this correcting entry.

This correcting entry is shown on Lines 13–14 of the form, page 233.

After all transactions for the previous day have been recorded on the journal entry transmittal, the junior accountant prepares a batch control sheet for the general transactions.

Batch control sheet for general transactions

The batch control sheet for general transactions provides summary totals of the entries recorded on the journal entry transmittal. The batch control sheet for the November 1, 1978, general transactions is shown below. The data necessary to complete the batch control sheet are obtained from the journal entry transmittal on page 233.

BATCH CONTROL SHEET

DATE _____11/01/78_____

1	TOTAL NUMBER OF BATCHES	5
2	TOTAL NUMBER OF TRANSACTION ENTRIES	14
3	TOTAL OF DOCUMENT NUMBERS	3,314
4	TOTAL OF ACCOUNT NUMBERS	32,625,975
5	TOTAL DEBITS	$ 497.48
6	TOTAL CREDITS	$ 497.48

CONTROL TOTALS FOR:	_____ Purchases _____ Cash Payments _____ Sales	✓ Cash Receipts ✓ General	PREPARED BY Carol Severson

Batch control sheet for general transactions

The steps in completing the batch control sheet from the journal entry transmittal on page 233 are:

☐ **1** Write the date, 11/01/78.

☐ **2** Write the number of batches.

☐ **3** Write the total number of transaction entries by adding the total number of entries for each batch of data.

☐ **4** Write the total of document numbers by adding all entries in the document number column.

☐ **5** Write the total of account numbers by adding the entries in the account number column.

☐ **6** Write the total debits by adding all entries in the debit column.

☐ **7** Write the total credits by adding all entries in the credit column.

☐ **8** Place a check mark (√) next to the type of data the control totals are summarizing.

The completed journal entry transmittal and batch control sheet for general transactions are given to one of the coding clerks for an accuracy check. The coding clerk re-adds the columns on the journal entry transmittal to verify the totals on the batch control sheet. The two forms are then returned to the junior accountant.

CONTROL SHEETS FOR SUBSIDIARY LEDGERS

The data for the subsidiary ledgers are also stored on magnetic disk storage connected to the computer system in the data processing department. The batch control sheets provide a record that summarizes the data on the three journal entry transmittals — purchases and cash payments, sales and cash receipts, and general transactions. To provide additional control for the automated data processing system, the junior accountant for Harrod's also prepares control sheets for accounts payable and accounts receivable. The three journal entry transmittals are used to prepare the control sheets for the subsidiary ledgers.

Accounts payable control sheet

A form for recording control totals for accounts payable is called an accounts payable control sheet. The accounts payable control sheet shows the latest condition of accounts payable. The accounts payable control sheet for November 1, 1978, is shown below.

<table>
<tr><td colspan="8" align="center">ACCOUNTS PAYABLE CONTROL SHEET</td></tr>
<tr><td colspan="8">MONTH OF November, 1978</td></tr>
<tr><td></td><td></td><td>1</td><td>2</td><td>3</td><td>4</td><td>5</td><td>6</td></tr>
<tr><td></td><td>DATE</td><td>BEGINNING BALANCE</td><td>PURCHASES CREDIT A/P</td><td>PURCH. RET. & ALLOWANCES DEBIT A/P</td><td>PURCHASES DISCOUNT DEBIT A/P</td><td>CASH PAID DEBIT A/P</td><td>ENDING BALANCE</td></tr>
<tr><td>1</td><td>11 1</td><td>4 38 6 80</td><td>2 79 0 00</td><td>2 18 00</td><td>33 35</td><td>2 62 1 65</td><td>4 30 3 80</td></tr>
<tr><td>32</td><td></td><td></td><td></td><td></td><td></td><td></td><td></td></tr>
<tr><td colspan="8">PREPARED BY Carol Severson</td></tr>
</table>

Accounts payable control sheet

At the beginning of each accounting period, the balance in the accounts payable account is entered in the Beginning Balance column, Column 1, on the control sheet. Each day the transactions affecting accounts payable are recorded on the control sheet in summary form.

The summary totals, recorded on the accounts payable control sheet, are obtained from the journal entry transmittals for purchases and cash payments, page 215, and general transactions, page 233. The batch data totals are identified in the explanation column of the transmittals.

The balance in the accounts payable controlling account contains the total of all the purchases of merchandise on account. The balance also includes other purchases on account, such as supplies. Therefore, the total purchases of merchandise on account and the total of other purchases on account are added together and recorded on the accounts payable control sheet as a combined total.

The total purchases of merchandise on account, purchases discount, and cash payments on account are obtained from the journal entry transmittal, page 215. Line 1, Column 7, contains the total purchases of merchandise on account, $2,679.00. Line 15, Column 8, contains the total purchases discount, $33.35, and Line 16, Column 8, contains the total cash payments on account, $2,621.65.

The total purchases returns and allowances and purchases of supplies on account are obtained from the journal entry transmittal for general transactions, page 233. Line 3, Column 8, contains the total purchases returns and allowances, $218.00. Line 4, Column 7, contains the total purchases of supplies on account, $111.00. The total purchases of merchandise on account, $2,679.00, and purchases of supplies on account, $111.00, are added together to obtain the total purchases on account for the day ($2,679.00 + $111.00 = $2,790.00).

The ending balance is figured on the accounts payable control sheet as follows:

BEGINNING BALANCE (Column 1).........................	$ 4,386.80
Plus purchases on account (Column 2)	+ 2,790.00
	$ 7,176.80
Minus purchases returns and allowances (Column 3)....	– 218.00
	$ 6,958.80
Minus purchases discount (Column 4).......................	– 33.35
	$ 6,925.45
Minus cash payments on account (Column 5)	– 2,621.65
Equals ENDING BALANCE (Column 6)	$ 4,303.80

Accounts receivable control sheet

A form for recording control totals for accounts receivable is called an accounts receivable control sheet. The accounts receivable control sheet shows the latest condition of accounts receivable. The accounts receivable control sheet used by Harrod's is shown on page 238.

At the beginning of each accounting period, the balance in the accounts receivable account is entered in the Beginning Balance column, Column 1, on the control sheet. Each day the transactions affecting accounts receivable are recorded on the control sheet in summary form.

The summary totals, recorded on the accounts receivable control sheet, are obtained from the journal entry transmittals for sales and cash receipts, page 227, and general transactions, page 233. The batch data totals are identified in the explanation column, Column 6, of the transmittals.

```
┌──────────────────────────────────────────────────────────────────────────┐
│              ACCOUNTS RECEIVABLE CONTROL SHEET                             │
│                                                                            │
│   MONTH OF  November, 1978                                                 │
│                 1              2              3            4          5     │
│  ┌──────────┬────────────┬────────────┬─────────────┬──────────┬─────────┐│
│  │          │ BEGINNING  │   SALES    │ SALES RET. &│   CASH   │ ENDING  ││
│  │   DATE   │  BALANCE   │ DEBIT A/R  │ ALLOWANCES  │ RECEIVED │ BALANCE ││
│  │          │            │            │ CREDIT A/R  │CREDIT A/R│         ││
│  ├──────────┼────────────┼────────────┼─────────────┼──────────┼─────────┤│
│1 │  11  1   │   6343 60  │   511 68   │    64 48    │ 422 38   │ 6368 42 ││ 1
│  ├──────────┼────────────┼────────────┼─────────────┼──────────┼─────────┤│
│32│          │            │            │             │          │         ││ 32
│  └──────────┴────────────┴────────────┴─────────────┴──────────┴─────────┘│
│                                        │ PREPARED BY                       │
│                                        │   Carol Severson                  │
└──────────────────────────────────────────────────────────────────────────┘
```

Accounts receivable
control sheet

The total sales on account and cash received on account are obtained from the journal entry transmittal for sales and cash receipts, page 227. The total sales on account include both the value of the merchandise sold plus the amount of sales tax charged. Therefore, Line 5, Column 8 (Sales Tax Payable), plus Line 6, Column 8 (Sales), contain the total sales on account, $511.68 ($19.68 + $492.00). Line 7, Column 7, contains the total cash received on account, $422.38.

The balance in the accounts receivable controlling account contains the total of all merchandise sold on account. The balance also includes the total of all sales tax charged to each sale. Therefore, the total of the sales returns and allowances recorded on the accounts receivable control sheet must also include the total of the sales tax that was charged.

The total sales returns and allowances and sales tax payable are obtained from the journal entry transmittal for general transactions, page 233. Line 9, Column 7, contains the total sales returns and allowances, $62.00. Line 10, Column 7, contains the sales tax payable, $2.48. The two totals are added together to obtain the total that is deducted from the accounts receivable as a result of sales returns and allowances ($62.00 + $2.48 = $64.48).

The ending balance is figured on the accounts receivable control sheet as follows:

BEGINNING BALANCE (Column 1)..........................	$6,343.60
Plus sales on account (Column 2)...............................	+ 511.68
	$6,855.28
Minus sales returns and allowances (Column 3).............	− 64.48
	$6,790.80
Minus cash received on account (Column 4)	− 422.38
Equals ENDING BALANCE (Column 5)....................	$6,368.42

After the two subsidiary control sheets are prepared, the junior accountant sends the following to the data processing department: all journal entry transmittals; all batch control sheets for purchases and cash payments, sales and cash receipts, and general transactions; and the subsidiary control sheets. The data processing department converts the data on the transmittals to input media (punched cards). The input media are then processed by the computer system according to instructions in the computer program. These procedures are described in Chapter 14.

After sending the data to the data processing department, the junior accountant files for future reference the source documents for general transactions.

SUMMARY

The procedures for recording daily transactions are summarized in the block diagram below.

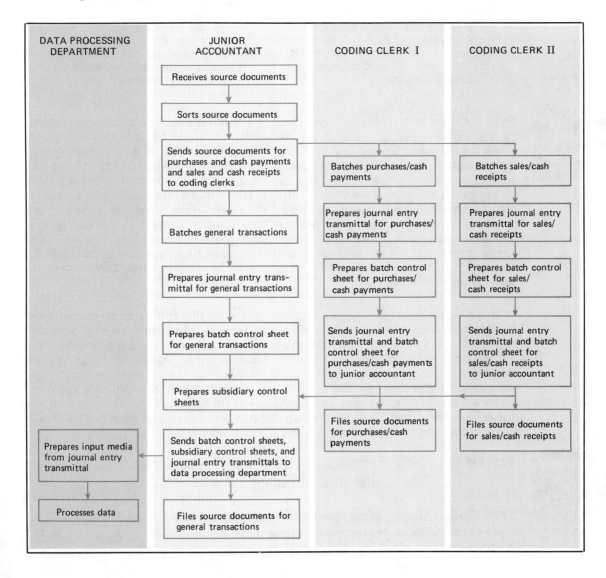

DATA PROCESSING DEPARTMENT	JUNIOR ACCOUNTANT	CODING CLERK I	CODING CLERK II
	Receives source documents		
	Sorts source documents		
	Sends source documents for purchases and cash payments and sales and cash receipts to coding clerks	Batches purchases/cash payments	Batches sales/cash receipts
	Batches general transactions	Prepares journal entry transmittal for purchases/cash payments	Prepares journal entry transmittal for sales/cash receipts
	Prepares journal entry transmittal for general transactions	Prepares batch control sheet for purchases/cash payments	Prepares batch control sheet for sales/cash receipts
	Prepares batch control sheet for general transactions	Sends journal entry transmittal and batch control sheet for purchases/cash payments to junior accountant	Sends journal entry transmittal and batch control sheet for sales/cash receipts to junior accountant
	Prepares subsidiary control sheets	Files source documents for purchases/cash payments	Files source documents for sales/cash receipts
Prepares input media from journal entry transmittal	Sends batch control sheets, subsidiary control sheets, and journal entry transmittals to data processing department		
Processes data	Files source documents for general transactions		

✦ What is the meaning of each of the following?

● accounts payable control sheet

● accounts receivable control sheet

1. What is the source document for all sales on account?
2. On the journal entry transmittal on page 227, how many entries are included in batch number 1?
3. On the journal entry transmittal on page 227, what batch number contains the transactions for cash receipts on account?
4. What does the coding clerk for Harrod's do with the completed journal entry transmittal and batch control sheet for sales and cash receipts?
5. On the block diagram on page 231, who files the source documents for sales and cash receipts?

6. Who prepares the batch control sheets for Harrod's?
7. Where is the data stored for the subsidiary ledgers of Harrod's automated accounting system?
8. Who prepares the control sheets for the subsidiary ledgers?
9. From where is the information needed to prepare the control sheets for the subsidiary ledgers obtained?
10. Who sends the batch control sheets and the journal entry transmittals to the data processing department?
11. What does the data processing department do with the data on the journal entry transmittals?

CASE 1 Clinton Valdez, junior accountant for Superior Advertising, prepares control sheets for the subsidiary ledgers. The data for the control sheets are obtained from journal entry transmittals sent to him by coding clerks. The journal entry transmittal used by Superior Advertising has an Explanation column for identifying the type of data within each batch of data. As an explanation is optional for an automated accounting system, the coding clerks have been leaving the column blank.

The junior accountant has requested that the coding clerks begin writing an explanation of each batch of data in the Explanation column of the journal entry transmittal. He contends that this explanation will make it easier to prepare the control sheets for the subsidiary ledgers. The coding clerks have objected to the request. They feel that writing an explanation would be a waste of time, as all data necessary to complete the control sheets are provided. With whom do you agree and why?

CASE 2 Mrs. Jameson has decided to open an additional department store in a shopping center. An automated accounting system will be used for both stores. The data processing facilities and accounting staff are to remain in the downtown store.

The accounting department has been journalizing daily transactions for the automated accounting system by batching and

recording the entries on a journal entry transmittal. Mrs. Jameson has requested that the accounting department make the necessary changes in procedures to allow identification of each store when recording daily transactions. She wants the computer printouts to reflect the operations of the two stores separately. What factors should be considered?

PROBLEM 13-1 Recording sales and cash receipts for an automated accounting system

The Garcia Office Systems Company completed the following sales and cash receipts transactions on November 16 of the current year. All transactions are sorted by groups before being recorded.

Nov. 16. Summary of sales of merchandise on account, total of $632.00, plus sales tax of $25.28; sold merchandise on account to:

Donna Bedford, $138.00, plus sales tax of $5.52. S783.
Kim Ellis, $88.00, plus sales tax of $3.52. S784.
John Zackery, $406.00, plus sales tax of $16.24. S785.

Nov. 16. Summary of cash receipts on account, total of $866.00; received cash on account from:

Jamie Casas, $66.00. R911.
Dave Hammond, $345.00. R912.
Pamela Werner, $115.00. R913.
Phyllis Kline, $340.00. R914.

Nov. 16. Summary of cash sales:

Cash sales for the day, $1,636.00, plus sales tax of $65.44. T298.

Instructions: □ **1.** Record the sales and cash receipts on a journal entry transmittal. Use the account numbers from the chart of accounts prepared in Problems 12-1 and 12-2, pages 222 and 223. Include a description of each data batch in the Explanation column.

□ **2.** Prepare a batch control sheet for the sales and cash receipts.

The journal entry transmittal prepared in Instruction 1 will be needed to complete Problems 13-3 and 13-4.

PROBLEM 13-2 Recording general transactions for an automated accounting system

The Garcia Office Systems Company completed the following general transactions on November 16 of the current year. All transactions are sorted by groups before being recorded.

Nov. 16. Summary of purchases returns and allowances, total of $211.00; returned merchandise to:

Balboa Supply, $66.00. DM205.
Hunter Machines, $145.00. DM206.

Nov. 16. Summary of office supplies bought on account, total of $33.00; bought office supplies on account from:

Lopez Enterprises, $15.00. M503.
Morates Office Supply, $18.00. M504.

Nov. 16. Summary of withdrawals of merchandise by owner.

Teresa Garcia, owner, withdrew merchandise for personal use, $76.00. M505.

Nov. 16. Summary of sales returns and allowances, total of $90.00, plus sales tax of $3.60; granted credit for merchandise returned to:

Joanna Durfee, $30.00, plus sales tax of $1.20. CM326.
Julio Valdez, $60.00, plus sales tax of $2.40. CM327.

Nov. 16. Summary of correcting entries affecting customers' accounts.

Discovered that a sale of merchandise on account to Eva Gilbert was incorrectly charged to the account of Dave Hammond, $83.00. M506.

Instructions: □ **1.** Record the general transactions on a journal entry transmittal. Use the account numbers from the chart of accounts for Garcia Office Systems Company prepared in Problems 12-1 and 12-2, pages 222 and 223. Include a description of each data batch in the Explanation column.

□ **2.** Prepare a batch control sheet for the general transactions.

The journal entry transmittal prepared in Instruction 1 will be needed to complete Problems 13-3 and 13-4.

PROBLEM 13-3 Preparing an accounts payable control sheet

The journal entry transmittals prepared in Problems 12-3, 13-1, and 13-2 are needed to complete this problem.

Instructions: Prepare an accounts payable control sheet. The beginning balance in the accounts payable controlling account was $6,445.75.

PROBLEM 13-4 Preparing an accounts receivable control sheet

The journal entry transmittals prepared in Problems 13-1 and 13-2 are needed to complete this problem.

Instructions: Prepare an accounts receivable control sheet. The beginning balance in the accounts receivable controlling account was $9,350.65.

Optional Problems   **MASTERY PROBLEM 13-M** Recording cash receipts for an automated accounting system

Morris Automotive Supply had the following cash receipts transactions on December 15 of the current year.

Dec. 15. Summary of cash receipts on account, total of $457.82; received cash on account from:

Diana Leyba, $166.54. R344.
Cira Miguel, $87.66. R345.
Ken Ruback, $106.44. R346.
Jane Scholl, $33.76. R347.
Adolf Soto, $63.42. R348.

Dec. 15. Summary of cash sales:

Cash sales for the day, $985.50, plus sales tax of $39.42. T288.

Instructions: ☐ **1.** Record the cash receipts on a journal entry transmittal. Include a description of each data batch in the Explanation column. The account numbers needed to complete the journal entry transmittal are given below.

Cash	11 01000	Cira Miguel	10 00750
Sales Tax Payable	21 03000	Ken Ruback	10 00875
Sales	41 01000	Jane Scholl	10 00950
Diana Leyba	10 00600	Adolf Soto	10 00975

☐ **2.** Prepare a batch control sheet for the cash receipts.

**BONUS
PROBLEM 13-B**   Preparing an accounts
payable control sheet

Cedar Furniture completed journal entry transmittals for purchases and cash payments and general transactions on November 14 of the current year. The following totals were obtained from the two journal entry transmittals:

> Purchases, $2,345.00.
> Purchases returns and allowances, $169.50.
> Purchases discount, $48.40.
> Cash payments on account, $1,985.60.

Instructions: Prepare an accounts payable control sheet. The beginning balance in the accounts payable controlling account was $4,620.50.

14

Processing Daily Transactions and End-of-Fiscal-Period Work

The procedures followed by Harrod's accounting department for recording its daily transactions for an automated accounting system are described in Chapters 12 and 13. The completed journal entry transmittals and batch control sheets prepared by the two coding clerks and by the junior accountant are sent to the data processing department. This chapter describes (a) the automated accounting system, (b) the procedures for converting data from journal entry transmittals to input media, and (c) the preparation of daily and end-of-fiscal-period reports.

THE AUTOMATED ACCOUNTING SYSTEM

The major objective of an automated accounting system is to obtain accurate, up-to-date facts as quickly and as economically as possible. The type of automated data processing system selected is based on (a) the amount of data to be recorded and reported, (b) the types of reports required, (c) the types of data to be included in each report, and (d) the frequency of the reports (daily, weekly, bi-weekly, monthly, quarterly, yearly).

Computerized accounting reports

The accounting department has the responsibility for determining the type, design, and number of accounting reports to be prepared by the data processing department. These reports provide checks on the accuracy of data stored in the computer system and provide the financial information necessary for decision making.

The source documents for data reported should be easily located. The result of accounting procedures that allow the tracing of data on reports back to the original source documents is called an audit trail. Every accounting system must include the procedures and reports necessary to form an audit trail. Harrod's requires the following reports:

1. Reports prepared daily by the computer:
   Entry register listing all daily transactions recorded on journal entry transmittals.
   Accounts payable register listing all increases and decreases in individual creditors' accounts in the accounts payable ledger.
   Accounts receivable register listing all increases and decreases in individual customers' accounts in the accounts receivable ledger.
2. Reports prepared monthly by the computer:
   Schedules of accounts payable and accounts receivable.
   Trial balance.
   Financial statements including an income statement, a capital statement, and a balance sheet.
   Post-closing trial balance.

Accounting procedures in an EDP system

Harrod's uses an electronic data processing system to process its accounting data. Many of the steps in the automated accounting cycle (input, processing, storage, and output) are done by specialized machines used to prepare and process the data. A chart, such as the one on page 209, is prepared to show how the data for Harrod's flow through a computer system. A chart of symbols showing the sequence of steps necessary to complete all or part of a data processing system is called a systems flowchart. The flowchart for Harrod's EDP system is shown on page 246, and the symbols are shown and explained below.

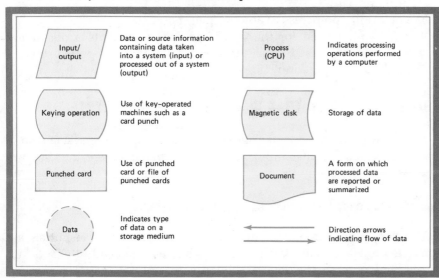

Input/output	Data or source information containing data taken into a system (input) or processed out of a system (output)	Process (CPU)	Indicates processing operations performed by a computer
Keying operation	Use of key-operated machines such as a card punch	Magnetic disk	Storage of data
Punched card	Use of punched card or file of punched cards	Document	A form on which processed data are reported or summarized
Data	Indicates type of data on a storage medium	⟵ ⟶	Direction arrows indicating flow of data

Flowchart symbols

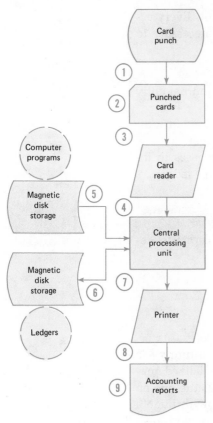

Systems flowchart

1. A card punch machine is used to convert data from the journal entry transmittals into input media.
2. The punched cards prepared on a card punch machine are represented in the flowchart by a punched card symbol. Harrod's uses an 80-column punched card for its input media.
3. The data on the punched cards are "read" by a card reader machine.
4. The data read by the card reader are transferred by the computer to the central processing unit (CPU). All processing takes place within the computer's central processing unit. The CPU controls all parts of the computer system. The CPU can multiply, divide, add, subtract, rearrange, and summarize data in the order needed.
5. The computer programs that provide the step-by-step instructions for each of Harrod's data processing jobs are stored on magnetic disk storage. The computer transfers the computer program for the job from storage to the CPU.
6. Data for the general ledger and subsidiary ledgers of Harrod's are also stored on magnetic disk storage. Based on instructions in the computer programs, data may be posted by the computer to accounts in the ledgers. Data may also be read from magnetic disk storage into the CPU, calculated, rearranged, and summarized.
7. The processed data are sent by the CPU to a machine known as a printer.
8. The printer prepares the accounting reports.
9. The symbol used for the processed data represents a document. This symbol is used for all processed data that are reported or summarized in paper form.

PROCESSING DAILY TRANSACTIONS IN AN EDP SYSTEM

Harrod's automated accounting procedures shown in the systems flowchart above require that input media be prepared before the data are processed by the computer.

Recording the daily transactions for computer processing

The daily transactions recorded on the journal entry transmittals are converted to 80-column punched cards. The data punched into cards are in the same order as the data on the journal entry transmittals.

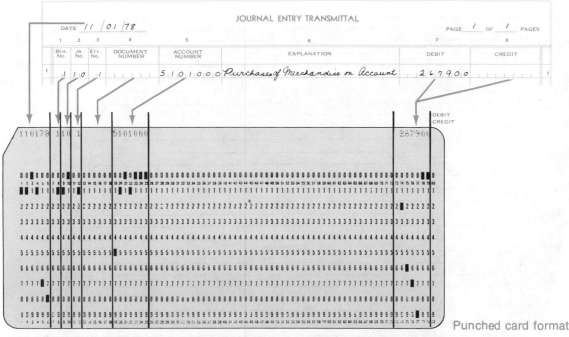

Punched card format

The location of the data on the punched cards must be the same from card to card. For example, if the date is to be punched in card columns 1–6 on one card, the date must also be punched in the same location on all remaining cards. The punched card columns reserved for the recording of specific data, such as the date, are called fields. A field may vary in length from one column to several columns, depending on the specific data desired. The punched card fields used for all punched cards prepared for Harrod's automated accounting system are:

Card Columns 1–6	Date
Card Columns 7–8	Batch Number
Card Columns 9–10	Journal Number
Card Columns 11–12	Entry Number
Card Columns 13–18	Document Number
Card Columns 19–25	Account Number
Card Columns 73–79	Amount
Card Column 80	Indicates whether amount is a debit or credit

The amount field is the same for both debits and credits. This is possible by showing the status of the amount field in card column 80. If the amount is a debit, card column 80 is left blank. If the amount is a credit, a dash (—) is punched in card column 80.

The punched cards for the November 1, 1978, transactions are illustrated on page 248. One card is punched for each line on the journal entry transmittals.

The journal number is written only once on the journal entry transmittal. However, a journal number is punched on each card.

```
110178 110 1     5101000                                    267900
110178  10 2  7432000300                                    48500-
110178  10 3  7442000500                                    35900-
110178  10 4  7452000750                                   120000-
110178  10 5  7462000800                                    26000-
110178  10 6  7472091000                                    37500-
110178 220 1  8626107000                                   120000
110178  20 2  8631107000                                     3600
110178  20 3  8646104000                                     8200
110178  20 4     1101000                                   131800-
110178 320 1  8652000100                                    48000
110178  20 2  8662000200                                    87500
110178  20 3  8672000300                                    55000
110178  20 4  8682001400                                    75000
110178  20 5     5103000                                     3335-
110178  20 6     1101000                                   262165-
110178 130 1  9231000200                                     3744
110178  30 2  9241000412                                     9152
110178  30 3  9251000800                                    31200
110178  30 4  9261001400                                     7072
110178  30 5     2104000                                     1968-
110178  30 6     4101000                                    49200-
110178 240 1     1101000                                    42238
110178  40 2  5661000100                                    13852-
110178  40 3  5671000950                                     7438-
110178  40 4  5681001350                                     8266-
110178  40 5  5691001800                                    12682-
110178 340 1  2631101000                                   133952
110178  40 2     2104000                                     5152-
110178  40 3     4101000                                   128800-
110178 150 1  2352000600                                    13000
110178  50 2  2362000800                                     8800
110178  50 3     5102000                                    21800-
110178 250 1     1106000                                    11100
110178  50 2  5162001200                                     9300-
110178  50 3  5172001400                                     1800-
110178 350 1  5183102000                                     5000
110178  50 2     5101000                                     5000-
110178 450 1     4102000                                     6200
110178  50 2     2104000                                      248
110178  50 3  3861000900                                     4160-
110178  50 4  3871001700                                     2288-
110178 550 1  5191001400                                     5400
110178  50 2     1000975                                     5400-
```

Daily transaction
cards

Preparing daily accounting reports in an EDP system

The data from the punched cards prepared from the journal entry transmittals are read and processed by Harrod's computer system, illustrated in the systems flowchart, page 246. Three daily accounting reports are prepared by the computer system — entry register, accounts payable register, and accounts receivable register.

Entry Register. This report includes a listing of all daily transactions and all batch control totals. The batch control totals are computed by the computer system as the transactions are being processed. The data for each daily transaction are also posted by the computer to the accounts in the general ledger and subsidiary ledgers stored on magnetic disk storage. The entry register for the November 1, 1978, transactions is illustrated on page 250.

As entries are posted to individual accounts in the subsidiary ledgers, the computer adds the individual amounts together. After posting is completed the total is posted to the appropriate controlling account in the general ledger. For example, the entry register, page 250, Lines 1–6, shows that batch 1, journal 10, has six entries for purchases of merchandise on account. Entries 2–6 represent credits to individual accounts in the accounts payable subsidiary ledger. The total of entries 2–6, $2,679.00, is posted to the controlling account in the general ledger, Accounts Payable.

The account titles are not recorded on the journal entry transmittals or on the input media (punched cards). The account titles for all accounts in the general ledger and subsidiary ledgers are stored on magnetic disk storage. Therefore, the account titles that appear on the entry register must be read from magnetic disk storage before being printed.

Batch control totals are computed by the computer system and printed on the entry register. The totals are identified on the entry register with an asterisk (*) printed next to each total. The totals are compared with the summary totals recorded on the batch control sheets prepared by the accounting department. This comparison is made to prove the accuracy of the input media.

The batch control totals for purchases and cash payments, journal numbers 10 and 20, are compared with the batch control sheet, page 219. The batch control totals for sales and cash receipts, journal numbers 30 and 40, are compared with the batch control sheet, page 230. The batch control totals for general transactions, journal number 50, are compared with the batch control sheet, page 235. The control totals are the same. Therefore, the input is assumed to be correct.

```
                                    ENTRY REGISTER
   DATE  11/01/78                   DAILY TRANSACTIONS                              PAGE 1


   BATCH   JOURNAL   ENTRY   DOCUMENT   ACCOUNT
   NO.     NO.       NO.     NO.        NO.          DESCRIPTION            DEBIT         CREDIT

    1       10        1                 5101000    PURCHASES            $2,679.00
            10        2       743       2000300    BALDWIN SUPPLY                      $    485.00
            10        3       744       2000500    GREENE GIFTWARE                          359.00
            10        4       745       2000750    RAMOS FASHIONS                         1,200.00
            10        5       746       2000800    STARK GIFTWARE                           260.00
            10        6       747       2001000    TROST MANUFACTURING                      375.00
    2       20        1       862       6107000    RENT EXPENSE          1,200.00
            20        2       863       1107000    OFFICE SUPPLIES           36.00
            20        3       864       6104000    MISCELLANEOUS EXPENSE     82.00
            20        4                 1101000    CASH                                   1,318.00
    3       20        1       865       2000100    AGREN MANUFACTURING CO.  480.00
            20        2       866       2000200    AMERICAN FURNITURE CO.   875.00
            20        3       867       2000800    STARK GIFTWARE           550.00
            20        4       868       2001400    YATES SUPPLIERS          750.00
            20        5                 5103000    PURCHASES DISCOUNT                        33.35
            20        6                 1101000    CASH                                   2,621.65

    3ᵡ               16ᵡ     9780ᵡ    43729850ᵡ   BATCH CONTROL TOTALS    6,652.00ᵡ     6,652.00ᵡ

    1       30        1       923       1000200    RONALD ADAMS         $    37.44
            30        2       924       1000412    CAROL BEARD               91.52
            30        3       925       1000800    CONNIE FABER             312.00
            30        4       926       1001400    JOHN RAMOS                70.72
            30        5                 2104000    SALES TAX PAYABLE                   $     19.68
            30        6                 4101000    SALES                                    492.00
    2       40        1                 1101000    CASH                     422.38
            40        2       566       1000100    NANCY ADAMS                              138.52
            40        3       567       1000950    JANICE KLINE                              74.38
            40        4       568       1001350    DORIS PRICE                               82.66
            40        5       569       1001800    DENNIS YOUNG                             126.82
    3       40        1       263       1101000    CASH                   1,339.52
            40        2                 2104000    SALES TAX PAYABLE                         51.52
            40        3                 4101000    SALES                                  1,288.00

    3ᵡ               14ᵡ     6231ᵡ    22619012ᵡ   BATCH CONTROL TOTALS    2,273.58ᵡ     2,273.58ᵡ

    1       50        1       235       2000600    MILES SUPPLY         $   130.00
            50        2       236       2000800    STARK GIFTWARE            88.00
            50        3                 5102000    PURCHASES RET. & ALLOW.             $    218.00
    2       50        1                 1106000    STORE SUPPLIES           111.00
            50        2       516       2001200    WAGNER SUPPLY                             93.00
            50        3       517       2001400    YATES SUPPLIERS                           18.00
    3       50        1       518       3102000    SAAD ARRIFAY, DRAWING     50.00
            50        2                 5101000    PURCHASES                                 50.00
    4       50        1                 4102000    SALES RETURNS & ALLOW.    62.00
            50        2                 2104000    SALES TAX PAYABLE          2.48
            50        3       386       1000900    OLGA HEINRICH                             41.60
            50        4       387       1001700    ROBERT WYSONG                             22.88
    5       50        1       519       1001400    JOHN RAMOS                54.00
            50        2                 1000975    JOHN LAROSE                               54.00

    5ᵡ               14ᵡ     3314ᵡ    32625975ᵡ   BATCH CONTROL TOTALS      497.48ᵡ       497.48ᵡ
```

Entry register

Accounts payable register. The data read and processed by the computer system to prepare the entry register are also used to prepare the accounts payable register. This report shows (a) the beginning balance in the accounts payable controlling account in the general ledger stored on magnetic disk storage, (b) the individual debit and credit entries for the day that have been posted to the accounts payable subsidiary ledger, and (c) the ending balance in the accounts payable controlling account in the general ledger after the total of the individual entries has been posted. The accounts payable register is shown below.

```
                        ACCOUNTS PAYABLE REGISTER
   DATE  11/01/78                                              PAGE 1


   BEGINNING    VENDOR        VENDOR            A/P       A/P      ENDING
    BALANCE     NUMBER         NAME            DEBIT     CREDIT    BALANCE

   $4,386.80

               2000300   BALDWIN SUPPLY                  $ 485.00
               2000500   GREENE GIFTWARE                   359.00
               2000750   RAMOS FASHIONS                  1,200.00
               2000800   STARK GIFTWARE                    260.00
               2001000   TROST MANUFACTURING               375.00
               2000100   AGREN MANUFACTURING CO.  $480.00
               2000200   AMERICAN FURNITURE CO.    875.00
               2000800   STARK GIFTWARE            550.00
               2001400   YATES SUPPLIERS           750.00
               2000600   MILES SUPPLY              130.00
               2000800   STARK GIFTWARE            88.00
               2001200   WAGNER SUPPLY                      93.00
               2001400   YATES SUPPLIERS                    18.00

                                                            $4,303.80
```

Accounts payable register

The beginning and ending balances printed on the above accounts payable register are computed to prove the accuracy of the data posted to the magnetic disk storage. The proof is obtained by comparing the accounts payable register with the accounts payable control sheet, page 236, prepared by the accounting department. The beginning and ending balances on the two forms must be the same.

Accounts receivable register. The data read and processed by the computer system to prepare the entry register are also used to prepare the accounts receivable register. This report shows (a) the beginning balance in the accounts receivable controlling account in the general ledger stored on magnetic disk storage, (b) the individual debit and credit entries for the day that have been posted to the accounts receivable subsidiary ledger, and (c) the ending balance in the accounts receivable controlling account after the total of the individual entries has been posted. The accounts receivable register is shown below.

```
                         ACCOUNTS RECEIVABLE REGISTER
          DATE  11/01/78                                        PAGE 1


          BEGINNING   CUSTOMER    CUSTOMER      A/R      A/R      ENDING
           BALANCE     NUMBER       NAME       DEBIT    CREDIT   BALANCE

          $6,343.60

                      1000200    RONALD ADAMS  $ 37.44

                      1000412    CAROL BEARD     91.52

                      1000800    CONNIE FABER   312.00

                      1001400    JOHN RAMOS      70.72

                      1000100    NANCY  ADAMS            $138.52

                      1000950    JANICE KLINE             74.38

                      1001350    DORIS PRICE              82.66

                      1001800    DENNIS  YOUNG           126.82

                      1000900    OLGA HEINRICH            41.60

                      1001700    ROBERT WYSONG            22.88

                      1001400    JOHN RAMOS      54.00

                      1000975    JOHN LAROSE              54.00

                                                        $6,368.42
```

Accounts receivable register

The beginning and ending balances printed on the above accounts receivable register are computed to prove the accuracy of the data posted to the magnetic disk storage. The proof is obtained by comparing the accounts receivable register with the accounts receivable control sheet, page 238, prepared by the accounting department. The beginning and ending balances must be the same.

The three daily accounting reports provide proof of the accuracy of the input media and the posting of the entries to the ledgers stored on magnetic disk storage. Any errors that are discovered as a result of the accuracy check must be located and corrected.

Errors in posting indicate instruction errors in the computer program. Errors in posting may also result from failure of the machines to operate properly. Regardless of the cause, errors must be corrected. New punched cards must be prepared for all input media errors. The automated procedures are then repeated until all summary totals on the reports agree with the control sheets prepared by the accounting department. A summary of the accuracy check of input media and posting procedures is illustrated below.

CONTROL SHEETS PREPARED BY ACCOUNTING DEPARTMENT		REGISTERS PREPARED BY COMPUTER SYSTEM
Batch Control Sheet Purchases and Cash Payments (page 219)	ACCURACY CHECK SUMMARY TOTALS	Entry Register Journals 10 and 20 Batch Control Totals (page 250)
Batch Control Sheet Sales and Cash Receipts (page 230)	ACCURACY CHECK SUMMARY TOTALS	Entry Register Journals 30 and 40 Batch Control Totals (page 250)
Batch Control Sheet General Transactions (page 235)	ACCURACY CHECK SUMMARY TOTALS	Entry Register Journal 50 Batch Control Totals (page 250)
Accounts Payable Control Sheet (page 236)	ACCURACY CHECK SUMMARY TOTALS	Accounts Payable Register (page 251)
Accounts Receivable Control Sheet (page 238)	ACCURACY CHECK SUMMARY TOTALS	Accounts Receivable Register (page 252)

Accuracy check summary

After accuracy has been determined, the journal entry transmittals, the control sheets, and the three accounting reports are forwarded by the ADP department to the accounting department. The junior accountant inspects and files the transmittals, control sheets, and computer printouts for future reference.

Processing the end-of-fiscal-period work in an EDP system

At the end of each monthly fiscal period, the schedules and financial statements are prepared by the computer system in the data processing department. The computer system prepares (a) a schedule of accounts receivable and a schedule of accounts payable, (b) a trial balance, (c) an income statement, (d) a capital statement, (e) a balance sheet, and (f) a post-closing trial balance.

Preparing the subsidiary schedules in an EDP system

The subsidiary ledgers for Harrod's are stored on magnetic disk storage connected to the computer system. Data for the subsidiary schedules are read from the magnetic disk storage, processed by the central processing unit, and printed by the printer connected to the computer. The subsidiary schedules prepared by the computer are forwarded to the accounting department. The totals computed on each of the schedules must balance with the ending balance on the accounts payable and accounts receivable control sheets prepared by the accounting department on the last business day of the month.

The accountant analyzes the subsidiary schedules, makes recommendations to management, and files the schedules for future reference. The subsidiary schedules are shown below.

HARROD'S
SCHEDULE OF ACCOUNTS RECEIVABLE
NOVEMBER 30, 1978

RONALD ADAMS	$ 93.56
MILDRED ADKINS	325.42
TAMMIE BAUER	132.68
CAROL BEARD	691.52
PATRICIA BURNS	1,669.46
DAVID COTTER	146.60
BERNICE DURFEE	560.92
CONNIE FABER	364.48
OLGA HEINRICH	93.20
JANICE KLINE	236.83
JOHN LAROSE	87.38
SAMMY PITT	609.80
JOHN RAMOS	70.72
JODY VINCENT	936.62
VIRGINIA WHITNEY	380.63
ROBERT WYSONG	83.32
DENNIS YOUNG	144.52
TOTAL ACCOUNTS RECEIVABLE	$6,627.66

HARROD'S
SCHEDULE OF ACCOUNTS PAYABLE
NOVEMBER 30, 1978

BALDWIN SUPPLY	$ 965.80
CALVO WOMEN'S FASHIONS	833.75
GREENE GIFTWARE	359.00
MILES SUPPLY	635.85
RAMOS FASHIONS	1,200.00
STARK GIFTWARE	260.00
TROST MANUFACTURING	580.40
WAGNER SUPPLY	93.00
YATES SUPPLIERS	18.00
TOTAL ACCOUNTS PAYABLE	$4,945.80

Subsidiary schedules

Preparing the trial balance in an EDP system

The trial balance provides the proof of the equality of debits and credits in the general ledger. The trial balance is recorded directly on the work sheet in a manual accounting system.

In an automated accounting system, a work sheet is not required. The general ledger data for Harrod's are stored on magnetic disk storage in the data processing department. All computations are done by the computer system according to instructions in the stored computer program.

Data for the trial balance are read from the magnetic disk storage, processed by the central processing unit, and printed by the printer connected to the computer. The trial balance prepared by the computer is forwarded to the accounting department. This trial balance is illustrated below.

```
                                    HARROD'S
                                  TRIAL BALANCE
                        FOR MONTH ENDED NOVEMBER 30, 1978


   1101000   CASH                                        $  8,347.30
   1102000   PETTY CASH                                       250.00
   1103000   ACCOUNTS RECEIVABLE                            6,627.66
   1104000   ALLOWANCE FOR UNCOLLECTIBLE ACCOUNTS                        $     238.98
   1105000   MERCHANDISE INVENTORY                         91,460.30
   1106000   STORE SUPPLIES                                 1,425.00
   1107000   OFFICE SUPPLIES                                  630.45
   1108000   PREPAID INSURANCE                                385.00
   1201000   STORE EQUIPMENT                                4,360.00
   1202000   ACCUMULATED DEPRECIATION--STORE EQUIPMENT                        983.40
   1203000   OFFICE EQUIPMENT                               1,875.50
   1204000   ACCUMULATED DEPRECIATION--OFFICE EQUIPMENT                         93.60
   2101000   ACCOUNTS PAYABLE                                               4,945.80
   2102000   EMPLOYEES INCOME TAX PAYABLE--FEDERAL                          3,326.30
   2103000   PAYROLL TAXES PAYABLE                                         1,260.00
   2104000   SALES TAX PAYABLE                                             1,680.42
   3101000   SAAD ARRIFAY, CAPITAL                                        93,757.33
   3102000   SAAD ARRIFAY, DRAWING                          1,000.00
   4101000   SALES                                                        41,000.00
   4102000   SALES RETURNS AND ALLOWANCES                     280.20
   5101000   PURCHASES                                     18,625.40
   5102000   PURCHASES RETURNS AND ALLOWANCES                                 280.40
   5103000   PURCHASES DISCOUNT                                              160.78
   6104000   MISCELLANEOUS EXPENSE                            130.20
   6106000   PAYROLL TAXES EXPENSE                            630.00
   6107000   RENT EXPENSE                                   1,200.00
   6108000   SALARY EXPENSE                                10,500.00

             TOTALS                                     $147,727.01    $147,727.01
```

Trial balance

The trial balance is used by the junior accountant to plan the adjusting entries and then filed for future reference.

Planning and recording the adjusting entries in an EDP system

At the end of a fiscal period, certain general ledger accounts need to be brought up to date. Adjustments to these accounts are planned and recorded on a journal entry transmittal. The data needed for the adjustments are:

Additional allowance for uncollectible accounts .... $ 180.00
Ending merchandise inventory 94,380.00
Store supplies used during November 325.00
Office supplies used during November 230.00
Insurance used during November 35.00
Additional depreciation of office equipment 93.60
Additional depreciation of store equipment 135.25

The completed journal entry transmittal for the adjusting entries of Harrod's is shown below.

JOURNAL ENTRY TRANSMITTAL

DATE 11/30/78 PAGE 1 OF 1 PAGES

	1 BCH. No.	2 JR. No.	3 ETY. No.	4 DOCUMENT NUMBER	5 ACCOUNT NUMBER	6 EXPLANATION	7 DEBIT	8 CREDIT	
1	1	50	1		6101000	Adjusting Entries	18000		1
2			2		1104000			18000	2
3			3		3103000		9146030		3
4			4		1105000			9146030	4
5			5		1105000		9438000		5
6			6		3103000			9438000	6
7			7		6109000		32500		7
8			8		1106000			32500	8
9			9		6105000		23000		9
10			10		1107000			23000	10
11			11		6103000		3500		11
12			12		1108000			3500	12
13			13		6102000		9360		13
14			14		1204000			9360	14
15			15		6102500		13525		15
16			16		1202000			13525	16
40									40

JOURNAL NUMBERS

PURCHASES = 10
CASH PAYMENTS = 20
SALES = 30
CASH RECEIPTS = 40
GENERAL = 50

PREPARED BY Carol Severson

Journal entry transmittal for adjusting entries

Account numbers are used in place of account titles on the journal entry transmittal above prepared by the junior accountant. The account numbers are found by referring to the chart of accounts, page 206. The form of the adjusting entries on this journal entry transmittal is similar to the Adjustments columns columns of the work sheet, page 48.

After the adjusting entries have been recorded on the journal entry transmittal, the junior accountant prepares a batch control sheet.

Batch control sheet for adjusting entries

The batch control sheet for the adjusting entries provides summary totals of the entries recorded on the journal entry transmittal. The batch control sheet for the November 30, 1978, adjusting entries is shown on page 257.

The data necessary to complete the batch control sheet are obtained from the journal entry transmittal above. After the journal entry transmittal and batch control sheet are prepared, the junior accountant forwards the two forms to the data processing department.

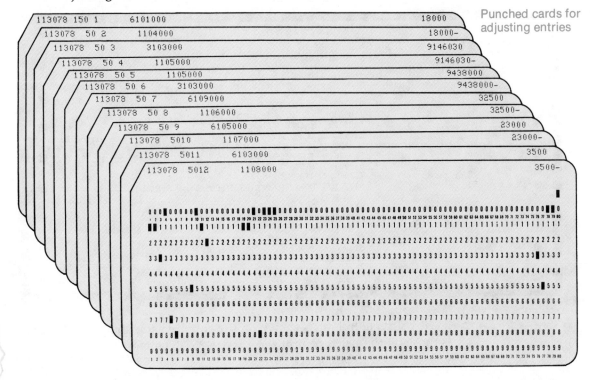

BATCH CONTROL SHEET

DATE ___11/30/78___

1	TOTAL NUMBER OF BATCHES	1
2	TOTAL NUMBER OF TRANSACTION ENTRIES	16
3	TOTAL OF DOCUMENT NUMBERS	
4	TOTAL OF ACCOUNT NUMBERS	51,869,500
5	TOTAL DEBITS	$186,839.15
6	TOTAL CREDITS	$186,839.15

CONTROL TOTALS FOR: ___ Purchases ___ Cash Payments ___ Sales ✓ Cash Receipts ✓ General

PREPARED BY
Carol Severson

Batch control sheet
for adjusting entries

Recording the adjusting entries for computer processing

The data processing department converts the data on the journal entry transmittal to input media (punched cards). One card is punched for each line on the journal entry transmittal, page 256. The punched cards for the adjusting entries are shown below and on page 258.

Punched cards for
adjusting entries

```
113078 150 1     6101000                                    18000
113078  50 2     1104000                                    18000-
113078  50 3     3103000                                    9146030
113078  50 4     1105000                                    9146030-
113078  50 5     1105000                                    9438000
113078  50 6     3103000                                    9438000-
113078  50 7     6109000                                    32500
113078  50 8     1106000                                    32500-
113078  50 9     6105000                                    23000
113078 5010      1107000                                    23000-
113078 5011      6103000                                    3500
113078 5012      1108000                                    3500-
```

Punched cards for
adjusting entries

The data from the punched cards for the adjusting entries prepared
from the journal entry transmittal are read and processed by the computer. An entry register is prepared listing all adjusting entries and all
batch control totals. The batch control totals are computed by the computer as the transactions are being processed. The data for each adjusting
entry are also posted by the computer to the accounts in the general ledger. The entry register for the adjusting entries is illustrated below.

| | | | | | ENTRY REGISTER | | |
| | | | | | ADJUSTING ENTRIES | | |

DATE   11/30/78   PAGE 1

BATCH NO.	JOURNAL NO.	ENTRY NO.	DOCUMENT NO.	ACCOUNT NO.	DESCRIPTION	DEBIT	CREDIT
1	50	1		6101000	BAD DEBTS EXPENSE	$ 180.00	
	50	2		1104000	ALLOW. FOR UNCOLL. ACCTS.		$ 180.00
	50	3		3103000	INCOME SUMMARY	91,460.30	
	50	4		1105000	MERCHANDISE INVENTORY		91,460.30
	50	5		1105000	MERCHANDISE INVENTORY	94,380.00	
	50	6		3103000	INCOME SUMMARY		94,380.00
	50	7		6109000	STORE SUPPLIES EXPENSE	325.00	
	50	8		1106000	STORE SUPPLIES		325.00
	50	9		6105000	OFFICE SUPPLIES EXPENSE	230.00	
	50	10		1107000	OFFICE SUPPLIES		230.00
	50	11		6103000	INSURANCE EXPENSE	35.00	
	50	12		1108000	PREPAID INSURANCE		35.00
	50	13		6102000	DEPR. EXP.--OFF. EQUIP.	93.60	
	50	14		1204000	ACCUM. DEPR.--OFF. EQUIP.		93.60
	50	15		6102500	DEPR. EXP.--STORE EQUIP.	135.25	
	50	16		1202000	ACCUM. DEPR.--STORE EQUIP.		135.25
1*		16*		51869500*	BATCH CONTROL TOTALS	186,839.15*	186,839.15*

Entry register for adjusting entries

The batch control totals shown on the entry register above are the same
as those on the batch control sheet, page 257. Therefore, the entry register is assumed to be correct.

Preparing financial statements in an EDP system

After accuracy has been determined, the computer system prepares the income statement, capital statement, and balance sheet. These statements are shown below and on page 260.

The journal entry transmittal, batch control sheet, entry register, and financial statements prepared by the computer are forwarded to the accounting department. The junior accountant inspects the reports to determine the necessary closing entries. The junior accountant then files the journal entry transmittal, batch control sheet, and entry register for future reference. The financial statements are given to the accountant to analyze for possible management recommendations. The accountant then files the financial statements for future reference.

Income statement

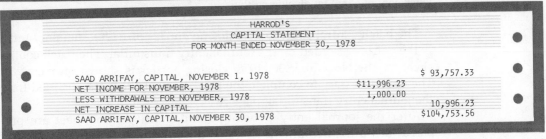

```
                                 HARROD'S
                             INCOME STATEMENT
                       FOR MONTH ENDED NOVEMBER 30, 1978


OPERATING REVENUE
  SALES                                              $ 41,000.00
  LESS SALES RETURNS AND ALLOWANCES                       280.20
  NET SALES                                                            $40,719.80
COST OF MERCHANDISE SOLD
  MERCHANDISE INVENTORY, NOVEMBER 1, 1978            $ 91,460.30
  PURCHASES                             $18,625.40
  LESS PURCHASES RETURNS AND ALLOWANCES    $280.40
       PURCHASES DISCOUNT                  160.78       441.18
  NET PURCHASES                                        18,184.22
  TOTAL COST OF MDSE. AVAIL. FOR SALE                 $109,644.52
  LESS MDSE. INVENTORY, NOV. 30, 1978                  94,380.00
  COST OF MERCHANDISE SOLD                                             15,264.52
GROSS PROFIT ON OPERATIONS                                            $25,455.28
OPERATING EXPENSES
  BAD DEBTS EXPENSE                                  $    180.00
  DEPRECIATION EXPENSE--OFFICE EQUIPMENT                   93.60
  DEPRECIATION EXPENSE--STORE EQUIPMENT                   135.25
  INSURANCE EXPENSE                                        35.00
  MISCELLANEOUS EXPENSE                                   130.20
  OFFICE SUPPLIES EXPENSE                                 230.00
  PAYROLL TAXES EXPENSE                                   630.00
  RENT EXPENSE                                          1,200.00
  SALARY EXPENSE                                       10,500.00
  STORE SUPPLIES EXPENSE                                  325.00
  TOTAL OPERATING EXPENSES                                             13,459.05

NET INCOME                                                           $11,996.23
```

```
                                 HARROD'S
                             CAPITAL STATEMENT
                       FOR MONTH ENDED NOVEMBER 30, 1978


  SAAD ARRIFAY, CAPITAL, NOVEMBER 1, 1978              $ 93,757.33
  NET INCOME FOR NOVEMBER, 1978             $11,996.23
  LESS WITHDRAWALS FOR NOVEMBER, 1978        1,000.00
  NET INCREASE IN CAPITAL                              10,996.23
  SAAD ARRIFAY, CAPITAL, NOVEMBER 30, 1978            $104,753.56
```

Capital statement

```
                              HARROD'S
                           BALANCE SHEET
                         NOVEMBER 30, 1978


                  ASSETS

     CURRENT ASSETS
        CASH                                      $ 8,347.30
        PETTY CASH                                    250.00
        ACCOUNTS RECEIVABLE           $6,627.66
           LESS ALLOW. FOR UNCOLL. ACCTS.  418.98   6,208.68
        MERCHANDISE INVENTORY                      94,380.00
        STORE SUPPLIES                              1,100.00
        OFFICE SUPPLIES                               400.45
        PREPAID INSURANCE                             350.00
        TOTAL CURRENT ASSETS                                   $111,036.43
     PLANT ASSETS
        STORE EQUIPMENT              $4,360.00
           LESS ACCUM. DEPR.--STORE EQUIP.  1,118.65  $ 3,241.35
        OFFICE EQUIPMENT            $1,875.50
           LESS ACCUM. DEPR.--OFF. EQUIP.    187.20    1,688.30
        TOTAL PLANT ASSETS                                       4,929.65
     TOTAL ASSETS                                              $115,966.08


                  LIABILITIES
     CURRENT LIABILITIES
        ACCOUNTS PAYABLE                          $ 4,945.80
        EMPLOYEES INCOME TAX PAYABLE                 3,326.30
        PAYROLL TAXES PAYABLE                        1,260.00
        SALES TAX PAYABLE                            1,680.42
        TOTAL LIABILITIES                                      $ 11,212.52


                  CAPITAL
     SAAD ARRIFAY, CAPITAL                                      104,753.56
     TOTAL LIABILITIES AND CAPITAL                             $115,966.08
```

Balance sheet

Recording the closing entries in an EDP system

The computer program used for the processing of the financial statements does not include the instructions necessary to make the closing entries. Therefore, the junior accountant recorded the closing entries on a journal entry transmittal as shown on page 261.

After the closing entries have been recorded on the journal entry transmittal, the junior accountant prepares a batch control sheet.

Batch control sheet for closing entries

The batch control sheet for the closing entries provides summary totals of the entries recorded on the journal entry transmittal. The batch control sheet for the November 30, 1978, closing entries is shown on page 261. The data necessary to complete the batch control sheet are obtained from the journal entry transmittal, page 261.

After the journal entry transmittal and batch control sheet are prepared, the junior accountant forwards the two forms to the data processing department.

JOURNAL ENTRY TRANSMITTAL

DATE 11/30/78   PAGE 1 OF 1 PAGES

	Bch. No.	Jr. No.	Ety. No.	DOCUMENT NUMBER	ACCOUNT NUMBER	EXPLANATION	DEBIT	CREDIT	
1	1 5 0		1		4 1 0 1 0 0 0	Closing Entries	4 1 0 0 0 0 0		1
2			2		5 1 0 2 0 0 0		2 8 0 4 0		2
3			3		5 1 0 3 0 0 0		1 6 0 7 8		3
4			4		3 1 0 3 0 0 0			4 1 4 4 1 1 8	4
5			5		3 1 0 3 0 0 0		3 2 3 6 4 6 5		5
6			6		4 1 0 2 0 0 0			2 8 0 2 0	6
7			7		5 1 0 1 0 0 0			1 8 6 2 5 4 0	7
8			8		6 1 0 1 0 0 0			1 8 0 0 0	8
9			9		6 1 0 2 0 0 0			9 3 6 0	9
10			1 0		6 1 0 2 5 0 0			1 3 5 2 5	10
11			1 1		6 1 0 3 0 0 0			3 5 0 0	11
12			1 2		6 1 0 4 0 0 0			1 3 0 2 0	12
13			1 3		6 1 0 5 0 0 0			2 3 0 0 0	13
14			1 4		6 1 0 6 0 0 0			6 3 0 0 0	14
15			1 5		6 1 0 7 0 0 0			1 2 0 0 0 0	15
16			1 6		6 1 0 8 0 0 0			1 0 5 0 0 0 0	16
17			1 7		6 1 0 9 0 0 0			3 2 5 0 0	17
18			1 8		3 1 0 1 0 0 0		1 0 0 0 0 0		18
19			1 9		3 1 0 2 0 0 0			1 0 0 0 0 0	19
20			2 0		3 1 0 3 0 0 0		1 1 9 9 6 2 3		20
21			2 1		3 1 0 1 0 0 0			1 1 9 9 6 2 3	21
22									22
40									40

JOURNAL NUMBERS

PURCHASES = 10   CASH RECEIPTS = 40
CASH PAYMENTS = 20   GENERAL = 50
SALES = 30

PREPARED BY

Carol Severson

Journal entry transmittal
for closing entries

BATCH CONTROL SHEET

DATE 11/30/78

1	TOTAL NUMBER OF BATCHES	1
2	TOTAL NUMBER OF TRANSACTION ENTRIES	21
3	TOTAL OF DOCUMENT NUMBERS	—
4	TOTAL OF ACCOUNT NUMBERS	103,169,500
5	TOTAL DEBITS	$ 86,802.06
6	TOTAL CREDITS	$ 86,802.06

CONTROL TOTALS FOR: ___ Purchases   ___ Cash Receipts
___ Cash Payments   ✓ General
___ Sales

PREPARED BY

Carol Severson

Batch control sheet
for closing entries

Recording the closing entries for computer processing

The data processing department converts the data on the journal entry transmittal to input media (punched cards). One card is punched for each line on the journal entry transmittal, page 261. The punched cards for the closing entries are shown below.

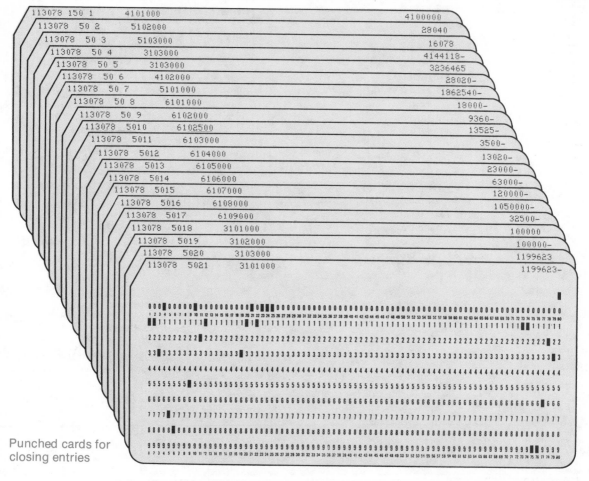

Punched cards for
closing entries

The data from the punched cards for the closing entries are read and processed by the computer system. An entry register is prepared listing all closing entries and all batch control totals. The batch control totals are computed by the computer system as the transactions are being processed. The data for each closing entry are also posted by the computer to the accounts in the general ledger. The entry register for the closing entries is shown on page 263.

The batch control totals printed on the entry register are compared with the summary totals recorded on the batch control sheet, page 261. This comparison is made to prove the accuracy of the input media.

```
                                        ENTRY REGISTER
    DATE   11/30/78                      CLOSING ENTRIES                                    PAGE 1


  BATCH  JOURNAL  ENTRY  DOCUMENT  ACCOUNT
   NO.     NO.     NO.     NO.       NO.        DESCRIPTION          DEBIT        CREDIT

    1       50      1              4101000  SALES                $41,000.00
            50      2              5102000  PURCHASES RET. & ALLOW.   280.40
            50      3              5103000  PURCHASES DISCOUNT        160.78
            50      4              3103000  INCOME SUMMARY                        $41,441.18
            50      5              3103000  INCOME SUMMARY        32,364.65
            50      6              4102000  SALES RETURNS AND ALLOW.                   280.20
            50      7              5101000  PURCHASES                               18,625.40
            50      8              6101000  BAD DEBTS EXPENSE                          180.00
            50      9              6102000  DEPR. EXP.--OFF. EQUIP.                     93.60
            50     10              6102500  DEPR. EXP.--STORE EQUIP.                   135.25
            50     11              6103000  INSURANCE EXPENSE                           35.00
            50     12              6104000  MISCELLANEOUS EXPENSE                      130.20
            50     13              6105000  OFFICE SUPPLIES EXPENSE                    230.00
            50     14              6106000  PAYROLL TAXES EXPENSE                      630.00
            50     15              6107000  RENT EXPENSE                             1,200.00
            50     16              6108000  SALARY EXPENSE                          10,500.00
            50     17              6109000  STORE SUPPLIES EXPENSE                     325.00
            50     18              3101000  SAAD ARRIFAY, CAPITAL  1,000.00
            50     19              3102000  SAAD ARRIFAY, DRAWING                    1,000.00
            50     20              3103000  INCOME SUMMARY        11,996.23
            50     21              3101000  SAAD ARRIFAY, CAPITAL                   11,996.23

    1*              21*           103169500* BATCH CONTROL TOTALS  86,802.06*    86,802.06*
```

Entry register for closing entries

Preparing a post-closing trial balance in an EDP system

After accuracy has been determined, the computer system prepares the post-closing trial balance. The post-closing trial balance is below.

```
                                    HARROD'S
                         POST-CLOSING TRIAL BALANCE
                            NOVEMBER 30, 1978


       CASH                                     $  8,347.30
       PETTY CASH                                    250.00
       ACCOUNTS RECEIVABLE                         6,627.66
       ALLOWANCE FOR UNCOLLECTIBLE ACCOUNTS                        $     418.98
       MERCHANDISE INVENTORY                       94,380.00
       STORE SUPPLIES                               1,100.00
       OFFICE SUPPLIES                                400.45
       PREPAID INSURANCE                              350.00
       STORE EQUIPMENT                              4,360.00
       ACCUMULATED DEPRECIATION--STORE EQUIPMENT                        1,118.65
       OFFICE EQUIPMENT                             1,875.50
       ACCUMULATED DEPRECIATION--OFFICE EQUIPMENT                         187.20
       ACCOUNTS PAYABLE                                                 4,945.80
       EMPLOYEES INCOME TAX PAYABLE                                     3,326.30
       PAYROLL TAXES PAYABLE                                            1,260.00
       SALES TAX PAYABLE                                               1,680.42
       SAAD ARRIFAY, CAPITAL                                          104,753.56

       TOTALS                                    $117,690.91      $117,690.91
```

Post-closing trial balance

The journal entry transmittal, batch control sheet, entry register, and post-closing trial balance are forwarded to the accounting department. The junior accountant inspects and files the reports for future reference.

SUMMARY

The complete automated accounting system of Harrod's is summarized in the chart below. The chart shows the forms, media, and reports prepared daily and at the end of the fiscal period by the accounting department and the data processing department.

AUTOMATED ACCOUNTING SYSTEM FORMS, MEDIA, AND REPORTS	PREPARED DAILY	PREPARED END OF FISCAL PERIOD	PREPARED BY ACCOUNTING DEPARTMENT	PREPARED BY DATA PROCESSING DEPARTMENT
Journal entry transmittals and batch control sheets for daily transactions	X		X	
Accounts payable control sheet	X		X	
Accounts receivable control sheet	X		X	
Input media (punched cards) for daily transactions	X			X
Entry register for daily transactions	X			X
Accounts payable register	X			X
Accounts receivable register	X			X
Schedule of accounts receivable		X		X
Schedule of accounts payable		X		X
Trial balance		X		X
Journal entry transmittal and batch control sheet for adjusting entries		X	X	
Input media (punched cards) for adjusting entries		X		X
Entry register for adjusting entries		X		X
Income statement		X		X
Capital statement		X		X
Balance sheet		X		X
Journal entry transmittal and batch control sheet for closing entries		X	X	
Input media (punched cards) for closing entries		X		X
Entry register for closing entries		X		X
Post-closing trial balance		X		X

Summary of automated accounting system

✦ What is the meaning of each of the following?

● audit trail

● systems flowchart

● fields

1. What is the major objective of an automated accounting system?
2. What four factors determine the type of automated data processing system to select?
3. What department has the responsibility for determining the type, design, and number of accounting reports to be prepared?
4. What type of punched card does Harrod's use in its automated accounting system?
5. In an automated accounting system, where does the processing of data take place?
6. In Harrod's automated accounting

system, where are the general ledger and subsidiary ledgers stored?
7. What are the three daily accounting reports prepared by Harrod's computer system?
8. Where does the computer system obtain the account titles that appear on the entry register?
9. How are the batch control totals on the entry register identified?
10. How does the junior accountant use the trial balance?
11. Where does the junior accountant obtain the data necessary to record the closing entries?

CASE 1 Tienda Office Supply uses an automated accounting system. Journal entry transmittals and batch control sheets are prepared for the daily transactions. The data processing department prepares punched cards from the journal entry transmittals and processes an entry register, accounts payable register, and accounts receivable register. The general ledger and subsidiary ledgers are stored on magnetic disk storage. As the data stored on mag-

netic disk are not visible, all punched cards have been kept because the punched cards can be visually read. Space for storing the large number of punched cards is becoming a problem. The manager says the punched cards must be kept indefinitely. The accountant says the punched cards can be destroyed after the accuracy of the input media and posting has been determined. With whom do you agree and why?

CASE 2 Eva Robelo owns and operates the Robelo Department Store. An electronic computer system is used to process the accounting data. Journal entry transmittals and batch control sheets are prepared for the daily transactions. The accounting reports currently being prepared by the data

processing department combine the business activity for the entire business. Ms. Robelo has requested that the accounting system be changed to allow reporting of revenue and expenses by department. What changes would be required to report the business activity by department?

PROBLEM 14-1 Recording adjusting entries for computer processing

On November 30 of the current year, the end of a fiscal period, the data necessary to prepare the adjusting entries for the Garcia Office Systems Company appear as shown on page 266.

Merchandise inventory: Beginning $78,500.00
                        Ending 81,300.00
Additional allowance for uncollectible accounts 630.00
Store supplies used during November... 380.00
Office supplies used during November.. 195.00
Insurance used during November.. 75.00
Additional depreciation of store equipment 115.00
Depreciation of office equipment.. 85.00

Instructions: □ **1.** Record the adjusting entries on a journal entry transmittal. Use the account numbers from the chart of accounts for Garcia Office Systems Company prepared in Problem 12-1, page 222.

□ **2.** Prepare a batch control sheet for the adjusting entries.

PROBLEM 14-2 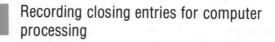 Recording closing entries for computer processing

The income statement and capital statement of Garcia Office Systems Company for the month ended November 30 of the current year are given below and on page 267.

```
                        GARCIA OFFICE SYSTEMS COMPANY
                              INCOME STATEMENT
                        FOR MONTH ENDED NOVEMBER 30, 19--


OPERATING REVENUE
   SALES                                              $33,593.50
   LESS SALES RETURNS AND ALLOWANCES                      165.00
   NET SALES                                                        $33,428.50
COST OF MERCHANDISE SOLD
   MERCHANDISE INVENTORY, NOVEMBER 1, 19--            $78,500.00
   PURCHASES                             $12,300.00
   LESS PURCHASES RETURNS AND ALLOWANCES    $225.00
          PURCHASES DISCOUNT                160.20      385.20
   NET PURCHASES                                       11,914.80
   TOTAL COST OF MDSE. AVAIL. FOR SALE                 $90,414.80
   LESS MERCHANDISE INVENTORY, NOV. 30, 19--           81,300.00
   COST OF MERCHANDISE SOLD                                          9,114.80
GROSS PROFIT ON OPERATIONS                                         $24,313.70
OPERATING EXPENSES
   BAD DEBTS EXPENSE                                  $    630.00
   DEPRECIATION EXPENSE--OFFICE EQUIPMENT                  85.00
   DEPRECIATION EXPENSE--STORE EQUIPMENT                  115.00
   INSURANCE EXPENSE                                       75.00
   MISCELLANEOUS EXPENSE                                   58.00
   OFFICE SUPPLIES EXPENSE                                195.00
   PAYROLL TAXES EXPENSE                                  630.00
   RENT EXPENSE                                           900.00
   SALARY EXPENSE                                      10,500.00
   STORE SUPPLIES EXPENSE                                 380.00
   TOTAL OPERATING EXPENSES                                         13,568.00

NET INCOME                                                         $10,745.70
```

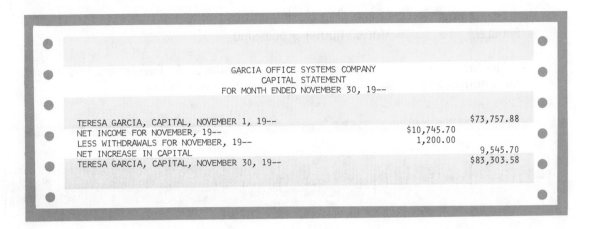

```
                    GARCIA OFFICE SYSTEMS COMPANY
                          CAPITAL STATEMENT
                    FOR MONTH ENDED NOVEMBER 30, 19--

TERESA GARCIA, CAPITAL, NOVEMBER 1, 19--                          $73,757.88
NET INCOME FOR NOVEMBER, 19--                      $10,745.70
LESS WITHDRAWALS FOR NOVEMBER, 19--                 1,200.00
NET INCREASE IN CAPITAL                                            9,545.70
TERESA GARCIA, CAPITAL, NOVEMBER 30, 19--                        $83,303.58
```

Instructions: □ **1.** Record the closing entries on a journal entry transmittal. Use the account numbers from the chart of accounts for Garcia Office Systems Company prepared in Problem 12-1, page 222.

□ **2.** Prepare a batch control sheet for the closing entries.

MASTERY PROBLEM 14-M ## Recording adjusting entries for computer processing

Optional Problems

On December 31 of the current year, the beginning and ending inventories and the value of the prepaid insurance of the Westside Hardware Company are shown below.

	Beginning Balance	Ending Balance
Merchandise Inventory	$64,500.00	$67,350.00
Store Supplies	986.00	745.00
Office Supplies	480.00	265.00
Prepaid Insurance	625.00	410.00

Instructions: □ **1.** Record the adjusting entries on a journal entry transmittal. Use the account numbers given below:

Merchandise Inventory	11 05000
Store Supplies	11 06000
Office Supplies	11 07000
Prepaid Insurance	11 08000
Income Summary	31 02000
Insurance Expense	61 03000
Office Supplies Expense	61 05000
Store Supplies Expense	61 08000

□ **2.** Prepare a batch control sheet for the adjusting entries.

**BONUS
PROBLEM 14-B**   ● Recording closing entries
for computer processing

The income statement and capital statement of the A. P. Furniture Company for the month ended October 31 of the current year are given below.

```
                    A. P. FURNITURE COMPANY
                       INCOME STATEMENT
                 FOR MONTH ENDED OCTOBER 31, 19--


OPERATING REVENUE
    SALES                                                    $24,750.75
COST OF MERCHANDISE SOLD
    MERCHANDISE INVENTORY, OCTOBER 1, 19--       $58,670.00
    PURCHASES                                     18,250.00
    TOTAL COST OF MERCHANDISE AVAILABLE FOR SALE  $76,920.00
    LESS MERCHANDISE INVENTORY, OCTOBER 31, 19--  61,200.00
    COST OF MERCHANDISE SOLD                                  15,720.00
GROSS PROFIT ON OPERATIONS                                   $ 9,030.75
OPERATING EXPENSES
    DEPRECIATION EXPENSE--OFFICE EQUIPMENT        $    87.50
    DEPRECIATION EXPENSE--STORE EQUIPMENT             362.00
    INSURANCE EXPENSE                                 45.00
    MISCELLANEOUS EXPENSE                             63.00
    SALARY EXPENSE                                 1,600.00
    SUPPLIES EXPENSE                                 120.00
    TOTAL OPERATING EXPENSES                                   2,277.50

NET INCOME                                                   $ 6,753.25
```

```
                    A. P. FURNITURE COMPANY
                       CAPITAL STATEMENT
                 FOR MONTH ENDED OCTOBER 31, 19--


A. P. ACOSTA, CAPITAL, OCTOBER 1, 19--                       $48,350.00
NET INCOME FOR OCTOBER, 19--                     $6,753.25
LESS WITHDRAWALS FOR OCTOBER, 19--               1,000.00
NET INCREASE IN CAPITAL                                        5,753.25
A. P. ACOSTA, CAPITAL, OCTOBER 31, 19--                      $54,103.25
```

Instructions: □ **1.** Record the closing entries on a journal entry transmittal. Use the account numbers given below.

A. P. Acosta, Capital	31 01000	Depreciation Expense —	
A. P. Acosta, Drawing	31 02000	Store Equipment	61 02000
Income Summary	31 03000	Insurance Expense	61 03000
Sales	41 01000	Miscellaneous Expense	61 04000
Purchases	51 01000	Salary Expense	61 05000
Depreciation Expense —		Supplies Expense	61 06000
Office Equipment	61 01000		

□ **2.** Prepare a batch control sheet for the closing entries.

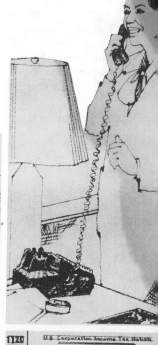

7

CORPORATION ACCOUNTING

MANY BUSINESSES ARE ORGANIZED AS CORPORATIONS.
A corporation is formed by receiving approval from a state or
federal agency. A corporation can buy, own, and sell
property as well as incur liabilities and enter into contracts
in its own name. A corporation may sell ownership in itself
in the form of capital stock to individuals or other corporations.
The corporation can then use the proceeds from the sale of
its capital stock to operate the corporation. Frequently
corporations are formed because many owners can provide
larger amounts of capital than one individual owner.

CORPORATIONS HAVE UNIQUE CAPITAL ACCOUNTS.
The principal difference between the accounting records of a
sole proprietorship, a partnership, and a corporation is in
the capital accounts. A corporation has a separate capital
account for each kind of stock it issues and for the earnings
that it keeps in the business.

Part 7 of this textbook describes how *Amcar Corporation*
is formed, issues capital stock, returns some of the profits
to owners, and prepares financial statements.

AMCAR CORPORATION
CHART OF ACCOUNTS

Balance Sheet Accounts

(1) ASSETS

	Account Number
11 _Current Assets_	
Cash	1101
Petty Cash	1102
Accounts Receivable	1103
Allowance for Uncollectible Accounts	1103.1
Subscriptions Receivable	1104
Merchandise Inventory	1105
Supplies — Sales	1106
Supplies — Office	1107
Prepaid Insurance	1108
12 _Long-Term Investment_	
Bond Sinking Fund	1201
13 _Plant Assets_	
Store Equipment	1301
Accumulated Depreciation — Store Equipment	1301.1
Delivery Equipment	1302
Accumulated Depreciation — Delivery Equipment	1302.1
Office Equipment	1303
Accumulated Depreciation — Office Equipment	1303.1
14 _Intangible Asset_	
Organization Costs	1401

(2) LIABILITIES

21 _Current Liabilities_	
Accounts Payable	2101
Employees Income Tax Payable	2102
FICA Tax Payable	2103
Unemployment Tax Payable — Federal	2104
Unemployment Tax Payable — State	2105
Federal Income Tax Payable	2106
Dividends Payable — Preferred	2107
Dividends Payable — Common	2108
22 _Long-Term Liability_	
Bonds Payable	2201

(3) STOCKHOLDERS' EQUITY

Capital Stock — Preferred	3101
Capital Stock — Common	3201
Treasury Stock	3201.1
Additional Paid-in Capital	3202
Paid-in Capital from Sale of Treasury Stock	3301
Common Stock Subscribed	3401
Retained Earnings	3501
Income Summary	3601

Income Statement Accounts

(4) OPERATING REVENUE

	Account Number
Sales	4101
Sales Returns and Allowances	4101.1

(5) COST OF MERCHANDISE

Purchases	5101
Purchases Returns and Allowances	5101.1
Purchases Discount	5101.2

(6) OPERATING EXPENSES

61 _Selling Expenses_	
Advertising Expense	6101
Delivery Expense	6102
Depreciation Expense — Delivery Equipment	6103
Depreciation Expense — Store Equipment	6104
Miscellaneous Expense — Sales	6105
Salary Expense — Sales	6106
Supplies Expense — Sales	6107
62 _Administrative Expenses_	
Bad Debts Expense	6201
Depreciation Expense — Office Equipment	6202
Insurance Expense	6203
Miscellaneous Expense — Administrative	6204
Payroll Taxes Expense	6205
Rent Expense	6206
Salary Expense — Administrative	6207
Supplies Expense — Office	6208

(7) OTHER REVENUE

Interest Income	7101

(8) OTHER EXPENSES

Interest Expense	8101
Organization Expense	8102

(9) INCOME TAX

Federal Income Tax	9101

The chart of accounts for the Amcar Corporation is illustrated above for ready reference in your study of Part 7 of this textbook.

Forming a Corporation

15

Businesses may be organized as sole proprietorships, as partnerships, or as corporations. Corporations differ from sole proprietorships principally in the nature of ownership and management.

ORGANIZATION OF A CORPORATION

An organization that has a legal right to act as "one person" and which may be owned by many persons is called a corporation.

Structure of a corporation

Some corporations are organized to conduct business and earn a profit for the owners. Other corporations are organized for non-profit purposes. For example, the American Red Cross is organized as a corporation for charitable and social purposes. Some foundations are incorporated to promote educational and research activities. Governmental units, such as cities or towns, may be incorporated to better serve the needs of their residents. Non-profit corporations depend upon gifts, dues, or taxes for their support.

The ownership of a corporation is divided into units. Each unit of ownership in a corporation is called a share of stock. The owner of one or more shares of a corporation is called a stockholder. The evidence of the number of shares each stockholder owns in a corporation is called a stock certificate. The total shares of ownership in a corporation are called the capital stock.

A corporation may have many owners. Therefore, the owners elect a small group to represent the owners' interests and to be responsible for the management of the corporation. The group of persons elected by the stockholders to manage a corporation is called the board of directors. The board of directors determines the corporate policies and selects the officers to whom the day-to-day management is delegated.

The following typical organization chart indicates the lines of authority extending from the stockholder to the directors to the president and other officers.

Typical organization
chart of a corporation

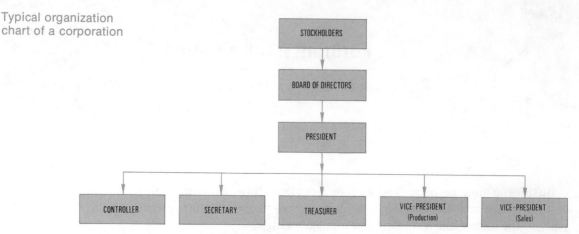

The chief accounting officer of a corporation is often called a controller. The controller supervises a staff of accountants, junior accountants, and accounting clerks. The treasurer has custody of the corporation's funds. The secretary keeps the minutes of the meetings of directors and stockholders and often represents the company in legal matters. One officer may serve as both treasurer and secretary.

Legal requirements to form a corporation

To form a corporation, a properly signed application must be submitted to the designated officials of the state in which the company is to be incorporated. A written application to the proper state or federal agency requesting permission to form a corporation is called the articles of incorporation. When the application is approved, the corporation comes into existence. The approved articles of incorporation are called a charter. A charter is sometimes known as a certificate of incorporation.

The articles of incorporation usually contain the following:

1. Name of the corporation.
2. Purpose of the corporation.
3. Kinds and total number of shares of stock authorized, and the par value of these shares.
4. Amount of capital stock initially subscribed.
5. Term of existence of the corporation.
6. Place where the principal business is to be transacted.
7. Names and addresses of members of first board of directors.

The articles of incorporation for Amcar Corporation are shown on pages 276–277.

Before making application to incorporate, the incorporators give a written promise to buy stock in the corporation. Persons who promise to buy stock of a corporation are called subscribers. The articles of incorporation must state the amount of stock that is subscribed.

When the charter for Amcar Corporation is received by the incorporators, the five persons listed as the first board of directors will hold a meeting. At this meeting, officers of the corporation will be elected.

Characteristics of a corporation

Corporations have some characteristics that differ from sole proprietorships and partnerships.

Advantages of a corporation. The important advantages of a corporation include the following:

1. *Separate legal existence.* With a legal right to act as an artificial "person," a corporation may buy, own, and sell property in its corporate name. A corporation also may incur liabilities and enter into contracts.

2. *Continuous existence.* Stockholders may buy and sell shares without affecting the existence of the corporation, as would be the case in a partnership or sole proprietorship. Thus the life of a corporation can be independent of its owners. A corporation's life may be for a specified time, which is renewable, or it may be unlimited.

3. *Limited liability of the owners.* Unlike a sole proprietor or a partner, a stockholder in a corporation is not liable for the debts of the corporation. Thus a stockholder can never lose more than the amount invested.

Disadvantages of a corporation. The significant disadvantages of a corporation include the following:

1. *Higher taxes.* A corporation must pay a higher rate of taxes on its net income than do the owners of most sole proprietorships. The net income of a corporation, after payment of its income tax, may be distributed to the owners. This net income distribution is considered personal income to the stockholders and is subject to personal income tax. Thus the net income of a corporation is subject to double taxation — first as corporation income and later as personal income when distributed to the stockholders. This taxation differs from that of sole proprietorships and partnerships where net income is taxed only as the personal income of the owners.

2. *Government regulations.* Because corporations come into existence under the terms of state and federal laws, corporations are said to be "creatures of the state." As such, they are subject to much closer governmental control and supervision than are sole proprietorships and partnerships. For example, corporations are generally required to prepare more reports for both federal and state governments.

ARTICLES OF INCORPORATION
OF
AMCAR CORPORATION

The undersigned, for the purpose of forming a corporation for profit under the laws of the State of Florida, hereby adopt the following Articles of Incorporation:

Article I - Name

The name of this corporation is Amcar Corporation.

Article II - Nature of Business

This corporation may engage in any activity or business permitted under the laws of the United States and of the State of Florida.

Article III - Capital Stock

1. The maximum authorized shares of common stock is 10,000 shares at a stated value of $100.00 per share. Each share of common stock will have one vote on every matter coming before the stockholders.
2. The maximum authorized shares of preferred stock is 4,000 shares of 6%, cumulative, nonparticipating preferred stock at a par value of $100.00 per share.

Article IV - Initial Capital

The amount of capital with which this corporation will begin business is not less than Two Hundred Fifty Thousand Dollars ($250,000.00).

Article V - Term

This corporation shall have perpetual existence.

Article VI - Address

1. The present address of the principal office of this corporation in the State of Florida is 4330 North Canal Street, Jacksonville, Florida.
2. The Board of Directors of this corporation may from time to time move its principal office in the State of Florida to any other place in this state.

Article VII - Directors

The number of directors of this corporation shall be determined in accordance with the by-laws but shall never be less than three.

Article VIII - Initial Directors

The names and street addresses of the members of the first Board of Directors of this corporation are:

Janis McCready	18 La Mesa Drive	Jacksonville, FL 32217
N. S. Floyd	6834 Barnett Street	Jacksonville, FL 32209
David C. Adkins	1373 Arbor Circle	Orange Park, FL 32073
Mary L. Deaux	3369 Tara Drive	Jacksonville, FL 32216
Allen Silverstein	986 Cheryl Drive	Jacksonville, FL 32217

Articles of incorporation

CAPITAL STOCK OF A CORPORATION

A corporation's charter indicates the kind and the total amount of capital stock that may be issued.

Article IX - Subscribers

The names and street addresses of the persons signing these articles of incorporation as subscribers are:

Janis McCready	18 La Mesa Drive	Jacksonville, FL 32217
N. S. Floyd	6834 Barnett Street	Jacksonville, FL 32209
David C. Adkins	1373 Arbor Circle	Orange Park, FL 32073
Mary L. Deaux	3369 Tara Drive	Jacksonville, FL 32216
Allen Silverstein	986 Cheryl Drive	Jacksonville, FL 32217

Article X - Beginning of Corporate Existence

Corporate existence shall begin when these articles of incorporation have been filed with and approved by the State of Florida and all filing fees and taxes have been paid.

Article XI - Amendment

This corporation reserves the right to amend or repeal any provisions contained in these articles of incorporation, or any amendment thereto, and any right conferred upon the stockholders is subject to this reservation.

IN WITNESS WHEREOF, we have executed and acknowledged these articles of incorporation this 15th day of December, 1978.

Janis McCready   _Mary G. Deaux_

N. S. Floyd   _Allen Silverstein_

David C. Adkins

STATE OF FLORIDA)
COUNTY OF DUVAL) ss:

Before me, an officer duly authorized in the State and County aforesaid, to take acknowledgments, personally appeared Janis McCready, N. S. Floyd, David C. Adkins, Mary L. Deaux, Allen Silverstein to me known to be the persons described in and who executed the foregoing instrument and they acknowledged before me that they executed the same.

WITNESS my hand and official seal in the County and State aforesaid, this 15th day of December, 1978.

Patricia Wiltse
Notary Public, State of Florida

(SEAL)

My Commission Expires June 30, 1979

Articles of incorporation

The total amount of stock that a corporation may issue is called the authorized capital stock. The total amount of stock that a corporation has sold is called issued capital stock. Occasionally a corporation may buy back some of its issued capital stock. The total amount of capital stock currently owned by stockholders is called outstanding capital stock.

Values of stock certificates

Shares of capital stock are frequently assigned a value and this value is printed on the stock certificate. A money value printed on a stock certificate is called the par value. For example, the charter of Amcar Corporation, pages 276–277, shows that the corporation may issue a total of 4,000 shares of preferred stock for a total value of $400,000.00. Therefore, the par value of each share of preferred stock is $100 ($400,000.00 ÷ 4,000 = $100.00) per share. A share of stock that has an authorized (par) value stated on the stock certificate is called par-value stock.

A share of stock that has no authorized value stated on the stock certificate is called no-par-value stock. Many states require that no-par-value stock be assigned a stated or specified value. No-par-value stock that is assigned a value by the corporation's board of directors is called stated-value stock. Stated-value stock is similar to par-value stock except the amount is not printed on the stock certificate.

Kinds of stock

Owners of stock may have certain basic rights, including:

1. The right to vote at stockholders' meetings.

2. The right to share in earnings of the corporation.

3. The right to maintain the same percentage of ownership in the corporation. If additional stock is issued, existing stockholders have first choice to buy additional shares to maintain their same percentage of ownership. For example, Margaret Zarb owns 100 shares of Ray Corporation. A total of 1,000 shares has been issued. Ms. Zarb owns 10 percent of the corporation. Ray Corporation offers for sale 200 new shares of stock. Ms. Zarb must be given first choice to buy 10 percent, 20 shares, of the new issue. In this way Ms. Zarb can maintain, if she desires, the same percentage of ownership.

4. The right to share in assets of the corporation if it ceases operations and sells all its assets.

Common stock. If a corporation issues only one class of stock, all stockholders have equal rights. Stock that does not give the stockholder any special preferences is called common stock.

If a corporation issues only common stock, the common stockholders are entitled to all the earnings distributed to stockholders. Earnings distributed to stockholders are called dividends.

Preferred stock. In order to attract more investors, a corporation may offer additional kinds of stock with preferences in some of the basic rights. Stock that gives stockholders preference in earnings or other rights is called preferred stock. One or more kinds of preferred stock may be issued, depending upon the basic rights to be given to the preferred stockholders. However the most common preferential treatment is the right to receive dividends before the common stockholders.

Some common types of preferred stock are:

1. *Cumulative preferred stock*. Preferred stock with a provision that the dividends will accumulate from one year to another until they are paid is called cumulative preferred stock. For example, Jardo Corporation has 6% cumulative preferred stock, par value $100.00 a share. The annual dividend should therefore be $6.00 a share. In 1978 the board of directors declared dividends of only $4.00 a share on the preferred stock. No dividends were declared on the common stock. In 1979 the preferred stockholders must receive a total of $8.00 ($2.00 per share unpaid in 1978 plus the total 1979 dividend of $6.00) before a dividend may be paid to the common stockholders.

> Preferred dividends may be stated as a percentage of par value or an amount per share.

2. *Noncumulative preferred stock*. Preferred stock that does not provide that the dividends will accumulate from one year to another is called noncumulative preferred stock. For example, Curtiss Corporation has issued 7% noncumulative preferred stock, par value $100.00 a share. In 1978 the preferred stockholders received $3.00 as dividends. The common stockholders received no share of the earnings in 1978 because the preferred stockholders had not received the full $7.00 a share. Nevertheless, in 1979 the preferred stockholders are entitled to only $7.00 per share of preferred stock. Inasmuch as dividends do not accumulate on the preferred stock of Curtiss Corporation, the common stockholders may receive dividends in any year that the $7.00 dividend to preferred stockholders is paid.

3. *Participating preferred stock*. A corporation may be authorized to issue participating or nonparticipating preferred stock. Preferred stock that is given a right to share with the common stock in profits above a certain amount is called participating preferred stock. Unless designated as being cumulative, participating preferred stock is assumed to be noncumulative.

Disco Corporation has 10,000 shares of 5% participating preferred stock, par value $100.00 a share, and 15,000 shares of no-par-value common stock. The preferred stock is to participate with common stock at an equal rate per share after $5.00 a share has been paid on each kind of stock. The corporation has $140,000.00 available in 1978 to be paid out as dividends. The calculation to determine how much is to be paid per share on each kind of stock is shown on page 280.

Total amount available for dividends	$140,000.00
Regular dividend on preferred stock ($5.00 × 10,000 shares)	50,000.00
Balance remaining..	$ 90,000.00
Dividend on common stock at the rate of $5.00 a share ($5.00 × 15,000)	75,000.00
Amount to be divided at an equal rate per share between the preferred and common stockholders...................................	$ 15,000.00
Participating dividend per share ($15,000.00 ÷ 25,000 shares, the total number of shares of both preferred and common stock)...	$ .60

Summary:
  Preferred stock:

Regular dividend	$5.00	
Participating dividend.......................................	.60	
Total dividend per share	$	5.60

  Common stock:

Total dividend per share ($5.00 + $.60)............................	$	5.60

If the total amount available for dividends in 1979 is $65,000.00, the dividends will be divided as follows:

Total amount available for dividends	$ 65,000.00
Regular dividend on preferred stock. ($5.00 × 10,000 shares)	50,000.00
Balance remaining..	$ 15,000.00
Dividend on common stock ($15,000.00 ÷ 15,000 shares)..........	$ 1.00

Summary:

Preferred stock, regular dividend......................................	$	5.00
Common stock, total dividend per share............................	$	1.00

The preferred stockholders receive only the basic regular dividend of $5.00 per share because a total of $5.00 in dividends has not been paid to the common stockholders.

The preferred stockholders received $5.60 per share in 1978 and only $5.00 per share in 1979. The common stockholders received $5.60 per share in 1978 and only $1.00 per share in 1979.

4. *Nonparticipating preferred stock*. Preferred stock that is not given the right to share in profits with the common stock above a certain amount is called nonparticipating preferred stock. If preferred stock is nonparticipating, the common stock may receive a higher rate of dividend than does the preferred. For example, Warren Corporation has 10,000 shares of 5% nonparticipating preferred stock, par value $100.00 a share, and 15,000 shares of common stock. The corporation has $140,000.00 available to be paid out as dividends. The calculation to determine how much is to be paid on each kind of stock is shown on page 281.

Total amount available for dividends	$140,000.00
Regular dividend on preferred stock ($5.00 × 10,000 shares)	50,000.00
Balance remaining...	$ 90,000.000
Balance remaining divided by total number of shares of common stock ($90,000.00 ÷ 15,000 shares).............................	$ 6.00

Summary:

Preferred stock, regular 5% dividend	$ 5.00
Common stock dividend	$ 6.00

From the viewpoint of the preferred stockholder, cumulative and participating features are most desirable. However every gain of the preferred stockholder comes at the expense of the common stockholder. Therefore, the number of preferential features included in preferred stock issues normally is determined by the demand for the stock and the need for additional capital. The lower the demand, the more important it will be to add desirable features to new preferred stock issues.

CAPITAL ACCOUNTS OF A CORPORATION

Separate capital accounts are kept in the general ledger for each owner of a sole proprietorship or a partnership. However, in a corporation a separate capital account is not kept in the general ledger for each stockholder. Instead a single capital account is kept for each kind of stock issued. When a corporation issues only common stock, all stock issued is recorded in a single capital stock account. When a corporation issues both preferred and common stock, two types of capital stock accounts are used: Capital Stock — Preferred and Capital Stock — Common.

The amount earned by a corporation and not yet distributed to stockholders is called retained earnings. Other terms used instead of retained earnings are earnings retained in the business, retained income, accumulated earnings, and earned surplus.

In a sole proprietorship or a partnership, the net income for a fiscal period is credited to the owner's capital account. However, in a corporation the net income is credited to the general ledger account Retained Earnings. In this way, the amount of net income is kept separate from the recorded values of issued capital stock. If a net loss results from the operations of a fiscal period, the amount is debited to Retained Earnings. If at any time the retained earnings account has a debit balance, the balance is often referred to as a deficit.

The T accounts at the right show the capital of a corporation that has issued $2,000,000.00 of preferred stock and $4,000,000.00 of common stock. The retained earnings account has a credit balance of $1,500,000.00. The total capital of the corporation is $7,500,000.00 ($2,000,000.00 + $4,000,000.00 + $1,500,000.00).

Capital Stock — Preferred 3101
2,000,000.00

Capital Stock — Common 3201
4,000,000.00

Retained Earnings 3501
1,500,000.00

TRANSACTIONS WHEN STARTING A CORPORATION

The incorporators of Amcar Corporation, whose articles of incorporation are shown on pages 276–277, received a charter from the State of Florida. After a charter is granted, a corporation has legal approval for transacting business in the name of the corporation. Like any other business, the corporation needs assets and capital to start functioning.

Amcar Corporation is authorized to issue 10,000 shares of common stock with a stated value of $100.00 a share. Also authorized is 4,000 shares of 6%, cumulative, nonparticipating preferred stock with a par value of $100.00 a share. Each of the five incorporators promises to buy 500 shares of common stock at the stated value. Because the five incorporators promise to buy stock when the corporation is formed, they are also considered subscribers. Thus, a total of 2,500 shares, $250,000.00, was subscribed at the time the application for a charter was made.

Issuing the initial capital stock

On December 15, 1978, the newly formed Amcar Corporation received $250,000.00 from the five subscribers in payment for the common stock they had promised to buy. In return, the corporation issued 500 shares of common stock to each of the five subscribers.

> December 15, 1978. Received cash from five subscribers in full payment for 2,500 shares of common stock at $100.00 a share, $250,000.00. Receipts No. 1–5.

The entry in the cash receipts journal to record the receipt of cash for 2,500 shares of common stock at $100.00 a share is shown below.

	DATE	ACCOUNT TITLE	DOC. NO.	POST. REF.	GENERAL DEBIT	GENERAL CREDIT	SALES CREDIT	ACCOUNTS RECEIVABLE CREDIT	CASH DEBIT	
	1978 Dec. 15	Capital Stock - Common	R1-5			25000000			25000000	1

CASH RECEIPTS JOURNAL   PAGE 1

Entry to record cash received for capital stock

Cash is debited for the amount of cash received, $250,000.00. Capital Stock — Common is credited for the stated value of the stock issued, $250,000.00.

Corporate records of stock issued

The corporation issues a stock certificate to each of the subscribers as they pay for their stock. The stock certificate usually contains a certificate number, the number of shares, the name and address of the owner of the shares, and the date of issue. The stock certificate issued to Janis McCready is shown below.

This Certifies that -----------------Janis McCready----------------- *is the owner of* -----------------five hundred----------------- *fully paid and non-assessable shares without par value of* AMCAR CORPORATION *transferable only on the books of the Corporation by the holder hereof in person or by duly authorized Attorney upon surrender of this Certificate properly endorsed.* Witness *the seal of the Corporation and the signatures of its duly authorized officers.* Dated December 15, 1978

Allen Silverstein *Secretary*

Janis McCready *President*

Stock certificate

A record is also kept showing the stock that is issued to each stockholder. Some corporations handle the transfer and issuance of the new stock certificates as well as the record of stock ownership. Many corporations, however, employ a transfer agent to issue the certificates and keep the stock ownership records.

Subscribing for capital stock and receiving payment on the installment plan

Frequently corporations contract with investors for the sale of capital stock with payment to be received at a later date. When an investor enters into an agreement with a corporation to buy capital stock and pay at a later date, the process is called subscribing for capital stock . The payment may be made all at one time or on the installment plan.

When a corporation receives subscriptions for capital stock to be paid for on the installment plan, each subscription is recorded as follows. The current asset account Subscriptions Receivable is debited and the capital account Capital Stock Subscribed is credited. The asset account Subscriptions Receivable shows the unpaid amount of all subscriptions. The capital account Capital Stock Subscribed shows the total amount of stock subscribed but not issued. This capital account is used because stock certificates are issued only when the stock is fully paid for.

Corporations that sell stock on the installment plan frequently use a special ledger for subscriptions receivable. Each subscriber for capital stock has a separate account in the subscriptions receivable ledger. The subscriptions receivable ledger is similar to an accounts receivable ledger since it shows amounts owed to the business by a number of individuals. The asset account Subscriptions Receivable is a controlling account in the general ledger. Subscriptions Receivable is listed in the chart of accounts under the heading "Current Assets."

Recording a stock subscription. On December 30, 1978, Lee Colclasure subscribed for 200 shares of common stock of Amcar Corporation at $100.00 a share. He agreed to pay $10,000.00 at the time of the subscription and $10,000.00 not later than March 30, 1979.

> *December 30, 1978. Received a subscription from Lee Colclasure for 200 shares of common stock at $100.00 a share, $20,000.00. Subscription No. 1.*

The entry in the general journal to record Mr. Colclasure's subscription for 200 shares of stock is shown below.

Entry to record a subscription receivable

Subscriptions Receivable is debited for $20,000.00, the amount to be received from the subscriber. The account for Lee Colclasure in the subscriptions receivable ledger is also debited for $20,000.00. Common Stock Subscribed is credited for $20,000.00 to show the amount of stock that is to be issued when fully paid.

Recording cash received on a stock subscription. Amcar Corporation received a cash payment from Lee Colclasure in accordance with his agreement to pay half the cost of the stock at the time of the subscription.

> *December 30, 1978. Received cash from Lee Colclasure in part payment of his stock subscription, $10,000.00. Receipt No. 11.*

The entry in the cash receipts journal to record the part payment of Mr. Colclasure's subscription for 200 shares of stock is shown on page 285.

	CASH RECEIPTS JOURNAL				PAGE /

Entry to record cash received on a stock subscription

Cash is debited and Subscriptions Receivable is credited for $10,000.00. Lee Colclasure's account in the subscriptions receivable ledger is also credited for $10,000.00.

A similar entry is made in the cash receipts journal for each installment of cash received on a stock subscription.

> If Amcar Corporation had many entries for subscriptions receivable, the company might have a special column for Subscriptions Receivable Credit in the cash receipts journal. Since the corporation does not expect many entries of this type, a special column is not used.

Recording the issuance of stock previously subscribed. When a subscription is paid in full, a stock certificate is issued to the subscriber.

> *March 30, 1979. Received cash from Lee Colclasure as the final installment on his stock subscription, $10,000.00. Receipt No. 36. Issued a stock certificate for 200 shares. Stock Certificate No. 20.*

The entry to record the receipt of cash is made in the cash receipts journal as illustrated above. Cash is debited and Subscriptions Receivable is credited for $10,000.00. The account of Lee Colclasure is credited for $10,000.00.

The entry in the general journal to record the issuance of stock to Lee Colclasure is shown below.

	GENERAL JOURNAL				PAGE 6

Entry to record the issuance of stock previously subscribed

Common Stock Subscribed is debited for $20,000.00, the total amount of the subscription. Capital Stock — Common is credited for $20,000.00, the total amount of the 200 shares of stock issued. The common stock account is increased by $20,000.00, the amount of the 200 shares of stock issued to Mr. Colclasure.

ORGANIZATION COSTS OF A CORPORATION

The necessary costs of forming a corporation include: (a) an incorporation fee paid to the state; (b) a fee paid to an attorney for preparing the articles of incorporation; and (c) possible travel costs and incidental expenses prior to approval of the articles of incorporation.

Fees and other expenses of organizing a corporation are called organization costs. After the charter has been issued, the corporation normally reimburses the incorporators for the organization costs.

While Amcar Corporation was being formed, Janis McCready, one of the principal incorporators, agreed to pay all of the organization costs.

On December 15, 1978, Ms. McCready submitted a statement of the total costs, $970.00, that she had incurred in connection with starting the corporation.

December 15, 1978. Reimbursed Janis McCready for organization costs, $970.00. Check No. 1.

The entry in the cash payments journal to record this cash payment is shown below.

					GENERAL		ACCOUNTS PAYABLE DEBIT	PURCHASES DISCOUNT CREDIT	CASH CREDIT	
	DATE	ACCOUNT TITLE	CHECK No.	POST. REF.	DEBIT	CREDIT				
1	1978 Dec. 15	Organization Costs	1		97000				97000	1
2										2
3										3
4										4
5										5
6										6

CASH PAYMENTS JOURNAL   PAGE 1

Entry to record payment of organization costs

Organization Costs is debited for $970.00 to record the amount of the costs. **Cash** is credited for $970.00 to record the amount of the check issued to Ms. McCready.

A corporation cannot be formed without organization costs. These costs are as necessary as plant and equipment. To handle organization costs as an expense in the year in which a corporation is formed could unreasonably reduce the net income from operations during the first year of existence. Furthermore, the benefits derived from these expenditures extend over the entire life of the corporation. As a result, these costs are considered to be an asset instead of an expense.

Assets of a nonphysical nature that have value for the business are called intangible assets. The account Organization Costs appears in the chart of accounts under the heading "Intangible Asset."

The adjusting entry to write off organization costs is described in Chapter 17.

BALANCE SHEET OF A CORPORATION

The balance sheet of a corporation is similar to the balance sheet of a sole proprietorship or a partnership. All balance sheets show the assets, liabilities, and capital of a business on a specific date after all accounts have been brought up to date.

The balance sheet of Amcar Corporation on December 31, 1978, is shown below.

```
                          Amcar Corporation
                           Balance Sheet
                         December 31, 1978


                              ASSETS

Current Assets:
  Cash . . . . . . . . . . . . . . . . . . . .  $259,030.00
  Subscriptions Receivable . . . . . . . . . .    10,000.00
  Total Current Assets . . . . . . . . . . . .                $269,030.00

Intangible Asset:
  Organization Costs . . . . . . . . . . . . .                     970.00

Total Assets . . . . . . . . . . . . . . . . .                            $270,000.00

                             CAPITAL

Paid-In Capital:
  Common stock, $100 stated
    value (10,000 shares
    authorized, 2,500 shares
    issued) . . . . . . . . . . . . . . . . .                $250,000.00
  Common stock subscribed . . . . . . . . . .                  20,000.00
  Total Paid-In Capital . . . . . . . . . . .                             $270,000.00

  Total Liabilities and Capital . . . . . . . .                           $270,000.00
```

Balance sheet of corporation

This balance sheet is similar to balance sheets prepared for sole proprietorships and partnerships with the following exception:
1. Subscriptions Receivable is listed in the "Current Assets" section.
2. The capital section for Amcar Corporation contains one account relating to the capital paid in by the stockholders. Capital accounts of

other corporations may include one or more classes of preferred stock as well as common stock.

Corporations use an account, **Retained Earnings**, in the "Capital" section to record the amount of earnings that has been kept in the business. After Amcar Corporation has been in operation and a net income has been earned, the balance sheet will list the retained earnings account in the "Capital" section.

Using Business Terms

✦ What is the meaning of each of the following?

- corporation
- share of stock
- stockholder
- stock certificate
- capital stock
- board of directors
- controller
- articles of incorporation
- charter
- subscribers
- authorized capital stock

- issued capital stock
- outstanding capital stock
- par value
- par-value stock
- no-par-value stock
- stated-value stock
- common stock
- dividends
- preferred stock
- cumulative preferred stock

- noncumulative preferred stock
- participating preferred stock
- nonparticipating preferred stock
- retained earnings
- subscribing for capital stock
- organization costs
- intangible assets

Questions for Individual Study

1. What part do stockholders have in the operation of a corporation?
2. What is the major responsibility of a corporation's board of directors?
3. What kinds of information are contained in the articles of incorporation?
4. What are the advantages of a corporation?
5. What are the disadvantages of a corporation?
6. How does "issued capital stock" differ from "outstanding capital stock"?
7. What basic rights do stockholders normally have?
8. What is the advantage of owning cumulative rather than noncumulative preferred stock?

9. What is the advantage of owning participating preferred stock?
10. What accounts are debited and credited when a corporation receives cash for shares of capital stock?
11. What does a stockholder receive as evidence of the stock purchased?
12. What accounts are debited and credited when a person subscribes for shares of capital stock that are to be paid for at a later date?
13. What account is debited and what account is credited when a corporation receives a partial payment for a stock subscription?
14. After a stock subscription has been paid completely, what accounts are debited and credited to recognize the issuance of the stock?

Cases for Management Decision

CASE 1 Joyce Bolser and Fred Simmons are partners in a department store. They plan to add two more stores in nearby cities. They consider the merits of forming a corporation. They ask you, their accountant, for your recommendation. Should they retain the partnership or form a corporation? Give your recommendation and the reasons for it.

CASE 2 Gary Corbett is considering buying some shares of stock as an investment. He has asked you whether he should buy Crissup Corporation common stock or cumulative, nonparticipating preferred stock. What factors should Mr. Corbett consider in deciding which kind of stock to buy?

PROBLEM 15-1 Recording investments to establish a corporation

Northcut Corporation received its charter January 2 of the current year with authorization to issue 10,000 shares of common stock, stated value $50.00.

Instructions: □ **1.** Record the following selected transactions. Use page 6 of a cash receipts journal, page 5 of a cash payments journal, and page 9 of a general journal similar to the ones illustrated in this chapter.

Jan. 2. Received cash, $150,000.00, from the subscribers in full payment for stock as follows:
   Alvin Brahkage, 3960 Forest Avenue, St. Louis, MO 63119, 1,000 shares, $50,000.00. R1.
   Sondra Jasinski, 5915 Eastern Avenue, St. Louis, MO 63135, 1,000 shares, $50,000.00. R2.
   R. L. Woods, 6461 Woods Street, St. Louis, MO 63122, 1,000 shares, $50,000.00. R3.
   5. Reimbursed Alvin Brahkage for organization costs, $675.00. Ck1.
  16. Received stock subscription from Yvonne Reed, 800 shares at stated value, $40,000.00. Subscription No. 1.

Instructions: □ **2.** Prepare a balance sheet for Northcut Corporation as of January 31 of the current year.

□ **3.** Record the following additional selected transactions.

Feb. 16. Received cash from Yvonne Reed in part payment of her stock subscription, $20,000.00. R8.
Mar. 16. Received cash from Yvonne Reed as the final installment on her stock subscription, $20,000.00. R21. Issued a stock certificate for 800 shares. Stock Certificate No. 50.

PROBLEM 15-2 Calculating the dividends of a corporation

The board of directors of Emick's Corporation approved the following amounts for dividends in four successive years:

| First year | $28,000.00 | Third year | $20,000.00 |
| Second year | 42,000.00 | Fourth year | 70,000.00 |

Emick's Corporation has outstanding 5,000 shares of 6% preferred stock, par value $100.00 a share, and 3,000 shares of no-par-value common stock.

Instructions: □ **1.** Calculate the total amount of dividends paid each year on preferred stock and on common stock if the preferred stock is noncumulative and nonparticipating.

□ **2.** Calculate the total amount of dividends paid each year on preferred stock and on common stock if the preferred stock is cumulative but nonparticipating.

☐ **3.** Calculate the total amount of dividends paid each year on preferred stock and on common stock if the preferred stock is noncumulative but participates at an equal rate per share with common stock after $6.00 a share has been paid on both kinds of stock.

☐ **4.** Calculate the total amount of dividends paid each year on preferred stock and on common stock if the preferred stock is cumulative and participates equally with common stock after $6.00 per share has been paid on both kinds of stock each year.

Optional Problems

MASTERY PROBLEM 15-M Division of corporate income

Janzen Corporation has issued 3,000 shares of 6% cumulative, nonparticipating preferred stock, par value $100.00 a share. It has also issued 4,000 shares of common stock, par value $100.00 a share. The results of operations over a 6 year period are as follows:

1973	$50,000.00	net income	1976	$20,000.00	net income
1974	6,000.00	net income	1977	50,000.00	net income
1975	6,000.00	net loss	1978	45,000.00	net income

At the end of each year in which there are earnings, the board of directors:

(1) Applies the earnings to the accumulated deficit if there is a deficit.
(2) Pays the regular dividend on preferred stock if the balance of the retained earnings account plus the net income for the year is sufficient. No partial payments are made. If there is not a sufficient amount to pay the total dividend to preferred stockholders, no dividend is paid in that year and the current net income is transferred to the retained earnings account.
(3) Pays a 6% dividend on common stock whenever the balance of the retained earnings account plus the net income for the year minus the dividend to preferred stockholders results in a balance of $24,000.00 or more.

The credit balance of the retained earnings account at the beginning of 1973 is $4,000.00. No dividends on the preferred stock have been accumulated to this date.

Instructions: Show the distribution of the net income or loss for each year on columnar paper with the following headings: (a) Year, (b) Net Income, (c) Total of Retained Earnings plus Net Income, (d) Paid to Preferred Stockholders, (e) Paid to Common Stockholders, and (f) Balance of Retained Earnings. (Note: If there are minus items to be written in any column, enclose them with parentheses.)

BONUS PROBLEM 15-B Division of corporate income

Reddick Corporation has issued 4,000 shares of 6% cumulative, participating preferred stock, par value $100.00 a share. Also issued are 10,000 shares of no-par-value common stock. The results of operations over a 6-year period are as follows:

1973	$ 32,000.00	net loss	1976	$150,000.00	net income
1974	34,000.00	net income	1977	170,000.00	net income
1975	110,000.00	net income	1978	230,000.00	net income

At the end of each year in which there are earnings, the board of directors:

(1) Applies the earnings to the accumulated deficit if there is a deficit.

(2) Pays dividends on the preferred stock to the extent that the current net income plus the balance of the retained earnings account permit such payments. No partial payments are made. If the total earnings available are not sufficient to pay the total amount of dividends owed for preferred stock, no dividends are paid that year and the current net income is transferred to the retained earnings account.

(3) When the total amount due for accumulated regular dividends on preferred stock is paid in a year, distributes the balance of the net income for that year as follows: 1/4 as an additional dividend on preferred stock; 1/2 as a dividend on common stock; and 1/4 to retained earnings.

The credit balance of the retained earnings account at the start of 1973 is $3,000.00. No dividends on the preferred stock have been accumulated to this date.

Instructions: □ **1.** Show the distribution of the net income or loss for each year on columnar paper that has the following headings: (a) Year, (b) Income, (c) Paid to Preferred Stockholders — Regular Dividends, (d) Balance Due to Preferred Stockholders, (e) Paid to Preferred Stockholders — Additional Dividends, (f) Paid to Common Stockholders, (g) Transferred to Retained Earnings, (h) Balance of Retained Earnings, (i) Dividends Paid on Each Share of Preferred Stock, and (j) Dividends Paid on Each Share of Common Stock. (Note: If there are minus items to be written in any column, enclose them with parentheses.)

□ **2.** Total the columns Paid to Preferred Stockholders — Regular Dividends and Paid to Preferred Stockholders — Additional Dividends. Add the two totals and divide the sum by 6 years to determine the average amount of dividends paid to preferred stockholders per year.

□ **3.** Determine the average dividend per share of preferred stock per year.

□ **4.** Total the column Paid to Common Stockholders. Divide the total by 6 years to determine the average amount of dividends paid to common stockholders per year.

□ **5.** Determine the average dividend per share of common stock per year.

16

Acquiring Capital for a Corporation

A corporation, like sole proprietorships and partnerships, has three principal sources of capital. Investors may contribute capital by buying stock, the company may retain earnings in the business, or the company may borrow money. However, because of the characteristics of a corporation, discussed in Chapter 15, the processes for acquiring capital for a corporation may be different.

ADDITIONAL CAPITAL STOCK

According to Amcar Corporation's charter, pages 276–277, the corporation is authorized to issue 10,000 shares of common stock and 4,000 shares of preferred stock. Ordinarily a corporation requests authorization to issue more shares than it expects to sell immediately after incorporation. The corporation can then periodically issue more stock as it grows and needs more capital.

Issuing capital stock at par value

On March 10, 1980, Amcar Corporation received $40,000.00 in payment for 400 shares of $100.00 par-value preferred stock.

> *March 10, 1980. Received cash from Jay Sheehan in full payment for 400 shares of preferred stock at $100.00 a share, $40,000.00. Receipt No. 418.*

The entry in the cash journal to record the receipt of cash for 400 shares of preferred stock at $100.00 a share is shown on page 293.

		CASH RECEIPTS JOURNAL			PAGE *18*				
					1	2	3	4	5
					GENERAL		SALES CREDIT	ACCOUNTS RECEIVABLE CREDIT	CASH DEBIT
	DATE	ACCOUNT TITLE	DOC. NO.	POST. REF.	DEBIT	CREDIT			
22	10	*Capital Stock—Preferred*	R418			40 00000			40 00000	22
23										23

Entry to record cash received
for preferred stock at par value

Mr. Sheehan bought and paid for the stock at one time. The stock was not subscribed and paid for at a future date. Therefore, **Subscriptions Receivable** is not affected.

Cash is debited for the amount of cash received, $40,000.00. Capital Stock — Preferred is credited for the par value of the issued stock, $40,000.00.

Issuing capital stock with no par value

Par or stated values of stock may or may not equal the market value of the stock. Since par or stated value is not necessarily the amount paid for the stock, no-par-value stock is becoming more popular. With no-par-value capital stock, the entire amount paid by the investor is recorded in the capital stock account.

Seestra Corporation received $10,000.00 in full payment of 100 shares of no-par-value common stock.

> *May 2, 1980. Received cash from Kevin Behrens in full payment for 100 shares of no-par-value common stock, $10,000.00. Receipt No. 97.*

The entry in the cash receipts journal to record the receipt of cash for the May 2 stock issue is shown below.

		CASH RECEIPTS JOURNAL			PAGE *1*				
					1	2	3	4	5
					GENERAL		SALES CREDIT	ACCOUNTS RECEIVABLE CREDIT	CASH DEBIT
	DATE	ACCOUNT TITLE	DOC. NO.	POST. REF.	DEBIT	CREDIT			
1	*1980 May 2*	*Capital Stock—Common*	R97			10 00000			10 00000	1
2										2

Entry to record cash received
for no-par-value common stock

Three months later the company received $12,000.00 in full payment of an additional 100 shares of no-par-value common stock.

> *August 2, 1980. Received cash from Edith Meramar in full payment for 100 shares of no-par-value common stock, $12,000.00. Receipt No. 124.*

The entry in the cash receipts journal to record the receipt of cash for the August 2 stock issue is shown below.

									GENERAL		SALES CREDIT	ACCOUNTS RECEIVABLE CREDIT	CASH DEBIT		

CASH RECEIPTS JOURNAL — PAGE 5

	DATE	ACCOUNT TITLE	DOC. NO.	POST. REF.	GENERAL DEBIT	GENERAL CREDIT	SALES CREDIT	ACCOUNTS RECEIVABLE CREDIT	CASH DEBIT	
1	1980 Aug. 2	Capital Stock - Common	R124			1200000			1200000	1

Entry to record cash received
for no-par-value common stock

In both entries Cash is debited and Capital Stock — Common is credited for the full amount received.

Issuing capital stock at amounts in addition to par or stated value

Par- or stated-value stock frequently is issued for amounts different from the assigned value. The market value of stock is determined more by how potential investors view the future of the corporation than the assigned par or stated value. The amount above par or stated value paid for capital stock is called additional paid-in capital.

Amcar Corporation has achieved excellent growth and profitability during its first two years. Because of Amcar's success, ownership of the stock is more appealing to potential stockholders in 1980 than in 1978. Consequently potential investors are now willing to pay more for Amcar stock than when the company was first formed.

On August 15, 1980, Amcar Corporation received $60,000.00 in payment for 500 shares of $100.00 stated-value common stock.

> August 15, 1980. Received cash from Susanne Wyer in full payment for 500 shares of common stock at $120.00 a share, $60,000.00. Receipt No. 683.

The entry in the cash receipts journal to record the receipt of cash for 500 shares of common stock at $120.00 a share is shown below.

CASH RECEIPTS JOURNAL — PAGE 28

	DATE	ACCOUNT TITLE	DOC. NO.	POST. REF.	GENERAL DEBIT	GENERAL CREDIT	SALES CREDIT	ACCOUNTS RECEIVABLE CREDIT	CASH DEBIT	
22	15	Capital Stock - Common	R683			5000000			6000000	22
23		Additional Paid-in Capital				1000000				23
24										24

Entry to record cash received for common
stock in addition to stated value

Cash is debited for the amount received, $60,000.00. Capital Stock — Common is credited for the stated value of the stock issued, $50,000.00. Additional Paid-in Capital is credited for the amount above stated value,

$10,000.00. The excess of $10,000.00, although placed in a separate account, is a part of the stockholder's investment. Therefore, the excess is part of the corporation's capital.

Issuing capital stock at a discount

The amount below par or stated value paid for capital stock is called a discount on capital stock. The legal treatment of discounts on capital stock varies from state to state. In some states, the stockholder may be held liable for the amount of the discount if the corporation is unable to pay creditors. In other states, the stockholder is not liable for the amount of discount. If the stockholder is not liable for the amount of discount, the discount is not entered in the accounts.

Hiers Corporation received $18,000.00 in full payment for 2,000 shares of $10.00 par-value common stock.

> *April 1, 1980. Received cash from Deborah Philbin in full payment for 2,000 shares of common stock at $9.00 a share, $18,000.00. Receipt No. 49.*

The entry in the cash receipts journal to record the receipt of cash for 2,000 shares of common stock discounted at $9.00 a share is shown below.

		DATE	ACCOUNT TITLE	DOC. NO.	POST. REF.	GENERAL DEBIT	GENERAL CREDIT	SALES CREDIT	ACCOUNTS RECEIVABLE CREDIT	CASH DEBIT	
						1	2	3	4	5	
1	1980 apr. 1		Capital Stock - Common	R49			20 00000			18 00000	1
2			Discount on Common Stock			2 00000					2

CASH RECEIPTS JOURNAL — PAGE 1

Entry to record cash received for common stock at a discount

Cash is debited for the amount received, $18,000.00. Capital Stock — Common is credited for the par value of the stock issued, $20,000.00. Discount on Common Stock is debited for the amount that cash received is below par, $2,000.00. A discount on capital stock is a contra account and must be deducted from the capital account to determine the amount invested by stockholders.

> Hiers Corporation records discount on capital stock in separate accounts for each class of stock — common and preferred.

Issuing capital stock for assets other than cash

Frequently small corporations may issue capital stock in exchange for assets other than cash. When other assets are exchanged for capital stock, the investor and corporation must agree upon the value of the other assets.

Amcar Corporation agreed with Sheila Paulkavich to issue 100 shares of preferred stock in exchange for two delivery trucks.

> *September 20, 1980. Received two delivery trucks from Sheila Paul-kavich at an agreed value of $10,000.00 in full payment for 100 shares of $100.00 par-value preferred stock. Memorandum No. 19.*

Since cash is not involved in this entry, the general journal is used to record the transaction as shown below.

Entry to record assets other than cash received for capital stock

ACCOUNTS PAYABLE DEBIT	GENERAL DEBIT	DATE	ACCOUNT TITLE	POST. REF.	GENERAL CREDIT	ACCOUNTS RECEIV. CREDIT
	1000000	1980 Sept. 20	Delivery Equipment			
			Capital Stock—Preferred		1000000	
			Receipt of 2 delivery			
			trucks in exchange			
			for 100 shares of preferred			
			stock. Memo. No. 19.			

GENERAL JOURNAL — PAGE 25

Delivery Equipment is debited for the agreed upon amount, $10,000.00. Capital Stock — Preferred is credited for $10,000.00, which is the par value for the preferred stock issued.

TREASURY STOCK

A corporation may buy back some of its own outstanding stock. For example a corporation may buy its own stock so that shares of stock will be available to the corporation's employees under a bonus plan.

A corporation's own stock that has been issued and reacquired but not canceled is called treasury stock. Treasury stock is not an asset. When a corporation buys its own stock, the capital account and the number of shares outstanding are reduced. Therefore the debit balance of the treasury stock account is a deduction from the credit balance of the capital stock account. Treasury Stock thus is a *contra* account and is listed in the chart of accounts, page 272, immediately following Capital Stock.

Since treasury stock is not owned by a stockholder, no one has voting rights for the shares of treasury stock. Also dividends are not paid on treasury stock. However, the treasury stock may be resold at any time unless the stock is canceled. The stock is known as treasury stock only as long as the stock is owned by the corporation. When treasury stock is reissued, the stock again becomes outstanding.

> Generally, preferred stock is not purchased by a corporation as treasury stock. Therefore, treasury stock usually refers to common stock.

Purchasing treasury stock

Normally treasury stock is recorded at the price paid for it by the corporation. On June 2, 1980, Amcar Corporation bought 30 shares of its common stock from Louise Henry for $110.00 a share, $3,300.00.

> June 2, 1980. Paid $3,300.00 to Louise Henry for 30 shares of common stock, $100.00 stated value. Check No. 476.

The entry in the cash payments journal to record the buying of treasury stock is shown below.

					CASH PAYMENTS JOURNAL					PAGE *20*
					1	2	3	4	5	
	DATE	ACCOUNT TITLE	CHECK No.	POST. REF.	GENERAL DEBIT	GENERAL CREDIT	ACCOUNTS PAYABLE DEBIT	PURCHASES DISCOUNT CREDIT	CASH CREDIT	
3	2	*Treasury Stock*	476		3 3 0 0 00				3 3 0 0 00	3

Entry to record acquisition of treasury stock

Treasury Stock is debited and Cash is credited for $3,300.00. Treasury Stock is debited for the full amount paid, $3,300.00, regardless of the amount received for the stock when it was first issued. When this entry is posted, Treasury Stock has a debit balance of $3,300.00.

Selling treasury stock

Treasury stock may be sold at any time and at any price agreed upon by a buyer. The price received may be greater than, less than, or the same as the amount that was paid for the stock.

Selling treasury stock for the cost price. On June 21, 1980, Amcar Corporation sold to Randy Cook 10 shares of the treasury stock purchased June 2, 1980.

> June 21, 1980. Received $1,100.00 cash from Randy Cook for 10 shares of treasury stock at $110.00 a share. Treasury stock was bought June 2, 1980, at $110.00 a share. Receipt No. 581.

The entry in the cash receipts journal to record this sale of treasury stock is shown below.

					CASH RECEIPTS JOURNAL					PAGE *24*
					1	2	3	4	5	
	DATE	ACCOUNT TITLE	DOC. NO.	POST. REF.	GENERAL DEBIT	GENERAL CREDIT	SALES CREDIT	ACCOUNTS RECEIVABLE CREDIT	CASH DEBIT	
15	21	*Treasury Stock*	R581			1 1 0 0 00			1 1 0 0 00	15

Entry to record sale of treasury stock for the cost price

Cash is debited for $1,100.00. Treasury Stock is credited for $1,100.00, the amount Amcar Corporation paid for the treasury stock. Since both amounts are the same, no other accounts are affected.

Selling treasury stock above the cost price. On August 22, 1980, Amcar Corporation sold to Jiles Gwaltney 10 shares of the treasury stock purchased June 2, 1980.

> August 22, 1980. Received $1,200.00 cash from Jiles Gwaltney for 10 shares of treasury stock at $120.00 a share. Treasury stock was bought June 2, 1980, at $110.00 a share. Receipt No. 699.

The entry in the cash receipts journal to record this sale of treasury stock is shown below.

				GENERAL		SALES CREDIT	ACCOUNTS RECEIVABLE CREDIT	CASH DEBIT	
DATE	ACCOUNT TITLE	DOC. NO.	POST. REF.	DEBIT	CREDIT				
22 Treasury Stock		R699			110000			120000	10
Paid-in Capital from Sale									11
of Treasury Stock					10000				12

CASH RECEIPTS JOURNAL — PAGE 29

Entry to record sale of
treasury stock above cost price

Cash is debited for $1,200.00. Paid-in Capital from Sale of Treasury Stock is credited for $100.00. Treasury Stock is credited for $1,100.00, the amount originally paid for the stock (10 shares @ $110.00 a share).

The difference between purchase costs of treasury stock and the amount the stock is sold for is credited to a paid-in capital account. The paid-in capital from sale of treasury stock account is listed in the capital section of the chart of accounts, as shown on page 272.

Selling treasury stock below the cost price. On December 15, 1980, Amcar Corporation sold to Hilda Martz 10 shares of the treasury stock purchased June 2, 1980.

> December 15, 1980. Received $1,050.00 cash from Hilda Martz for 10 shares of treasury stock at $105.00 a share. Treasury stock was bought June 2, 1980, at $110.00 a share. Receipt No. 880.

The entry in the cash receipts journal to record this sale of treasury stock is shown on page 299.

Cash is debited for $1,050.00, Paid-in Capital from Sale of Treasury Stock is debited for $50.00, and Treasury Stock is credited for $1,100.00. Less money is received for the treasury stock than was paid. Therefore the difference is debited to Paid-in Capital from Sale of Treasury Stock.

						GENERAL		SALES CREDIT	ACCOUNTS RECEIVABLE CREDIT	CASH DEBIT	
CASH RECEIPTS JOURNAL						1	2	3	4	5	PAGE *37*
DATE	ACCOUNT TITLE		DOC. NO.	POST. REF.		DEBIT	CREDIT				
3	15 Treasury Stock		R880				110000			105000	3
4	Paid-in Capital from Sale										4
5	of Treasury Stock					5000					5

Entry to record sale of treasury
stock below the cost price

When treasury stock transactions occur, no entry is made in the capital stock accounts. Treasury stock is still considered to be issued stock. The difference between the balances of the capital stock accounts and the treasury stock account is the value of the outstanding stock.

CORPORATE BONDS PAYABLE

A corporation's president or board of directors will decide whether to issue additional stock or to borrow money to expand and develop the business. Several factors will determine which source of money is better. However, an important factor is the cost of borrowing versus the corporation's profitability.

If the decision is to borrow, a corporation may need to borrow a large sum of money for a long period of time. Large loans are sometimes difficult to obtain from one bank or one individual. Therefore, corporations frequently divide the total amount of a large loan into a series of "promises to pay" in $100.00 to $1,000.00 amounts.

A printed promise of a corporation to pay a specified amount at a specified date one or more years in the future and to pay interest at stated intervals is called a bond. Bonds are like promissory notes because they are written promises to pay creditors. However, bonds differ from notes in that they generally run for a long period of time — 5, 10, 20, or more years.

> Corporations borrow money for short periods as well as long periods of time. Normally notes payable are used for short-term borrowing and bonds payable for long-term borrowing.

Obtaining cash by selling bonds is called floating a loan. All the bonds representing the total amount of a loan are called a bond issue. When floating a bond issue, a corporation usually prepares a mortgage in favor of a bank. A note accompanied by a pledge of specified assets to settle the liability if the loan is not paid is called a mortgage. The bank holding a mortgage as security for corporate bonds issued is called a trustee. A bond issue is usually sold to a securities dealer, who then sells individual bonds to the public.

Issuing bonds payable

On June 30, 1980, Amcar Corporation decided to borrow $100,000.00 to construct a new warehouse. The corporation issued 100, 8% interest-bearing mortgage bonds with a par value of $1,000.00. The bonds are to mature in 10 years. The issue was sold at par value to a local securities dealer.

> June 30, 1980. Received cash for the face value of a bond issue of 100 10-year, 8% bonds, par value $1,000.00, $100,000.00. Receipt No. 610.

The entry in the cash receipts journal to record the sale of the bond issue is shown below.

	DATE	ACCOUNT TITLE	DOC. NO.	POST. REF.	GENERAL DEBIT	GENERAL CREDIT	SALES CREDIT	ACCOUNTS RECEIVABLE CREDIT	CASH DEBIT	
22	30	Bonds Payable	R610			100000 00			100000 00	22

CASH RECEIPTS JOURNAL PAGE 25

Entry to record sale of bond issue

In this entry the account **Bonds Payable** is credited for $100,000.00. This credit represents the corporation's promise to pay the bondholders $100,000.00 ten years after the date of issue. Since the bonds will not mature for ten years, **Bonds Payable** is listed in the chart of accounts, page 272, under the caption "Long-Term Liability."

Paying interest on bonds payable

The interest on the bonds issued by Amcar Corporation is payable semiannually. Twice a year the corporation sends a check for $4,000.00 to the trustee to pay the semiannual interest on the bonds.

> December 31, 1980. Paid $4,000.00 to the bond trustee for semiannual interest on bonds payable. Check No. 672.

The entry in the cash payments journal to record this payment of interest on bonds is shown below.

CASH PAYMENTS JOURNAL PAGE 26

	DATE	ACCOUNT TITLE	CHECK NO.	POST. REF.	GENERAL DEBIT	GENERAL CREDIT	ACCOUNTS PAYABLE DEBIT	PURCHASES DISCOUNT CREDIT	CASH CREDIT	
28	31	Interest Expense	672		4000 00				4000 00	28

Entry to record payment of semi-annual interest on bonds

Interest Expense is debited and **Cash** is credited for $4,000.00, the amount of the semiannual interest on the bond issue. The trustee uses the $4,000.00 to issue separate interest payments to each bondholder.

Depositing cash with a trustee for a bond sinking fund

Investors generally want assurance that the bond issue will be paid when due. Amcar Corporation agreed to deposit with the bond trustee each year for ten years an amount of cash equal to 1/10 of the total bond issue. This money is to be used by the trustee solely for paying the bonds at maturity. An amount set aside to pay a bond issue when due is called a bond sinking fund.

> *June 30, 1981. Paid $10,000.00 to the bond trustee for annual deposit to the bond sinking fund. Check No. 891.*

The entry in the cash payments journal to record this deposit to the bond sinking fund is shown below.

| | | | | | GENERAL | | ACCOUNTS PAYABLE DEBIT | PURCHASES DISCOUNT CREDIT | CASH CREDIT | |
| | | | | | 1 | 2 | 3 | 4 | 5 | |
DATE	ACCOUNT TITLE	CHECK No.	POST. REF.		DEBIT	CREDIT				
30	Bond Sinking Fund	891			1000000				1000000	29
										30
										31

In this entry **Bond Sinking Fund** is debited and **Cash** is credited for $10,000.00, the amount of the payment to the bond sinking fund. When the entry is posted, the balance of the account **Bond Sinking Fund** shows that $10,000.00 has been paid to the bond trustee. At the end of the second year, the balance of **Bond Sinking Fund** will be $20,000.00. The bond sinking fund account is an asset. The account is usually listed in the chart of accounts, page 272, immediately preceding the plant assets under the caption "Long-Term Investment."

Entry to record payment to trustee for bond sinking fund

> The bond sinking fund for Amcar Corporation must be increased $10,000.00 every year. However, the trustee invests the bond sinking fund, and any earnings reduce the amount Amcar must contribute to the fund. In future years, the trustee will notify Amcar Corporation how much must be paid into the bond sinking fund for each year.

Retiring bonds payable

Cancellation of a bond issue by paying the bonds at maturity is called retirement of a bond issue. When the bonds of Amcar Corporation mature on June 30, 1990, the bond trustee will use the bond sinking fund to retire the bonds outstanding.

> *June 30, 1990. Received notice from the bond trustee that the bond issue had been retired by using the bond sinking fund to pay the face value of the bonds, $100,000.00. Memorandum No. 143.*

The entry in the general ledger to record the retirement of the entire bond issue is shown below.

				GENERAL JOURNAL			PAGE 33
1	2					3	4
ACCOUNTS PAYABLE DEBIT	GENERAL DEBIT	DATE		ACCOUNT TITLE	POST. REF.	GENERAL CREDIT	ACCOUNTS RECEIV. CREDIT
	10000000	30		Bonds Payable			
				Bond Sinking Fund		10000000	
				Retired issue of first			
				mortgage bonds.			
				Memorandum No. 143.			

Entry to record retirement of bond issue

In this entry Bonds Payable is debited for $100,000.00, the total amount of the bond issue. Bond Sinking Fund is credited for $100,000.00, the total amount previously paid to the trustee bank for retirement of the bond issue. When this entry is posted, both the bonds payable account and the bond sinking fund account will be in balance and the bond issue will be retired.

The bonds issued by Amcar are all due June 30, 1990. Bond issues that are retired on a single date are known as term bonds. For some bond issues, a portion of the issue is retired each year. These bonds are known as serial bonds. For example, 20-year bonds may be issued with 1/10 of the bonds being retired each year beginning with the tenth year.

Capital stock compared with bonds payable as a means of raising capital for a corporation

A comparison of both capital stock and bonds payable is shown in the following chart:

Capital Stock	Bonds Payable
Stockholders are owners of a corporation.	Bondholders are creditors of a corporation.
As owners, stockholders have secondary claims against the assets of a corporation.	As creditors, bondholders have first claim against the assets of a corporation.
Capital Stock is a capital account.	Bonds Payable is a long-term liability account.
Dividends paid to stockholders are distributions of net income of a corporation.	Interest paid to bondholders is an expense of a corporation.
Dividends are not fixed charges that must be paid periodically. Dividends on both common and preferred stock depend upon sufficient earnings to pay dividends.	Interest on bonds is a fixed charge that must be paid periodically and for which the corporation is legally liable. (Bond interest does not depend upon earnings.)

✦ What is the meaning of each of the following?

- additional paid-in capital
- discount on capital stock
- treasury stock
- bond

- floating a loan
- bond issue
- mortgage

- trustee
- bond sinking fund
- retirement of a bond issue

1. What are the three principal sources of capital for a corporation?
2. What portion of the amount received for a share of no-par-value capital stock is recorded in the account Capital Stock?
3. What accounts are debited and credited if a corporation receives $120.00 for one share of $100.00 par-value capital stock?
4. What accounts are debited and credited if a corporation receives $80.00 as a payment in full for one share of $100.00 par-value capital stock?
5. What kind of account is Treasury Stock and where is it listed on the balance sheet?
6. When does treasury stock cease to be called "treasury stock"?

7. What accounts are debited and credited if a corporation receives $120.00 for one share of treasury stock for which the corporation paid $100.00?
8. What entries are made in the account Capital Stock when treasury stock transactions occur?
9. How are bonds and promissory notes similar? How are they different?
10. In which sections of the chart of accounts are (a) the bonds payable account and (b) the bond sinking fund account?
11. Why would a corporation deposit money in a bond sinking fund if the bond payable is not due for 10 years?
12. What accounts are debited and credited when a corporation with a bond sinking fund retires a bond issue?

CASE 1 Arid Corporation needs an additional $200,000.00 with which to expand its business. The board of directors is considering two alternative sources of additional capital: issue bonds or sell additional common stock. The current interest rate on long-term bonds is 8 percent. The company has been paying and expects to continue to pay 5 percent annual dividends on outstanding common stock. The production manager estimates that the expansion will increase net income $20,000.00 annually before taxes and before any interest or dividends on the additional investment. The corporation's income tax rate is 50 percent of net income before taxes. Interest may be deducted from income before the tax rate is applied. To assist the board of directors in making a decision, you are asked to identify the factors that should be considered. Also you are asked for your recommendation and the reasons for it.

CASE 2 Inez Moody owns 100 shares of Amcar Corporation's $100.00 stated-value common stock. If she sells her Amcar Corporation stock to George Adkinson for $120.00 per share, what effect will this transaction have on the corporation's records?

CASE 3 The board of directors of Normal Corporation votes to have the corporation buy 1,000 shares of the corporation's common stock. The board asks you, the controller, if the purchase could be recorded as a debit to the account Investments and a credit to Cash. What is your reply? Explain your reasons.

PROBLEM 16-1 Sale of capital stock

Industrial Supply Corporation began operations two years ago with an authorization to issue 4,000 shares of $50.00 par-value common stock. Currently 2,000 shares have been issued and are outstanding.

Industrial Supply Corporation uses three accounts relating to capital stock:

    Capital Stock   Additional Paid-in Capital   Discount on Capital Stock

Instructions: Record the following selected transactions on page 6 of a cash receipts journal and page 15 of a general journal.

Jan. 5. Received cash from Patty Hutson in full payment for 200 shares of stock, $10,000.00. R219.

Mar. 12. Received cash from J. H. Carter in full payment for 100 shares of stock, $4,900.00. R241.

Apr. 10. Received cash from Opal Hopper in full payment for 150 shares of stock, $7,500.00. R253.

June 5. Received cash from Allen Nicholas in full payment for 200 shares of stock, $10,200.00. R270.

July 2. Received 5 acres of land from Bill Snodgrass in full payment for 200 shares of stock. The land is appraised by an independent appraiser at a value of $10,000.00. M192.

Aug.30. Received cash from Rose Lanham in full payment for 150 shares of stock, $7,800.00. R292.

Nov. 4. Received 2 metal lathes from Lloyd Roush in full payment for 50 shares of stock. The agreed upon value of the 2 lathes is $2,650.00. M215.

PROBLEM 16-2 Transactions for treasury stock

McFarland Manufacturing Company has 10,000 shares of $100.00 stated-value common stock authorized, issued, and outstanding.

Instructions: Record the following selected transactions. Use page 4 of a cash receipts journal and page 10 of a cash payments journal similar to the ones illustrated in this chapter.

Jan. 15. Paid Willard Somers for 50 shares of McFarland Manufacturing Company's common stock, $4,900.00. Ck189.

Jan. 25. Received cash from Tom Parnell for 30 shares of treasury stock, $2,940.00. Treasury stock was bought January 15. R153.

Mar. 12. Paid Lindel McCollum for 100 shares of McFarland Manufacturing Company's common stock, $10,200.00. Ck268.

Apr. 4. Received cash from Bernice Eldred for 20 shares of treasury stock, $2,040.00. Treasury stock was bought January 15. R178.

July 22. Received cash from Hazel Reames for 50 shares of treasury stock, $5,200.00. Treasury stock was bought March 12. R219.

Sept. 5. Received cash from Dixie Blackledge for 50 shares of treasury stock, $5,050.00. Treasury stock was bought March 12. R234.

Oct. 11. Paid Charles Milacek for 200 shares of McFarland Manufacturing Company's common stock, $20,000.00. Ck547.

Dec. 14. Received cash from Alice Sartain for 50 shares of treasury stock, $5,200.00. Treasury stock was bought October 11. R346.

PROBLEM 16-3 Transactions for corporate bonds payable

At the beginning of the annual fiscal period, July 1, 1978, Scofield Company receives $240,000.00 in cash from a 10-year, 8% bond issue. The bond agreement provides that a bond sinking fund is to be set up. The fund is to be increased $24,000.00 at the end of each of the 10 years.

Instructions: □ **1.** Record in a cash receipts journal, page 9, the cash received for the bond issue on July 1, 1978. R1.

□ **2.** Record in a cash payments journal, page 4, the first two semiannual interest payments. Ck223 and Ck418.

□ **3.** Record in the cash payments journal, page 4, the annual amounts transferred to the trustee bank for the bond sinking fund for the first two years. The first payment, June 30, 1979, is $24,000.00. The trustee notifies Scofield Company that the amount due for the June 30, 1980, payment is $22,320.00 ($24,000.00 increase in fund less $1,680.00 interest earned by the fund). Ck419 and Ck792.

□ **4.** In a general journal, page 12, record the retirement of the bond issue at maturity. All interest payments and transfers to the bond sinking fund have been made. M397.

MASTERY PROBLEM 16-M Sale of common and preferred stocks

Santa Fe Corporation is authorized to issue 10,000 shares of no-par-value common stock, of which 5,000 shares were outstanding at the beginning of the year. The corporation is also authorized to issue 5,000 shares of 6% preferred stock, par value $100.00, of which 3,000 shares were outstanding at the beginning of the year.

Santa Fe Corporation uses four accounts relating to capital stock:

Capital Stock — Preferred   Additional Paid-in Capital
Capital Stock — Common   Discount on Capital Stock

Instructions: Record the following selected transactions. Use a cash receipts journal, page 2, and a general journal, page 8, similar to the ones illustrated in this chapter.

Jan. 10. Received cash from Louis Roper in full payment for 200 shares of preferred stock, $20,000.00. R487.

Feb. 15. Received cash from Alvina Meisner in full payment for 100 shares of common stock, $9,600.00. R513.

Mar. 28. Received cash from C. H. Gardner in full payment for 50 shares of preferred stock, $4,900.00. R539.

May 4. Received cash from Rita Cornelsen in full payment for 300 shares of common stock, $30,000.00. R601.

July 9. Received cash from Jack Allison in full payment for 150 shares of preferred stock, $15,150.00. R636.

July 28. Received 15 new office desks from Allied Office Supplies in full payment for 50 shares of preferred stock. The agreed upon value for the 15 desks is $5,150.00. M59.

Oct. 12. Received cash from Harold Kusch in full payment for 200 shares of common stock, $20,500.00. R735.

Nov. 2. Received one used delivery truck from Irvin Pryor in full payment for 40 shares of common stock. The truck is appraised by an independent appraiser at a value of $4,250.00, which is the agreed upon value. M86.

Dec. 16. Received cash from Russell West in full payment for 100 shares of preferred stock, $10,200.00. R811.

BONUS PROBLEM 16-B

Transactions for corporate bonds payable

At the beginning of the annual fiscal period on January 1, 1979, Kimball Corporation receives $1,500,000.00 in cash for a 5-year, 8% bond issue. As part of the bond agreement, the corporation is to increase a bond sinking fund by $300,000.00 each year for 5 years.

Instructions: ☐ **1.** On page 1 of a cash receipts journal like the one shown in this chapter, record the cash received for the bond issue on January 1, 1979. R1.

☐ **2.** On page 5 of a cash payments journal like the one shown in this chapter, record the annual interest payments on December 31 of 1979 and 1980. Ck356 and Ck593.

☐ **3.** On page 5 of the cash payments journal, record the transfer of cash to the bond sinking fund on December 31 of the first two years. The first payment, December 31, 1979, is $300,000.00. The trustee notifies Kimball Corporation that the amount due for the December 31, 1980, payment is $279,000.00 ($300,000.00 increase in fund less $21,000.00 interest earned by the fund). Ck357 and Ck594.

☐ **4.** On page 7 of a general journal, record the retirement of the bond issue at maturity. All interest payments and transfers to the bond sinking fund have been made. M237.

Financial Analysis and Reporting of a Corporation

17

Financial information of a business should be analyzed and reported to persons who have an interest in the welfare of the business. The interested persons in a sole proprietorship and a partnership are often limited to the owners and possibly to some creditors. Those persons interested in the financial condition and progress of a corporation may number in the thousands. One group is the board of directors and officers, who need financial reports to help make sound management decisions. Another group is the stockholders and prospective owners, who need to know how sound the corporation is as an investment. A third group is the bondholders and other creditors, who need to know how well the corporation is meeting its credit obligations.

CORPORATE WORK SHEET

Work sheets for sole proprietorships, partnerships, and corporations generally are similar. Regardless of the type of business, a work sheet is used to plan adjustments and to provide summarized information needed in preparing the income statement and the balance sheet.

The work sheet prepared for Amcar Corporation, pages 308 and 309, is for the fiscal year ended December 31, 1981. Only those adjustments peculiar to Amcar Corporation will be discussed in this chapter. These include two adjustments made only for corporations — corporate organization costs and corporate federal income tax.

Adjustment for writing off organization costs

Federal income tax laws permit organization costs of a newly formed corporation to be treated as an intangible asset. The laws also provide that organization costs may be written off in not less than 5 years. Most corporations do not carry organization costs in the accounts as an asset for an indefinite period of time. The reason for this policy is the true

Amcar Corporation
Work Sheet
For Year Ended December 31, 1981

	ACCT. NO.	TRIAL BALANCE DEBIT	TRIAL BALANCE CREDIT	ADJUSTMENTS DEBIT	ADJUSTMENTS CREDIT	INCOME STATEMENT DEBIT	INCOME STATEMENT CREDIT	BALANCE SHEET DEBIT	BALANCE SHEET CREDIT	
Cash	1101	5822340						5822340		1
Petty Cash	1102	50000						50000		2
Accounts Receivable	1103	8297690						8297690		3
Allow. for Uncoll. Accts.	1103.1		52500		(a) 282880				335380	4
Subscriptions Receivable	1104	200000						200000		5
Merchandise Inventory	1105	17997360		(c) 5079370	(b) 17997360			5079370		6
Supplies - Sales	1106	774980			(d) 452550			522430		7
Supplies - Office	1107	509000			(e) 206220			302780		8
Prepaid Insurance	1108	1470000			(f) 490000			980000		9
Bond Sinking Fund	1201	1000000						1000000		10
Store Equipment	1301	6315000						6315000		11
Accum. Depr.-Store Equip.	1301.1		575000		(g) 337500				912500	12
Delivery Equipment	1302	2625000						2625000		13
Accum. Depr.-Del. Equip.	1302.1		692200		(h) 400000				1092200	14
Office Equipment	1303	1464000						1464000		15
Accum. Depr.-Office Equip.	1303.1		120000		(i) 78150				198150	16
Organization Costs	1401	58200			(j) 19400			38800		17
Accounts Payable	2101		2609050						2609050	18
Employees Inc. Tax Pay.	2102		363070						363070	19
FICA Tax Payable	2103		169650						169650	20
Unempl. Tax Pay.-Federal	2104		6960						6960	21
Unempl. Tax Pay.-State	2105		39150						39150	22
Fed. Inc. Tax Payable	2106				(k) 257444				257444	23
Dividends Pay. -Preferred	2107									24
Dividends Pay.-Common	2108									25
Bonds Payable	2201		10000000						10000000	26
Capital Stock - Preferred	3101		10000000						10000000	27
Capital Stock - Common	3201		48000000						48000000	28
Treasury Stock	3201.1	625000						625000		29
Addl. Paid-in Capital	3202		3000000						3000000	30

	Account	No.							
31	Paid-in Cap. from Sale of Tr. St.	3301							12000
32	Common Stock Sub.	3401							300000
33	Retained Earnings	3501	2326500	(A)					2326500
34	Income Summary	3601	1797360	5040937 0	1797360	5040937 0	1797360 5040937 0		
35	Sales	4101	4347300				4347300		
36	Sales Returns + Allow.	4101.1	378370				378370		
37	Purchases	5101	4293610				4293610		
38	Purch. Returns + Allow.	5101.1	602250					602250	
39	Purchases Discount	5101.2	489120					489120	
40	Advertising Expense	6101	2150000				2150000		
41	Delivery Expense	6102	2670880				2670880		
42	Depr. Exp.- Delivery Equip.	6103		(A) 400000			400000		
43	Depr. Exp.- Store Equip.	6104		(A) 337500			337500		
44	Misc. Expense- Sales	6105	212600				212600		
45	Salary Expense- Sales	6106	9115000				9115000		
46	Supplies Expense- Sales	6107		(A) 252550			252550		
47	Bad Debts Expense	6201		(A) 282880			282880		
48	Depr. Exp.- Office Equip.	6202		(A) 78150			78150		
49	Insurance Expense	6203		(A) 490000			490000		
50	Misc. Expense- Admin.	6204	287020				287020		
51	Payroll Taxes Expense	6205	1099550				1099550		
52	Rent Expense	6206	1800000				1800000		
53	Salary Expense- Admin.	6207	6375000				6375000		
54	Supplies Exp.- Office	6208		(A) 206220			206220		
55	Interest Income	7101	5850						5850
56	Interest Expense	8101	400000				400000		
57	Organization Expense	8102		(A) 9400			9400		
58	Federal Income Tax	9101	2420000	(C) 257440			2677440		
59			24110600 24110600	14749917 34 14749917 34	17 415 3890	786524 10	7819035 4		
60					5462056		5462056		
61	Net Income After 3 Fed. Inc. Tax			17415389 0 17415389 0	786524 10 786524 10				
62									
63									
64									
65									

Work sheet of a corporation

value of an intangible asset that has existed for a number of years is too difficult to determine.

When organization costs are written off, Organization Expense is debited and Organization Costs is credited for the amount to be written off. Organization Expense is not a typical expense caused by business operations. Therefore, Organization Expense appears in the chart of accounts under the heading "Other Expenses." Organization Costs appears under the heading "Intangible Asset" at the end of the asset section.

Amcar Corporation incurred total organization costs of $970.00. The share of the organization costs to be written off each year by Amcar is $194.00 ($970.00 ÷ 5 years = $194.00 a year). In each of the previous years, 1979 and 1980, organization costs of $194.00 were written off, leaving a balance in the organization costs account of $582.00. The 1981 adjustment for writing off organization costs is shown as adjustment (j) in the Adjustments columns of the work sheet, pages 308 and 309. Organization Expense is debited and Organization Costs is credited for $194.00.

Estimated federal income tax

Corporations that anticipate federal income taxes of $40.00 or more are required to estimate their tax. The estimated income tax is paid in quarterly installments in April, June, September, and December. Even though a corporation is on a pay-as-you-go basis, the actual income tax must be figured at the end of the fiscal year. Based on these actual results for the year the corporation must file an annual return. Any tax due but not paid at the end of the year must be paid when the tax return is filed by the corporation. Any overpayment of income tax is refunded to the corporation by the federal government.

Amcar Corporation estimated $24,200.00 federal income tax for 1981 and paid $6,050.00 in each quarterly installment for a total of $24,200.00. Each payment is recorded in the cash payments journal as a debit to Federal Income Tax and a credit to Cash.

Adjustment for federal income tax

Federal income tax is an expense of a corporation. However, the amount of tax depends on the net income before the tax is recorded. To figure the amount of federal income tax and record the adjustment on the work sheet, pages 308 and 309, the following six steps are taken:

☐ 1 Complete all adjustments on the work sheet except the adjustment for federal income tax.

☐ 2 Extend all amounts except the balance of the federal income tax account to the appropriate Income Statement columns or Balance Sheet columns.

☐ **3** Foot the Income Statement columns of the work sheet and find the difference between the two footings. The amount of this difference is the net income before federal income tax. The calculations for Amcar Corporation are as follows:

Footing of Income Statement Credit column $1,947,538.90
Footing of Income Statement Debit column 1,868,460.90
Net income before federal income tax................................. $ 79,078.00

☐ **4** Figure the amount of the federal income tax using the tax rate table furnished by the Internal Revenue Service. The amount of the federal income tax for Amcar Corporation for 1981 is $24,457.44.

> Tax rate tables are distributed by the Internal Revenue Service showing income tax rates for corporations. Each corporation should check a current table to find the applicable rates. Federal income tax rates for corporations at the time this text was written were used to figure federal income taxes for Amcar Corporation.

☐ **5** Record the adjustment for the federal income tax owed in the Adjustments columns of the work sheet. The difference, $257.44, between the total federal income tax and the estimated tax already paid ($24,457.44 − $24,200.00 = $257.44) is shown as adjustment (k) on the work sheet. Federal Income Tax is debited for $257.44 and Federal Income Tax Payable is credited for the same amount.

> Federal Income Tax, an expense account, appears under the special heading "Income Tax" as the last item in the chart of accounts, page 272. Federal Income Tax Payable, a liability account, appears under the heading "Current Liabilities."

☐ **6** Extend the balance of the federal income tax account to the Income Statement Debit column. Extend the balance of the federal income tax payable account to the Balance Sheet Credit column.

Completing the corporate work sheet

The Income Statement columns are totaled and the totals are written as illustrated on page 309. The Income Statement Credit column total is $54,620.56 more than the Income Statement Debit column total. This amount, $54,620.56, is written in the Income Statement Debit column. "Net Income After Federal Income Tax" is written in the Account Title column on the same line as the amount. The Income Statement columns are then totaled and ruled.

The Balance Sheet columns are totaled and the totals are written as shown on page 309. The amount of the net income after federal income tax, $54,620.56, is written in the Balance Sheet Credit column. The Balance Sheet columns are then totaled and ruled.

CORPORATE FINANCIAL STATEMENTS

Amcar Corporation prepares three important financial statements for distribution to interested persons: the income statement, the statement of stockholders' equity, and the balance sheet.

Income statement of a corporation

The income statement is prepared from data in the Income Statement columns of the work sheet. The income statement for the year ended December 31, 1981, is shown on page 313.

Amcar Corporation's income statement differs very little from income statements prepared for sole proprietorships and for partnerships. The three main differences are:

1. **Organization Expense**, which shows the amount of organization costs written off for the period, is reported under the heading "Other Expenses."
2. "Net Income Before Federal Income Tax" is shown.
3. "Net Income After Federal Income Tax" is reported.

   Federal income tax takes a large share of a corporation's total net income. Corporate income statements, therefore, show the net income both before and after federal income tax has been deducted to better report the progress of the business.

Statement of stockholders' equity

The stockholders' equity statement shows the changes that have occurred in the equity of a corporation during a fiscal period. The stockholders' equity statement is similar to the capital statement of a sole proprietorship or a partnership. However, more details are reported in an equity statement than in a capital statement.

A stockholders' equity statement normally reports the equity accounts in two major sections: (a) those relating to paid-in capital and (b) those relating to the profits retained in the corporation. The statement of stockholders' equity of Amcar Corporation for the year ended December 31, 1981, is shown on page 314.

This stockholders' equity statement shows that Amcar started the fiscal year on January 1, 1981, with $380,120.00 "paid-in" capital. This paid-in capital consisted of 500 shares of preferred stock, $50,000.00; 3,200 shares of common stock, $320,000.00; $10,000.00 of additional paid-in capital; and $120.00 of paid-in capital from sale of treasury stock.

During the year, Amcar received $168,000.00 paid-in capital. This addition consisted of $50,000.00 for 500 shares preferred stock, $98,000.00 for 980 shares common stock, and $20,000.00 additional paid-in capital. During the year, however, Amcar paid $6,250.00 for 60 shares of its own

Amcar Corporation
Income Statement
For Year Ended December 31, 1981

Operating Revenue:			
Sales		$1,432,473.00	
Less Sales Returns & Allowances . . .		3,783.70	
Net Sales			$1,428,689.30
Cost of Merchandise Sold:			
Merchandise Inventory, January 1, 1981		$ 179,973.60	
Purchases	$1,422,936.10		
Less: Purch. Ret. & Allow. $6,022.50			
Purchases Discount . 4,891.20	10,913.70		
Net Purchases		1,412,022.40	
Total Cost of Mdse. Avail. for Sale .		$1,591,996.00	
Less Mdse. Inventory, Dec. 31, 1981 .		504,093.70	
Cost of Merchandise Sold			1,087,902.30
Gross Profit on Operations			$ 340,787.00
Operating Expenses:			
Selling Expenses:			
Advertising Expense	$ 21,500.00		
Delivery Expense	26,708.80		
Depreciation Exp.--Delivery Equip. .	4,000.00		
Depreciation Exp.--Store Equip. . .	3,375.00		
Miscellaneous Expense--Sales	2,126.00		
Salary Expense--Sales	91,150.00		
Supplies Expense--Sales	2,525.50		
Total Selling Expenses		$ 151,385.30	
Administrative Expenses:			
Bad Debts Expense	$ 2,828.80		
Depreciation Exp.--Office Equipment	781.50		
Insurance Expense	4,900.00		
Miscellaneous Exp.--Administrative .	2,870.20		
Payroll Taxes Expense	10,995.50		
Rent Expense	18,000.00		
Salary Expense--Administrative . . .	63,750.00		
Supplies Expense--Office	2,062.20		
Total Administrative Expenses . . .		106,188.20	
Total Operating Expenses			257,573.50
Income from Operations			$ 83,213.50
Other Revenue:			
Interest Income		$ 58.50	
Other Expenses:			
Interest Expense	$ 4,000.00		
Organization Expense	194.00		
Total Other Expenses		4,194.00	
Net Deduction			4,135.50
Net Income Before Federal Income Tax . .			$ 79,078.00
Less Federal Income Tax			24,457.44
Net Income After Federal Income Tax . .			$ 54,620.56

Income statement of a corporation

common stock. Thus, at the end of the fiscal year, Amcar Corporation
had paid-in capital outstanding of $541,870.00 ($380,120.00 beginning
paid-in capital plus $168,000.00 additions less $6,250.00 treasury stock on
hand at cost).

```
                              Amcar Corporation
                        Statement of Stockholders' Equity
                        For Year Ended December 31, 1981
```

Paid-in Capital:			
Capital Stock:			
Preferred 6%, $100 Par (4,000 Shares			
Authorized)			
Jan. 1, 1981, 500 Shares Issued	$ 50,000.00		
Issued during 1981, 500 Shares	50,000.00		
Balance, Dec. 31, 1981, 1,000 Shares Issued		$100,000.00	
Common, $100 Stated Value (10,000 Shares			
Authorized)			
Jan. 1, 1981, 3,200 Shares Issued	$320,000.00		
Issued during 1981, 980 Shares	98,000.00		
Balance, Dec. 31, 1981, 4,180 Shares Issued		418,000.00	
Other Capital:			
Additional Paid-in Capital:			
Jan. 1, 1981	$ 10,000.00		
Received during 1981	20,000.00		
Balance, Dec. 31, 1981		30,000.00	
Paid-in Capital from Sale of Treasury Stock,			
Balance, Dec. 31, 1981		120.00	
Total Paid-in Capital on Stock Issued		$548,120.00	
Less Treasury Stock:			
Purchased during 1981 (at Cost)	$ 6,250.00		
Balance, Dec. 31, 1981 (60 Common Shares) . .		6,250.00	
Paid-in Capital Outstanding, Dec. 31, 1981 . .		$541,870.00	
Plus Common Stock Subscribed, Dec. 31, 1981 . .		3,000.00	
Total Paid-in Capital Outstanding and			
Subscribed			$544,870.00
Retained Earnings:			
Jan. 1, 1981		$ 36,865.00	
Plus Net Income After Taxes for 1981	$ 54,620.56		
Less Dividends Declared during 1981	13,600.00		
Net Increase during 1981		41,020.56	
Balance, Dec. 31, 1981			77,885.56
Total Stockholders' Equity, Dec. 31, 1981			$622,755.56

Statement of stockholders' equity of a corporation

✳ The changes in the equity accounts during the year are obtained from
the accounts in the general ledger and the work sheet.

On December 31, 1981, Amcar has $3,000.00 of common stock sub-
scribed. This stock has not yet been paid for in full and the shares have
not been issued. The amount of the common stock subscribed increased
the capital and is therefore added to the amount of paid-in capital outstanding. The amount of paid-in capital outstanding, $541,870.00, plus
the amount of common stock subscribed, $3,000.00, equals the total paid-
in capital outstanding and subscribed on December 31, 1981,
$544,870.00.

For the fiscal year ended December 31, 1981, Amcar Corporation
earned a net income after federal income tax of $54,620.56. This amount
is obtained from the line on the work sheet titled "Net Income After
Federal Income Tax." During the year, dividends of $13,600.00 were de-
clared and paid. This amount is obtained from the general ledger account, **Retained Earnings**. The amount of retained earnings on January 1,

1981, $36,865.00, plus the net income after taxes, $54,620.56, less the dividends declared, $13,600.00, equals the amount of retained earnings on December 31, 1981, $77,885.56. This amount will be the balance in the retained earnings account after all adjusting and closing entries are posted.

The amount of paid-in capital outstanding and subscribed, $544,870.00, plus the amount of retained earnings, $77,885.56, equals the total stockholders' equity of Amcar Corporation on December 31, 1981, $622,755.56.

Balance sheet of a corporation

The balance sheet of a corporation reports the assets, the liabilities, and the stockholders' equity of the business on a specific date, after all accounts have been brought up to date.

The balance sheet of Amcar Corporation on December 31, 1981, is shown on page 316. This balance sheet is similar to those prepared for sole proprietorships and partnerships with the following exceptions.

1. Subscriptions Receivable is listed in the assets section of the balance sheet under the heading "Current Assets."
2. Bond Sinking Fund is listed in the assets section under the heading "Long-Term Investment."
3. Organization Costs is listed in the assets section under the heading "Intangible Asset."
4. The stockholders' equity section contains accounts relating to paid-in capital and to earnings kept in the business. For Amcar Corporation these accounts include Capital Stock — Preferred, Capital Stock — Common, Treasury Stock, Additional Paid-in Capital, Paid-in Capital from Sale of Treasury Stock, Common Stock Subscribed, and Retained Earnings.

When the retained earnings account has a debit balance, the amount of this deficit may be shown in the stockholders' equity section of the balance sheet as a deduction from paid-in capital. For example, at the end of a fiscal period, Huskey Company has a deficit of $13,782.60. The stockholders' equity section of the balance sheet for this company could be shown as follows:

Stockholders' Equity		
Paid-in Capital	$250,000.00	
Less Deficit	13,782.60	
Total Stockholders' Equity		236,217.40
Total Liabilities and Stockholders' Equity . .		$325,410.80

Deficit on a corporate balance sheet

Amcar Corporation
Balance Sheet
December 31, 1981

ASSETS

Current Assets:

Cash		$ 58,223.40
Petty Cash		500.00
Accounts Receivable	$82,976.90	
Less Allowance for Uncollectible Accounts . .	3,353.80	79,623.10
Subscriptions Receivable		2,000.00
Merchandise Inventory		504,093.70
Supplies--Sales		5,224.30
Supplies--Office		3,027.80
Prepaid Insurance		9,800.00
Total Current Assets		$662,492.30

Long-Term Investment:

Bond Sinking Fund		10,000.00

Plant Assets:

Store Equipment	$63,150.00	
Less Accumulated Depr.--Store Equipment . . .	9,125.00	$ 54,025.00
Delivery Equipment	$26,250.00	
Less Accumulated Depr.--Delivery Equipment . .	10,922.00	15,328.00
Office Equipment	$14,640.00	
Less Accumulated Depr.--Office Equipment . . .	1,981.50	12,658.50
Total Plant Assets		82,011.50

Intangible Asset:

Organization Costs		388.00

Total Assets		$754,891.80

LIABILITIES

Current Liabilities:

Accounts Payable	$ 26,090.50	
Employees Income Tax Payable	3,630.70	
FICA Tax Payable	1,696.50	
Unemployment Tax Payable--Federal	69.60	
Unemployment Tax Payable--State	391.50	
Federal Income Tax Payable	257.44	
Total Current Liabilities		$ 32,136.24

Long-Term Liability:

Bonds Payable		100,000.00

Total Liabilities		$132,136.24

STOCKHOLDERS' EQUITY

Total Paid-in Capital	$544,870.00	
Retained Earnings	77,885.56	
Total Stockholders' Equity		622,755.56
Total Liabilities and Stockholders' Equity		$754,891.80

Balance sheet of a corporation

END-OF-PERIOD WORK FOR A CORPORATION

End-of-period work for a corporation, except for differences in the equity accounts, is the same as the work for sole proprietorships and partnerships. After corporate financial statements are prepared, the following end-of-period work must be completed.

1. Journalize and post the adjusting entries.
2. Journalize and post the closing entries.
3. Prepare a post-closing trial balance.

Adjusting entries for a corporation are made from the Adjustments columns of the work sheet as they are for a sole proprietorship or a partnership. The adjusting entries for Amcar Corporation for December 31, 1981, taken from the work sheet, pages 308 and 309, are shown below.

ACCOUNTS PAYABLE DEBIT	GENERAL DEBIT	DATE	ACCOUNT TITLE	POST. REF.	GENERAL CREDIT	ACCOUNTS RECEIV. CREDIT
			Adjusting Entries			
	282880	1981 Dec. 31	Bad Debts Expense			
			Allow. for Uncoll. Accts.		282880	
	17997360	31	Income Summary			
			Merchandise Inventory		17997360	
	50409370	31	Merchandise Inventory			
			Income Summary		50409370	
	252550	31	Supplies Expense—Sales			
			Supplies—Sales		252550	
	206220	31	Supplies Expense—Office			
			Supplies—Office		206220	
	490000	31	Insurance Expense			
			Prepaid Insurance		490000	
	337500	31	Depr. Exp.—Store Equipment			
			Accum. Depr.—Store Equip.		337500	
	400000	31	Depr. Exp.—Delivery Equip.			
			Accum. Depr.—Delivery Equip.		400000	
	78150	31	Depr. Exp.—Office Equipment			
			Accum. Depr.—Office Equip.		78150	
	19400	31	Organization Expense			
			Organization Costs		19400	
	25744	31	Federal Income Tax			
			Federal Income Tax Pay.		25744	

Adjusting entries of a corporation

The closing entries for a corporation are made from the Income Statement columns of the work sheet. However, the final closing entry for a corporation differs from those previously studied. After all revenue and expense balances have been closed to Income Summary, the balance of the income summary account is closed to Retained Earnings. The closing entries for Amcar Corporation on December 31, 1981, are shown below.

| | GENERAL JOURNAL | | | | | PAGE 44 | |
| 1 | 2 | | | | 3 | 4 | |
ACCOUNTS PAYABLE DEBIT	GENERAL DEBIT	DATE	ACCOUNT TITLE	POST. REF.	GENERAL CREDIT	ACCOUNTS RECEIV. CREDIT	
			Closing Entries				1
	4924730 0	1981 Dec. 31	Sales				2
	602250		Purchases Ret. and Allow.				3
	489120		Purchases Discount				4
	5850		Interest Income				5
			Income Summary		4434452 0		6
	17294474	31	Income Summary				7
			Sales Ret. and Allow.		378370		8
			Purchases		4229361 0		9
			Advertising Expense		215000 0		10
			Delivery Expense		267088 0		11
			Depr. Exp.-Delivery Equip.		40000 0		12
			Depr. Exp.-Store Equip.		33750 0		13
			Miscellaneous Exp.-Sales		21260 0		14
			Salary Expense-Sales		911500 0		15
			Supplies Expense-Sales		252550		16
			Bad Debts Expense		282880		17
			Depr. Exp.-Office Equip.		78150		18
			Insurance Expense		49000 0		19
			Miscellaneous Exp.-Admin.		287020		20
			Payroll Taxes Expense		109955 0		21
			Rent Expense		180000 0		22
			Salary Expense-Admin.		637500 0		23
			Supplies Expense-Office		206220		24
			Interest Expense		40000 0		25
			Organization Expense		19400		26
			Federal Income Tax		244574 4		27
	5462056	31	Income Summary				28
			Retained Earnings		5462056		29

After the adjusting and closing entries have been posted, a post-closing trial balance is made to check the accuracy of the journal entries and postings. The account balances for the post-closing trial balance are taken from the general ledger accounts. The post-closing trial balance for Amcar Corporation is shown below.

ACCOUNT TITLE	ACCT. NO.	DEBIT	CREDIT
Amcar Corporation			
Post-Closing Trial Balance			
December 31, 1981			
Cash	1101	5822340	
Petty Cash	1102	50000	
Accounts Receivable	1103	8297690	
Allowance for Uncollectible Accounts	1103.1		335380
Subscriptions Receivable	1104	200000	
Merchandise Inventory	1105	50409370	
Supplies—Sales	1106	522430	
Supplies—Office	1107	302780	
Prepaid Insurance	1108	980000	
Bond Sinking Fund	1201	1000000	
Store Equipment	1301	6315000	
Accumulated Depreciation—Store Equipment	1301.1		912500
Delivery Equipment	1302	2625000	
Accumulated Depreciation—Delivery Equipment	1302.1		1092200
Office Equipment	1303	1464000	
Accumulated Depreciation—Office Equipment	1303.1		198150
Organization Costs	1401	38800	
Accounts Payable	2101		2609050
Employees Income Tax Payable	2102		363070
FICA Tax Payable	2103		169650
Unemployment Tax Payable—Federal	2104		6960
Unemployment Tax Payable—State	2105		39150
Federal Income Tax Payable	2106		25744
Bonds Payable	2201		10000000
Capital Stock—Preferred	3101		10000000
Capital Stock—Common	3201		41800000
Treasury Stock	3201.1	625000	
Additional Paid-in Capital	3202		3000000
Paid-in Capital from Sale of Treasury Stock	3301		12000
Common Stock Subscribed	3401		300000
Retained Earnings	3501		7788556
		78652410	78652410

FEDERAL INCOME TAX RETURN FOR A CORPORATION

A business operating as a corporation must file a federal income tax return (Form 1120) and pay income taxes. The data needed for Form 1120 are taken from the income statement prepared by the corporation. The Form 1120 prepared by Amcar Corporation for the year ended December 31, 1981, is shown below.

Form **1120**	**U.S. Corporation Income Tax Return**	**1981**
Department of the Treasury Internal Revenue Service	For calendar year 1981 or other taxable year beginning ....Jan. 1......., 1981, ending ...Dec. 31......., 19 81 (PLEASE TYPE OR PRINT)	

Check if a—	Name	D Employer identification number
A Consolidated return ☐	Amcar Corporation	74-1324457
B Personal Holding Co. ☐	Number and street	E Date incorporated
C Business Code No. (See page 7 of instructions)	4330 North Canal Street	Dec. 15, 1978
	City or town, State, and ZIP code	F Enter total assets from line 14, column (D), Schedule L (See instruction R)
	Jacksonville, FL 32209	$ 754,891.80

IMPORTANT—Fill in all applicable lines and schedules. If the lines on the schedules are not sufficient, see instruction N.

GROSS INCOME

1 Gross receipts or gross sales...1,432,473.00....Less: Returns and allowances....3,783.70..........	1	1,428,689.30
2 **Less:** Cost of goods sold (Schedule A) and/or operations (attach schedule)	2	1,087,902.30
3 Gross profit	3	340,787.00
4 Dividends (Schedule C)	4	
5 Interest on obligations of the United States and U.S. instrumentalities	5	
6 Other interest	6	58.50
7 Gross rents	7	
8 Gross royalties	8	
9 (a) Net capital gains (attach separate Schedule D)	9(a)	
(b) Ordinary gain or (loss) from Part II, Form 4797 (attach Form 4797)	9(b)	
10 Other income (see instructions—attach schedule)	10	
11 TOTAL income—Add lines 3 through 10	11	340,845.50

DEDUCTIONS

12 Compensation of officers (Schedule E)	12	50,000.00
13 Salaries and wages (not deducted elsewhere)	13	104,900.00
14 Repairs (see instructions)	14	
15 Bad debts (Schedule F if reserve method is used)	15	2,828.80
16 Rents	16	18,000.00
17 Taxes (attach schedule)	17	10,995.50
18 Interest	18	4,000.00
19 Contributions (**not over 5% of line 30 adjusted per instructions—attach schedule**)	19	
20 Amortization (attach schedule)	20	194.00
21 Depreciation (Schedule G)	21	8,156.50
22 Depletion	22	
23 Advertising	23	21,500.00
24 Pension, profit-sharing, etc. plans (see instructions) (enter number of plans ▶ ....) . .	24	
25 Employee benefit programs (see instructions)	25	
26 Other deductions (attach schedule)	26	41,192.70
27 TOTAL deductions—Add lines 12 through 26	27	261,767.50
28 Taxable income before net operating loss deduction and special deductions (line 11 less line 27)	28	79,078.00
29 **Less:** (a) Net operating loss deduction (see instructions—attach schedule) . . │29(a)│		
(b) Special deductions (Schedule I) . . . . │29(b)│		
30 Taxable income (line 28 less line 29)	30	79,078.00
31 TOTAL TAX (Schedule J)	31	24,457.44

Section of Form 1120, U.S. Corporation Income Tax Return

In addition to filing an income tax return with the Internal Revenue Service, a corporation is required to file several other tax-information forms each year. As an employer, the corporation must file a statement showing the total earnings of each employee and the amounts withheld for taxes. The corporation must also file a tax-information form showing the total annual dividends paid to stockholders.

CORPORATE DIVIDENDS

Earnings retained by a corporation are credited to the account Retained Earnings. A corporation frequently retains a part of its earnings to expand and improve the business. Most corporations also try to return a part of their earnings to the stockholders. Corporation earnings distributed to stockholders are known as dividends.

The board of directors of a corporation has the sole authority to distribute dividends to stockholders. The action of the board of directors to distribute a definite amount of corporate earnings to stockholders on a specific date is called declaring a dividend. The board of directors determines when and what amount of dividends will be declared based upon the profitability and future plans of the corporation.

There are three important dates involved in paying a dividend: (1) the date of declaration, (2) the date of record, and (3) the date of payment. The date on which the board of directors of a corporation votes to distribute a specific amount of corporation earnings to stockholders is called the date of declaration. The dividend is paid to stockholders who own stock as of a specific date. The date that determines which stockholders are to receive dividends is called the date of record. The date on which dividends are paid to the stockholders is called the date of payment.

Ordinarily the date of payment is several weeks after the date of record. Thus, the corporation has time to determine who is to receive the dividends, to prepare the dividend checks, and to mail the checks on the date of payment.

Accounting transactions are made on two of the three dates affecting dividends: (a) the date of declaration and (b) the date of payment.

Declaring a dividend

When the board of directors of a corporation declares a dividend, the corporation is obligated to pay the dividend in the future. A liability is incurred by the corporation. This liability must be recorded in the accounting records of the corporation.

> *February 15, 1982. The board of directors of Amcar Corporation voted to declare a dividend of $6.00 a share to preferred and $5.00 a share to common stockholders of record on March 1, 1982. Date of payment is March 15, 1982. Common stock outstanding is 4,120 shares and preferred stock, 1,000 shares. Corporate Minutes, February 15, 1982.*

The entry in the general journal to record the declaration of a dividend is shown on the next page. The amount declared is $6,000.00 ($6.00 a share for 1,000 shares) for preferred stock and $20,600.00 ($5.00 a share for 4,120 shares) for common stock.

			GENERAL JOURNAL			PAGE 46
1	2				3	4
ACCOUNTS PAYABLE DEBIT	GENERAL DEBIT	DATE	ACCOUNT TITLE	POST. REF.	GENERAL CREDIT	ACCOUNTS RECEIV. CREDIT
2660000		*1982* Feb. 15	Retained Earnings			
			Dividends Payable - Preferred		600000	
			Dividends Payable - Common		2060000	
			Corporate Minute Book,			
			board of dir., Feb. 15, 1982.			

Entry to record the declaration of
a dividend by a corporation

Retained Earnings is debited for $26,600.00 to record the reduction in retained earnings. Dividends Payable — Preferred is credited for $6,000.00 and Dividends Payable — Common for $20,600.00 to record the liability the corporation now has for the dividends declared.

Paying a dividend

On March 15, 1982, the date of dividend payment, Amcar Corporation issues one check for the amount of the total dividend.

> March 15, 1982. Paid $26,600.00 cash to stockholders of record as of March 1, 1982, for dividend declared February 15, 1982. Check No. 1207.

This check is deposited in a special dividend checking account. Individual checks for each stockholder are drawn on this special account. The special account is used to avoid a large number of entries in the cash payments journal.

> The special dividend checking account also reserves cash specifically for the paying of dividends. A check is often drawn and given to an agent, such as a bank, who handles the details of sending dividend checks to individual stockholders.

The entry in the cash payments journal to record the payment of $26,600.00 in dividends is shown below.

					GENERAL		ACCOUNTS PAYABLE DEBIT	PURCHASES DISCOUNT CREDIT	CASH CREDIT
CASH PAYMENTS JOURNAL					1	2	3	4	PAGE 40
	DATE	ACCOUNT TITLE	CHECK NO.	POST. REF.	DEBIT	CREDIT			
	15	Dividends Payable - Preferred	1207		600000				2660000
		Dividends Payable - Common			2060000				

Entry to record the payment of dividends

Dividends Payable — Preferred is debited for the amount of preferred dividends paid, $6,000.00. Dividends Payable — Common is debited for the amount of common dividends paid, $20,600.00. Cash is credited for the total amount of cash paid out, $26,600.00. When these entries are posted, the dividends payable accounts are closed.

ANALYSIS OF THE EQUITY OF A CORPORATION

Many persons, especially stockholders and prospective stockholders, may be interested in how well a corporation is progressing and its financial strength. An income statement and a balance sheet give financial information about a corporation. However, a person considering a small investment in a large corporation has difficulty relating corporate financial statements to a few shares of stock. Therefore corporations may report some financial information that is relative to one share of stock, such as equity per share, earnings per share, and price-earnings ratio.

Equity per share

The amount of the total stockholders' equity that belongs to a single share of stock is called equity per share. Equity per share is also known as book value.

If a corporation issues only common stock, the equity per share of stock is figured by dividing the total stockholders' equity of the corporation by the number of shares outstanding.

Deaton Corporation has total stockholders' equity of $250,000.00. The company has 5,000 shares of common stock outstanding and no preferred stock. Equity per share is figured as follows:

Total Stockholders' Equity ÷ Shares Outstanding = Equity per share
$250,000.00 ÷ 5,000 shares = $50.00

Corporations with common and preferred stock must allocate the total equity between the two classes of stock before figuring equity per share. The preferential rights of the preferred stockholders are considered in allocating the equity. Frequently these rights permit the preferred stockholder to share first in assets of the corporation if it ceases to operate. Generally, these preferential rights are par value or some amount above par value. The exact amount is stated on the preferred stock certificate.

On December 31, 1981, Amcar Corporation has $622,755.56 total stockholders' equity with 1,000 shares of preferred stock. The corporation also has 4,120 shares of common stock outstanding (4,180 shares issued less 60 shares treasury stock). Rights of the preferred stock are par value of $100.00 per share. Equity per share for Amcar Corporation is figured as shown on page 324.

Allocation of Total Stockholders' Equity

Total Stockholders' Equity... $622,755.56
Allocated to Preferred Stock:
  1,000 shares × $100.00 par value............................... 100,000.00
Allocated to Common Stock.. $522,755.56

Equity Per Share

Preferred Stock: $100,000.00 ÷ 1,000 shares = $100.00
Common Stock: $522,755.56 ÷ 4,120 shares = $126.88

Earnings per share

The amount of net income earned on one share of common stock during a fiscal period is called earnings per share. Earnings per share are figured by dividing a corporation's net income for a fiscal period by the number of shares of stock outstanding.

For the year ended December 31, 1981, Nuney Corporation earned $100,000.00. Outstanding capital stock was 4,000 shares. Earnings per share are figured as follows:

$100,000.00 net income ÷ 4,000 outstanding shares = $25.00 earnings per share

Preferred stockholders normally have preference rights to receive their dividends first. These rights are printed on the preferred stock certificates. Therefore, preferred stockholders know what their dividends will be if declared. The common stock certificates do not include specific data about dividends to be paid. Therefore, earnings per share are reported on a corporation income statement for common stock only. In this way, the common stockholders are informed about their possible dividends.

Sources of information to figure earnings per share are as follows: (a) net income from the income statement, (b) number of shares outstanding and the preferred dividend requirement from the stockholders' equity statement or the balance sheet. Information needed to figure earnings per share for Amcar Corporation is taken from pages 313 and 314.

Earnings per share of Amcar Corporation common stock for the year ended December 31, 1981, are figured as shown below:

Net income... $54,620.56
Preferred stock dividend requirement (1,000 shares @
  $6.00)... 6,000.00
Net income after preferred dividends............................ $48,620.56

$48,620.56 ÷ 4,120 shares common stock outstanding = $11.80 earnings per share on common stock

Amcar Corporation may list its earnings per share of common stock immediately below the listing of "net income after federal income tax" on its income statement as shown on page 325.

Net Income After Federal Income Tax . .	$	54,620.56
Earnings Per Share on Common Stock . . .	$	11.80

Portion of corporation income statement showing earnings per share on common stock

The earnings per share reported by Amcar Corporation mean that the corporation earned $11.80 for each share of common stock outstanding. Stockholders normally can relate earnings per share more closely than total corporate income to the profitability of the corporation.

Market value per share

Market value of stock is determined by how much a buyer is willing to pay for the stock. Therefore market value is established by persons buying and selling the stock. The market value, however, is never recorded in the corporation's accounts. The amount the corporation receives for the stock when first issued is the amount recorded in the corporation's accounts.

The value at which a share of stock may be sold is called the market value. If the business is profitable, the market value may be higher than the equity per share or the par value. If the business is not profitable, the market value may be lower than the equity per share or the par value.

The illustration at the right shows a section of the financial page of a newspaper. This section reports the market values of stock being bought and sold on the stock market.

Column 1. Name of company and amount of last dividend paid. (General Electric, dividend $1.80.)

Column 2. Hundreds of shares sold on day reported on. (1386 times one hundred shares, or 138,600 shares.)

Column 3. Highest price paid for stock on day reported on. (Highest price paid for General Electric stock is $53.875.)

Column 4. Lowest price paid on stock that day. (Lowest price paid for General Electric stock is $53.25.)

Column 5. Price being paid for stock when stock market activities stopped for the day. (Closing price for General Electric stock is $53.875.)

Column 6. The amount of change, in dollars, in the price from the end of the previous day to the end of the current day. (The change in General Electric stock was +5/8. That is, it increased 62 1/2¢ per share.)

1		2	3	4	5	6
Stocks	Div.	Sales 100s	High	Low	Close	Net Chg.
GenEl	1.80	1386	53 7/8	53 1/4	53 7/8	+ 5/8
GnFood	1.64	284	31 7/8	31 5/8	31 3/4	+ 1/8
GnGth	1.38e	10	23 3/8	23 1/4	23 3/8	− 1/8
GenHost	.60	7	12 1/2	12 1/2	12 1/2	+ 1/8
GenInst	.22t	132	20 1/2	19 7/8	20 1/4	+ 1/4
GnInstr	pf 3	2	36 7/8	36 5/8	36 5/8	− 1/4
GenMed	.30	100	19 1/2	19 1/8	19 1/4	......
GenMills	.88	237	28 1/8	27 5/8	28 1/8	+ 5/8
GnMot	5.80e	2365	67 1/4	65 7/8	66 1/2	+ 1/4
GMot	pf 3.75	1	52	52	52	......
GMot	pf 5	2	70	70	70	......
GenPort		58	7 1/2	7 3/8	7 3/8	− 1/8
GPU	1.68	234	19 1/8	18 7/8	18 7/8	− 1/4
GenRefr	.10e	108	9 1/4	8 3/4	9	+ 3/8
GnSignl	1.04	254	52 7/8	52 1/4	52 5/8	+ 1 1/4
GenSteel		18	6 1/8	6	6 1/8	......
GTelEl	2	950	30 3/8	30	30 1/4	+ 1/4
GTIEl	pf2.50	1	34 1/2	34 1/2	34 1/2	− 1/2
GTIEl	pf2.48	10	28 3/8	28 3/8	28 3/8	− 1/8
GTFl	pf 1.30	y10	16	16	16	+ 5/8
GTFl	pf 8.16	y2000	99 5/8	99 1/2	99 1/2	+ 1 1/8
GTire	1.20b	159	26 7/8	26 1/2	26 1/2	− 1/4
Genesco		207	6 3/8	6 1/8	6 3/8	+ 3/8
Genstar	1.40	4	22	21 5/8	22	+ 1/8
GenuPts	.90	121	32	31 5/8	31 5/8	− 3/8
GaPac	.80b	298	33 5/8	33	33 5/8	+ 1/2
GaPw	pf2.52	2	27 1/2	27 1/2	27 1/2	+ 1/8
GaPw	pf2.75	15	29 3/8	29 1/8	29 3/8	+ 1/8
Gerber	1.30	3056	39 1/2	38 3/4	38 3/4	+ 5 1/2
GettyO	2.70e	55	186	182 1/2	186	+ 2

Price-earnings ratio

Investors normally try to buy stock in companies that are earning a reasonable amount of net income. A price-earnings ratio may be computed as one measure of profitability in relation to investment. The relationship between the earnings per share and the market value per share of stock is called the price-earnings ratio.

Amcar Corporation's earnings per share for 1981 as shown on page 324 are $11.80. If the market price for one share of Amcar common stock is $125.00, the price-earnings ratio per share is figured as follows:

Market price for One Share ÷ Earnings per Share = Price-Earnings Ratio
$125.00 ÷ $11.80 = 10.59 to 1

A price-earnings ratio of 10.59 to 1 means that one share of stock costs 10.59 times what one share earned in the most recent fiscal year. The lower the ratio the more profitable the stock is. Therefore if an investor is comparing Amcar Corporation stock with Largo Corporation Stock with a price-earnings ratio of 20 to 1, Amcar stock would have a preferred price-earnings ratio. A person buying Amcar Corporation stock has a chance of receiving greater dividends than a person buying Largo Corporation stock.

Using Business Terms

✦ What is the meaning of each of the following?

- declaring a dividend
- date of declaration
- date of record
- date of payment
- equity per share
- earnings per share
- market value
- price-earnings ratio

Questions for Individual Study

1. What groups of persons are most likely to be interested in the financial reports of a corporation? For what purpose does each group need them?
2. What account titles on the corporate work sheet, pages 308 and 309, are different from those of a partnership or a sole proprietorship?
3. What are the steps in figuring the federal income tax and recording the adjustment on a corporate work sheet?
4. What are the three main differences between an income statement for Amcar Corporation and an income statement for a sole proprietorship or partnership?
5. What statement of a sole proprietorship or partnership is similar to a corporation's statement of stockholders' equity?
6. A stockholders' equity statement normally reports the equity accounts in which two major sections?
7. In what four ways does the balance sheet of Amcar Corporation on page 316 differ from balance sheets previously studied?

8. When the retained earnings account of a corporation has a deficit, how is the deficit shown on the balance sheet?

9. What is the source of information required to make the closing entries for a corporation?

10. What is the normal source of data needed to prepare a corporation's federal income tax return?

11. Why do corporations usually not pay all of their earnings to their stockholders?

12. What action must be taken and by whom before a corporation can pay a dividend?

13. How is "equity per share" figured for a corporation that has only common stock?

14. How are "earnings per share" figured for a corporation?

15. What is the relationship between a corporation's "equity per share" and its "market value per share"?

Cases for Management Decision

CASE 1 The president of Fannen Corporation makes the following suggestion to you, the corporation's controller. "I think we should drop the statement of stockholders' equity from our financial statements. Stockholders' equity is already shown on our balance sheet and the income statement tells us what we have done for the year. I think the equity statement is unnecessary duplication." Do you agree or disagree? Give reasons for your response.

CASE 2 On December 15, 1978, the board of directors of Owens Corporation votes to pay a $5.00 per share dividend. The dividend is to be paid on February 15, 1979, to stockholders of record on January 15, 1979. After the close of business December 31, 1978, data on the financial statements show that the corporation had a deficit for the year. One of the board members suggests the declared dividends not be paid since there is no legal obligation for corporations to pay dividends. As the accountant for the corporation, what is your response to the board member's suggestion?

CASE 3 Jose Garcia is considering buying some shares of stock in a corporation as an investment. He has narrowed his choice to two companies. Mr. Garcia asks for your recommendation. Data on the two companies are shown at the right.

Give your recommendation and reasons.

	Jackson Corporation	Winston Corporation
Market value per share	$100.00	$50.00
Equity per share	125.00	45.00
Earnings per share	9.00	5.00
Price-earnings ratio	11.1 to 1	10.0 to 1

PROBLEM 17-1 Preparing a work sheet for a corporation

Problems for Applying Concepts

If the workbook correlating with the textbook is not available, complete Review Problem 17-R 1 instead of this problem.

The trial balance of Fashion Fabrics Corporation on December 31 of the current year is given in the Trial Balance columns of an eight-column work sheet in the workbook.

Instructions: Complete the work sheet for the year ended December 31 of the current year. The additional data needed are listed below.

Additional allowance for uncollectible accounts, 3% of balance in Accounts Receivable.
Merchandise inventory, December 31, $137,848.00.
Supplies — Sales inventory, December 31, $503.90.
Supplies — Office inventory, December 31, $581.00.
Value of insurance policies, December 31, $2,700.00.
Annual depreciation on store and office equipment, 10%.
Annual depreciation on delivery equipment, 20%.
Organization costs to be written off, $400.00.
Federal income tax for the year, 22% of net income before federal income tax.

The work sheet prepared in this problem should be retained by the student for use in completing Problems 17-2 and 17-4.

PROBLEM 17-2 ● Preparing financial reports for a corporation

Instructions: □ **1.** From the work sheet completed in Problem 17-1 prepare an income statement for the fiscal period ended December 31 of the current year.

□ **2.** Prepare a stockholders' equity statement. The additional information needed is:

January 1 balance of capital stock account, $140,000.00. (Par value $10.00; 20,000 shares authorized; 14,000 shares issued.)
January 1 balance of additional paid-in capital account, $3,000.00.
January 1 balance of treasury stock account, $2,400.00. (200 shares.)
January 1 balance of retained earnings account, $18,135.12.
Issued 1,000 shares of $10.00 par-value capital stock for $11,000.00 cash on January 2.
Sold one half of treasury stock (100 shares) at cost on January 10.
Dividend of 30 cents per share declared February 15. Dividend paid on April 15 to stockholders of record on March 15, $4,470.00.

□ **3.** Prepare a balance sheet as of December 31.

The financial reports prepared in this problem should be retained by the student for use in completing Problem 17-3.

PROBLEM 17-3 ● Analyzing the equity of a corporation

Instructions: □ **1.** From the financial reports completed in Problem 17-2, figure the equity per share as of December 31.

□ **2.** Figure the earnings per share for the current year.

□ **3.** Figure the price-earnings ratio for the current year. Market value of the stock on December 31 was $14.50 per share.

PROBLEM 17-4 Recording adjusting and closing entries for
a corporation

Instructions: □ **1.** From the work sheet prepared in Problem 17-1, record the adjusting entries on page 14 of a general journal.

□ **2.** Record the closing entries on page 15 of a general journal.

CUSTOM ★ AUTO CENTER
A Business Simulation

You are ready to apply the accounting principles you have learned to the realistic situations included in the Custom Auto Center business simulation. The corporation distributes automobile parts and accessories and uses a voucher accounting system. The books of account are shown above. A symbolic flowchart of the accounting cycle is shown on page 331. A pictorial flowchart is shown on pages 332 and 333.

(The narrative is provided in the set from the publisher.)

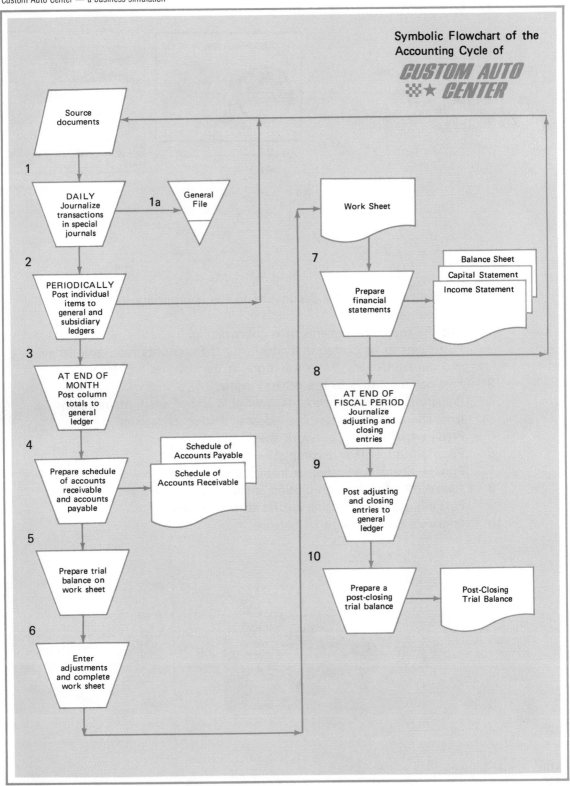

Symbolic Flowchart of the
Accounting Cycle of

CUSTOM AUTO
★ CENTER

Source documents

1 DAILY Journalize transactions in special journals

1a General File

2 PERIODICALLY Post individual items to general and subsidiary ledgers

3 AT END OF MONTH Post column totals to general ledger

4 Prepare schedule of accounts receivable and accounts payable

Schedule of Accounts Payable
Schedule of Accounts Receivable

5 Prepare trial balance on work sheet

6 Enter adjustments and complete work sheet

Work Sheet

7 Prepare financial statements

Balance Sheet
Capital Statement
Income Statement

8 AT END OF FISCAL PERIOD Journalize adjusting and closing entries

9 Post adjusting and closing entries to general ledger

10 Prepare a post-closing trial balance

Post-Closing Trial Balance

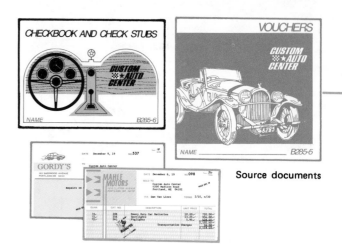

Source documents

Pictorial Flowchart of the Accounting Cycle of

1   Journalize from source documents to the appropriate special journals and registers.

1a   File the source documents after journalizing.

2   Post items to be posted individually to the accounts receivable ledger and general ledger. Enter notations in the voucher register.

3   Post column totals to the general ledger.

4   Prepare schedules of accounts receivable and of accounts payable from the accounts receivable ledger and voucher register.

5   Prepare trial balance on work sheet.

6   Enter adjustments and complete work sheet.

7   Prepare financial statements from the work sheet.

8   Journalize adjusting and closing entries from work sheet.

9   Post adjusting and closing entries to the general ledger.

10   Prepare a post-closing trial balance.

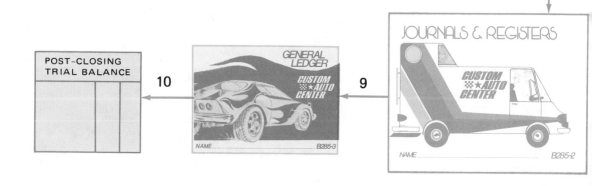

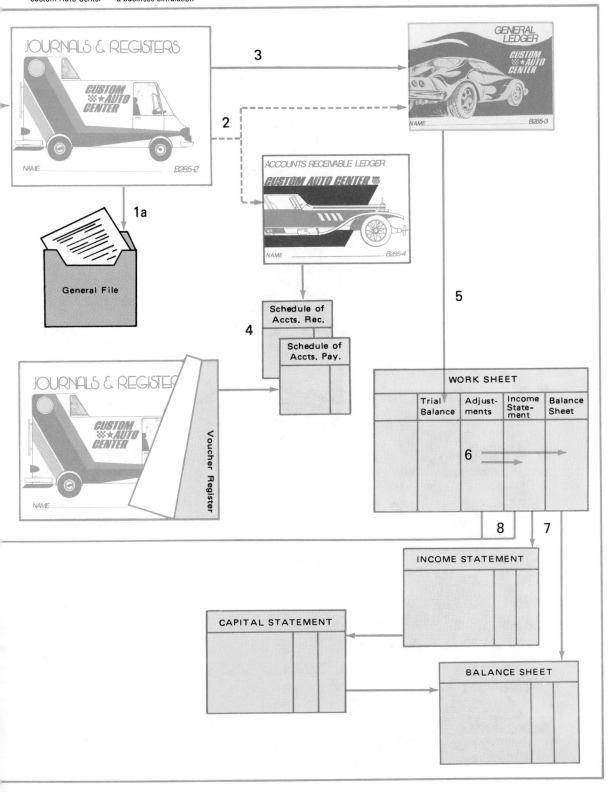

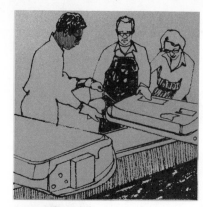

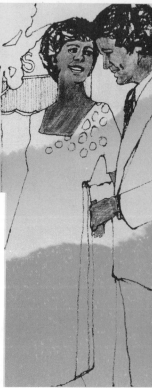

COST ACCOUNTING CLERKS

BUSINESSES USE COST INFORMATION TO CONTROL COSTS. Cost must be controlled for a business to be competitive and to earn net income. Controlling cost requires planned accounting and management practices: (a) managers are responsible for controlling specific costs, (b) cost accounting clerks record each element of cost, and (c) cost accounting clerks prepare cost summaries or reports to be presented to the responsible managers.

COST ACCOUNTING VARIES FOR DIFFERENT TYPES OF BUSINESSES. Merchandising businesses normally emphasize the cost elements (a) cost of goods sold, (b) selling expenses, and (c) administrative expenses. Merchandising businesses may also record cost data separately by departments so cost responsibility can be assigned to departmental managers. Manufacturing businesses normally emphasize the cost elements (a) direct materials, (b) direct labor, and (c) factory overhead in addition to the cost elements of merchandising businesses.

Part 8 of this textbook describes procedures used by two different types of businesses. *Tanler Appliances*, a merchandising business, uses a cost accounting system described in Chapter 18. *Carefree Trailer Company*, a manufacturing business, uses a cost accounting system described in Chapters 19 and 20.

CAREFREE TRAILER COMPANY
CHART OF ACCOUNTS

Balance Sheet Accounts

(1000) ASSETS — Account Number

1100 *Current Assets*

Cash	1101
Petty Cash	1102
Accounts Receivable	1103
Allowance for Uncollectible Accounts	1103.1
Materials	1104
Work in Process	1105
Finished Goods	1106
Prepaid Insurance	1107
Supplies — Factory	1108
Supplies — Sales	1109
Supplies — Office	1110

1200 *Plant Assets*

Factory Equipment	1201
Accumulated Depreciation — Factory Equipment	1201.1
Store Equipment	1202
Accumulated Depreciation — Store Equipment	1202.1
Office Equipment	1203
Accumulated Depreciation — Office Equipment	1203.1
Building	1204
Accumulated Depreciation — Building	1204.1
Land	1205

(2000) LIABILITIES

2100 *Current Liabilities*

Vouchers Payable	2101
Employees Income Tax Payable	2102
FICA Tax Payable	2103
Unemployment Tax Payable — Federal	2104
Unemployment Tax Payable — State	2105
Property Tax Payable	2106
Income Tax Payable — Federal	2107

2200 *Long-Term Liability*

Mortgage Payable	2201

(3000) CAPITAL

Capital Stock	3100
Retained Earnings	3200
Income Summary	3300

Income Statement Accounts

(4000) OPERATING REVENUE — Account Number

Sales	4101
Sales Discount	4101.1

(5000) MANUFACTURING COST

Depreciation Expense — Building	5101
Depreciation Expense — Factory Equipment	5102
Factory Overhead	5103
Heat, Light, and Power	5104
Insurance Expense — Factory	5105
Miscellaneous Expense — Factory	5106
Payroll Taxes Expense — Factory	5107
Property Tax Expense — Factory	5108
Supplies Expense — Factory	5109

(6000) OPERATING EXPENSE

(6100) *Selling Expenses*

Advertising Expense	6101
Delivery Expense	6102
Depreciation Expense — Store Equipment	6103
Misc. Expense — Sales	6104
Salary Expense — Sales	6105
Supplies Expense — Sales	6106

(6200) *Administrative Expenses*

Bad Debts Expense	6201
Depreciation Expense — Building	6202
Depreciation Expense — Office Equipment	6203
Insurance Expense — Office	6204
Miscellaneous Expense — Administrative	6205
Payroll Taxes Expense — Operating	6206
Property Tax Expense — Operating	6207
Salary Expense — Administrative	6208
Supplies Expense — Office	6209

(7000) OTHER REVENUE

Gain on Plant Assets	7101

(8000) OTHER EXPENSES

Interest Expense	8101
Loss on Plant Assets	8102

(9000) INCOME TAX

Federal Income Tax	9101

The chart of accounts for Carefree Trailer Company is illustrated above for ready reference as you study Chapters 19 and 20 in Part 8 of this textbook.

Cost Accounting for a
Merchandising Business

18

A society providing consumers an opportunity to select a product from many choices is dependent upon many types of businesses. Manufacturers make the product. Wholesale distributors store large amounts of the product until needed by retailers. Transportation firms move the product from manufacturers to wholesalers, to retailers, and eventually to consumers. Merchandising businesses gather many products in one location so that consumers may make selections from among the products.

COSTS OF DEPARTMENTALIZED MERCHANDISING BUSINESSES

Costs of operating retail merchandising businesses consist of two kinds: (a) cost of merchandise to be sold, and (b) expenses of operating the business.

Merchandisers buy and resell merchandise as quickly as possible to help consumers and to make a profit. The more quickly a specific piece of merchandise is sold, the greater the possibilities for increased profits. For example, if a furniture store sells one chair every 15 days, the store can sell two chairs in a month. However, if the store can sell one chair every 10 days, three chairs will be sold in a month. Thus, if the store can sell one chair within 10 days of the time the chair is purchased, more profit can be made than if it takes 15 days to sell the chair.

Sometimes a business can sell more merchandise by using an aggressive advertising program to bring more buying customers into the store.

A business may reduce prices to be more competitive and attract new customers. In addition, a business may reduce costs and expenses to realize a greater profit. Merchandising managers must be able to control sales, costs, and expenses in order to increase profits.

The typical income statement for a merchandising business shows net income earned during a fiscal period. However, the income statement does not show data about the departmental profits of the business. Therefore, merchandising businesses often prepare departmental statements to show how each department is contributing to the net income earned by the total business. Assigning control of revenues, costs, and expenses of a business is called responsibility accounting. In responsibility accounting, operating expenses are classified as either direct or indirect expenses. An operating expense chargeable to the operation of a single, specific department is called a direct expense. An operating expense chargeable to the overall operation of the entire business and usually not identified with a single, specific department is called an indirect expense. The cost of supplies used by a specific department is an example of a direct expense. The cost of electricity used by the entire business is an example of an indirect expense.

The revenue earned by a department less its cost of merchandise sold and less its direct expenses is called departmental margin. A statement that reports the departmental margin for a single, specific department is called a departmental margin statement.

Tanler Appliances uses responsibility accounting to help control costs and expenses of the business. Tanler Appliances has two departments: Small Appliances and Large Appliances. Costs of merchandise sold and the direct expenses for each department are recorded in separate general ledger accounts for each department. The general ledger includes the usual accounts plus some that are divided by departments as shown in the portion of the chart of accounts on page 339.

WORK SHEET FOR A DEPARTMENTALIZED MERCHANDISING BUSINESS USING RESPONSIBILITY ACCOUNTING

Tanler Appliances uses an expanded work sheet to help sort data needed for the departmental margin statements. The twelve-column work sheet prepared on April 30, 1979, is shown on pages 340 and 341.

Eight of the amount columns on the work sheet are the same as on work sheets studied previously. Four additional columns are used by Tanler Appliances: Departmental Margin Statement — Small Appliances Debit and Credit; and Departmental Margin Statement — Large Appliances Debit and Credit. Data in these four additional columns are used to prepare departmental margin statements.

TANLER APPLIANCES

Chart of Accounts

(3000) CAPITAL	Account Number
Capital Stock.....................................	3101
Retained Earnings	3201
Income Summary — Small Appliances...	3301
Income Summary — Large Appliances...	3302
Income Summary — General...............	3303

(4000) REVENUE

	Account Number
Sales — Small Appliances....................	4101
Sales Returns and Allowances — Small Appliances....................................	4101.1
Sales — Large Appliances....................	4201
Sales Returns and Allowances — Large Appliances....................................	4201.1

(5000) COST OF MERCHANDISE

	Account Number
Purchases — Small Appliances	5101
Purchases Returns and Allowances — Small Appliances............................	5101.1
Purchases — Large Appliances.............	5201
Purchases Returns and Allowances — Large Appliances............................	5201.1

(6000) DIRECT EXPENSES	Account Number
Advertising Expense — Small Appliances.....................................	6001
Depr. Expense — Store Equipment, Small Appliances............................	6002
Insurance Expense — Small Appliances..	6003
Payroll Taxes Expense — Small Appliances.....................................	6004
Salary Expense — Small Appliances.......	6005
Supplies Expense — Small Appliances ...	6006
Advertising Expense — Large Appliances.....................................	6101
Bad Debts Expense — Large Appliances.	6102
Delivery Expense — Large Appliances...	6103
Depr. Expense — Delivery Equipment, Large Appliances...........................	6104
Depr. Expense — Store Equipment, Large Appliances...........................	6105
Insurance Expense — Large Appliances .	6106
Payroll Taxes Expense — Large Appliances.....................................	6107
Salary Expense — Large Appliances	6108
Supplies Expense — Large Appliances...	6109

(6200) INDIRECT EXPENSES	
Depr. Expense — Office Equipment.......	6201
Insurance Expense — Administrative	6202
Miscellaneous Expense........................	6203
Payroll Taxes Expense — Administrative	6204
Rent Expense	6205
Salary Expense — Administrative	6206
Supplies Expense — Administrative......	6207
Utilities Expense	6208

Portion of chart of accounts for merchandising business using responsibility accounting

Trial balance columns on a twelve-column work sheet

A trial balance is prepared by Tanler Appliances in the same way as previously studied for other kinds of businesses. The trial balance prepared by Tanler Appliances, April 30, 1979, is shown on the work sheet, pages 340 and 341. All accounts in the general ledger are listed whether the accounts have balances or not. Note that there are three income summary accounts. Two are used for summarizing accounts relating to separate departments. Income Summary — General is used for closing indirect expense accounts and departmental margin accounts.

Tanler Appliances
Work Sheet
For Month Ended April 30, 1979

Account Title	Acct. No.	Trial Balance Debit	Trial Balance Credit	Adjustments Debit	Adjustments Credit	Dept. Margin — Small Appliances Debit	Dept. Margin — Small Appliances Credit	Dept. Margin — Large Appliances Debit	Dept. Margin — Large Appliances Credit	Income Statement Debit	Income Statement Credit	Balance Sheet Debit	Balance Sheet Credit
Cash	1101	9384080										9384080	
Accounts Receivable	1102	9021780										9021780	
Allow. for Uncoll. Accts.	1102.1		17840		(a) 90420								108260
Merchandise Inv.-Sm. Appl.	1103	17933400		(b) 19368070	(b) 17933400							19368070	
Merchandise Inv.-Lg. Appl.	1104	18742400		(c) 19341790	(c) 18742400							19341790	
Prepaid Insurance	1105	1860000			(f) 155000							1705000	
Supplies	1106	553500			293000							260500	
Delivery Equipment	1201	2450000										2450000	
Accum. Depr.-Delivery Equip.	1201.1		735000		(d) 40915								775915
Office Equipment	1202	4325000										4325000	
Accum. Depr.-Office Equip.	1202.1		64875		(c) 3590								68465
Store Equip.-Small Appl.	1203	2184000										2184000	
Accum. Depr.-St. Eq.-Sm. Ap.	1203.1		655000		36470								691670
Store Equip.-Large Appl.	1204	548000										548000	
Accum. Depr.-St. Eq.-Lg. Ap.	1204.1		164400		(e) 4550								168950
Accounts Payable	2101		8445630										8445630
Salaries Payable	2102												
Employees Inc. Tax Pay.	2103		854000										854000
FICA Tax Payable	2104		60600										60600
Unempl. Tax Pay.-Federal	2105		10500										10500
Unempl. Tax Pay.-State	2106		22500										22500
Income Tax Pay.-Federal	2107				(d) 613805								613805
Sales Tax Payable	2108		857120										857120
Capital Stock	3101		30000000										30000000
Retained Earnings	3201		17146985										17146985
Income Summary-Sm. Appl.	3301			(b) 17933400	(b) 19368070	17933400	19368070						
Income Summary-Lg. Appl.	3302			(c) 18742400	(c) 18741790			18742400	18741790				
Income Summary-General	3303												
Sales-Small Appliances	4101		9963170				9963170						
Sales-Large Appliances	4101.1	42040				42040							

No.	Account Title	Acct. No.	Trial Balance Dr	Trial Balance Cr	Adjustments (Dr)	Dept. — Small Appl.	Dept. — Large Appl.	Income Statement	Balance Sheet / Other
31	Sales – Large Appliances	4201		1145 1950			1145 1950 (Cr)		
32	Sales Ret.+Allow. – Lg. Appl.	4201.1	549 15				549 15		
33	Purchases – Small Appliances	5101.1	6675220			6675220			
34	Purch. Ret.+Allow. – Sm. Appl.	5101.1		29650		29650 (Cr)			
35	Purchases – Large Appliances	5201	6785000				6785000		
36	Purch. Ret.+Allow. – Lg. Appl.	5201.1		27460			27460 (Cr)		
37	Advertising Exp. – Sm. Appl.	6001	124820			124820			
38	Depr. Exp.–St. Eq. – Sm. Appl.	6002			(p) 36470	36470			
39	Insurance Exp. – Sm. Appl.	6003			(f) 84800	84800			
40	Payroll Taxes Exp. – Sm. Appl.	6004	132388			132388			
41	Salary Exp. – Small Appl.	6005	1439000			1439000			
42	Supplies Exp. – Small Appl.	6006			(q) 117200	117200			
43	Advertising Exp. – Lg. Appl.	6101	176500				176500		
44	Bad Debts Exp. – Lg. Appl.	6102	108260		(a) 90420		198680		
45	Delivery Exp. – Lg. Appl.	6103	293750				293750		
46	Depr. Exp.–Del. Eq. – Lg. Appl.	6104			(b) 409 15		409 15		
47	Depr. Exp.–St. Eq. – Lg. Appl.	6105			(d) 4550		4550		
48	Insurance Exp. – Lg. Appl.	6106			(f) 68200		68200		
49	Payroll Taxes Exp. – Lg. Appl.	6107	123372				123372		
50	Salary Exp. – Large Appl.	6108	1341000				1341000		
51	Supplies Exp. – Large Appl.	6109			(q) 102550		102550		
52	Depr. Exp. – Office Equip.	6201			(c) 3590			3590	
53	Insurance Exp. – Admin.	6202			(f) 2000			2000	
54	Miscellaneous Expense	6203	381640					381640	
55	Payroll Taxes Exp. – Admin.	6204	158240					158240	
56	Rent Expense	6205	1500000					1500000	
57	Salary Expense – Admin.	6206	1720000					1720000	
58	Supplies Expense – Admin.	6207			(q) 73250			73250	
59	Utilities Expense	6208	572475					572475	
60			7913280	7913280		2316 0890	2932 1200	2337 1200	67123410 / 67123410
61	Dept. Margin – Sm. Appl.					2775552		2775552	
62	Dept. Margin – Lg. Appl.						3389368	3389368	
63						2316 0890 2932 1200	2337 1200 2316 0890	3389368 / 3389368	
64	Federal Income Tax	8001			(l) 6138 05			6138 05	44 1195 / 6164920
65								5025000 6164920	49 5720 / 50 5558 00
66	Net Income after Fed. Inc. Tax							1399 20	1399 20
67								6164920 49 5720	60 19 5720
68									

Twelve-column work sheet

Adjustments columns of a twelve-column work sheet

The adjustments planned on a twelve-column work sheet are recorded on the work sheet in the same way as previously studied for other kinds of businesses. However, some adjustments for Tanler Appliances are split between the small appliances and large appliances departments. For example, an adjusting entry for beginning merchandise inventory is made for each of the two departments.

Merchandise Inventory — Small Appliances	1103
Bal. 179,334.00	Adj. 179,334.00

Income Summary — Small Appliances	3301
Adj. 179,334.00	

The balance shown in the trial balance for the account Merchandise Inventory — Small Appliances is $179,334.00. The adjusting entry for this account is shown in the T accounts at the left. This adjustment is shown on the work sheet, pages 340–341, on Lines 4 and 26. A similar adjustment is made for the beginning merchandise inventory of the large appliances department. This adjustment is shown on the work sheet, Lines 5 and 27.

The following adjustments are also split between the two departments:

Item Adjusted	Lines on work sheet
Ending merchandise inventory	Lines 4, 5, 26, and 27
Insurance expense	Lines 6, 39, 48, and 53
Supplies expense	Lines 7, 42, 51, and 58

The remaining adjustments for Tanler Appliances are made on the work sheet in the same way as previously studied. The Adjustments columns are not totaled and ruled until the adjustment for Federal Income Tax is figured. Compare the work sheet for Tanler Appliances, pages 340–341, with the work sheet shown in Chapter 17, pages 308–309.

Completing a twelve-column work sheet

The following basic steps are followed in completing a twelve-column work sheet:

☐ **1** Extend the balance sheet items to the Balance Sheet Debit and Credit columns. (Lines 1–25 of the work sheet, pages 340–341.)

The procedure for extending the balance sheet items is the same as previously studied. When an account is not affected by an adjustment, the amount in either the Trial Balance Debit or Credit column is extended to either the Balance Sheet Debit or Credit column. When an account is affected by an adjustment, the new balance is figured. The new balance is extended to either the Balance Sheet Debit or Credit column.

☐ **2** Extend the revenue, cost, and direct expense items for the small appliances department to the Departmental Margin — Small Appliances Debit and Credit columns. (Lines 26, 29, 30, 33, 34, and 37–42 of the work sheet, pages 340–341.)

The procedure for extending these items is the same as previously studied for income statement items. The exception is that the amounts are extended to the Departmental Margin Statements — Small Appliances Debit and Credit columns.

☐ **3** Extend the revenue, cost, and direct expense items for the large appliances department to the Departmental Margin Statements — Large Appliances Debit and Credit columns. (Lines 27, 31, 32, 35, 36, and 43–51 of the work sheet, pages 340–341.)

The procedure for extending these items is the same as that for the items applying to the small appliances department described in Step 2.

☐ **4** Extend the remaining expense items to the Income Statement Debit columns. (Lines 52–59 of the work sheet, pages 340–341.)

☐ **5** Figure the departmental margin for each department. (Lines 61 and 62 of the work sheet, pages 340–341.)

Rule a single line across the Departmental Margin Statements — Small Appliances Debit and Credit columns on the line with the last account not including Federal Income Tax. Add each column and write the totals under the ruled line. (Line 60 of the work sheet.) Subtract the smaller total from the larger total ($293,608.90 − $265,853.38 = $27,755.52). Write the difference, $27,755.52, in the Departmental Margin Statements — Small Appliances Debit column on the next line. Also, write the same amount in the Income Statement Credit column. Write the words *Dept. Margin — Sm. Appl.* on the same line in the Account Title column. The amount written on this line, $27,755.52, is the departmental margin for the small appliances department for the month ended April 30, 1979.

The same procedure is followed to find the departmental margin for the large appliances department. This departmental margin is recorded on the work sheet in the Departmental Margin Statements — Large Appliances Debit column and in the Income Statement Credit column. The totals, Large Appliances Debit and Credit columns are begun on the same line as the small appliances totals. The departmental margin is entered on the next line under the departmental margin for small appliances. (Lines 60–62 of the work sheet.)

The Departmental Margin Statement columns for the two departments are totaled and ruled as shown on Line 63 of the work sheet.

☐ **6** Figure the expense for federal income tax by footing the Income Statement columns and finding the tax on the difference between the two column totals. Enter the proper amount for the tax liability in the Adjustments columns. (See Chapter 17, pages 310–311, for an explanation of this adjustment.) Total and rule the Adjustments columns. Extend the federal income tax liability balance to the Balance Sheet columns. Extend the federal income tax expense balance to the Income Statement columns.

☐ **7** Figure the net income in the Income Statement columns of the work sheet. Rule a single line across the Income Statement Debit and Credit columns below the last amount recorded in these columns. (Line 64 of the work sheet, pages 340–341.) The two Income Statement columns are totaled as shown on Line 65 of the work sheet. The difference between the two totals is found ($61,649.20 − $50,250.00 = $11,399.20). The difference, $11,399.20, is the net income after taxes for the total business for the month ended April 30, 1979. Write the difference on the next line in the Income Statement Debit column (the column with the smaller total). Write the words *Net Income After Fed. Inc. Tax* in the Account Title column on the same line as the amount of net income. The two Income Statement columns are totaled again and ruled as shown on Line 67 of the work sheet. The procedure for totaling and ruling the Income Statement columns is the same as for work sheets previously studied.

☐ **8** Complete the Balance Sheet columns of a work sheet. The amount of net income figured for the Income Statement columns is written in the Balance Sheet Credit column. The Balance Sheet columns are totaled and ruled in the same manner as on work sheets previously studied. (Line 67 of the work sheet, pages 340–341.)

Generally the procedures for completing a twelve-column work sheet are the same as for work sheets previously studied. The differences are in: (a) extending amounts to the Departmental Margin Statements columns, (b) figuring departmental margin, and (c) completing the Income Statement columns.

FINANCIAL STATEMENTS FOR A MERCHANDISING BUSINESS USING RESPONSIBILITY ACCOUNTING

Tanler Appliances prepares the usual financial statements at the end of a fiscal period: income statement, stockholders' equity statement, and balance sheet. In addition, Tanler Appliances prepares two responsibility statements: (a) departmental margin statement — small appliances and (b) departmental margin statement — large appliances. Financial statements showing revenue, costs, and direct expenses that are under the control of a specific department are called responsibility statements. The two departmental margin statements prepared by Tanler Appliances are responsibility statements.

Departmental margin statements

Major responsibility for improving the financial condition of Tanler Appliances rests with the departmental managers. To help these managers make management decisions, two responsibility statements are prepared to provide data about the progress of the two departments.

Tanler Appliances' departmental margin statement — small appliances, shown for the month ended April 30, 1979, is below. The data for this statement are taken from the Departmental Margin — Small Appliances columns of the work sheet, pages 340 and 341.

The departmental margin statement includes data about revenue, cost of merchandise sold, and the *direct expenses* which can be identified with the small appliances department. The departmental margin statement is a type of income statement for the small appliances department. The statement is prepared in much the same form as an income statement. However, only direct expenses for the small appliances department are included on the statement.

```
                              Tanler Appliances                        Schedule A
                   Departmental Margin Statement--Small Appliances
                          For Month Ended April 30, 1979


                                                                         *% of
                                                                       Net Sales
  Revenue:
    Sales  . . . . . . . . . . . . . . . . . .   $ 99,631.70             100.4
    Less Sales Returns and Allowances  . . . . . .    420.40               0.4
    Net Sales . . . . . . . . . . . . . . . . .               $99,211.30  100.0
  Cost of Merchandise Sold:
    Merchandise Inventory, April 1, 1979 . . . . .  $179,334.00           180.8
    Purchases . . . . . . . . . . . . . .  $66,752.20                      67.3
    Less Purchases Returns and Allowances    296.50                         0.3
    Net Purchases . . . . . . . . . . . . .        66,455.70               67.0
    Total Cost of Merchandise Available for Sale . . $245,789.70          247.7
    Less Merchandise Inventory, April 30, 1979 . . .  193,680.70          195.2
    Cost of Merchandise Sold . . . . . . . . . . .              52,109.00   52.5
  Gross Profit . . . . . . . . . . . . . . . .                 $47,102.30   47.5
  Direct Departmental Expenses:
    Advertising Expense  . . . . . . . . . . . . . $  1,248.20              1.3
    Depreciation Expense--Store Equipment  . . . . .   364.70               0.4
    Insurance Expense . . . . . . . . . . . . . . .    848.00               0.9
    Payroll Taxes Expense . . . . . . . . . . . . .  1,323.88               1.3
    Salary Expense . . . . . . . . . . . . . . . .  14,390.00              14.5
    Supplies Expense . . . . . . . . . . . . . . .   1,172.00               1.2
    Total Direct Departmental Expenses . . . . . . .            19,346.78   19.5
  Departmental Margin . . . . . . . . . . . . . .              $27,755.52   28.0


  *Each item rounded to nearest 0.1%
```

Tanler Appliances includes a Percentage of Net Sales column on the departmental margin statements to help interpret data. The amounts in this column are figured by dividing the amount on each line by the amount of departmental *net* sales. For example, on the departmental margin statement — small appliances, page 345, the cost of merchandise sold percentage is figured as:

Cost of Merchandise Sold   ÷   Net Sales   =   Percentage of Net sales

$52,109.00   ÷ $99,211.30   =   52.5%

This percentage is interpreted as 52.5% of the revenue received from net sales is needed to cover the cost of the merchandise sold. More than half, 52.5%, of the revenue from net sales is needed to purchase the merchandise that was sold to produce the revenue.

Percentages for the current fiscal period are compared to similar percentages for previous fiscal periods. For example, the manager of the small appliances department finds these figures on departmental margin statements:

	Percentages for		
	April, 1979	March, 1979	February, 1979
Cost of Merchandise Sold	52.5%	53.7%	55.6%

The manager reaches a conclusion from these percentages. A smaller percentage of the revenue from net sales is needed to purchase the merchandise sold than was needed for each of the past two months. The percentage has gone from 55.6% in February to 52.5% in April. A greater amount of the revenue, therefore, is available to pay for direct expenses or to increase the amount of departmental margin for the department. The goal is always to decrease the percentage of costs and expenses so that net income increases.

When changes in percentages occur for an item on the departmental margin statement, the departmental manager seeks the reasons for the changes. If the changes are good, the policies resulting in the favorable changes are continued. If the changes are not good, the manager seeks to change policies to prevent the unfavorable changes.

Sometimes sales revenue increases because of special sales and advertising programs. Sometimes the cost of merchandise percentages change because lower prices are obtained when merchandise is purchased. At other times the percentages change because of a drop in sales or because of a general increase in the cost of merchandise purchased. Without the data on the departmental margin statements, the departmental manager will not know which policies to continue and which to change.

Tanler Appliances prepares a departmental margin statement for the large appliances department as well as for the small appliances department. The departmental margin statement — large appliances for the month ended April 30, 1979, is shown on page 347.

Tanler Appliances   Schedule B
Departmental Margin Statement--Large Appliances
For Month Ended April 30, 1979

			*% of Net Sales
Revenue:			
Sales	$114,519.50		100.5
Less Sales Returns and Allowances	549.15		0.5
Net Sales		$113,970.35	100.0
Cost of Merchandise Sold:			
Merchandise Inventory, April 1, 1979	$137,424.00		120.6
Purchases	$67,850.00		59.5
Less Purchases Returns and Allowances	274.60		0.2
Net Purchases	67,575.40		59.3
Total Cost of Merchandise Available for Sale	$204,999.40		179.9
Less Merchandise Inventory, April 30, 1979	148,417.90		130.2
Cost of Merchandise Sold		56,581.50	49.6
Gross Profit		$ 57,388.85	50.4
Direct Departmental Expenses:			
Advertising Expense	$ 1,765.00		1.5
Bad Debts Expense	1,986.80		1.7
Delivery Expense	2,937.50		2.6
Depreciation Expense--Delivery Equipment	409.15		0.4
Depreciation Expense--Store Equipment	45.50		0.0
Insurance Expense	682.00		0.6
Payroll Taxes Expense	1,233.72		1.1
Salary Expense	13,410.00		11.8
Supplies Expense	1,025.50		0.9
Total Direct Departmental Expenses		23,495.17	20.6
Departmental Margin		$ 33,893.68	29.7

*Rounded to nearest 0.1%

Departmental margin statement for a
merchandising business

Income statement

An income statement for Tanler Appliances reports revenues, cost of
merchandise sold, gross profit, direct expenses, departmental margin, indirect expenses, federal income tax, and net income. The income statement for Tanler Appliances prepared on April 30, 1979, is shown on page
348.

The data for the income statement are taken from the departmental
margin statements for the two departments and from the Income Statement columns of the work sheet, pages 340–341. The income statement is
prepared as follows:

1. Write the *heading*. Use the same format as for income statements previously studied.

2. Prepare the *net sales* section. Data are taken from the two departmental margin statements.

3. Prepare the *cost of merchandise sold* section. Data are taken from the
   two departmental margin statements.

```
                              Tanler Appliances
                              Income Statement
                         For Month Ended April 30, 1979

                                                                    % of Net
                                                  Amounts           Sales

Net Sales:
   Small Appliances Department  . . .    $ 99,211.30
   Large Appliances Department  . . .     113,970.35
   Total Net Sales                                    $213,181.65     100.0

Cost of Merchandise Sold:
   Small Appliances Department  . . .    $ 52,109.00
   Large Appliances Department  . . .      56,581.50
   Total Cost of Merchandise Sold . .                  108,690.50      51.0

Gross Profit:
   Small Appliances Department  . . .    $ 47,102.30
   Large Appliances Department  . . .      57,388.85
   Total Gross Profit . . . . . . . .                 $104,491.15      49.0

Direct Departmental Expenses:
   Small Appliances Department  . . .    $ 19,346.78
   Large Appliances Department  . . .      23,495.17
   Total Direct Departmental Expenses                   42,841.95      20.1

Departmental Margin:
   Small Appliances Department  . . .    $ 27,755.52
   Large Appliances Department  . . .      33,893.68
   Total Departmental Margin  . . . .                 $ 61,649.20      28.9

Indirect Expenses:
   Depreciation Exp.--Office Equip. .    $     35.90
   Insurance Expense--Administrative.          20.00
   Miscellaneous Expense  . . . . . .       3,816.40
   Payroll Taxes Expense--Admin.  . .       1,582.40
   Rent Expense . . . . . . . . . . .      15,000.00
   Salary Expense--Administrative . .      17,200.00
   Supplies Expense--Administrative .         732.50
   Utilities Expense  . . . . . . . .       5,724.75
   Total Indirect Expenses  . . . . .                   44,111.95      20.7

Net Income Before Federal Income Tax                  $ 17,537.25       8.2
Less Federal Income Tax  . . . . . .                     6,138.05       2.9

Net Income After Federal Income Tax.                  $ 11,399.20       5.3
```

Income statement for a merchandising business

4. Prepare the *gross profit* section. Data are taken from the departmental margin statements.

5. Prepare the *direct expenses* section. Data are taken from the departmental margin statements.

   Bad Debts Expense is included in the direct departmental expenses section of the departmental margin statement — large appliances of Tanler Appliances because only large appliances are sold on credit. Therefore, bad debts expense is charged only to this department. In some companies bad debts expense is divided among the various departments. In other companies, bad debts expense is considered an administrative expense and is listed in the indirect expenses section of the income statement.

6. Prepare the *departmental margin* section. Data are taken from the departmental margin statements.

7. Prepare the *indirect expenses* section. Names of accounts and account balances are taken from the Income Statement columns of the work sheet, pages 340–341. All expense account titles and their balances are listed. The total amount of indirect expenses is shown on the income statement.

   Details for the direct expenses are not listed. If the managers need these figures, they refer to the departmental margin statements.

8. Complete the income statement. The procedure is the same as for income statements previously studied. Tanler Appliances has no items to include under the headings *Other Revenue* or *Other Expenses*. However, if these items were to be included, the same procedure as was previously studied would be followed.

9. Prepare the *Percentage of Net Sales* column. The procedure is the same as figuring the percentage of net sales on the departmental margin statements.

✦ What is the meaning of each of the following?

Using
Business
Terms

- responsibility accounting
- direct expense
- indirect expense
- departmental margin
- departmental margin statement
- responsibility statements

Questions
for
Individual
Study

1. How does a merchandising business serve consumers?
2. What are the two kinds of costs of operating a merchandising business?
3. What is the major difference between a direct expense and an indirect expense?
4. How are supplies that are a direct expense for a specific department accounted for differently from supplies for the entire business?
5. Why is there a difference between the work sheet for a departmentalized merchandising business and a non-departmentalized business?
6. How do adjustments on a work sheet

for a departmentalized merchandising business differ from those of a non-departmentalized merchandising business?
7. To which columns on a work sheet would a balance be extended for the account Insurance Expense — Jewelry Department?
8. What is the difference between "gross profit on operations" and "departmental margin"?
9. What information is given in departmental margin statements that is not given in a non-departmentalized income statement?

CASE 1 Marons Department Store has three departments: furniture, appliances, and lighting fixtures. The departmental margins reported for the three departments for the year ended December 31 are: furniture, $43,278.80; appliances, $51,483.75; lighting fixtures, $1,216.30. These amounts are similar to the departmental margins reported for the past four years. David Maron, the president, is considering closing the lighting fixtures department because of the consistently low departmental margin. Before taking action, he asks for your recommendation. What is your reply? What factors should be considered before a decision is made to close the department?

CASE 2 Vargas Corporation, an automotive supply company, prepares departmental margin statements for each of its four departments. Tsai Wu, a new tax accountant for the company, has listed as net income on the tax return the sum of the departmental margins. Denise Pierce, the company controller, asks you to verify the correctness of the tax return. Did Mr. Wu prepare the tax return correctly? Explain.

PROBLEM 18-1 Preparing a twelve-column work sheet for a departmentalized merchandising business

Burk Hardware uses an accounting system that provides the data to prepare departmental margin statements as well as an income statement and a balance sheet. The company has two departments: hardware and appliances.

Burk Hardware's trial balance for the current year ended December 31, is shown below.

Account Title	Acct. No.	Trial Balance Debit	Credit
Cash	1101	$ 34,643.20	
Accounts Receivable	1102	28,043.60	
Allowance for Uncollectible Accounts	1102.1		$ 71.40
Merchandise Inventory — Hardware	1103	35,866.80	
Merchandise Inventory — Appliances	1104	27,484.80	
Prepaid Insurance	1105	7,440.00	
Supplies	1106	8,856.00	
Delivery Equipment	1201	9,800.00	
Accum. Depr. — Delivery Equipment	1201.1		2,940.00
Office Equipment	1202	2,575.00	
Accum. Depr. — Office Equipment	1202.1		386.25
Store Equipment — Hardware	1203	8,736.00	
Accum. Depr. — Store Equip., Hardware	1203.1		2,620.80
Store Equipment — Appliances	1204	2,192.00	
Accum. Depr. — Store Equip., Appliances	1204.1		657.60
Accounts Payable	2101		16,891.30
Salaries Payable	2102		——
Employees Income Tax Payable	2103		629.30
FICA Tax Payable	2104		420.00
Unemployment Tax Payable — Federal	2105		45.00
Unemployment Tax Payable — State	2106		243.00
Income Tax Payable	2107		——
Sales Tax Payable	2108		1,714.20
Capital Stock	3101		100,000.00
Retained Earnings	3201		15,896.85
Income Summary — Hardware	3301	——	——
Income Summary — Appliances	3302	——	——
Income Summary — General	3303	——	——

Account Title	Acct. No.	Trial Balance Debit	Trial Balance Credit
Sales — Hardware	4101		$246,116.10
Sales Returns and Allow. — Hardware	4101.1	$ 1,009.00	
Sales — Appliances	4201		282,846.80
Sales Returns and Allow. — Appliances	4201.1	1,317.90	
Purchases — Hardware	5101	160,205.30	
Purchases Returns and Allow. — Hardware	5101.1		711.60
Purchases — Appliances	5201	162,840.00	
Purchases Returns and Allow. — Appliances	5201.1		659.10
Advertising Expense — Hardware	6001	2,995.70	
Depreciation Expense — Store Equip., Hardware	6002	——	
Insurance Expense — Hardware	6003	——	
Payroll Taxes Expense — Hardware	6004	3,177.31	
Salary Expense — Hardware	6005	34,536.00	
Supplies Expense — Hardware	6006	——	
Advertising Expense — Appliances	6101	4,236.00	
Delivery Expense — Appliances	6102	7,050.00	
Depreciation Expense — Del. Equip., Appliances	6103	——	
Depreciation Expense — Store Equip., Appliances	6104	——	
Insurance Expense — Appliances	6105	——	
Payroll Taxes Expense — Appliances	6106	2,960.93	
Salary Expense — Appliances	6107	32,184.00	
Supplies Expense — Appliances	6108	——	
Bad Debts Expense	6201	2,598.20	
Depreciation Expense — Office Equipment	6202	——	
Miscellaneous Expense	6203	14,759.40	
Payroll Taxes Expense — Administrative	6204	3,797.76	
Rent Expense	6205	21,600.00	
Salary Expense — Administrative	6206	41,280.00	
Supplies Expense — Administrative	6207	——	
Utilities Expense	6208	6,539.40	
Federal Income Tax	8001	4,125.00	
		$672,849.30	$672,849.30

Additional data needed to make adjustments are listed below.

Additional bad debts expense for the period	$ 2,170.10
Merchandise inventories on December 31:	
Hardware Department	38,736.20
Appliances Department	29,683.60
Value of insurance policies, December 31	3,720.00
Insurance expense charged as follows:	
Hardware Department — 60%	
Appliances Department — 40%	
Supplies inventory, December 31	1,824.00
Supplies were used as follows:	
Hardware Department — 40%	
Appliances Department — 35%	
Administrative — 25%	
Depreciation for the year:	
Delivery Equipment	982.00
Office Equipment	129.25
Store Equipment — Hardware	875.30
Store Equipment — Appliances	109.20
Federal Income Tax:	
25% of Net Income Before Federal Income Tax	

Instructions: □ **1.** Prepare a trial balance on a twelve-column work sheet. Be sure to list *all* accounts with or without a balance. Skip four lines after Utilities Expense before entering Federal Income Tax on the work sheet.

□ **2.** Make adjusting entries on the work sheet.

□ **3.** Complete the work sheet. Be sure to extend proper amounts to the Departmental Margin Statements columns for Hardware Department and Appliances Department plus the Income Statement columns and the Balance Sheet columns. All accounts beginning with the number 62 are classified as indirect expenses.

The work sheet prepared in this problem will be used in Problems 18-2 and 18-3.

PROBLEM 18-2 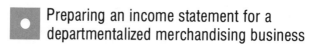 Preparing departmental margin statements

The work sheet prepared in Problem 18-1 is needed for Problem 18-2.

Instructions: Using the work sheet prepared in Problem 18-1, prepare departmental margin statements for the hardware department and the appliances department. Prepare statements similar to the ones on pages 345 and 347. Figure the percentage of net sales.

The statements prepared in Problem 18-2 are needed for Problem 18-3.

PROBLEM 18-3 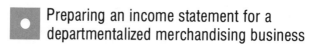 Preparing an income statement for a departmentalized merchandising business

The work sheet prepared in Problem 18-1 and statements prepared in Problem 18-2 are needed for Problem 18-3.

Instructions: Using the work sheet prepared in Problem 18-1 and the statements prepared in Problem 18-2, prepare an income statement. Prepare an income statement similar to the one on page 348. Figure the percentage of net sales.

PROBLEM 18-4 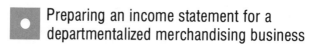 Preparing departmental margin statements

Cindy's Cycle Shop sells and repairs motorcycles. The company prepares departmental margin statements for each of its two departments — sales and service. The Departmental Margin Statements columns from the completed work sheet for May are shown on page 353.

Instructions: Prepare departmental margin statements similar to the ones on pages 345 and 347 for each of the two departments — sales department and service department. Figure the percentage of net sales.

	Departmental Margin Statements			
	Sales Department		Service Department	
	Debit	Credit	Debit	Credit
Income Summary — Sales Dept.	35,866.80	38,736.10		
Income Summary — Service Dept.			13,742.40	14,841.80
Income Summary — General.......................				
Sales — Sales Dept.		19,926.30		
Sales Returns & Allow. — Sales Dept...........	84.00			
Sales — Service Dept.				11,451.95
Sales Returns & Allow. — Service Dept........			54.90	
Purchases — Sales Dept...........................	13,350.40			
Purchases Returns & Allow. — Sales Dept.		59.30		
Purchases — Service Dept.........................			5,088.75	
Purchases Returns & Allow. — Service Dept.				20.60
Advertising Expense — Sales Dept..............	249.60			
Bad Debts Expense — Sales Dept.	198.60			
Delivery Expense — Sales Dept.	587.50			
Depr. Exp. — Delivery Equip., Sales Dept....	81.80			
Depr. Exp. — Store Equip., Sales Dept.	73.00			
Insurance Expense — Sales Dept.................	173.60			
Payroll Taxes Exp. — Sales Dept.	264.78			
Salary Exp. — Sales Dept..........................	2,878.00			
Supplies Exp. — Sales Dept.	234.40			
Advertising Expense — Service Dept...........			176.50	
Bad Debts Expense — Service Dept.			99.30	
Depr. Exp. — Shop Equip., Service Dept.			48.50	
Insurance Expense — Service Dept.............			68.20	
Payroll Taxes Exp. — Service Dept.			185.06	
Salary Exp. — Service Dept.......................			2,011.50	
Supplies Exp. — Service Dept.			102.55	
	54,042.48	58,721.70	21,577.66	26,314.35
Departmental Margin — Sales	4,679.22			
Departmental Margin — Service			4,736.69	
	58,721.70	58,721.70	26,314.35	26,314.35

MASTERY PROBLEM 18-M		Preparing a work sheet and end-of-period statements for a departmentalized merchandising business

The account balances for Hammack's Office Furniture and Supplies are shown below for the current year ended December 31.

Account Title	Acct. No.	Trial Balance	
		Debit	Credit
Cash...	1101	$ 46,920.60	
Accounts Receivable	1102	45,108.90	
Allow. for Uncollectible Accounts.......................	1102.1		$ 708.30
Merchandise Inventory — Furniture Dept.	1103	120,974.40	
Merchandise Inventory — Supplies Dept.	1104	73,261.30	
Prepaid Insurance..	1105	10,400.00	
Supplies..	1106	5,535.00	

Account Title	Acct. No.	Trial Balance Debit	Trial Balance Credit
Delivery Equipment — Furniture Dept.	1201	$ 8,750.00	
Accum. Depr. — Delivery Equip.........................	1201.1		$ 1,750.00
Office Equipment	1202	9,057.20	
Accum. Depr. — Office Equip.	1202.1		1,358.60
Store Equipment — Furniture Dept.	1203	6,792.90	
Accum. Depr. — Store Equip., Furniture Dept.	1203.1		2,037.90
Store Equipment — Supplies Dept.	1204	18,114.40	
Accum. Depr. — Store Equip., Supplies Dept.	1204.1		5,434.30
Accounts Payable	2101		42,325.60
Salaries Payable..	2102		——
Employees Income Tax Payable.........................	2103		425.60
FICA Tax Payable	2104		215.00
Unemployment Tax Pay. — Federal.....................	2105		90.00
Unemployment Tax Pay. — State	2106		486.00
Income Tax Payable	2107		2,730.00
Sales Tax Payable..	2108		3,026.50
Property Tax Payable.....................................	2109		1,155.00
Capital Stock...	3101		200,000.00
Retained Earnings	3201		72,835.65
Income Summary — Furniture Dept.	3301	——	——
Income Summary — Supplies Dept.	3302	——	——
Income Summary — General.............................	3303	——	——
Sales — Furniture Dept.	4101		687,117.70
Sales Ret. and Allow. — Furniture Dept.	4101.1	3,294.90	
Sales — Supplies Dept.	4201		597,790.20
Sales Ret. and Allow. — Supplies Dept.	4201.1	2,516.40	
Purchases — Furniture Dept.	5101	495,408.60	
Purch. Ret. and Allow. — Furniture Dept.............	5101.1		5,289.00
Purchases — Supplies Dept.	5201	454,162.80	
Purch. Ret. and Allow. — Supplies Dept.	5201.1		1,885.50
Advertising Exp. — Furniture Dept.....................	6001	4,608.65	
Delivery Exp. — Furniture Dept.	6002	11,728.60	
Depr. Exp. — Deliv. Equip., Furniture Dept.	6003	——	
Depr. Exp. — Store Equip., Furniture Dept.	6004	——	
Insurance Expense — Furniture Dept....................	6005	——	
Payroll Taxes Exp. — Furniture Dept.	6006	8,478.72	
Salary Exp. — Furniture Dept...........................	6007	92,160.00	
Supplies Exp. — Furniture Dept.	6008	——	
Advertising Exp. — Supplies Dept.	6101	3,072.40	
Delivery Exp. — Supplies Dept..........................	6102	5,864.30	
Depr. Exp. — Store Equip., Supplies Dept.	6103	——	
Insurance Expense — Supplies Dept.....................	6104	——	
Payroll Taxes Exp. — Supplies Dept.	6105	7,418.88	
Salary Exp. — Supplies Dept............................	6106	80,640.00	
Supplies Exp. — Supplies Dept.	6107	——	
Bad Debts Expense	6201	2,163.50	
Depreciation Exp. — Office Equip......................	6202	——	
Insurance Expense — Administrative	6203	——	
Miscellaneous Expense	6204	11,782.60	
Payroll Taxes Exp. — Administrative....................	6205	3,974.40	
Property Tax Expense	6206	1,155.00	
Rent Expense...	6207	36,000.00	
Salary Exp. — Administrative	6208	43,200.00	
Supplies Exp. — Administrative.........................	6209	——	
Utilities Expense	6210	6,236.40	
Federal Income Tax	8101	7,880.00	
		$1,626,660.85	$1,626,660.85

Additional data needed to make adjustments are listed below.

Additional bad debts expense		$ 751.10
Merchandise inventories on December 31:		
Furniture Dept.		130,917.75
Supplies Dept.		96,371.40
Value of insurance policies December 31		5,580.00
Insurance expense charged as follows:		
Furniture Dept.	50%	
Supplies Dept.	40%	
Administrative	10%	
Supplies inventory, December 31		926.50
Supplies were used as follows:		
Furniture Dept.	30%	
Supplies Dept.	40%	
Administrative	30%	
Depreciation for the year:		
Delivery Equipment		875.00
Office Equipment		679.30
Store Equipment — Furniture Dept.		905.70
Store Equipment — Supplies Dept.		1,811.45
Federal Income Tax:		
25% of Net Income Before Federal Income Tax		

Instructions: □ **1.** Prepare a trial balance in the Trial Balance columns of a twelve-column work sheet. Be sure to list *all* accounts with or without a balance. Skip four lines after Utilities Expense before entering Federal Income Tax.

□ **2.** Make adjusting entries on the work sheet.

□ **3.** Complete the work sheet. Extend proper amounts to debit and credit columns for Departmental Margin Statement — Furniture, Departmental Margin Statement — Supplies, Income Statement, and Balance Sheet. All accounts beginning with the number 62 are classified as indirect expenses.

□ **4.** Prepare a departmental margin statement — furniture department and a departmental margin statement — supplies department for the year ended December 31. Figure the percentage of net sales.

□ **5.** Prepare an income statement for the year ended December 31. Figure the percentage of net sales.

BONUS PROBLEM 18-B Analyzing a departmental margin statement

The departmental margin statements for the fuel department of Monahan Ice and Fuel Company for the years 1978 and 1979 are shown on page 356. The company has set a goal for the fuel department to contribute a minimum of 20.0% departmental margin. For the years 1974 through 1978, the departmental margin for the fuel department has varied from 20.0% to 21.9% of net sales.

MONAHAN ICE AND FUEL COMPANY
Departmental Margin Statement — Fuel
For Years Ended June 30, 1979 and 1978

	1979		% of Net Sales	1978		% of Net Sales
	Amounts			Amounts		
Revenue:						
Sales...................	$264,308.00			$238,146.50		100.5
Less Sales Ret. and Allowances..............	1,314.90			1,215.80		0.5
Net Sales.................		$262,993.10			$236,930.70	100.0
Cost of Merchandise						
Merch. Inv., January 1..	$ 29,452.40			$ 26,775.70		11.3
Purchases.................	172,870.30			142,465.80		60.1
Total Cost of Merch. Available.................	$202,322.70			$169,241.50		71.4
Less Merch. Inv., December 31............	32,692.20			29,452.40		12.4
Cost of Merch. Sold......		169,630.50			139,789.10	59.0
Gross Profit.................		$ 93,362.60			$ 97,141.60	41.0
Direct Dept. Expenses:						
Advertising Exp.	$ 2,630.00			$ 2,606.20		1.1
Bad Debts Exp.............	2,630.00			2,132.40		0.9
Delivery Exp..............	5,522.80			5,212.50		2.2
Depr. Exp. — Delivery Equip.	3,317.00			3,317.00		1.4
Depr. Exp. — Storage Equip.	2,132.40			2,132.40		0.9
Insurance Exp.	1,841.00			1,658.50		0.7
Payroll Taxes Exp.........	2,594.70			2,215.15		0.9
Salary Expense............	28,929.40			25,588.50		10.8
Supplies Expense.........	1,840.10			1,895.40		0.8
Total Direct Dept. Exp.		51,437.40			46,758.05	19.7
Departmental Margin......		$ 41,925.20			$ 50,383.55	21.3

Instructions: ☐ **1.** Figure the percentage of net sales for each item on the 1979 Departmental Margin Statement — Fuel. Round to one decimal place.

☐ **2.** Figure the changes in "% of Net Sales" from 1978 to 1979 for the following items: (a) cost of merchandise sold, (b) gross profit, (c) total direct departmental expenses, and (d) departmental margin.

☐ **3.** From an analysis of the departmental margin statements and the amounts obtained from Instructions 1 and 2, answer the following questions:
  a. Is the departmental margin for the fuel department at a satisfactory percentage of sales? Explain why it is or is not satisfactory.
  b. Is the trend of the cost of merchandise sold percentage favorable or unfavorable? Explain why it is or is not favorable. Can you suggest some possible reasons for the change in cost of merchandise sold from 1978 to 1979?
  c. Is the trend of the total direct departmental expenses percentage favorable or unfavorable? Explain why the trend is or is not favorable.

Cost Accounting for a Manufacturing Business 19

A merchandising business purchases products and, without changing their form, sells those products to customers. A department store and an auto supply store are examples of merchandising businesses.

A manufacturing business buys materials and by using labor and machines, changes the form of the materials into finished products. Carefree Trailer Company manufactures and sells travel and camper trailers. The company buys wood, aluminum siding, and other materials to make travel and camper trailers.

A merchandising business keeps records of merchandise purchases so the cost of merchandise sold can be figured. A manufacturing company also needs to know the cost of finished products sold. However, to know how much the finished products cost, a manufacturing business must keep records of all the costs involved in making the products.

Selling and administrative activities of a manufacturing business normally are similar to a merchandising business. Procedures for recording the selling and administrative expenses are also similar in both types of businesses.

ELEMENTS OF MANUFACTURING COST

The manufacturing cost of any finished product is made up of three elements. These are (a) direct materials, (b) direct labor, and (c) factory overhead.

Direct materials

Materials that become an identifiable part of a finished product are called direct materials. These include all materials used in the manufacturing process that are of sufficient value to justify charging the cost directly to the product. Examples of direct materials are the wood and aluminum siding used in the manufacture of the trailers. On the other hand, nails used on each job may not have sufficient value to justify keeping a separate record.

Direct labor

The wages of workers who make a product are called direct labor. Direct labor includes only the wages of persons working directly on a product. Wages of supervisors, maintenance workers, and others whose efforts do not apply directly to the manufacture of a product are not direct labor.

Factory overhead

All expenses other than direct materials and direct labor that apply to the making of products are called factory overhead. Factory overhead includes all labor other than direct labor, all materials other than direct materials, and all other manufacturing expenses such as rent, depreciation, and insurance.

INVENTORIES FOR A MANUFACTURING BUSINESS

A merchandising business normally has one general ledger account for merchandise inventory. However, a manufacturing business has three inventory accounts related to the products manufactured: (a) materials, (b) work in process, and (c) finished goods.

The materials inventory account shows the costs of raw materials on hand that have not yet been used in making a product. Products that are being manufactured but are not yet complete are called work in process. The work in process inventory account therefore has all the costs that have been spent on products that are not yet complete. All products completed are called finished goods. The finished goods inventory account therefore includes the costs of completed products still on hand and unsold.

The flow of costs through the manufacturing inventory accounts is shown on page 359.

Accounting for the costs of manufacturing a product follows the same sequence as the manufacturing process. (a) Direct materials are purchased and used. (b) Direct labor is used. (c) Factory overhead costs are incurred. As these three manufacturing cost elements are used in the manufacturing process, they are said to be "in process." (d) The costs are accumulated for each product. When the product is completed, all of the accumulated costs of making that product are debited to the inventory account Finished Goods. (e) When the completed product is sold, the accumulated cost of the product is transferred from Finished Goods to cost of goods sold.

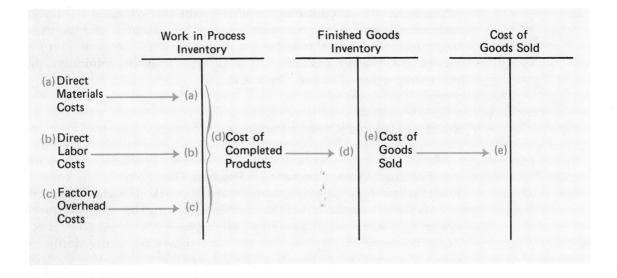

RECORDS FOR DIRECT MATERIALS

A manufacturing business should have a record of charges made for direct materials used in the manufacturing process. In addition, sufficient direct materials should be on hand so that the manufacturing process will not be interrupted. On the other hand, too great a stock of materials requires needless investment in inventory. To provide a perpetual inventory and detailed cost information about direct materials, Carefree Trailer Company keeps a record of each kind of material. The record showing the quantity and value of each kind of direct material is called a materials ledger.

Preparing a materials ledger

A materials ledger contains a form for each kind of direct material kept in the storeroom. A materials ledger card is shown below.

ARTICLE S460 Prefinished Plywood Paneling, 1.2 x 2.4 meters	NO. 268
Maximum 500	Minimum 90	Location Area A-32

ORDER			RECEIVED					ISSUED					BALANCE			
Date	Purchase Order No.	Quantity	Date	Purchase Order No.	Quantity	Unit Price	Value	Date	Requisition No.	Quantity	Unit Price	Value	Date	Quantity	Unit Price	Value
													1979 Jan. 2	90	8.70	783.00
1979 Jan. 2	721	400	1979 Jan. 18	721	400	8.70	3,480.00						18	490	8.70	4,263.00

An account in the materials ledger

The name and account number of the item are written at the top of each account card in the materials ledger. The maximum and the minimum quantities that should be maintained in stock are shown on the second line. When the number on hand approaches the minimum, the purchasing agent is notified by the materials clerk and a new order is placed.

Recording purchases of direct materials

On January 2 the company orders 400 sheets of prefinished plywood paneling from Ozark Company on Purchase Order No. 721. A copy of this purchase order is given to the materials clerk. The materials clerk records the date of the order, the purchase order number, and the quantity on a materials ledger account shown on page 359. Information about quantities ordered is posted to the card to avoid placing duplicate orders.

When the items ordered have been received, the approved invoice is sent to the materials clerk. The materials clerk makes the entry that is shown in the Received columns in the account on page 359. The quantity and value are added to the previous balance and extended into the Balance columns.

The relation of the general ledger accounts to the forms discussed in this chapter will be explained in Chapter 20.

RECORDS FOR WORK IN PROCESS

During the manufacturing process, all costs of making the products must be recorded.

The form on which all charges for direct materials, direct labor, and factory overhead for a particular job are recorded is known as a cost sheet. A cost sheet is maintained for each manufacturing job in the factory. A job order number is recorded on each cost sheet to identify the specific job.

Preparing cost sheets

When a factory department is ready to start a new job, the factory department supervisor requests a job number from the cost accounting department. A cost accounting clerk assigns the next number following the last job. The cost accounting clerk notifies the factory department supervisor of the job number and prepares a cost sheet for the job. All costs then can be charged to a specific job number.

On January 4 Carefree Trailer Company starts Job Order No. 724 for 5 No. CF-18 Travel Trailers. The heading of the cost sheet for Job No. 724, as prepared by the cost accounting clerk, is shown on page 361.

COST SHEET

Job. No. _724_   Date _January 4, 1979_

Item _CF-18 Travel Trailers_   Date wanted _January 29, 1979_

No. of items_ 5_   Date completed _____

Ordered for_ Stock_

Direct Materials		Direct Labor				Summary	
Req. No.	Amount	Date	Amount	Date	Amount	Item	Amount

Cost sheet

Recording requisitions of direct materials

When direct materials are needed in the factory, they are requested from the storeroom. A materials requisition form is used to authorize transfer of items from the storeroom to the factory. The materials requisition is prepared in triplicate and signed by a person in authority, usually the factory superintendent or factory department supervisor.

A materials requisition for 40 sheets of paneling, prepared by a factory department supervisor, is shown below.

MATERIALS REQUISITION

Requisition No. 823   Date _January 22_   19 _79_

Requisitioned By _L. H. Brittain_   Position _Supervisor_

JOB ORDER NO.	QUANTITY	DESCRIPTION	UNIT PRICE	AMOUNT
724	40	5460 - Prefinished Plywood Paneling, 1.2 × 2.4 meters		

Materials Issued _____ 19 ___   Recorded:

By _____
Materials Clerk

Materials requisition prepared by a factory supervisor

After a materials requisition is prepared, one copy is kept for the factory; two copies are given to the materials clerk in the storeroom. The materials clerk records the unit price and total cost of the order on both copies of the requisition. The clerk also records the date on which the materials are issued and initials the requisition to show that the materials have been issued. The materials clerk retains a copy of the requisition as a record and sends the original copy to the cost accounting clerk. The completed Materials Requisition No. 823 is shown on page 362.

Completed materials
requisition form

From the copy of the materials requisition, the materials clerk makes
an entry in the materials ledger. The entry for Materials Requisition No.
823 is shown in the materials ledger account below. The requisition is
first summarized in the Issued columns. Then the quantity and value
entered in the Issued columns are subtracted from the amounts in the
Balance columns to show the new balance.

Materials ledger account after
entering a materials requisition

Recording direct materials costs on the cost sheet

The cost accounting clerk receives the original copy of each materials
requisition from the materials clerk. As the requisitions are received, the
cost accounting clerk records them on the cost sheets for the jobs to be
charged. For example, Materials Requisition No. 823 is for direct materials, $348.00, for Job Order No. 724. The entries for direct materials are
shown in the Direct Materials columns on the cost sheet, page 364.

Recording direct labor costs on the cost sheet

Each worker in the factory, in the course of a day, may work on a number of different job orders. Therefore, a job-time record is kept showing the amount of time spent on each job. At the end of the day the time clerk summarizes all job-time records and reports to the cost accounting clerk the total direct labor cost for each job. A job-time record for one employee working 4 hours on Job Order No. 724 is shown below.

JOB – TIME RECORD

Employee Number _16_   Job Number _724_

Date ___1/18/79___

Time started _8 a.m._

Time finished _12 noon_

Total time spent on Job . . . . _4.0 hrs._

Job-time record

The January direct labor costs for Job Order No. 724 are shown in the Direct Labor columns on the cost sheet, page 364.

Distributing factory overhead among all jobs

The cost of direct materials and direct labor are an important part of the cost of each factory job. A manufacturing business also has other expenses that must be included in the total cost of each manufacturing job.

Some workers in the factory devote their time to supervisory, clerical, and maintenance tasks necessary to the operation of the factory. Such workers include time clerks, supervisors, maintenance people, receiving clerks, and inspectors. The wages paid to workers who are not actually making products but who are working in the factory are called indirect labor.

Some of the other costs incurred in the manufacturing process are: (a) supplies used in the factory; (b) depreciation of factory buildings and equipment; (c) repairs on the factory buildings and equipment; (d) insurance on the building, equipment, and stock; (e) taxes on property owned; and (f) heat, light, and power. All of the above expenses, including indirect labor, make up factory overhead.

Some factory overhead expenses occur regularly throughout the fiscal period while others occur irregularly. Also the amounts of many factory overhead expenses are not known until the end of the fiscal period. Therefore, factory overhead expenses normally are charged to jobs by using a distribution rate based on a known cost such as direct labor. This method distributes the factory overhead expenses to all the jobs and permits the company to record overhead on a cost sheet as soon as the job is completed.

Carefree Trailer Company's cost accountant compares total factory overhead for the past several fiscal periods with the total direct labor costs. The cost accountant finds that the total factory overhead has regularly been about 60% of the total direct labor costs. The company decides, therefore, to use 60% of the direct labor cost on each job as the estimate of factory overhead to be recorded on each cost sheet.

Completing the cost sheet

The completed cost sheet for Job Order No. 724 with the factory overhead added is shown below.

COST SHEET

Job. No. _724_

Item _CF-18 Travel Trailers_

No. of items_ 5 _

Ordered for _Stock_

Date _January 4, 1979_

Date wanted _January 29, 1979_

Date completed _January 26, 1979_

Direct Materials		Direct Labor				Summary	
Req. No.	Amount	Date	Amount	Date	Amount	Item	Amount
803	$1,218.00	Jan. 4	$ 112.00	Jan. 20	$ 156.00	Direct Materials	$ 4,486.00
809	927.00	5	247.50	23	159.40	Direct Labor	2,780.50
816	874.00	8	190.40	24	152.50	Factory Overhead	
823	348.00	9	158.00	25	163.20	(60% of direct	
826	1,119.00	10	136.30	26	57.40	labor costs)	1,668.30
	$4,486.00	11	175.00		$2,780.50	Total Cost	$ 8,934.80
		12	186.40				
		13	193.70			No. units finished	5
		15	185.50			Cost per unit	$ 1,786.96
		17	181.40				
		18	165.20				
		19	160.60				

Completed cost sheet

To determine the cost of each travel trailer manufactured in Job Order No. 724, the total cost is divided by the number of trailers produced. The unit cost is $1,786.96, ($8,934.80 ÷ 5 units).

RECORDS FOR FINISHED GOODS

After a job is completed, the finished goods are placed in the finished goods stockroom until they are shipped to customers.

Some manufacturing businesses maintain a perpetual inventory for finished goods. A finished goods ledger form is maintained for each kind of item included in the inventory. The forms containing a record of all finished goods are called a finished goods ledger. This ledger is similar to the materials ledger described earlier in this chapter. A perpetual inventory of finished goods is valuable to a manufacturing business needing a continuous record of the goods available for sale.

Using Business Terms

✦ What is the meaning of each of the following?

- direct materials
- direct labor
- factory overhead
- work in process
- finished goods
- materials ledger
- indirect labor
- finished goods ledger

Questions for Individual Study

1. How is a merchandising business different from a manufacturing business?
2. For what kind of expenses are the recording procedures similar in both merchandising and manufacturing businesses?
3. What are the three elements of manufacturing cost of any finished product?
4. What three inventory accounts are unique to a manufacturing business?
5. Why do manufacturers usually maintain records that will show at any time the quantity and the value of the direct materials on hand?
6. What information is maintained on each card in the materials ledger?
7. What information is shown on the materials requisition prepared in the factory?
8. After a materials requisition is approved in the factory, what information does the materials clerk record on the two copies of the requisition sent to the storeroom?
9. What information is recorded daily on each cost sheet?
10. Where is the information obtained for the Direct Materials section of each cost sheet?
11. Where is the information obtained for the Direct Labor section of each cost sheet?
12. What are some of the overhead expenses incurred in manufacturing?
13. Normally how are factory overhead expenses distributed to a specific job?

Cases for Management Decision

CASE 1 The cost accounting clerk for Zollar Corporation uses the following procedure for charging factory overhead to specific jobs. The cost accounting clerk waits until after the end of the month before adding up all the factory overhead expenses. The total factory overhead costs are then evenly divided among the jobs completed that month. Is this a satisfactory procedure for distributing the factory overhead? Explain your answer.

CASE 2 The Easystep Shoe Company manufactures shoes. During the current year expenditures were made for the items listed below. Classify each item as (a) direct materials, (b) direct labor, or (c) factory overhead. Give reasons for your classification.
1) Leather to be used in the shoes.
2) Oil for the machinery.
3) Thread to be used in stitching the shoes.
4) Wages of the factory superintendent.
5) Sweeping compound to clean the factory floors.
6) Wages of the operator of a polishing machine.
7) Rent of the factory building.

CASE 3 The Kenyon Candy Company has found that the total factory overhead is usually about 100% of the cost of all the direct labor.

The business has three manufacturing departments: A, B, and C. In Department A, much expensive machinery is used. In Department B, some machinery is used. In Department C, virtually no machinery is used, all the work being hand work. There is a great difference in the amount of time required to process various jobs in the different departments.

Under these circumstances do you believe that the company should charge factory overhead to each job at the rate of 100% of direct labor? If not, what would you recommend?

Problems for Applying Concepts

PROBLEM 19-1 Preparing a cost sheet

On April 15 of the current year, Monford Company began work on Job Order No. 956. The order was for 20 No. 3060 executive desks for stock, to be completed by April 26 of the current year.

Instructions: ▫ **1.** Open a cost sheet similar to the one shown on page 364 and record the following items:

Apr. 15. Direct materials, $324.00. Requisition No. 783.
    15. Direct labor, $53.00. Daily summary of Job-Time Records.
    16. Direct labor, $62.00. Daily summary of Job-Time Records.
    17. Direct materials, $116.00. Requisition No. 789.
    17. Direct labor, $98.00. Daily summary of Job-Time Records.
    18. Direct labor, $112.00. Daily summary of Job-Time Records.
    19. Direct materials, $74.00. Requisition No. 798.
    19. Direct labor, $114.00. Daily summary of Job-Time Records.
    22. Direct materials, $103.00. Requisition No. 803.
    22. Direct labor, $108.00. Daily summary of Job-Time Records.
    23. Direct materials, $97.00. Requisition No. 812.
    23. Direct labor, $94.00. Daily summary of Job-Time Records.
    24. Direct materials, $43.00. Requisition No. 818.
    24. Direct labor, $89.00. Daily summary of Job-Time Records.
    25. Direct labor, $48.00. Daily summary of Job-Time Records.

Instructions: ▫ **2.** Complete the cost sheet, recording factory overhead at the rate of 80% of direct labor costs.

Optional Problems

MASTERY PROBLEM 19-M Preparing a cost sheet

On April 10, Ingersoll Company began work on Job Order No. 427. The order was for 50 No. 30E E-Z Way lawn mowers for stock, to be completed by April 19.

Instructions: ▫ **1.** Open a cost sheet similar to the one shown on page 364 and record the following items:

Apr. 10. Direct materials, $211.00. Requisition No. 298.
  10. Direct labor, $76.00. Daily summary of Job-Time Records.
  11. Direct labor, $122.00. Daily summary of Job-Time Records.
  12. Direct materials, $426.00. Requisition No. 307.
  12. Direct labor, $109.00. Daily summary of Job-Time Records.
  15. Direct labor, $118.00. Daily summary of Job-Time Records.
  16. Direct labor, $122.00. Daily summary of Job-Time Records.
  17. Direct materials, $188.00. Requisition No. 324.
  17. Direct labor, $103.00. Daily summary of Job-Time Records.
  18. Direct labor, $97.00. Daily summary of Job-Time Records.
  19. Direct labor, $51.00. Daily summary of Job-Time Records.

Instructions: □ **2.** Complete the cost sheet, recording factory overhead at the rate of 120% of direct labor costs.

BONUS Recording entries in a
PROBLEM 19-B   materials ledger

Instructions: □ **1.** Prepare a materials ledger sheet for G240 high pressure industrial hose, 2 cm. The hose is Item No. 183. Maximum Quantity is set at 4,000 meters, minimum at 500 meters. Inventory location is in Area B-24.
  Whenever the balance reaches the minimum, make an entry in the Order column. Number the purchase orders consecutively, starting with Purchase Order No. 844. G240 hose is sold in 500 meter coils only. Order enough full coils to get as close to the maximum as possible without exceeding it. Record the receipt of the order fifteen days later.

□ **2.** Record the beginning balance on February 1 of the current year of 250 meters at a unit price of $1.20 per meter. Although this balance is below the minimum, an order was placed for more hose in the previous month when the minimum balance was reached.

□ **3.** Record the following transactions:

Feb. 2. Issued 50 meters G240 hose. Materials Requisition No. 581.
  5. Received 3,500 meters G240 hose which had been ordered on January 21 on Purchase Order No. 843. Also received notice from the supplier that for future orders the price will be $1.50 per meter. Note that this new price will apply only to hose received which has been ordered at this new price.
  6. Issued 2,100 meters G240 hose. Materials Requisition No. 597.
  10. Issued 1,200 meters G240 hose. Materials Requisition No. 605.
  13. Issued 250 meters G240 hose. Materials Requisition No. 622.
  22. Issued 50 meters G240 hose. Materials Requisition No. 655.

End-of-Fiscal-Period Work for a Manufacturing Business

The procedure for recording costs on a cost sheet was described in Chapter 19. However, few of the costs are recorded in the general ledger as a product is being manufactured. A manufacturing business therefore makes entries at the end of a fiscal period to update the general ledger manufacturing accounts.

The adjusting entries made in the manufacturing inventory accounts are similar to the adjustments made to Merchandise Inventory in a merchandising business. A manufacturing business, however, has three inventory accounts: Materials, Work in Process, and Finished Goods. Therefore, a separate statement normally is prepared. A statement that gives information about the costs of finished goods is called a statement of cost of goods manufactured. This statement shows the details of the cost elements — materials, direct labor, and factory overhead — spent on the goods completed in the fiscal period.

VOUCHER REGISTER FOR A MANUFACTURING BUSINESS

Carefree Trailer Company controls all expenditures by using a voucher system. The company's voucher register is shown on pages 370–371.

A voucher is prepared for each expenditure. The vouchers are numbered consecutively each year and the voucher number is recorded in the Voucher No. column of the voucher register. A missing number in the Voucher No. column calls attention to any omission of a voucher entry.

The amount of each voucher is recorded in the Vouchers Payable Credit column. Unless a voucher requires more than one line of writing, there are no blank lines in the Vouchers Payable Credit column.

In the Distribution section of the voucher register, special columns are provided for the accounts that are debited frequently. The account number of each of these accounts is printed as part of the heading of the column. The account number in the column heading makes it easier to locate the account in the ledger when the transactions are posted.

Entries that affect accounts for which no special columns are provided are recorded in the General section of the voucher register. The name of each account and the amounts are recorded. If more than one line is used, a brace ({) is placed in the date column to show that the entries on these lines belong to the same transaction.

Each voucher is paid by check when due. The date of payment and the check number are recorded in the Paid columns of the voucher register. Therefore, the accountant can determine easily which vouchers are unpaid.

Each amount in the General Debit and General Credit columns is posted individually during the month.

At the end of the month the voucher register is totaled and proved. The totals of the special columns are then posted to the proper accounts in the general ledger.

RECORDING THE PAYROLL COSTS

Carefree Trailer Company pays all factory employees twice each month. At the end of each pay period, the amounts on all time cards for factory employees are totaled. These totals are the basis for preparing the factory payroll. Sales and administrative personnel are paid only once each month.

A payroll register shows the distribution of the payroll to the proper general ledger accounts. The factory payroll is recorded separately in the payroll register since it is paid twice a month. A voucher is prepared for each factory payroll debiting the two factory accounts, **Work in Process** for direct labor and **Factory Overhead** for indirect labor. Two withholding accounts are credited, **Employees Income Tax Payable** and **FICA Tax Payable**. **Vouchers Payable** is credited for the net amount.

During January, Carefree Trailer Company prepared factory payroll vouchers on January 15 and January 31. The two entries in the voucher register are shown on pages 370–371.

PAGE *12*	VOUCHER REGISTER					
				PAID		VOUCHERS PAYABLE CREDIT (2101)
DATE	CREDITOR	VCHR. NO.	DATE	CK. NO.		
1979 Jan. 2 Schubert Steel Co.		1	Jan. 10	1391	2880 00	1
3 Padgett Equipment Co.		2			308 25	2
4 Jerry Chambliss		3	Jan. 4	1387	3 50	3
4 McMillan Lumber Co.		4	Jan. 12	1401	23 30	4
15 Factory Payroll		39	Jan. 15	1432	9535 45	21
						22
						23
						24
31 Factory Payroll		91	Jan. 31	1463	11632 47	35
						36
						37
						38
31 Totals					6660 24	39
					(2101)	40

Voucher register of a manufacturing business (left page)

When the factory payroll entries in the voucher register are posted to the general ledger, the accounts are affected as shown in the T accounts below.

Work in Process	1105
Bal. 8,167.32	
Jan. 15 8,285.20	
Jan. 31 10,544.80	

Vouchers Payable	2101
	Jan. 15 9,535.45
	Jan. 31 11,632.47

Factory Overhead	5103
Jan. 15 3,203.30	
Jan. 31 3,470.22	

Employees Income Tax Payable	2102
	Jan. 15 1,263.74
	Jan. 31 1,541.65

FICA Tax Payable	2103
	Jan. 15 689.31
	Jan. 31 840.90

Amounts in the Vouchers Payable T account are shown to illustrate the complete entries. In practice, only the sum of all amounts in the Vouchers Payable column would be posted to **Vouchers Payable**.

FOR MONTH OF *January* 1979   PAGE *12*

MATERIALS DEBIT (1104)	SUPPLIES—FACTORY DEBIT (1108)	MISC. EXP.—FACTORY DEBIT (5106)	MISC. EXP.—SALES DEBIT (6104)	MISC. EXP.—ADMIN. DEBIT (6205)	ACCOUNT	POST REF.	DEBIT	CREDIT	
2880 00									1
					Factory Equip.	1201	308 25		2
		3 50							3
	23 30								4
					Work in Process	1105	8285 20		21
					Factory Overhead	5103	3203 30		22
					Empl. Inc. Tax Pay.	2102		1263 74	23
					FICA Tax Pay.	2103		689 31	24
					Work in Process	1105	10544 80		35
					Factory Overhead	5103	3470 22		36
					Empl. Inc. Tax Pay.	2102		1541 65	37
					FICA Tax Pay.	2103		840 90	38
31327 02	721 75	220 52	635 06	660 92			87646 57	4611 60	39
(1104)	(1108)	(5106)	(6104)	(6205)			(✓)	(✓)	40

Voucher register of a manufacturing business (right page)

SUMMARIZING THE MATERIALS COSTS

The amount of materials purchased and the amount used are recorded in the general ledger account Materials.

Materials purchases

Carefree Trailer Company records each purchase invoice in a voucher register. All purchases of direct materials are debited to Materials in the general ledger. Since purchases of direct materials are frequent, a special column headed Materials Debit is provided in the voucher register. An entry for direct materials is shown on Line 1 of the voucher register above and on page 370.

At the end of the month, the totals of the special columns in the voucher register are posted to the proper accounts in the general ledger. The effect of posting the January total of the Materials Debit column in the voucher register to Materials is shown at the right.

Materials	1104
Bal. 16,698.52	
Jan. 31 31,327.02	

The debit balance of $16,698.52 on January 1 is the amount of the direct materials inventory at the beginning of the month. The debit of $31,327.02 on January 31 is the total posted from the Materials Debit column of the voucher register. This last entry is the total cost of direct materials purchased for which an invoice was received during the month.

Materials requisitions

Each materials requisition is for direct materials used on a specific job order. After a materials requisition is recorded on a cost sheet, the requisition is placed in the materials requisitions file. At the end of the month, all requisitions in the materials requisitions file are totaled. The total for January, $30,202.40, is the amount of all direct materials transferred from the storeroom to the factory. The following summarizing entry is made in the general journal:

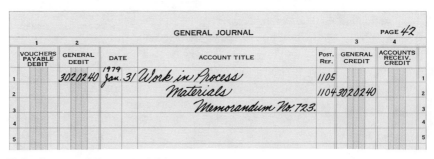

Entry to record the materials requisitions for the month

The effect of posting this journal entry is shown in the T accounts at the left.

Work in Process	1105
Balance 8,167.32	
Dir. Lab. 8,285.20	
Dir. Lab. 10,544.80	
Dir. Mat. 30,202.40	

Materials	1104
Balance 16,698.52	Used 30,202.40
Pur. 31,327.02	

The first debit amount in the work in process account is the inventory of work in process at the beginning of the month. The last debit amount is the total of direct materials placed in process on all jobs during the month.

The first debit amount in the materials account is the inventory of direct materials at the beginning of the month. The second debit amount is the total amount of materials purchased during the month. The credit amount is the total of all direct materials placed in process on all jobs during the month.

Materials account

The materials account in the general ledger is a controlling account for the materials ledger described in Chapter 19. The total of all purchases of direct materials as shown in the voucher register is debited to the general ledger account Materials. Each individual purchase of direct materials is also recorded in the Received columns of an account in the materials ledger after the invoice has been received.

The total of all requisitions for direct materials is recorded in the general journal as a credit to the general ledger account Materials. Each individual requisition for direct materials is recorded in the Issued columns of an account in the materials ledger. Therefore, the balance of the general ledger account Materials should equal the sum of the balances of all the accounts in the materials ledger.

DETERMINATION OF FACTORY OVERHEAD

Factory overhead is made up of various indirect expenses such as indirect labor, taxes, depreciation, and insurance. Actual factory overhead expenses are summarized in an account called Factory Overhead.

Recording actual overhead

Indirect labor is posted directly to the factory overhead account from the factory payroll recorded in the voucher register. The other indirect expenses are charged to expense accounts with appropriate titles. At the end of the month, these indirect expenses are all transferred to the factory overhead account. Then the actual overhead can be compared with the estimated amount of overhead recorded on the job cost sheets. The entry in the general journal to transfer actual overhead expenses to the factory overhead account is shown below.

GENERAL JOURNAL						PAGE 42	
1	2					3	4
VOUCHERS PAYABLE DEBIT	GENERAL DEBIT	DATE	ACCOUNT TITLE	POST. REF.		GENERAL CREDIT	ACCOUNTS RECEIV. CREDIT
	442444	Dec. 31	Factory Overhead	5103			
			Depreciation Exp.-Building	5101		25000	
			Depr. Exp.-Factory Equip.	5102		47650	
			Heat, Light, + Power	5104		132212	
			Insurance Exp.-Factory	5105		4147	
			Miscellaneous Exp.-Factory	5106		15562	
			Payroll Taxes Exp.-Factory	5107		153021	
			Property Tax Exp.-Factory	5108		14366	
			Supplies Expense-Factory	5109		50506000000	
			Memorandum No. 724.				

Entry to transfer actual overhead expenses
for the month to the factory overhead account

After posting the voucher register, pages 370–371, and the entry, page 373, all of the factory overhead expense accounts are summarized in the factory overhead account. The factory overhead account is debited for the actual overhead expenses for the month, indirect labor of $3,203.30 and $3,470.22, plus the other actual expenses of $4,424.64. The effect of these entries on the factory overhead account is shown in the T account at the left.

Factory Overhead	5103
Ind. labor 3,203.30	
Ind. labor 3,470.22	
Act. exp. 4,424.64	

Recording overhead applied to jobs in process

Carefree Trailer Company distributes the estimated factory overhead, as explained in Chapter 19. Overhead is applied to each job at the rate of 60% of the direct labor charges on the cost sheet.

At the end of the month, the factory overhead recorded on all job cost sheets during the month is debited to the work in process account. The amount of this debit is figured from the total amount of direct labor recorded in the work in process account. The applied overhead cost is 60% of $18,830.00, or $11,298.00. The following entry is recorded in the general journal:

GO

GREEN

VOUCHERS PAYABLE DEBIT	GENERAL DEBIT	DATE	GENERAL JOURNAL — ACCOUNT TITLE	POST. REF.	GENERAL CREDIT	ACCOUNTS RECEIV. CREDIT	PAGE 42
	1 29800	31	Work in Process	1105			14
			Factory Overhead	5103	1 29800		15
			Memorandum No. 725.				16

Entry to record applied overhead

Work in Process	1105
Balance 8,167.32	
Dir. Lab. 8,285.20	
Dir. Lab. 10,544.80	
Dir. Mat. 30,202.40	
Applied Fac. Overhead	
11,298.00	

Factory Overhead		5103	
Actual	11,098.16	Applied	11,298.00

The effect of this entry is shown in the T accounts at the left. The work in process account now shows the beginning inventory, the direct labor cost, the direct materials cost, and the applied factory overhead.

The debit in the factory overhead account is the total actual factory overhead expense for the month. The credit is the amount of overhead recorded on job cost sheets during the month. The credit balance of the factory overhead account is $199.84. This credit balance resulted from recording more applied overhead than the amount of actual overhead expense.

Overapplied and underapplied overhead

The estimated amount of applied overhead recorded on the various job cost sheets during the month is $199.84 larger than the actual overhead. The amount by which applied overhead is more than actual overhead is called overapplied overhead. The overapplied overhead of Carefree Trailer Company for the month of January is therefore $199.84.

Applied overhead may be estimated carefully and be almost the same as the actual overhead. However, there will usually be a remaining balance in the factory overhead account. This balance is closed to the income summary account. On January 31, the company's factory overhead account has a credit balance. The entry in the general journal to close the factory overhead account at the end of January is shown below.

	VOUCHERS PAYABLE DEBIT	GENERAL DEBIT	DATE	ACCOUNT TITLE	POST. REF.	GENERAL CREDIT	ACCOUNTS RECEIV. CREDIT	
17		199 84	Dec 31	Factory Overhead	5103			17
18				Income Summary	3300	199 84		18
19				Memorandum No. 726.				19
20								20
21								21
22								22
23								23
24								24

GENERAL JOURNAL   PAGE 42

1984

Entry to close the factory overhead
account when there is overapplied overhead

A debit balance in the factory overhead account indicates that applied overhead is less than actual overhead. The amount by which applied overhead is less than actual overhead is called underapplied overhead.

If the factory overhead account has a debit balance, Income Summary is debited and Factory Overhead is credited for the amount of underapplied overhead.

RECORDING THE COSTS OF FINISHED GOODS MANUFACTURED

After a cost sheet is completed, the sheet is filed. At the end of the month, the total amounts on all cost sheets completed during the current month are added. The total of all completed cost sheets for January, $54,518.81, is the value of work finished during the month. This total value is transferred from Work in Process to Finished Goods. The transfer is recorded by the entry in the general journal shown on page 376.

			GENERAL JOURNAL			PAGE 42
1	2				3	4
VOUCHERS PAYABLE DEBIT	GENERAL DEBIT	DATE	ACCOUNT TITLE	POST. REF.	GENERAL CREDIT	ACCOUNTS RECEIV. CREDIT
20	54518 81	31 Finished Goods		1106		20
21		Work in Process		1105	54518 81	21
22		Memorandum No. 727.				22
23						23
24						24
25						25

Entry to record finished goods
manufactured during the month

The effect of this entry is shown in the T accounts below. The first debit in the finished goods account is the beginning inventory of Finished Goods. The second debit is the value of goods finished during the month and placed in the finished goods stockroom. The credit to Work in Process is the value of finished goods transferred from the factory to the stockroom. The balance of the work in process account is the ending inventory of Work in Process.

Finished Goods	1106
Balance 15,518.76	
Completed Cost Sheets 54,518.81	

Work in Process	1105
Balance 8,167.32	Finished Goods 54,518.81
Dir. Lab. 8,285.20	
Dir. Lab. 10,544.80	
Dir. Mat. 30,202.40	
Applied Fac. Overhead 11,298.00	

MANUFACTURING ACCOUNTS IN THE GENERAL LEDGER

After the entries described in this chapter are all posted, the manufacturing accounts in the general ledger appear as shown below and on page 377.

ACCOUNT **Materials**   ACCOUNT NO. 1104

DATE	ITEM	POST. REF.	DEBIT	CREDIT	BALANCE DEBIT	BALANCE CREDIT
1979 Jan. 1	Balance	✓			16 698 52	
31		VR 14	31 327 02		48 025 54	
31		J 42		30 202 40	17 823 14	

Manufacturing
accounts

Manufacturing accounts

ACCOUNT **Work in Process** ACCOUNT NO. **1105**

DATE	ITEM	POST. REF.	DEBIT	CREDIT	BALANCE DEBIT	BALANCE CREDIT
1979 Jan. 1	Balance	✓			816732	
15		VR13	828520		1645252	
31		VR14	1054480		2699732	
31		J42	3020240		5719972	
31		J42	1129800		6849772	
31		J42		5451881	1397891	

ACCOUNT **Finished Goods** ACCOUNT NO. **1106**

DATE	ITEM	POST. REF.	DEBIT	CREDIT	BALANCE DEBIT	BALANCE CREDIT
1979 Jan. 1	Balance	✓			1551876	
31		J42	5451881		7003757	

ACCOUNT **Factory Overhead** ACCOUNT NO. **5103**

DATE	ITEM	POST. REF.	DEBIT	CREDIT	BALANCE DEBIT	BALANCE CREDIT
1979 Jan. 15		VR13	320330		320330	
31		VR14	347022		667352	
31		J42	442464		1109816	
31		J42		1129800		19984
31		J42	19984			

ADJUSTMENTS FOR INVENTORIES

The balance of each inventory account needs to be brought up to date at the end of each fiscal period. The inventory accounts of Carefree Trailer Company that need to be adjusted are Materials, Work in Process, and Finished Goods.

Materials and work in process

The balances of the materials account and the work in process account are the inventories that should be on hand on January 31. To prove the accuracy of these two account balances, a periodic inventory is taken of direct materials and of work in process. If there is a significant difference between the account balance and the periodic inventory, an adjusting entry is made.

If the periodic materials inventory is more than the materials account balance, the difference is debited to Materials and credited to Income Summary. If the periodic materials inventory is less than the materials account balance, the difference is debited to Income Summary and credited to Materials. Similar adjusting entries are made for differences between the account balance and the periodic inventory of work in process.

Finished goods

The finished goods account shows the beginning balance and the total value of all job orders completed during the month. At the end of the month, a periodic inventory of the finished goods is taken. This finished goods inventory is similar to the merchandise inventory of a merchandising business. The difference between this finished goods periodic inventory and the debit balance of the finished goods account is then found. This difference is the cost of goods sold. An adjusting entry is made by debiting Income Summary and crediting Finished Goods for $42,879.41, the amount of difference, as shown below.

VOUCHERS PAYABLE DEBIT	GENERAL DEBIT	DATE	ACCOUNT TITLE	POST. REF.	GENERAL CREDIT	ACCOUNTS RECEIV. CREDIT	
	4287941	31	*Income Summary*	3300			23
			Finished Goods	1106	4287941		24
			Memorandum No. 728.				25
							26

GENERAL JOURNAL   PAGE *42*

Adjusting entry for finished goods

The effect of this entry is shown in the T accounts below. The debits in the finished goods account are the beginning inventory and the value of work completed during the period. The credit to Finished Goods and debit to Income Summary is the amount of finished goods sold during the period. The balance of the finished goods account, $27,158.16, is now the ending inventory of Finished Goods.

Finished Goods	1106		Income Summary	3300
Balance 15,518.76	Cost of Goods Sold 42,879.41		Cost of Goods Sold 42,879.41	
Completed Cost Sheets 54,518.81				

FISCAL-PERIOD STATEMENTS

A manufacturing business prepares fiscal-period statements similar to those of other businesses. Carefree Trailer Company prepares a statement of cost of goods manufactured, an income statement, and a balance sheet.

Statement of cost of goods manufactured

A statement of cost of goods manufactured supplements the income statement and may be attached as a schedule. A statement of cost of goods manufactured for Carefree Trailer Company is on page 379.

```
                      Carefree Trailer Company              Schedule A
                  Statement of Cost of Goods Manufactured
                     For Month Ended January 31, 1979
═══════════════════════════════════════════════════════════════════════

   Direct Materials:
      Materials Inventory, January 1, 1979 . . . . . . .   $16,698.52
      Materials Purchased  . . . . . . . . . . . . . . .    31,327.02
      Total Materials Available During the Period  . . .   $48,025.54
      Less Materials Inventory, January 31, 1979 . . .     17,823.14
      Cost of Direct Materials Placed in Process . . . .                  $30,202.40

   Direct Labor . . . . . . . . . . . . . . . . . . . .                    18,830.00

   Factory Overhead Applied . . . . . . . . . . . . . .                    11,298.00

   Total Cost of Work Placed in Process . . . . . . . .                   $60,330.40
      Add Work in Process Inventory, January 1, 1979 . .                    8,167.32

   Total Cost of Work in Process During the Period  . .                   $68,497.72
      Less Work in Process Inventory, January 31, 1979 .                   13,978.91

   Cost of Goods Manufactured . . . . . . . . . . . . .                    $54,518.81
```

Statement of cost of goods manufactured

Data for the statement above come from three sources. Materials inventory and work in process inventory come from the general ledger accounts, pages 376–377. Materials purchased and direct labor come from the voucher register, pages 370–371. The amount of factory overhead, $11,298.00, is the total estimate recorded on cost sheets and not the actual overhead debited to Factory Overhead. The total amount to be included in cost of goods manufactured is therefore the total applied overhead and not the actual overhead.

Income statement of a manufacturing business

The income statement of Carefree Trailer Company on January 31 is shown on the next page. This income statement differs in two ways from the income statements of merchandising businesses shown in previous chapters.

First, cost of goods manufactured is used instead of purchases. Reference is made to Schedule A, the statement of cost of goods manufactured, where the details of the cost of goods manufactured are given.

Second, the amount of overapplied overhead, $199.84, is subtracted from the cost of goods sold. The amount is subtracted because applied overhead, $11,298.00, is more than the actual overhead, $11,098.16.

If there had been underapplied overhead, the overhead included in the cost of goods manufactured would have been less than the actual overhead expenses. In that case, the amount of the underapplied overhead would have been added to the cost of goods sold on the income statement.

Carefree Trailer Company
Income Statement
For the Month Ended January 31, 1979

Revenue from Sales:		
Sales	$64,574.75	
Less Sales Discount	645.32	
Net Sales		$63,929.43
Cost of Goods Sold:		
Finished Goods Inventory, January 1, 1979	$15,518.76	
Cost of Goods Manufactured (Schedule A)	54,518.81	
Total Cost of Finished Goods Available for Sale .	$70,037.57	
Less Finished Goods Inventory, January 31, 1979 .	27,158.16	
Cost of Goods Sold	$42,879.41	
Less Overapplied Overhead	199.84	
Net Cost of Goods Sold		42,679.57
Gross Profit on Operations		$21,249.86
Operating Expenses:		
Selling Expenses:		
Advertising Expense	$1,022.65	
Delivery Expense	2,512.10	
Depreciation Expense--Store Equipment	26.17	
Miscellaneous Expense--Sales	635.06	
Salary Expense--Sales	4,911.90	
Supplies Expense--Sales	568.64	
Total Selling Expenses	$ 9,676.52	
Administrative Expenses:		
Bad Debts Expense	$ 322.82	
Depreciation Expense--Building	49.41	
Depreciation Expense--Office Equipment	29.00	
Insurance Expense--Office	16.51	
Miscellaneous Expense--Administrative	660.92	
Payroll Taxes Expense--Operating	947.74	
Property Tax Expense--Operating	39.18	
Salary Expense--Administrative	6,480.40	
Supplies Expense--Office	144.32	
Total Administrative Expenses	8,690.30	
Total Operating Expenses		18,366.82
Net Income from Operations		$ 2,883.04
Other Revenue:		
Gain on Plant Assets	$ 66.00	
Other Expense:		
Loss on Plant Assets	104.00	
Net Deduction		38.00
Net Income Before Federal Income Tax		$ 2,845.04
Less Federal Income Tax		625.91
Net Income After Federal Income Tax		$ 2,219.13

Income statement of a manufacturing business

Balance sheet of a manufacturing business

The balance sheet prepared by Carefree Trailer Company on January 31 is shown on the next page. Except for the listing of inventories, the balance sheet of a manufacturing business is similar to the balance sheet of a merchandising business. In a manufacturing business, the current assets section of the balance sheet lists three types of inventories: (a) Materials, (b) Work in Process, and (c) Finished Goods.

```
                    Carefree Trailer Company
                         Balance Sheet
                       January 31, 1979
```

ASSETS

Current Assets:			
Cash			$ 25,156.15
Petty Cash			200.00
Accounts Receivable	$47,410.62		
Less Allowance for Uncollectible Accounts . .	1,447.44		45,963.18
Materials			17,823.14
Work in Process			13,978.91
Finished Goods			27,158.16
Prepaid Insurance			558.91
Supplies--Factory			999.81
Supplies--Sales			712.56
Supplies--Office			210.40
Total Current Assets			$132,761.22
Plant Assets:			
Factory Equipment	$41,616.00		
Less Accumulated Depr.--Factory Equipment . .	11,360.00	$ 30,256.00	
Store Equipment	$ 3,140.00		
Less Accumulated Depr.--Store Equipment . . .	1,174.30	1,965.70	
Office Equipment	$ 3,480.00		
Less Accumulated Depr.--Office Equipment . . .	1,146.58	2,333.42	
Building	$96,000.00		
Less Accumulated Depr.--Building	9,600.00	86,400.00	
Land		40,000.00	
Total Plant Assets			160,955.12
Total Assets			$293,716.34

LIABILITIES

Current Liabilities:		
Vouchers Payable	$ 5,840.52	
Employees Income Tax Payable	3,037.54	
FICA Tax Payable	3,048.88	
Unemployment Tax Payable--Federal	177.48	
Unemployment Tax Payable--State	261.04	
Property Tax Payable	840.64	
Income Tax Payable--Federal	1,297.92	
Total Current Liabilities		$ 14,504.02
Long-Term Liability:		
Mortgage Payable		20,000.00
Total Liabilities		$ 34,504.02

STOCKHOLDERS' EQUITY

Capital Stock	$200,000.00	
Retained Earnings	59,212.32	
Total Stockholders' Equity		259,212.32
Total Liabilities and Stockholders' Equity		$293,716.34

Balance sheet of a manufacturing business

Using Business Terms

✦ What is the meaning of each of the following?

- statement of cost of goods manufactured
- overapplied overhead
- underapplied overhead

Questions for Individual Study

1. Where are the specific cost elements for manufacturing an individual job recorded?
2. What three inventory accounts does a manufacturing business have?
3. What are the three cost elements of manufacturing a product?
4. When a factory payroll is entered in the voucher register, what accounts are debited and what accounts normally are credited?
5. How is a specific job charged with the amount of direct labor actually used to manufacture that job?
6. When the total of all direct materials requisitions is recorded in the general journal at the end of the month, what account is debited and what account is credited?
7. After all journals have been posted, what amounts are debits in the factory overhead account?
8. How does the cost accounting clerk for Carefree Trailer Company distrib-

ute the estimated factory overhead to the job orders?
9. What entry is made at the end of the month to record the applied overhead for the month?
10. When there is overapplied overhead at the end of a month, does the factory overhead account have a debit balance or a credit balance?
11. What entry is made at the end of the month to close the factory overhead account when there is underapplied overhead?
12. How does the cost accounting clerk for Carefree Trailer Company determine the amount of work finished during the month?
13. What entry is made at the end of the month to record the finished goods manufactured during the month?
14. In the factory overhead account on page 377, what is represented by (a) the credit entry, and (b) the last debit entry?

Cases for Management Decision

CASE 1 Cole Corporation records factory overhead at the rate of 75% of the direct labor charges on each job order. At the end of March, the total of all direct labor charges recorded on cost sheets for jobs processed during the month is $10,260.00.

The total of the balances of all factory overhead expense accounts is $7,830.00. (1) Is the factory overhead for the month overapplied or underapplied? (2) How will the balance of the factory overhead account be listed on the income statement for March?

CASE 2 Avery Corporation is a small manufacturing company. During 1978 the company had underapplied and overapplied overhead as follows:

Underapplied		Overapplied	
January	$320.00	April	$235.00
February	205.00	May	340.00
March	20.00	June	720.00
November	230.00	July	165.00
December	400.00	August	540.00
		September	310.00
		October	50.00
	$1,175.00		$2,360.00

Avery Corporation closes the books and prepares statements at the end of each calendar year. (1) On December 31 is the factory overhead for 1978 underapplied or overapplied? (2) How will the balance of the factory overhead account be listed on the income statement for 1978?

In 1976 and 1977, the company had underapplied and overapplied overhead amounts as follows:

	Underapplied	Overapplied
1976	$1,025.00	$1,740.00
1977	1,140.00	1,950.00

(3) Considering the relationship between underapplied and overapplied overhead for the three years, as the cost accounting clerk would you make any recommendations to the controller and to the factory manager? Explain.

PROBLEM 20-1 **Recording journal entries in a voucher register of a manufacturing business**

Problems for Applying Concepts

Instructions: □ **1.** Record on page 11 of a voucher register, similar to the one shown on pages 370–371, the following transactions of the Copeland Electrical Company. The source document voucher is abbreviated V.

May 1. Purchased direct materials on account from Martin's Electric Company, $6,347.60. V1116.

2. Bought supplies on account from Village Supply Company as follows: factory supplies, $326.40; office supplies, $49.75. V1117.

6. Received bill from the Sailmaker Restaurant, to entertain a customer, $46.20. V1118. (Miscellaneous Expense — Sales)

8. Purchased direct materials on account from Southern Electrical Company, $2,462.65. V1119.

10. Received bill from Marconi Sheet Metal Company for machinery repairs, $124.35. V1120. (Miscellaneous Expense — Factory)

13. Bought factory supplies on account from Shaw's, $275.30. V1121.

15. Received bill from Economy Printing Company for advertising, $217.40. V1122. (Advertising Expense)

17. Purchased direct materials on account from Collins, Inc., $929.80. V1123.

20. Received bill from Gordon Paints for painting the office, $175.00. V1124. (Miscellaneous Expense — Administrative)

24. Bought a new wiring machine from Krueger Machinery Company, $923.50. V1125. (Factory Equipment)

27. Received bill from Delgado Typewriter Company for typewriter repairs, $27.00. V1126. (Miscellaneous Expense — Administrative)

28. Bought decorations for an electrical display from Simmons Company, $26.35. V1127. (Miscellaneous Expense — Sales)

31. Monthly payroll data: Direct labor, $3,400.00; Indirect labor, $1,315.00; Employees Income Tax Payable $754.40; FICA Tax Payable, $282.90. V1128.

31. Replenished the petty cash fund as follows: Supplies — Factory, $28.30; Supplies — Office, $6.45; Miscellaneous Expense — Factory, $38.20; Miscellaneous Expense — Sales, $22.05; Advertising Expense, $33.25. V1129.

Instructions: □ **2.** Foot, prove, total, and rule the voucher register.

PROBLEM 20-2 **Journalizing the entries that summarize the cost records at the end of the month**

Completed Problem 20-2 will be needed for Problem 20-3.

On March 31 of the current year, Wilton Company has the information listed on page 384.

(a) The various accounts in the general ledger used in recording the actual factory overhead expenses during the month have the following balances:

Depreciation Expense — Building	5101	$1,334.00
Depreciation Expense — Factory Equipment	5102	4,890.00
Heat, Light, and Power	5104	3,704.00
Insurance Expense — Factory	5105	624.00
Miscellaneous Expense — Factory	5106	3,596.00
Payroll Taxes Expense — Factory	5107	5,500.00
Property Tax Expense — Factory	5108	2,424.00
Supplies Expense — Factory	5109	5,156.00

(b) Inventory account balances are:

Materials, $118,550.00. (March 1 balance, $88,730.00, plus March purchases, $29,820.00.) Account No. 1104.
Work in Process, March 1 balance, $11,398.00. Account No. 1105.
Finished Goods, March 1 balance, $100,126.00. Account No. 1106.

(c) The following accounts are needed for completing the posting (no beginning balances are needed):

Factory Overhead	5103
Employees Income Tax Payable	2102
FICA Tax Payable	2103
Income Summary	3300

(d) The total factory payroll for the month according to the payroll register is $78,544.00.

Payroll distribution is:	Work in Process	$65,800.00
	Factory Overhead	12,744.00
	Vouchers Payable	65,191.36
	Employees Income Tax Payable	8,640.00
	FICA Tax Payable	4,712.64

(e) The total of all requisitions of direct materials issued during the month is $86,372.00.
(f) The factory overhead to be charged to Work in Process is 60% of the direct labor cost.
(g) The total of all cost sheets completed during the month is $185,374.00.

Instructions: ▫ **1.** Open ledger accounts and record balances for information items (a), (b), and (c).

▫ **2.** Record the factory payroll entry on page 19 of a voucher register. V55. Post the general debit and general credit entries.

▫ **3.** Record the following entries on page 23 of a general journal. Post the entries.
   (a) An entry to transfer the total of all direct materials requisitions from Materials to Work in Process. M984.
   (b) An entry to transfer the balances of all individual factory overhead expense accounts to Factory Overhead. M985.

(c) An entry to transfer the applied factory overhead from Factory Overhead to Work in Process. M986.

□ **4.** Record and post the entry to transfer the balance of the factory overhead account to Income Summary. M987.

□ **5.** Record and post the entry to transfer the total of all cost sheets completed from Work in Process to Finished Goods. M988.

PROBLEM 20-3 Preparing a statement of cost of goods manufactured

Completed Problem 20-2 is needed for Problem 20-3.

Instructions: Prepare a statement of cost of goods manufactured, similar to the one illustrated on page 379, for Wilton Company for the month ended March 31 of the current year. Use the data in completed Problem 20-2.

MASTERY PROBLEM 20-M Journalizing the entries that summarize the cost records at the end of the month and preparing a statement of cost of goods manufactured

Optional Problems

On February 28 of the current year, McWilliams Company has the following information:

(a) The various accounts in the general ledger used in recording the actual factory overhead expenses during the month have the following balances:

Depreciation Expense — Building	5101	$1,867.60
Depreciation Expense — Factory Equipment	5102	6,846.00
Heat, Light, and Power	5104	5,185.60
Insurance Expense — Factory	5105	873.60
Miscellaneous Expense — Factory	5106	5,034.40
Payroll Taxes Expense — Factory	5107	7,700.00
Property Tax Expense — Factory	5108	3,393.60
Supplies Expense — Factory	5109	7,218.40

(b) Inventory account balances are:

Materials, $165,970.00. (February 1 balance, $124,222.00, plus February purchases, $41,748.00.) Account No. 1104.

Work in Process, February 1 balance, $15,957.20. Account No. 1105.

Finished Goods, February 1 balance, $141,032.00. Account No. 1106.

(c) The following accounts are needed for completing the posting (no beginning balances are needed):

Factory Overhead	5103
Employees Income Tax Payable	2102
FICA Tax Payable	2103
Income Summary	3300

(d) The total factory payroll for the month according to the payroll register is $109,961.60. Payroll distribution is:

Work in Process................	$92,120.00	Employees Income Tax Payable.	$12,096.00
Factory Overhead..............	17,841.60	FICA Tax Payable	6,597.70
Vouchers Payable..............	91,267.90		

(e) The total of all requisitions of direct materials issued during the month is $120,920.80.

(f) The factory overhead to be charged to Work in Process is 60% of the direct labor cost.

(g) The total of all cost sheets completed during the month is $259,523.60.

Instructions: □ **1.** Open ledger accounts and record balances for information items (a), (b) and (c).

□ **2.** Record the entry for the factory payroll on page 6 of a voucher register. V47. Post general debit and general credit entries.

□ **3.** Record the following entries on page 14 of a general journal. Post the entries.

   (a) An entry to transfer the total of all direct materials requisitions from Materials to Work in Process. M623.

   (b) An entry to transfer the balances of all individual factory overhead expense accounts to Factory Overhead. M624.

   (c) An entry to transfer the applied factory overhead from Factory Overhead to Work in Process. M625.

□ **4.** Record and post the entry to transfer the balance of the factory overhead account to Income Summary. M626.

□ **5.** Record and post the entry to transfer the total of all cost sheets completed from Work in Process to Finished Goods. M627.

□ **6.** Prepare a statement of cost of goods manufactured, similar to the one illustrated on page 379, for McWilliams Company for the month ended February 28 of the current year.

**BONUS
PROBLEM 20-B**   Journalizing the entries that summarize the cost records at the end of the month

On April 30 of the current year, Mato Company has the following information:

(a) The various accounts in the general ledger used in recording the actual factory overhead expenses during the month have the following balances:

Depreciation Expense — Building	5101	$ 720.00
Depreciation Expense — Factory Equipment.........................	5102	1,472.00
Heat, Light, and Power..	5104	2,310.00
Insurance Expense — Factory..	5105	384.00
Miscellaneous Expense — Factory.......................................	5106	4,320.00
Payroll Taxes Expense — Factory	5107	5,490.00
Property Tax Expense — Factory	5108	1,812.00
Supplies Expense — Factory	5109	4,608.00

(b) Inventory account balances are:

Materials, $138,900.00. (April 1 balance, $77,316.00, plus April purchases, $61,584.00.) Account No. 1104.
Work in Process, April 1 balance, $48,960.00. Account No. 1105.
Finished Goods, April 1 balance, $36,450.00. Account No. 1106.

(c) The following accounts are needed for completing the posting (no beginning balances are needed):

Factory Overhead 5103
Employees Income Tax Payable.. 2102
FICA Tax Payable 2103
Income Summary... 3300

(d) The total factory payroll for the month according to the payroll register is $78,432.00. Payroll distribution is:

Work in Process................. $58,260 .00   Employees Income Tax Payable. $ 8,628.00
Factory Overhead..............   20,172.00   FICA Tax Payable 4,705.92
Vouchers Payable..............   65,098.08

(e) The total of all requisitions of direct materials issued during the month is $64,344.00.
(f) The factory overhead to be charged to Work in Process is 72% of the direct labor cost.
(g) The total of all cost sheets completed during the month is $159,000.00.

Instructions: □ **1.** Open ledger accounts and record balances for information items (a), (b) and (c).
□ **2.** Record the entry for the factory payroll on page 3 of a voucher register. V150. Post general debit and general credit entries.
□ **3.** Record the following entries on page 7 of a general journal. Post the entries.
  (a) An entry to transfer the total of all direct materials requisitions from Materials to Work in Process. M1057.
  (b) An entry to transfer the balances of all individual factory overhead expense accounts to Factory Overhead. M1058.
  (c) An entry to transfer the applied factory overhead from Factory Overhead to Work in Process. M1059.
□ **4.** Record and post the entry to transfer the balance of the factory overhead account to Income Summary. M1060.
□ **5.** Record and post the entry to transfer the total of all cost sheets completed from Work in Process to Finished Goods. M1061.
□ **6.** Prepare a statement of cost and goods manufactured, similar to the one on page 379, for Mato Company for the month ended April 30 of the current year.
□ **7.** Record and post the general journal entry to transfer the cost of goods sold from Finished Goods to Income Summary. April 30 Finished Goods inventory is $28,600.00. M1062.

JUNIOR ACCOUNTANTS

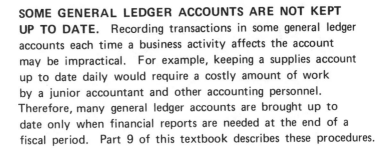

SOME GENERAL LEDGER ACCOUNTS ARE NOT KEPT UP TO DATE. Recording transactions in some general ledger accounts each time a business activity affects the account may be impractical. For example, keeping a supplies account up to date daily would require a costly amount of work by a junior accountant and other accounting personnel. Therefore, many general ledger accounts are brought up to date only when financial reports are needed at the end of a fiscal period. Part 9 of this textbook describes these procedures.

JUNIOR ACCOUNTANTS DO MANY KINDS OF ACCOUNTING WORK. Their work may include supervising other accounting personnel. Junior accountants are also often responsible for the end-of-fiscal-period work of a business.

SOME BUSINESSES USE CASH–BASIS ACCOUNTING. Some businesses engage in a relatively small number of transactions. The nature of the business and the small number of transactions make the use of several special journals and several kinds of ledgers unnecessary. A system is sufficient if a record is kept of cash received, cash paid, and the reasons for the receipts and payments. Therefore, many businesses choose to keep accounting records on a cash basis.

In Part 9 of this textbook, Chapters 21, 22, and 23, as most earlier chapters, describe businesses that keep records on an accrual basis. All transactions, whether they affect cash or not, are recorded. Chapter 24, however, describes a business that keeps records on a cash basis using a simple form of transaction register.

Balance Sheet Accounts

(1000) ASSETS	Account Number
1100 Current Assets	
Cash	1101
Petty Cash	1102
Accounts Receivable	1103
Allowance for Uncollectible Accounts	1103.1
Notes Receivable	1104
Merchandise Inventory	1105
Supplies — Sales	1106
Supplies — Warehouse	1107
Supplies — Office	1108
Prepaid Insurance	1109
Interest Receivable	1110
1200 Plant Assets	
Delivery Equipment	1201
Accumulated Depreciation — Delivery Equipment	1201.1
Warehouse Equipment	1202
Accumulated Depreciation — Warehouse Equipment	1202.1
Office Equipment	1203
Accumulated Depreciation — Office Equipment	1203.1
Building	1204
Accumulated Depreciation — Building	1204.1
Land	1205

(2000) LIABILITIES	
2100 Current Liabilities	
Accounts Payable	2101
Notes Payable	2102
Salaries Payable	2103
Employees Income Tax Payable — Federal	2104
FICA Tax Payable	2105
Unemployment Tax Payable — Federal	2106
Unemployment Tax Payable — State	2107
Rent Received in Advance	2108
Interest Payable	2109
Corporation's Income Tax Payable — Federal	2110
Property Tax Payable	2111
2200 Long-term Liability	
Mortgage Payable	2201

(3000) CAPITAL	
Capital Stock	3100
Retained Earnings	3200
Income Summary	3300

Income Statement Accounts

(4000) OPERATING REVENUE	Account Number
Sales	4001
Sales Returns and Allowances	4001.1
Sales Discount	4001.2

(5000) COST OF MERCHANDISE	
Purchases	5001
Purchases Returns & Allowances	5001.1
Purchases Discount	5001.2

(6000) OPERATING EXPENSES	
6100 Selling Expenses	
Advertising Expense	6101
Delivery Expense	6102
Depreciation Expense — Delivery Equipment	6103
Miscellaneous Expense — Sales	6104
Salary Expense — Sales	6105
Supplies Expense — Sales	6106
6200 Warehouse Expenses	
Depreciation Expense — Warehouse Equipment	6201
Miscellaneous Expense — Warehouse	6202
Salary Expense — Warehouse	6203
Supplies Expense — Warehouse	6204
6300 Administrative Expenses	
Bad Debts Expense	6301
Depreciation Expense — Office Equipment	6302
Depreciation Expense — Building	6303
Insurance Expense	6304
Miscellaneous Expense — Administrative	6305
Payroll Taxes Expense	6306
Salary Expense — Administrative	6307
Supplies Expense — Office	6308

(7000) OTHER REVENUE	
Gain on Plant Assets	7001
Interest Income	7002
Rent Income	7003

(8000) OTHER EXPENSES	
Interest Expense	8001
Loss on Plant Assets	8002

(9000) CORPORATION TAXES	
Federal Income Tax	9001
Property Tax	9002

The chart of accounts for Handley Corporation is illustrated above for ready reference in your study of Part 9 of this textbook.

21

Accounting for Uncollectible Accounts

The use of credit by businesses and individuals has contributed greatly to the expansion and strength of the American economy. However, no business wants to sell to a charge customer who might fail to pay what is owed. For this reason, most businesses investigate the credit rating of each new charge customer before selling on account.

Regardless of the care taken in granting credit to customers, there may be some charge customers from whom a business cannot collect what is due. Accounts receivable that cannot be collected are called uncollectible accounts. Uncollectible accounts are sometimes known as bad debts.

A business may use either of two methods in recording bad debts expense:

1. Recording the bad debts expense when the account is actually determined uncollectible, regardless of when the charge sale was made, is called the direct write-off method.

2. Recording an estimated amount for bad debts expense in the fiscal period in which the charge sales are made is called the allowance method.

The Internal Revenue Service permits a business to choose either of the two methods for recording bad debts expense for income tax purposes.

DIRECT WRITE-OFF METHOD OF RECORDING BAD DEBTS EXPENSE

Until a business discovers that a charge customer's account actually is uncollectible, the amount is recorded as an asset in Accounts Receivable. At the time it is determined that the account is uncollectible, the amount becomes an expense. A charge customer's account that is uncollectible should be closed. The account is no longer an asset of the business. Canceling the balance of a charge customer's account because the customer cannot or will not pay the amount due is called writing off an account. An uncollectible account is usually recorded as an expense in an account titled Bad Debts Expense.

The Cardinal Pet Shop sells only a small amount of merchandise on account. Therefore, the shop has few uncollectible accounts receivable. For this reason, the direct write-off method of recording bad debts expense is used. Bad debts expense is recorded only when the shop actually determines that a specific account receivable is uncollectible.

Writing off an account — direct write-off method

On March 6, 1978, the Cardinal Pet Shop learns that Jack Osgood, a charge customer, has died and apparently left no money to pay his debts. The balance of Mr. Osgood's account is $23.95. This amount is now determined to be uncollectible.

March 6, 1978. Wrote off the account of Jack Osgood as uncollectible, $23.95. Memorandum No. 15.

This transaction is analyzed in the T accounts below.

GENERAL LEDGER	ACCOUNTS RECEIVABLE LEDGER
Bad Debts Expense 6111	Jack Osgood
23.95	Balance 23.95 | 23.95
Accounts Receivable 1102	
23.95	

Bad Debts Expense is debited, $23.95, to show the increase in the balance of this expense account.

Accounts Receivable is credited, $23.95, to show the decrease in the balance of this asset account. Jack Osgood's account in the accounts receivable ledger is also credited for $23.95.

Collecting a written-off account — direct write-off method

An account that is written off in one fiscal period as uncollectible may be collected in a later fiscal period. When an account is written off, the amount becomes an expense. When an uncollectible account is later collected, the amount must be recorded as revenue for the fiscal period in which collected. On January 5, 1979, the Cardinal Pet Shop receives a check for $23.95 from the estate of Jack Osgood.

January 5, 1979. Received a check for $23.95 in full payment of Jack Osgood's account, previously written off as uncollectible. Memorandum No. 58 and Receipt No. 21.

The Cardinal Pet Shop wishes to have a complete record of accounts receivable. Therefore, when an account previously written off is collected, accounts receivable is recorded on the books again. The analysis of this transaction is shown in the T accounts below.

GENERAL LEDGER		ACCOUNTS RECEIVABLE LEDGER	
Accounts Receivable 1102		Jack Osgood	
23.95		Balance 23.95 23.95	23.95
Bad Debts Collected 7004			
	23.95		

Accounts Receivable and the charge customer's account are debited for $23.95 so that this account is restored to the records. Bad Debts Collected, an other revenue account, is credited for $23.95.

> The bad debts collected account is closed to **Income Summary** as part of the regular closing entries at the end of a fiscal period. The bad debts collected account is shown on the income statement under the heading Other Revenue.

After the account is restored to the records, the Cardinal Pet Shop records the receipt of cash to pay the account. This transaction is shown in the T accounts below.

GENERAL LEDGER		ACCOUNTS RECEIVABLE LEDGER	
Cash 1101		Jack Osgood	
23.95		Balance 23.95 23.95	23.95 23.95
Accounts Receivable 1102			
	23.95		

Cash is debited to show the receipt of cash. Accounts Receivable and the charge customer's account are credited for $23.95. The charge customer's account now shows a complete history including payment in full for the amount owed.

ALLOWANCE METHOD OF RECORDING BAD DEBTS EXPENSE

The Phillips Company has some bad debts expense. The bad debts expense is recorded in the fiscal period during which the uncollectible charge sales are made. In this way the company's balance sheet shows the portion of accounts receivable that is estimated to be collectible. Also, when an income statement is prepared, all the expenses of the fiscal period are shown.

At the time a charge sale is made there is usually no way of knowing for sure if the amount will be collectible. Therefore, only an estimate can be made of the uncollectible amounts owed by charge customers. In the allowance method, an estimate of probable bad debts expense is usually based on the past experience of a business. The past records are examined and one of two common methods of estimating the bad debts expense is used:

1. Take a percentage of a figure related to the charge sales. The figures used may be (a) net sales, or (b) net charge sales.

2. Take a percentage of a figure related to the amount owed by charge customers at the end of a fiscal period. The figures used may be (a) the balance of the general ledger accounts receivable account, or (b) the amounts to be collected from charge customers according to the length of time owed by the customers. Analyzing accounts receivable according to when the amounts are due is called aging accounts receivable.

Estimating bad debts expense based on aging accounts receivable

The Phillips Company ages its accounts receivable at the end of each fiscal period. On December 31, 1978, the junior accountant prepared the following schedule of accounts receivable by age.

		SCHEDULE OF ACCOUNTS RECEIVABLE BY AGE December 31, 19--				
Customer's Name	Account Balance	Age of Account Balance				
		Not yet due	1-30 days past due	31-60 days past due	61-90 days past due	Over 90 days past due
Nancy Addler Ronald Doall Darrel Foster	582.00 23.00 249.45	582.00	23.00			249.45
Lance Willard	138.94			138.94		
TOTALS	9,051.98	6,155.29	2,077.36	452.60	96.47	270.26

Schedule of accounts receivable by age

Based on past records, the Phillips Company has found that a portion of the balances owed in each "age" of accounts receivable will be uncollectible. The percentages are: (a) not yet due, 1%; (b) 1–30 days past due, 2%; (c) 31–60 days past due, 6%; (d) 61–90 days past due, 20%; and (e) over 90 days past due, 60%. Using the data from the schedule of accounts receivable by age above, the estimate of bad debts expense on December 31, 1978, is shown on page 395.

Of the $9,051.98 in accounts receivable on the records of the Phillips Company, the company estimates that $311.71 will be uncollectible. There is no attempt, however, to identify the specific accounts that are expected to be uncollectible. The estimated value of accounts receivable is $8,740.27 ($9,051.98 − $311.71 = $8,740.27). The difference between

Age of balance owed	Total in each age	Percentage uncollectible	Estimated amount of bad debts expense
Not yet due	$6,155.29	1%	$ 61.55
1–30 days past due	2,077.36	2%	41.55
31–60 days past due	452.60	6%	27.16
61–90 days past due	96.47	20%	19.29
Over 90 days past due	270.26	60%	162.16
Totals	$9,051.98		$311.71

the total amount of accounts receivable and the amount estimated to be uncollectible is called the book value of accounts receivable. The book value of accounts receivable is shown on the balance sheet of the Phillips Company. This provides a clearer picture of the estimated valuation of accounts receivable.

On December 31, 1978, Allowance for Uncollectible Accounts has a credit balance of $42.50. The estimated amount of uncollectible accounts figured above is $311.71. Therefore, the balance of the allowance account must be adjusted to bring the balance up to $311.71. The effect of the adjustment on the general ledger accounts is shown in the T accounts at the right.

Bad Debts Expense	6301
Adjusting 269.21	

Allowance for Uncollectible Accounts	1103.1
	Balance 42.50
	Adjusting 269.21

The amount for the adjustment, $269.21, is found by subtracting the balance of the allowance account from the estimated amount of uncollectible accounts ($311.71 − $42.50).

Bad Debts Expense is debited and Allowance for Uncollectible Accounts is credited for $269.21. The new balance of the allowance account is $311.71 ($42.50 + $269.21).

Estimating bad debts expense based on a percentage of charge sales

The Handley Corporation estimates its bad debts expense based on the total charge sales for a fiscal period. Past records of the corporation show that the bad debts expense is equal to about 1% of the total charge sales made in a fiscal period. For the year ended December 31, 1979, the Handley Corporation had total charge sales of $105,490.78. The corporation estimates its bad debts expense to be $1,054.91 ($105,490.78 × 1%).

At the end of each fiscal period, the Handley Corporation makes an adjusting entry to record the amount of bad debts expense. For the adjusting entry on December 31, 1979, the effect on the accounts is shown at the right.

Bad Debts Expense is debited for $1,054.91 to record the amount of bad debts for the fiscal period. Allowance for Uncollectible Accounts is credited for $1,054.91 to show this change in the contra asset account. The credit to Allowance for Uncollectible Accounts is added to any credit balance that already exists in the account to figure the new credit balance.

Bad Debts Expense	6301
1,054.91	

Allowance for Uncollectible Accounts	1103.1
	1,054.91

The balance of **Allowance for Uncollectible Accounts** may grow from year to year. This increase in the balance of the account may indicate that the percentage being used to estimate the amount of bad debts expense is wrong. When this occurs, the percentage should be corrected based on actual experience with uncollectible accounts for the past two or three years.

The corporation might have used the other method described on page 394 for estimating the amount of bad debts expense for a fiscal period. Regardless of the method used to estimate the amount, the accounts affected by the adjusting entry are the same.

Writing off an account — allowance method

When the amount of bad debts expense is estimated, the specific names of customers and amounts that will be uncollectible are unknown. When the names and amounts become specifically known to be uncollectible, the amounts are written off against the balance of **Allowance for Uncollectible Accounts.**

On February 5, 1980, the Handley Corporation learns that Ronald Doall has gone into bankruptcy and the balance of his account will be uncollectible, $23.00.

February 5, 1980. Wrote off the account of Ronald Doall as uncollectible, $23.00. Memorandum No. 16.

The analysis of this transaction is shown in the T accounts below. **Allowance for Uncollectible Accounts** is debited, $23.00, to show the decrease in the balance of this contra asset account. **Accounts Receivable** is credited, $23.00, to show the decrease in the balance of this asset account. The charge customer's account, **Ronald Doall**, is also credited for $23.00.

GENERAL LEDGER	ACCOUNTS RECEIVABLE LEDGER
Allowance for Uncollectible Accounts 1103.1	Ronald Doall
23.00	Balance 954.90	Balance 23.00	23.00
Accounts Receivable 1103	
	23.00	

The general journal entry to record the writing off of Ronald Doall's account is shown on page 397.

When this entry is posted, Ronald Doall's account is closed. The balance of the controlling account, **Accounts Receivable**, is reduced by $23.00. The balance of **Allowance for Uncollectible Accounts** is also reduced by $23.00. The new balance of the allowance account, $931.90, represents the amount of accounts receivable that Handley Corporation still estimates will be uncollectible.

			GENERAL JOURNAL			PAGE *3*

| 1 | 2 | | | 3 | 4 |
ACCOUNTS PAYABLE DEBIT	GENERAL DEBIT	DATE	ACCOUNT TITLE	POST. REF.	GENERAL CREDIT	ACCOUNTS RECEIV. CREDIT
16		2300	5 *Allow. for Uncollectible Accts.*				16
17			*Ronald Doall*			2300	17
18			*Memorandum No. 16.*				18
19							19

Entry to write off an uncollectible account — allowance method

The entry to write off an account is the same regardless of the method used to estimate bad debts expense.

Collecting a written-off account — allowance method

On August 23, 1980, Handley Corporation received payment in full for the account of Ronald Doall which had been written off.

> *August 23, 1980. Received a check in full payment of Ronald Doall's account, previously written off as uncollectible, $23.00. Memorandum No. 72 and Receipt No. 160.*

The two entries described on pages 392–393 for the direct write-off method are used by Handley Corporation. However, the accounts differ slightly. The first entry records the account receivable on the records again. The second entry records the receipt of cash on account.

Entry to reinstate an account previously written off as uncollectible. The analysis of the general journal entry to reinstate an account receivable previously written off as uncollectible is shown in the T accounts below.

The entry to reinstate the account is the reverse of the one made to write it off as uncollectible. Accounts Receivable and the charge customer's account are debited for $23.00. Allowance for Uncollectible Accounts is credited for $23.00. This entry restores the records to what they were before Ronald Doall's account was written off.

GENERAL LEDGER

Accounts Receivable   1103

23.00	

Allowance for
Uncollectible Accounts 1103.1

	23.00

ACCOUNTS RECEIVABLE LEDGER

Ronald Doall

Balance	23.00	23.00
	23.00	

The entry in the general journal to record the reinstatement of Ronald Doall's account is shown on page 398.

		GENERAL JOURNAL			PAGE *10*

Entry to reinstate an account receivable previously
written off as uncollectible — allowance method

Entry to record receipt of cash for an account previously written off as uncollectible. The second entry made to record cash received from Ronald Doall is shown in the T accounts below.

GENERAL LEDGER

Cash   1101
23.00 |

Accounts Receivable   1103
                              | 23.00

ACCOUNTS RECEIVABLE
LEDGER

Ronald Doall

Balance   23.00 | 23.00
           23.00 | **23.00**

This entry is the same as it would be for the receipt of cash from any charge customer to apply on account.

The entry in the cash receipts journal to record the receipt of cash from Ronald Doall is shown below.

					CASH RECEIPTS JOURNAL						PAGE *12*

Entry to record cash received on account from customer
previously written off as uncollectible — allowance method

After the two entries have been posted, Ronald Doall's account will again be closed. The amount received from him on account will be deducted from the accounts receivable account. The amount previously charged off as uncollectible will again be part of the balance of Allowance for Uncollectible Accounts.

ACCOUNTS RECEIVABLE TURNOVER

A business that sells on account desires to make prompt collection from charge customers. The seller wants to receive payment for the merchandise so that the cash is available to use again. If the amounts due from charge customers are not collected promptly, too large a share of the business assets are represented by accounts receivable.

One means of analyzing the efficiency of the collection methods is to figure the accounts receivable turnover rate. The number of times the average amount of accounts receivable is collected in a year is called the accounts receivable turnover rate.

Figuring the accounts receivable turnover rate

The accounts receivable turnover rate is figured by dividing the net charge sales for the year by the average book value of the accounts receivable for the year. If monthly balances of accounts receivable are available, they should be used in figuring the average. If they are not available, the balance of the accounts receivable account at the beginning and the end of the year may be used.

The accounts receivable turnover rate for Handley Corporation is figured as follows:

Net charge sales for the year 1980 .... $110,502.66

Book value of Accounts Receivable, beginning of 1980............ $ 13,081.98
Plus book value of Accounts Receivable at end of 1980............ 12,032.26

Equals Total.. $ 25,114.24

Total *divided* by 2 *equals* average book value of Accounts Receivable for 1980... $ 12,557.12
Net charge sales, $110,502.66, *divided* by average book value, $12,557.12, *equals* the accounts receivable turnover rate for 1980... 8.8

Analyzing the accounts receivable turnover rate

Handley Corporation sells to charge customers on terms of 1/10, n/30. The terms mean that charge customers are expected to pay the amount owed in 30 days or less. An accounts receivable turnover rate of 12 means that the amounts are collected in about one-twelfth of a year, or one month (30 days). An accounts receivable turnover rate of 12 indicates that charge customers are taking the full time allowed them in which to pay their accounts — one month (30 days).

Handley Corporation has an accounts receivable turnover rate of 8.8. This means that charge customers are taking an average of about 1 1/3 months (12 months ÷ 8.8), or 40 days, to pay their accounts. This is more than the 30 days stated in the credit terms.

Records of previous years for Handley Corporation show the following accounts receivable turnover rates:

1975	1976	1977	1978	1979	1980
8.0	8.1	7.9	8.0	8.3	8.8

The accounts receivable turnover rate has risen from 8.0 in 1975 to 8.8 in 1980. These turnover rates show a good trend. The trend shows that there is less time between the charge sale and receipt of cash in 1980 than there was in 1975. Also, the turnover rate has been slowly increasing over the past four years. This increase is favorable. However, 8.8 is short of the expected 12 rate. The Handley Corporation should plan ways to encourage customers to pay on account more quickly than they do. Also, the Handley Corporation should encourage more customers to pay cash instead of buying on account. Sometimes, however, a demand for quicker payment by charge customers could result in loss of their business. If this appears to be true, Handley Corporation needs to consider changing the credit terms.

Using Business Terms

✦ What is the meaning of each of the following?

- uncollectible accounts
- direct write-off method
- allowance method
- writing off an account

- aging accounts receivable
- book value of accounts receivable
- accounts receivable turnover rate

Questions for Individual Study

1. What is the major difference between the direct write-off method and the allowance method of recording bad debts expense?
2. When might a business decide to use the direct write-off method of recording bad debts expense?
3. In the direct write-off method, what accounts are affected and how are they affected when an account receivable is written off?
4. Why are two entries made when cash is received on account from a charge customer whose account has already been written off as uncollectible?
5. When the entry is made to reinstate a customer's account that has been written off as uncollectible, what accounts are affected if the direct write-off method is used?
6. Why is the amount charged to bad debts expense at the end of each fiscal period an estimate when using the allowance method?
7. What is the first step required in the method used by the Phillips Company, as described in this chapter, for estimating its bad debts expense?
8. What basis is used by Handley Corporation, as described in this chapter,

for estimating its bad debts expense?
9. What accounts are affected and how are they affected by the adjustment for bad debts expense made by the Handley Corporation as described in this chapter?
10. When the allowance method is used, what accounts are affected and how are they affected when it is determined that an account receivable is uncollectible?
11. What accounts are affected when an entry is made to reinstate an account receivable, which was previously written off as uncollectible, when using the allowance method?
12. In the table on page 399 showing the accounts receivable turnover rates for Handley Corporation: (a) in what two years was the rate the same? (b) in what year were the collections best? (c) in what year were the collections worst?
13. If a business had business terms of 1/10, n/30 for its charge customers, what would be an ideal accounts receivable turnover rate? If the terms were 1/20, n/60, what would be an ideal rate?

CASE 1 Mantle's Shop-and-Take Discount Store sells merchandise on account. The store maintains its own credit department and makes collections from charge customers. The business uses the allowance method of recording bad debts expense. Based on past experience, the store estimates bad debts expense each fiscal year as 1% of its net charge sales. The manager proposes to the board of directors that charge sales be eliminated and the business do strictly cash business with customers. The argument is that the expense for uncollectible accounts in the past year was $20,450.00. The manager believes that going to a strict cash sales basis will save that expense and thus increase the net income. The presiding officer of the board of directors does not want to eliminate charge sales. As the junior accountant for the store, which course of action would you recommend? Why?

CASE 2 On July 9 Brandt Clothing Store wrote off as uncollectible the account of Jason Gibbs. An entry was made to debit Allowance for Uncollectible Accounts and credit Accounts Receivable in the general ledger. On July 11 the store learned that a mistake had been made and Jason Gibbs' account was collectible. An entry was made to reinstate Mr. Gibbs' account. Accounts Receivable was debited and Bad Debts Expense was credited. What effect will these two entries have on the store's records?

PROBLEM 21-1   Direct write off of uncollectible accounts

The Dixie Company uses the direct write-off method of recording uncollectible accounts. Listed below are some selected transactions completed by the Dixie Company during the current year.

Instructions: Record all the necessary entries on page 14 of a cash receipts journal and page 21 of a general journal.

Feb. 19. Wrote off Ray Barella's account as uncollectible, $107.46. M14.

Mar. 28. Wrote off David Chou's account as uncollectible, $33.84. M22.

May 15. Received a check in full payment of Nancy Ling's account, $109.37. Ms. Ling's account had been written off in December of the previous year as uncollectible. M35 and R131.

July 31. Wrote off Wilma Strasser's account as uncollectible, $58.42. M69.

Nov. 7. Received a check from Ray Barella in full payment of his account, $107.46. His account had been written off in February of the current year as uncollectible. M105 and R177.

Dec. 3. Received a check from Botsworthy Company, $141.25. This business is bankrupt. There will be no additional payments on account from this company. The total owed by the company is $226.50. The difference between the amount owed and the amount received is written off as uncollectible. M119 and R201.

PROBLEM 21-2   Estimating the bad debts expense by aging accounts receivable

The junior accountant for Morristown Distributors prepares a schedule of accounts receivable by age at the end of each fiscal year. Part of the schedule prepared on December 31 of the current year is shown on page 402.

SCHEDULE OF ACCOUNTS RECEIVABLE BY AGE December 31, 19--							
Customer's name	Account balance	Age of account balance					
		Not yet due	1-30 days past due	31-60 days past due	61-90 days past due	91-120 days past due	Over 120 days past due
Ambrose Bartel	292.50				130.00	162.50	
Carmen Junco	225.00	225.00					
Abdulla Rafie	294.40	192.10	102.30				
Marty Youngblood	84.50						84.50
TOTALS	13,536.20	10,223.20	877.50	603.20	1,101.10	480.70	250.50
Estimated percent uncollectible	—	1	2	5	9	15	30

Instructions: ☐ **1.** Prepare a list of the amount of estimated uncollectible accounts for each of the age groups on the schedule above. Use a form for this list similar to the one shown on page 395.

☐ **2.** Record on page 58 of a general journal the adjusting entry for bad debts expense as of December 31 of the current year. The balance of Allowance for Uncollectible Accounts before this adjustment is $156.74.

PROBLEM 21-3 Using the allowance method of estimating and recording bad debts expense

The Manwell Company uses the allowance method of recording bad debts expense.

Instructions: ☐ **1.** Open accounts in a general ledger for Allowance for Uncollectible Accounts (Account No. 115.1) and Bad Debts Expense (Account No. 612). Record in the account the balance, as of January 1 of the current year, for Allowance for Uncollectible Accounts, $368.94.

☐ **2.** Use page 8 of a cash receipts journal and page 16 of a general journal. Record the necessary entries for each of the following transactions. After you record each transaction, post the amounts affecting the two accounts opened in the general ledger. All entries are made during the current year.

Jan. 18. Wrote off Wanda Rodriguez' account as uncollectible, $40.15. M11.
Mar. 31. Wrote off Bloomquists & Sons' account as uncollectible, $114.41. M54.
June 12. Received a check in full payment of Wanda Rodriguez' account, $40.15. This account was written off on January 18. M108 and R289.
Aug. 2. Wrote off Harry Oldman's account as uncollectible, $189.84. M308.

Dec. 31. Record the adjusting entry to bring the balance of Allowance for Uncollectible Accounts up to an amount equal to 2% of the balance of Accounts Receivable. The balance of Accounts Receivable on December 31 is $20,105.75.

Dec. 31. Record the closing entry for Bad Debts Expense.

| MASTERY PROBLEM 21-M | | Entries affecting Allowance for Uncollectible Accounts |

The Watkins Company makes adjusting entries on a quarterly fiscal period: March 31, June 30, September 30, and December 31. The company estimates the amount used in adjusting for bad debts expense as 1% of the net charge sales for the quarter.

Instructions: Record all the necessary entries for the following selected items. Use page 16 of a cash receipts journal and page 26 of a general journal.

Jan. 19. Write off Anslow Willard's account as uncollectible, $264.67. M11.

Mar. 31. Record the adjusting entry for bad debts expense. The net charge sales for the quarter are $20,163.73.

May 28. Write off the account of Chuck's Service Station as uncollectible, $178.11. M47.

June 30. Record the adjusting entry for bad debts expense. The net charge sales for the quarter are $17,006.27.

Sept. 7. Received a check in full payment of Anslow Willard's account, $264.67. This account had been written off on January 19. M93 and R618.

Sept. 24. Write off the account of Main Street Garage as uncollectible, $288.15. M95.

Sept. 30. Record the adjusting entry for bad debts expense. The net charge sales for the quarter are $16,255.00.

Dec. 17. Write off Antonio Franki's account as uncollectible, $278.52. M117.

Dec. 31. Record the adjusting entry for bad debts expense. The net charge sales for the quarter are $22,745.32.

| BONUS PROBLEM 21-B | | Entries affecting Allowance for Uncollectible Accounts |

Assume that in Mastery Problem 21-M the policy is to adjust the allowance for uncollectible accounts each quarter up to 1% of the net charge sales made to customers during the quarter.

Instructions: □ **1.** Open an account for Allowance for Uncollectible Accounts, Account No. 115.1, credit balance of $268.78 as of January 1 of the current year.

□ **2.** Record the entries for the transactions given in Mastery Problem 21-M. Use page 12 of a cash receipts journal and page 19 of a general journal. As each entry is recorded, post amounts affecting Allowance for Uncollectible Accounts.

22

Accounting for Plant Assets

Current assets are used up or converted to cash in a short period of time — usually within a year. Current assets include cash, accounts receivable, and supplies.

Some assets of a business will be used for longer than a year. Assets that will be used for a number of years in the operation of a business are called plant assets. Plant assets are sometimes known as fixed assets or long-term assets. Plant assets include office equipment, warehouse equipment, delivery equipment, manufacturing equipment, buildings, and land.

> An automobile agency sells automobiles and trucks. These items are considered by the agency to be merchandise inventory rather than plant assets. The automobiles and trucks are not used in the operation of the agency, but are available for sale to customers.

DEPRECIATION

Plant assets will not last forever. The plant assets wear out, may no longer be needed in the operation of the business, or may become outdated as better models become available. As plant assets wear out or grow older, they decrease in value. An automobile worth $4,000.00 in 1978 is normally worth less in 1979, in 1980, and in 1981. The decrease in value of a plant asset because of use and the passage of time is called depreciation. Land, because of its permanent nature, is not subject to depreciation. The increase or decrease in the value of land is usually recorded only at the time the land is sold or otherwise disposed of.

The amount that a plant asset depreciates each year is an expense of the business. Three factors used to determine the annual amount of depreciation for a plant asset are:

1. The *original cost* of a plant asset.
2. The estimated *salvage value* of the plant asset.
3. The estimated *useful life* of the plant asset.

Original cost of plant assets

The original cost of a plant asset includes all expenditures needed to get the plant asset into place and ready for use. For example, the original cost of a piece of machinery could include the invoice price, less any cash discount, plus freight charges and installation costs.

Salvage value of plant assets

When a plant asset is disposed of, some of the original cost value may still remain — the plant asset may still be worth something. The amount that the owner of a plant asset expects to receive at the end of the plant asset's useful life is called the salvage value. The salvage value is also known as the trade-in or scrap value.

At the time a plant asset is bought, a business may have difficulty determining what the item will be worth when it is disposed of. For this reason, the salvage value is an estimated amount. The exact salvage value will not be known until the plant asset is actually disposed of. However, at the time the plant asset is bought, a salvage value is needed to help figure depreciation. Therefore, the best possible estimate of the salvage value is made.

Useful life of plant assets

A plant asset will be useful to a business for a number of years. The number of years may differ from one person to another and from one business to another. For example, a person may buy a personal car and keep it for three to five years. A taxi company may find the useful life of a car only one year.

Most businesses use past experience as the basis for estimating the useful life of a plant asset. If a typewriter usually has been useful for six years, the company can use six years as the useful life of all typewriters it buys. Sometimes, however, a business has difficulty estimating a specific useful life for a plant asset. Guidelines are issued by the Internal Revenue Service which give the estimated useful life for many kinds of plant assets. The guidelines are based on the experience of a wide variety of businesses and on income tax regulations. Many businesses use these guidelines to determine the useful life of plant assets to assure that the figures used are within the tax regulations.

Regardless of the method used, the useful life decided upon at the time a plant asset is bought is still an estimate. The actual useful life will not be known until the plant asset is disposed of or replaced.

Figuring annual depreciation of plant assets

Depreciation of plant assets is an expense of a business. Depreciation of plant assets is therefore recorded each fiscal period. Charging the same amount of expense in each fiscal period of a plant asset's useful life is called the straight-line method of figuring depreciation. The Handley Corporation uses the straight-line method in figuring its annual depreciation expenses.

Other methods of figuring depreciation are described later in this chapter. Regardless of the method used to figure the depreciation, the accounts debited and credited will be the same.

The Handley Corporation bought a typewriter on January 4, 1978, $560.00, with an estimated salvage value of $60.00, and an estimated useful life of five years. The annual estimated depreciation is figured as:

Original cost	minus	Estimated salvage value	equals	Total amount of estimated depreciation
$560.00	−	$60.00	=	$500.00

Total amount of estimated depreciation	divided by	Years of estimated useful life	equals	Annual estimated depreciation
$500.00	÷	5	=	$100.00

If a plant asset were used until completely worn out, there would be no salvage value. The total depreciation would equal the original cost of the plant asset. However, many plant assets do have some value at the time they are discarded or replaced. The original cost minus the total amount of recorded depreciation of a plant asset is called the book value of a plant asset. For example, after two years, the Handley Corporation will have charged $200.00 depreciation on the typewriter bought on January 4, 1978. Thus, at the end of 1979, the typewriter is worth $360.00 (original cost, $560.00 − total depreciation recorded, $200.00 = book value, $360.00).

PLANT ASSETS RECORDS

· A business keeps a record of each plant asset owned in order to determine the book value at the time the asset is disposed of. Some businesses use a separate card form on which to record the original cost and depreciation history of each plant asset. This card form record is especially helpful when a business has many different kinds of plant assets and many individual items of each kind.

The Handley Corporation finds that keeping plant asset data on a single sheet is sufficient because of the relatively few items of each kind of plant asset. The form used is shown on pages 408 and 409.

The Handley Corporation classifies plant assets into several kinds: delivery equipment, warehouse equipment, office equipment, buildings, and land. Separate general ledger accounts are kept for each of these kinds of plant assets as shown on the chart of accounts, page 390. In addition, a separate sheet for each kind of plant asset is kept in a book.

Plant assets register

A book or record that contains the details of cost and depreciation of individual plant assets is called a plant assets register. The plant assets register used by Handley Corporation is shown on pages 408 and 409.

The left-hand page, Columns 1 to 7, of the plant assets register is completed for each plant asset at the time the asset is bought. For example, Line 32 of the plant assets register, page 408, shows depreciation information for a table. On August 28, 1978, the table was bought for a cost of $410.00, estimated salvage value is $50.00, and estimated life is 6 years. The total depreciation recorded over the useful life of the table is $360.00 ($410.00 − $50.00). The annual depreciation to be recorded is $60.00 ($360.00 ÷ 6).

The right-hand page, Columns 8 to 18, of the plant assets register is used to record the depreciation history for each plant asset. If a plant asset has a useful life of more than six years, the data will have to be continued on another sheet. For example, the desk shown on Line 6 of the register, page 409, was bought in 1974. Depreciation for one-half year was recorded on page 3 of the plant assets register for office equipment. The total, $28.00, was carried forward to page 4 of the register, and the data history continued.

Columns 16, 17 and 18, on the right-hand side of the plant assets register, are used to show the disposition of each plant asset. The data shown on Line 1 of the register indicate that the storage cabinet was disposed of on December 28, 1976, with a book value of $100.00. The book value at the time the cabinet was discarded was also the actual salvage value. At the time data are recorded in Columns 16, 17, and 18, a line is drawn through the description and cost of the asset in Columns 2 and 3. This procedure is shown for the storage cabinet on Line 1 of the plant assets register, pages 408 and 409.

The total of Column 3, not including any deletions, as shown on Line 1, gives the total cost of all office equipment still owned and in use. This total should be the same as the balance of the office equipment account in the general ledger. The total of each of the columns for depreciation expense (Columns 9, 10, 11, 12, 13, and 14) gives the amount of depreciation expense that was recorded in a specific year for office equipment.

PAGE 4		PLANT ASSETS REGISTER *Office Equipment*					
1	2	3	4	5	6	7
DATE BOUGHT	DESCRIPTION	COST	SALVAGE VALUE	USEFUL LIFE IN YEARS	AMOUNT OF DEPRECIATION	
					TOTAL	ANNUAL
1	01 02 67 *Storage Cabinet*	160000	10000	10	150000	15000	1
6	06 04 74 *Desk*	68000	12000	10	56000	5600	6
31	01 04 78 *Typewriter*	56000	6000	5	50000	10000	31
32	08 28 78 *Table*	41000	5000	6	36000	6000	32
33							33
34	12 31 79 *Totals*	6202400					34

Plant assets register, left-hand page

For example, in 1979 the total depreciation expense that was recorded was $961.00. The data for Column 13, 1979, were filled in at the end of the fiscal year, December 31, and the column totaled. At the end of the fiscal year, Column 3 is also totaled again to figure the new total after any plant assets were disposed of during the year.

The book value of a specific plant asset can be figured from the data on the plant assets register. The book value of the desk shown on Line 6 is figured as follows:

Cost (Column 3)..	$680.00
Minus total recorded depreciation, (total of Columns 8 to 14).........	308.00
Equals book value (at the end of 1979).......................................	$372.00

ADJUSTING ENTRY FOR DEPRECIATION

At the end of each fiscal period, the junior accountant for the Handley Corporation figures the depreciation on each plant asset. The total is then recorded in the appropriate column (Columns 9–14) on the plant assets register. As shown on the plant assets register, page 409, the amounts for 1978, Column 12, were figured as:

Line 1: No amount listed; this plant asset has been disposed of.

Line 6: The plant asset was used for the entire year; $56.00, the amount shown in Column 7, is recorded.

Line 31: The plant asset was used for the entire year; $100.00, the amount shown in Column 7, is recorded.

Line 32: The plant asset was bought on August 28, 1978. It was owned and used for only four months of the year. Therefore, only one third of a year's depreciation is recorded. One third of the amount in Column 7, $60.00, is $20.00. This amount, $20.00, is recorded in Column 12 for 1978.

PLANT ASSETS REGISTER *Office Equipment*									PAGE *4*	
8	9	10	11	12	13	14	15	16	17	18
ACCUM. DEPR. BROUGHT FORWARD	DEPRECIATION EXPENSE FOR THE YEAR						ACCUM. DEPR. CARRIED FORWARD	DISPOSITION		
	1975	1976	1977	1978	1979	1980		BOOK VALUE	DATE	COMMENTS
1 120000	15000	15000						10000	12 28 76	*Discarded* 1
6 2800	5600	5600	5600	5600	5600					6
31				10000	10000					31
32				2000	6000					32
33										33
34	112500	112500	115600	106700	96100					34

Plant assets register, right-hand page

Line 34: The column for 1978 is totaled. The total, $1,067.00, is the amount of additional depreciation expense on office equipment to be recorded at the end of 1978.

The Handley Corporation keeps a plant assets register for each kind of plant asset: delivery equipment, warehouse equipment, office equipment, and buildings. The same procedure described for office equipment is followed for each kind of plant asset. Land, because of its permanent nature, is not subject to depreciation. Therefore, this procedure is not used for the record kept of land owned.

Analyzing adjustment for depreciation expense

Using the total of the year column in the plant assets register, an adjusting entry is analyzed and recorded on the work sheet for the fiscal year. The effect of the depreciation expense of office equipment for 1979 is shown in the T accounts at the right.

Depreciation Expense — Office Equipment	6302
961.00	

Accumulated Depreciation — Office Equipment	1203.1
	961.00

Recording the adjusting entry for depreciation expense

The adjusting entry for the depreciation expense of office equipment is based on data taken from the Adjustments columns of the work sheet. This adjusting entry is shown in the general journal below.

			GENERAL JOURNAL			PAGE *16*	
1	2				3	4	
ACCOUNTS PAYABLE DEBIT	GENERAL DEBIT	DATE	ACCOUNT TITLE	POST. REF.	GENERAL CREDIT	ACCOUNTS RECEIV. CREDIT	
16	96100	31	*Depreciation Exp.- Office Equip.*				16
17			*Accum. Depr.- Office Equip.*		96100		17
18							18

Adjusting entry for depreciation of plant assets

A similar adjusting entry is made for each of the kinds of plant assets owned by the Handley Corporation: delivery equipment, warehouse equipment, office equipment, and buildings. No depreciation is recorded annually for land.

DISPOSING OF PLANT ASSETS

Plant assets may be disposed of by (a) discarding them, (b) selling them, or (c) trading them in for similar plant assets. When a plant asset is disposed of, its depreciation from the beginning of the current fiscal period to the date of the transaction is recorded. If the total accumulated depreciation on a plant asset is equal to the cost value, the plant asset has no salvage value.

Discarding a plant asset with no book value

The Handley Corporation discarded a plant asset as follows:

> June 26, 1979. Discarded a stenciling machine bought on June 25, 1974: cost, $500.00; total accumulated depreciation to January 1, 1979, $450.00. Memorandum No. 291.

The stenciling machine was used in the warehouse.

Recording depreciation expense for part of a year. Depreciation on the stenciling machine was last recorded on December 31, 1978. The machine was used for six months in 1979 before being discarded. Therefore, depreciation expense for one-half year, $50.00, must be recorded. The effect of the depreciation expense for 1979 is shown in the T accounts at the left.

The total accumulated depreciation recorded for the stenciling machine after this adjusting entry is posted is: Previous amount recorded, $450.00, *plus* additional amount recorded, $50.00, *equals* $500.00, total accumulated depreciation recorded.

Depreciation Expense —
Warehouse Equipment   6201

Adj. 50.00	

Accumulated Depreciation —
Warehouse Equipment 1202.1

	Bal. 450.00
	Adj. 50.00

Recording the discarding of a plant asset. At the time the stenciling machine is discarded, the total accumulated depreciation, $500.00, is equal to the cost, $500.00. Thus, the stenciling machine has no book value. The effect of discarding the stenciling machine is shown in the T accounts at the left.

The entry to record the discarding of the stenciling machine is shown in the general journal on page 411.

After the entry is made in the general journal, the junior accountant also records the data on the plant assets register for warehouse equipment.

Accumulated Depreciation —
Warehouse Equipment 1202.1

500.00	Bal. 450.00
	Adj. 50.00

Warehouse Equipment   1202

	500.00

			GENERAL JOURNAL			PAGE 24	
1	2				3	4	
ACCOUNTS PAYABLE DEBIT	GENERAL DEBIT	DATE	ACCOUNT TITLE	POST. REF.	GENERAL CREDIT	ACCOUNTS RECEIV. CREDIT	
19	50000	26	Accum. Depr.-Warehouse Equip!				19
20			Warehouse Equipment		50000		20
21			Memorandum No. 291.				21

Entry to record discarding a plant asset with no book value

Discarding a plant asset with a book value

The Handley Corporation discarded a small office chair as follows:

> January 9, 1979. Discarded an office chair bought on December 27, 1975: cost $77.00; total accumulated depreciation to January 1, 1979, $72.00. Memorandum No. 34.

The chair was discarded early in January, 1979. Therefore, no depreciation expense for part of a fiscal year needs to be recorded.

Analyzing the adjusting entry for discarding a plant asset with a book value. At the time the chair is discarded it still has a book value of $5.00 (cost, $77.00, *minus* accumulated depreciation, $72.00, *equals* book value, $5.00). The amount of the book value is recorded as an expense. The effect of discarding the chair with a book value is shown in the T accounts at the right.

The chair had a book value of $5.00 but no salvage value. This situation results in a loss on the records of the Handley Corporation equal to the book value of the discarded chair. A loss resulting from the disposition of plant assets is not an operating expense of the business. Therefore, the loss is recorded in an other expenses account titled Loss on Plant Assets.

Accumulated Depreciation — Office Equipment	1203.1
72.00	

Loss on Plant Assets	8002
5.00	

Office Equipment	1203
	77.00

Recording the discarding of a plant asset with a book value. The entry to record the discarding of a plant asset with a book value is shown in the general journal below.

			GENERAL JOURNAL			PAGE 17	
1	2				3	4	
ACCOUNTS PAYABLE DEBIT	GENERAL DEBIT	DATE	ACCOUNT TITLE	POST. REF.	GENERAL CREDIT	ACCOUNTS RECEIV. CREDIT	
17	7200	9	Accum. Depr.-Office Equip.				17
18	500		Loss on Plant Assets				18
19			Office Equipment		7700		19
20			Memorandum No. 34.				20

Entry to record discarding a plant asset with a book value

Selling a plant asset for less than its book value

The Handley Corporation sold a desk that was no longer needed.

March 23, 1979. Sold for $100.00 a desk bought on January 10, 1976: cost, $500.00; total accumulated depreciation to January 1, 1979, $360.00. Memorandum No. 129 and Receipt No. 240.

Recording depreciation expense for part of a year. The desk was owned and used by Handley Corporation from January 1 to March 23, 1979. Therefore, depreciation expense for three months, or one fourth of a year, $30.00, needs to be recorded. After depreciation for part of a year is recorded, the total accumulated depreciation for the desk is $390.00. The new total is figured as: previously recorded, $360.00, *plus* additional recorded, $30.00, *equals* total at time desk is sold, $390.00.

Analyzing the selling of a plant asset for less than its book value. The effect of selling the desk is shown in the T accounts at the left.

Cash	1101
100.00	

Accumulated Depreciation — Office Equipment	1203.1
390.00	

Loss on Plant Assets	8002
10.00	

Office Equipment	1203
	500.00

The cost of the desk, $500.00, *minus* the accumulated depreciation, $390.00, *equals* the book value at the time the desk is sold, $110.00. The book value, $110.00, *minus* the cash actually received, $100.00, *equals* the loss from the sale of the desk, $10.00.

Recording the selling of a plant asset for less than its book value. The entry to record the sale of the desk for less than its book value is shown in the cash receipts journal below.

After the entry is recorded in the cash receipts journal, the junior accountant records the data on the plant assets register for office equipment.

| | | | | | GENERAL | | SALES | SALES TAX | ACCOUNTS | SALES | CASH |
	DATE	ACCOUNT TITLE	Doc. No.	Post. Ref.	DEBIT	CREDIT	CREDIT	PAYABLE CREDIT	RECEIVABLE CREDIT	DISCOUNT DEBIT	DEBIT
32	23	Accum. Depr.-Office Equip.	R240		390 00						100 00
33		Loss on Plant Assets			10 00						
34		Office Equipment				500 00					

CASH RECEIPTS JOURNAL   PAGE 5

Entry to record sale of a plant asset for less than its book value

Selling a plant asset for more than its book value

When a plant asset is sold for less than its book value, a loss is recorded in the general ledger account, Loss on Plant Assets. Similarly, when a plant asset is sold for more than its book value, revenue is re-corded in an other revenue account titled Gain on Plant Assets.

The Handley Corporation sold the following plant asset:

January 10, 1979. Sold for $50.00 a loading cart bought in January, 1973: cost, $200.00; total accumulated depreciation to January 1, 1979, $180.00. Receipt No. 40.

The loading cart was used as part of the delivery equipment. Because the cart was sold during the first half of January, 1979, no additional depreciation needs to be recorded for 1979.

Analyzing the sale of a plant asset for more than its book value. The effect of this transaction on the accounts is shown in the T accounts at the right.

At the time of the sale, the loading cart had a book value of $20.00 (cost, $200.00, *minus* accumulated depreciation, $180.00). The cash received for the cart, $50.00, *minus* the book value, $20.00, *equals* the gain on the sale of the plant asset, $30.00.

Recording the sale of a plant asset for more than its book value. The entry to record this sale is shown in the cash receipts journal below.

Cash	1101
50.00	

Accumulated Depreciation — Delivery Equipment	1201.1
180.00	

Gain on Plant Assets	7001
	30.00

Delivery Equipment	1201
	200.00

						GENERAL		SALES CREDIT	SALES TAX PAYABLE CREDIT	ACCOUNTS RECEIVABLE CREDIT	SALES DISCOUNT DEBIT	CASH DEBIT	
		CASH RECEIPTS JOURNAL				1	2	3	4	5	6	PAGE 1 7	
	DATE	ACCOUNT TITLE	Doc. No.	Post. Ref.		DEBIT	CREDIT						
12	10	Accum. Depr.-Delivery Equip.	R40			18000						5000	12
13		Gain on Plant Assets					3000						13
14		Delivery Equipment					20000						14

Entry to record sale of a plant asset for more than its book value

After the entry is made in the cash receipts journal, the junior accountant records the data on the plant assets register for delivery equipment. Each time a plant asset is disposed of, a line is drawn through the Description and Cost columns, Columns 2 and 3, of the appropriate plant assets register. Then, the data are entered in the Disposition columns, Columns 16, 17, and 18, of that plant assets register.

Trading in a plant asset

Many times, instead of discarding or selling a plant asset, a business will trade it for a similar plant asset. For example, when a delivery truck becomes old enough to be inefficient or when a different truck is needed, the old truck is traded on a new truck.

According to Internal Revenue Service regulations, a loss or gain is not recognized when one plant asset is exchanged for another similar plant asset. The new plant asset is recorded at a cost value equal to the cash paid plus the book value of the old plant asset.

The Handley Corporation traded one delivery truck for another.

> June 28, 1979. Paid cash, $5,000.00, plus old delivery truck for a new delivery truck: cost of old delivery truck bought on January 2, 1976, $7,800.00; total accumulated depreciation to January 1, 1979, $4,080.00. Memorandum No. 294 and Check No. 450.

The old delivery truck was used for six months in 1979. Therefore, one half of the annual depreciation needs to be recorded for 1979, $680.00. After this additional depreciation is recorded, the total accumulated depreciation on the old delivery truck is $4,760.00 (previously recorded depreciation, $4,080.00, *plus* additional depreciation, $680.00).

Analyzing entry to record trading in one plant asset for another. The effect on the general ledger accounts of trading in one delivery truck for another is shown in the T accounts at the left.

Delivery Equipment	1201
New truck 8,040.00	Old truck 7,800.00

Accumulated Depreciation — Delivery Equipment	1201.1
4,760.00	

Cash	1101
	5,000.00

Delivery Equipment is debited for the cost value of the new delivery truck. The cost value, figured according to the IRS regulations, is:

Cost value of old delivery truck traded in	$7,800.00
Less accumulated depreciation	4,760.00
Equals book value of old delivery truck..............	$3,040.00
Plus cash paid for new delivery truck.................	5,000.00
Equals cost of new delivery truck......................	$8,040.00

Delivery Equipment is credited for the cost value of the old delivery truck. Accumulated Depreciation — Delivery Equipment is debited for the total depreciation recorded on the old truck up to the time it is traded in, $4,760.00. Cash is credited for the amount paid, $5,000.00.

Recording the entry for trading in one plant asset for another. The entry in the cash payments journal to record the trading of one delivery truck for another delivery truck is shown on page 415.

After the entry is made in the cash payments journal, data about the old and new trucks are recorded on the plant assets register for delivery equipment. A plant assets register like the one on pages 408 and 409 would be used. An indication of the disposition of the old delivery truck is made in Columns 16, 17, and 18. A line is drawn through the data for the old delivery truck in the Description and Cost columns, Columns 2 and 3. Columns 1 to 7 are completed on a new line for the new delivery truck. The new delivery truck is recorded at a cost of $8,040.00 regardless of the advertised selling price of the truck.

	CASH PAYMENTS JOURNAL								PAGE *12*	
				1	2	3	4	5	6	
DATE	ACCOUNT TITLE	CK. No.	POST. REF.	GENERAL		PURCHASES DEBIT	PURCHASES DISCOUNT CREDIT	ACCOUNTS PAYABLE DEBIT	CASH CREDIT	
				DEBIT	CREDIT					
28 Delivery Equipment		450		8 04 0 00					5 000 00	22
Accum. Depr.-Delivery Equip!				4 76 0 00						23
Delivery Equipment					7 8 0 0 00					24

Entry to record trading one
plant asset for another

Disposing of buildings

The depreciation rate for buildings is usually lower than for other kinds of plant assets. Buildings usually last for more years than most other kinds of plant assets. Buildings are seldom discarded. However, a building could become so old and useless that no one would want to buy it. In such circumstances, the building might be torn down and the materials sold or discarded. However, the entries to record the buying, depreciating, and selling of buildings are similar to those for any other plant asset. When a building is bought, the cost price is recorded, and the data are recorded on the plant assets register for buildings. When a building is disposed of, additional depreciation for the year is recorded if needed. Then an entry is made to show the selling or trading of the building. Buildings are not traded as often as many other kinds of plant assets. Usually, when being disposed of, a building is sold.

If a building is sold for more than its book value, the revenue is recorded in Gain on Plant Assets. If a building is sold for less than its book value, the loss is recorded in Loss on Plant Assets.

Disposing of land

Most businesses owning buildings also own the land on which the buildings stand. When land is bought, a plant asset account titled Land is debited for the cost price. No depreciation is recorded on land because land is not usually worn out through use.

The value of land may increase or decrease from year to year. No record is made of this change in value, however, until the land is actually disposed of. If the selling price of the land is greater than the cost, the gain is recorded in Gain on Plant Assets. If the selling price is less than the cost, the loss is recorded in Loss on Plant Assets.

OTHER METHODS OF FIGURING DEPRECIATION

The Handley Corporation figures depreciation on plant assets using the straight-line method. However, some plant assets depreciate faster in the early years of use than in later years. For example, automobiles usually depreciate more the first year than the second, more the second than the third, and more the third than the fourth. The straight-line method of figuring depreciation does not take into account this difference in the amount of depreciation from one year to the next. There are three popular methods of figuring depreciation that do take into consideration the differences from year to year. These three methods are: (a) the declining-balance method, (b) the sum-of-the-years-digits method, and (c) the production-unit method.

Declining-balance method of figuring depreciation

Multiplying the book value at the end of each fiscal period by a constant rate is called the declining-balance method of figuring depreciation. The rate is the same each year, but the book value used declines from one year to the next. The result is that the amount of depreciation in each year also is less than the year before. The greatest amount of depreciation expense is charged in the first year the plant asset is owned.

The depreciation rate for the declining-balance method is based on a straight-line rate. The steps in figuring the depreciation are:

1. Determine the three factors: cost, $5,000.00; salvage value, $250.00; useful life, 5 years.

2. Determine the straight-line depreciation rate: depreciation for 5 years would be at the straight-line rate of 20% (one fifth of the depreciation is charged to each year).

3. Multiply the straight-line rate by 2: 20% *times* 2 equals 40%, declining-balance depreciation rate.

4. Multiply the book value at the beginning of each year by the declining-balance depreciation rate:

Year	Book value beginning of year	Depreciation rate	Depreciation for year
1	$5,000.00	40%	$2,000.00
2	3,000.00	40%	1,200.00
3	1,800.00	40%	720.00
4	1,080.00	40%	432.00
5	648.00	40%	259.20

In the table above, the book value for the beginning of the second year is found: book value first year, $5,000.00, *minus* depreciation first year, $2,000.00, *equals* book value at the beginning of the second year, $3,000.00. This same procedure is used to find the book value for each of the remaining years in the table. Thus, the book value for the beginning of the fifth year is found: $1,080.00 − $432.00 = $648.00.

Once the amount of depreciation is figured in a specific year, the entry to record the depreciation expense is the same as that on page 409.

Sum-of-the-years-digits method of figuring depreciation

Using fractions based on the years of useful life of a plant asset is called the sum-of-the-years-digits method of figuring depreciation. With this method, the amount of depreciation expense recorded in the first year is greater than in later years.

The steps in determining the fractions for a plant asset with 5 years of useful life are shown at the right.

Year	Fraction
1	5/15
2	4/15
3	3/15
4	2/15
5	1/15

1. The number of years of useful life are listed in numerical sequence from 1 to 5. The numbers for the years (the digits) are totaled, *15*. The total, *15*, becomes the denominator for the fractions.

2. The fractions are listed with the year digits, in reverse order, becoming the numerators of the fractions: 5/15, 4/15, 3/15, 2/15, and 1/15.

The depreciation for each year is found by multiplying the total amount of depreciation to be recorded over the useful life by the year's fraction. This is shown below.

Cost, $5,000.00, *minus* salvage value, $250.00, *equals* total depreciation, $4,750.00.

Year	Fraction ×	Total depreciation =	Depreciation for year
1	5/15	$4,750.00	$1,583.33
2	4/15	4,750.00	1,266.67
3	3/15	4,750.00	950.00
4	2/15	4,750.00	633.33
5	1/15	4,750.00	316.67

Comparison of three methods of figuring depreciation

A comparison of the straight-line method, declining-balance method, and sum-of-the-years-digits method of figuring depreciation for the same plant asset is shown below.

Factors: Cost $5,000.00; salvage value, $250.00; useful life, 5 years.

YEAR	Straight-line		Declining-balance		Sum-of-the-years-digits	
	Rate	Amount	Rate	Amount	Fraction	Amount
1	20%	$ 950.00	40%	$2,000.00	5/15	$1,583.33
2	20%	950.00	40%	1,200.00	4/15	1,266.67
3	20%	950.00	40%	720.00	3/15	950.00
4	20%	950.00	40%	432.00	2/15	633.33
5	20%	950.00	40%	259.20	1/15	316.67
Totals		$4,750.00		$4,611.20		$4,750.00

The sum-of-the-years-digits method is more accurate than the declining-balance method (total depreciation is shown in the table as $4,750.00 vs. $4,611.20). However, the declining-balance method is easier to use. Nevertheless, many businesses still use the straight-line method because it is the easiest of *all* methods to figure.

Composite depreciation rate

Some businesses believe that the clerical expense of keeping detailed records of each plant asset is too costly. Instead of using a different rate of depreciation for each plant asset, a composite or single rate for each class of plant assets is used. A single rate is based on the average life of all items in each class of plant assets. Regardless of the actual estimated total depreciation and useful life of plant assets, the same rate of depreciation is used. For example, past records might show that delivery equipment depreciates at about an average of 6% a year. Therefore, at the end of a fiscal period, the depreciation expense for delivery equipment is figured as: balance of delivery equipment account *times* 6% *equals* depreciation expense.

Production-unit method of figuring depreciation

How rapidly some plant assets wear out depends upon how much the asset is used. For example, a delivery truck that is driven 50,000 miles in one year is wearing out faster than a delivery truck that is driven 30,000 miles in one year. The number of miles the truck is driven depends upon the amount of business in a fiscal year. In these circumstances, a business may figure the depreciation on the basis of the "production units" in a fiscal period. Figuring annual depreciation on the basis of the amount of production expected from a plant asset is called the production-unit method of figuring depreciation. An ice cream making machine may be depreciated on the basis of how many gallons of ice cream are produced; a printing machine may be depreciated on the basis of how many printing impressions are made.

The Barteau Delivery Service owns a truck: cost, $7,000.00; estimated salvage value, $1,000.00; useful life, estimated to be 60,000 miles. The rate of estimated depreciation is figured as:

Cost	*minus*	Estimated salvage value	*equals*	Total estimated depreciation
$7,000.00	−	$1,000.00	=	$6,000.00

Total estimated depreciation	*divided by*	Estimated useful life	*equals*	Estimated depreciation rate
$6,000.00	÷	60,000 miles	=	10¢ per mile

The depreciation for three years on the delivery truck is figured as:

Year ×	Depreciation factor	Mileage × that year =	Depreciation expense
1	10¢	20,000	$2,000.00
2	10¢	25,000	2,500.00
3	10¢	19,000	1,900.00
Total			$6,400.00

The book value at the end of the third year is: cost, $7,000.00, *minus* total depreciation to the end of the third year, $6,400.00, *equals* book value, $600.00.

DEPLETION

Some plant assets, such as standing timber and mineral deposits, decrease in value because of the removal of part of the valuable part of the asset. Timber is felled and turned into lumber. Mineral deposits, such as coal, are mined. Oil deposits are pumped out of the ground and sold. The decrease in the value of a plant asset because of its removal from the land is called depletion. Plant assets subject to depletion are almost always connected to land. Plant assets subject to depletion are sometimes known as wasting assets. The salvage value of the land and plant asset subject to depletion is the value of the land after the asset has been fully removed. Thus, after all the oil deposits have been pumped out, the salvage value will be the value of the land that remains.

Figuring depletion expense

The removal of parts of a wasting asset is usually not the same from one year to the next. Therefore, the depletion expense is based on the amount of the asset removed as compared to the cost of the plant asset. An estimated depletion expense per unit of the plant asset is figured. The number of units removed is multiplied by the estimated depletion expense per unit to figure the depletion expense for that fiscal period.

> The method of figuring depletion expense is very similar to the production-unit method of figuring depreciation expense.

The Merriweather Mining Company bought the Roundhill Copper Mine for $100,000.00. The company's engineers estimate that 2,000,000 metric tons of copper ore can be mined from the property. The value of the land after the ore is removed is estimated to be $20,000.00. The total value of depletion of the property by removing the copper ore is: cost, $100,000.00, *minus* salvage value, $20,000.00, *equals* depletion, $80,000.00. The depletion expense per metric ton of ore is: total depletion, $80,000.00, *divided by* total tonnage, 2,000,000, *equals* 4¢ per metric ton.

During the first year of operation, the company removes 50,000 metric tons of copper ore. The depletion expense for the year is figured as:

Tonnage removed, 50,000, *times* 4¢ *equals* depletion expense, $2,000.00.

Recording depletion expense

The effect of recording the depletion expense for Merriweather Mining Company for the first year the Roundhill Mine is in operation is shown in the T accounts below.

Depletion Expense — Roundhill Mine 6205	Accumulated Depletion — Roundhill Mine 1206.1
2,000.00	2,000.00

The entry to record the depletion expense for the Roundhill Mine at the end of the first fiscal year is shown in the general journal below.

Entry to record depletion

			GENERAL JOURNAL			PAGE *14*
ACCOUNTS PAYABLE DEBIT	GENERAL DEBIT	DATE	ACCOUNT TITLE	POST. REF.	GENERAL CREDIT	ACCOUNTS RECEIV. CREDIT
	2 000 00	31	Depletion Exp.- Roundhill Mine			
			Accum. Depl.- Roundhill Mine		2 000 00	

The book value of the Roundhill Mine at the end of the first year is figured as: cost, $100,000.00, *minus* accumulated depreciation — Roundhill Mine, $2,000.00, *equals* book value, $98,000.00.

Reporting depletion on the financial statements

The account Depletion Expense — Roundhill Mine is listed on the income statement along with the other operating expenses.

The balance of the plant asset account, Roundhill Mine, is listed in the plant assets section of the balance sheet. The balance of Accumulated Depletion — Roundhill Mine is subtracted from the balance of the plant asset account. The new balance shows the book value of this plant asset at the end of the fiscal period.

TAXES ON PLANT ASSETS

Legally there are two kinds of property: real and personal. Land and anything permanently attached to the land is called real property. Real property is sometimes known as real estate. All property not classified as real property is called personal property. Real property, such as land and buildings, cannot be moved. Personal property, such as equipment, merchandise, cars, clothes, bicycles, and cash, can be moved.

Figuring value of plant assets for tax purposes

Most local and state governments place a tax on real property. Many government units also tax personal property. The Handley Corporation pays taxes on real property only. The amount of tax to be paid on property depends on the tax rate and the assessed value of the property. A value placed on property by tax authorities for the purpose of figuring taxes is called the assessed value. The assessed value and the book value recorded by a business may not be the same. The assessed value is usually based on the judgment of persons known as assessors. Assessors are sometimes elected by citizens in a governmental unit, such as a city or county. Sometimes the assessors are trained persons employed by a governmental unit instead of being elected.

Handley Corporation's land and buildings have been assessed for: land, $7,500.00; buildings, $25,000.00; total, $32,500.00. The tax rate on property is 4% in the locality where Handley Corporation is located. The annual property tax is figured as: $32,500.00 *times* 4% *equals* $1,300.00. The local government sends a tax statement to Handley Corporation listing the amount of tax due. The corporation is required to pay the tax in two installments of $650.00 each, due on June 1 and December 1 of each year.

Paying property tax on plant assets

On December 1, 1979, the Handley Corporation paid the second installment of its property tax.

December 1, 1979. Paid second installment of property tax, $650.00. Check No. 825.

The first installment of the property tax is paid on June 1, 1979. The effect of the second installment payment, December 1, is shown in the T accounts below.

Property Tax	9002		Cash	1101
6/1 650.00			12/1 650.00	
12/1 650.00				

After the entry is posted on December 1, the balance of the property tax account is $1,300.00. This is the total amount of property tax paid during the year.

Some businesses consider property tax as an operating expense. The property tax may be listed in the chart of accounts as either an other expense or as an operating expense.

✦ What is the meaning of each of the following?

- plant assets
- depreciation
- salvage value
- straight-line method
- book value of a plant asset

- plant assets register
- declining-balance method
- sum-of-the-years-digits method
- production-unit method

- depletion
- real property
- personal property
- assessed value

1. Why is depreciation on plant assets recorded at the end of each fiscal period?
2. What are the three factors used in figuring the depreciation expense for a plant asset?
3. A business bought a typewriter that cost $400.00, had a salvage value estimated at $50.00, and had an estimated useful life of 5 years. The straight-line method of estimating depreciation is used. How much depreciation expense would be recorded for the typewriter at the end of each of the first three years?
4. For the typewriter described in question 3, what is the book value at the end of the third year?
5. What data are recorded in each column of the plant assets register, pages 408–409, for each plant asset?
6. What is the source of the depreciation expense amount used in the adjusting entry shown on page 409?
7. What two accounts are affected by an adjusting entry for depreciation for office equipment? For delivery equipment? For warehouse equipment? For buildings?
8. What are three ways a plant asset may be disposed of?
9. Why was an adjusting entry for depreciation expense made before the entry to record the discarding of the

plant asset, as described on page 410?
10. Why is there a loss recorded for the plant asset discarded with a book value, as described on page 411?
11. Why was a gain on plant assets recorded for the sale of a plant asset as described on pages 412 and 413?
12. Why is it that no gain or loss on plant assets is recorded when the new delivery truck is bought, as described on pages 413 and 414?
13. If a plant asset with a cost of $500.00 and a total accumulated depreciation of $400.00 is traded in on a similar plant asset plus payment of $150.00 in cash, what will be the cost of the new plant asset?
14. Why is depreciation not recorded for land?
15. Using the data in question 3, what is the amount of estimated depreciation for each of the first three years using the declining-balance method?
16. Using the data in question 3, what is the amount of estimated depreciation for each of the first three years using the sum-of-the-years-digits method?
17. What two accounts are used to record depletion expense on a wasting asset called the Back-Forty Timber?
18. What two accounts are used to record the payment of property taxes?

CASE 1 Beatrice Bloom owns and manages Bloom's Tree Surgery Service. The service has several trucks, some tree cutting equipment, and some office equipment. The service also owns the building in which it is headquartered. At present the straight-line

method of figuring depreciation is used for all plant assets. Mrs. Bloom asks what the advantages and disadvantages would be in using each of the three methods described in this chapter. What would you tell her?

CASE 2 William Blanchard bought a parcel of land for $5,000.00. He built a building on the land for $55,000.00. He recorded both amounts in an account titled Land and Buildings, which now has a balance of $60,000.00. He plans to record depreciation for the account using the straight-line method of 10% a year for 10 years. A certified public accountant, Miss Marguerita Lopez, advises Mr. Blanchard to separate the amounts into two accounts: (a) Land and (b) Buildings. Do you agree with Mr. Blanchard's procedures or with Miss Lopez's suggestion? Why?

CASE 3 On January 2, 1978, the Century Mining Company bought some land with mineral rights for $1,000,000.00. The engineers estimate that about 200,000 metric tons of ore can be taken from the land. The engineers also estimate it will take 10 years to mine all the ore. Estimates of the amount of ore to be extracted annually have been prepared for each of the 10 years. The junior accountant for the Century Mining Company figures depreciation at the end of 1978 by taking the cost, $1,000,000.00 times 10% and recording $10,000.00 as the depletion expense. Do you agree with this procedure? Explain your answer.

Problems
for
Applying
Concepts

PROBLEM 22-1 Figuring depreciation expense by three common methods

On January 2 of the current year, Chosin Tool and Die Company, owned by Hosan Chosin, bought a new machine for $7,500.00. The estimated useful life is 5 years. The estimated salvage value is $570.00.

Instructions: □ **1.** Prepare a table similar to the one below. Show the annual amount of depreciation for each year using each of the methods listed in the column headings.

Year	Straight-line depreciation		Declining-balance depreciation		Sum-of-the-years-digits depreciation	
	Rate	Amount	Rate	Amount	Fraction	Amount
1						
2						

Instructions: □ **2.** Also show the total depreciation for all five years and the ending book value for each of the three methods of figuring depreciation.

PROBLEM 22-2 Recording depreciation expense and property taxes

If the workbook for this textbook is not being used, complete Review Problem 22-R 2.

The office equipment plant assets register of Wesselberg Company, January 1 of the current year, is given in the workbook.

Instructions: Record the following selected entries in the plant assets register. Also record the necessary entries in the journals. Use page 5 of a cash payments journal and page 1 of a general journal.

Mar. 31. Record in the plant assets register the depreciation for the first quarter of the year. Enter the total of the First Quarter column on the total line at the bottom of the page.

Mar. 31. Record the general journal entry for the depreciation expense of the first quarter.

June 30. Record in the plant assets register the depreciation for the second quarter of the year. Enter the total of the Second Quarter column on the total line at the bottom of the page.

June 30. Record the general journal entry for the depreciation expense of the second quarter.

July 1. Paid property taxes due, $900.00. Ck307.

July 1. Enter in the plant assets register (Line 11) the purchase of a calculating machine.

> An old calculating machine (listed on Line 7) and $100.00 in cash are given for the new machine. It is estimated that the new machine has a useful life of 10 years and a salvage value of $70.00.

In the Disposition column, on Line 7, write the explanation "Traded, 7/1." Draw a line through the description of the old calculating machine in the Description column. Also, draw a line through the cost price in the Cost column.

July 1. Record in the cash payments journal the entry to trade in the old machine and buy the new calculating machine. Ck308.

Sept. 30. Record in the plant assets register the depreciation for the third quarter of the year. Enter the total on the total line.

Sept. 30. Record the general journal entry for the depreciation expense of the third quarter.

Nov. 15. Record in the general journal the depreciation for part of a year on the old typewriter (on Line 5) traded on this date. M82. (Do not enter this depreciation in the plant assets register.)

Nov. 15. Enter in the plant assets register (on Line 12) the purchase of a new typewriter.

> An old typewriter (listed on Line 5) and $270.00 cash are given for the new typewriter. The new typewriter has an estimated useful life of 5 years and a salvage value of $70.00.

Make the necessary entries in the plant assets register to show that the typewriter (on Line 5) has been disposed of.

Nov. 15. Record in the cash payments journal the entry to trade the old typewriter and buy the new typewriter. Ck441.

Dec. 31. Paid property taxes due, $900.00. Ck442.

Dec. 31. Complete the plant assets register for the fourth quarter.

Dec. 31. Record in the general journal the depreciation expense for the fourth quarter of the year.

Dec. 31. Complete the plant assets register for the year. Enter in the Carried Forward column the accumulated depreciation for each item. Enter in the Book Value column the book value of each item on December 31. Total the Cost column, the Carried Forward column, and the Book Value column. The Carried Forward column total *plus* the Book Value column total must equal the total of the Cost column.

| **MASTERY** | | Recording entries for depreciation |
| **PROBLEM 22-M** | | expense and for disposing of plant assets |

The Driscol Company bought a machine on January 3, 1977, for $5,000.00. The machine's estimated useful life is 3 years and the estimated salvage value is $500.00.

Instructions: □ **1.** Record on page 3 of a general journal the adjusting entries for depreciation expense on this machine for the following dates: (a) December 31, 1977; (b) December 31, 1978. Use the straight-line method.

□ **2.** Record the entries for the following on March 29, 1978:
  (a) General journal entry (page 3) to record depreciation to this date for part of 1978. M15.
  (b) Cash receipts journal entry (page 7) if the machine is sold on this date for $3,000.00. R159.

□ **3.** Record the entries if instead the machine is sold on March 29, 1978, for $3,150.00. R159 and M15.

□ **4.** Record the entries if instead the machine is traded on March 29, 1978. The old machine and $3,500.00 cash are given for a new machine.
  (a) Record the entry for the depreciation of part of a year. M15.
  (b) Record the trading of the old machine for the new machine. Ck143. (Use page 11 of a cash payments journal.)

| **BONUS** | | Using several methods to estimate and |
| **PROBLEM 22-B** | | record depreciation expense |

The Mercer Manufacturing Company bought a machine on January 3, 1977. The cost is $63,000.00. The estimated useful life of the machine will be the production of 90,000 units. The estimated salvage value of the machine is $9,000.00. It is estimated that the machine will be in use 12 years to produce 90,000 units.

Instructions: Determine how much depreciation expense to charge for the machine on December 31, 1977, in each of the following situations:
  (1) If the straight-line method of estimating depreciation expense is used.
  (2) If the declining-balance method is used.
  (3) If the sum-of-the-years-digits method is used.
  (4) If the production-unit method is used. Total units produced in 1977, 8,500.

23

Accounting for Prepaid and Accrued Items

Some businesses pay for expenses before the items actually become expenses. For example, a business may buy enough supplies to last for two months. However, only the supplies actually used in the first month are charged as expenses for that month. The value of supplies still on hand is an asset.

Sometimes a business receives revenue before it is earned. For example, one business may rent space in its building to another business. On the first day of a month when the rent is received in advance, none has been earned. The amount of rent not earned is a liability of the business receiving it.

PREPAID EXPENSES AND REVENUE

Expenses paid in one fiscal period but which do not become expenses until a later fiscal period are called prepaid expenses. Revenue that is received in one fiscal period but which is not earned until a later fiscal period is called revenue received in advance. Revenue received in advance is sometimes known as unearned revenue, prepaid revenue, or prepaid income.

Charging to a fiscal period all those revenues earned and expenses incurred, regardless of when cash is actually received or paid, is called accrual basis accounting. Charging to a fiscal period only those revenues actually received and expenses actually paid, regardless of when earned or incurred, is called cash basis accounting.

Accounting records kept on a cash basis are described in Chapter 24.

The Dubolt Company keeps accounting records on the accrual basis. When supplies are bought for cash, Supplies is debited and Cash is credited. When supplies are bought on account, Supplies is debited and Accounts Payable is credited. When rent is received in advance, Cash is debited and Rent Received in Advance is credited.

Prepaid expenses recorded initially as assets

The junior accountant for Dubolt Company finds the procedure too time consuming to record a change each time a small quantity of supplies is used. If this procedure were followed, several entries each day may have to be made as supplies are used. Instead, the junior accountant makes an adjusting entry at the end of each fiscal period to bring the supplies account up to date. The adjusting entry records the value of the supplies used as an expense.

Adjusting entry for supplies expense when recorded initially as an asset. An adjustment for supplies expense is analyzed and described in Chapter 3, page 50. Dubolt Company makes a similar adjusting entry. On March 31, 1979, Dubolt Company takes an inventory of supplies. The supplies inventory is $1,948.58. The balance of the supplies account in the general ledger is $5,135.60. An adjusting entry must be made to change the balance of the supplies account to the actual inventory, $1,948.58. The adjusting entry for supplies expense is shown on Lines 16–17 of the general journal below.

	ACCOUNTS PAYABLE DEBIT	GENERAL DEBIT	DATE	ACCOUNT TITLE	POST. REF.	GENERAL CREDIT	ACCOUNTS RECEIV. CREDIT	
	1	2			3	4		
1				*Adjusting Entries*				1
16		3187 02	31	Supplies Expense	6110			16
17				Supplies	1106	3187 02		17
18		980 00	31	Insurance Expense	6106			18
19				Prepaid Insurance	1107	980 00		19
20		1000 00	31	Rent Received in Advance	2108			20
21				Rent Income	7003	1000 00		21
22		525 00	31	Salary Expense	6109			22
23				Salaries Payable	2103	525 00		23
24		48 31	31	Payroll Taxes Expense	6108			24
25				FICA Tax Payable	2105	31 50		25
26				Unempl. Tax Pay. – Fed.	2106	2 63		26
27				Unempl. Tax Pay. – State	2107	14 18		27
28		5 75	31	Interest Expense	8002			28
29				Interest Payable	2109	5 75		29
30		16 10	31	Interest Receivable	1108			30
31				Interest Income	7002	16 10		31
32		951 00	31	Property Tax	9002			32
33				Property Tax Payable	2111	951 00		33
34		5205 14	31	Federal Income Tax	9001			34
35				Corp. Inc. Tax Pay. – Fed.	2110	5205 14		35
36								36
37								37

GENERAL JOURNAL PAGE 5

Adjusting entries

In the adjusting entry on Lines 16–17, Supplies is credited for $3,187.02 to bring the balance of this account to its correct amount ($5,135.60 − $3,187.02 = $1,948.58). In the same entry, Supplies Expense is debited for $3,187.02, the value of supplies used during the month.

Adjusting entry for prepaid insurance when recorded initially as an asset. An adjusting entry for insurance expense is analyzed and described in Chapter 3, page 50. On March 31, 1979, the junior accountant checks the Dubolt Company's insurance records. The value of unused insurance premiums on March 31 is $4,900.00. The prepaid insurance account in the general ledger has a debit balance of $5,880.00. The adjusting entry for prepaid insurance is shown on Lines 18–19 of the general journal, page 427.

In the adjusting entry on Lines 18–19, Prepaid Insurance is credited for $980.00 to bring this account balance to its correct amount ($5,880.00 − $980.00 = $4,900.00). In the same entry, Insurance Expense is debited for $980.00, the value of insurance used during the month.

Revenue received in advance and recorded initially as a liability

On March 1, 1979, Dubolt Company receives $2,000.00 in advance for two months' rent. Cash is debited and Rent Received in Advance is credited for $2,000.00. On March 31, 1979, one half of the revenue received in advance for rent, $1,000.00, has been earned. The other half, $1,000.00, remains as unearned revenue.

	Rent Received in Advance	2108
Adj.	1,000.00	Bal. 2,000.00

	Rent Income	7003
		Adj. 1,000.00

An adjusting entry is made to bring Rent Received in Advance up to date. The effect of this adjusting entry is shown in the T accounts at the left.

The adjusting entry for rent income is shown on Lines 20–21, of the general journal, page 427. Rent Received in Advance is debited for $1,000.00 to bring this account to its correct balance. Rent Income is credited for the same amount to record the rent income earned in March.

Similar adjusting entries are made for any other prepaid expenses or revenues. Dubolt Company has only prepaid expenses for supplies and insurance and prepaid revenue for rent.

ACCRUED EXPENSES AND REVENUE

At the end of a fiscal period a business may have some expenses that are owed but not yet paid. One example is the salaries earned by employees but not paid until the next pay day in the following fiscal period. Dubolt Company's pay period ends on Wednesday of each week. The payroll is actually paid to the employees on Friday of the same week. For this reason, on March 31, 1979, the company owes employees for work done on March 29–31. The amount owed for this period will be paid in the regular payroll on April 6. Expenses incurred in one fiscal period but not paid until a later fiscal period are called accrued expenses.

A business may also earn revenue in one fiscal period but not receive cash for the revenue until the next fiscal period. For example, Dubolt Company accepted a note receivable on March 16, 1979. The note is due in 30 days, or on April 15. On March 31, 1979, the company has earned interest on the note for 15 days, but the interest has not yet been received. Revenue earned in one fiscal period but not received until the next fiscal period is called accrued revenue.

Accrued expenses

Dubolt Company has two accrued expenses on March 31, 1979: (a) salaries owed to employees and the related payroll taxes; and (b) any interest due on notes payable.

Adjusting entry for accrued salary expense. On March 31, 1979, Dubolt Company owes employees $525.00 for salaries earned on March 29–31. An adjusting entry is made to record the accrued salary expense. The effect of the adjusting entry is shown in the T accounts at the right.

Salary Expense		6109
Bal.	5,425.00	
Adj.	525.00	

Salaries Payable		2103
	Adj.	525.00

The adjusting entry for accrued salary expense is shown on Lines 22–23 of the general journal, page 427.

The new balance for Salary Expense, $5,950.00, is the total salary expense for March, both actually paid and accrued. The adjusted balance of Salaries Payable is the amount owed to employees but not yet paid on March 31, 1979.

Adjusting entry for employer's accrued payroll taxes expense. In addition to the accrued salary expense on March 31, Dubolt Company has accrued payroll taxes for the same period of time. The employer's accrued payroll taxes expenses are: FICA tax, $31.50; federal unemployment tax, $2.63; state unemployment tax, $14.18; total, $48.31.

An adjusting entry is made to record the employer's accrued payroll taxes on March 31. The effect of this adjusting entry is shown in the T accounts on page 430.

> No adjusting entry is required to record the employees' income tax payable or the employees' share of FICA tax. These amounts will not become liabilities of the business until the payroll is actually paid and these amounts are withheld.

The adjusting entry for employer's accrued payroll taxes expense is shown on Lines 24–27 of the general journal, page 427.

Payroll Taxes Expense 6108		Unemployment Tax Payable — Federal 2106	
Bal.	499.10	Bal.	27.13
Adj.	48.31	Adj.	2.63

FICA Tax Payable 2105		Unemployment Tax Payable — State 2107	
	Bal.	651.00	Bal.	146.48
	Adj.	31.50	Adj.	14.18

Adjusting entry for accrued interest expense. An adjusting entry for accrued interest expense is analyzed and described in Chapter 3, page 51. On March 31, 1979, the junior accountant for Dubolt Company checks the records of outstanding notes payable. The interest owed as of March 31 for these notes totals $5.75. An adjusting entry is made to record this accrued interest expense. The adjusting entry for Dubolt Company on March 31 is shown on Lines 28–29 of the general journal, page 427.

Accrued revenue

Dubolt Company usually has only one source of accrued revenue at the end of a three-month fiscal period: interest on notes receivable. On March 31, 1979, the junior accountant for Dubolt Company inspects the records and figures the accrued interest income to be $16.10. An adjusting entry for accrued interest income is analyzed and described in Chapter 3, page 51. The adjusting entry made by Dubolt Company on March 31 is shown on Lines 30–31 of the general journal, page 427.

Accrued taxes

The Dubolt Company has employer's accrued payroll taxes to record at the end of each fiscal period. In addition, the company has accrued property taxes and accrued corporation income taxes to record.

Adjusting entry for accrued property tax. Property tax is described in Chapter 22, page 421. Dubolt Company's property tax totals $3,804.00 per year. On March 31, 1979, the company owes property tax for three months in 1979. The tax is due to be paid at a time set by the local governmental units later in 1979. Therefore, on March 31, the company has $951.00 in accrued property tax for the three months that have passed.

The effect of an adjusting entry to record accrued property tax is shown in the T accounts on page 431.

The credit balance in **Property Tax** is the result of a reversing entry. The reversing entry is explained later in this chapter.

Property Tax		9002		Property Tax Payable		2111
Adj.	951.00	Bal.	634.00		Adj.	951.00

The adjusting entry recorded by the junior accountant is shown on Lines 32–33 of the general journal, page 427. The resulting balance of Property Tax, $317.00 ($951.00 − $634.00), is the amount of property tax expense chargeable to March, 1979.

Adjusting entry for accrued federal income tax. Corporations pay federal income tax on net income the same as individuals pay income taxes on personal income. An adjusting entry to record estimated federal income tax owed by a corporation is described in Chapter 17, page 310.

The junior accountant for Dubolt Company estimates that the federal income tax owed for the first three months of 1979 is $5,205.14. The effect of the adjusting entry for accrued federal income tax is shown in the T accounts below.

Federal Income Tax		9001		Corporation's Income Tax Payable — Federal		2110
Adj.	5,205.14	Bal.	3,602.26		Adj.	5,205.14

The credit balance in Federal Income Tax is the result of a reversing entry. The reversing entry is explained later in this chapter.

The adjusting entry to record Dubolt Company's estimated federal income tax is shown on Lines 34–35 of the general journal, page 427. The new balance of Federal Income Tax, $1,602.88, is the portion of the tax chargeable to March, 1979 ($5,205.14 − $3,602.26).

PREPAID AND ACCRUED ITEMS ON FINANCIAL STATEMENTS

The expense and revenue accounts related to the prepaid and accrued items are shown on the income statement, page 432. The amounts used on the income statement are taken from the Income Statement columns of the work sheet prepared on March 31, 1979.

Supplies, Prepaid Insurance, and Interest Receivable are classified as current assets. Rent Received in Advance, Salaries Payable, Interest Payable, Property Tax Payable, and Corporation's Income Tax Payable — Federal are classified as current liabilities. The balance sheet for Dubolt Company, page 433, includes these prepaid and accrued items. The amounts used on the balance sheet are taken from the Balance Sheet columns of the work sheet and from the statement of stockholders' equity.

The work sheet prepared by Dubolt Company is similar to the one shown in Chapter 17, pages 308 and 309.

Dubolt Company
Income Statement
For Month Ended March 31, 1979

Operating Revenue:		
Sales		$485,175.02
Less: Sales Returns and Allowances	$ 1,513.48	
Sales Discount	2,093.57	3,607.05
Net Sales		$481,567.97
Cost of Merchandise Sold:		
Merchandise Inventory, March 1, 1979		$ 61,571.47
Purchases	$460,174.80	
Less: Purchases Returns and Allow. . $1,409.00		
Purchases Discount 2,844.40	4,253.40	
Net Purchases		455,921.40
Total Cost of Merchandise Available for Sale .		$517,492.87
Less Merchandise Inventory, March 31, 1979 . .		56,444.33
Cost of Merchandise Sold		461,048.54
Gross Profit on Operations		$ 20,519.43
Operating Expenses:		
Advertising Expense		$ 600.00
Bad Debts Expense		381.72
Delivery Expense		683.20
Depreciation Expense--Building		290.00
Depreciation Expense--Equipment		520.20
Insurance Expense		980.00
Miscellaneous Expense		1,998.40
Payroll Taxes Expense		547.41
Salary Expense		5,950.00
Supplies Expense		3,187.02
Total Operating Expenses		15,137.95
Income from Operations		$ 5,381.48
Other Revenue:		
Gain on Plant Assets	$ 345.00	
Interest Income	72.10	
Rent Income	1,000.00	
Total Other Revenue		$ 1,417.10
Other Expenses:		
Interest Expense	$ 18.07	
Loss on Plant Assets	52.00	
Total Other Expenses		70.07
Net Addition		1,347.03
Net Income Before Taxes		$ 6,728.51
Taxes:		
Federal Income Tax	$ 1,602.88	
Property Tax	317.00	
Total Taxes		1,919.88
Net Income After Taxes		$ 4,808.63

Income statement showing expenses and revenue
accounts related to prepaid and accrued items

CLOSING ENTRIES

The closing entries are recorded and posted for Dubolt Company in the
same manner as for any business. An example of closing entries for a

Dubolt Company
Balance Sheet
March 31, 1979

ASSETS

Current Assets:

Cash		$ 13,289.36
Petty Cash		400.00
Accounts Receivable	$33,190.76	
Less Allowance for Uncollectible Accounts	995.72	32,195.04
Notes Receivable		3,500.00
Merchandise Inventory		56,444.33
Supplies		1,948.58
Prepaid Insurance		4,900.00
Interest Receivable		16.10
Total Current Assets		$112,693.41

Plant Assets:

Equipment	$41,616.00		
Less Accumulated Depreciation--Equipment	6,069.00	$ 35,547.00	
Building	$70,000.00		
Less Accumulated Depreciation--Building	6,290.00	63,710.00	
Land		25,000.00	
Total Plant Assets			124,257.00
Total Assets			$236,950.41

LIABILITIES

Current Liabilities:

Accounts Payable	$ 10,436.00	
Notes Payable	2,100.00	
Salaries Payable	525.00	
Employees Income Tax Payable--Federal	759.50	
FICA Tax Payable	682.50	
Unemployment Tax Payable--Federal	29.76	
Unemployment Tax Payable--State	160.66	
Rent Received in Advance	1,000.00	
Interest Payable	5.75	
Corporation's Income Tax Payable--Federal	5,205.14	
Property Tax Payable	951.00	
Total Current Liabilities		$ 21,855.31

STOCKHOLDERS' EQUITY

Capital Stock	$200,000.00	
Retained Earnings	15,095.10	
Total Stockholders' Equity		215,095.10
Total Liabilities and Stockholders' Equity		$236,950.41

Balance sheet showing prepaid and accrued items

corporation is shown in Chapter 17, page 318. All accounts with balances recorded in the Income Statement Debit and Credit columns are closed. A final closing entry is made to close the income summary account and record the net income in the retained earnings account.

REVERSING ENTRIES

On April 6, 1979, Dubolt Company records a payroll with a total of $973.00. This amount covers the payroll period from March 29 to April 4. The payroll expenses for March 29–31, $525.00, are recorded through an adjusting entry at the end of March. If Dubolt Company records the entire April payroll on April 6 with a debit of $973.00 to Salary Expense, the $525.00 portion will be recorded twice. Therefore, a method must be used to avoid reporting the $525.00 expense in two different fiscal periods.

One way to avoid double recording the $525.00 is to split the payroll entry on April 6. The amount, $525.00, is recorded as a debit to Salaries Payable to cancel this liability. The remainder of the payroll, $448.00, is recorded as a debit to Salary Expense to show that this applies to April. Similar entries would have to be made in FICA Tax Payable, Unemployment Tax Payable — Federal, Unemployment Tax Payable — State, and Payroll Taxes Expense. Splitting an entry would also have to be done when property taxes and federal income taxes are paid.

To avoid splitting a later entry, the adjusting entries for these accounts are reversed on the first day of the new fiscal period. An entry made at the beginning of one fiscal period that is the opposite of an adjusting entry for a previous fiscal period is called a reversing entry.

Some adjusting entries for accrued items create balances in asset or liability accounts where no balances existed before the adjustment. For example, the adjusting entry for interest expense, page 430, creates a credit balance in Interest Payable. The same is true of the adjusting entry for salaries payable, page 429. When an adjusting entry creates a balance in an asset or liability account, that adjusting entry is reversed at the beginning of the next fiscal period.

Reversing entry for accrued payroll

Two reversing entries are needed to reverse the two adjusting entries made for payroll expense. The two payroll adjusting entries are shown on Lines 22–27 of the general journal, page 427.

The junior accountant prepares reversing entries for Dubolt Company on April 1. The reversing entry for the two payroll entries is shown on Lines 2–7 of the general journal on page 435.

On March 31, 1979, after the closing entries are posted, amounts in the salary expense account are as shown in the T account at the left.

Salary Expense		6109	
Balance	5,425.00	Closing	5,950.00
Adjusting	525.00		
	5,950.00		5,950.00

On April 1 the junior accountant makes a reversing entry for salary expense as shown on Lines 2–3 of the general journal, page 435. The effect of this entry is shown in the T accounts on page 435.

			GENERAL JOURNAL		PAGE 6	
1 ACCOUNTS PAYABLE DEBIT	2 GENERAL DEBIT	DATE	ACCOUNT TITLE	POST. REF.	3 GENERAL CREDIT	4 ACCOUNTS RECEIV. CREDIT
			Reversing Entries			
	52500	1979 Apr. 1	Salaries Payable	2103		
			Salary Expense	6109	52500	
	3150	1	FICA Tax Payable	2105		
	263		Unempl. Tax Payable-Federal	2106		
	1418		Unempl. Tax Payable-State	2107		
			Payroll Taxes Expense	6108	4831	
	575	1	Interest Payable	2109		
			Interest Expense	8002	575	
	1610	1	Interest Income	7002		
			Interest Receivable	1108	1610	
	95100	1	Property Tax Payable	2111		
			Property Tax	9002	95100	
	520514	1	Corp. Inc. Tax Pay'l-Federal	2110		
			Federal Income Tax	9001	520514	

Reversing entries for accrued revenues and expenses

Salaries Payable	2103		
Reversing 525.00	Adjusting	525.00	

Salary Expense			6109
Balance	5,425.00	Closing	5,950.00
Adjusting	525.00		
	5,950.00		5,950.00
		Reversing	525.00

On April 6 a payroll entry is made for the salaries paid on this date. In this entry, Salary Expense is debited for the full payroll expense, $973.00. The effect of this payroll entry on the salary expense account is shown in the T account at the right. The resulting balance, $448.00 ($973.00 − $525.00), is the balance of the account. The balance, $448.00, is the portion of the April 6 payroll that is an expense for April.

Salary Expense			6109
Balance	5,425.00	Closing	5,950.00
Adjusting	525.00		
	5,950.00		5,950.00
April 6	973.00	Reversing	525.00

The advantages in using reversing entries are:

1. Regular journal entries can be made during a month when expenses are paid and revenues are received. There is no need to split some entries at one time and not at others.

2. Accrued revenues and expenses recorded in one fiscal period are not included and reported in the next fiscal period. This situation is true even though the expenses may be paid or the revenue received in the next fiscal period.

Reversing entry for accrued interest expense

The adjusting entry for accrued interest expense is shown on Lines 28–29 of the general journal, page 427. The reversing entry for this expense is shown on Lines 8–9 of the general journal, above.

Reversing entry for accrued interest income

The adjusting entry for accrued interest income is shown on Lines 30–31 of the general journal, page 427. The reversing entry made by the junior accountant for interest income is shown on Lines 10–11 of the general journal, page 435.

Reversing entries for taxes

The adjusting entries for accrued property tax and federal income tax are shown on Lines 32–35 of the general journal, page 427. The reversing entries for these two accrued tax expenses are shown on Lines 12–15 of the general journal, page 435.

PREPAID ITEMS RECORDED INITIALLY AS REVENUES AND EXPENSES

When Dubolt Company buys supplies, the amount is recorded as a debit to the asset account, Supplies. Supplies eventually become expenses of the company. Some businesses prefer to record supplies initially as expenses. When this is done, Supplies Expense is debited at the time supplies are bought. When insurance premiums are paid, Insurance Expense is debited instead of Prepaid Insurance. When rent is received in advance, Rent Income is credited instead of Rent Received in Advance. When this method of recording prepaid items is used, the adjusting entries differ from those used by the Dubolt Company.

Adjusting entry when supplies are recorded initially as an expense

The Ling Restaurant records the buying of supplies as a debit to Supplies Expense. On January 31, 1979, the general ledger accounts show the following debit balances: Supplies, $92.00; Supplies Expense, $514.00.

No entries have been recorded in Supplies during the month of January. The balance in this account, $92.00, is the result of an adjusting entry at the end of December, 1978.

The supplies inventory for Ling Restaurant on January 31 is $225.00. Using both the data in the accounts and the supplies inventory, the following questions are answered:

1. What is the balance of the supplies account now?...................... $ 92.00
2. What should the balance be?... $225.00
3. What must be done to correct the account balance?..............Add $133.00
4. What adjusting entry must be made?..................Debit Supplies $133.00
                                       Credit Supplies Expense $133.00

The effect of the adjusting entry for supplies expense is shown in the T accounts on page 437.

After the adjusting entry is posted, Supplies has its correct balance, $225.00. Also, Supplies Expense has a new balance, $381.00 ($514.00 − $133.00). The new balance, $381.00, is the correct amount of the supplies expense for January.

Supplies			1106
Bal.	92.00		
Adj.	133.00		

Supplies Expense			6110
Bal.	514.00	Adj.	133.00

Adjusting entry when insurance is recorded initially as an expense

The Ling Restaurant records all payments for insurance as debits to Insurance Expense. On January 31, 1979, the general ledger accounts show the following debit balances: Prepaid Insurance, $432.00; Insurance Expense, $300.00.

A check of the insurance records on January 31, 1979, shows that the unused insurance totals $350.00. Using the data in the accounts and the insurance inventory, the following questions are answered:

1. What is the balance of the prepaid insurance account now? $432.00
2. What should the balance be?.. $350.00
3. What must be done to correct the account balance? ....Subtract $ 82.00
4. What adjusting entry must be made?...Debit Insurance Expense $ 82.00
   Credit Prepaid Insurance $ 82.00

The effect of the adjusting entry for insurance expense is shown in the T accounts at the right. After the entry is posted, Insurance Expense has a new balance of $382.00. This amount is the insurance expense chargeable to January, 1979. Prepaid Insurance has a new balance of $350.00 ($432.00 − $82.00). This new balance is the correct amount of prepaid insurance remaining at the end of January.

Insurance Expense			6106
Bal.	300.00		
Adj.	82.00		

Prepaid Insurance			1107
Bal.	432.00	Adj.	82.00

Adjusting entry when rent income received in advance is recorded initially as revenue

The Ling Restaurant owns the building in which the business is located. The restaurant rents an office in the building to a lawyer for $300.00 a month. The rental contract requires that the lawyer pay the rent for three months in advance. When cash is received for rent, Cash is debited and Rent Income is credited for $900.00.

On January 31, 1979, the account balances in the general ledger are: Rent Received in Advance, zero balance; Rent Income, $900.00.

On January 31 one month's rent has been earned, $300.00. The unearned balance remaining is $600.00. The questions asked are:

1. What is the balance of the rent received in advance account? ...... zero
2. What should the balance be?.. $600.00
3. What must be done to correct the account balance?..............Add $600.00
4. What adjusting entry must be made?............Debit Rent Income $600.00
   Credit Rent Received in Advance $600.00

Rent Income		7003
Adj.	600.00	Bal.	900.00

Rent Received in Advance		2108
		Adj.	600.00

The effect of this adjusting entry is shown in the T accounts at the left. After this adjusting entry is posted, the new balance of Rent Income is $300.00. This amount is the rent income earned in January, 1979. The new balance of Rent Received in Advance, $600.00, is the amount still prepaid.

Reversing entries when prepaid items are recorded initially as revenues and expenses

When prepaid expenses are recorded initially as expenses, the adjusting entries correct all account balances involved. The same is true for revenues received in advance. Therefore, when this method is used in initially recording the prepaid items, *no reversing entries are needed*. Because no reversing entries are needed, some accountants prefer this method to that used by the Dubolt Company described at the beginning of this chapter.

Using Business Terms

✦ What is the meaning of each of the following?

- prepaid expenses
- revenue received in advance
- accrual basis accounting
- cash basis accounting
- accrued expenses
- accrued revenue
- reversing entry

Questions for Individual Study

1. Why are supplies sometimes considered prepaid expenses?
2. When supplies are recorded initially as assets when bought, what two accounts are affected and how are they affected by the adjusting entry for supplies?
3. When insurance is recorded initially as an asset when paid, what two accounts are affected and how are they affected by the adjusting entry for insurance expense?
4. When rent received in advance is recorded initially as a liability when received, what two accounts are affected and how are they affected by the adjusting entry for rent income?
5. Why might salaries be considered accrued expenses?
6. Why did the Dubolt Company, described in this chapter, make an adjusting entry for interest expense on March 31?
7. What accounts are affected by the adjusting entry for property tax and how are they affected? For federal income tax on the corporation's earnings?

8. On the income statement, page 432, in which account would the balance shown include the following items: value of supplies that became an expense this fiscal period? accrued interest on notes receivable? accrued interest on notes payable? rent received in advance which became a revenue this fiscal period? amount of the company's federal income tax actually paid and accrued to date?
9. On the balance sheet, page 433, what is the name of the account related to each of the following items: interest receivable? salaries owed to employees but not yet paid? rent received but not yet earned? interest owed on notes payable but not yet paid? property taxes not yet paid? In which section of the balance sheet is each account listed?
10. For the Dubolt Company, a corporation, what account is credited when the closing entry is made to record the net income?
11. Why are reversing entries made?

12. For which items are the adjusting entries reversed by reversing entries on the records of the Dubolt Company?
13. When supplies bought for cash are recorded initially as expenses, what two accounts are affected?
14. What four questions are asked in figuring the adjusting entry for supplies when supplies are recorded initially as expenses?
15. Why is no reversing entry made for supplies expense when supplies are recorded initially as an expense?

CASE 1 Cynthia Abernathy owns several beauty shops. She prepares financial statements at the end of each month so that comparisons can be made from one month to the next. Ms. Abernathy uses accrual basis accounting. However, she makes no record of property taxes until she receives her tax statements in May and November of each year. What effect does this procedure have on the financial statements for Ms. Abernathy's businesses?

CASE 2 The junior accountant for Miller and Haymaker inspected the general ledger accounts at the end of a monthly fiscal period and found that the interest expense account had a debit balance of $12.55. The junior accountant also inspected the record of notes payable and found that during the fiscal period four notes had been paid. The total interest paid for all four notes was $18.55. Because of the difference between $12.55 and $18.55, the junior accountant made a correcting entry to debit interest expense for an additional $6.00. Should the junior accountant have made the correcting entry? Explain your answer.

CASE 3 Jason Bullock owns and manages a hardware store. On January 5, the first month of a new fiscal period, he inspects the general ledger accounts. Mr. Bullock finds that the other revenue account, Interest Income, has a debit balance. Mr. Bullock asks his accounting clerks to check the records, find the error, and correct it. What might cause the interest income account to have a debit balance? Explain your answer.

CASE 4 The Shapiro Apparel Store records the buying of supplies by debiting the general ledger account Supplies. The store also records the payment of insurance premiums by debiting Insurance Expense. Are these procedures acceptable? Explain your answer.

CASE 5 On June 18 of the current year, the Mason Store finds it necessary to borrow money from a bank. As part of the application for a loan, the store is required to include an up-to-date balance sheet and income statement. The store is on an annual fiscal period that ends in December. The junior accountant prepares a work sheet on June 18. Data from the work sheet are used to prepare an income statement and a balance sheet as of June 18. However, the junior accountant does not record adjusting and closing entries on June 18 and does not prepare a post-closing trial balance. Is this procedure correct? Explain your answer.

PROBLEM 23-1 Adjusting and reversing entries for prepaid and accrued items

The Zamora Company keeps its accounting records on the accrual basis. Prepaid items are recorded initially as assets or liabilities. A partial list of general ledger accounts and balances on December 31 of the current year is shown on page 440.

Account Title	Account Balances
Supplies	$ 2,067.00
Prepaid Insurance	3,194.00
Interest Receivable	——
Salaries Payable	——
Employees Income Tax Payable — Federal	$ 245.00
FICA Tax Payable..	90.00
Unemployment Tax Payable — Federal................................	7.50
Unemployment Tax Payable — State	40.50
Interest Payable	——
Rent Received in Advance	6,000.00
Corporation's Income Tax Payable — Federal	——
Property Tax Payable	——
Insurance Expense..	——
Payroll Taxes Expense	1,504.00
Salary Expense...	17,250.00
Supplies Expense	——
Interest Income	35.40
Rent Income..	——
Interest Expense..	48.50
Federal Income Tax..	2,213.75
Property Tax..	948.75

Instructions: ▫ **1.** On a work sheet, record the account titles. Record the account balances in the Trial Balance columns. (Do not total or rule the columns.)

▫ **2.** In the Adjustments columns of the work sheet, record the needed adjusting entries. The additional data needed are listed below. (Do not total or rule the Adjustments columns.)

Supplies inventory, December 31	$ 351.00
Value of insurance policies, December 31..	1,274.00
Accrued interest on notes receivable	12.50
Accrued salary expense on December 31	750.00
Employer's accrued payroll taxes:	
FICA tax..	45.00
Unemployment tax payable — federal..	3.75
Unemployment tax payable — state...	20.25
Rent received in advance and still unearned on December 31	500.00
Accrued interest on notes payable	6.40
Accrued corporation's federal income tax, December 31	201.25
Accrued property tax, December 31..	86.25

Instructions: ▫ **3.** Record the needed adjusting entries. Use page 14 of a general journal. The data needed for the adjusting entries are taken from the Adjustments columns of the work sheet prepared in Instruction 2.

▫ **4.** Record the needed reversing entries for the following: interest receivable, salaries payable, employer's accrued payroll taxes, interest payable, corporation's accrued income tax, and accrued property tax. Use page 15 of a general journal.

PROBLEM 23-2 Adjusting entries for prepaid and accrued items

The Delmario Company keeps its accounting records on the accrual basis. Prepaid items are recorded initially as revenue or expenses. A partial list of general ledger accounts and balances on December 31 of the current year is shown below.

Account Title	Account Balances	
	Debit	Credit
Supplies	$ 333.45	
Prepaid Insurance	1,210.30	
Interest Receivable	12.50	
Interest Payable		$ 6.00
Rent Received in Advance		500.00
Corporation's Income Tax Payable — Federal		197.23
Property Tax Payable		84.50
Insurance Expense..	3,130.00	
Supplies Expense	2,067.00	
Interest Income		34.60
Rent Income		7,200.00
Interest Expense...	———	
Federal Income Tax...	2,410.00	
Property Tax...	841.00	

Instructions: □ 1. Record the account titles in the Account Title column of a work sheet. Record the account balances in the Trial Balance columns of the work sheet. (Do not total or rule the Trial Balance columns.)

□ 2. Record the needed adjusting entries in the Adjustments columns of the work sheet.

> Before recording the adjustments on the work sheet, review the material, pages 436 to 438, about recording prepaid items as revenues or expenses. Use the same question format described on page 436 to determine the adjustment for each of the items.

The additional data needed for the adjusting entries are listed below. (Do not total or rule the Adjustments columns.)

Supplies inventory, December 31	$ 526.00
Value of insurance policies, December 31..	1,440.00
Accrued interest on notes receivable, December 31....................................	16.00
Rent received in advance and still unearned, December 31.	600.00
Accrued interest on notes payable, December 31.......................................	7.50
Accrued corporation's federal income tax, December 31	221.38
Accrued property tax, December 31...	94.88

Instructions: □ 3. Record the needed adjusting entries on page 12 of a general journal. Use the data from the Adjustments columns of the work sheet prepared in Instruction 2.

PROBLEM 23-3 End-of-fiscal-period work including prepaid and accrued items

The Wilcoxin Corporation keeps its accounting records on the accrual basis. Prepaid items are recorded initially as assets or liabilities. The accounts and balances in the general ledger on June 30 of the current year are as shown below and on the next page.

Account Title	Acct. Nos.	Debit	Credit
Cash	1101	$ 9,967.02	
Petty Cash	1102	300.00	
Accounts Receivable	1103	24,893.07	
Allowance for Uncollectible Accounts	1103.1		$ 460.50
Notes Receivable	1104	2,625.00	
Merchandise Inventory	1105	46,178.60	
Supplies	1106	3,851.70	
Prepaid Insurance	1107	4,410.00	
Interest Receivable	1108	——	
Equipment	1201	31,212.00	
Accumulated Depreciation — Equipment	1201.1		4,161.00
Building	1202	52,500.00	
Accumulated Depreciation — Building	1202.1		4,500.00
Land	1203	18,750.00	
Accounts Payable	2101		7,827.00
Notes Payable	2102		1,575.00
Salaries Payable	2103		——
Employees Income Tax Payable — Federal	2104		569.63
FICA Tax Payable	2105		488.25
Unemployment Tax Payable — Federal	2106		20.35
Unemployment Tax Payable — State	2107		109.86
Rent Received in Advance	2108		1,500.00
Interest Payable	2109		——
Corporation's Income Tax Payable — Federal	2110		——
Property Tax Payable	2111		——
Capital Stock	3010		150,000.00
Retained Earnings	3020		7,974.19
Income Summary	3090	——	——
Sales	4001		363,881.26
Sales Returns and Allowances	4001.1	1,135.10	
Sales Discount	4001.2	1,570.18	
Purchases	5001	338,776.70	
Purchases Returns and Allowances	5001.1		1,056.75
Purchases Discount	5001.2		2,133.30
Advertising Expense	6101	450.00	
Bad Debts Expense	6102	——	
Delivery Expense	6103	512.40	
Depreciation Expense — Building	6104	——	
Depreciation Expense — Equipment	6105	——	
Insurance Expense	6106	——	

Account Title	Acct. Nos.	Account Balances	
		Debit	Credit
Miscellaneous Expense	6107	$ 1,498.80	
Payroll Taxes Expense	6108	374.33	
Salary Expense	6109	4,068.75	
Supplies Expense	6110	——	
Interest Income	7001		$ 42.00
Rent Income	7002		——
Interest Expense	8001	9.24	
Loss on Plant Assets	8002	39.00	
Federal Income Tax	9001	2,701.70	
Property Tax	9002	475.50	

Instructions: □ **1.** Record the account titles in the Account Title column of a work sheet. Record the account balances in the Trial Balance columns of the work sheet. Total and rule the Trial Balance columns.

□ **2.** Record the needed adjustments in the Adjustments column of the work sheet. The additional data needed are listed below. Total, prove, and rule the Adjustments columns of the work sheet.

Bad debts expense: The balance of allowance for uncollectible accounts should equal 3% of the accounts receivable account balance.

Merchandise inventory, June 30	$42,333.25
Supplies inventory, June 30	1,461.44
Value of insurance policies, June 30	3,675.00
Accrued interest on notes receivable	12.08
Depreciation on equipment for June	460.10
Depreciation on building for June	912.00
Accrued salary expense	393.75
Employer's accrued payroll taxes:	
FICA tax	23.63
Unemployment tax — federal	1.97
Unemployment tax — state	10.63
Rent received in advance and still unearned, June 30	750.00
Accrued interest on notes payable	4.32
Accrued federal income tax to June 30	1,202.16
Accrued property tax to June 30	237.75

Instructions: □ **3.** Finish the work sheet and determine the net income for the month. Before completing the work sheet, review the material in Chapter 17, pages 307–311, on preparing a work sheet for a corporation.

□ **4.** Prepare an income statement from data in the Income Statement columns of the work sheet prepared in Instructions 1, 2, and 3.

□ **5.** Prepare a balance sheet from data in the Balance Sheet columns of the work sheet.

24 Accounting on a Cash Basis

Accounting records may be kept on an accrual basis or on a cash basis. When the accrual basis is used, all revenues, costs, and expenses are recorded in the fiscal period in which earned or incurred. On a cash basis, the revenues, costs, and expenses are recorded only when cash is actually received or paid out. Some small businesses choose the cash basis because the number of entries to be made is reduced. A comparison of the entries made on an accrual basis and on a cash basis for the purchase of merchandise is shown below.

Event	Accrual basis entry	Cash basis entry
Jan. 4. Received merchandise	No entry made	No entry made
Jan. 8. Received invoice	Debit Purchases and credit Accounts Payable	No entry made
Jan. 12. Issued check	Debit Accounts Payable and credit Cash	Debit Purchases and credit Cash

Most wage earners keep personal records and prepare individual income tax returns on a cash basis. Many small businesses selling only services also use the cash basis. Many small businesses selling merchandise for cash only use the cash basis.

Cheryl and Milton Robyn are married and both attend college. To earn a living, the Robyns operate a small business called the Key and Tag Shop. The business makes keys, small plastic signs, and other novelty items. The business is located in a suburban shopping area near the college attended by the two owners. All sales are for cash. The Robyns wait on customers and do not hire additional employees. The accounting records for the Key and Tag Shop are kept on the cash basis. The shop engages a junior accountant from a local public accounting firm part-time to keep most of the shop's accounting records. At the end of each week the source documents are taken to the junior accountant's office. The junior accountant verifies all source documents and records them in the records for the Key and Tag Shop.

RECORDING TRANSACTIONS ON A CASH BASIS

The junior accountant uses a single journal, known as a daily journal, to record all cash received and paid by the Key and Tag Shop. Subsidiary ledgers for accounts receivable and accounts payable are not used. The shop has no accounts receivable and very few accounts payable.

A daily journal

The daily journal for the Key and Tag Shop is shown below.

MONTH OF		DOC.			RECEIPTS			PAYMENTS				PAGE
CASH												
RECEIVED C-1	PAID C-2	NO.	DATE	ITEM	SALES R-1	SALES TAX R-2	OTHER R-3	PURCHASES P-1	SUPPLIES P-2	UTILITIES P-3	OTHER P-4	

A daily journal

The daily journal for the Key and Tag Shop has the following amount columns: (a) *Cash columns.* These two columns are used to record the amounts of cash received and paid out. (b) *Receipts columns.* These columns are for sales, sales tax, and other (or miscellaneous) receipts. These three columns are used to show the sources of cash received by the shop. (c) *Payments columns.* These columns are for purchases, supplies, utilities, and other (or miscellaneous) payments. These four columns are used to show the reasons for which cash is paid.

When money is received for cash sales, the amount is recorded on a cash register. Cash received for other than sales is recorded on a handwritten receipt form. On Friday of each week the junior accountant uses the cash register tape and the copies of receipts as source documents to record entries for revenue.

> If the number of transactions for revenue were greater, the source documents might be used to record revenue on a daily basis.

When cash is paid, except for small amounts, the owners write a check. The check stub is used by the junior accountant as the source document for cash payments transactions.

Memorandum entry in a daily journal

The junior accountant starts a new page in the daily journal for each month. On Line 1, page 1 of the daily journal for each month, a memorandum entry is made for the beginning cash balance.

January 1, 1979. Recorded beginning cash balance, $2,092.52. Memorandum No. 1.

The memorandum entry for the beginning cash balance is shown on Line 1 of the daily journal below.

	CASH		DOC. NO.	DATE	ITEM	RECEIPTS			PAYMENTS				
	RECEIVED C-1	PAID C-2				SALES R-1	SALES TAX R-2	OTHER R-3	PURCHASES P-1	SUPPLIES P-2	UTILITIES P-3	OTHER P-4	
1				1979 Jan. 1	Balance on hand, $2,092.52								1
2		50.00	Ck21	2	✓				50.00				2
3		75.00	Ck22	3	✓				75.00				3
4		150.00	Ck23	3	Rent							150.00	4
5		10.00	Ck24	4	✓					10.00			5
6	714.00		T6	6	✓	680.00	34.00						6
7	7.50		R1	8	Purchases Returns				7.50				7
8		255.10	Ck25	9	Sales Tax							255.10	8
9		300.00	Ck26	10	Withdrawal							300.00	9

MONTH OF *January* 19 79   DAILY JOURNAL   PAGE 1

Entries recorded in a daily journal

The memorandum entry for the beginning cash balance is made in the daily journal in much the same way as in any cash journal. Another example of a memorandum entry for a beginning cash balance is shown in Chapter 2, page 27.

Transactions related to purchases

Most merchandise purchased by the Key and Tag Shop is paid for at the time of purchase. Sometimes the shop receives merchandise on one day and pays for it a few days later when the invoice is received by mail. For any purchases transaction, however, no entry is made in the daily journal until a check is issued.

Cash purchases. On January 10 the shop receives merchandise ordered from a vendor. A check is issued and given to the vendor at the time the merchandise is delivered.

January 2, 1979. Purchased merchandise for cash, $50.00. Check No. 21.

The junior accountant makes the entry shown on Line 2 of the daily journal illustrated above. The amount of the check, $50.00, is written in the Cash Paid column. The same amount is written in the Purchases column to show the reason for the payment. A check mark is placed in the Item column to show that additional data do not need to be recorded for this transaction.

After the entry for purchases is made in the daily journal, the junior accountant marks the invoice *paid* and writes the check number on the invoice. The paid invoice is then filed in a paid invoices file. The invoices are filed alphabetically so that the shop has a record of the purchases made from each vendor.

Purchases on account. Once in a while the shop receives merchandise but does not pay for it until later in the month. Usually the payment is made within a week or two. When merchandise is paid for after it is received, no entry is made until the check is actually issued.

January 3, 1979. Issued a check to pay for merchandise received on December 30, 1978, $75.00. Check No. 22.

The entry for this transaction is recorded as a cash purchase. The entry in the daily journal is similar to the one on Line 2 of the daily journal, page 446. The entry for this January 3 transaction is shown on Line 3 of the daily journal, page 446.

When invoices are received but not paid until later, the unpaid invoices are temporarily filed in an unpaid invoices file. When an invoice is paid, it is removed from the unpaid invoices file, marked *paid*, and placed in the paid invoices file.

Purchases returns and allowances. Usually, the Key and Tag Shop pays cash for all merchandise purchased. For this reason, when merchandise is returned to a vendor, the shop usually receives cash in return.

January 8, 1979. Received cash for merchandise returned to a vendor, $7.50. Receipt No. 1.

The entry for this transaction is shown on Line 7 of the daily journal, page 446. The amount of cash received, $7.50, is written in the Cash Received column. The same amount is written in the Other Receipts column. Whenever an entry is made in the Other Receipts column, a notation is made in the Item column to show the source of cash. Therefore, the words *Purchases Returns* are written in the Item column.

Transactions related to sales

All merchandise is sold for cash by the Key and Tag Shop. All sales are final because the merchandise is specially prepared according to the wishes of customers. For this reason, the shop has no sales returns.

Cash sales. When merchandise is sold to customers, the sale is recorded on a cash register. The cash register prints the amount of the sale and sales tax on a paper tape inside the cash register. At the end of each week, the sales for the week are totaled on the cash register tape. The amounts for the weekly totals include the total sales, total sales tax collected, and the total of all cash received from these two sources. The cash register tape is the source document for recording cash sales.

> *January 6, 1979. Total weekly cash sales: sales, $680.00; sales tax, $34.00; total cash received, $714.00. Cash Register Tape No. 6.*

The entry to record weekly cash sales is shown on Line 6 of the daily journal, page 446. The total amount of cash received, $714.00, is written in the Cash Received column. The total amount of sales, $680.00, is written in the Sales column. The total amount of sales tax received, $34.00, is written in the Sales Tax column. The sum of the two amounts ($680.00 + $34.00) is equal to the amount recorded in the Cash Received column.

The amount of the sales tax collected from customers must be reported and forwarded periodically to the government. Such payment is discussed later in this chapter.

Transactions related to buying supplies

Usually a check is issued at the time supplies are bought. On a few occasions the shop buys supplies on one day and pays for the supplies on a later day. In either case, an entry is made only when a check is issued.

Buying supplies for cash. On January 4 the shop issues a check for supplies received the same day.

> *January 4, 1979. Issued a check for supplies bought, $10.00. Check No. 24.*

The entry for this transaction is shown on Line 5 of the daily journal, page 446. The amount of cash paid, $10.00, is written in the Cash Paid column. The same amount is written in the Supplies Payments column to show the reason for the payment.

Buying supplies on account. On January 23, 1979, the shop receives supplies bought from a vendor in another city. The invoice for the supplies is received by mail on January 27. On January 29, a check is issued to pay for the supplies invoice.

> *January 29, 1979. Issued a check for supplies received on January 23, $30.00. Check No. 40.*

No entry is made for this transaction until the check is actually issued on January 29. The entry to record this transaction is shown on Line 2 of the daily journal on page 449.

CASH RECEIVED C-1	CASH PAID C-2	DOC. NO.	DATE	ITEM	SALES R-1	SALES TAX R-2	OTHER R-3	PURCHASES P-1	SUPPLIES P-2	UTILITIES P-3	OTHER P-4	
459365	440426		Jan. 29	Brought Forward	435538	21777	2050	321267	23263	19000	76896	1
	3000	Ck40	29	✓					3000			2
	1200	Ck41	29	Advertising							1200	3
	22500	Ck42	30	Insurance							22500	4
	3200	Ck43	31	✓					2300			5
				Miscellaneous							900	6
	3500	Ck44	31	Telephone						3500		7
	4000	Ck45	31	Equipment							4000	8
39585		J31	31	✓	37700	1885						9
498950 498950	477826 477826		31	Totals	473238 473238	23662 23662	2050 2050	321267 321267	28563 28563	22500 22500	105496 105496	10
												11
												12
230376			31	Cash on hand								13
				Dist. of Other Revenue:								14
				Purchases Returns			2050					15
				Dist. of Other Payments:								16
				Advertising							1200	17
				Equipment							4000	18
				Insurance							22500	19
				Miscellaneous							7286	20
				Rent							15000	21
				Sales Tax							25510	22
				Withdrawal							30000	23
				Total Other Payments							105496	24

Page of daily journal showing end of month rulings

This entry for a supplies transaction is recorded in the same way as the entry shown on Line 5 of the daily journal, page 446.

Transactions related to expenses

The major expenses of the Key and Tag Shop are for rent and utilities plus the cost of supplies. Some other miscellaneous expenses are also paid each month.

Utilities expenses. The shop has several utilities expenses. All the utilities expenses are recorded in the Utilities Payments column in the daily journal.

> January 31, 1979. Issued a check to pay the telephone bill, $35.00. Check No. 44.

The entry for this expense transaction is shown on Line 7 of the daily journal above. The amount paid, $35.00, is written in the Cash Paid column. The same amount is written in the Utilities column to show the reason for the payment. To show which utility expense is paid, the word *Telephone* is written in the Item column.

The entry to record other utilities (water, electricity, and heat) is similar to the entry for telephone expense. The difference in recording other utilities is the explanation written in the Item column.

Rent expense. Some expenses occur only once each month. Some expenses occur only once or twice a year. For the infrequent expenses, a special Payments column is not used. If there is no special Payments column for a cash payment, the amount is recorded in the Other Payments column.

Rent expense is a relatively large expense compared to many of the other individual expenses. However, rent is recorded only once each month. Therefore, no special Payments column is used for rent payments made by the Key and Tag Shop.

January 3, 1979. Issued a check in payment of January rent, $150.00. Check No. 23.

The entry for this transaction is recorded on Line 4, page 1 of the daily journal, page 446. The amount, $150.00, is written in the Cash Paid column. The same amount is written in the Other Payments column. The explanation, *Rent*, is written in the Item column.

The entry for payment of insurance is recorded in the same way as the entry for rent. An entry for insurance expense is shown on Line 4, page 3 of the daily journal, page 449.

Paying the sales tax liability

The amount of sales tax collected from customers must be reported and forwarded monthly (quarterly in some cases) to the proper governmental unit. At the end of the month the total of the Sales Tax column indicates the amount of sales tax payable. Such payments are made the month following the period in which the taxes are collected.

January 9, 1979. Paid state sales tax liability for December, $255.10. Check No. 25.

The entry to record the payment of the sales tax liability for December is shown on Line 8 of the daily journal, page 446.

Withdrawals by the owner

Withdrawals by the owner are recorded in the daily journal. The entry for a cash withdrawal by the owner is similar to the entries in the daily journal for other cash payments.

January 10, 1979. The owner withdrew cash for personal use, $300.00. Check No. 26.

The entry to record this withdrawal of cash is shown on Line 9 of the daily journal, page 446.

Buying equipment

The Key and Tag Shop buys equipment only when there is sufficient money on hand to pay cash for the equipment.

> *January 31, 1979. Issued a check for a display rack, $40.00. Check No. 45.*

The entry for this transaction is shown on Line 8, page 3 of the daily journal, page 449. The amount of the check, $40.00, is written in the Cash Paid column. The amount is written in the Other Payments column. The explanation, *Equipment*, is written in the Item column.

Replenishing petty cash

The Key and Tag Shop has a petty cash fund of $100.00. The petty cash fund is used to make change and small payments of $2.00 or less. When cash payments are made from the petty cash fund, a paid-out voucher is prepared and placed in the cash register drawer. The petty cash fund is replenished whenever the fund falls below $45.00. However, the fund is always replenished at the end of each month regardless of the amount remaining.

A check of the petty cash fund on January 31, 1979, showed that $68.00 remained in the fund. The junior accountant used the paid-out vouchers to prepare the following summary:

SUMMARY OF PETTY CASH PAID — OUT VOUCHERS January 31, 1979	
REASONS FOR PAYMENTS	AMOUNT
Supplies	$23.00
Miscellaneous	9.00
Total paid out	$32.00

A check is issued on January 31 to replenish the petty cash fund.

> *January 31, 1979. Issued a check to replenish petty cash fund: Supplies, $23.00; Miscellaneous, $9.00; total, $32.00. Check No. 43.*

The entry to record this transaction is shown on Lines 5–6, page 3 of the daily journal, page 449. The amount of the check, $32.00, is written in the Cash Paid column. On the same line, the amount, $23.00, is written in the Supplies column. The amount, $9.00, is written in the Other Payments column on the next line. The word *Miscellaneous* is written on the same line in the Item column. A brace ({) is placed in the Date column around Lines 5 and 6 to show that the data on the two lines belong to a single entry.

COMPLETING A DAILY JOURNAL AT THE END OF A MONTH

At the end of each month, the junior accountant completes the daily journal. The junior accountant foots the daily journal, proves cash, totals and rules the daily journal, and analyzes the amounts recorded in the Other Receipts and Other Payments columns.

Proving cash

After footing the Cash columns on the daily journal, page 449, the junior accountant prepares the following cash proof on scratch paper:

Cash balance, January 1, 1979 .... $2,092.52
Plus total cash received (column C-1) 4,989.50

Equals total cash available during January $7,082.02
Minus total cash paid (column C-2) 4,778.26

Equals cash balance, January 31, 1979 .... $2,303.76

The balance shown on the last used check stub is $2,303.76. This amount is the same balance as that shown in the cash proof above. Cash is proved. The amount of the cash balance on January 31 is written in the daily journal as shown on Line 13, page 3 of the journal, page 449.

Totaling and ruling a daily journal

The daily journal is footed, totaled, and ruled as shown on Line 10, page 3 of the journal, page 449. The junior accountant checks the accuracy of the totals by:

(1) Adding the totals of the three Receipts columns ($4,732.38 + $236.62 + $20.50). The total, $4,989.50, is compared to the total of the Cash Received column. The two amounts must be the same.

(2) Adding the totals of the four Payments columns ($3,212.67 + $285.63 + $225.00 + $1,054.96). The total, $4,778.26, is compared to the total of the Cash Paid column. The two figures must be the same.

The totals shown on Line 10, page 3 of the daily journal, page 449, do prove as described above. Therefore, the junior accountant is reasonably sure that the work has been done correctly.

Analyzing the Other Receipts and Other Payments columns

Sources of revenue for which no special column is provided in the daily journal are recorded in the Other Receipts column. The amounts in the Other Receipts column need to be analyzed to determine the total amounts of like kinds of receipts. For example, all the purchases returns are recorded in the Other Receipts column. The amounts need to be summarized to show the total of the purchases returns separately from other receipts recorded in the Other column. The only receipts recorded in the Other Receipts column were for purchases returns. Therefore, the amount, $20.50, is written in the Other Receipts column. An explanation is written in the Item column. This analysis is shown on Lines 14–15, page 3 of the daily journal, page 449.

The amounts in the Other Payments column are also analyzed. The analysis prepared by the junior accountant on January 31, 1979, is shown on Lines 16–24, page 3 of the daily journal, page 449. The total of this analysis, shown on Line 24, $1,054.96, is the same as the total of the Other Payments column, shown on Line 10.

The analysis shown on Lines 14–21 of the daily journal, page 449, provides data needed in preparing the income statement. The analysis shown on Lines 13 and 23 provides data needed in preparing the balance sheet. The amount of Line 22, $255.10, is not needed for any reports but must be included so the total of the analysis and the total of the Other Payments column will balance. The use of this data is explained later in this chapter.

PREPARING FINANCIAL STATEMENTS

The Key and Tag Shop prepares two major financial statements at the end of each month: an income statement and a balance sheet. To help summarize data needed for the two statements, the junior accountant also prepares a summary report. The data for the summary report are taken from records of the shop other than the daily journal.

Summary report

The summary report prepared by the junior accountant on January 31, 1979, is shown below.

SUMMARY REPORT	Prepared on _Jan. 31_ 19 _79_		
Value of equipment (plant assets file)	$	2,440.00	S-1
Unpaid payable invoices, total amount		235.00	S-2
Merchandise inventory, end of last month		2,846.38	S-3
Merchandise inventory, end of this month		2,991.42	S-4
Capital, end of last month		6,988.80	S-5

Summary report

Each line on the summary report is given a code number. The code number is shown at the right of each line on the summary report, page 453. These code numbers help in preparing the financial reports. The use of the code numbers is explained later in this chapter.

The source of data for each of the lines on the summary report is:

Line S-1. This amount is taken from the plant assets file records. The Key and Tag Shop keeps a plant assets file showing the value of each piece of equipment owned by the business.

Line S-2. The amount on this line is found by adding the amounts of all invoices in the unpaid invoices file. These unpaid invoices represent amounts owed to creditors.

Line S-3. The amount on this line is taken from Line S-4 of the summary report prepared at the end of the previous month. The beginning merchandise inventory in January is the ending inventory listed on Line S-4 of the December 31 summary report.

Line S-4. The amount for this line is found by making a periodic inventory of all merchandise on hand at the end of the month.

Line S-5. The amount of capital at the end of last month is taken from the balance sheet prepared for the previous month. The amount on Line S-5 of the summary report, page 453, $6,988.80, is taken from the balance sheet prepared on December 31, 1978.

The summary report is not a financial statement. However, the junior accountant files each summary report in case some of the amounts need to be verified at a later date.

Income statement

The nature of the Key and Tag Shop's business is just about the same from one month to the next. The kinds of expenses and sources of revenue do not change. For this reason, the junior accountant for the shop has had blank income statement forms printed. A copy of the form is completed each month to provide an income statement. The completed form prepared on January 31, 1979, is shown on page 455.

> Expenses that occur regularly each month are printed in alphabetic order. An expense that occurs only once or twice a year would be entered on a blank line under Other.

Many of the blank lines on the income statement form are coded. The code numbers correspond to the same numbers on the daily journal and on the summary report. The code numbers show where the data are obtained for each of the blank lines on the form. If a blank line has no code number, the amount for this space is figured as the income statement is prepared. For example, the blank line for Sales is coded R-1. This is the

KEY AND TAG SHOP
Income Statement
For Month Ended _January 31_   19_79_

OPERATING REVENUE:		
Sales.		$4,732.38 R-1
COST OF MERCHANDISE:		
Merchandise Inventory, end of last month	$2,846.38 S-3	
Purchases $3,212.67 P-1		
Less Purchases Returns 20.50 R-3		
Net Purchases	3,192.17	
Total Merchandise Available for Sale.	$6,038.55	
Less Merchandise Inventory, end of this month. . .	2,991.42 S-4	
Cost of Merchandise Sold.		3,047.13
GROSS PROFIT ON OPERATIONS		$1,685.25
EXPENSES:		
Equipment	$ 40.00 P-4	
Insurance	225.00 P-4	
Miscellaneous.	72.86 P-4	
Rent	150.00 P-4	
Supplies	285.63 P-2	
Utilities.	225.00 P-3	
Other (list below):		
Advertising	12.00 P-4	
	P-4	
	P-4	
	P-4	
	P-4	
Total Expenses.		1,010.49
NET INCOME.		$ 674.76

Income statement

code number of the Sales column in the daily journal, page 449. The monthly total of the Sales column is placed in this blank space. The line for the Gross Profit on Operations has no code number. The amount for this space is figured from data already entered on the income statement form. Lines coded with an _R_ use data from the Receipts columns of the daily journal. Lines coded with a _P_ use data from the Payments columns of the daily journal. Not all the amounts in the Other Payments column appear on the income statement. Such amounts as sales tax and withdrawals appear on the balance sheet. Lines coded with an _S_ use data from the summary report.

The amount of net income reported on the income statement is used in preparing the balance sheet for the Key and Tag Shop. For this reason, the junior accountant prepares the income statement before the balance sheet is prepared.

Balance sheet

The balance sheet for the Key and Tag Shop is also prepared on a printed form. The explanation of the code letters for the blank lines on the income statement apply also to the balance sheet. C-1 is the code for the Cash Received column of the daily journal. However, for the balance sheet this identifies the location of the ending cash balance entered in the summary section after cash was proved. The total of the column is not to be used. The balance sheet prepared by the junior accountant on January 31, 1979, is shown below.

KEY AND TAG SHOP
Balance Sheet
January 31, 1979

ASSETS:
Cash	$ 2,303.76	C-1
Petty Cash	100.00	
Merchandise Inventory	2,991.42	S-4
Equipment	2,440.00	S-1
Other (list below):		
Total Assets	$ 7,835.18	

LIABILITIES:
Accounts Payable	$ 235.00	S-2
Sales Tax	236.62	R-2
Other (list below):		
Total Liabilities	$ 471.62	

CAPITAL:
Capital, end of last month	$ 6,988.80	S-5
Plus: Additional Investment		R-3
Net Income of this month	674.76	
Less: Withdrawals of this month	300.00	P-4
Capital, end of this month	7,363.56	
TOTAL LIABILITIES AND CAPITAL	$ 7,835.18	

Balance sheet

The junior accountant uses data from the daily journal, page 449, the summary report, page 453, and the income statement, page 455, in preparing the balance sheet.

Annual financial statements

In addition to preparing monthly financial statements, the junior accountant prepares annual financial statements for the Key and Tag Shop.

The owners, assisted by the junior accountant, compare data on the monthly financial statements to determine how the business is doing from one month to the next. Comparisons are also made between one month this year with the same month a year ago. The same comparisons are made on the annual financial statements. The figures on the annual statements for 1979 can be compared with the figures on the annual statements for 1978.

Annual income statement. The Key and Tag Shop's fiscal year is from January 1 to December 31 of each calendar year. On December 31 of each year a monthly income statement is prepared as usual. Then, the data are summarized from the twelve monthly income statements to prepare an annual income statement for the fiscal year. The annual income statement prepared for the year ended December 31, 1979, is shown below.

```
                        Key and Tag Shop
                        Income Statement
                  For Year Ended December 31, 1979

Operating Revenue:
  Sales . . . . . . . . . . . . . . .                        $47,421.23

Cost of Merchandise:
  Merchandise Inventory, January 1, 1979.       $ 2,846.38
  Purchases . . . . . . . . . . . . .  $32,769.23
  Less Purchases Returns . . . . . . .     209.10
  Net Purchases . . . . . . . . . .                32,560.13
  Total Mdse. Available for Sale  . . . .        $35,406.51
  Less Mdse. Inventory, Dec. 31, 1979 . .          3,888.85
  Cost of Merchandise Sold . . . . . .                          31,517.66

Gross Profit on Operations . . . . . . .                        $15,903.57

Expenses:
  Equipment . . . . . . . . . . . . . .         $    250.00
  Insurance . . . . . . . . . . . . . .              472.50
  Miscellaneous . . . . . . . . . . . .            1,123.67
  Rent  . . . . . . . . . . . . . . . .            1,800.00
  Supplies  . . . . . . . . . . . . . .            3,741.75
  Utilities . . . . . . . . . . . . . .            2,317.50
  Other:
    Advertising . . . . . . . . . . . .              200.00
    Dues, Merchants Association . . . . .            180.00
  Total Expenses . . . . . . . . . . .                           10,085.42

Net Income  . . . . . . . . . . . . . .                         $ 5,818.15
```

Annual income statement

Annual balance sheet. Balance sheets are prepared as of a specific date. For this reason, the monthly balance sheet prepared on December 31, 1979, is both a monthly balance sheet and an annual balance sheet. Therefore, no additional annual balance sheet is prepared. The one balance sheet serves both purposes.

Using the financial statements

The junior accountant and the owners of the Key and Tag Shop compare financial statements regularly. The comparisons are made to judge how well the shop is doing. The kinds of comparisons made include:

1. Compare the income statement and the balance sheet for this month with the same statements prepared for the same month a year ago.

2. Compare the annual income statement and balance sheet prepared on December 31 of each year with the annual statements prepared on December 31 a year before.

3. Compare figures on the financial statements with national figures for similar businesses. The junior accountant supplies these figures from data received as part of the normal work of the public accounting firm.

Chapter 27 includes some ways in which financial statements may be analyzed and compared.

Questions for Individual Study

1. When a business keeps records on a cash basis, when are entries made in the records?
2. What is the difference in the number of entries needed to record a purchase on account on the accrual basis and on the cash basis?
3. What is the difference in the number of entries needed to record a payment on account on the accrual basis and on the cash basis?
4. What is the name of the journal used by the Key and Tag Shop described in Chapter 24?
5. What kinds of amount columns are in the journal used by the Key and Tag Shop?
6. How does the Key and Tag Shop make an initial record of each cash received transaction?
7. What are the source documents prepared by the Key and Tag Shop for cash payments transactions?
8. In what amount column of the daily journal, page 449, are entries written for each of the following transactions?

a. Cash purchases
b. Purchases returns
c. Total weekly cash sales
d. Buying supplies for cash
e. Paying cash for a utility expense
f. Paying cash for monthly rent
g. Buying equipment for cash

9. How is the accuracy of the column totals of the daily journal, page 449, checked?
10. Why is the Other Payments column analyzed and the amounts written as shown on Lines 16–24 of the daily journal, page 449?
11. Why is the summary report, page 453, prepared?
12. Why are code numbers shown next to some of the blank lines on the printed income statement form, page 455? What do the code numbers mean?
13. What is the source of data used to prepare the annual income statement, page 457?
14. How are the financial statements used to analyze the operations of the Key and Tag Shop?

Cases for Management Decision

CASE 1 Don Wiltshire owns and operates a beauty shop. He has been keeping accounting records on the accrual basis. He consults with a public accountant about the possibility of changing to the cash basis. If you were the public accountant he contacted, what would you advise him?

CASE 2 Norma Jean Beck owns and operates a small gasoline station. She keeps records on a cash basis much the same as those described in this chapter for the Key and Tag Shop. Miss Beck does not prepare monthly financial statements. She believes that looking at the totals in the daily journal provides all the needed data about the operation of the business. Mrs. Wanda Mentoza, a junior accountant with a local public accounting firm, recommends that Miss Beck prepare or have prepared monthly financial statements. With whom do you agree and why?

PROBLEM 24-1   Recording transactions on a cash basis

Problems for Applying Concepts

Bobbie June Mason owns Mason's Leather Goods. She uses a cash basis accounting system similar to that described in Chapter 24. The transactions below were completed during July of the current year.

Instructions: □ **1.** Record the transactions starting on page 11 of a daily journal similar to the one shown on page 449. The source documents are listed as: check, Ck; cash register tape, T; receipt, R.

July 1. Beginning cash balance, $3,236.00.
       5. Purchased merchandise for cash, $60.00. Ck342.
       5. Issued a check for July rent, $300.00. Ck343.
       6. Purchased merchandise for cash, $55.00. Ck344.
       7. Issued a check to pay for merchandise received on June 30, $26.25. Ck345.
       8. Total weekly cash sales: sales, $816.00; sales tax, $40.80; total cash received, $856.80. T8.
      10. Issued a check for withdrawal of cash by owner, $500.00. Ck346.
      10. Purchased merchandise for cash, $47.50. Ck347.
      11. Issued a check to pay for merchandise received on July 7, $22.30. Ck348.
      11. Issued a check for supplies bought today, $24.00. Ck349.
      12. Issued a check to pay sales tax liability, $221.50. Ck350.
      12. Issued a check to pay for merchandise received on July 10, $219.50. Ck351.
      13. Purchased merchandise for cash, $9.50. Ck352.
      13. Received cash for merchandise returned to a vendor, $9.00. R53.
      13. Issued a check to replenish petty cash fund: supplies, $17.50; miscellaneous, $10.40; total $27.90. Ck353.
      14. Issued a check to pay for merchandise received on July 12, $421.00. Ck354.
      15. Total weekly cash sales: sales, $1,224.00; sales tax, $61.20; total cash received, $1,285.20. T15.
      17. Issued a check to pay for merchandise received on July 15, $209.50. Ck355.
      18. Purchased merchandise for cash, $13.50. Ck356.
      19. Issued a check to pay for merchandise received on July 15, $356.50. Ck357.
      20. Issued a check for supplies bought today, $21.60. Ck358.
      22. Total weekly cash sales: sales, $1,346.40; sales tax, $67.32; total cash received, $1,413.72. T22.
      24. Received cash for merchandise returned to a vendor, $5.75. R54.
      24. Issued a check to pay the telephone bill, $32.00. Ck359.
      24. Issued a check to pay for merchandise received on July 22, $125.00. Ck360.

July 25. Issued a check to pay for miscellaneous expenses, $14.70. Ck361.

25. Issued a check to pay for merchandise received on July 21, $417.75. Ck362.

26. Purchased merchandise for cash, $290.00. Ck363.

26. Issued a check to pay the electric bill, $95.00. Ck364.

28. Purchased merchandise for cash, $358.50. Ck365.

28. Issued a check to pay the gas bill, $24.00. Ck366.

29. Total weekly cash sales: sales, $1,162.80; sales tax, $58.14; total cash received, $1,220.94. T29.

29. Issued a check to pay for merchandise received on July 28, $624.00. Ck367.

31. Cash sales for the day: sales, $51.00; sales tax, $2.55; total cash received, $53.55. T31.

31. Issued a check for supplies bought on July 29, $35.50. Ck368.

31. Issued a check to pay the water bill, $35.25. Ck369.

31. Issued a check to replenish the petty cash fund: miscellaneous, $9.88; total, $9.88. Ck370.

31. Purchased merchandise for cash, $375.00. Ck371.

31. Issued a check to pay for newspaper advertising, $50.00. Ck372.

31. Issued a check to pay for miscellaneous expenses, $21.50. Ck373.

Instructions: □ **2.** Pencil foot the daily journal, prove cash, and prove the daily journal. The check stub balance after the last check was written on July 31, 1979, is $3,037.33.

□ **3.** Total and rule the daily journal in the same manner shown for the daily journal on page 449.

□ **4.** Analyze the Other Receipts and Other Payments columns in the same ways shown on page 449. Write the results of the analysis at the top of a new page of the daily journal.

PROBLEM 24-2 Preparing financial statements from records kept on a cash basis

Rita Mancelleo owns the Cycle Shop. Accounting records for the shop are kept on a cash basis. Data from the daily journal on May 31 of the current year are:

Cash balance on May 1, 19—..	$2,954.08
Column totals from the daily journal are:	
(C-1) Cash Received column..	3,891.81
(C-2) Cash Paid column..	4,198.61
(R-1) Sales column..	3,691.26
(R-2) Sales Tax column	184.56
(R-3) Distribution of Other Receipts column:	
Purchases Returns	15.99
(P-1) Purchases column..	2,505.88
(P-2) Supplies column..	222.79
(P-3) Utilities column..	175.50

(P-4) Distribution of Other Payments column:

Equipment	$ 31.00
Insurance	170.00
Miscellaneous	66.19
Rent	200.00
Advertising	36.75
Sales tax	190.50
Withdrawal	600.00

The summary report prepared on May 31, 19——, includes:

(S-1)	Value of equipment	$1,406.72
(S-2)	Unpaid invoices total	183.30
(S-3)	Merchandise inventory, end of last month	2,220.18
(S-4)	Merchandise inventory, end of this month	2,333.31
(S-5)	Capital, end of last month	6,207.18

Instructions: □ **1.** Prove cash. The check stub balance after the last check was written on May 31, 19——, is $2,647.28.

□ **2.** Prepare an income statement similar to the one shown on page 455.

□ **3.** Prepare a balance sheet similar to the one shown on page 456.

PROBLEM 24-3 Recording transactions and preparing financial statements on a cash basis

Marvin Beardsley owns and operates a small leather belt and pocketbook shop. The shop is called the Leather Corner. Accounting records for the business are kept on a cash basis. The transactions below were completed during March of the current year. Source documents are referred to as: checks, Ck; cash register tapes, T; and receipts, R.

Instructions: □ **1.** Record the transactions beginning on page 9 of a daily journal similar to the one shown on page 449.

Mar. 1. Beginning cash balance, $3,041.94.
  2. Issued a check for March rent, $350.00. Ck171.
  2. Purchased merchandise for cash, $72.60. Ck172.
  3. Issued a check to pay for merchandise received on February 28, $31.75. Ck173.
  3. Purchased merchandise for cash, $65.70. Ck174.
  3. Total weekly cash sales: sales, $987.36; sales tax, $49.37; total cash received, $1,036.73. T3.
  5. Purchased merchandise for cash, $57.00. Ck175.
  6. Issued a check to pay for newspaper advertising, $61.00. Ck176.
  6. Issued a check for supplies bought today, $30.00. Ck177.
  7. Issued a check to pay for merchandise received on March 6, $26.98. Ck178.
  8. Issued a check to pay for miscellaneous expenses, $26.00. Ck179.

Mar. 8. Issued a check to pay for merchandise received on March 7, $265.60. Ck180.
   9. Purchased merchandise for cash, $11.50. Ck181.
   10. Received cash for merchandise returned to a vendor, $10.89. R26.
   10. Total weekly cash sales: sales, $1,481.04; sales tax, $74.05, total cash received, $1,555.09. T10.
   10. Issued a check to replenish petty cash fund: supplies, $22.90; miscellaneous, $12.58; total, $35.48. Ck182.
   12. Issued a check to pay for merchandise received on March 9, $509.41. Ck183.
   13. Issued a check to pay for merchandise received on March 12, $253.50. Ck184.
   14. Purchased merchandise for cash, $16.34. Ck185.
   15. Issued a check to pay for merchandise received on March 10, $431.37. Ck186.
   16. Issued a check for supplies bought today, $26.14. Ck187.
   16. Purchased merchandise for cash, $26.00. Ck188.
   17. Total weekly cash sales: sales, $1,629.14; sales tax, $81.46; total cash received, $1,710.60. T17.
   18. Issued a check to pay the telephone bill, $38.72. Ck189.
   19. Received cash for merchandise returned to a vendor, $6.96. R27.
   20. Issued a check to pay for merchandise received on March 17, $151.25. Ck190.
   21. Issued a check to pay for merchandise received on March 19, $505.48. Ck191.
   21. Issued a check to pay for miscellaneous expenses, $17.79. Ck192.
   22. Purchased merchandise for cash, $350.90. Ck193.
   22. Purchased supplies for cash, $145.00. Ck194.
   23. Purchased merchandise for cash, $433.75. Ck195.
   23. Issued a check to pay the electric bill, $114.95. Ck196.
   24. Issued a check to pay the gas bill, $29.00. Ck197.
   24. Total weekly cash sales: sales, $1,406.90; sales tax, $70.35; total cash received, $1,477.25. T24.
   27. Issued a check to pay for merchandise received on March 23, $755.00. Ck198.
   28. Issued a check for supplies bought today, $42.96. Ck199.
   29. Issued a check to pay the water bill, $42.50. Ck200.
   29. Purchased merchandise for cash, $453.75. Ck201.
   30. Issued a check for sales tax liability, $320.20. Ck202.
   30. Issued a check for withdrawal of cash by owner, $1,200.00. Ck203.
   30. Issued a check to replenish petty cash fund: supplies, $15.50; miscellaneous, $11.95; total, $27.45. Ck204.
   31. Total weekly cash sales: sales, $1,881.66; sales tax, $94.08, total cash received, $1,975.74. T31.

Instructions: □ **2.** Pencil foot the daily journal, prove cash, and prove the daily journal. The check stub for Ck204 shows a remaining balance of $3,890.13.

☐ **3.** Total and rule the daily journal as shown on page 449. Analyze the Other Receipts and the Other Payments columns. Write the results of the analysis at the top of a new page of the daily journal as shown on page 449.

☐ **4.** Using the data from the daily journal and the data below, prepare an income statement similar to the one shown on page 455.

Summary Report
Prepared on March 31, 19––

Value of equipment (plant assets file)	$1,602.13 (S-1)
Unpaid invoices, total	221.79 (S-2)
Merchandise inventory, end of last month	2,686.42 (S-3)
Merchandise inventory, end of this month	2,823.31 (S-4)
Capital, end of last month	6,888.50 (S-5)

☐ **5.** Using the data from the daily journal and the data given in Instruction 4 above, prepare a balance sheet similar to the one shown on page 456. Leather Corner has a petty cash fund of $100.00.

The Trade Winds Marine business simulation provides a review of the accounting principles that apply to a manufacturing corporation. The set illustrates the use of job-order-cost records of a small manufacturer. The business maintains perpetual inventories of direct materials, work in process, and finished goods. The symbolic flowchart of the accounting cycle is shown on page 465. A pictorial flowchart is shown on pages 466 and 467.

(The narrative is provided in the set available from the publisher.)

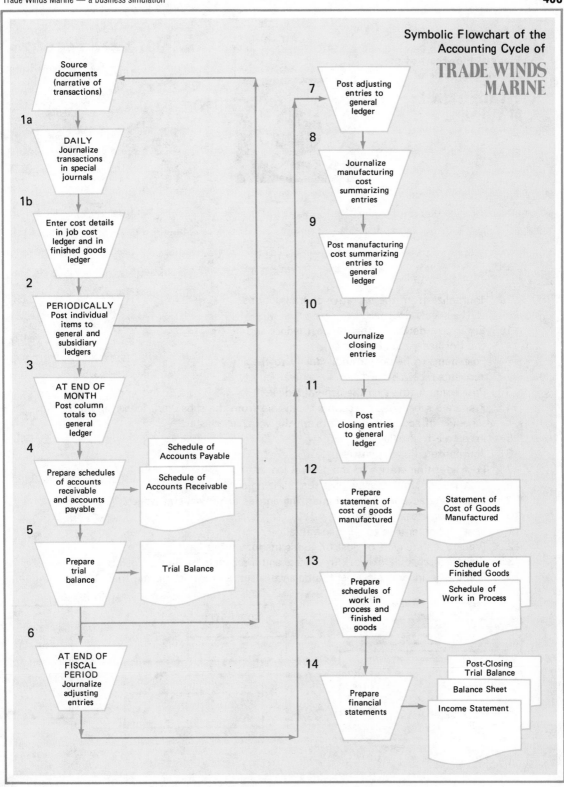

Symbolic Flowchart of the
Accounting Cycle of

TRADE WINDS MARINE

**Pictorial Flowchart of the
Accounting Cycle of**

TRADE WINDS
MARINE

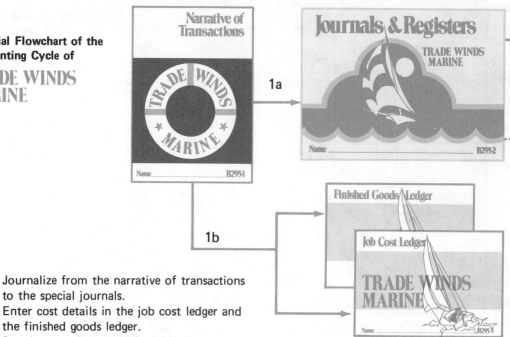

1a Journalize from the narrative of transactions
to the special journals.
1b Enter cost details in the job cost ledger and
the finished goods ledger.
2 Post items to be posted individually to the
accounts receivable ledger and general ledger.
3 Post column totals to the general ledger.
4 Prepare a schedule of accounts receivable from the subsidiary ledger and a
schedule of accounts payable from the voucher register.
5 Prepare a trial balance.
6 Journalize adjusting entries.
7 Post adjusting entries to the general ledger.
8 Journalize manufacturing cost summarizing entries.
9 Post manufacturing cost summarizing entries to the general ledger.
10 Journalize closing entries.
11 Post closing entries to the general ledger.
12 Prepare a statement of cost of goods manufactured.
13 Prepare a schedule of work in process and a schedule of finished goods.
14 Prepare an income statement, a balance sheet, and a post-closing trial balance.

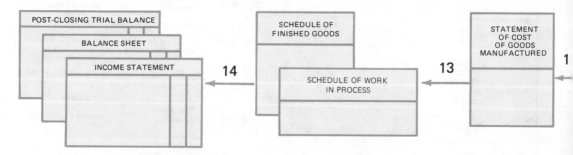

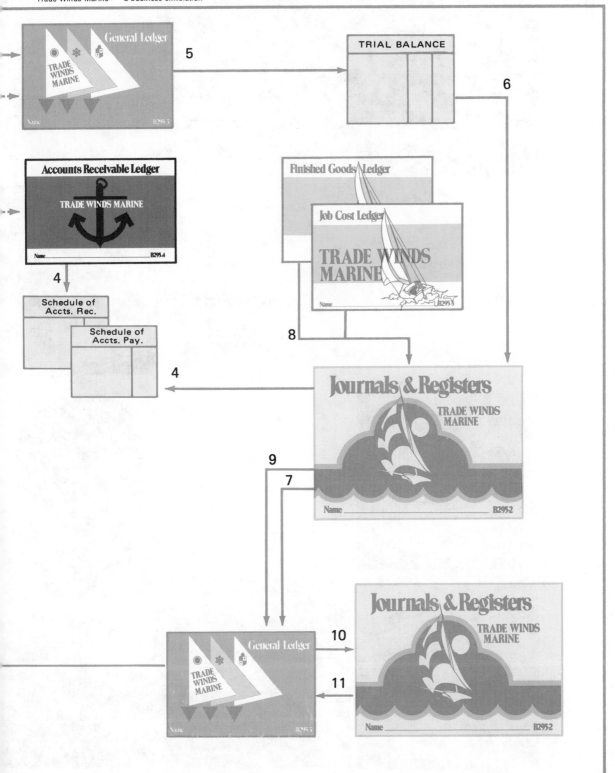

Newberg
Fence
Company

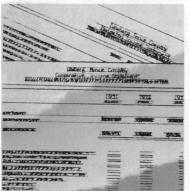

ASSISTANT ACCOUNTANTS

ACCOUNTING INFORMATION IS IMPORTANT FOR PLANNING AND CONTROLLING BUSINESS OPERATIONS. Accounting data are analyzed and interpreted to provide much of the information successful businesses use to plan and control their business operations. Part 10 describes some of the accounting information used by these businesses. Some concepts presented are: a budget is a financial plan that shows the expected course of action for a business; analyses of sales and cost data help managers plan the most profitable amount and type of products to manufacture and/or sell; analyses of financial statements help managers identify financial strengths and weaknesses of a business so improvements can be made; a statement of changes in financial position shows how a business provided funds, how it used funds, and the resulting increase or decrease in funds.

In Part 10 of this textbook, Chapters 25 and 26 describe how the assistant accountant at the *Newberg Fence Company* coordinates the preparation of the budget and analyzes cost data used in management decisions. Chapters 27 and 28 describe the analyses of financial statements and the preparation of the statement of changes in financial position at *Barcelona Corporation*.

NEWBERG FENCE COMPANY
CHART OF ACCOUNTS

Balance Sheet Accounts

(1000) ASSETS	Account Number
11 *Current Assets*	
Cash	1101
Petty Cash	1102
Notes Receivable	1103
Interest Receivable	1104
Accounts Receivable	1105
Allowance for Uncollectible Accounts	1105.1
Merchandise Inventory	1106
Supplies — Sales	1107
Supplies — Office	1108
Prepaid Insurance	1109
12 *Plant Assets*	
Delivery Equipment	1201
Accumulated Depreciation — Delivery Equipment	1201.1
Warehouse Equipment	1202
Accumulated Depreciation — Warehouse Equipment	1202.1
Office Equipment	1203
Accumulated Depreciation — Office Equipment	1203.1

(2000) LIABILITIES

21 *Current Liabilities*	
Notes Payable	2101
Interest Payable	2102
Accounts Payable	2103
Employees Income Tax Payable — Federal	2104
Employees Income Tax Payable — State	2105
FICA Tax Payable	2106
Unemployment Tax Payable — Federal	2107
Unemployment Tax Payable — State	2108
Income Tax Payable — Federal	2109
Income Tax Payable — State	2110

22 *Long-Term Liability*	
Mortgage Payable	2201

(3000) CAPITAL

Capital Stock	3010
Retained Earnings	3020
Income Summary	3030

Income Statement Accounts

(4000) OPERATING REVENUE	Account Number
Sales	4101
Sales Returns and Allowances	4101.1
Sales Discount	4101.2

(5000) COST OF MERCHANDISE	
Purchases	5101
Purchases Returns and Allowances	5101.1
Purchases Discount	5101.2

(6000) OPERATING EXPENSES

61 *Selling Expenses*	
Advertising Expense	6101
Delivery Expense	6102
Depreciation Expense — Delivery Equipment	6103
Depreciation Expense — Warehouse Equipment	6104
Miscellaneous Expense — Sales	6105
Salary Expense — Commissions	6106
Salary Expense — Regular	6107
Supplies Expense — Sales	6108

62 *Administrative Expenses*	
Bad Debts Expense	6201
Depreciation Expense — Office Equipment	6202
Insurance Expense	6203
Miscellaneous Expense — Administrative	6204
Payroll Taxes Expense	6205
Rent Expense	6206
Salary Expense — Administrative	6207
Supplies Expense — Office	6208
Utilities Expense	6209

(7000) OTHER REVENUE	
Gain on Plant Assets	7101
Interest Income	7102

(8000) OTHER EXPENSES	
Interest Expense	8101
Loss on Plant Assets	8102

(9000) TAX	
Income Tax — Federal	9101
Income Tax — State	9102

The chart of accounts for Newberg Fence Company is illustrated above for ready reference in your study of Part 10 of this textbook.

25

Budgetary Planning and Control

Successful businesses determine their goals, then plan ways to accomplish those goals. One of the major goals of most businesses is to earn a reasonable amount of profit. Therefore, financial planning should be an important part of a company's overall plan. Planning the financial operations of a business is called budgeting. A written financial plan of a business for a specific period of time, expressed in dollars, is called a budget.

DEFINING THE ROLE OF A BUDGET

Budgets are estimates of what will happen in the future. Predicting the future precisely is impossible. However, a carefully prepared budget reflects the best predictions possible by those persons who prepare the plan. A completed budget, then, shows the expected course of action for the business.

A budget can serve three important roles for management: (a) a planning guide, (b) an operational control guide, and (c) a departmental coordination guide.

Planning guide

Preparing a budget requires managers to anticipate what will probably happen in the future. This advance look at the future helps the manager plan for actions that should accomplish desired goals. In effect, the budgeting process forces the manager to decide what goals to work toward.

Operational control guide

A thoughtfully prepared budget includes what the business expects to accomplish — the kind as well as the amount of activities expected. By comparing the amount actually produced with the amount expected to be produced, a manager can judge how well the business is doing.

By comparing actual expenses with expected or budgeted expenses, a business also can identify where action is needed to control expenses. The comparison of actual with budgeted amounts identifies items for which costs are higher than expected.

Departmental coordination guide

Profitable growth of a business requires that those personnel who make management decisions be aware of the company's plans for the future. The budget reflects these plans. Each phase of a business operation must be coordinated with all other related phases. For example, if estimated sales are to be achieved, the purchasing department must know when and how much merchandise to purchase. Therefore, all management personnel must help plan and use a budget as a guide to control and to coordinate revenue and expenses.

DESIGNING A BUDGET

A budget is a look into the future, a plan of expected financial activities. Therefore, budget preparation begins with company goals. Are the company goals to increase sales 10 percent, to reduce cost of goods sold 2 percent, to increase net income 3 percent? All of these goals affect budget preparation because the budget is a financial plan for the business.

Selecting the time period

The length of time covered by a budget is called the budget period. Usually this period is one year. Some companies also prepare a long-range budget of five years or more for special projects and plant and equipment purchases. However, the annual budget is the one that is used to compare current performance with budget plans.

An annual budget normally is prepared for a company's fiscal year. The annual budget commonly is divided into quarterly and monthly budgets. Such budget subdivisions provide many opportunities to evaluate how actual operations are comparing with budgeted operations.

A budget must be prepared in sufficient time to be communicated to the appropriate managers prior to the beginning of a budget period. If a company is large and complex, gathering budget data will begin long before the beginning of the new budget year. Gathering the data, making analyses, making decisions, preparing the budget, and approving and communicating the budget take time.

Determining the type of budget to prepare

Businesses frequently prepare two types of annual budgets: (a) a budgeted income statement and (b) a cash budget.

Budgeted income statement. A budgeted income statement is an estimate of a business's expected revenue, expenses, and net income for a fiscal period. The budgeted income statement is similar to a regular income statement and is sometimes known as an operating budget or a revenue and expense budget.

Cash budget. A cash budget is an estimate of a business's expected cash receipts and payments for a fiscal period. For example, a cash budget shows an expected cash shortage as of May 31. Therefore, the company makes arrangements to borrow enough cash to cover the expected shortage. If the cash budget shows an expected surplus of cash on June 30, the company plans how to invest the extra cash.

Identifying the sources of data for preparing a budget

A budget should be based on data from company records of past operations, current general economic information, consultation with staff members, and good judgment. A budget cannot be exact since only expected revenue and expenses are reflected. However, a company's best estimate of what will occur in future operations should be shown. Vague guessing has no place in the preparation of a realistic budget.

Company records. Much of the information from which a budget is prepared exists in a company's accounting and sales records. Actual accounting data about a company's operations during previous years are used to determine trends in sales, purchases, and operating expenses. Information such as price changes, sales promotion plans, and market research studies also is important in predicting activity during the budget period.

General economic information. General economic information also may influence budget decisions. A general slowdown or speedup in the national economy may affect budget decisions. A labor strike may affect some related industry and thus affect company operations. New product development, changes in consumer buying habits, availability of merchandise, international trade, and general business conditions all must be considered when preparing a budget.

Consultation with company staff and managers. Sales personnel may be asked to estimate the amount of sales they expect. Executives and department heads should be asked what they anticipate as essential budget items for the new budget period. Because of their knowledge of the business's operations, the executives can provide information that may not otherwise be available.

Good judgment. In the final analysis, the good judgment of the individuals preparing the budget is essential to a realistic budget. Even after evaluating all available data, there is seldom an obvious answer to many of the budget questions. Since some information will be in conflict with other information, budget decisions are based finally on good judgment.

Using past records in obtaining data for budgeting

Comparing budgets and actual operating results for previous years provides much useful information in preparing a budget for a new budget period.

Comparison of previous year's budget with actual amounts. A comparison of budgeted and actual revenue and expense amounts for the year immediately preceding the new budget period is important. Such a comparison may reveal differences between the planned operations and the actual operations of the business that will require adjustment in the new budget. A comparison of Newberg Fence Company's budgeted income statement with the actual income statement for 1978 is shown on page 475.

> Sometimes parentheses are used to indicate an alternate item as in Other Revenue (Expenses) and Net Addition (Deduction). Actual and budgeted amounts for an alternate item are placed in parentheses as shown in the illustration on page 475.

The first amount column of the comparison shows the amounts budgeted for 1978. The second amount column shows the actual revenue, costs, and expenses for 1978. The third amount column shows how much the actual amount is an increase or a decrease from the budgeted amount. All amounts are rounded to the nearest ten dollars for ease in making comparisons. The fourth column shows the percent the actual amount increased or decreased from the budgeted amount.

Each variation (increase or decrease) in the budgeted amounts is studied carefully. An explanation for the unfavorable variation of any item is required from those persons responsible. In planning the 1979 budget, the actual amounts and the variations in the budgeted amounts for 1978 and the amounts available for 1979 are considered.

Newberg Fence Company
Comparison of Budgeted Income Statement
With Actual Income Statement
For Year Ended December 31, 1978

	Budget 1978	Actual 1978	Increase/ Decrease From Budget	% of Increase/ Decrease From Budget
Operating Revenue:				
Sales	$1,080,000.00	$1,089,000.00	+ 9,000.00	+ 0.8%
Cost of Merchandise Sold . . .	462,000.00	484,000.00	+ 22,000.00	+ 4.8%
Gross Profit on Operations . . .	$ 618,000.00	$ 605,000.00	- 13,000.00	- 2.1%
Operating Expenses:				
Selling Expenses:				
Advertising Expense	$ 9,000.00	$ 8,900.00	- 100.00	- 1.1%
Delivery Expense	17,000.00	17,500.00	+ 500.00	+ 2.9%
Depr. Exp.--Delivery Equip..	13,000.00	13,000.00		
Depr. Exp.--Warehouse Equip.	8,500.00	9,000.00	+ 500.00	+ 5.9%
Misc. Expense--Sales	6,000.00	6,000.00		
Salary Expense--Commissions.	86,400.00	87,120.00	+ 720.00	+ 0.8%
Salary Expense--Regular . .	200,000.00	201,800.00	+ 1,800.00	+ 0.9%
Supplies Expense--Sales . .	19,400.00	19,800.00	+ 400.00	+ 2.1%
Total Selling Expenses . . .	$ 359,300.00	$ 363,120.00	+ 3,820.00	+ 1.1%
Administrative Expenses:				
Bad Debts Expense	$ 5,400.00	$ 5,450.00	+ 50.00	+ 0.9%
Depr. Expense--Office Equip.	4,300.00	4,300.00		
Insurance Expense	1,100.00	1,200.00	+ 100.00	+ 9.1%
Misc. Expense--Admin. . . .	2,550.00	2,500.00	- 50.00	- 2.0%
Payroll Taxes Expense . . .	32,880.00	33,130.00	+ 250.00	+ 0.8%
Rent Expense	18,000.00	18,000.00		
Salary Expense--Admin. . . .	71,000.00	71,200.00	+ 200.00	+ 0.3%
Supplies Expense--Office . .	2,200.00	2,200.00		
Utilities Expense	4,600.00	4,700.00	+ 100.00	+ 2.2%
Total Admin. Expenses . . .	$ 142,030.00	$ 142,680.00	+ 650.00	+ 0.5%
Total Operating Expenses	$ 501,330.00	$ 505,800.00	+ 4,470.00	+ 0.9%
Income From Operations	$ 116,670.00	$ 99,200.00	- 17,470.00	- 15.0%
Other Revenue (Expenses):				
Interest Expense	$ (1,200.00)	$ (1,400.00)	+ 200.00	+ 16.7%
Net Addition (Deduction)	$ (1,200.00)	$ (1,400.00)	+ 200.00	+ 16.7%
Net Income Before Taxes	$ 115,470.00	$ 97,800.00	- 17,670.00	- 15.3%
Income Taxes	41,930.00	33,440.00	- 8,490.00	- 20.2%
Net Income After Taxes	$ 73,540.00	$ 64,360.00	- 9,180.00	- 12.5%
Units (m^2) of Fencing Sold . . .	120,000	121,000	+ 1,000	+ 0.8%

Comparison of budgeted income statement
with actual income statement

Comparison of several previous years' income statements. An income
statement containing revenue, cost, and expense data for several years is
called a comparative income statement. Such a statement is prepared to
show trends that may be taking place in certain revenue or expense

items. The comparative income statement of Newberg Fence Company is shown below.

Newberg Fence Company
Comparative Income Statement
For Years Ended December 31, 1976, 1977, and 1978

	1976 Actual	1977 Actual	1978 Actual	1979 Budget
Operating Revenue:				
Sales	$906,100	$977,500	$1,089,000	$1,193,800
Cost of Merchandise Sold	381,230	414,000	484,000	531,460
Gross Profit on Operations	$524,870	$563,500	$ 605,000	$ 662,340
Operating Expenses:				
Selling Expenses:				
Advertising Expense	$ 8,000	$ 8,100	$ 8,900	$ 9,000
Delivery Expense	15,700	16,500	17,500	18,500
Depreciation Expense--Delivery Equip..	12,000	12,500	13,000	13,500
Depreciation Expense--Warehouse Equip..	8,000	8,500	9,000	9,000
Miscellaneous Expense--Sales	5,000	5,500	6,000	6,500
Salary Expense--Commissions	72,490	78,200	87,120	95,500
Salary Expense--Regular	159,500	175,500	201,800	222,000
Supplies Expense--Sales	16,700	18,000	19,800	21,400
Total Selling Expenses	$297,390	$322,800	$ 363,120	$ 395,400
Administrative Expenses:				
Bad Debts Expense	$ 4,530	$ 4,890	$ 5,450	$ 5,970
Depreciation Expense--Office Equipment.	3,600	4,300	4,300	4,300
Insurance Expense	1,000	1,000	1,200	1,500
Miscellaneous Expense--Administrative .	2,150	2,350	2,500	2,640
Payroll Taxes Expense	26,850	29,290	33,130	36,160
Rent Expense	15,000	15,000	18,000	18,000
Salary Expense--Administrative	59,900	64,700	71,200	75,500
Supplies Expense--Office	2,000	2,100	2,200	2,300
Utilities Expense	4,200	4,400	4,700	5,400
Total Administrative Expenses	$119,230	$128,030	$ 142,680	$ 151,770
Total Operating Expenses	$416,620	$450,830	$ 505,800	$ 547,170
Income from Operations	$108,250	$112,670	$ 99,200	$ 115,170
Other Revenue (Expenses):				
Interest Expense	$(1,000)	$(1,200)	$ (1,400)	$ (800)
Net Addition (Deduction)	$(1,000)	$(1,200)	$ (1,400)	$ (800)
Net Income Before Taxes	$107,250	$111,470	$ 97,800	$ 114,370
Income Taxes	37,980	40,010	33,440	41,400
Net Income After Taxes	$ 69,270	$ 71,460	$ 64,360	$ 72,970
Net Income % of Sales	7.6%	7.3%	5.9%	6.1%
% of Increase (Decrease) in Net Income . .		3.2%	(9.9)%	13.4%
Units (m²) of Fencing Sold	110,500	115,000	121,000	127,000
% Increase in Units Sold		4.1%	5.2%	5.0%

Comparative income statement

Newberg's comparative income statement shows that net sales have increased from $906,100.00 in 1976 to $1,089,000.00 in 1978, a 20.2% increase over two years. However, net income after taxes has decreased from $69,270.00 in 1976 to $64,360.00 in 1978. This change is a 7.1% decrease over two years.

PLANNING A BUDGETED INCOME STATEMENT

After analyzing records of previous years and estimates of future trends, a business may prepare estimates of revenue, costs, and expenses for the year immediately ahead. Newberg Fence Company prepares separate schedules for the major parts of the budgeted income statement. Separate schedules are prepared for sales, purchases, selling expenses, administrative expenses, and other revenue and expenses. To permit more frequent comparisons with budgeted amounts, schedules for the budget are separated into quarterly estimates.

At Newberg Fence Company, Diane Harris, assistant accountant, is responsible for coordinating the budget preparation. The sales manager is responsible for the sales, purchases, and selling expenses budget schedules. The administrative manager is responsible for the administrative expenses budget and the other revenue and expenses budget. However, the assistant accountant helps both managers assemble the necessary information and prepares the budget schedules for both managers. Ms. Harris then prepares the budgeted income statement from the budget schedules and sends the completed budget with attached schedules to the budget committee. This budget is reviewed and approved by the budget committee consisting of the president, the sales manager, the administrative manager, and the controller.

Sales budget schedule

The sales budget schedule shows the estimated sales for a budget period. This budget schedule is usually the first one prepared because the other schedules are affected by the expected revenue from sales. Before a business can estimate the merchandise to purchase, a reasonably accurate estimate is made of the expected sales. The expected sales generally determine the amount that may be spent for salaries, advertising, and other selling and administrative expenses.

Newberg Fence Company's sales manager, with the assistance of sales representatives and the assistant accountant, prepares a sales budget schedule. In preparing a sales budget schedule, sales during the previous years and trends in sales for a period of several years are considered. Also considered are general economic conditions, consumer buying trends, competition, new products on the market, and activities such as special sales planned.

A review of previous years' income statements, page 476, was the basis for the sales staff's estimate that there would be about a 5 percent increase in fencing sales each year. Economic and competitive conditions seem to support a similar sales trend. Sales personnel also estimate a 5 percent increase for 1979 in units of fencing sales expected. After reviewing competitors' selling prices and expected costs of merchandise, the sales manager increases the planned sales price for 1979 from $9.00 to $9.40. When all factors that may affect sales have been considered, the sales budget schedule is prepared by the assistant accountant. The units are rounded to the nearest hundreds. The 1979 sales budget schedule for Newberg Fence Company is shown below.

	Newberg Fence Company Sales Budget Schedule For Year Ended December 31, 1979			Schedule 1
	1978 Units (m^2) @9.00	Actual Amount	1979 Units (m^2) @9.40	Estimated Amount
1st Quarter	22,990	$ 206,910.00	24,100	$ 226,540.00
2d Quarter	37,510	337,590.00	39,400	370,360.00
3d Quarter	36,300	326,700.00	38,100	358,140.00
4th Quarter	24,200	217,800.00	25,400	238,760.00
	121,000	$1,089,000.00	127,000	$1,193,800.00

Sales budget schedule

Once the budget is approved, the sales manager knows the company's goal is to sell the number of units shown for 1979. For example, 24,100 units of fencing must be sold at $9.40 per unit during the first quarter. Sales activities will be planned to achieve this goal.

Purchases budget schedule

A purchases budget schedule shows the anticipated amount of purchases that will be required during a budget period. Since the amount of purchases depends on estimated sales, the purchases budget schedule is prepared after the sales budget schedule.

In planning a purchases budget schedule, the following factors are considered:

1. The estimate of net sales as shown in the sales budget schedule.
2. The quantity of merchandise on hand at the beginning of the budget period.
3. The quantity of merchandise needed to fill expected sales without having too much inventory on hand at any one time.
4. The price trends of merchandise to be purchased.

The cost of purchases is estimated as follows:

	Estimated ending inventory in units
Plus	Estimated sales in units
Equals	Total number of units needed
Minus	Beginning inventory in units
Equals	Estimated purchases in units
Times	Estimated unit cost
Equals	Estimated cost of purchases

Enough total units are needed to meet sales demands while new units are being purchased. Estimated sales in units are found in the sales budget schedule (rounded to the nearest hundreds). Beginning inventory is the same amount as the ending inventory for the previous period. Estimated units of purchases are multiplied by the estimated cost per unit to figure the estimated cost of purchases.

At Newberg Fence Company, the sales manager estimates that materials will cost about $4.20 per square meter in 1979. The sales manager also estimates that the desired number of units for ending inventory should be about 40 percent of the number of units estimated to be sold in the next quarter. The sales manager and the assistant accountant prepare the 1979 purchases budget schedule shown below.

Newberg Fence Company   Schedule 2
Purchases Budget Schedule
For Year Ended December 31, 1979

Period	Ending Inventory	+ Sales	= Total Needed	− Beginning Inventory	= Purchases	× Unit Cost	= Purchases
1st Quarter	15,800	24,100	39,900	9,700	30,200	$4.20	$126,840.00
2d Quarter	15,300	39,400	54,700	15,800	38,900	4.20	163,380.00
3d Quarter	10,200	38,100	48,300	15,300	33,000	4.20	138,600.00
4th Quarter	10,200	25,400	35,600	10,200	25,400	4.20	106,680.00
Year	10,200	127,000	137,200	9,700	127,500	4.20	535,500.00

Purchases budget schedule

A purchases budget schedule follows the same pattern as a sales budget schedule. However, purchases are made in advance of sales to allow for delivery of the merchandise. For example, merchandise that is to be sold in April must be ordered in an earlier month. The exact date depends on the time required for delivery.

Selling expense budget schedule

A selling expense budget schedule shows the expected expenditures for a budget period for expenses related directly to the selling operation. The sales manager estimates the information for the selling expense budget schedule. However, other sales personnel may provide certain specific information. For example, the advertising manager may supply much of the data for advertising expense. After the selling expense data have been estimated, the assistant accountant assembles the data and prepares the selling expense budget schedule.

Some expenses in a selling expense budget are relatively stable and require little budget planning. For example, depreciation expense on warehouse equipment is reasonably stable from year to year. On the other hand, several selling expenses increase and decrease somewhat in relation to sales increases and decreases. Newberg Fence Company has a seasonal business with higher sales during the second and third quarters. The company hires more people and spends more for advertising and sales supplies during the heavy sales season. Also the delivery equipment is used more during the spring and summer, so the trucks are depreciated by the miles driven. All of these factors are considered in making a selling expense budget schedule. The 1979 selling expense budget schedule for Newberg Fence Company is shown below.

Newberg Fence Company   Schedule 3
Selling Expense Budget Schedule
For Year Ended December 31, 1979

	1978 Actual	1979 Budget	1979 - By Quarters			
			1st	2d	3d	4th
Advertising Exp.	$ 8,900.00	$ 9,000.00	$ 2,000.00	$ 3,000.00	$ 3,000.00	$ 1,000.00
Delivery Expense	17,500.00	18,500.00	3,510.00	5,740.00	5,550.00	3,700.00
Depr. Expense-- Delivery Equip.	13,000.00	13,500.00	2,560.00	4,190.00	4,050.00	2,700.00
Depr. Expense-- Warehouse Equip.	9,000.00	9,000.00	2,250.00	2,250.00	2,250.00	2,250.00
Misc. Exp.--Sales	6,000.00	6,500.00	1,230.00	2,010.00	1,960.00	1,300.00
Salary Exp.--Comm.	87,120.00	95,500.00	18,120.00	29,630.00	28,650.00	19,100.00
Salary Exp.--Reg.	201,800.00	222,000.00	46,000.00	65,500.00	63,500.00	47,000.00
Supp. Exp.--Sales	19,800.00	21,400.00	4,050.00	6,630.00	6,420.00	4,300.00
Total Selling Exp.	$363,120.00	$395,400.00	$79,720.00	$118,950.00	$115,380.00	$81,350.00

Selling expense budget schedule

The sales manager at Newberg Fence Company uses a number of approaches to estimate the various 1979 selling expenses. For example, the advertising expense estimate is based on planned advertising for the year. The sales manager plans about the same amount of advertising in 1979 as was used in 1978. However, a check with the newspaper indicates costs for advertising are expected to increase about 1 percent. Depreciation expenses are determined by reviewing the depreciation schedules for delivery equipment and warehouse equipment.

Several selling expenses increase each year about the same percent over the previous year. Based upon previous years' increases, the sales manager estimates the following amounts: delivery expense up 5.7% to $18,500.00; miscellaneous expense up 8.3% to $6,500.00; regular salary expense up 10% to $222,000.00; and supplies expense up 8.1% to $21,400.00. Each of the estimates was reviewed carefully after considering expected increases in costs in 1979. For example, miscellaneous expense has been increasing each year but the increase is smaller each year. From 1976 to 1977, the increase was 10%. From 1977 to 1978, the increase was 9.1%. Therefore, the sales manager anticipates another reduction in the rate of change. Regular salaries have been increasing about 10% for several years. Last year the increase was 15% because of an unusually large increase in wage rates. However, the sales manager expects the wage rate increase to be 10% again in 1979. Supplies expense has increased about 8% until last year when extra costs caused a 10%

increase. However, the increase is expected to be 8% again in 1979. Miscellaneous expense has usually been a consistent 0.55% of sales. Salary commissions are 8% of sales. Therefore, this rate is used for 1979.

Administrative expense budget schedule

An administrative expense budget schedule shows the expected expenses for the budget period for all operating expenses not directly related to the selling operation. The administrative manager is responsible for estimating most of the information that goes into this budget. Data for this schedule come from a study of past records, an evaluation of company plans, the sales budget schedule, and discussions with other managers. After the administrative expenses have been estimated, the assistant accountant assembles the data and prepares the administrative expense budget schedule.

Several administrative expenses are fixed so that the amounts are known or can be estimated at the beginning of a year. For example, Newberg Fence Company leases the building in which it is located. The company pays annual rent of $18,000.00. Since the amount is known, rent expense can be budgeted accurately at $4,500.00 each quarter and $18,000.00 a year. A few administrative expenses need to be budgeted as a percent of another amount. For example, the amount of bad debts expense probably will be related to the amount of sales. Payroll taxes will be related to the amount of salary expenses. Utilities will be determined by the amount of power, heat, and other utilities used.

The administrative manager at Newberg Fence Company uses a number of approaches to estimate expenses that have proven in the past to be reasonably accurate. The 1979 administrative expenses at Newberg are estimated in the following manner. Bad debts expenses are estimated to be 0.5% of sales. Depreciation expense amounts are taken from the depreciation schedule. Insurance premiums are paid in advance. Therefore, the amount of quarterly expense is known. Miscellaneous expenses are estimated to be 3.5% of administrative salaries. Payroll taxes are 9.2% of all salaries, selling and administrative. The amount of rent expense is stated on the lease contract. The administrative manager does not expect to add any personnel to the administration department but a 6% salary increase is planned. Therefore, salary expense is estimated to increase approximately 6%. Supplies expense has been increasing 4.5 to 5% annually for several years. A 4.5% increase is estimated for 1979. A 15% increase in utilities expense is estimated. This increase is based upon a utility company's announced rate increase of 10%, plus a 5% estimated increase in usage caused by a 5% increase in fencing units sold.

After the administrative manager at Newberg Fence Company has completed the expense estimates, the assistant accountant prepares the administrative expense budget schedule. The 1979 administrative expense budget schedule for Newberg Fence Company is shown below.

	1978 Actual	1979 Budget	1979 - By Quarters			
			1st	2d	3d	4th
Bad Debts Expense	$ 5,450.00	$ 5,970.00	$ 1,130.00	$ 1,850.00	$ 1,790.00	$ 1,200.00
Depr. Exp.--Off. Equip.	4,300.00	4,300.00	1,075.00	1,075.00	1,075.00	1,075.00
Insurance Expense	1,200.00	1,500.00	375.00	375.00	375.00	375.00
Misc. Expense--Admin.	2,500.00	2,640.00	500.00	820.00	790.00	530.00
Payroll Taxes Expense	33,130.00	36,160.00	7,220.00	10,900.00	10,560.00	7,480.00
Rent Expense	18,000.00	18,000.00	4,500.00	4,500.00	4,500.00	4,500.00
Salary Expense--Admin.	71,200.00	75,500.00	14,300.00	23,400.00	22,600.00	15,200.00
Supplies Exp.--Office	2,200.00	2,300.00	450.00	700.00	700.00	450.00
Utilities Expense	4,700.00	5,400.00	1,250.00	1,450.00	1,450.00	1,250.00
Total Admin. Expenses	$142,680.00	$151,770.00	$30,800.00	$45,070.00	$43,840.00	$32,060.00

Newberg Fence Company
Administrative Expense Budget Schedule
For Year Ended December 31, 1979   Schedule 4

Administrative expense budget schedule

Other revenue and expense budget schedule

An other revenue and expense budget schedule shows the expected revenue and expenses during the budget period from activities other than normal operations. Typical items in this budget are interest income, interest expense, and gains or losses on the sale of plant assets. The 1979 other revenue and expense budget schedule for Newberg Fence Company is shown below.

Newberg Fence Company
Other Revenue and Expense Budget Schedule
For Year Ended December 31, 1979   Schedule 5

	1978 Actual	1979 Budget	1979 - By Quarters			
			1st	2d	3d	4th
Other Revenue (Expenses):						
Interest Expense	($1,400.00)	($800.00)		($400.00)	($400.00)	
Net Other Revenue (Expenses)	($1,400.00)	($800.00)		($400.00)	($400.00)	

Other revenue and expense budget schedule

The administrative manager at Newberg Fence Company is responsible for estimating most of the information in the other revenue and expense budget schedule. Interest expense, the only item in the 1979 budget, is estimated on a short-term $20,000.00 loan that will be needed during the second and third quarters.

Budgeted income statement

A budgeted income statement shows the estimated sales, costs, expenses, and net income of a company. The assistant accountant prepares the budgeted income statement for Newberg Fence Company from the data in the sales, purchases, selling expense, administrative expense, and other revenue and expense budget schedules. Since the budget schedules contain detail items, Newberg Fence Company prepares a shortened budgeted income statement and then attaches the budget schedules.

The 1979 budgeted income statement for Newberg Fence Company is shown below.

Budgeted income statement

Newberg Fence Company
Budgeted Income Statement
For Year Ended December 31, 1979

	Total For Year	1979--By Quarters			
		1st	2d	3d	4th
Operating Revenue:					
Sales (Schedule 1)	$1,193,800	$226,540	$370,360	$358,140	$238,760
Cost of Merchandise Sold:					
Beginning Inventory (Schedule 2)	*$ 38,800	*$ 38,800	$ 66,360	$ 64,260	$ 42,840
Purchases (Schedule 2)	535,500	126,840	163,380	138,600	106,680
Total Merchandise Available . .	$ 574,300	$165,640	$229,740	$202,860	$149,520
Less Ending Inventory (Sched. 2)	42,840	66,360	64,260	42,840	42,840
Cost of Merchandise Sold	$ 531,460	$ 99,280	$165,480	$160,020	$106,680
Gross Profit on Operations	$ 662,340	$127,260	$204,880	$198,120	$132,080
Operating Expenses:					
Selling Expenses (Schedule 3) .	$ 395,400	$ 79,720	$118,950	$115,380	$ 81,350
Admin. Expenses (Schedule 4) . .	151,770	30,800	45,070	43,840	32,060
Total Operating Expenses	$ 547,170	$110,520	$164,020	$159,220	$113,410
Income from Operations	$ 115,170	$ 16,740	$ 40,860	$ 38,900	$ 18,670
Net Addition (Deduction)(Sched. 5)	$ (800)		$ (400)	$ (400)	
Net Income Before Taxes	$ 114,370	$ 16,740	$ 40,460	$ 38,500	$ 18,670
Income Taxes	41,400	** 10,350	** 10,350	** 10,350	** 10,350
Net Income After Taxes	$ 72,970	$ 6,390	$ 30,110	$ 28,150	$ 8,320

* Inventory January 1 cost $4.00 per unit
  All other inventories $4.20 per unit

** Quarterly estimate of income taxes

Comparison of budgeted income statement with actual income statement

At the end of each quarter, a business compares the income statement containing actual amounts with the budgeted income statement for that period. This comparison shows variations between actual and budgeted items. Steps can then be taken at once to correct any unfavorable situations. If significant conditions change, the budget for the remainder of the year can be revised.

At the end of each quarter, Newberg's assistant accountant prepares a statement comparing budgeted income with actual income. This statement is sent to the sales manager and the administrative manager. Significant differences between budgeted and actual amounts help the managers identify areas that need to be reviewed. By identifying large cost variations early, the managers may be able to make changes that will correct negative effects on net income. For the first quarter, 1979, the assistant accountant prepares the statement shown below.

Newberg Fence Company
Comparison of Budgeted Income Statement
With Actual Income Statement
For Quarter Ended March 31, 1979

	Budget 1979 1st Qtr.	Actual 1979 1st Qtr.	Increase/ Decrease From Budget	% of Increase/ Decrease From Budget
Sales (m²)	24,100	24,300	+ 200	+ 0.8%
Operating Revenue:				
Sales	$226,540.00	$228,420.00	+ 1,880.00	+ 0.8%
Cost of Merchandise Sold . . .	99,280.00	102,260.00	+ 2,980.00	+ 3.0%
Gross Profit on Operations . . .	$127,260.00	$126,160.00	- 1,100.00	- 0.9%
Operating Expenses:				
Selling Expenses:				
Advertising Expense	$ 2,000.00	$ 2,000.00		
Delivery Expense	3,510.00	3,540.00	+ 30.00	+ 0.9%
Depr. Exp.--Delivery Equip .	2,560.00	2,560.00		
Depr. Exp.--Warehouse Equip.	2,250.00	2,250.00		
Misc. Expense--Sales	1,230.00	1,220.00	- 10.00	- 0.8%
Salary Expense--Commissions.	18,120.00	18,274.00	+ 154.00	+ 0.8%
Salary Expense--Regular . .	46,000.00	46,000.00		
Supplies Expense--Sales . .	4,050.00	4,090.00	+ 40.00	+ 1.0%
Total Selling Expenses . . .	$ 79,720.00	$ 79,934.00	+ 214.00	+ 0.3%
Administrative Expenses:				
Bad Debts Expense	$ 1,130.00	$ 1,140.00	+ 10.00	+ 0.9%
Depr. Exp.--Office Equip. .	1,075.00	1,075.00		
Insurance Expense	375.00	375.00		
Misc. Expense--Admin. . . .	500.00	490.00	- 10.00	- 2.0%
Payroll Taxes Expense . . .	7,220.00	7,230.00	+ 10.00	+ 0.1%
Rent Expense	4,500.00	4,500.00		
Salary Expense--Admin. . . .	14,300.00	14,300.00		
Supplies Expense--Office . .	450.00	445.00	- 5.00	- 1.1%
Utilities Expense	1,250.00	1,310.00	+ 60.00	+ 4.8%
Total Admin. Expenses . . .	$ 30,800.00	$ 30,865.00	+ 65.00	+ 0.2%
Total Operating Expenses	$110,520.00	$110,799.00	+ 279.00	+ 0.3%
Net Income Before Taxes	$ 16,740.00	$ 15,361.00	- 1,379.00	- 8.2%
Income Taxes	10,350.00	10,350.00		
Net Income After Taxes	$ 6,390.00	$ 5,011.00	- 1,379.00	- 21.6%

Comparison of budgeted income statement
with actual income statement

Differences between budgeted and actual amounts appear to be insignificant except for two items, cost of merchandise sold and utilities expense. This statement alerts the sales manager that cost of merchandise is rising faster than sales. The company may need to increase the selling price of fencing or find a less expensive source of materials. Whatever the cause of the increased costs, the trend must be corrected to avoid further decreases in net income.

The administrative manager also needs to review the reason for the rapid rise in utility costs. If the cost of utility service has increased, the manager cannot change that. However, if power is being wasted, procedures may be changed to avoid the waste.

PLANNING THE CASH BUDGET

Good management requires the planning and controlling of cash so that cash will be available to meet obligations when due. Reliable cash management requires a knowledge of beginning cash balances, expected cash receipts during a period, and expected cash payments during that same budget period.

The cash budget for Newberg Fence Company is planned by the treasurer in consultation with the budget committee. The assistant accountant then figures the amounts and prepares the cash budget. Planning the cash budget requires a detailed analysis of expected receipts from cash sales, receipts from customers on account, and receipts from other sources. The cash budget also requires an analysis of the expected cash payments for ordinary expenses such as rent, payroll, and payments to creditors on account. In addition, consideration is given to other cash payments, such as buying plant assets or supplies. Since a cash budget reports estimated cash receipts and payments, Newberg Fence Company prepares two schedules, one for cash receipts and one for cash payments. Total amounts are then entered in the cash budget.

Cash receipts schedule

A cash receipts schedule shows expected cash receipts for a budget period. The following estimates are made in preparing a cash receipts schedule:

1. An estimate of cash sales for each month or quarter of the year.
2. An estimate of collections from customers on account for each month or quarter of the year. The amounts received from customers will not be the same as the amount of sales on account. Normally, cash is received for sales on account made during the previous one or two months. Also, there are likely to be some sales returns and allowances. Sometimes there will also be some uncollectible accounts.
3. An estimate of the cash to be received from other sources.

The 1979 cash receipts schedule for Newberg Fence Company is shown on page 486.

An analysis of sales for previous years shows the following pattern of total sales. In a quarter, about 10 percent of all sales are cash sales. About

Newberg Fence Company   Schedule A
Cash Receipts Schedule
For Year Ended December 31, 1979

| | Quarters | | | |
	1st	2d	3d	4th
From Sales:				
Cash Sales	$ 22,654.00	$ 37,036.00	$ 35,814.00	$ 23,876.00
Accts. Rec. Collection--				
This Qtr. Sales	90,616.00	148,144.00	143,256.00	95,504.00
Accts. Rec. Collection--				
Last Qtr. Sales	107,811.00	112,137.00	183,328.00	177,279.00
Total Receipts from Sales.	$221,081.00	$297,317.00	$362,398.00	$296,659.00
From Other Sources:				
Note Payable to Bank . . .		20,000.00		
Total Cash Receipts	$221,081.00	$317,317.00	$362,398.00	$296,659.00

Cash receipts schedule

40 percent are sales on account collected in the quarter. About 49.5 percent are collected in the following quarter. About 0.5 percent are sales on
account that prove to be uncollectible, or are sales returns and allowances. For example, an analysis of cash receipts from sales for the first
quarter, 1979, shows expected cash receipts of $221,081.00. This amount
is figured as follows:

10% × $226,540 (First quarter sales from budgeted income
  statement, page 483) = $ 22,654.00

40% × $226,540 (First quarter sales from budgeted income
  statement, page 483) = 90,616.00

49.5% × $217,800 (Fourth quarter sales from last year's in-
  come statement) = 107,811.00

Estimated total cash to be received in first quarter $221,081.00

Other potential sources of revenue should be determined. After pre-
liminary planning of estimated cash receipts and cash payments, the
treasurer determines that cash on hand will be reduced in the second
quarter to an unusually low level. This condition could prevent the company from making timely payments on accounts payable. Therefore, the
treasurer plans to borrow $20,000.00 on a short-term promissory note
during the second quarter.

Cash payments schedule

A cash payments schedule shows expected cash payments for a budget
period. To prepare a cash payments schedule, the assistant accountant
and the treasurer estimate the cash payments to be made in each month
or quarter. The following factors are considered in preparing the cash
payments schedule:

1. The estimated amount of cash to be paid out for each expense item
   each period. This requires an analysis of the selling expense, administrative expense, and other revenue and expense budgets.

2. The estimated amount of cash to be paid to creditors on account or on notes each period.
3. The estimated amount of cash to be paid for buying equipment and other assets.
4. The estimated amount of cash to be paid for dividends.

The 1979 cash payments schedule for Newberg Fence Company is shown below.

Newberg Fence Company
Cash Payments Schedule
For Year Ended December 31, 1979

Schedule B

	Quarter			
	1st	2d	3d	4th
For Merchandise:				
Cash Purchases.	$ 12,684	$ 16,338	$ 13,860	$ 10,668
Payment on A/P--This Quarter Purchases . . .	76,104	98,028	83,160	64,008
Payment on A/P--Last Quarter Purchases . . .	29,040	38,052	49,014	41,580
Total Cash Purchases	$117,828	$152,418	$146,034	$116,256
For Operating Expenses:				
Cash Selling Expenses:				
Advertising Expense	$ 2,000	$ 3,000	$ 3,000	$ 1,000
Delivery Expense	3,510	5,740	5,550	3,700
Miscellaneous Expense--Sales	1,230	2,010	1,960	1,300
Salary Expense--Commissions	18,120	29,630	28,650	19,100
Salary Expense--Regular	46,000	65,500	63,500	47,000
Supplies Expense--Sales	4,050	6,630	6,420	4,300
Total Cash Selling Expenses	$ 74,910	$112,510	$109,080	$ 76,400
Cash Administrative Expenses:				
Insurance Expense	$ 375	$ 375	$ 375	$ 375
Miscellaneous Expense--Administrative . . .	500	820	790	530
Payroll Taxes Expense	7,220	10,900	10,560	7,480
Rent Expense	4,500	4,500	4,500	4,500
Salary Expense--Administrative	14,300	23,400	22,600	15,200
Supplies Expense--Office	450	700	700	450
Utilities Expense	1,250	1,450	1,450	1,250
Total Cash Administrative Expenses	$ 28,595	$ 42,145	$ 40,975	$ 29,785
For Other Cash Payments:				
Income Tax	$ 10,350	$ 10,350	$ 10,350	$ 10,350
Buy New Truck		11,000		
Pay Cash Dividend				25,000
Pay Note Payable and Interest			20,800	
Total Other Cash Payments	$ 10,350	$ 21,350	$ 31,150	$ 35,350
Total Cash Payments	$231,683	$328,423	$327,239	$257,791

Cash payments schedule

The selling expense schedule, page 480, and the administrative expense schedule, page 482, include estimated items for which cash will not be paid. For example, cash will not be paid for the amounts budgeted for depreciation or for bad debts expense. Therefore, these items do not appear in the cash payments schedule.

The purchases schedule, page 479, shows estimated purchases for the first quarter, 1979, to be $126,840.00. An analysis of past records for payments to creditors on account shows the following cash payment pattern.

About 10 percent of all purchases are cash purchases. About 60 percent are purchases on account paid for in the quarter. About 30 percent are purchases on account paid for in the following quarter.

Newberg Fence Company is also planning for cash payments other than for merchandise, selling expenses, and administrative expenses. An estimate is made of the 1979 income tax, and regular cash payments will be made throughout the year. The company also plans in the second quarter to buy a new truck for $11,000.00. Plans call for repaying at the end of the third quarter the promissory note and interest, $20,800.00. In the fourth quarter the company expects to pay a $25,000.00 cash dividend to the stockholders.

The last line of the cash payments schedule shows the total cash payments expected each quarter. This total indicates the amount of cash that must be available each quarter to make the expected payments.

Cash budget

A cash budget shows for each month or quarter the estimated beginning cash balance, the estimated cash receipts and cash payments, and the estimated ending cash balance. The assistant accountant prepares Newberg Fence Company's cash budget from the data in the cash receipts schedule and the cash payments schedule. The 1979 cash budget for Newberg Fence Company is shown below.

Newberg Fence Company
Cash Budget
For Year Ended December 31, 1979

	Quarters			
	1st	2d	3d	4th
Cash Balance--Beginning. . . .	$ 33,200.00	$ 22,598.00	$ 11,492.00	$ 46,651.00
Add Cash Receipts:				
(Schedule A)	221,081.00	317,317.00	362,398.00	296,659.00
Cash Available	$254,281.00	$339,915.00	$373,890.00	$343,310.00
Less Cash Pay. (Schedule B) .	231,683.00	328,423.00	327,239.00	257,791.00
Cash Balance--Ending	$ 22,598.00	$ 11,492.00	$ 46,651.00	$ 85,519.00

Cash budget

At the end of each quarter of a budget period, Newberg Fence Company compares the actual cash balance with the estimated cash balance as shown in the cash budget. If the actual cash balance is less than the estimated balance, the reasons for the decrease are determined and action is taken to correct the problem. One reason may be that some customers are not paying their accounts when they should. Another may be that expenses are exceeding budget estimates. If the decrease continues, the company could have a quarter in which there is not enough cash to make all the required cash payments. If this shortage does occur, the business will have to borrow money until receipts and payments are brought into balance.

✦What is the meaning of each of the following?

- budgeting
- budget
- budget period
- comparative income statement

1. A budget serves what three roles for management?
2. What does a completed budget show?
3. How does preparing a budget force a manager to plan?
4. How does the budgeting process help control expenses?
5. When designing a company budget, what information should be considered first?
6. Why is a one-year budget often divided into quarterly and monthly budgets?
7. In relation to a budget year, when should a budget be prepared?
8. What is a budgeted income statement?
9. What is a cash budget?
10. What are the four main sources of data for budgeting?

11. Why is the sales budget prepared first?
12. What factors are considered in preparing the sales budget?
13. What factors are considered in preparing the purchases budget?
14. Why do some items in a selling expense budget stay about the same from period to period, while other items vary a great deal?
15. Why is a cash budget important?
16. What estimates are made in preparing the cash receipts schedule?
17. What factors are considered in preparing the cash payments schedule?
18. Why, at the end of each quarter, is the actual cash balance compared with the estimated cash balance as shown in the summary cash budget?

CASE 1 Fred McCort was recently promoted to sales manager for Fitzpatrick's Glass Company. You, the assistant accountant, are responsible for coordinating the preparation of the annual company budget. As one of the first steps, you request that Mr. McCort prepare a sales budget for the coming year. Mr. McCort says he cannot prepare a sales budget until he knows how much the merchandise is going to cost, how much the company will be able to spend for advertising, and how many sales personnel will be hired. Is Mr. McCort correct? How would you answer?

CASE 2 Dorothy Kohn owns and manages an appliance store. She states that, because the business is small, she does not prepare a budgeted income statement. She does not think the time spent in the extra activity is justified since she has not needed a budget in the past. What is Miss Kohn overlooking in her consideration of a budgeted income statement?

CASE 3 The controller, Betty Tarver, and the treasurer, Kurt Easton, of Sykes Corporation have been debating the value of budgeted income statements versus cash budgets. Mrs. Tarver believes the budgeted income statement is most important to management. Mr. Easton believes the cash budget is most important. Who is correct? Discuss the arguments in favor of each statement.

PROBLEM 25-1   Preparing a sales budget schedule and a purchases budget schedule

At the end of 1978, Hewitt Company plans to prepare a sales budget schedule and a purchases budget schedule for 1979. The accounting records show that sales units have increased about 5 percent each year over the past four years. This increase is expected to continue in 1979. After reviewing the trends in prices, the sales manager estimates that Hewitt Company will need to increase its sales price per unit of merchandise from $5.00 to $5.25 in 1979.

The sales manager, after checking with the company's merchandise suppliers, estimates that the cost of merchandise will increase from the 1978 cost of $3.00 per unit to $3.20 per unit in 1979.

The accounting records show the following quarterly unit sales in 1978:

1st quarter	12,200 units	3d quarter	13,800 units
2d quarter	13,600 units	4th quarter	15,600 units
1978 ending inventory	6,400 units		

After considering the time required to reorder merchandise, the sales manager established the following desired levels of quarterly ending inventories for 1979:

1st quarter	7,000 units	3d quarter	8,000 units
2d quarter	7,200 units	4th quarter	6,800 units

Instructions: □ **1.** Prepare a sales budget schedule for the year ended December 31, 1979, similar to the one on page 478. Round your estimates to the nearest $10.00.

□ **2.** Prepare a purchases budget schedule for the year ended December 31, 1979, similar to the one on page 479. Round your estimates to the nearest $10.00.

PROBLEM 25-2 Preparing a budgeted income statement

The sales manager and administrative manager of Zyvoloski Company have made the following estimates to be used in preparing a budgeted income statement for the current calendar year:

(a) Total net sales for the current year are estimated to be $766,800.00.
(b) Cost of merchandise sold is estimated to be 70 percent of the net sales.
(c) Expenses for the year are estimated as shown below. (Percentages are based on the net sales estimated for the current year.)

Selling Expenses

Advertising Expense	1.6%
Delivery Expense	.6%
Depreciation Expense — Delivery Equipment	$2,100.00
Depreciation Expense — Store Equipment	$3,200.00
Miscellaneous Exp. — Sales	.4%
Salary Expense — Sales	5.0%
Supplies Expense — Sales	.8%

Administrative Expense

Bad Debts Expense	.5%
Depreciation Expense — Office Equipment	$ 2,250.00
Insurance Expense	.8%
Miscellaneous Exp. — Admin.	.5%
Rent Expense	$12,000.00
Salary Expense — Admin.	4.2%
Supplies Expense — Office	.6%
Utilities Expense	1.8%

(d) Income taxes are 30% of estimated net income.

Instructions: Prepare a budgeted income statement for the current year ended December 31. Use the 1979 Budget column of the comparative income statement, page 476, as your guide. Round amounts to the nearest $10.00. First, prepare selling and administrative expense budget schedules similar to those on pages 480 and 482.

PROBLEM 25-3 Preparing a cash budget

The following table shows the estimated sales, purchases, and cash payments for expenses for Abdullah Company for 1979.

Quarter	Estimated Sales	Estimated Purchases	Estimated Cash Payments for Expenses
1st	$516,300.00	$411,460.00	$59,360.00
2d	532,300.00	427,200.00	64,960.00
3d	520,240.00	417,760.00	76,300.00
4th	538,600.00	436,800.00	71,120.00

Actual amounts for the 4th quarter of 1978 are as follows:

Sales	Purchases	Cash Payments for Expenses
$490,600.00	$397,000.00	$67,800.00

Instructions: Prepare a cash budget for the four quarters ending December 31, 1979. Make the budget similar to the one shown on page 488. Round all amounts to the nearest $10.00. A cash receipts schedule (A) and a cash payments schedule (B) similar to those on pages 486 and 487 must be prepared first.

In preparing the cash budget, assume the following:

(a) The balance of cash on hand on January 1, 1979, is $22,180.00.

(b) In each quarter, the cash received from cash sales and from collections of accounts receivable is equal to 60% of the sales for the current quarter plus 40% of the sales for the preceding quarter.

(c) In each quarter, cash payments for cash purchases and accounts payable are equal to 50% of the purchases for the current quarter plus 50% of the purchases of the preceding quarter.

(d) There will be no other cash receipts and no other cash payments except those listed in the Cash Payments for Expenses column above.

MASTERY PROBLEM 25-M Preparing a cash budget

Instructions: Prepare a cash budget for Abdullah Company for the four quarters ending December 31, 1979. Use the data for sales, purchases, and cash payments for expenses given in the table in Problem 25-3. Make the budget similar to the one shown on page 488. Round all amounts to the nearest $10.00. A cash receipts schedule (A) and a cash payments schedule (B) similar to those on pages 486 and 487 must be prepared first.

In preparing this cash budget, assume the following:

(a) The cash balance on January 1, 1979, is $42,200.00.

(b) In each quarter, the cash received from cash sales and from collections of accounts receivable is equal to 50% of the sales for the current quarter plus 49% of the sales for the preceding quarter. One percent of the sales are uncollectible.

(c) In each quarter, the cash payments for cash purchases and accounts payable are equal to 60% of the purchases for the current quarter plus 40% of the purchases for the preceding quarter.

(d) In the first quarter, $20,000.00 is borrowed on a promissory note. In the second quarter, equipment costing $15,000.00 will be purchased for cash. In the third quarter, the promissory note plus interest, $21,000.00, will be repaid. In the fourth quarter, dividends amounting to $20,000.00 will be paid in cash. The other cash payments are those listed in the Cash Payments for Expenses column in the table given in Problem 25-3.

**BONUS
PROBLEM 25-B**   Preparing a sales budget schedule and a purchases budget schedule

On December 31, 1978, the accounting records of Rhodes Company show the following unit sales for 1978:

1st quarter	81,500 units	3d quarter	79,700 units
2d quarter	83,400 units	4th quarter	87,300 units
1978 ending inventory	46,200 units		

The records also show that sales units have increased about 6 percent each year over the past five years. This increase is expected to continue in 1979.

The sales manager, after reviewing price trends and checking with the company's merchandise suppliers, estimates the cost of merchandise will increase from the 1978 cost of $2.40 per unit to $2.50 per unit in 1979. Because of the increase in costs, the company increases selling prices from the 1978 price of $3.80 to $4.00 for 1979.

After considering the time required to reorder merchandise, the sales manager establishes the following desired levels of quarterly ending inventories for 1979:

1st quarter	55,000 units	3d quarter	57,400 units
2d quarter	52,600 units	4th quarter	56,800 units

Instructions: ☐ **1.** Prepare a sales budget schedule for the year ended December 31, 1979, similar to the one on page 478. Round your estimates to the nearest 10 for both dollars and units.

☐ **2.** Prepare a purchases budget schedule for the year ended December 31, 1979, similar to the one on page 479. Round your estimates to the nearest 10 for both dollars and units.

Accounting Information for Management Decisions

26

Owners of business organizations normally operate their businesses to make a profit. The soundness of management decisions frequently determines whether a business operates profitably. Since earning a satisfactory net income is one of the major objectives for most managers, many of their decisions relate to revenues and costs. Therefore, accounting information is one of the most valuable sources of information for management decisions.

COST CHARACTERISTICS THAT INFLUENCE DECISIONS

A manager increases company net income by making decisions that: (a) increase revenues, and/or (b) decrease costs. A manager, working with the company accountant, identifies some of the strengths and weaknesses of a company by analyzing sales and cost data. One report on which a manager can base decisions is the income statement. The income statement includes information about sales, cost of merchandise sold, gross profit, selling and administrative expenses, and net income. All of these items are important indicators to the manager of a company. However, if net income is going down, the income statement may not help the manager identify the problem. The manager may need greater detail about unit costs, variable costs, and fixed costs than the typical financial reports contain.

Total costs versus unit cost

All the costs for a specific period of time are called total costs. The cost of merchandise sold, as shown in the income statement below, is $32,000.00. This amount is the total cost of merchandise sold for the period of time, October 1 through October 31. The selling expenses of $28,000.00 are another kind of total cost. The $28,000.00 represents the total selling costs for the month of October. Total costs show how many total dollars were spent for specific activities during a specific period of time.

```
                          Newberg Fence Company
                            Income Statement
                     For Month Ended October 31, 1978


Sales . . . . . . . . . . . . . . . . . . . . . .          $72,000.00

Cost of Merchandise Sold . . . . . . . . . . . .           32,000.00

Gross Profit on Operations . . . . . . . . . . .          $40,000.00

Operating Expenses:
  Selling Expenses . . . . . . . . . . . . . .   $28,000.00
  Administrative Expenses . . . . . . . . . .     7,600.00
Total Operating Expenses . . . . . . . . . . .             35,600.00

Income from Operations . . . . . . . . . . . .            $ 4,400.00

Other Expenses . . . . . . . . . . . . . . . .                125.00

Net Income Before Taxes . . . . . . . . . . . .           $ 4,275.00
Income Taxes . . . . . . . . . . . . . . . . .                900.00

Net Income After Taxes . . . . . . . . . . . .            $ 3,375.00
```

Abbreviated income statement

The amount spent for a specific product or service is called a unit cost. Newberg Fence Company sold 8,000 square meters of fencing in October at a total cost of $32,000.00. The unit cost of each square meter of fence is $4.00 (total cost, $32,000.00 ÷ 8,000 square meters).

Newberg Fence Company's sales personnel made 400 sales contacts during October to sell fence. The selling expense per sales contact for fencing is $28,000.00 total selling expenses ÷ 400 contacts = $70.00 selling expense per sales contact.

Units may be expressed in many different terms. However, they should be expressed in terms that are meaningful to the people who are responsible for the costs. Some examples of other unit terms are gallons, liters, pounds, kilograms, feet, yards, meters, and hours. A knowledge of unit costs can be helpful to the manager in setting the unit selling price and in planning the control of costs.

Variable costs

Costs may be separated into two parts: variable and fixed. Costs which change in direct proportion to the change in the number of units are called variable costs.

For example, a roll of camera film costs $1.50. After deciding to enter an amateur picture contest, a customer returns to buy five more rolls of film. The price is $7.50 (5 × $1.50). The cost of film is a variable cost. The change in cost is the same percentage of increase as the percentage of increase in the number of units. The first purchase was one roll for $1.50; the second purchase, five rolls for $7.50. The second purchase is five times the first purchase in both units and total cost.

Fence purchases made by Newberg Fence Company for the months January through June are shown below.

<table>
<tr><td colspan="4" align="center">NEWBERG FENCE COMPANY
Fence Material Purchases</td></tr>
<tr><th>Month</th><th>Units Purchased</th><th>Unit Cost</th><th>Total Cost</th></tr>
<tr><td>January</td><td>4,800 m²</td><td>$4.00 per m²</td><td>$19,200.00</td></tr>
<tr><td>February</td><td>5,400 m²</td><td>$4.00 per m²</td><td>$21,600.00</td></tr>
<tr><td>March</td><td>7,800 m²</td><td>$4.00 per m²</td><td>$31,200.00</td></tr>
<tr><td>April</td><td>12,000 m²</td><td>$4.00 per m²</td><td>$48,000.00</td></tr>
<tr><td>May</td><td>14,400 m²</td><td>$4.00 per m²</td><td>$57,600.00</td></tr>
<tr><td>June</td><td>15,600 m²</td><td>$4.00 per m²</td><td>$62,400.00</td></tr>
</table>

The symbol for square meters is m².

The volume of fencing purchased ranges from a low of 4,800 square meters in January to a high of 15,600 square meters in June. However, the price paid per square meter (unit cost) remained at $4.00 throughout the six month period. A comparison of the relationship of *total cost* per month to *usage* per month shows that both change in the same proportion. For example, the 12,000 units purchased in April is 2 1/2 times greater than the 4,800 units purchased in January (12,000 ÷ 4,800 = 2 1/2). The $48,000.00 paid for the April purchases is also 2 1/2 times greater than the $19,200.00 paid for the January purchases ($19,200.00 × 2 1/2 = $48,000.00). This is true because the unit cost is $4.00 per square meter in each instance. These costs, then, have the characteristics of variable costs.

If the monthly costs of Newberg's fence purchases are plotted on a graph, as shown on page 496, a line drawn between the plotted points is a straight, sloped line.

The line is straight because Newberg's unit cost per square meter remained the same even though the number of units purchased per month varied. The change is in *direct proportion* to the quantities purchased. This situation results in a straight line.

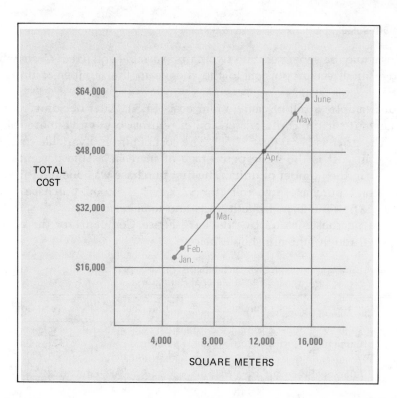

Characteristic of
variable costs

Fixed costs

Costs that remain constant regardless of change in business activity are called fixed costs. For example, if building rent for Newberg Fence Company is $1,500.00 per month, the cost is a fixed cost. The building rent is *fixed* because the amount has been set at $1,500.00 per month regardless of how many square meters of fence are sold. If each monthly rental cost is plotted on a graph and connected, the chart will appear as shown below. Notice that the fixed cost line becomes a straight line parallel with the base of the graph.

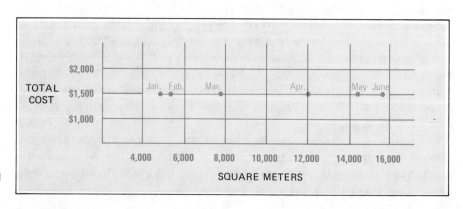

Characteristic of fixed
costs

Contribution margin versus gross profit on operations

The usual income statement reports gross profit on operations and net income. Revenue determined by subtracting cost of merchandise sold from sales is called gross profit on operations. On the normal income statement, below, the costs are shown as cost of merchandise sold, selling expenses, and administrative expenses.

```
                          Newberg Fence Company
                            Income Statement
                     For Month Ended October 31, 1978


Operating Revenue:
   Sales 8,000 m² fence @ $9.00 . . . . . .              $72,000.00
   Cost of Merchandise Sold 8,000 m² @ $4.00             32,000.00

Gross Profit on Operations . . . . . . . .               $40,000.00

Operating Expenses:
   Selling Expenses:
      Sales Commission 8,000 m² @ $.72 . . .  $ 5,760.00
      Installation Costs 8,000 m² @ $1.00 . .   8,000.00
      Other Selling Expenses . . . . . . . .   14,240.00  $28,000.00

   Administrative Expenses:
      Rent . . . . . . . . . . . . . . . . .  $ 1,500.00
      Insurance . . . . . . . . . . . . . .      100.00
      Other Administrative Expenses . . . . .   6,000.00    7,600.00
   Total Operating Expenses . . . . . . . .                          35,600.00

Income from Operations . . . . . . . . . .                          $ 4,400.00

Other Expenses . . . . . . . . . . . . .                               125.00

Net Income Before Taxes . . . . . . . . .                           $ 4,275.00
Income Taxes . . . . . . . . . . . . . .                               900.00

Net Income After Taxes . . . . . . . . .                            $ 3,375.00
```

Abbreviated income statement
with gross profit on operations

Income determined by subtracting all variable costs from sales revenue is called contribution margin. Contribution margin is also known as marginal income. The income statement shown on page 498 reports contribution margin and net income by grouping expenses into two categories: variable costs and fixed costs.

The manager of Newberg Fence Company can determine, from the income statement, page 498, that $2.70 contribution margin will be earned for every square meter of fence that is sold. This amount consists of the $9.00 per square meter selling price less the per square meter costs of $4.00 for materials, $.72 sales commission, $1.00 installation costs, and $.58 other variable costs. The manager also knows that the company will have $18,225.00 fixed costs each month even if no fence is sold. These fixed costs consist of $1,500.00 rent, $100.00 insurance, and $16,625.00 other fixed costs.

```
                            Newberg Fence Company
                              Income Statement
                       For Month Ended October 31, 1978


    Sales 8,000 m2 fence @ $9.00  . . . . . . . . .                    $72,000.00
    Less Variable Costs:
      Fence Materials 8,000 m2 @ $4.00  . . . . . .    $32,000.00
      Sales Commission 8,000 m2 @ $.72  . . . . . .      5,760.00
      Installation Costs 8,000 m2 @ $1.00 . . . . .      8,000.00
      Other Variable Costs 8,000 m2 @ $.58  . . . .      4,640.00
      Total Variable Costs . . . . . . . . . . . .                     50,400.00

    Contribution Margin . . . . . . . . . . . . . .                   $21,600.00

    Less Fixed Costs:
      Rent  . . . . . . . . . . . . . . . . . . . .    $ 1,500.00
      Insurance . . . . . . . . . . . . . . . . . .        100.00
      Other Fixed Costs . . . . . . . . . . . . . .     16,625.00
      Total Fixed Costs . . . . . . . . . . . . . .                    18,225.00

    Net Income  . . . . . . . . . . . . . . . . . .                   $ 3,375.00
```

Abbreviated income statement
with contribution margin

DECISIONS THAT AFFECT INCOME

If a manager is to make decisions that will yield favorable profits for
the company, two important kinds of facts are needed: (a) What amount
of merchandise or services must the company sell to make a reasonable
profit? and (b) Which factors are contributing most to company profits?

Figuring the breakeven point

The volume point at which the revenue from sales is exactly the same
as the total costs is called the breakeven point. At the breakeven point
there will be neither net income nor net loss. At Newberg Fence Company, the assistant accountant figures the breakeven point to determine
how many dollars worth of merchandise or services must be sold before
the company makes a net income.

The data required to figure the breakeven point are:

1. Total revenue.
2. Total variable costs.
3. Total fixed costs.

The breakeven point is figured in three steps.

Step 1: Figure the contribution margin. The contribution margin for
Newberg Fence Company for October is shown on the income statement
above. The amount of the contribution margin is figured as:

Revenue	−	Total Variable Costs	=	Contribution Margin
$72,000.00	−	$50,400.00	=	$21,600.00

Step 2: Figure the contribution margin rate. The contribution margin rate is figured as:

Contribution Margin   ÷   Total Revenue   =   Contribution Margin Rate
$21,600.00   ÷ $72,000.00   =   .30 or 30%

Variable costs change in direct proportion to changes in sales activity. Therefore, the contribution margin rate means that for every $1.00 of revenue, 70¢ is required for variable costs. Also for every $1.00 of revenue, 30¢ is contribution margin. The contribution margin is for fixed costs and net income.

Step 3: Figure the breakeven point. The breakeven point is where the entire contribution margin is used to pay for fixed costs. The contribution margin rate for Newberg Fence Company is 30 percent. The breakeven point is figured as:

Total Fixed Costs   ÷   Contribution Margin Rate   =   Breakeven Point
$18,225.00   ÷   .30 or 30%   = $60,750.00

The Newberg Fence Company must have total sales revenue of $60,750.00 just to recover the costs of doing business. The manager of the company knows that more than $60,750.00 in sales must be made if the company is to earn any net income.

Breakeven point in sales dollars versus breakeven point in units. Occasionally a manager may be more interested in how many units of merchandise must be sold to break even. The process is:

Step 1: Determine Sales Price Per Unit from income statement
Step 2: Determine Variable Costs Per Unit from income statement
Step 3: Figure the Contribution Margin Per Unit = Sales Price Per Unit − Variable Costs Per Unit
Step 4: Figure the Breakeven Point in Units = Total Fixed Costs ÷ Contribution Margin Per Unit

Using the data from the income statement on page 498, the breakeven point in units for Newberg Fence Company is figured as follows:

Step 1: Sales Price Per m^2		$9.00
Step 2: Variable Costs:		
Fence Materials Per m^2	$4.00	
Sales Commission Per m^2	.72	
Installation Costs Per m^2	1.00	
Other Variable Costs Per m^2	.58	
Variable Costs Per m^2		$6.30
Step 3: Sales Price Per m^2		$9.00
Less Variable Costs Per m^2		6.30
Contribution Margin Per m^2		$2.70

Step 4: Breakeven Point in Units = $18,225.00 ÷ $2.70 = 6,750 m^2

The business must sell more than 6,750 square meters of fencing per month before the company begins to make any net income.

Verification of the breakeven point computations. The simplest way to verify the accuracy of breakeven figures is to prepare an income statement using the breakeven point numbers. If the breakeven point is accurate, the net income will be zero. The breakeven income statement, below, shows the proof for the breakeven point figures of Newberg Fence Company.

```
                        Newberg Fence Company
                      Breakeven Income Statement
                         For a Projected Month


Sales 6,750 m2 fence @ $9.00  . . . . . . . . .              $60,750.00
Less Variable Costs:
  Fence Materials 6,750 m2 @ $4.00  . . . . . .  $27,000.00
  Sales Commission 6,750 m2 @ $.72  . . . . . .    4,860.00
  Installation Costs 6,750 m2 @ $1.00 . . . . .    6,750.00
  Other Variable Costs 6,750 m2 @ $.58  . . . .    3,915.00
  Total Variable Costs . . . . . . . . . . . .                42,525.00

Contribution Margin . . . . . . . . . . . . .                $18,225.00

Less Fixed Costs:
  Rent  . . . . . . . . . . . . . . . . . . . .   $ 1,500.00
  Insurance . . . . . . . . . . . . . . . . . .      100.00
  Other Fixed Costs . . . . . . . . . . . . . .   16,625.00
  Total Fixed Costs . . . . . . . . . . . . . .                18,225.00

Net Income  . . . . . . . . . . . . . . . . . .                    -0-
```

Proof of breakeven point figures

The breakeven point in units (6,750 square meters) times the normal sales price per unit ($9.00 per square meter) equals the breakeven point in sales dollars ($60,750.00). Also, the contribution margin of $18,225.00 is 30 percent of sales ($60,750.00). This verifies the contribution margin rate of 30 percent for Newberg Fence Company.

Determining the effect of changes on net income

Knowing the breakeven point for October will not help the manager plan business activities for October. However, the October information may have implications for November activity. Managers making decisions about future activities need information that helps predict future events. Since actual data are not available for the future, the next best thing, data from the past, is used.

Newberg's manager needs estimated answers to the following questions: What will be the net income if 6,000 square meters of fence are sold rather than 8,000 square meters? What will happen to the net income if the price per square meter is increased from $9.00 to $10.00?

Effect of changes in volume (number of units sold). The relationship of sales to cost and profit is:

$$\text{Sales} = \text{Variable Costs} + \text{Fixed Costs} + \text{Profit}$$

Also, variable costs are always a percentage of each sales dollar regardless of the amount of sales. The remainder, contribution margin, is available to pay fixed costs and contribute to net income. Fixed costs must be paid first and any amount remaining is net income.

The illustration below shows how net income changes as the units of products sold changes.

	Per Unit	6,000 m²	6,750 m²	7,500 m²
Sales..............................	$9.00	$54,000.00	$60,750.00	$67,500.00
Variable Costs..................	6.30	37,800.00	42,525.00	47,250.00
Contribution Margin.........	$2.70	$16,200.00	$18,225.00	$20,250.00
Fixed Costs.....................		18,225.00	18,225.00	18,225.00
Net Income (Loss).............		($ 2,025.00)	$ –0–	$ 2,025.00

Comparison of volume of sales
to net income earned

From every square meter of fence sold by Newberg Fence Company, $2.70 contribution margin is available for fixed costs and profit. The manager knows that there are $18,225.00 fixed costs each month. Therefore, the entire $2.70 per square meter contribution margin will be applied to fixed costs until the $18,225.00 has been paid. For every square meter of fence sold above 6,750 (the breakeven point), the $2.70 per square meter contribution margin will be net income. Therefore, when 7,500 square meters of fence are sold, contribution margin from the first 6,750 units will pay the fixed costs. Contribution margin from the remaining 750 square meters of fence will result in a net income of $2,025.00 (750 square meters × $2.70).

If only 6,000 square meters of fence are sold during the month, the contribution margin of $16,200.00 will not cover the fixed costs of $18,225.00. At this volume of sales a net loss of $2,025.00 will result.

The graph, page 502, shows the relationship of sales, costs, and profit as the volume of units changes. The sales line, beginning at zero, represents unit sales price times number of units sold. The line starting at $18,225.00 (the total fixed costs) represents the total amount of cost involved per number of units sold. The variable cost area represents 70 percent of sales regardless of volume. The fixed costs are $18,225,00. No matter what the sales volume is, the fixed costs remain constant, as shown by the horizontal line at the bottom of the graph.

If 6,750 square meters of fence are sold for $60,750.00, the variable costs are $42,525.00 and fixed costs are $18,225.00. No net income is earned. If 7,500 square meters of fence are sold for $67,500.00, the

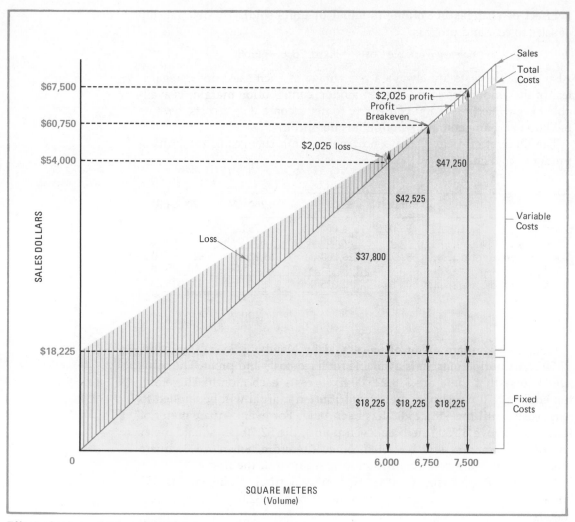

Effect of sales volume on net income

$67,500.00 is composed of $47,250.00 variable costs and $18,225.00 fixed costs, with the remainder, $2,025.00, for net income. If only 6,000 square meters of fence are sold for $54,000.00, the variable costs are $37,800.00 and fixed costs are $18,225.00. A net loss of $2,025.00 results. More than 6,750 units of fencing must be sold to earn a net income.

Effect of changes in costs. There are two types of costs that influence the decisions a manager may make. Variable costs increase or decrease as sales increase or decrease. Fixed costs remain constant regardless of the amount of sales.

The manager of Newberg Fence Company is considering a sales alternative. The company is only three years old and is expanding each year. The company has been buying precut wood fence materials and then paying a crew $1.00 per square meter to install the fence. The manager is considering buying standard length materials, cutting and assembling fence sections, and then installing the fence for customers. The manager believes this new method will make assembly more efficient and permit regular employees to continue assembling sections during slow-selling periods. However, the new method will require an additional building and additional equipment. The manager also estimates that installation costs will be reduced from $1.00 to $0.55 per square meter of fence. The assistant accountant makes an analysis of costs for the two alternatives which shows:

Alternative 1: Buy precut materials. Variable costs per square meter of fence are $6.30. Fixed costs are $18,225.00 per month.

Alternative 2: Cut and assemble sections. Variable costs per square meter of fence are estimated to be $5.85. Fixed costs are estimated to be $21,825.00 per month.

Sales are estimated to average 8,000 square meters of fence per month. The cost comparisons are shown below.

	Precut			Cut/Assemble in Plant		
	Per Unit	Units Sold	Total	Per Unit	Units Sold	Total
Sales.........................	$9.00	8,000	$72,000.00	$9.00	8,000	$72,000.00
Variable Costs............	6.30	8,000	50,400.00	5.85	8,000	46,800.00
Contribution Margin...	$2.70		$21,600.00	$3.15		$25,200.00
Fixed Costs...............			18,225.00			21,825.00
Net Income...............			$ 3,375.00			$ 3,375.00

Effect of variable and fixed costs — average volume

At a sales level of 8,000 units of fence, the net income is the same for both alternatives. With Alternative 2, the contribution margin is higher, but the fixed costs also are higher. Thus the higher fixed costs cancel out the higher contribution margin.

If the Newberg Fence Company's prospects look bright for increased sales, a cost comparison may be made for a higher sales rate. Cost comparisons with a 15 percent sales increase to 9,200 units are shown below.

	Precut			Cut/Assemble in Plant		
	Per Unit	Units Sold	Total	Per Unit	Units Sold	Total
Sales.........................	$9.00	9,200	$82,800.00	$9.00	9,200	$82,800.00
Variable Costs............	6.30	9,200	57,960.00	5.85	9,200	53,820.00
Contribution Margin...	$2.70		$24,840.00	$3.15		$28,980.00
Fixed Costs...............			18,225.00			21,825.00
Net Income...............			$ 6,615.00			$ 7,155.00

Effect of variable and fixed costs — above average volume

With the increased sales volume, Alternative 2 earns a higher net income. If the manager believes sales are going to increase, Alternative 2 is more profitable than Alternative 1.

However, if there is doubt whether sales will increase, the results could be much different. From the previous cost comparison, a manager may conclude that Alternative 2 will earn approximately 8 percent more than Alternative 1. However, if the number of units actually sold is 15 percent less (6,800 units) than previous average sales, the results will favor Alternative 1. At the lower volume, shown below, Alternative 1 will earn $135.00 net income while Alternative 2 will incur a $405.00 net loss.

	Precut			Cut/Assemble in Plant		
	Per Unit	Units Sold	Total	Per Unit	Units Sold	Total
Sales.........................	$9.00	6,800	$61,200.00	$9.00	6,800	$61,200.00
Variable Costs............	6.30	6,800	42,840.00	5.85	6,800	39,780.00
Contribution Margin...	$2.70		$18,360.00	$3.15		$21,420.00
Fixed Costs...............			18,225.00			21,825.00
Net Income (Loss).......			$ 135.00			($ 405.00)

Effect of variable and fixed costs —
below average volume

What is the reason for the change in favorable alternatives? The contribution margin rate favors Alternative 2.

	Alternative 1		Alternative 2	
	Precut		Cut and Assemble	
	Dollars	Percent	Dollars	Percent
Sales................................	$72,000.00	100%	$72,000.00	100%
Variable Costs....................	50,400.00	70%	46,800.00	65%
Contribution Margin...........	$21,600.00	30%	$25,200.00	35%

Effects of contribution margin rate

The figures above show that the contribution margin rate for Alternative 1 is 30 percent ($21,600.00 ÷ $72,000.00) versus 35 percent ($25,200.00 ÷ $72,000.00) for Alternative 2. This means that for every $1.00 of sales from Alternative 1, 30 cents is available for fixed costs and net income. But for every $1.00 of sales from Alternative 2, 35 cents is available for fixed costs and net income.

A high contribution margin rate is desirable. However, fixed costs must also be reasonable since the contribution margin must cover the fixed costs before any net income is earned. The contribution margin rate for the cut and assemble method is more favorable (35 percent). But, in the illustration of decreased volume, page 504, fixed costs are $21,825.00, $3,600.00 more than fixed costs for the precut method. Thus, if sales volume is reduced as shown, the contribution margin is not enough to pay fixed costs and a loss is incurred. By comparison, the precut method with a lower fixed cost is still a profitable operation when sales volume declines 15 percent.

A manager's logical conclusion then may be: "Everything else being equal, the activity with the higher contribution margin rate is the more profitable." If "everything else" *is* equal, selecting the more profitable choice is very simple. However, the alternatives normally are not that simple because fixed costs probably will differ for each alternative. Therefore, an effective manager looks for the best combination of fixed and variable costs.

Effect of unit price on net income. Setting the selling price of products is an extremely important job for a manager who expects to make a reasonable net income. If the price is set too high, potential customers will buy from someone else. If the price is set too low, the company may lose money. The objective then is to set selling prices to include a reasonable amount of net income while keeping competitive prices.

The following example shows the estimated net income on 8,000 units at the current price.

Product	Per Unit			No. Units Sold	Total		
	Sales Price	Variable Cost	Contr. Margin		Sales	Variable Costs	Contr. Margin
Fence, m²	$9.00	$6.30	$2.70	8,000	$72,000.00	$50,400.00	$21,600.00
Less Fixed Costs							18,225.00
Net Income							$ 3,375.00

Net income at current price

The manager of Newberg Fence Company decides that although a monthly net income of $3,375.00 is acceptable, an increase in net income is more desirable. The manager reviews company prices and those of competitors. The manager then assumes that a 10 percent reduction in selling price will result in a 20 percent increase in the number of units sold. The assistant accountant prepares a schedule to estimate the effect of this price change on the sales volume and net income. The schedule is shown on page 506. A 10 percent reduction in unit price and a 20 percent increase in volume results in a net loss.

Price cutting can be dangerous. In October, Newberg Fence Company had a contribution margin per square meter of fence sold of $2.70. A total of 8,000 units was sold resulting in $21,600.00 total contribution margin.

Product	Per Unit			No. Units Sold	Total		
	Sales Price	Variable Costs	Contr. Margin		Sales	Variable Costs	Contr. Margin
Fence, m²	$8.10	$6.30	$1.80	9,600	$77,760.00	$60,480.00	$17,280.00
Less Fixed Costs							18,225.00
Net Income (Loss)							($ 945.00)

Effect of 10 percent reduction in sales price
and 20 percent increase in units sold

A price reduction of 10 percent (90 cents per unit) will reduce the contribution margin to $1.80. The contribution margin would be reduced 33 1/3 percent (from $2.70 to $1.80) even though the total selling price would be reduced only 10 percent.

The potential results of a price cut can be figured as follows: Divide the total contribution margin (or desired contribution margin) by the contribution margin per unit to determine the number of units to be sold.

October Contribution Margin	÷	New Contribution Margin Per Unit	=	Units Required to Maintain Contribution Margin
$21,600.00	÷	$1.80	=	12,000 units

A decrease in price from $9.00 to $8.10 is estimated to increase sales from 8,000 to 9,600 units. However, at $8.10, a total of 12,000 units would have to be sold to maintain the same income as current sales at the $9.00 price. Apparently, reducing the selling price by 90 cents would not be a profitable decision if only 9,600 units can be sold.

Effect of sales mix on net income. If price increases could be freely made, each product could be priced to yield a reasonable amount of net income.

However, competition frequently prevents a desired price increase. For example, a furniture store prices a chair at $35.00. A chair of similar quality is priced at $25.00 by competitors. The first store probably will not sell many chairs at $35.00.

The relative distribution of sales among various products is called sales mix. A company's sales mix is determined by figuring the relationship that the sales of each product bear to total sales. Sales mix becomes important in maintaining net income. If those products which have the highest contribution margin can be identified and sales increased for those products, overall net income should increase.

Newberg Fence Company sold only wood fences the first three years of the company's existence. Sales are always low during the winter months. In an effort to increase sales, the company started selling chain-link metal fence. The calculations for determining net income for January, 1979, the first month wood and metal fences were sold, is shown on page 507.

| Product | Per Unit | | | | Total | | |
	Sales Price	Variable Costs	Contr. Margin	No. Units Sold	Sales	Variable Costs	Contr. Margin
Wood Fence...............	$9.00	$6.30	$2.70	5,000	$45,000.00	$31,500.00	$13,500.00
Metal Fence	6.00	3.30	2.70	1,000	6,000.00	3,300.00	2,700.00
Totals					$51,000.00	$34,800.00	$16,200.00
Less Fixed Costs.........							18,225.00
Net Income (Loss).........							($ 2,025.00)

Effect of sales mix on net income

Newberg Fence Company lost $2,025.00 during January operations. After reviewing the January contribution margin and net loss, Newberg's manager concluded that:

1. An increase in the price of fencing was unacceptable because competitors would then be selling similar fencing at a lower price.
2. Variable costs were as low as possible.
3. Fixed costs could not be reduced.

Can Newberg Fence Company operate profitably during the winter months? The manager noticed that each unit of wood fencing sold for $9.00 and earned $2.70 contribution margin — a contribution margin of 30 percent. However, each unit of metal fence sold for only $6.00 and also earned $2.70 contribution margin — a contribution margin of 45 percent. Why not, during the slow, winter months, change the sales emphasis to sell more metal fences? Newberg decided to change the sales mix. A larger variety of metal fencing was stocked in inventory. Advertising emphasis for February was changed from wood to metal fences. Sales personnel started calling on more potential metal-fence customers. After changing the sales emphasis, Newberg Fence Company's net income for February appeared as shown below.

| Product | Per Unit | | | | Total | | |
	Sales Price	Variable Cost	Contr. Margin	No. Units Sold	Sales	Variable Cost	Contr. Margin
Wood Fence...............	$9.00	$6.30	$2.70	3,400	$30,600.00	$21,420.00	$ 9,180.00
Metal Fence	6.00	3.30	2.70	3,400	20,400.00	11,220.00	9,180.00
Totals					$51,000.00	$32,640.00	$18,360.00
Less Fixed Costs.........							18,225.00
Net Income...............							$ 135.00

Effect of change in sales mix

Newberg Fence Company's sales for February were the same as January's sales, $51,000.00. The unit sales prices, variable costs, and fixed costs remained the same. The only change was the sales mix. Fewer units of wood fence were sold but more units of metal fence, with a higher contribution margin rate, were sold. The change in sales mix changed operating results from a $2,025.00 net loss to a $135.00 net income.

Using Business Terms

✦ What is the meaning of each of the following?

- total costs
- unit cost
- variable costs

- fixed costs
- gross profit on operations

- contribution margin
- breakeven point
- sales mix

Questions for Individual Study

1. What information does a manager need to make sound decisions?
2. How can a manager increase company net income?
3. What are the differences between variable and fixed costs?
4. If total monthly variable costs for a company were plotted on a graph for six months, what kind of line would connect the plotted points? Would the line be parallel to the base or sloped? Explain why.
5. If total monthly fixed costs for a company were plotted on a graph for six months, what kind of line would connect the plotted points? Would the line be parallel to the base or sloped? Explain why.

6. What financial data are required to compute the breakeven point?
7. How is the contribution margin rate figured?
8. How does gross profit on operations differ from contribution margin?
9. How is the breakeven point figured?
10. What does the contribution margin rate represent? Why is the knowledge of the rate helpful to a manager?
11. Which of the following changes will have the most significant effect on net income?
    (a) 10% reduction in sales price.
    (b) 10% increase in variable costs.
    (c) 10% increase in fixed costs.

Cases for Management Decision

CASE 1 Huxham Auto Paint Company has been earning approximately $10,000.00 per month. A typical monthly income statement is shown below:

Sales...	$80,000.00
Variable Costs............................	60,000.00
Contribution Margin..................	$20,000.00
Fixed Costs...............................	10,000.00
Net Income...............................	$10,000.00

A new paint process has just been introduced. The manager at Huxham considers changing to the new paint process but asks you, the assistant accountant, to evaluate the financial effects. At the same level of sales, variable costs will be reduced to $48,000.00 but fixed costs will increase to $25,000.00. What is your recommendation? Explain your reasons. Under what conditions would you recommend the change?

CASE 2 Joanne Eckart manages an automobile service station. She has been selling about 20,000 gallons of gasoline each month at 60 cents per gallon. Her variable costs are 50 cents per gallon and fixed costs are $1,000.00 per month. Miss Eckart is searching for a way to improve sales volume and net income. She estimates that cutting the unit price of gasoline about 10 percent (60 cents to 55 cents), will increase sales 15 percent (20,000 to 23,000 gallons). Is this a wise decision? Explain.

PROBLEM 26-1 Figuring the contribution margin; figuring the contribution margin rate; figuring the breakeven point

Vollar Air Conditioning Company sells a home air conditioning unit. The company recorded the following sales and costs for last year:

Sales — 400 units @ $1,500.00
Variable costs — 400 units @ $1,125.00
Fixed costs — $100,000.00

Instructions: ☐ **1.** Figure the contribution margin.

☐ **2.** Figure the contribution margin rate.

☐ **3.** Figure the breakeven point (a) in sales dollars and (b) in units.

PROBLEM 26-2 Figuring the breakeven point; figuring plans for net income

Mr. DeSandro, Lorenz Chair Company, is planning his net income potential for the coming year. Sales prices and expenses for last year are as follows:

Variable Data	Per Chair	
Selling price...	$	24.00
Cost of chairs	$	16.80
Sales commission		1.20
Total variable costs	$	18.00

Annual Fixed Costs	
Rent	$15,000.00
Salaries	60,000.00
Miscellaneous	15,000.00
Total fixed costs	$90,000.00

Use the preceding data as a basis for net income planning. Treat each part below independently.

Instructions: ☐ **1.** Figure the breakeven point for the year (a) in total sales dollars and (b) in number of chairs.

☐ **2.** If a $30,000.00 annual net income is desired, figure the required (a) sales dollars and (b) number of chairs to be sold.

☐ **3.** Figure the breakeven point (a) in sales dollars and (b) in number of chairs if the manager decides that an additional $36,000.00 in salaries will be paid in place of the $1.20 per chair sales commission.

PROBLEM 26-3 Figuring unit selling price; unit variable
costs; total fixed costs

The Dedra Grill Company sold 50,000 barbecue grills last year with the following
results:

Dedra Grill Company
Income Statement
For Year Ended December 31, 19——

Sales — 50,000 grills @ $20.00	$1,000,000
Less Variable Costs — 50,000 grills @ $12.00................................	600,000
Contribution Margin...	$ 400,000
Less Fixed Costs	320,000
Net Income...	$ 80,000

Ann Sherri, manager of Dedra Grill Company, is anticipating rapidly increasing
prices next year; so, she is doing some advance planning.

Instructions: Figure the new net income for each of the following changes. Consider each case independently.
   (a) Unit selling price increases 20%.
   (b) Unit variable costs increase 20%.
   (c) Total fixed costs increase 20%.
   (d) All changes of Parts (a), (b), and (c) occur.

Analyses of Financial Statements

Financial information about a business is important to several groups of people. Managers use financial information to help them make better decisions about operating the business. Owners and potential owners use the information to help them decide whether to buy, sell, or keep their investment. Banks and lending agencies use the information to decide whether to loan money to a business. Each of these groups may need different financial information about a business. Therefore, each group analyzes and evaluates the financial data that will provide the most help in making decisions.

FINANCIAL ANALYSIS

Decisions needed to effectively analyze financial data include: (a) What are the objectives for making the analysis? (b) What are the sources of data needed to make the analysis? (c) What kind of analysis is to be made? (d) What is an acceptable level of performance?

Objectives for analyzing financial data

The objective for analyzing financial data is determined by the characteristics and achievements of a business that are important to the person making the analysis. The data are analyzed to give more knowledge about the various strengths and weaknesses of the business. Common objectives for analyzing financial data are to determine: (a) the profitability of a business, and (b) the financial strength of a business.

Sources of financial data

Financial statements, with supporting schedules, are the primary sources of data to be analyzed. Financial statements for Barcelona Corporation are shown on pages 512 and 513. For each statement, data for the current year and the two preceding years are given. Financial statements containing data for each of several years are called comparative financial statements. Showing data for several years permits the statement reader to compare differences from year to year. Both the income statement and the balance sheet are given in condensed form. For example, on the comparative income statement below, a number of selling expenses are combined in the caption "Other Selling Expenses." Also, a number of administrative expenses are combined in the caption "Other Administrative Expenses." Similarly, on the comparative balance sheet, page 513, accounts receivable is given as a "net" amount (accounts receivable minus the allowance for uncollectible accounts). Also, plant assets is given as a "net" amount (plant assets minus the accumulated depreciation).

BARCELONA CORPORATION
Comparative Income Statement
For Years Ended December 31, 1977, 1978, and 1979

	1979		1978		1977	
	Amount	%	Amount	%	Amount	%
Operating Revenue:						
Net Sales	$2,207,000	100.0	$1,682,000	100.0	$1,294,000	100.0
Cost of Merchandise Sold:						
Merchandise Inv., Jan. 1 .	$ 55,200	2.5	$ 41,800	2.5	$ 32,800	2.5
Net Purchases	1,193,900	54.1	938,500	55.8	702,600	54.3
Cost of Mdse. Available . .	$1,249,100	56.6	$ 980,300	58.3	$ 735,400	56.8
Less Mdse. Inv., Dec. 31 .	70,600	3.2	55,200	3.3	41,800	3.2
Cost of Merchandise Sold .	$1,178,500	53.4	$ 925,100	55.0	$ 693,600	53.6
Gross Profit on Operations . .	$1,028,500	46.6	$ 756,900	45.0	$ 600,400	46.4
Operating Expenses:						
Selling Expenses:						
Advertising Expense	$ 22,100	1.0	$ 15,100	0.9	$ 10,300	0.8
Delivery Expense	35,300	1.6	26,900	1.6	20,700	1.6
Salary Expense	483,300	21.9	368,400	21.9	284,700	22.0
Supplies Expense	39,700	1.8	30,300	1.8	23,300	1.8
Other Selling Expenses . .	55,200	2.5	42,000	2.5	33,600	2.6
Total Selling Expenses . .	$ 635,600	28.8	$ 482,700	28.7	$ 372,600	28.8
Administrative Expenses:						
Bad Debts Expense	$ 13,200	0.6	$ 8,400	0.5	$ 6,500	0.5
Salary Expense	147,900	6.7	114,400	6.8	90,600	7.0
Other Admin. Expenses . . .	117,000	5.3	94,200	5.6	72,500	5.6
Total Admin. Expenses . . .	$ 278,100	12.6	$ 217,000	12.9	$ 169,600	13.1
Total Operating Expenses . . .	$ 913,700	41.4	$ 699,700	41.6	$ 542,200	41.9
Net Income Before Fed. Inc. Tax	$ 114,800	5.2	$ 57,200	3.4	$ 58,200	4.5
Less Federal Income Tax	41,600	1.9	14,000	0.8	14,400	1.1
Net Income After Fed. Inc. Tax.	$ 73,200	3.3	$ 43,200	2.6	$ 43,800	3.4

Comparative income statement

BARCELONA CORPORATION
Comparative Statement of Owners' Equity
December 31, 1977, 1978, and 1979

	1979	1978	1977
Capital Stock, January 1	$200,000.00	$200,000.00	$200,000.00
Capital Stock Issued	50,000.00	-0-	-0-
Capital Stock, December 31	$250,000.00	$200,000.00	$200,000.00
Retained Earnings, January 1	$107,800.00	$ 84,600.00	$ 65,800.00
Net Income After Federal Income Tax . .	73,200.00	43,200.00	43,800.00
Total	$181,000.00	$127,800.00	$109,600.00
Less Dividends Declared	25,000.00	20,000.00	25,000.00
Retained Earnings, December 31	$156,000.00	$107,800.00	$ 84,600.00
Total Owners' Equity, December 31 . . .	$406,000.00	$307,800.00	$284,600.00

Comparative statement of owners' equity

BARCELONA CORPORATION
Comparative Balance Sheet
December 31, 1977, 1978, and 1979

	1979	1978	1977
ASSETS			
Current Assets:			
Cash	$103,400.00	$ 51,800.00	$ 63,600.00
Accounts Receivable (Net)	296,100.00	347,300.00	126,100.00
Merchandise Inventory	70,600.00	55,200.00	41,800.00
Other Current Assets	12,700.00	10,200.00	6,100.00
Total Current Assets	$482,800.00	$464,500.00	$237,600.00
Plant Assets (Net)	400,000.00	300,000.00	280,000.00
Total Assets	$882,800.00	$764,500.00	$517,600.00
LIABILITIES			
Current Liabilities:			
Notes Payable	$ 80,000.00	$119,700.00	$ 20,000.00
Interest Payable	6,300.00	9,600.00	1,600.00
Accounts Payable	170,100.00	206,000.00	87,800.00
Income Tax Payable - Federal . .	5,600.00	1,100.00	1,500.00
Other Current Liabilities	2,800.00	4,300.00	2,100.00
Total Current Liabilities	$264,800.00	$340,700.00	$113,000.00
Long-Term Liability:			
Mortgage Payable	212,000.00	116,000.00	120,000.00
Total Liabilities	$476,800.00	$456,700.00	$233,000.00
OWNERS' EQUITY			
Capital Stock	$250,000.00	$200,000.00	$200,000.00
Retained Earnings	156,000.00	107,800.00	84,600.00
Total Owners' Equity	$406,000.00	$307,800.00	$284,600.00
Total Liabilities and Owners' Equity	$882,800.00	$764,500.00	$517,600.00
Capital Stock Shares Outstanding	2,500	2,000	2,000

Comparative balance sheet

Procedures for analyzing financial data

Comparative financial statements are reports of a business's current and past activities. However, most readers of financial statements are also interested in how well the business will continue to perform. Therefore, financial statements generally are analyzed to help predict how well the business will perform in the future.

Several different kinds of comparisons may be used to analyze financial statements. Three most commonly used comparisons are (a) trend analysis, (b) component percentage analysis, and (c) ratio analysis.

Trend analysis. Trends in the financial condition and the operating results of a business are not apparent from the financial data for a single year. Data for several fiscal periods must be compared to determine whether a business is making satisfactory progress. Comparing the relationship between one item on a financial statement and the same item on a previous year's financial statement is called trend analysis. A trend analysis can be done for any item on the income statement. For example, according to the comparative income statement illustrated on page 512, Barcelona Corporation had net sales of $1,294,000.00, $1,682,000.00, and $2,207,000.00 in the years 1977, 1978, and 1979 respectively. A comparison of changes in net sales is figured as follows:

Change in Net Sales ÷ Net Sales Previous Year = % Increase or Decrease in
                                                 Net Sales
1978: $388,000.00 Increase ÷ $1,294,000.00   = 29.98% Increase
1979: $525,000.00 Increase ÷ $1,682,000.00   = 31.21% Increase

A review of the trend in Barcelona sales the past three years indicates net sales are increasing about 30 percent each year.

Component percentage analysis. The percentage relationship between one item on a financial statement and the total that includes that item is called a component percentage. The relationship between each item and net sales is shown in a separate percentage column. For example, the income statement column for 1979 on the statement, page 512, shows that cost of merchandise sold was 53.4 percent of net sales. Also, the total operating expenses were 41.4 percent of net sales.

In addition, component percentages on comparative statements show changes in a specific item from year to year. For example, cost of merchandise sold at Barcelona Corporation was 53.6 percent, 55.0 percent, and 53.4 percent of net sales for the years 1977, 1978, and 1979 respectively. A review of these percentages suggests that something occurred in 1978 to cause the cost of merchandise sold to be higher than what appears to be normal. A closer examination of the cost data for 1978 shows that unit costs of merchandise purchased increased more than the increase in selling prices.

Ratio analysis. An expression of the numeric relationship between two amounts is called a ratio. A ratio is a stated comparison between two numbers showing how many times one number exceeds the other. A ratio also may be expressed as a percentage or a fraction. Assume that a business has sales of $1,000,000.00 and net income of $100,000.00. This relationship may be stated as any of the following types of ratios:

(a) Sales ÷ Net Income = Stated Ratio
    $1,000,000.00 ÷ $100,000.00 = 10 (often stated as 10 to 1 or 10:1)

(b) Net Income ÷ Sales = Percentage Ratio
    $100,000.00 ÷ $1,000,000.00 = .10 or 10%

(c) Net Income ÷ Sales = Fractional Ratio
    $100,000.00 ÷ $1,000,000.00 = 1/10

The relationship is expressed as: (a) the ratio of sales to net income is 10 to 1, or (b) net income is 10 percent of sales, or (c) net income is one tenth of sales. All three methods of figuring and expressing ratios are correct and essentially the same. Ten percent expressed as a fraction is 1/10. The method selected is usually determined by the preference of the users of the statements.

Determination of acceptable levels of performance

Analyzing financial data shows relationships among the data analyzed. However, to be useful, a company needs to know what level of performance is acceptable for each analysis made. For example, Schrall Grocery considers a 3 percent rate of return on sales very good. But Schroeder Manufacturing Company considers a 9 percent rate of return on sales unacceptable. The two companies have different acceptable rates of return because they have different financial characteristics. The grocery company has low investment in plant assets and sells its inventory quickly. The manufacturing company has high investment in plant assets and holds its inventory much longer because of the time required to manufacture a finished product. Because of the larger investment required per sales dollar by the manufacturing company, the company must receive a higher rate of return on sales. The management of each company must determine the acceptable levels of performance for each financial analysis the company makes.

Many businesses use two major guides to determine acceptable levels of performance. (a) Trends in results are compared with previous performances of the business. (b) Company results are compared with industry performance standards (published by organizations of industry).

Other frequently used sources of performance guides are: (a) financial and credit reporting companies such as Dun and Bradstreet, (b) the company's planned requirements, and (c) current interest rates.

With the assistance of accounting personnel, the management of each company should determine the acceptable levels of performance for each financial analysis made by the company.

ANALYSIS OF EARNINGS PERFORMANCE

The amount and consistency of earnings are important measures of a business's success. Earnings must be satisfactory for a business to continue to operate. Consequently, managers, owners, and creditors are interested in an analysis of earnings performance. Barcelona Corporation figures four ratios for the three most recent years.

Rate of return on average total assets

A business uses its assets to earn net income. If all assets are used as efficiently as possible, the business should earn the best possible net income. The rate found by dividing net income after federal income tax by average total assets is called the rate of return on average total assets. The rate of return on average total assets shows how well a business is using its assets to earn a profit.

Based on data from the income statement and balance sheet, pages 512 and 513, the assistant accountant figures the 1979 rate of return on average total assets for Barcelona Corporation as:

$$\text{Net Income After Federal Income Tax} \div \text{Average Total Assets} = \text{Rate of Return on Average Total Assets}$$

$$\$73,200.00 \div \frac{\$882,800.00 + \$764,500.00}{2} = 8.9\%$$

Average total assets are the average amount of assets held during a year. The average is figured by dividing by two the sum of total assets owned at the beginning and at the end of the year being analyzed.

A rate of return on average total assets of 8.9 percent means that for each $1.00 in assets the business earned 8.9 cents. The following rates of return on average total assets for Barcelona Corporation were figured from data on the financial statements, pages 512 and 513. (Some data for 1977 are taken from 1976 financial statements that are not illustrated.)

	1979	1978	1977
Net Income After Federal Income Tax..............	$73,200.00	$43,200.00	$43,800.00
Average Total Assets.........	$882,800.00 +764,500.00 ÷ 2	$764,500.00 +517,600.00 ÷ 2	$517,600.00 +499,400.00 ÷ 2
Rate of Return on Average Total Assets..............	8.9%	6.7%	8.6%

Barcelona Corporation determines an acceptable rate of return on total assets by reviewing the company's previous results and comparing rates of return on alternative investment sources. The goal at Barcelona is to earn on average total assets a rate of return at least as high as other investments available. For example if the company can make more by placing extra cash in savings and loan deposits or government bonds, the company is not competing very well for investment money.

Currently investment sources comparable to Barcelona are earning 8.5 percent. Also, the trend in rate of return, except for 1978, is up. Therefore, Barcelona Corporation believes a rate of return on total assets of 8.9 percent is satisfactory.

Rate of return on average owners' equity

Owners are particularly interested in knowing how much net income their investment is earning. Also potential investors may compare the rate of return on owners' equity for several businesses to determine which business to invest in. The rate found by dividing net income after federal income tax by average owners' equity is called the rate of return on average owners' equity.

The assistant accountant makes the following analysis from Barcelona Corporation's 1979 owners' equity statement and income statement on pages 512 and 513.

Net Income After ÷ Federal Income Tax	Average Owners' Equity	=	Rate of Return on Average Owners' Equity
$73,200.00	$\div \dfrac{\$406,000.00 + \$307,800.00}{2} =$		20.5%

The average owners' equity is figured by dividing by two the sum of owners' equity at the beginning and end of the year.

From the data on Barcelona's financial statements, rates of returns on average owners' equity is figured for 1979, 1978, and 1977.

	1979	1978	1977
Net Income After Federal Income Tax..................	$73,200.00	$43,200.00	$43,800.00
Average Owners' Equity ...	$406,000.00 +307,800.00 ÷ 2	$307,800.00 +284,600.00 ÷ 2	$284,600.00 +265,800.00 ÷ 2
Rate of Return on Average Owners' Equity.............	20.5%	14.6%	15.9%

Barcelona Corporation determines an acceptable rate of return on owners' equity by reviewing the company's previous results. The company also compares its rate of return on owners' equity with rates earned by other companies in the same industry. Minimum industry standards for the last three years have been 15 percent.

A review of the analysis shows 1978 did not meet the minimum acceptable rate of return on owners' equity. However, the trend, except for 1978, is up. Based upon the trend and comparison with industry standards, Barcelona Corporation achieved an excellent rate of return on owners' equity in 1979.

Rate of return on net sales

A business that carefully controls costs should earn about the same or higher percentage of net income compared to sales dollar from year to year. However, if costs suddenly change, the rate of return on net sales will change also. The rate found by dividing net income after federal income tax by net sales is called the rate of return on net sales.

The assistant accountant figures the 1979 rate of return on net sales for Barcelona Corporation as:

$$\begin{array}{ccc} \text{Net Income After} \\ \text{Federal Income Tax} \end{array} \div \begin{array}{c} \text{Net} \\ \text{Sales} \end{array} = \begin{array}{c} \text{Rate of Return} \\ \text{on Net Sales} \end{array}$$

$$\$73,200.00 \div \$2,207,000.00 = 3.3\%$$

The following rates of returns on net sales for Barcelona Corporation were figured from data on the income statement, page 512.

	1979	1978	1977
Net Income After Federal Income Tax	$73,200.00	$43,200.00	$43,800.00
Net Sales	$2,207,000.00	$1,682,000.00	$1,294,000.00
Rate of Return on Net Sales	3.3%	2.6%	3.4%

When evaluating an acceptable rate of return on sales, Barcelona Corporation considers what is normal for other similar businesses as well as the company's own past experience.

Businesses similar to Barcelona Corporation have been earning about a 3.1% rate of return on sales for the last three or four years. Based on a comparison with similar businesses, Barcelona had an unsatisfactory rate of return on sales in 1978. The trend in rate of return, although down from 1977, has risen from the 1978 rate of return. This trend should be watched closely for any future declines. When the rate of return on sales declines, the company must increase sales or reduce costs to overcome the lower rate of return on net income.

Earnings per share

The amount of net income earned on one share of common stock during a fiscal period is known as earnings per share. Earnings per share is most important to owners of stock. However, management also frequently uses earnings per share as a measure of success. As earnings per share increases, more people become interested in buying some of the stock. This demand causes the price of stock to go up, and the company finds it easier to issue stock or borrow money. Earnings per share also is described in Chapter 17.

The assistant accountant at Barcelona Corporation figures the 1979 earnings per share as:

$$\frac{\text{Net Income After}}{\text{Federal Income Tax}} \div \frac{\text{Shares of Stock}}{\text{Outstanding}} = \frac{\text{Earnings}}{\text{Per Share}}$$

$$\$73,200.00 \quad \div \quad 2,500 \quad = \quad \$29.28$$

From data on the statements, pages 512 and 513, the assistant accountant at Barcelona Corporation figures the earnings per share as follows:

	1979	1978	1977
Net Income After Federal Income Tax	$73,200.00	$43,200.00	$43,800.00
Shares of Stock Outstanding............	2,500	2,000	2,000
Earnings Per Share........................	$29.28	$21.60	$21.90

A trend of increasing earnings per share is important to stockholders. This trend is one signal to stockholders that the company is continuing to increase the net income earned for each share. Therefore, Barcelona Corporation considers a trend of increasing earnings per share important to the company. Earnings per share decreased slightly in 1978, a bad result. However the trend is up dramatically in 1979, a very encouraging change.

Other analyses of earnings performance

Net income is the result of four major components: sales, cost of merchandise sold, operating expenses, and income tax. A company's management should work toward maintaining or reducing costs and expenses as a percentage of sales from year to year.

A comparison of the component percentages for several years may reveal potential trouble spots. Component percentages from Barcelona Corporation's comparative income statement, page 512, are shown below:

	1979	1978	1977
Net Sales	100.0%	100.0%	100.0%
Cost of Merchandise Sold...........................	53.4%	55.0%	53.6%
Operating Expenses	41.4%	41.6%	41.9%
Federal Income Tax	1.9%	0.8%	1.1%
Net Income...	3.3%	2.6%	3.4%

A review of the component percentages reveals that cost of merchandise sold was about 1.5 percent higher in 1978 than in either 1977 or 1979. Operating expenses have been steadily declining. Therefore, a reasonable conclusion is that cost of merchandise purchased in 1978 rose before an adequate increase was made in selling prices. Management should be alert for this kind of situation to avoid declining revenues resulting in a loss.

ANALYSIS OF SHORT-TERM FINANCIAL STRENGTH

A successful business needs adequate capital. A business gets capital as: (a) money invested by owners, and (b) money borrowed. A business acquires some capital, either invested or borrowed, to be used for long periods of time. Also, some capital is borrowed for short periods of time. A business can invest long-term capital in some assets (such as equipment and buildings) for long periods of time. A business also invests in assets (such as merchandise) that will be converted back to cash in a short period of time. Short-term assets are known as operating assets because they are used for the business's daily activities. Long-term assets are known as plant assets and are used over a long period of time.

Barcelona Corporation uses two common ratios to analyze short-term financial strength: the current ratio and the acid-test ratio.

Current ratio

A ratio that shows the numeric relationship of current assets to current liabilities is called the current ratio. The normal expectation is that current liabilities will be paid from the cash on hand plus cash soon to be received from other current assets.

The current ratio is figured by dividing the total current assets by the total current liabilities. Based on the balance sheet data on page 513, the assistant accountant figured the current ratio of Barcelona Corporation for 1979 as:

Current Assets	÷	Current Liabilities	=	Current Ratio
$482,800.00	÷	$264,800.00	=	1.8:1

The current ratio of 1.8:1 means that Barcelona Corporation owns $1.80 in current assets for each $1.00 needed to pay the current liabilities.

A current ratio becomes more meaningful when compared to current ratios for other years. From the balance sheet data on page 513, the following are current ratios of Barcelona Corporation for the three years:

	1979	1978	1977
Total Current Assets.................	$482,800.00	$464,500.00	$237,600.00
Total Current Liabilities............	264,800.00	340,700.00	113,000.00
Current Ratio	1.8:1	1.4:1	2.1:1

Businesses similar to Barcelona Corporation try to maintain a current ratio of 2:1. If the ratio goes higher than 1:1, a company is holding more current assets than are necessary to pay current liabilities. However, experience in the industry has shown that if a business does not have a current ratio of at least 2:1, the company will have difficulty raising ready cash to pay the current liabilities on time. At the same time, industry experience shows that a current ratio can be too high (3:1 for example). If the current ratio is 3:1, the business has too much capital invested in current assets which are not needed to run the business.

In 1977, Barcelona Corporation had a current ratio of 2.1:1. The last two years have been below the satisfactory level with 1978 dangerously low. The current ratio for 1979 does show signs of recovery. A review of other financial data suggests that part of the reason for the lower current ratio is the company's fast expansion. Frequently, when a business expands too rapidly, money is borrowed to buy more inventory and to pay more employees. The rate of increased costs for merchandise and payroll may be greater than the rate of increase in sales.

Acid-test ratio

Those current assets that are cash or that can be quickly turned into cash are called quick assets. Quick assets include cash, receivables, and marketable securities, but not merchandise or prepaid expenses. Merchandise inventory is a current asset that is expected to be turned into cash. The merchandise first has to be sold and then receivables have to be collected before cash is available. Therefore, merchandise inventory is not considered to be a quick asset. Also prepaid expenses will seldom be converted to cash.

The ratio that shows the numeric relationship of quick assets to current liabilities is called the acid-test ratio. This ratio shows the ability of the business to pay all current liabilities almost immediately if necessary.

Based on the balance sheet data on page 513, the assistant accountant figures the acid-test ratio of Barcelona Corporation for 1979 as:

(Cash + Accounts Receivable) ÷ Total Current Liabilities = Acid-Test Ratio
($103,400.00 + $296,100.00) ÷ $264,800.00 = 1.5:1

The ratio indicates that for each $1.00 needed to pay current liabilities, Barcelona Corporation has available $1.50 in quick assets.

Based on the balance sheet data, page 513, the acid-test ratios for the three years are:

	1979	1978	1977
Total Quick Assets	$399,500.00	$399,100.00	$189,700.00
Total Current Liabilities	264,800.00	340,700.00	113,000.00
Acid-Test Ratio........................	1.5:1	1.2:1	1.7:1

For companies similar to Barcelona Corporation, the desired industry standard for a quick-assets ratio is between 1.5:1 and 1.6:1. Barcelona

Corporation's quick-asset ratios show considerable change in the three previous years. The ratio in 1977 was acceptable. In 1978, the ratio dipped to a dangerously low level but returned to a satisfactory level in 1979.

Using Business Terms

✦ What is the meaning of each of the following?

- comparative financial statements
- trend analysis
- component percentage
- ratio

- rate of return on average total assets
- rate of return on average owners' equity

- rate of return on net sales
- current ratio
- quick assets
- acid-test ratio

Questions for Individual Study

1. Why are financial data of a business analyzed?
2. What are two common objectives for analyzing financial data of a business?
3. What are the primary sources of data needed to analyze how well a business is doing financially?
4. How can trends in financial condition and operating results of a business be determined?
5. How may ratios be expressed?
6. What are four ratios that can be used to analyze earnings performance of a business?
7. What does a rate of return on average total assets show?

8. What can be learned by reviewing a comparison of component percentages of a comparative income statement?
9. What two ratios can be used to analyze short-term financial strength?
10. Would the trend in the following current ratios be considered favorable or unfavorable? Why?

	Current Ratio
1979	.9:1
1978	1.4:1
1977	2.0:1

11. What is the major difference between current assets and quick assets?

Cases for Management Decision

CASE 1 Mr. Fred White considers buying some stock in Bannister Corporation. Before making the purchase, he asks you to take the latest financial statements for the corporation, analyze them, and make a recommendation. From the statements, you figure the ratios shown below.

After reviewing your analysis, do you recommend that Mr. White buy the stock or not? Why? What additional data should you have before making a definite recommendation?

Rate of return on average total assets ..	16%
Rate of return on average owners' equity	16%
Rate of return on net sales	8%
Current ratio	1:1
Acid-test ratio	.5:1

CASE 2 Irwin Corporation has had declining net income the past four years. The company president employs you as a consultant to review the company's operations in an effort to identify the reason for the decline. As part of your analysis, you make a component percentage analysis of the company's four most recent income statements. A part of that analysis is shown below.

	1978	1977	1976	1975
Cost of Merchandise Sold	64.5%	60.8%	57.6%	54.9%
Total Selling Expenses	10.2%	11.9%	13.6%	15.3%

Are there implications from the data on the preceding page? Are any problems or potential problems evident from this analysis?

If so, what are they? What are your suggestions to the company?

PROBLEM 27-1   Preparing comparative financial statements

Problems
for
Applying
Concepts

The following data are taken from the financial records of Ismail Corporation on December 31, 1979 and 1978:

	1979	1978
Cash	$ 40,600.00	$ 34,100.00
Notes Receivable	48,600.00	15,800.00
Interest Receivable	200.00	100.00
Accounts Receivable (Net)	57,000.00	37,100.00
Merchandise Inventory	242,000.00	160,500.00
Other Current Assets	7,400.00	6,600.00
Plant Assets (Net)	129,800.00	116,200.00
Notes Payable	59,400.00	10,600.00
Accounts Payable	113,400.00	48,200.00
Income Tax Payable — Federal	3,600.00	2,400.00
Other Current Liabilities	14,500.00	7,900.00
Mortgage Payable (Long-Term Liability)	66,000.00	52,800.00
Capital Stock	238,000.00	238,000.00
Retained Earnings	30,700.00	10,500.00
Net Sales	633,600.00	422,400.00
Net Purchases	598,800.00	437,900.00
Advertising Expense	12,800.00	9,500.00
Salary Expense — Sales	35,400.00	25,300.00
Other Selling Expenses	3,600.00	3,100.00
Bad Debts Expense	6,100.00	2,700.00
Salary Expense — Administrative	12,000.00	10,600.00
Other Administrative Expenses	7,000.00	5,400.00
Income Tax — Federal	8,168.00	4,980.00
Shares of capital stock outstanding	23,800	23,800

Additional Data:

Merchandise Inventory, January 1, 1978	$ 63,500.00
Total Assets, January 1, 1978	246,400.00
Total Owners' Equity, January 1, 1978	230,600.00

Instructions: □ **1.** Prepare a comparative income statement, similar to the one on page 512, for the two years 1979 and 1978. You need not show percentages; show the amounts only.

□ **2.** Prepare a comparative balance sheet, similar to the one shown on page 513, for the two years 1979 and 1978.

The two comparative financial statements prepared in Problem 27-1 will be needed to complete Problems 27-2, 27-3, and 27-4.

PROBLEM 27-2 Analyzing a comparative income statement

The comparative income statement prepared in Problem 27-1 is needed to complete Problem 27-2.

Instructions: ☐ **1.** Based on the comparative income statement for the years ended December 31, 1979 and 1978, prepared for Ismail Corporation in Problem 27-1, figure for each year the percentage of net sales each of the following is:

(a) Cost of merchandise sold.
(b) Gross profit on operations.
(c) Total operating expenses.
(d) Net income after federal income tax.

☐ **2.** For each of the percentages figured above, indicate if there appears to be a favorable or unfavorable trend from 1978 to 1979. Give reasons for your answers.

PROBLEM 27-3 Analyzing earnings performance from comparative financial statements

The comparative statements prepared in Problem 27-1 are needed to complete Problem 27-3.

Instructions: ☐ **1.** Based on the comparative financial statements for the years ended December 31, 1979 and 1978, for Ismail Corporation prepared in Problem 27-1, figure for each year the following percentages and amount:

(a) Rate of return on average total assets.
(b) Rate of return on average owners' equity.
(c) Rate of return on net sales.
(d) Earnings per share.

☐ **2.** For each of the above, indicate if there appears to be a favorable or an unfavorable trend from 1978 to 1979. Give reasons for your answers.

PROBLEM 27-4 Analyzing short-term financial strength from a comparative balance sheet

The comparative statements prepared in Problem 27-1 are needed to complete Problem 27-4.

Instructions: ☐ **1.** Based on the comparative balance sheet as of December 31, 1979 and 1978, prepared for Ismail Corporation in Problem 27-1, figure for each year the following ratios:

(a) Current ratio.
(b) Acid-test ratio.

☐ **2.** For each ratio figured above, indicate if there appears to be a favorable or an unfavorable trend from 1978 to 1979. Give reasons for your answers.

MASTERY
PROBLEM 27-M

Preparing and analyzing
comparative financial statements

The following data are taken from the financial records of Volinski Corporation
on December 31, 1979 and 1978:

	1979	1978
Cash	$ 11,100.00	$ 22,700.00
Notes Receivable	32,400.00	10,500.00
Interest Receivable	80.00	80.00
Accounts Receivable (Net)	38,000.00	24,720.00
Merchandise Inventory	177,360.00	106,960.00
Other Current Assets	4,960.00	4,400.00
Plant Assets (Net)	86,560.00	79,440.00
Notes Payable	39,600.00	7,040.00
Accounts Payable	75,600.00	32,160.00
Income Tax Payable — Federal	2,400.00	1,600.00
Other Current Liabilities	9,680.00	5,280.00
Mortgage Payable (Long-Term Liability)	44,000.00	35,200.00
Capital Stock	150,000.00	150,000.00
Retained Earnings	29,180.00	17,520.00
Net Sales	422,400.00	281,600.00
Net Purchases	419,200.00	291,920.00
Advertising Expense	8,560.00	6,320.00
Salary Expense — Sales	23,600.00	16,880.00
Other Selling Expenses	2,400.00	2,080.00
Bad Debts Expense	4,080.00	1,760.00
Salary Expense — Administrative	8,000.00	7,040.00
Other Administrative Expenses	4,640.00	3,600.00
Income Tax — Federal	4,460.00	3,330.00
Shares of capital stock outstanding	15,000	15,000

Additional Data:

Merchandise Inventory, January 1, 1978	$ 42,320.00
Total Assets, January 1, 1978	165,000.00
Total Owners' Equity, January 1, 1978	160,600.00

Instructions: □ **1.** Prepare a comparative income statement, similar to the one on
page 512, for the two years 1979 and 1978. You need not show percentages; show
the amounts only.

□ **2.** Prepare a comparative balance sheet, similar to the one shown on page 513,
for the two years 1979 and 1978.

□ **3.** Based on the comparative income statement for the years ended December 31,
1979 and 1978, figure for each year the percentage of net sales each of the following
is:

(a) Cost of merchandise sold.
(b) Gross profit on operations.

(c) Total operating expenses.
(d) Net income after federal income tax.

□ **4.** For each of the percentages figured in Instruction 3, indicate if there appears to be a favorable or unfavorable trend from 1978 to 1979. Give reasons for your answers.

□ **5.** Based on the comparative financial statements for the years ended December 31, 1979 and 1978, figure for each year the following percentages and amount:

    (a) Rate of return on average total assets.
    (b) Rate of return on average owners' equity.
    (c) Rate of return on net sales.
    (d) Earnings per share.

□ **6.** For each of the percentages and amount figured above, indicate if there appears to be a favorable or an unfavorable trend from 1978 to 1979. Give reasons for your answers.

□ **7.** Based on the comparative balance sheet as of December 31, 1979 and 1978, figure for each year the following ratios: (a) current ratio and (b) acid-test ratio.

□ **8.** For each ratio figured above, indicate if there appears to be a favorable or an unfavorable trend from 1978 to 1979. Give reasons for your answers.

BONUS   Preparing and analyzing
PROBLEM 27-B   comparative financial statements

The following data are taken from the financial records of Metcalf Corporation on December 31, 1979 and 1978:

	1979	1978
Cash	$ 19,980.00	$ 45,400.00
Notes Receivable	58,320.00	21,000.00
Interest Receivable	140.00	80.00
Accounts Receivable (Net)	68,400.00	49,440.00
Merchandise Inventory	301,510.00	213,920.00
Other Current Assets	8,930.00	8,800.00
Plant Assets (Net)	155,810.00	158,880.00
Notes Payable	71,280.00	28,160.00
Accounts Payable	136,080.00	106,870.00
Income Tax Payable — Federal	4,320.00	1,800.00
Other Current Liabilities	17,420.00	10,560.00
Mortgage Payable (Long-Term Liability)	79,200.00	70,400.00
Capital Stock	200,000.00	200,000.00
Retained Earnings	104,790.00	79,730.00
Net Sales	760,320.00	563,200.00
Net Purchases	680,550.00	583,840.00
Advertising Expense	17,800.00	12,640.00
Salary Expense — Sales	49,090.00	33,760.00
Other Selling Expenses	4,990.00	4,160.00

	1979	1978
Bad Debts Expense..	$ 8,490.00	$ 3,520.00
Salary Expense — Administrative............................	16,640.00	14,080.00
Other Administrative Expenses................................	9,650.00	7,200.00
Income Tax — Federal	15,636.00	6,822.00
Shares of capital stock outstanding	20,000	20,000

Additional Data:

Merchandise Inventory, January 1, 1978...........................	$ 84,640.00
Total Assets, January, 1, 1978	405,440.00
Total Owners' Equity, January 1, 1978	264,670.00

Instructions: □ **1.** Prepare a comparative income statement, similar to the one on page 512, for the two years 1979 and 1978. You need not show percentages; show the amounts only.

□ **2.** Prepare a comparative balance sheet, similar to the one shown on page 513, for the two years 1979 and 1978.

□ **3.** Based on the comparative income statement for the years ended December 31, 1979 and 1978, figure for each year the percentage of net sales each of the following is:

(a) Cost of merchandise sold.
(b) Gross profit on operations.
(c) Total operating expenses.
(d) Net income after federal income tax.

□ **4.** For each of the percentages figured above, indicate if there appears to be a favorable or unfavorable trend from 1978 to 1979. Give reasons for your answers.

□ **5.** Based on the comparative financial statements for the years ended December 31, 1979 and 1978, figure for each year the following percentages and amount:

(a) Rate of return on average total assets.
(b) Rate of return on average owners' equity.
(c) Rate of return on net sales.
(d) Earnings per share.

□ **6.** For each of the percentages and amount figured above, indicate if there appears to be a favorable or an unfavorable trend from 1978 to 1979. Give reasons for your answers.

□ **7.** Based on the comparative balance sheet as of December 31, 1979 and 1978, figure for each year the following ratios: (a) current ratio and (b) acid-test ratio.

□ **8.** For each ratio figured above, indicate if there appears to be a favorable or an unfavorable trend from 1978 to 1979. Give reasons for your answers.

28 Statement of Changes in Financial Position

Financial progress and strength of a business can be reviewed by analyzing comparative balance sheets, income statements, and statements of stockholders' equity. An income statement shows how much net income a business has earned during a fiscal period. A statement of stockholders' equity shows how much the stockholders' equity of a business has changed from the beginning to the end of a fiscal period. A balance sheet shows the amount of a business's assets, liabilities, and stockholders' equity at the end of a fiscal period. However, these statements do not show what caused the changes in the financial position of a business. For this reason, many businesses provide additional analyses by preparing statements of changes in financial position.

A financial statement showing the sources, the uses, and the resulting increase or decrease in funds is called a statement of changes in financial position. This statement is also known as a statement of source and application of funds or a statement of resources provided and applied. Other names for the statement are a statement of changes in working capital and a funds statement.

WORKING CAPITAL FUNDS

In accounting, the term "funds" has a number of meanings. In previous chapters the term was used in such expressions as "petty cash funds" and "bond sinking funds." The assistant accountant for Barcelona Corporation prepares a statement of changes in financial position to show changes in "working capital funds." The excess of a business's total current assets over its total current liabilities is called the working capital.

Current assets are cash and those assets that are expected to be converted into cash or to be used up during a business operating cycle of one year. Some of the common current assets in addition to cash are notes and accounts receivable, inventories of merchandise and manufacturing materials, and prepaid expenses.

Current liabilities are those obligations that are expected to be paid out of current assets during the next twelve months. Some common current liabilities are notes and accounts payable, salaries payable, taxes payable, and the current portion of long-term bonds or mortgages payable.

Barcelona Corporation's statement of changes in financial position identifies those transactions that "brought in" and those transactions that "used up" the company's working capital.

Sources of working capital funds

Funds flow into and out of a company because of the many financial transactions that occur every day. For example, sales are made, merchandise and supplies are purchased, and expenses are paid. All of these transactions affect the level of the working capital funds existing within a business.

Transactions that increase working capital are called sources of working capital. The most common sources of working capital are (a) funds provided from the normal operations of a business and (b) funds provided from sources other than normal operations.

Funds from normal operations of a business. The net income figure shown on the income statement of a business is a source of working capital funds. However, because the net income figure does not show all funds provided by operations, some adjustments ordinarily must be made to the net income. The most common adjustment is for depreciation. On the income statement of a business, all costs are deducted from sales to obtain net income. These costs include cost of merchandise sold, selling expenses, administrative expenses, and other expenses. All of these costs, except depreciation, use funds and therefore reduce the funds from sales. While annual depreciation is deducted as an expense on the income statement, this expense does not use funds during the current year.

Plant assets are purchased at various times in previous periods. The costs of the plant assets are distributed over the entire period of time they are used. The plant assets are depreciated annually over their estimated life. The funds are used at the time the plant assets are bought, not during the year when depreciation is recorded. Depreciation is deducted as an expense on the income statement in determining net income. Depreciation does not use funds in the current year. Therefore, the amount of depreciation must be added back to the net income figure to obtain the total amount of funds provided from net income.

Funds from sources other than normal operations. Other sources of working capital funds are provided by transactions other than normal operations such as sales and operating expense transactions. These other sources of funds are classified in terms of their effects on noncurrent balance sheet accounts. All balance sheet accounts not classified as current are called noncurrent accounts. Sources of fund transactions that affect noncurrent accounts are:

1. Transactions that *decrease* noncurrent assets (all assets other than current assets). Examples are sale of plant assets or sale of long-term investments (stocks and bonds) held by the business.
2. Transactions that *increase* noncurrent liabilities (all liabilities other than current liabilities). Examples are the issuance of bonds payable and long-term notes payable or mortgages payable.
3. Transactions that *increase* capital. Examples are the sale of additional capital stock of a corporation or an additional investment by owners of a sole proprietorship or a partnership.

Uses of working capital funds

A business must continually bring in funds. A prosperous business also must use funds effectively. Both owners and management are interested in seeing how funds have been used during each fiscal period.

Transactions that decrease working capital are called uses of working capital. The most common uses of working capital by transactions other than normal operations are classified in terms of their effects on noncurrent accounts. These are:

1. Transactions that *increase* noncurrent assets. Examples are purchases of plant assets and purchases of long-term investments such as stocks and bonds to be held for more than one year.
2. Transactions that *decrease* noncurrent liabilities. Examples are the payment of mortgages and long-term notes payable or the retirement of bonds payable.
3. Transactions that *decrease* capital. Examples are declaration of cash dividends, purchase of treasury stock, and withdrawals of invested capital by owners of a sole proprietorship or a partnership.

STATEMENT OF CHANGES IN FINANCIAL POSITION

A statement of changes in financial position shows what transactions during a fiscal period caused the changes in working capital. To prepare this statement, the balances of the balance sheet accounts are needed for both the beginning and the end of the fiscal period. The most readily available source of these account balances is the comparative balance sheet for the current period and the previous period. From the comparative balance sheet, a schedule of changes in working capital is prepared to show the net change in working capital. From this schedule, the comparative balance sheet, and other data found in the accounting records, a statement of changes in financial position is prepared.

Preparing a schedule of changes in working capital

A report showing increases and decreases in current assets, current liabilities, and working capital is called a schedule of changes in working capital.

The comparative balance sheet of Barcelona Corporation as of December 31, 1979, is shown on page 513 of Chapter 27. From this comparative balance sheet, the assistant accountant prepares the schedule of changes in working capital shown below.

BARCELONA CORPORATION
Schedule of Changes in Working Capital
For Year Ended December 31, 1979

	Balances December 31		Increase/ Decrease
	1979	1978	
Current Assets:			
Cash	$103,400.00	$ 51,800.00	+$51,600.00
Accounts Receivable (Net)	296,100.00	347,300.00	- 51,200.00
Merchandise Inventory	70,600.00	55,200.00	+ 15,400.00
Other Current Assets	12,700.00	10,200.00	+ 2,500.00
Total Current Assets	$482,800.00	$464,500.00	+$18,300.00
Current Liabilities:			
Notes Payable	$ 80,000.00	$119,700.00	-$39,700.00
Interest Payable	6,300.00	9,600.00	- 3,300.00
Accounts Payable	170,100.00	206,000.00	- 35,900.00
Income Tax Payable - Federal . . .	5,600.00	1,100.00	+ 4,500.00
Other Current Liabilities	2,800.00	4,300.00	- 1,500.00
Total Current Liabilities	$264,800.00	$340,700.00	-$75,900.00
Working Capital	$218,000.00	$123,800.00	+$94,200.00

Schedule of changes in working capital

The balances of the accounts at the beginning and the end of the fiscal period are given in the first two columns. (The balances at the end of 1978 are also the balances at the beginning of 1979.) Either the increase or the decrease in each item is listed in the third column of the schedule. The total current liabilities are deducted from the total current assets to obtain the amount of working capital for the year. The difference between the working capital at the beginning of the year and the working capital at the end of the year is the net change in working capital. In the illustration above, the working capital on December 31, 1979, is $218,000.00; the working capital on December 31, 1978, is $123,800.00. The net change in working capital is therefore an increase of $94,200.00 ($218,000.00 − $123,800.00). This net change is the final amount shown in the Increase/Decrease column.

Identifying sources and uses of working capital

The schedule of changes in working capital, page 531, shows a net increase in working capital for Barcelona Corporation of $94,200.00. However, the schedule does not show what caused this change in working capital. To identify the transactions that provided and used working capital, changes in the noncurrent accounts must be analyzed.

Barcelona Corporation's comparative balance sheet for the years ended December 31, 1979 and 1978, is shown below. Working capital and noncurrent accounts are shown.

BARCELONA CORPORATION
Comparative Balance Sheet with Working Capital
December 31, 1979 and 1978

| | Balances December 31 | | | |
	1979		1978	
Working Capital		$218,000.00		$123,800.00
Noncurrent Assets:				
Plant and Equipment	$510,000.00		$380,000.00	
Less Accum. Depreciation . .	110,000.00	400,000.00	80,000.00	300,000.00
Total Working Capital and				
Noncurrent Assets		$618,000.00		$423,800.00
Noncurrent Liabilities and				
Stockholders' Equity:				
Mortgage Payable		$212,000.00		$116,000.00
Capital Stock ($10 Par) . .		250,000.00		200,000.00
Retained Earnings		156,000.00		107,800.00
Total Noncurrent Liabilities				
and Stockholders' Equity .		$618,000.00		$423,800.00

Comparative balance sheet with working capital

The working capital balances are obtained from the schedule of changes in working capital, page 531. The noncurrent account balances are obtained from the comparative balance sheet, page 513.

The use of a work sheet is helpful in identifying the transactions that affected working capital. The information necessary to prepare a statement of changes in financial position can then be taken from the completed work sheet. The steps in this procedure are described below.

☐ 1 Prepare a work sheet for analyzing changes in financial position as shown on page 533. The work sheet has four amount columns: Beginning Account Balances, Debit Transactions for 1979, Credit Transactions for 1979, and Ending Account Balances. The work sheet is separated into two major parts: (a) the top part is for balance sheet accounts, and (b) the lower part is for changes in working capital. Each of these parts is separated into two parts. Balance sheet accounts are separated into debit balance and credit balance accounts. Changes in working capital is separated into a section for sources of working capital and a section for uses of working capital.

BARCELONA CORPORATION
Work Sheet for Analyzing Changes in Financial Position
For Year Ended December 31, 1979

Balance Sheet Accounts	Beginning Account Balances	Analysis of Transactions for 1979		Ending Account Balances
		Debit	Credit	
Changes in Working Capital				
Sources of Working Capital:				
Uses of Working Capital:				

Work sheet format for analyzing
changes in financial position

☐ **2** Enter in the Beginning Account Balances column the balances at the beginning of the fiscal period. (Beginning balances are the same as the ending balances of the preceding period.) Record the beginning balances by listing asset accounts as debits and liability and equity accounts as credits.

The working capital balance is obtained from the schedule of changes in working capital. The noncurrent balances are obtained from the comparative balance sheet.

The beginning balances for Barcelona Corporation are entered as shown below.

BARCELONA CORPORATION
Work Sheet for Analyzing Changes in Financial Position
For Year Ended December 31, 1979

Balance Sheet Accounts	Beginning Account Balances	Analysis of Transactions for 1979		Ending Account Balances
		Debit	Credit	
Debits				
Working Capital	123,800.00			
Plant and Equipment	380,000.00			
Totals	503,800.00			
Credits				
Accumulated Depreciation . . .	80,000.00			
Mortgage Payable	116,000.00			
Capital Stock, $10 Par	200,000.00			
Retained Earnings	107,800.00			
Totals	503,800.00			

Partial work sheet for analyzing changes in financial
position showing beginning account balances

□ **3** Enter in the Ending Account Balances column the account balances
at the end of the fiscal period. The working capital balance is obtained from the schedule of changes in working capital. The noncurrent balances are obtained from the comparative balance sheet.

The ending balances for Barcelona Corporation are entered as
shown below.

BARCELONA CORPORATION
Work Sheet for Analyzing Changes in Financial Position
For Year Ended December 31, 1979

Balance Sheet Accounts	Beginning Account Balances	Analysis of Transactions for 1979		Ending Account Balances
		Debit	Credit	
Debits				
Working Capital	123,800.00			218,000.00
Plant and Equipment	380,000.00			510,000.00
Totals	503,800.00			728,000.00
Credits				
Accumulated Depreciation . . .	80,000.00			110,000.00
Mortgage Payable	116,000.00			212,000.00
Capital Stock, $10 Par	200,000.00			250,000.00
Retained Earnings	107,800.00			156,000.00
Totals	503,800.00			728,000.00

Partial work sheet for analyzing changes in financial
position showing beginning and ending account balances

After these entries have been made, the difference between the
beginning and ending balances in each account represents the
changes that have occurred in that account during the fiscal period.

□ **4** Identify the activities that occurred during the year that affected
working capital. This identification may be made by examining the
comparative balance sheet, the comparative income statement, the
general ledger accounts, and any other necessary records. The assistant accountant for Barcelona Corporation identified the following
transactions during 1979 that affected working capital:

(a) Net income for the year, $73,200.00.
(b) Depreciation on plant assets for the year, $30,000.00.
(c) Plant assets bought, $130,000.00.
(d) Proceeds from addition to mortgage payable, $100,000.00.
(e) Payments on mortgage payable during the year, $4,000.00.
(f) Dividends on capital stock declared and paid to stockholders,
$25,000.00.
(g) Sale of additional capital stock, $50,000.00.

□ **5** Analyze each of the transactions in Step 4 to determine the effect on
working capital. Each transaction is analyzed by making an adjusting entry on the work sheet similar to the original transaction that
caused the change in the account.

Transactions that increase working capital are sources of working capital. Transactions that decrease working capital are uses of working capital. Several lines on the work sheet should be allowed below the "sources" section and the "uses" section. As each transaction is analyzed, an adjusting entry is made in the Analysis of Transactions columns of the work sheet as shown on page 536. The adjusting entry consists of an entry to the affected balance sheet account and an entry, describing the change, to the changes in working capital section. The assistant accountant analyzes the entries affecting working capital as follows:

(a) Net income for the year, $73,200.00: increases Retained Earnings, a capital account, and increases Working Capital, an asset account. The increase in Working Capital shows net income is a source of working capital.

Thus in the changes in working capital section, Net Income from Operations is debited. In the balance sheet account section, Retained Earnings is credited.

Source of Working Capital:
Net Income from Operations 73,200.00
    Retained Earnings 73,200.00

(b) Depreciation for the year, $30,000.00: was deducted as an expense in determining net income but did not use working capital. Therefore the depreciation expense for the year must be added back to net income to show the correct amount net income affects working capital.

Thus in the changes in working capital section, Depreciation Expense is debited. In the balance sheet section, Accumulated Depreciation is credited as the account was credited when the original entry was made.

Source of Working Capital (adjustment to net income):
Depreciation Expense................................. 30,000.00
    Accumulated Depreciation 30,000.00

(c) Plant and equipment bought, $130,000.00: uses working capital to acquire plant assets, a noncurrent asset.

Thus in the balance sheet account section, Plant and Equipment is debited. In the changes in working capital section, Bought New Equipment is credited.

Use of Working Capital:
Plant and Equipment 130,000.00
    Bought New Equipment 130,000.00

(d) Proceeds from addition to mortgage payable, $100,000.00: increases Mortgage Payable, a noncurrent liability, and therefore is a source of working capital.

Thus, in the changes in working capital section, Borrowed on Mortgage Payable is debited. In the balance sheet section, Mortgage Payable is credited.

Source of Working Capital:

Borrowed on Mortgage Payable.................	100,000.00	
Mortgage Payable		100,000.00

BARCELONA CORPORATION
Work Sheet for Analyzing Changes in Financial Position
For Year Ended December 31, 1979

Balance Sheet Accounts	Beginning Account Balances	Analysis of Transactions for 1979		Ending Account Balances
		Debit	Credit	
Debits				
Working Capital	123,800.00	(h) 94,200.00		218,000.00
Plant and Equipment	380,000.00	(c) 130,000.00		510,000.00
Totals	503,800.00			728,000.00
Credits				
Accumulated Depreciation . . .	80,000.00		(b) 30,000.00	110,000.00
Mortgage Payable	116,000.00	(e) 4,000.00	(d) 100,000.00	212,000.00
Capital Stock, $10 Par	200,000.00		(g) 50,000.00	250,000.00
Retained Earnings	107,800.00	(f) 25,000.00	(a) 73,200.00	156,000.00
Totals	503,800.00	253,200.00	253,200.00	728,000.00
Changes in Working Capital				
Sources of Working Capital:				
Net Income from Operations		(a) 73,200.00		
Depreciation Expense		(b) 30,000.00		
Borrowed on Mortgage Payable		(d) 100,000.00		
Issued 5,000 Shares Capital Stock . . .		(g) 50,000.00		
Uses of Working Capital:				
Bought New Equipment			(c) 130,000.00	
Paid on Mortgage Payable			(e) 4,000.00	
Paid Cash Dividend			(f) 25,000.00	
		253,200.00	159,000.00	
Increase in Working Capital in 1979 . . .			(h) 94,200.00	
Totals		253,200.00	253,200.00	

Completed work sheet for analyzing
changes in financial position

(e) Payments on mortgage payable, $4,000.00: uses working capital to pay off a mortgage payable, a noncurrent liability. Thus in the balance sheet section, Mortgage Payable is debited. In the changes in working capital section, Paid on Mortgage Payable is credited.

Use of Working Capital:

Mortgage Payable...	4,000.00	
Paid on Mortgage Payable.............................		4,000.00

(f) Dividends declared and paid, $25,000.00: decreases Retained Earnings, a capital account, and uses working capital to pay a dividend. Thus in the balance sheet section, Retained Earnings is debited. In the changes in working capital section, Paid Cash Dividend is credited.

Use of Working Capital:
Retained Earnings	25,000.00	
Paid Cash Dividend		25,000.00

(g) Additional capital stock sold, $50,000.00: increases Capital Stock, a capital account, and increases working capital from cash received for the capital stock. Thus in the changes in working capital section, Issued 5,000 Shares Capital Stock is debited. In the balance sheet section, Capital Stock is credited.

Source of Working Capital:
Issued 5,000 Shares Capital Stock	50,000.00	
Capital Stock		50,000.00

The transactions entered in the changes in working capital section of the work sheet show all the information necessary to prepare the statement of changes in financial position. If the total sources of working capital exceed the total uses, working capital has increased. If the total uses of working capital exceed the total sources, working capital has decreased.

(h) Change in working capital recorded, $94,200.00: After all known transactions that affected working capital have been entered in the Analysis columns, an accuracy check can be made. Check each balance sheet account to see if the beginning account balance plus or minus the adjustments equals the ending account balance. For example, a debit balance account, Plant and Equipment, on the work sheet, page 536, is checked as follows:

Beginning account balance	$380,000.00
Add debit adjustment	130,000.00
Equals ending account balance	$510,000.00

The ending account balance figured above is the same as the amount in the Ending Account Balance column of the work sheet. Therefore the accuracy of the plant and equipment account is proved.

A credit balance account, Mortgage Payable, on the work sheet, page 536, is checked as follows:

Beginning account balance	$116,000.00
Subtract debit adjustment	(4,000.00)
Add credit adjustment	100,000.00
Equals ending account balance	$212,000.00

The ending account balance is the same as the amount in the Ending Account Balance column of the work sheet. Therefore the accuracy of the mortgage payable account is proved.

After all non-working capital accounts have been proved, an adjusting entry is made for the change in working capital. The amount of increase, $94,200.00, shown in the schedule of changes in working capital, page 531, is debited to the balance sheet account Working Capital. In the changes in working capital section, Increase in Working Capital is credited, $94,200.00. If working capital decreases, the amount of change is credited to Working Capital and debited to Decrease in Working Capital.

After the adjustment to working capital has been entered and the accuracy proved, information is available to prepare the statement of changes in financial position.

Change in Working Capital:
Working Capital...	94,200.00	
Increase in Working Capital		94,200.00

Preparing a statement of changes in financial position

There are many possible variations in the form of the statement of changes in financial position. Ordinarily, however, the first section of the statement lists the sources of working capital, with net income from operations as the first item. The second section of the statement lists the uses of working capital. The difference between the total of the source section and the total of the use section is the increase or decrease in working capital.

The changes in working capital section of the work sheet provides the information to prepare the statement of changes in financial position. From the work sheet, page 536, the assistant accountant at Barcelona Corporation prepared the statement shown on page 539.

The increase in working capital for Barcelona Corporation for the year ended December 31, 1979, as shown on the statement of changes in financial position, page 539, is $94,200.00. The increase in working capital as shown on the schedule of changes in working capital, page 531, is also $94,200.00. Since the two amounts agree, the work is considered to be proved. The two statements together provide a complete picture of the inflow and the outflow of working capital for the fiscal period.

Using Business Terms

✦ What is the meaning of each of the following?

- statement of changes in financial position
- working capital

- sources of working capital
- noncurrent accounts

- uses of working capital
- schedule of changes in working capital

```
                        BARCELONA CORPORATION
                 Statement of Changes in Financial Position
                      For Year Ended December 31, 1979


   Sources of Working Capital:
     Net Income from Operations  . . . . . . . .        $ 73,200.00
     Add Expenses Not Using Working Capital:
       Depreciation Expense  . . . . . . . . .            30,000.00
     Working Capital Provided by Operations  . .        $103,200.00
     Borrowed on Mortgage Payable  . . . . . .           100,000.00
     Issued 5,000 Shares Capital Stock . . . . .          50,000.00
     Total Sources of Working Capital  . . . . .        $253,200.00

   Uses of Working Capital:
     Bought New Equipment  . . . . . . . . . .  $130,000.00
     Paid on Mortgage Payable  . . . . . . . . .   4,000.00
     Paid Cash Dividend  . . . . . . . . . . . .  25,000.00
     Total Uses of Working Capital . . . . . .                      159,000.00

   Increase in Working Capital in 1979 . . . . .                    $ 94,200.00
```

Statement of changes in financial position

1. What information does a statement of changes in financial position show that is not shown on a balance sheet or an income statement?
2. Barcelona Corporation prepares a statement of changes in financial position to show changes in what kind of funds?
3. What are the most common sources of working capital?
4. To be successful, how should a business manage its working capital funds?
5. When the net income figure is used as a source of working capital funds, why must depreciation be added back to the net income figure?
6. What are the most common uses of working capital?
7. What data are shown on a schedule of changes in working capital?
8. What are the steps in identifying sources and uses of working capital to obtain information for preparing the statement of changes in financial position?
9. After the analyzed working capital transactions have been entered in the changes in working capital section of the work sheet, (a) what do the debit entries represent, and (b) what do the credit entries represent?
10. What data are shown on a statement of changes in financial position?

CASE 1 On January 1, 1979, Southern Corporation and Universal Corporation had exactly the same working capital position as well as the same current asset and liability account balances. At the end of the year, both corporations had increased their working capital $10,000.00. However, the condition of individual current account balances of the two corporations was no longer similar as shown on the schedules of changes in working capital, page 540.

Both corporations increased their working capital from $50,000.00 to $60,000.00 during the fiscal period. From the information given in the two schedules, do you consider the current financial progress of each corporation to be equally strong? Explain your answer.

SOUTHERN CORPORATION
Schedule of Changes in Working Capital
For Year Ended December 31, 1979

	Balances on December 31		Increase/
	1979	1978	Decrease
Current Assets:			
Cash	$ 30,000.00	$ 20,000.00	+10,000.00
Accounts Receivable (Net)	30,000.00	40,000.00	−10,000.00
Merchandise Inventory	40,000.00	40,000.00	No change
Total Current Assets	$100,000.00	$100,000.00	No change
Current Liabilities	$ 40,000.00	$ 50,000.00	−10,000.00
Working Capital	$ 60,000.00	$ 50,000.00	+10,000.00

UNIVERSAL CORPORATION
Schedule of Changes in Working Capital
For Year Ended December 31, 1979

	Balances on December 31		Increase/
	1979	1978	Decrease
Current Assets:			
Cash	$ 10,000.00	$ 20,000.00	−10,000.00
Accounts Receivable (Net)	70,000.00	40,000.00	+30,000.00
Merchandise Inventory	40,000.00	40,000.00	No change
Total Current Assets	$120,000.00	$100,000.00	+20,000.00
Current Liabilities	$ 60,000.00	$ 50,000.00	+10,000.00
Working Capital	$ 60,000.00	$ 50,000.00	+10,000.00

CASE 2 The statement of changes in financial position based on working capital prepared for Wegman Company at the end of the fiscal year on December 31, 1979, is shown below.

WEGMAN COMPANY
Statement of Changes in Financial Position
For Year Ended December 31, 1979

Sources of Working Capital:		
Proceeds from Sale of Land	$ 8,000	
Proceeds from Securing Mortgage Payable	10,000	
Additional Investment in Business by Owner	10,000	
Total Working Capital Provided in 1979		$28,000
Uses of Working Capital:		
Net Loss from Operations	$18,000	
Payment of Long-Term Note Payable	8,000	
Total Working Capital Applied in 1979		26,000
Increase in Working Capital		$ 2,000

(1) From a review of the statement of changes in financial position, what can you determine about the financial condition of the Wegman Company? Give reasons for your answer.

(2) If the company continues the present trend for the next five years, what effect will this have on the company's (a) employees, (b) owner, (c) creditors, and (d) customers?

CASE 3 Judy Robertson, the manager of Fenner Corporation, has been examining the financial statements prepared for the company at the end of the current fiscal year. She has asked you to explain the reasons for the situations in the following items:

(1) The beginning and ending balances of the plant and equipment account are both $100,000.00. Yet the statement of changes in financial position shows

"Bought Equipment, $10,000.00," under the caption Uses of Working Capital.

(2) The income statement reports a net loss of $3,000.00 from normal operations for the current year. The statement of changes in financial position, however, reports operations during the year as a $2,000.00 source of working capital.

Give reasons for these situations.

PROBLEM 28-1 Preparing a statement of changes in financial position

The comparative balance sheet for Goforth Corporation for the years ended December 31, 1979 and 1978, is given on page 542.

Additional data needed are:

(a) Net income for the year, $16,000.00.
(b) Depreciation on plant assets for the year, $16,000.00.
(c) Plant assets were bought for $24,000.00.
(d) Cash received from addition to mortgage payable, $32,000.00.
(e) Payments made on mortgage during year, $16,000.00.
(f) Dividends declared and paid, $12,800.00.
(g) Additional capital stock issued for $32,000.00.

Instructions: □ **1.** Prepare a schedule of changes in working capital similar to the one shown on page 531.

□ **2.** Prepare a work sheet for analyzing changes in financial position. Enter in the work sheet the beginning balances and the ending balances of the working capital and noncurrent accounts.

□ **3.** Analyze the transactions that affected working capital. Prepare an adjusting entry in the work sheet for each transaction analyzed to show its effect on working capital. Complete the work sheet.

□ **4.** Prepare a statement of changes in financial position similar to the one shown on page 539.

GOFORTH CORPORATION
Comparative Balance Sheet
December 31, 1979 and 1978

	1979		1978	
Assets				
Current Assets:				
Cash..	$ 33,600.00		$ 38,400.00	
Accounts Receivable (Net).............	112,000.00		96,000.00	
Merchandise Inventory.................	208,000.00		192,000.00	
Other Current Assets	6,400.00		9,600.00	
Total Current Assets....................		$360,000.00		$336,000.00
Noncurrent Assets:				
Plant Assets..............................	$216,000.00		$192,000.00	
Less Accum. Depr. — Plant Assets.	96,000.00		80,000.00	
Total Noncurrent Assets		120,000.00		112,000.00
Total Assets		$480,000.00		$448,000.00
Liabilities				
Current Liabilities:				
Accounts Payable	$ 88,000.00		$101,000.00	
Income Tax Payable — Federal	12,800.00		16,000.00	
Other Current Liabilities	8,000.00		11,000.00	
Total Current Liabilities...............		$108,800.00		$128,000.00
Long-Term Liability:				
Mortgage Payable.......................		128,000.00		112,000.00
Total Liabilities.............................		$236,800.00		$240,000.00
Stockholders' Equity				
Capital Stock................................	$224,000.00		$192,000.00	
Retained Earnings	19,200.00		16,000.00	
Total Stockholders' Equity...............		243,200.00		208,000.00
Total Liab. and Stockholders' Equity..		$480,000.00		$448,000.00

**MASTERY
PROBLEM 28-M** Preparing a schedule of changes
in working capital

The comparative balance sheet for Burlison Corporation for the years ended December 31, 1979 and 1978, is shown on page 543.

Additional data needed are:
  (a) Net income for the year, $9,600.00.
  (b) Depreciation on plant assets for the year, $13,200.00.
  (c) Plant assets were bought for $24,000.00.
  (d) Fully depreciated plant asset originally costing $5,000.00 was disposed of. No cash was received. (The cost and amount of accumulated depreciation must appear on the partial work sheet for balancing purposes.)
  (e) Cash received from addition to mortgage payable, $36,000.00.
  (f) Payments made on the mortgage during year, $12,000.00.
  (g) Dividends declared and paid, $6,000.00.
  (h) Additional capital stock issued for $12,000.00.

BURLISON CORPORATION
Comparative Balance Sheet
December 31, 1979 and 1978

	1979		1978	
Assets				
Current Assets:				
Cash...	$ 18,000.00		$ 24,000.00	
Accounts Receivable (Net).............	30,000.00		48,000.00	
Merchandise Inventory.................	150,000.00		120,000.00	
Other Current Assets	3,600.00		2,400.00	
Total Current Assets.....................		$201,600.00		$194,400.00
Noncurrent Assets:				
Plant Assets...............................	$163,000.00		$144,000.00	
Less Accum. Depr. — Plant Assets .	16,600.00		8,400.00	
Total Noncurrent Assets		146,400.00		135,600.00
Total Assets.................................		$348,000.00		$330,000.00
Liabilities				
Current Liabilities:				
Accounts Payable	$ 30,000.00		$ 52,800.00	
Income Tax Payable — Federal.......	6,000.00		3,600.00	
Other Current Liabilities	6,000.00		7,200.00	
Total Current Liabilities...............		$ 42,000.00		$ 63,600.00
Long-Term Liability:				
Mortgage Payable		96,000.00		72,000.00
Total Liabilities		$138,000.00		$135,600.00
Stockholders' Equity				
Capital Stock...............................	$192,000.00		$180,000.00	
Retained Earnings	18,000.00		14,400.00	
Total Stockholders' Equity...............		210,000.00		194,400.00
Total Liab. and Stockholders' Equity..		$348,000.00		$330,000.00

Instructions: Prepare a schedule of changes in working capital similar to the one shown on page 531.

BONUS PROBLEM 28-B Preparing a statement of changes in financial position

Prepare a statement of changes in financial position for the year ended December 31, 1979, using the comparative balance sheet given in Mastery Problem 28-M.

Instructions: □ **1.** Prepare a work sheet for analyzing changes in financial position. Enter in the work sheet the beginning balances and the ending balances of the working capital and noncurrent accounts.

□ **2.** Analyze the transactions that affected working capital. Prepare an adjusting entry in the work sheet for each transaction analyzed to show its effect on working capital. Complete the work sheet.

□ **3.** Prepare a statement of changes in financial position similar to the one shown on page 539.

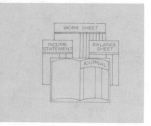

Review Problems

Note: No review problems for Chapter 1 are provided.

**REVIEW
PROBLEM 2-R 1**  Journalizing transactions

Marilyn Martinez owns and operates MM Gifts, a small, self-service gift and card store. The transactions listed below were completed in May of the current year.

Instructions: □ **1.** Record the transactions in a sales journal (page 7), purchases journal (page 8), cash receipts journal (page 6), cash payments journal (page 5), and general journal (page 3) like the ones shown in Chapter 2. MM Gifts uses a sales tax rate of 5%.

The listing of source documents is abbreviated as follows: check, Ck; purchase invoice, P; sales invoice, S; receipt, R; cash register tape, T; debit memorandum, DM; credit memorandum, CM.

May 1. Record the memorandum entry for beginning cash, $3,375.92.
    1. Paid May rent, $400.00. Ck52.
    2. Paid for cash purchase of merchandise, $69.30. Ck53.
    3. Paid cash for supplies, $25.20. Ck54.
    6. Purchased merchandise on account from Jason Miller, $522.00. P23.
    7. Sold merchandise on account to Billy Jackson, $37.80 plus sales tax of $1.89. S146.
    9. Paid to Marilyn Martinez for cash withdrawal, $320.00. Ck55.
   10. Returned merchandise to Charles Beckwith for credit, $19.00. DM6.
   14. Received on account from Delbert Monwith, $27.19. R66.
   15. Sold merchandise on account to Ella Mansing, $272.79 plus sales tax of $13.64. S147.
   16. Paid on account to Jason Miller, $522.00. Ck56.
   17. Received for cash sales, May 1–17, $3,866.31 plus sales tax of $193.32. T17.

Proving the journals and cash: Pencil foot the following journals: cash receipts, cash payments, general journal. Prove equality of debits and credits in these three journals. Prove cash. The cash balance is $6,126.24.

May 21. Granted credit to Ella Mansing for merchandise returned, $37.80 plus sales tax of $1.89. CM10.
　23. Purchased merchandise on account from Nancy Cheng, $488.25. P24.
　24. Sold merchandise on account to Georgia Watkins, $151.20 plus sales tax of $7.56. S148.
　28. Returned merchandise to Nancy Cheng for credit, $34.65. DM7.
　30. Paid for miscellaneous expenses, $41.08. Ck57.
　31. Paid for advertising expenses, $94.50. Ck58.
　31. Received on account from Grace Levi, $21.50. R67.
　31. Paid a cash refund to a cash customer for merchandise returned, $10.00 plus sales tax of $0.50. Ck59.
　31. Purchased merchandise on account from Jason Miller, $521.00. P25.
　31. Received for cash sales, May 19–31, $3,603.60 plus sales tax of $180.18. T31.

Proving journals and cash: Pencil foot the following journals: cash receipts, cash payments, general journal. Prove equality of debits and credits in these three journals. Prove cash. The cash balance is $9,785.44.

Instructions: ☐ **2.** Total and rule all of the journals.

REVIEW PROBLEM 3-R 1 End-of-fiscal-period work

On December 31 of the current year, the account balances for Dimitri's Store are as shown below and on page 546. December 31 is the end of a yearly fiscal period.

Cash	$10,657.92
Accounts Receivable	17,229.66
Allowance for Uncollectible Accounts	344.61
Notes Receivable	600.00
Merchandise Inventory	3,361.48
Supplies	1,113.00
Prepaid Insurance	966.00
Interest Receivable	——
Equipment	7,560.00
Accumulated Depreciation — Equipment	1,512.00
Accounts Payable	8,761.20
Notes Payable	500.00
Sales Tax Payable	386.09
Interest Payable	——
Dimitri Polski, Capital	26,384.16
Dimitri Polski, Drawing	6,000.00
Income Summary	——

Sales	$73,595.35
Sales Returns and Allowances	798.00
Purchases	57,584.10
Purchases Returns and Allowances	661.50
Bad Debts Expense	——
Depreciation Expense — Equipment	——
Insurance Expense	——
Miscellaneous Expense	891.27
Rent Expense	5,400.00
Supplies Expense	——
Interest Income	17.75
Interest Expense	1.23

Additional data:

Additional bad debts expense	$ 257.25
Merchandise inventory, December 31	3,632.06
Supplies inventory, December 31	335.90
Value of insurance policies, December 31	230.00
Depreciation on equipment for the year	378.00
Interest on notes receivable earned but not yet received	2.76
Interest on notes payable owed but not yet paid	2.88

Instructions: □ **1.** Prepare a trial balance in the Trial Balance columns of a work sheet. Be sure to list all accounts with or without a balance.

□ **2.** Complete the work sheet.

□ **3.** Prepare an income statement.

□ **4.** Prepare a capital statement. The balance of the capital account on January 1 of the current year was $16,384.16. An additional investment of $10,000.00 was made during the year.

□ **5.** Prepare a balance sheet.

□ **6.** On page 14 of a general journal like the one shown on page 55, record the adjusting entries.

□ **7.** Record the closing entries.

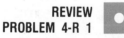

REVIEW PROBLEM 4-R 1 Forming a partnership; assets and liabilities invested by one partner, and only cash invested by another partner

On June 1 of the current year, Oscar Lummas and Sandra Bach form a partnership. The partnership takes over the assets and assumes the liabilities of Mr.

Lummas' existing sole proprietorship. Mrs. Bach invests cash equal to Mr. Lummas' capital.

The trial balance shown below contains the balances of the accounts in the general ledger of Mr. Lummas' business.

Instructions: Use page 1 of a general journal. Record the opening entries for the investment of each partner in the new partnership. M1 and M2.

	Oscar Lummas Trial Balance May 31, 19—	
Cash	1,948.35	
Notes Receivable	392.00	
Accounts Receivable	3,615.92	
Allowance for Uncollectible Accounts		108.15
Supplies	91.84	
Prepaid Insurance	114.80	
Office Equipment	4,121.00	
Accumulated Depreciation — Office Equip.		182.40
Notes Payable		300.00
Accounts Payable		693.36
Oscar Lummas, Capital		9,000.00
	10,283.91	10,283.91

REVIEW PROBLEM 4-R 2 Admission of a new partner with no increase in partnership capital

Ada Alonso and Carmen Laredo have $15,000.00 each invested in a partnership. Each of the partners sells one third of her interest in the partnership to Nilda Moreno. The agreement is that Ms. Moreno will have one third of the capital in the partnership.

Instructions: Use the current date. Record on page 8 of a general journal the journal entry to admit Ms. Moreno as a partner. M1. (The cash paid is between the individuals and is not recorded on the partnership books.)

REVIEW PROBLEM 5-R 1 Recording the division of net income by a combination of methods

On December 31 of the current year, the partnership of Lowell, Pappas, and Seigel has the following investments: Jerry Lowell, $11,500.00; John Pappas, $9,200.00;

and Joseph Seigel, $8,000.00. The income statement for the fiscal year, ended December 31 of the current year, shows a net income of $28,123.00. The articles of partnership include a statement that each partner is to receive 5% interest on invested capital. In addition, monthly salaries are to be paid as follows: Lowell, $700.00; Pappas, $500.00; Seigel, $400.00. The remaining net income or loss is divided equally. The partners' salaries are treated as withdrawals.

Instructions: □ **1.** Prepare a distribution of net income statement.

□ **2.** Use page 25 of a general journal. Record the entry to close the income summary account and distribute the net income to the partners' capital accounts.

REVIEW
PROBLEM 6-R 1   ●   Partnership end-of-fiscal-period work

The fiscal period for the partnership of Kiosko and Downing ends on December 31 of each year. The general ledger account balances on December 31 of the current year are:

Cash	$ 4,022.54
Petty Cash	250.00
Accounts Receivable	15,881.04
Allowance for Uncollectible Accounts	165.44
Notes Receivable	1,800.00
Merchandise Inventory	67,364.71
Supplies	862.72
Prepaid Insurance	738.00
Interest Receivable	——
Equipment	5,500.00
Accumulated Depreciation — Equipment	733.00
Accounts Payable	9,798.80
Notes Payable	1,900.00
Employees Income Tax Payable — Federal	208.98
FICA Tax Payable	139.32
Unemployment Tax Payable — Federal	5.81
Unemployment Tax Payable — State	31.93
Sales Tax Payable	500.48
Interest Payable	——
Gloria Downing, Capital	33,025.46
Gloria Downing, Drawing	8,100.00
Michael Kiosko, Capital	43,128.79
Michael Kiosko, Drawing	10,578.00
Income Summary	——
Sales	110,104.55
Sales Returns and Allowances	1,247.48

Purchases	$64,226.16
Purchases Returns and Allowances	2,974.22
Advertising Expense..	819.18
Delivery Expense	489.11
Miscellaneous Expense — Sales...	409.71
Salary Expense — Sales...	9,504.00
Bad Debts Expense...	——
Depreciation Expense — Equipment......................................	——
Insurance Expense..	——
Miscellaneous Expense — Administrative...............................	385.35
Payroll Taxes Expense...	1,288.27
Rent Expense...	4,800.00
Salary Expense — Administrative..	4,428.00
Supplies Expense	——
Interest Income...	26.38
Interest Expense...	48.89

Instructions: ☐ **1.** Prepare a trial balance in the Trial Balance columns of a work sheet. Complete the work sheet using the following data:

Additional bad debts expense	$ 237.85
Interest earned but not received on notes receivable	9.47
Merchandise inventory, December 31, 19--	67,010.40
Supplies inventory, December 31, 19--	189.54
Value of insurance policies, December 31, 19--	184.00
Additional depreciation of equipment......................................	288.00
Interest owed but not paid on notes payable..............................	7.55

☐ **2.** Prepare an income statement.

☐ **3.** Prepare a distribution of net income statement. The partnership agreement includes provisions for:

Salaries: Michael Kiosko, $11,000.00 per year; Gloria Downing, $8,500.00 per year.
3% interest on investment at the beginning of the year.
Share remaining net income or loss equally.

☐ **4.** Prepare a capital statement. No additional investments were made during the current year by either of the partners.

☐ **5.** Prepare a balance sheet.

☐ **6.** On page 12 of a general journal, record the adjusting entries. Use the data from the work sheet.

☐ **7.** On page 13 of a general journal, record the closing entries. Use the data from the work sheet and from the distribution of net income statement.

REVIEW Recording purchases and cash payments
PROBLEM 7-R 1   of a departmental business

Baldwin's operates two departments: Furniture and Carpeting. The purchases journal used by the store is similar to the one shown on page 114 except that there are only two departments. The cash payments journal is similar to the one shown on page 119 except that there is a purchases discount column for each of the two departments.

All purchases of merchandise on account are subject to a 2% discount if payment is made within 15 days.

Instructions: □ **1.** Record the following selected transactions for March of the current year on page 8 of a purchases journal and on page 12 of a cash payments journal.

Mar. 1. Purchased furniture on account from Sotelo Furniture, $2,352.00. P173.
      3. Paid March rent, $650.00. Ck635.
      3. Purchased carpeting on account from Quist Rug Corporation, $683.50. P174.
      5. Paid advertising expense, $62.40. Ck636.
      7. Purchased furniture on account from Garcia Furniture Co., $1,945.00. P175.
      8. Purchased carpeting on account from Price Mills, Inc., $1,080.00. P176.
     10. Paid on account to Sotelo Furniture, $2,304.96, covering P173 less discount. Ck637.
     11. Purchased furniture on account from Valdez Furniture Co., $886.20. P177.
     14. Purchased carpeting on account from Harria Carpeting, $930.60. P178.
     14. Bought supplies for cash from Ivory Supply Company, $23.75. Ck638.
     15. Received a bank statement showing a service charge for the checking account, $4.73. M7.
     15. Paid on account to Quist Rug Corporation, $669.83, covering P174 less discount. Ck639.
     16. Paid on account to Price Mills, Inc., $1,058.40, covering P176 less discount. Ck640.
     17. Purchased carpeting on account from Price Mills, Inc., $956.30. P179.
     18. Purchased carpeting on account from Lucio Carpeting Company, $844.85. P180.
     18. Paid on account to Garcia Furniture Co., $1,906.10, covering P175 less discount. Ck641.
     19. Purchased furniture on account from Doyle Furniture, $620.00. P181.
     22. Paid on account to Valdez Furniture Co., $868.48, covering P177 less discount. Ck642.
     23. Paid on account to Harria Carpeting, $911.99, covering P178 less discount. Ck643.
     24. Paid miscellaneous expense, $63.55. Ck644.

Mar. 28. Paid on account to Price Mills, Inc., $937.17, covering P179 less discount. Ck645.

31. Paid on account to Lucio Carpeting Company, $827.95, covering P180 less discount. Ck646.

Instructions: ☐ **2.** Foot the columns in the two journals. Prove the equality of debits and credits in the two journals.

☐ **3.** Total and rule the two journals.

REVIEW PROBLEM 7-R 2 Reconciling a bank statement

On May 1 of the current year, Eastside Sport Center received its bank statement from the First National Bank and Trust Company. With the statement were the canceled checks and a charge slip showing that a service charge of $3.86 had been deducted from the account.

Instructions: ☐ **1.** Record the service charge on page 6 of a cash payments journal similar to the one explained on page 122. M9.

☐ **2.** Prepare a reconciliation of the bank statement in the same form as that shown on page 121.

(a) The checkbook balance at the close of business on April 30 was $1,574.59.

(b) The balance shown on the bank statement was $1,822.54.

(c) A deposit of $286.35, made on April 30, was not shown on the bank statement.

(d) Outstanding checks were: No. 273, $253.90; No. 281, $111.66; No. 282, $172.60.

REVIEW PROBLEM 8-R 1 Recording sales on account and sales returns and allowances for a departmental business

The Abernathy Hardware Store has three departments: Hardware, Sporting Goods, and Appliances. The selected transactions listed on page 552 were completed during January of the current year.

Instructions: ☐ **1.** Record the following transactions on page 10 of a sales journal and on page 7 of a sales returns and allowances journal similar to those shown on page 129 and page 132.

Jan. 2. Sold sporting goods to Meala Doyle, $38.50, plus sales tax, $1.54; total, $40.04. S1.

4. Sold an appliance to Tawanna Gibson, $88.00, plus sales tax, $3.52; total, $91.52. S2.

9. Sold hardware to Lionel Rodriguez, $21.35, plus sales tax, $.85; total, $22.20. S3.

12. Granted an allowance to Tawanna Gibson for damaged appliance, $15.00, plus sales tax on the allowance, $.60; total, $15.60. CM1.

12. Granted credit to Meala Doyle for sporting goods returned, $12.95, plus sales tax on returned sporting goods, $.52; total, $13.47. CM2.

16. Sold an appliance to Grover Dotson, $369.00, plus sales tax, $14.76; total, $383.76. S4.

18. Sold sporting goods to Bertha Gomez, $16.95, plus sales tax, $.68; total, $17.63. S5.

20. Sold hardware to Grover Dotson, $33.40, plus sales tax, $1.34; total, $34.74. S6.

23. Granted credit to Bertha Gomez for sporting goods returned, $16.95, plus sales tax, $.68; total, $17.63. CM3.

26. Sold on account to Lionel Rodriguez: hardware, $43.50; sporting goods, $25.00; plus sales tax, $2.74; total, $71.24. S7.

28. Sold an appliance to Grover Dotson, $45.75, plus sales tax, $1.83; total, $47.58. S8.

31. Granted credit to Lionel Rodriguez for hardware returned, $9.00, plus sales tax on returned hardware, $.36; total, $9.36. CM4.

Instructions: □ **2.** Foot the amount columns of the sales journal, prove the equality of debits and credits, and total and rule the journal.

□ **3.** Foot the amount columns of the sales returns and allowances journal, prove the equality of debits and credits, and total and rule the journal.

REVIEW 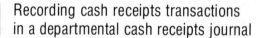 Recording cash receipts transactions
PROBLEM 8-R 2   in a departmental cash receipts journal

The Salinas Shoe Store has three departments: Women's Shoes, Men's Shoes, and Children's Shoes. The selected cash receipts transactions listed below were completed during February of the current year.

Instructions: □ **1.** Record the following cash receipts transactions on page 10 of a cash receipts journal similar to the one shown on page 133.

Feb. 1. Recorded the cash balance on February 1 as a memorandum entry in the cash receipts journal, $1,833.55.

1. Received on account from Anita Andrews, $33.46. R53.

Feb. 3. Received on account from Herminio Nevarez, $24.63. R54.

3. Cash sales for February 1–3: Women's Shoes, $287.77; Men's Shoes, $314.40; Children's Shoes, $264.63; plus sales taxes of $34.67; total, $901.47. T3.

7. Received on account from Maria Valdez, $63.56. R55.

9. Received on account from Otela Zamora, $18.47. R56.

10. Cash sales for February 5–10: Women's Shoes, $613.58; Men's Shoes, $565.39; Children's Shoes, $586.47; plus sales taxes of $70.62; total, $1,836.06. T10.

14. Received on account from Carlos Leyba, $28.44. R57.

16. Received on account from Berta Ortez, $33.64. R58.

17. Cash sales for February 12–17: Women's Shoes, $596.00; Men's Shoes, $613.55; Children's Shoes, $605.00; plus sales taxes of $72.58; total, $1,887.13. T17.

21. Received on account from Bruno Angula, $22.88. R59.

24. Cash sales for February 19–24: Women's Shoes, $614.50; Men's Shoes, $603.00; Children's Shoes, $577.55; plus sales taxes of $71.80; total, $1,866.85. T24.

27. Received from the telephone company for share of public telephone receipts, $6.33. R60.

28. Cash sales for February 26–28: Women's Shoes, $316.00; Men's Shoes, $296.44; Children's Shoes, $274.00; plus sales taxes of $35.46; total, $921.90. T28.

Instructions: □ **2.** Foot the amount columns of the cash receipts journal and prove the equality of debits and credits.

□ **3.** Total and rule the cash receipts journal.

REVIEW PROBLEM 9-R 1 Pricing an inventory by the fifo and lifo methods

The inventory clerk for Sykes Sound Center obtained the following information from the records of the business concerning the purchases of stereo players during the current year.

Model	Beginning Inventory Jan. 1	First Purchase	Second Purchase	Third Purchase	Inventory Count Dec. 31
520	4 @ $105	5 @ $100	9 @ $ 85	4 @ $ 81	6
521	2 @ $100	4 @ $100	6 @ $105	6 @ $108	2
522	6 @ $120	3 @ $125	2 @ $130	4 @ $135	7
660	8 @ $155	3 @ $145	12 @ $150	6 @ $155	8
661	2 @ $175	4 @ $180	2 @ $195	7 @ $200	10
662	1 @ $325	3 @ $325	6 @ $333	5 @ $318	6

Instructions: □ **1.** Use an inventory sheet with the following column headings:

Model	Number of Units on Hand	Unit Cost	Value

□ **2.** Figure the total amount of the inventory on December 31 according to the *fifo* method. Proceed as follows:

(a) Record the model number and number of units of each model on hand on December 31.

(b) Record the unit cost of each model. If more than one unit cost must be used, list the number of units on hand with the unit cost applicable to each on separate lines.

(c) Figure the total value of each model and write the amount in the Value column.

(d) Add the Value column to determine the total amount of the inventory.

□ **3.** On another inventory sheet, figure the total amount of the inventory according to the *lifo* method. Follow the steps given in Instruction 2.

□ **4.** Compare the total amount of the inventory obtained in Instructions 2 and 3 above. Which method, *fifo* or *lifo*, resulted in the lower total amount for the inventory?

**REVIEW
PROBLEM 9-R 2**   ● Pricing the inventory at lower of cost or market

Part of the inventory sheet of the Alonzo Appliance Store on September 30 of the current year is shown below.

Article	No. of Units on Hand	Unit Cost Price	Current Unit Market Price
A	30	$3.10	$2.85
B	100	2.50	3.10
C	50	1.00	1.10
D	60	1.75	1.85
E	90	1.75	1.45
F	35	3.25	3.00
G	45	1.25	1.05
H	40	2.60	2.55
I	90	2.15	2.15
J	35	3.40	3.70

Instructions: □ **1.** Copy the inventory data given on page 554 on an inventory sheet with the following column headings:

Article	No. of Units on Hand	Unit Cost Price	Current Unit Market Price	Unit Price to be Used	Value

□ **2.** Figure the value of each kind of merchandise at lower of cost or market. Record the value in the last amount column.

□ **3.** Total the Value column to determine the amount of the ending merchandise inventory.

REVIEW PROBLEM 9-R 3 Preparing an interim departmental statement of gross profit

Watley Furniture has three departments: Appliances, Carpeting, and Furniture. The accounting clerk obtained the following data from the accounting records at the end of January of the current year.

Beginning inventory, January 1: Appliance Department $26,200.00
Carpeting Department............................ 19,800.00
Furniture Department 58,300.00

Net purchases for January: Appliance Department................................. $ 3,460.00
Carpeting Department................................. 1,880.00
Furniture Department................................. 7,620.00

Net sales for January: Appliance Department... $ 8,930.00
Carpeting Department 4,270.00
Furniture Department 10,140.00

Gross profit on sales ....30% of sales

Instructions: □ **1.** Estimate the value of the ending inventory for January of the current year for each department. Use the gross profit method of estimating an inventory.

□ **2.** Prepare an interim departmental statement of gross profit for the month ended January 31 of the current year.

REVIEW
PROBLEM 10-R 1   ●   Preparing a payroll register
and recording the payroll entries

The Montgomery Company has two sales departments: Textbooks and School Supplies. Salesclerks and employees in the accounting department are paid on an hourly basis and receive 1½ times the regular hourly pay rate for all hours worked over 40 each week. Departmental supervisors are paid on a weekly basis and receive monthly commissions of 1% of net sales. Payroll data about the 11 employees for the week ended April 1 of the current year are shown below.

Empl. No.	Name	Job Title	Dept.	Marital Status	Number of Exemptions	Total Hours Worked	Regular Hourly Pay Rate	Weekly Wages
1	Atkins, Carl	Salesclerk	Supplies	S	1	40	$3.50	
2	Baker, Nancy	Supervisor	Books	M	2	—	—	$175.00
3	Ellis, Greg	Salesclerk	Supplies	M	3	43	$3.50	
4	Heard, Cedric	Salesclerk	Books	M	2	42	$3.60	
5	Greer, Deborah	Accountant	Acct.	S	1	44	$4.50	
6	Lucio, Peter	Salesclerk	Supplies	S	1	40	$3.50	
7	Pernell, Alice	Salesclerk	Books	M	2	44	$3.80	
8	Sanders, Jean	Supervisor	Supplies	M	3	—	—	$175.00
9	Tapia, Cindy	Salesclerk	Supplies	S	1	41	$4.00	
10	Tovar, Kathy	Salesclerk	Books	M	2	43	$3.80	
11	Valdez, Christina	Payroll Clerk	Acct.	S	1	40	$4.00	

All earnings on the April 1 payroll are subject to both FICA tax and unemployment compensation tax.

Instructions: □ **1.** Prepare a commissions record for each departmental supervisor, similar to the one on page 163, for the month of March. Additional data needed are:
(a) Books: charge sales, $5,396.25; cash sales, $7,493.40; sales returns and allowances, $135.60.
(b) Supplies: charge sales, $5,740.65; cash sales, $7,930.75; sales returns and allowances, $177.85.

□ **2.** Prepare a payroll register, similar to the one on pages 164 and 165, for the week ended April 1. Additional data needed are:
(a) A deduction is to be made from each employee's pay for federal income tax. Use the appropriate income tax withholding table on page 167.
(b) A deduction of 3% is to be made from each employee's pay for state income tax.
(c) A deduction of 6% is to be made from each employee's pay for FICA tax.
(d) A deduction of $6.00 is to be made from each single employee's pay and a deduction of $8.50 is to be made from each married employee's pay for hospital insurance.

□ **3.** Make the entry on page 13 of a cash payments journal like the one on page 173 to record the payroll for the week ended April 1. Check No. 433 for the net amount of the payroll has been issued and deposited in the special payroll bank account.

□ **4.** Make an entry on page 11 of a general journal like the one on page 45 to record the employer's payroll taxes expenses on the April 1 payroll. The FICA tax rate for the employer is 6%. The federal unemployment tax rate is 0.5%, and the state unemployment tax rate is 2.7%. M42.

□ **5.** Complete the payroll register by inserting the payroll check numbers, beginning with Ck246.

REVIEW Recording transactions when a
PROBLEM 11-R 1 voucher system is used

The Lozoria Company has two departments: Fabric and Notions. The company uses a voucher register similar to the one shown on pages 190 and 191 and a check register similar to the one shown on page 194.

Instructions: □ **1.** Record the following transactions completed during February of the current year. Use page 8 of a voucher register and page 4 of a check register. Source documents are abbreviated as: check, Ck; debit memorandum, DM; voucher, V.

Feb. 1. Recorded the cash balance on February 1 as a memorandum entry in the check register, $12,523.68.
 1. Received bill for February rent owed to Hernandez Rental, $700.00. V93.
 1. Paid V93, $700.00. Ck76.
 4. Purchased merchandise on account from Perez Company as follows: Fabric, $630.00; Notions, $768.40. V94.
 6. Purchased merchandise on account from Ostro Company as follows: Fabric, $1,977.00; Notions, $987.25. V95.
 7. Bought supplies on account from Bonner Supply Co. as follows: store supplies, $284.50; office supplies, $124.00. V96.
 8. Issued DM68 to Perez Company for the return of merchandise purchased for Notions, $80.00. Canceled V94 and issued V97.
 8. Received monthly bill from General Telephone Company, $63.00. V98. (Miscellaneous Expense)
 8. Paid V98, $63.00. Ck77.
 11. Received monthly statement from Daily Times News for newspaper advertising, $44.50. V99.
 11. Paid V99, $44.50. Ck78.
 13. Paid V95, $2,964.25, less purchases discount as follows: Fabric, $39.54; Notions, $19.75. Ck79.
 13. Purchased merchandise on account from Butler Fabrics as follows: Fabric, $2,465.40; Notions, $2,177.00. V100.

Feb. 14. Paid V97, $1,318.40, less purchases discount as follows: Fabric, $6.30; Notions, $6.88. Ck80.

14. Made a deposit in the bank, $5,683.66.

15. Paid V96, $408.50; no discount. Ck81.

15. The payroll register for the semimonthly payroll showed the following: Salary Expense — Delivery, $288.00; Salary Expense — Store, $1,522.60; Salary Expense — Administrative, $540.00; Employees Income Tax Payable — Federal, $314.20; Employees Income Tax Payable — State, $102.30; FICA Tax Payable, $141.04. V101.

15. Paid V101, $1,793.06. Ck82.

18. Bought office supplies from Bonner Supply Co., $233.75. V102.

20. Bought a desk from Pernell Company, $450.00. V103.

21. Paid V100, $4,642.40, less purchases discount as follows: Fabric, $24.65; Notions, $21.77. Ck83.

25. Purchased merchandise on account from Ellis Company as follows: Fabric, $1,120.00; Notions, $1,325.00. V104.

25. Paid V102, $233.75; no discount. Ck84.

25. Bought store supplies from Ashley Supply, $320.75. V105.

25. Paid V103, $450.00; no discount. Ck85.

28. Replenished the petty cash fund as follows: Store Supplies, $8.20; Office Supplies, $11.40; Advertising Expense, $7.30; Delivery Expense, $19.35. V106.

28. Paid V106, $46.25. Ck86.

28. The payroll register showed the following: Salary Expense — Delivery, $288.00; Salary Expense — Store, $1,635.40; Salary Expense — Administrative, $563.60; Employees Income Tax Payable — Federal, $338.60; Employees Income Tax Payable — State, $108.19; FICA Tax Payable, $149.22. V107.

28. Paid V107, $1,890.99. Ck87.

28. Made a deposit in the bank, $8,936.55.

Instructions: □ **2.** Foot, prove, total, and rule the voucher register and the check register.

REVIEW PROBLEM 12-R 1 Adding new accounts to the general ledger chart of accounts

The general ledger chart of accounts for the Westside Plumbing Co. is given on page 559.

Instructions: □ **1.** On a sheet of paper copy the names of the following new accounts that are being added to the general ledger chart of accounts.

Allowance for Uncollectible Accounts	Bad Debts Expense
Office Supplies	Office Supplies Expense
Sales Tax Payable	Rent Expense

Account Number	ASSETS	Account Number	OPERATING REVENUE
	Current Assets	41 01000	Sales
11 01000	Cash	41 02000	Sales Returns and Allowances
11 02000	Petty Cash		
11 03000	Accounts Receivable		**COST OF MERCHANDISE**
11 04000	Merchandise Inventory	51 01000	Purchases
11 04500	Store Supplies	51 02000	Purchases Returns and
11 05000	Prepaid Insurance		Allowances
		51 03000	Purchases Discount
	Plant Assets		
12 01000	Store Equipment		**OPERATING EXPENSES**
12 02000	Accumulated Depreciation — Store Equipment	61 01000	Depreciation Expense— Store Equipment
	LIABILITIES	61 02000	Insurance Expense
	Current Liabilities	61 02500	Payroll Taxes Expense
21 01000	Accounts Payable	61 03000	Salary Expense
		61 04000	Store Supplies Expense
	CAPITAL		
31 01000	Wilmer Smith, Capital		
31 02000	Wilmer Smith, Drawing		
31 03000	Income Summary		

Instructions: □ **2.** Assign account numbers to the new accounts. Refer to the chart of accounts for Harrod's, page 206, for the proper order of general ledger accounts. Use the "unused middle number" method of assigning new account numbers. (Assume that the first number assigned to operating expenses is 61 00000. Do not assign this number.)

□ **3.** On a second sheet of paper prepare a new chart of accounts for the general ledger. Include the new accounts with their respective account numbers.

The chart of accounts prepared in Instruction 3 will be needed to complete Review Problem 13-R1.

REVIEW PROBLEM 12-R 2   Adding new accounts to the accounts receivable subsidiary ledger

The chart of accounts for the accounts receivable subsidiary ledger of Westside Plumbing Co. is given below.

Customer Number	Customer Name	Customer Number	Customer Name
10 00100	Wayne Ackerman	10 00450	Vicki Layfield
10 00200	Vernon Allen	10 00500	Jerald McCoy
10 00250	Guido Banvelos	10 00600	Carol Palmer
10 00300	Gail Franklin	10 00650	Sarah Redmond
10 00400	Rosa Lamas	10 00700	Nora Valle

Instructions: ☐ **1.** On a sheet of paper copy the names of the following accounts that are being added to the accounts receivable subsidiary ledger on page 559.

Mary Allbee	Lillian Kato
John Dunbar	Carmen Picelli
Delio Hernandez	

☐ **2.** Assign account numbers to the new accounts. Use the "unused middle number" method of assigning new account numbers.

☐ **3.** On a second sheet of paper prepare a new chart of accounts for the accounts receivable ledger. Include the new accounts with their respective account numbers.

The chart of accounts prepared in Instruction 3 will be needed to complete Review Problem 13-R1.

REVIEW Recording sales and cash receipts for
PROBLEM 13-R 1   an automated accounting system

The charts of accounts prepared in Instruction 3, Review Problems 12-R 1 and 12-R 2, are needed to complete this problem.

Westside Plumbing Co. completed the following sales and cash receipts transactions on December 17 of the current year. All transactions are sorted by groups before being recorded.

Dec. 17. Summary of sales of merchandise on account, total of $372.40, plus sales tax of $14.90; sold merchandise on account to:
Vernon Allen, $154.00, plus sales tax of $6.16. S668.
Gail Franklin, $88.40, plus sales tax of $3.54. S669.
Nora Valle, $130.00, plus sales tax of $5.20. S670.

Dec. 17. Summary of cash receipts on account, total of $936.00; received cash on account from:
Wayne Ackerman, $78.00. R634.
Rosa Lamas, $144.75. R635.
Carol Palmer, $713.25. R636.

Dec. 17. Summary of cash sales:
Cash sales for the day, $879.00, plus sales tax of $35.16. T321.

Instructions: ☐ **1.** Record the sales and cash receipts on a journal entry transmittal. Use the account numbers from the charts of accounts prepared in Review Problems 12-R 1 and 12-R 2. Include a description of each data batch in the Explanation column.

☐ **2.** Prepare a batch control sheet for the sales and cash receipts.

REVIEW PROBLEM 13-R 2   Preparing an accounts receivable control sheet

Cedar Furniture completed journal entry transmittals for sales and cash receipts and general transactions on November 14 of the current year. The following totals were obtained from the two journal entry transmittals:

> Sales on account, $645.00.
> Sales returns and allowances, $56.00.
> Cash receipts on account, $533.00.

Instructions: Prepare an accounts receivable control sheet. The beginning balance in the accounts receivable controlling account was $5,245.50.

REVIEW PROBLEM 14-R 1   Recording adjusting entries for computer processing

On January 31 of the current year, the beginning and ending inventories and the value of the prepaid insurance of the Bellview Plumbing Company are shown below.

	Beginning Balance	Ending Balance
Merchandise Inventory	$36,500.00	$38,250.00
Store Supplies	383.00	252.00
Office Supplies	215.00	183.00
Prepaid Insurance	425.00	345.00

Instructions: □ **1.** Record the adjusting entries on a journal entry transmittal. Use the account numbers given below.

Merchandise Inventory	11 05000
Store Supplies	11 07000
Office Supplies	11 08000
Prepaid Insurance	11 09000
Income Summary	31 03000
Insurance Expense	61 03000
Office Supplies Expense	61 05000
Store Supplies Expense	61 08000

□ **2.** Prepare a batch control sheet for the adjusting entries.

REVIEW PROBLEM 15-R 1   Division of corporate income

LeGrand Corporation has issued 900 shares of 5% participating, noncumulative preferred stock, par value $100.00 per share. The corporation has also issued 1,500 shares of no-par-value common stock. The results of operations over the last 10 years are as follows:

1969	$9,000.00	net income	1974	$ 9,000.00	net income
1970	7,500.00	net loss	1975	15,300.00	net income
1971	6,000.00	net income	1976	24,000.00	net income
1972	3,000.00	net income	1977	21,000.00	net income
1973	6,000.00	net loss	1978	25,500.00	net income

At the end of each year in which there are earnings, the board of directors:

(1) Applies the earnings to the accumulated deficit if there is a deficit.
(2) Pays dividends on the preferred stock to the extent that the current net income plus the balance of the retained earnings account permit such payments. No partial payments are made. If the total earnings available are not sufficient to pay the total amount of dividends owed for preferred stock, no dividends are declared that year and the current net income is transferred to the retained earnings account.
(3) When the total amount due for regular dividends to preferred stock is paid in a year, distributes the balance of the net income for that year as follows: 1/4 as an additional dividend on preferred stock; 1/2 as a dividend on common stock; and 1/4 to Retained Earnings. The credit balance of the retained earnings account at the start of 1969 was $1,125.00.

Instructions: Show the distribution of the net income or loss for each year on columnar paper with the following headings: (a) Year, (b) Net Income, (c) Paid to Preferred Stockholders — Regular Dividend, (d) Paid to Preferred Stockholders — Additional Dividend, (e) Paid to Common Stockholders, (f) Transferred to Retained Earnings, (g) Balance of Retained Earnings. (Note: If there are minus items to be written in any column, enclose them with parentheses.)

REVIEW PROBLEM 16-R 1 Transactions for capital stock and treasury stock

D & K Metal Products Company begins business on January 2. The company is authorized to issue 20,000 shares of $50.00 par-value common stock and 5,000 shares of $100.00 par-value preferred stock.

D & K Metal Products Company uses the following accounts relating to the stockholders' equity:

Capital Stock — Preferred
Capital Stock — Common
Treasury Stock
Additional Paid-in Capital
Paid-in Capital from Sale of Treasury Stock
Capital Stock Subscribed — Preferred
Capital Stock Subscribed — Common

Instructions: Record the following selected transactions. Use page 7 of a cash receipts journal, page 3 of a cash payments journal, and page 11 of a general journal similar to the ones illustrated in Chapter 16.

Jan. 2. Received cash, $150,000.00, from the incorporators in full payment for common stock as follows:

Beulah Preson, 1,500 shares, $75,000.00. R1.
Dale Minton, 1,000 shares, $50,000.00. R2.
Kay Sikes, 500 shares, $25,000.00. R3.

Jan. 11. Received a subscription from Albert Gill for 500 shares of preferred stock at par value, $50,000.00. Preferred Stock Subscription No. 1.

Jan. 29. Received cash from Richard Lawson in full payment for 100 shares of preferred stock, $10,100.00. R15.

Feb. 11. Received cash from Albert Gill as first installment on his preferred stock subscription, $25,000.00. R19.

Mar. 1. Received cash from Roger Hays in full payment for 100 shares of common stock, $5,100.00. R25.

Mar. 11. Received cash from Albert Gill as final installment on his preferred stock subscription, $25,000.00. R28. Issued a stock certificate for 500 shares. Stock Certificate No. 30.

July 25. Paid Roger Hays for 50 shares of D & K Metal Products Company's common stock, $2,600.00. Ck85.

Aug. 5. Received a subscription from Bruce Parks for 500 shares of common stock, $25,000.00. Common Stock Subscription No. 5.

Aug. 29. Received cash from J. L. Bowen for 30 shares of treasury stock, $1,590.00. Treasury stock was bought July 25. R83.

Sept. 5. Received cash from Bruce Parks as first installment on his common stock subscription, $12,500.00. R88.

| **REVIEW** | | End-of-period work for |
| **PROBLEM 17-R 1** | | a corporation |

The trial balance for Roffler Corporation on June 30 of the current year, the end of a quarterly fiscal period, is shown on page 564.

Instructions: □ 1. Prepare a work sheet for Roffler Corporation for the quarterly fiscal period ended June 30 of the current year. Additional data needed for completing the work sheet are listed below.

Additional allowance for uncollectible accounts, 1/2% of charge sales of $68,659.20.
Merchandise inventory, June 30, $38,418.40.
Supplies inventory, June 30, $757.00.
Value of insurance policies, June 30, $560.00.
Quarterly rate of depreciation on equipment, 2%.
Quarterly rate of depreciation on building, 0.5%.
Organization costs to be written off, $80.00.
Estimated property tax for the period, $1,430.20.
Federal income tax for the period, 22% of net income before federal income tax.

	Account Title	Acct. No.	Trial Balance Debit	Trial Balance Credit
1	Cash	1101	16,065.56	
2	Accounts Receivable	1102	7,043.60	
3	Allowance for Uncollectible Accounts	1102.1		155.20
4	Merchandise Inventory	1103	30,429.60	
5	Supplies	1104	3,571.00	
6	Prepaid Insurance	1105	1,600.00	
7	Equipment	1201	32,000.00	
8	Accumulated Depreciation — Equipment	1201.1		2,640.00
9	Building	1202	120,000.00	
10	Accumulated Depreciation — Building	1202.1		4,400.00
11	Land	1203	10,000.00	
12	Organization Costs	1301	240.00	
13	Accounts Payable	2101		5,230.40
14	Employees Income Tax Payable	2102		1,527.20
15	FICA Tax Payable	2103		1,404.00
16	Unemployment Tax Payable — Federal	2104		181.36
17	Unemployment Tax Payable — State	2105		979.30
18	Property Tax Payable	2106		——
19	Federal Income Tax Payable	2107		
20	Dividends Payable	2108		1,680.00
21	Capital Stock	3101		178,000.00
22	Retained Earnings	3201		6,961.40
23	Income Summary	3202	——	
24	Sales	4101		176,398.74
25	Sales Returns and Allowances	4101.1	526.00	
26	Purchases	5101	110,814.30	
27	Purchases Returns and Allowances	5101.1		2,420.00
28	Purchases Discount	5101.2		1,550.80
29	Advertising Expense	6101	4,800.00	
30	Delivery Expense	6102	1,410.00	
31	Miscellaneous Expense — Sales	6103	619.60	
32	Salary Expense — Sales	6104	17,270.00	
33	Bad Debts Expense	6201	——	
34	Depreciation Expense — Building	6202	——	
35	Depreciation Expense — Equipment	6203	——	
36	Insurance Expense	6204	——	
37	Miscellaneous Expense — Administrative	6205	884.30	
38	Payroll Taxes Expense	6206	3,282.44	
39	Property Tax Expense	6207	——	
40	Salary Expense — Administrative	6208	19,000.00	
41	Supplies Expense	6209	——	
42	Interest Income	7101		28.00
43	Organization Expense	8101	——	
44	Federal Income Tax	9101	4,000.00	
			383,556.40	383,556.40

Instructions: ☐ **2.** Prepare an income statement.

☐ **3.** Prepare a stockholders' equity statement. Roffler Corporation has 1,780 shares of $100.00 stated-value common stock issued and outstanding. The ledger accounts show that there has been no change in the capital stock account. The only change in the retained earnings account during the fiscal period was the declaration of the dividend of $1,680.00 on May 15. The dividend is to be paid July 30 to stockholders of record on June 30.

□ **4.** Prepare a balance sheet.

□ **5.** Analyze the equity of Roffler Corporation by figuring the following:

a. Equity per share as of June 30.
b. Earnings per share for the current quarter.
c. Price-earnings ratio for the current quarter. Market value of the stock on June 30 was $102.00 per share.

□ **6.** Record the adjusting entries on page 18 of a general journal.

□ **7.** Record the closing entries on page 19 of a general journal.

REVIEW PROBLEM 18-R 1 Work sheet and end-of-period statements for a departmentalized merchandising business

The account balances for Thrift-Wise Grocery are shown on page 566 for the current year ended December 31.

Instructions: □ **1.** Prepare a trial balance on a twelve-column work sheet similar to the one shown on pages 340–341. Skip four lines after Utilities Expense before entering Federal Income Tax.

□ **2.** Make adjusting entries on the work sheet. Additional data needed to make adjustments are listed below.

Additional bad debts expense	$ 58.60
Merchandise inventories on December 31:	
Grocery Dept.	65,458.90
Meat Dept.	38,548.55
Value of insurance policies, December 31	2,790.00
Insurance expense charged as follows:	
Grocery Dept. ... 40%	
Meat Dept. ... 50%	
Administrative ... 10%	
Supplies inventory, December 31	463.10
Supplies were used as follows:	
Grocery Dept. ... 50%	
Meat Dept. ... 30%	
Administrative ... 20%	
Depreciation for the year:	
Office Equipment	437.50
Store Equip. — Grocery Dept.	1,086.80
Store Equip. — Meat Dept.	2,173.75
Federal income tax for the year:	2,150.00

Account Title	Acct. No.	Balances Debit	Balances Credit
Cash	1101	$ 21,585.30	
Accounts Receivable	1102	2,255.45	
Allow. for Uncollectible Accounts	1102.1		$ 45.10
Merchandise Inventory — Grocery Dept.	1103	60,487.20	
Merchandise Inventory — Meat Dept.	1104	29,304.50	
Prepaid Insurance	1105	5,200.00	
Supplies	1106	2,767.50	
Office Equipment	1201	4,528.60	
Accum. Depr. — Office Equip.	1201.1		679.30
Store Equip. — Grocery Dept.	1202	8,151.50	
Accum. Depr. — Store Equip., Grocery Dept.	1202.1		2,445.50
Store Equip. — Meat Dept.	1203	21,737.30	
Accum. Depr. — Store Equip., Meat Dept.	1203.1		6,521.50
Accounts Payable	2101		21,162.80
Salaries Payable	2102		———
Employees Income Tax Payable	2103		1,680.30
FICA Tax Payable	2104		540.00
Unemployment Tax Payable — Federal	2105		45.00
Unemployment Tax Payable — State	2106		243.00
Income Tax Payable	2107		———
Sales Tax Payable	2108		1,513.25
Property Tax Payable	2109		1,386.00
Capital Stock	3101		100,000.00
Retained Earnings	3201		17,581.50
Income Summary — Grocery Dept.	3301	———	———
Income Summary — Meat Dept.	3302	———	———
Income Summary — General	3303	———	———
Sales — Grocery Dept.	4101		343,558.85
Sales Ret. and Allow. — Grocery Dept.	4101.1	1,647.45	
Sales — Meat Dept.	4201		239,116.10
Sales Ret. and Allow. — Meat Dept.	4201.1	1,006.60	
Purchases — Grocery Dept.	5101	247,704.30	
Purch. Ret. and Allow. — Grocery Dept.	5101.1		2,644.50
Purchases — Meat Dept.	5201	181,665.10	
Purch. Ret. and Allow. — Meat Dept.	5201.1		754.20
Advertising Exp. — Grocery Dept.	6001	2,304.30	
Depr. Exp. — Store Equip., Grocery Dept.	6002	———	
Insurance Exp. — Grocery Dept.	6003	———	
Payroll Taxes Exp. — Grocery Dept.	6004	4,239.36	
Salary Exp. — Grocery Dept.	6005	46,080.00	
Supplies Exp. — Grocery Dept.	6006	———	
Advertising Exp. — Meat Dept.	6101	1,229.00	
Depr. Exp. — Store Equip., Meat Dept.	6102	———	
Insurance Exp. — Meat Dept.	6103	———	
Payroll Taxes Exp. — Meat Dept.	6104	3,709.44	
Salary Exp. — Meat Dept.	6105	40,320.00	
Supplies Exp. — Meat Dept.	6106	———	
Bad Debts Expense	6201	136.30	
Depr. Exp. — Office Equip.	6202	———	
Insurance Exp. — Administrative	6203	———	
Miscellaneous Expense	6204	5,891.30	
Payroll Taxes Exp. — Administrative	6205	1,987.20	
Property Tax Expense	6206	1,386.00	
Rent Expense	6207	18,000.00	
Salary Exp. — Administrative	6208	21,600.00	
Supplies Exp. — Administrative	6209	———	
Utilities Expense	6210	3,118.20	
Federal Income Tax	8101	1,875.00	
		$739,916.90	$739,916.90

Instructions: □ **3.** Complete the work sheet. Extend proper amounts to debit and credit columns for Departmental Margin Statement — Grocery, Departmental Margin Statement — Meat, Income Statement, and Balance Sheet. All accounts with account numbers beginning with the number 62 are classified as indirect expenses.

□ **4.** Prepare a departmental margin statement — grocery department and a departmental margin statement — meat department for the year ended December 31. Figure the percentage of net sales. Use the statements on pages 345 and 347 as your guide.

□ **5.** Prepare an income statement similar to the one on page 348 for the year ended December 31. Figure the percentage of net sales.

REVIEW
PROBLEM 19-R 1 Preparing a cost sheet

On May 1, McDuff Company began work on Job Order No. 773. The order was for 25 No. 42JW dining tables for stock, to be completed by May 10.

Instructions: □ **1.** Open a cost sheet similar to the one shown on page 364 and record the following items:

May 1. Direct materials, $512.00. Requisition No. 497.
     1. Direct labor, $202.00. Daily summary of Job-Time Records.
     2. Direct labor, $214.00. Daily summary of Job-Time Records.
     3. Direct labor, $208.00. Daily summary of Job-Time Records.
     6. Direct materials, $58.00. Requisition No. 516.
     6. Direct labor, $74.00. Daily summary of Job-Time Records.
     7. Direct labor, $78.00. Daily summary of Job-Time Records.
     8. Direct materials, $135.00. Requisition No. 525.
     8. Direct labor, $125.00. Daily summary of Job-Time Records.
     9. Direct labor, $62.00. Daily summary of Job-Time Records.
   10. Direct labor, $44.00. Daily summary of Job-Time Records.

Instructions: □ **2.** Complete the cost sheet, recording factory overhead at the rate of 125% of direct labor costs.

REVIEW
PROBLEM 20-R 1 Journalizing the entries that summarize the cost records at the end of the month

On December 31 of the current year, W. W. Houston Company has the information listed on page 568.

(a) The various accounts in the general ledger used in recording the actual factory overhead expense during the month have the following balances:

Depreciation Expense — Building	5101	$ 480.00
Depreciation Expense — Factory Equipment	5102	982.00
Heat, Light, and Power	5104	1,540.00
Insurance Expense — Factory	5105	256.00
Miscellaneous Expense — Factory	5106	2,880.00
Payroll Taxes Expense — Factory	5107	3,660.00
Property Tax Expense — Factory	5108	1,208.00
Supplies Expense — Factory	5109	3,072.00

(b) Inventory account balances are:

Materials, $92,600.00. (December 1 balance, $51,544.00, plus December purchases, $41,056.00.) Account No. 1104.
Work in Process, December 1 balance, $32,640.00. Account No. 1105.
Finished Goods, December 1 balance, $80,500.00. Account No. 1106.

(c) The following accounts are needed for completing the posting (no beginning balances are needed):

Factory Overhead	5103	FICA Tax Payable	2103
Employees Income Tax Payable	2102	Income Summary	3300

(d) The total factory payroll for the month according to the payroll register is $52,288.00. Payroll distribution is:

Work in Process	$38,848.00	Employees Income Tax	
Factory Overhead	13,440.00	Payable	$ 5,750.00
Vouchers Payable	43,400.72	FICA Tax Payable	3,137.28

(e) The total of all requisitions of direct materials issued during the month is $42,896.00.
(f) The factory overhead to be charged to Work in Process is 70% of the direct labor cost.
(g) The total of all cost sheets completed during the month is $106,000.00.

Instructions: ☐ **1.** Open ledger accounts and record the balances for information items (a), (b), and (c).

☐ **2.** Record the entry for the factory payroll on page 11 of a voucher register. V186. Post general debit and general credit entries.

☐ **3.** Record the following entries on page 18 of a general journal. Post the entries.

(a) An entry to transfer the total of all direct materials requisitions from Materials to Work in Process. M723.
(b) An entry to transfer the balances of all individual factory overhead expense accounts to Factory Overhead. M724.
(c) An entry to transfer the applied factory overhead from Factory Overhead to Work in Process. M725.

□ **4.** Record and post the entry to transfer the balance of the factory overhead account to Income Summary. M726.

□ **5.** Record and post the entry to transfer the total of all cost sheets completed from Work in Process to Finished Goods. M727.

□ **6.** Prepare a statement of cost of goods manufactured, similar to the one illustrated on page 379, for W. W. Houston Company for the month ended December 31 of the current year.

REVIEW PROBLEM 21-R 1 Using the allowance method of recording bad debts expense

The Bushido Company uses the allowance method of recording bad debts expense. The company makes adjusting entries for bad debts expense quarterly: March 31, June 30, September 30, and December 31. The amount of bad debts expense for each quarter is estimated as 1% of the net sales for the quarter.

Instructions: Record the necessary entries for the following selected transactions. Use page 30 of a cash receipts journal and page 51 of a general journal. Use the current year in the dates.

Jan.   17. Write off Allen Blake's account as uncollectible, $73.40. M6.
Mar.   6. Write off Melva Dario's account as uncollectible, $41.97. M38.
Mar. 31. Record the adjusting entry for bad debts expense. The net sales for the quarter are $23,071.11.
Apr. 30. Write off Bill's Pet Grooming Shop account as uncollectible, $45.30. M49.
June 30. Record the adjusting entry for bad debts expense. The net sales for the quarter are $22,214.63.
July   1. Received a check from Bill's Pet Grooming Shop in full payment of account, $45.30. This account had been written off on April 30. M63 and R369.
Sept. 30. Record the adjusting entry for bad debts expense. The net sales for the quarter are $21,788.77.
Nov. 18. Write off the account of Gonzales and Espejo as uncollectible, $177.61. M127.
Dec. 31. Record the adjusting entry for bad debts expense. The net sales for the quarter are $23,738.87.

REVIEW PROBLEM 22-R 1 Figuring depreciation expense by three methods

On January 6 of the current year, Milligan Company bought a new machine. Cost of the machine is $12,000.00; estimated useful life is 6 years; and estimated salvage value is $1,200.00.

Instructions: Prepare a table similar to the one on page 417. Show the annual depreciation for each year using each of the following methods:

(1) Straight-line method.
(2) Declining-balance method (at twice the straight-line rate).
(3) Sum-of-the-years-digits method.

REVIEW
PROBLEM 22-R 2   Recording depreciation expense

Marilyn Kan, owner of Kan-dells Gift Shop, keeps a plant assets register. The section of the plant assets register for store equipment is shown below as of January 1, 1978.

Item No.	Description	Date of Purchase	Cost	Estimated Salvage Value	Years Useful Life	Annual Depr. Rate	Accum. Depreciation Years	Accum. Depreciation Amount
		1975						
1	Display case	Jan. 2	$420.00	$20.00	10	10%	3	$120.00
2	Scale	2	200.00	20.00	10	10%	3	54.00
3	Counter	2	310.00	10.00	20	5%	3	45.00
4	Table	2	65.00	5.00	10	10%	3	18.00
5	Shelves	2	400.00	——	20	5%	3	60.00
		1977						
6	Counter	Jan. 2	190.00	30.00	20	5%	1	8.00

Instructions: Use page 5 of a general journal and page 16 of a cash payments journal. Record the following transactions:

Mar. 31, 1978. Record the total depreciation expense for the first quarter of 1978.
June 30, 1978. Record the total depreciation expense for the second quarter of 1978.
July 1, 1978. Bought a new scale. Gave the old scale (item No. 2) and $100.00 cash in payment. Ck201. (Estimated useful life of new scale, 10 years; estimated salvage value, $25.00)
Sept. 30, 1978. Record the total depreciation expense for the third quarter of 1978.
Dec. 31, 1978. Record the total depreciation expense for the last quarter of 1978.

REVIEW
PROBLEM 23-R 1   Adjusting and reversing entries for prepaid and accrued items

Adronia Corporation keeps its records on the accrual basis. Prepaid items are recorded initially as assets or liabilities. A partial list of general ledger accounts and balances on December 31 of the current year is shown on page 571.

Account Title	Account Balances
Supplies	$ 2,687.10
Prepaid Insurance	4,152.20
Interest Receivable	——
Salaries Payable	——
Employees Income Tax Payable — Federal	$ 318.50
FICA Tax Payable	117.00
Unemployment Tax Payable — Federal...............................	9.75
Unemployment Tax Payable — State	52.65
Interest Payable	
Rent Received in Advance	7,800.00
Corporation's Income Tax Payable — Federal	——
Property Tax Payable	——
Insurance Expense...	——
Payroll Taxes Expense	1,955.00
Salary Expense..	22,425.00
Supplies Expense	——
Interest Income	——
Rent Income	——
Interest Expense...	63.05
Federal Income Tax...	2,877.58
Property Tax...	1,233.38

Instructions: □ **1.** Record the account titles in the Account Title column of a work sheet. Record the account balances in the Trial Balance columns of the work sheet. (Do not total or rule the Trial Balance columns.)

□ **2.** Record the needed adjustments on the work sheet. The additional data needed are listed below. (Do not rule the Adjustments columns.)

Supplies inventory, December 31	$ 456.30
Value of insurance policies, December 31..	1,656.20
Accrued interest on notes receivable	16.25
Accrued salary expense, December 31:	975.00
Employer's accrued payroll taxes:	
FICA tax..	58.50
Unemployment tax payable — federal..	4.88
Unemployment tax payable — state	26.33
Rent received in advance and still unearned, December 31	650.00
Accrued interest on notes payable	8.32
Accrued corporation's federal income tax, December 31	261.63
Accrued property tax, December 31..	112.13

Instructions: □ **3.** Record the needed adjusting entries on page 16 of a general journal. Use the data from the work sheet completed in Instruction 2.

□ **4.** Record the needed reversing entries for interest receivable, salaries payable, employer's accrued payroll taxes, interest payable, corporation's accrued federal income tax, and accrued property tax. Use page 17 of a general journal.

Adjusting entries for prepaid and
accrued items

Wait-o-Dix Corporation keeps its records on the accrual basis. Prepaid items are recorded initially as revenue or expenses. A partial list of general ledger accounts and balances on December 31 of the current year is shown below.

	Account Balances	
Account Title	Debit	Credit
Supplies	$ 468.83	
Prepaid Insurance	1,694.40	
Interest Receivable	17.50	
Interest Payable		$ 8.40
Rent Received in Advance		700.00
Corporation's Income Tax Payable — Federal		276.12
Property Tax Payable		118.30
Insurance Expense	4,382.00	
Supplies Expense	2,893.80	
Interest Income		48.40
Rent Income		10,080.00
Interest Expense	65.80	
Federal Income Tax	3,374.00	
Property Tax	1,446.00	

Instructions: □ **1.** Record the account titles in the Account Title column of a work sheet. Record the account balances in the Trial Balance columns of the work sheet. (Do not total or rule the Trial Balance columns.)

□ **2.** Record the needed adjusting entries in the Adjustments columns of the work sheet.

> Before recording the adjustments on the work sheet, review the material on pages 436–438 about recording prepaid items as revenues or expenses. Use the same question format described on these pages to determine the adjustment for each of the items.

The additional data needed for the adjustments are listed below. (Do not total or rule the Adjustments columns.)

Supplies inventory, December 31	$ 736.40
Value of insurance policies, December 31	2,016.00
Accrued interest on notes receivable	22.40
Rent received in advance and still unearned, December 31	840.00
Accrued interest on notes payable	10.50
Accrued corporation's federal income tax, December 31	309.93
Accrued property tax, December 31	132.83

Instructions: □ **3.** Record the needed adjusting entries on page 14 of a general journal. Use the data in the Adjustments columns of the work sheet prepared in Instruction 2.

Recording transactions and preparing
financial statements on a cash basis

Chin Shyu Ling owns and operates a small gift shop in a resort inn. The business is called Oriental Jewels. The accounting records for the business are kept on a cash basis. The transactions listed below and on page 574 were completed during November of the current year. Source documents are referred to as: checks, Ck; cash register tapes, T; and receipts, R.

Instructions: ☐ **1.** Record the transactions beginning on page 24 of a daily journal similar to the one shown on page 446.

Nov. 1. Beginning cash balance, $2,889.84.
2. Issued a check for March rent, $332.50. Ck470.
2. Purchased merchandise for cash, $68.97. Ck471.
3. Issued a check to pay for merchandise received on October 29, $30.16. Ck472.
3. Purchased merchandise for cash, $62.42. Ck473.
3. Total weekly cash sales: sales, $937.99; sales tax, $46.90; total cash received, $984.89. T3.
5. Purchased merchandise for cash, $54.15. Ck474.
6. Issued a check to pay sales tax liability, $301.20. Ck475.
6. Issued a check for supplies bought today, $28.50. Ck476.
7. Issued a check to pay for merchandise received on November 5, $25.63. Ck477.
7. Issued a check to pay for merchandise received on November 6, $252.32. Ck478.
8. Issued a check to pay for miscellaneous expenses, $24.40. Ck479.
9. Received cash for merchandise returned to a vendor, $10.34. R80.
10. Purchased merchandise for cash, $10.93. Ck480.
10. Issued a check to replenish petty cash fund: supplies, $21.76; miscellaneous, $11.95; total, $33.71. Ck481.
10. Total weekly cash sales: sales, $1,406.99; sales tax, $70.35; total cash received, $1,477.34. T10.
12. Issued a check to pay for merchandise received on November 10, $483.94. Ck482.
13. Issued a check to pay for merchandise received on November 12, $240.85. Ck483.
14. Purchased merchandise for cash, $15.52. Ck484.
15. Issued a check for supplies bought today, $24.83. Ck485.
16. Issued a check to pay for merchandise received on November 15, $409.80. Ck486.
16. Purchased merchandise for cash, $24.70. Ck487.
17. Total weekly cash sales: sales, $1,547.68; sales tax, $77.38; total cash received, $1,625.06. T17.
18. Received cash for merchandise returned to a vendor, $6.61. R81.
19. Issued a check to pay the telephone bill, $36.00. Ck488.

Nov. 20. Issued a check to pay for merchandise received on November 18, $143.69. Ck489.

21. Issued a check to pay for miscellaneous expenses, $16.90. Ck490.

21. Issued a check to pay for merchandise received on November 20, $480.21. Ck491.

22. Purchased supplies for cash, $137.75. Ck492.

23. Purchased merchandise for cash, $333.35. Ck493.

23. Issued a check to pay the electric bill, $109.20. Ck494.

24. Purchased merchandise for cash, $412.06. Ck495.

24. Issued a check to pay the gas bill, $27.55. Ck496.

24. Total weekly cash sales: sales, $1,336.50; sales tax, $66.83; total cash received, $1,403.33. T24.

27. Issued a check to pay the water bill, $41.38. Ck497.

28. Issued a check for supplies bought today, $40.81. Ck498.

29. Issued a check to pay for merchandise received on November 24, $717.25. Ck499.

30. Purchased merchandise for cash, $431.06. Ck500.

30. Issued a check to replenish petty cash fund: supplies, $14.75; miscellaneous, $11.53; total, $26.28. Ck501.

30. Issued a check to pay for newspaper advertising, $57.95. Ck502.

30. Issued a check for withdrawal of cash by owner, $500.00. Ck503.

30. Total weekly cash sales: sales, $1,787.58; sales tax, $89.38; total cash received, $1,876.96. T30.

Instructions: □ **2.** Pencil foot the daily journal, prove cash, and prove the daily journal. The check stub for Ck504 shows a remaining balance of $4,338.40.

□ **3.** Total and rule the daily journal as shown on page 449. Analyze the Other Receipts and Other Payments columns in the same way as shown on page 449. Write the results of the analysis at the top of a new page of the daily journal.

□ **4.** Using the data from the daily journal and the data below, prepare an income statement similar to the one shown on page 455.

Summary Report Prepared on November 30, 19——	
Value of equipment (plant assets file)	$1,617.00 (S-1)
Unpaid invoices, total	210.70 (S-2)
Merchandise inventory, end of last month	2,552.10 (S-3)
Merchandise inventory, end of this month	2,682.14 (S-4)
Capital, end of last month	6,597.04 (S-5)

□ **5.** Using the data from the daily journal and the data given in Instruction 4 above, prepare a balance sheet similar to the one shown on page 456. Oriental Jewels has a petty cash fund of $50.00.

REVIEW
PROBLEM 25-R 1 ● Preparing a budgeted income statement

The sales manager and administrative manager of Centennial Company have made the following estimates to be used in preparing a budgeted income statement for the current year ended December 31.

(a) Quarterly net sales for year are estimated as follows:

1st quarter	$202,100.00	3d quarter	$252,700.00
2d quarter	252,700.00	4th quarter	303,200.00

(b) Cost of merchandise sold is estimated to be 60 percent of the net sales.
(c) The estimated expenses for the year are as shown below. (Percentages are based on the net sales expected for each quarter in the current year.)

Selling Expenses

Advertising Expense	2.0%
Delivery Expense	1.2%
Depreciation Expense — Delivery Equipment	$2,350.00
Depreciation Expense — Store Equipment	$3,140.00
Miscellaneous Expense — Sales....	1.2%
Salary Expense — Sales	7.5%
Supplies Expense — Sales	.9%

Administrative Expense

Bad Debts Expense	.5%
Depreciation Expense — Office Equipment	$2,620.00
Insurance Expense	1.0%
Miscellaneous Expense — Admin.	1.8%
Payroll Taxes Expense	.8%
Rent Expense	$15,000.00
Salary Expense — Admin.	7.1%
Utilities Expense	2.4%

(d) Income taxes are 30% of estimated net income.

Instructions: Prepare a budgeted income statement for Centennial Company for the current year ended December 31 similar to the one on page 483. Round amounts for the estimates to the nearest $10.00. Selling and administrative expense budget schedules similar to those on pages 480 and 482 must be prepared first.

REVIEW
PROBLEM 26-R 1 ● Figuring plans for net income

Miss Souder, manager of Parrish Slacks Company, is planning her net income potential for the coming year. Sales prices and expenses for last year are as follows:

Variable Data	Per Pair	Annual Fixed Costs	
Selling price	$ 20.00	Rent	$ 20,000.00
Cost of slacks	$ 12.00	Salaries	80,000.00
Sales commission	2.00	Miscellaneous	20,000.00
Total variable costs	$ 14.00	Total fixed costs	$120,000.00

Use the preceding data as a basis for net income planning. Treat each part on page 576 independently.

Instructions: □ **1.** Figure the breakeven point for the year (a) in total sales dollars and (b) in number of slacks.

□ **2.** If a $30,000.00 annual net income is desired, figure the required (a) sales dollars and (b) number of slacks.

□ **3.** Figure the breakeven point (a) in sales dollars and (b) in number of slacks if an additional $60,000.00 in salaries is paid in place of the $2.00 sales commission per pair of slacks.

REVIEW PROBLEM 27-R 1 ● Preparing comparative financial statements

The following data are taken from the financial records of Laporte Corporation on December 31, 1979 and 1978:

	1979	1978
Cash	$ 70,800.00	$ 34,400.00
Notes Receivable	33,000.00	101,400.00
Accounts Receivable (Net)	77,200.00	118,800.00
Merchandise Inventory	566,200.00	554,200.00
Other Current Assets	13,200.00	15,400.00
Plant Assets (Net)	242,000.00	270,600.00
Notes Payable	142,000.00	112,200.00
Accounts Payable	130,400.00	225,000.00
Income Tax Payable — Federal	4,800.00	7,400.00
Other Current Liabilities	23,000.00	25,800.00
Mortgage Payable (Long-Term Liability)	88,000.00	132,000.00
Capital Stock	500,000.00	500,000.00
Retained Earnings	114,200.00	92,400.00
Net Sales	1,070,000.00	1,320,000.00
Net Purchases	912,200.00	1,303,600.00
Advertising Expense	19,800.00	26,600.00
Salary Expense — Sales	52,800.00	73,800.00
Other Selling Expenses	6,600.00	7,400.00
Bad Debts Expense	3,400.00	7,800.00
Salary Expense — Administrative	21,800.00	25,000.00
Other Administrative Expenses	21,875.00	14,925.00
Income Tax — Federal	9,075.00	30,520.00
Shares of capital stock outstanding	5,000	5,000

Additional Data:

Merchandise Inventory, January 1, 1978	$334,200.00
Total Assets, January 1, 1978	524,200.00
Total Owners' Equity, January 1, 1978	570,600.00

Instructions: ▢ **1.** Prepare a comparative income statement, similar to the one on page 512, for the two years 1979 and 1978. You need not show percentages; show the amounts only.

▢ **2.** Prepare a comparative balance sheet, similar to the one shown on page 513, for the two years 1979 and 1978.

The two comparative financial statements prepared in Review Problem 27-R 1 will be needed to complete Review Problems 27-R 2, 27-R 3, and 27-R 4.

**REVIEW
PROBLEM 27-R 2** Analyzing a comparative income statement

The comparative income statement prepared in Review Problem 27-R 1 is needed to complete Review Problem 27-R 2.

Instructions: ▢ **1.** Based on the comparative income statement prepared for Laporte Corporation in Review Problem 27-R 1, figure for each year the percentage of net sales each of the following is:

(a) Cost of merchandise sold.
(b) Gross profit on operations.
(c) Total operating expenses.
(d) Net income after federal income tax.

▢ **2.** For each of the percentages figured above, indicate if there appears to be a favorable or unfavorable trend from 1978 to 1979. Give reasons for your answers.

**REVIEW
PROBLEM 27-R 3** Analyzing earnings performance from comparative financial statements

The comparative financial statements prepared in Review Problem 27-R 1 are needed to complete Review Problem 27-R 3.

Instructions: ▢ **1.** Based on the comparative financial statements for the years ended December 31, 1979 and 1978, prepared for Laporte Corporation in Review Problem 27-R 1, figure for each year the following percentages and amount:

(a) Rate of return on average total assets.
(b) Rate of return on average owners' equity.
(c) Rate of return on net sales.
(d) Earnings per share.

▢ **2.** For each of the percentages and amount figured above, indicate if there appears to be a favorable or an unfavorable trend from 1978 to 1979. Give reasons for your answers.

REVIEW
PROBLEM 27-R 4
Analyzing short-term financial strength
from a comparative balance sheet

The comparative financial statements prepared in Review Problem 27-R 1 are needed to complete Review Problem 27-R 4.

Instructions: □ **1.** Based on the comparative balance sheet as of December 31, 1979 and 1978, prepared for Laporte Corporation in Review Problem 27-R1, figure for each year the following ratios:

(a) Current ratio.
(b) Acid-test ratio.

□ **2.** For each ratio figured above, indicate if there appears to be a favorable or an unfavorable trend from 1978 to 1979. Give reasons for your answers.

REVIEW
PROBLEM 28-R 1
Preparing a statement of changes
in financial position

The comparative balance sheet for Ostendorf Corporation for the year ended December 31, 1979, is shown on page 579.

Additional data needed are:
(a) Net income for the year, $16,000.00.
(b) Depreciation on plant assets for the year, $22,000.00.
(c) Plant assets bought for $40,000.00.
(d) Cash received from addition to mortgage payable, $60,000.00.
(e) Payments made on mortgage during year, $20,000.00.
(f) Dividends declared and paid, $10,000.00.
(g) Additional capital stock issued for $20,000.00.

Instructions: □ **1.** Prepare a schedule of changes in working capital similar to the one shown on page 531.

□ **2.** Prepare a work sheet for analyzing changes in financial position. Enter in the work sheet the beginning balances and the ending balances of the working capital and noncurrent accounts.

□ **3.** Analyze the transactions that affected working capital. Prepare an adjusting entry in the work sheet for each transaction analyzed to show its effect on working capital. Complete the work sheet.

□ **4.** Prepare a statement of changes in financial position similar to the one shown on page 539.

OSTENDORF CORPORATION
Comparative Balance Sheet
December 31, 1979 and 1978

	1979		1978	
Assets				
Current Assets:				
Cash...	$ 30,000.00		$ 40,000.00	
Accounts Receivable (Net)............	50,000.00		80,000.00	
Merchandise Inventory................	250,000.00		200,000.00	
Other Current Assets	6,000.00		4,000.00	
Total Current Assets...................		$336,000.00		$324,000.00
Noncurrent Assets:				
Plant Assets..............................	$280,000.00		$240,000.00	
Less Accum. Depr.— Plant Assets .	36,000.00		14,000.00	
Total Noncurrent Assets		244,000.00		226,000.00
		$580,000.00		$550,000.00
Liabilities				
Current Liabilities:				
Accounts Payable	$ 50,000.00		$ 85,000.00	
Income Tax Payable — Federal......	10,000.00		6,000.00	
Other Current Liabilities	10,000.00		15,000.00	
Total Current Liabilities...............		$ 70,000.00		$106,000.00
Long-Term Liability:				
Mortgage Payable		160,000.00		120,000.00
Total Liabilities		$230,000.00		$226,000.00
Stockholders' Equity				
Capital Stock................................	$320,000.00		$300,000.00	
Retained Earnings	30,000.00		24,000.00	
Total Stockholders' Equity..............		350,000.00		324,000.00
Total Liab. and Stockholders' Equity.		$580,000.00		$550,000.00

Index